Politics of the Possible

THE DECADE OUR AMERICAN DEMOCRACY WORKED

A view from the inside

MARY ELLEN McCAFFREE

and ANNE McNAMEE CORBETT

FIRST EDITION PAPERBACK
ISBN 978-0-9835127-9-0

Printed in the United States of America

Library of Congress Control Number: 2011905829
McCaffree, Mary Ellen and Anne McNamee Corbett
Politics of the Possible / Mary Ellen McCaffree and Anne McNamee Corbett

Text design, cover design and cover photo by Anne McNamee Corbett / Island Penworks
Previous special edition hardcover © 2010 ISBN: 978-0-9835127-2-1

To our children and grandchildren...

who keep us young and growing,
and who have inspired this inside view
of our democratic process

CONTENTS

PREFACE

THIS IS A REFRESHING GOVERNMENT SUCCESS STORY in which the winners are 'We the people'. It happened one decade, in one state in our nation's far northwest nearly two hundred years after our colonies agreed to unite.

More than a history, it affirms what is possible here and now: *Politics of the Possible* provides living proof that politics can be positive, government progress is possible, and a focus on responsive governing can overcome partisan ills. It demonstrates that strong leaders can possess — and sustain — integrity, and that one citizen can honestly enter in and make a difference. In this story, no scandal rocked a single member of the leadership team, nor their central opponents, throughout an entire decade of high profile, high-powered, high intensity political conflict and compromise. The capitol press corps hovered close: They could vouch for it.

This book is intended to serve as a guide for citizens today or down the road — a map for the disillusioned, the disenfranchised, anyone who is disappointed with politics or feels alienated from our government at any level. It is equally apropos for those enamored with political strategy and effect.

In the Prologue you'll meet both co-authors and learn why we teamed to re-tell this particular chapter of Mary Ellen McCaffree's life. The Epilogue returns us to today, suggesting how we can draw from this story to keep our ships of state on course.

Though this book is sufficiently detailed to deliver a solid lesson in legislative work, we as authors opted to avoid the textbook approach in favor of a lively narrative complete with dialogue, political intrigue, honest admissions and amusing episodes to recreate the experience — to make it real. We researched legislative journals (each encounter on the floor of the House and Senate is drawn directly from these), and consulted news clippings, oral history accounts, Mary Ellen's personal files and her political papers archived at the University of Washington. We interviewed key players and plumbed Mary Ellen's remarkable recall. And we were faithful to her open-minded perspective.

The movers and shakers in *Politics of the Possible* could easily have hailed from either party. Republicans and Democrats alike will recognize themselves among this leadership team we track. We cheer both sides when they play at politics fair and square and when they keep their eyes and actions on governing – with the people's interests firmly center.

Our hero is not a person, but the democratic process within the system of government designed to serve us all. Mary Ellen McCaffree, our narrator, entered this process as a mother of five actively seeking to fix the problem of her children's ill-funded schools. We join her journey to the inside as she experiences the intricacies essential to our government functioning well. We travel deeper inside the process than journalists are ever allowed, entering locked caucus doors, campaign headquarters, the governor's office, lobbyist parties, late-night legislative haunts and, more publicly, committee meetings and hearings, and action within a state Senate and House.

We grow with the narrator as she progresses from her humble start as a minority freshman, through an early coalition and coup, to her central role in an arduous redistricting battle that revitalizes her state's two-party system and, more importantly, re-establishes one-man, one-vote. Once her state is back on a balanced track, a series of elections (hers and others) lands Mary Ellen inside the state leadership team, where she ultimately works within the majority's inner circle and soon agrees to lead a major state reform.

Along the way we witness her party ousting its crippling radical fringe, revisit the turbulence of the 1960's, and hear a sole black legislator's lonely plea for civil rights. We experience abortion picketers, Black Panthers, an earthquake and two views on university unrest: From her professor husband and their student son.

We follow a steady political resurgence that finally produces bi-partisan teamwork on an astonishing sweep of major, progressive reforms. Within this decade, this team re-claims and reforms their state government to better serve its citizens. It was remarkable but not miraculous. It can happen again.

Our goal in recounting this story is to embolden more citizens to participate in the process of our government. We've de-mystified the gears of governing, stripped the political process bare, and delved into the particulars of this dynamic decade in the hope that readers will no longer shy from active involvement. The process is in place for us, and it works.

While this is not intended to be a technical manual on legislation, we spare few technicalities as we trace the actual legislative path. There is no detour around the reality that creating and passing good laws is complex, formal, often time-consuming and, yes, political.

Our narrator takes us on an inside legislative track. More uniquely, we're permitted inside a private home and into a marriage that delicately reconciles a mother and wife's public service with her devotion to her family.

Because we are devotees of our nation's history as well, we detour briefly into precedents laid by our founders — the 'whys' behind our government's design. This success story owes a major debt to the earliest families who settled America and then fought, literally, to defend their revolutionary notion that all people deserve equality and respect. They designed our federal government — not a national government, but a federation of individual states — to allow our states to remain central in our lives. Each state is unique, and each is ours. In this book we celebrate one state's renaissance, made possible by the system of governing we've inherited.

In one pivotal decade, by respecting this system and its tenets of equality and respect, the team Mary Ellen joined was able to move their state to the head of the nation with a host of cutting edge policies and reforms. They were named one of the most effective state governments of the 20th Century.

This story deserves to be told... and retold.

PROLOGUE

I'T'S FAIR TO ACCUSE ME OF ADMIRING Mary Ellen McCaffree immensely, though she'll whisk away adulation — she's too busy 'doing' to stop for praise. Problem-solving and taking action are what Mary Ellen does, and she's been doing both, now, for more than nine decades. This book highlights one: A distinctive decade when our political system functioned exactly as our forefathers designed, driven by a group of people (Mary Ellen among them) who said, "Our government isn't working for us!" — then rolled up their sleeves, jumped in and made a difference. My life has intersected with Mary Ellen McCaffree at four important junctures that collectively illustrate who she is, why we chose to write this personal slice of her history, and why it matters so much today.

ENCOUNTER 1: THE KITSAP LAND TRUST

I CLEARLY RECALL THAT AUTUMN DAY in 1991 when Mary Ellen walked into my living room and inextricably entered my life. I had recently returned from two years in Japan to give birth to my third child, a third daughter.

Before I'd left the U.S., a professional project led me to create the Kitsap Land Trust, a non-profit which I had then entrusted to my co-founders when it was six months young so that I could venture abroad. I wanted to slow my life and to focus on my family. I'd returned to a smaller American town, content to suckle my newborn and tend my brood. I had consciously abandoned my previous driven intensity. I wanted to mother.

And so on that day, I opened my door to Mary Ellen, determined to be polite but not to bend to her mission. She'd telephoned the week before.

"Hello, Anne?" A voice of age. "This is Mary Ellen McCaffree. I'm on the board of the Kitsap Land Trust and I'd like to come talk with you."

My gut reacted — mixed. I was glad the land trust was thriving. But how did they know I was back? How did they find me? And who was this Mary Ellen?

"I'm sorry," I told her by telephone. "I don't have time to serve on the land trust board. I've just had a baby, you see…"

"I just want to talk to you," she said.

And so I agreed. Though business-like, she sounded warm. Unpretentious. Someone whose word you could trust.

Mary Ellen walked into my small living room, a bit unsteadily due to a recent operation on her knee. After I cleared away the burp cloth and baby blanket, she took a seat on my couch. I excused myself and nursed right there, to emphasize my point: I was glad the land trust was moving along, glad they remembered me fondly, but I wasn't going back. I have a baby.

"They respect you," Mary Ellen told me. "They have confidence in your leadership. They want you back on the board. I told them I'd talk to you."

I changed the subject. How had she become involved? She'd worked in her own small community to protect local land. *How nice*, I thought, *what a nice thing to do in retirement. Better than knitting.* We talked about babies and gardening. I didn't know who she was.

"You should consider coming back on the board," she said again.

I switched my baby to the other side: "No, I can't. Really. I don't have the time. I edit part time and that's all I can handle."

"Is this editing interesting to you? Meaningful?"

"It helps pay the bills."

Undeterred, she asked me again to consider.

"Are you willing to let the land trust falter?" she asked, noting my silent concern and adding, "Some things you do for your soul, some for community."

And as the sunlight streamed in my living room and crossed my baby's warm body and mine, I knew she was right. I cared about this community project to protect an urban salmon stream. She was right... and I resented it. How do you feed your soul — out there in the world — and still have time to snuggle and nurture your babies?

"Do you have children?" I asked, defensive now.

"Yes," she smiled. "Five."

"Oh."

And I don't recall what she told me next — a grandchild, perhaps a first great-grandchild, on its way — but I softened to this woman whose heart seemed to warm so fully to family. I felt safe. She wouldn't push me. She understood. I breathed, relieved, and stroked my baby.

"Will you consider the land trust?" she asked again.

I helped her to her feet, perplexed by this woman who was so soft, warm and womanly, yet so determined to pull me from my home and into the world.

But she was right. And within three months, I was back on the board of the land trust. Within the next year I attended a national conference on land conservation and formed a working bond with Mary Ellen McCaffree, having found a kindred spirit in community work. Together we tended the nuts and bolts and networking of our growing organization.

Over the next several years, the two of us shared rides, ideas and legwork. And her history leaked out, never from her, though — only from others. I learned that Mary Ellen McCaffree was a former four-term state legislator and a key player on Governor Dan Evans' famously effective legislative team. And as for her hounding our land trust about accurate accounting and a perpetual financial base, well… she had previously run our state's Department of Revenue!

These facts astonished me as much as her never mentioning them.

To Mary Ellen, past accomplishments were not important, except as they served to actively address her local community's problems of the day. Lesson 1.

ENCOUNTER 2: A 60-YEAR MARRIAGE

AS HER 60TH WEDDING ANNIVERSARY APPROACHED, Mary Ellen and her husband Ken asked me early in 2001 to help them compile a small book.

"We want a little something to share with our grandchildren. It's a surprise."

Ironically, after nineteen years of marriage, my husband had departed that New Year's Day. I was alone in caring for my three daughters as well as a "foster" daughter of sorts, while simultaneously nursing a heavy, heavy heart. Working with the McCaffrees gave me a positive partnership to celebrate — a timely blessing, indeed, if ever there was one.

Through this project, which swelled from a small collection of their favorite quotes to a full-fledged life history and a 200-page hardback, I came to know Ken and Mary Ellen as a team… one that was fully functional and remarkably healthy. They worked both independently and together, argued frankly, spoke their minds. Through compromise, they eventually struck a reasonable balance to get the job done.

"We don't need to write about our courtship," she said.

He wholeheartedly disagreed.

"Fine," she said. "You do it."

And he did.

"Do we have to write about the locusts?" he asked. "What does that have to do with us?"

"It's important," she said.

"If you say so, love," said he, and the locusts joined their story.

I learned about these two as individuals — from their Kansas family farm roots to two separate distinguished public careers. And I learned the history of this amazing team — husband and wife, with their five children firmly center.

It began to dawn on me how this mother of five had been able to move such big mountains — she belonged to a marriage and a family and an ancestry built on honesty, teamwork, equality and respect. The McCaffrees worked side-by-side, focused not on self, but on community, whether it was the community of marriage, family, neighborhood or beyond... all that cradled their lives.

August 29, 2001 marked the McCaffree's 60th anniversary. At a weekend-long celebration, among their five children (and spouses), fourteen grandchildren (and five in-laws by marriage), and three great-grandchildren to date, Mary Ellen and Ken presented their hardbound gift.

As their book reported: *There are basically two approaches to life — building up or tearing down. Our goal was to be a family of builders.* Lesson 2.

ENCOUNTER 3: THE MORNING OF SEPTEMBER 11, 2001

I WATCHED THE EVENTS UNFOLD ON TV with my three daughters huddled around me. Then I kissed my girls good-bye and, cell phone in hand, left for my late-morning meeting across town.

This was the day 83-year-old Mary Ellen and I were to begin planning to write about her political history. She wanted to write for her grandchildren again, this time to help them understand why as citizens they must work at making our democracy work. She wanted to inspire them to join in the process.

And I wanted to write about her, about how a woman balances family and public service, and also to illustrate that our political process does indeed work, with the proper ingredients — which I felt would be clear if we simply recounted Mary Ellen's particular path.

I arrived at 11 that morning at the home of this "Greatest Generation" couple.

Ken had served on a Mediterranean minesweeper in World War II, while Mary Ellen held down the home front and tended their babies. After the war, the young family of five inhabited old barracks at the University of Chicago, where they soon became six while Ken attained his doctorate in economics, courtesy of the G.I. Bill. Next they moved to Seattle for a faculty post at the University of Washington, and midway through that first school year, they became seven.

Gracious as always on that September morning, Ken and Mary Ellen greeted me warmly and offered their traditional tea and cookies before we buckled down to work. Their relaxed demeanors didn't jive with the day's events. I realized they hadn't heard the news.

When I told them America had been attacked, they didn't believe me. We turned on their TV and they both sank.

Dead silence. More silence. The agenda for the day was set aside.

Mary Ellen's response in the ensuing months was telling.

She studied.

Islam. Muslim communities. Emerging democracies in Afghanistan, Somalia, Sierra Leone. Emerging markets. Globalization. More buzz words.

She read voraciously: Dozens of books, a range of periodicals and several daily newspapers — local, national, global. She also consulted public radio and several formats of TV. She dug into every source of information she could think of, in search of answers to two perturbing questions: How did this happen? How can we fix it?

"We need the skills to co-exist with other cultures," she said. "This is not just a matter of national survival, but global survival."

All eyes were on us. How would America lead?

"We have to continue to build our democracy within the framework of a world that is not secure, within the framework of the global community," she said. "We need to be as good an example as possible, and still be compassionate, tolerant, understanding. We need to co-exist."

Her focus temporarily shifted — away from prodding her grandchildren to become more involved, and onto contemplating our role as the world's most visible democracy. What was democracy, really? Government of the people. But what kind of government? That varied. How was ours distinct? What made it stay afloat?

We met each week, with Mary Ellen reflecting, the two of us discussing, me taking notes. She redirected her aim again, this time at our forefathers.

"The founding fathers intended our government to be responsive to the needs of the people. But they didn't use the word democracy — that word isn't in the constitution. They talked about liberty, personal freedoms, and equality in terms of justice for all — ideas that were absolutely revolutionary! Then they emphasized our collective responsibility to keep those rights alive. It took the colonies 150 years of experimentation to arrive at our form of government — one that responds to us, but only *if* we remain involved.

"Independence and equality come with a price, and that's responsibility. In a representative democracy, you have a responsibility to be a part of the process. This is our government, not the government of someone higher up. But we have to stay involved."

I just kept scribbling.

"Participation depends largely on education about our political system, and that's one place I think we fall short. Education is the basis for an effective democracy. Freedom, open elections and education — the three are all woven together."

Gradually, we laid the conceptual groundwork for our book.

As for the terrorist attacks, she continued to contemplate, and after five months concluded, "In the U.S., our biggest threat is not terrorism, but a failure of our democracy."

A year after 9/11, she continued to mull.

"All these other countries are picking up democracy's words: Independence, human rights, equality… If we believe in these principles, we have to keep working at the functioning of our government here at home.

"Some countries want democracy because they see our material wealth more than the actual cultural and spiritual wealth of this government — our founding principles. Some other countries look at our wealth as a negative."

This dawned on her when her granddaughter Jessica returned from Croatia with some surprising stories from the international study program she'd attended. She had befriended students from all over the world, who told her repeatedly they don't want their countries to be like America — "because all Americans care about is being rich."

Mary Ellen's response, upon reflecting on this: "I think in Arab countries, particularly, that's how they see us. As greedy. And that's what they're against," she said, searching for the root of the problem — the basis of a solution — rather than an enemy to hate.

"From the outside, people may look at our country's capitalistic excesses and fraud, and mistakenly equate capitalism with democracy. They are not one and the same. Democracy is not meant to serve self-interest, influence or greed. Democracy is people looking after people, and protecting our freedoms together.

"At every crucial time in our history, we've had leaders able to expand on and move forward on the principles of our founding fathers and the colonies. But now we seem to be stepping backwards and that worries me. For example, this war on terror is going to limit our individual freedom. That's a fact. I believe it's necessary for collective security and welfare, but it is not a principle upon which our country is based.

"Democracy is a principle, not a form of governing per se. It means different things in different countries. Our Bill of Rights is what democracy means here. There's not just one way to govern democratically. What works in America may not work somewhere else, and maybe it shouldn't. Globally, the focus has to be humanity.

"Globally, if the US can be a good example of human rights — rather than just talking about human rights — *then* others will follow. Words are not important. Actions are. And no better place to start than on your own street."

Ah — the crux of her message.

"If you believe the process of self-government is a growing thing, democracy will continue to work. From our constitution on, it's an ever, ever, ever — even today — an ever-growing thing. It takes people willing to discuss and compromise and debate — they must be willing to look at what's going on to provide the best good for the most people.

"I've always felt that if you could communicate with other people, there's a possibility of living together peaceably. Any group of people can get something done if they share a commitment to the principles of individual freedom and justice for all." Lesson 3.

ENCOUNTER 4: THE McCAFFREE FAMILY GATHERS ROUND

STACEY, 31, A ZOO EDUCATOR and marine biologist, came to lunch with her grandmother at the McCaffree condo in April 2002, coinciding with one of our weekly 'book' workdays. While I continued reading through Mary Ellen's files, I caught snippets of their intergenerational dialogue in the next room — a lively, congenial jousting between peers. Another vibrant McCaffree relationship.

"Honestly, people my age don't know how it's supposed to run, or why we should vote, or who we should vote for," Stacey says without apology for her ignorance. "I don't really follow candidates and issues. Personally, I'm curious, though — I mean, you hear about the legislature trying to pass bills and get things done, and then they can't — there's a stalemate or an extension — and I just wonder, 'What are they doing?!' I really have no idea."

Mary Ellen can't believe this is Stacey speaking. Her get-it-done grand-daughter Stacey.

"That's my beef with education," she tells Stacey as they share homemade potato salad and sandwiches (BLT).

"The truth is, Grandma, I didn't learn anything about it in high school."

If it was up to Mary Ellen, high schools would teach the founding principles, then require students to intern in their communities — to participate, to learn how government works. She realizes that her grandchildren embody what's wrong with government today: A disconnection and disenchantment between the government and the people, when in fact our government *IS* — or at least should reflect — the people.

Not long after her lunch with Stacey, Mary Ellen sends an email.

"Dear Grandchildren: As most of you know I am working on writing my own political story. In order to make it meaningful to your generation, I need your help…"

She's been spurred by another granddaughter, Alison, an entrepreneurial engineer who is trying to learn more about government mechanics as she launches a company of her own. Alison consults the best political authority she knows:

Her grandmother. And between them, a lively correspondence course in U.S. civics ensues, which continues to this day.

They begin with America's election process and two-party system. Mary Ellen defends our two-party tradition, pointing Alison to the scholarly writing of political journalist Joseph Harsch, who noted: "The system has its drawbacks, and at times even unsightly characteristics, as when a winner oversteps the bounds in his profit taking, or a loser in his abuse of those in office. Anyone tempted to regard the price (of the two-party system) as too high need only reflect for a moment on the higher price other peoples have paid, and pay today, for a monopoly…" Mary Ellen wraps up the three-page private lesson with, "All for now. Hope to hear from you soon. Love, Grandmother McCaffree."

After her initial email, we created a questionnaire for her grandchildren, and they responded with words that caused her further dismay. They know so little, feel so removed, think of government as "them" not "us" — and a mighty disreputable 'them' at that.

"How does the government *actually* function?" asks Shayna, a professional counselor, who suggests they meet as a group to talk this through. "It appears so complicated and convoluted that to understand what exactly one is voting for is pretty overwhelming… I haven't studied government in detail. I don't feel my education comes close to helping me understand… The majority of my friends don't think a whole lot about the government 'out there' — they're just trying to find jobs and a way to survive."

Or as Carey, the oldest McCaffree grandchild — a geophysicist with a young family — writes frankly, "I consider myself an uninformed and disinterested citizen. Raising three kids seems to take all my time."

If Mary Ellen had general concerns about our government and democracy before her survey, this growing message from her grandchildren made it clear: Newer Americans don't know enough to keep our government healthy. Nor do they realize that even the smallest involvement — volunteering in the community, serving on a local committee or board — counts as participation in our government. It does make a difference.

"I was shocked by the reactions of my grandchildren," she said. "I was amazed at the extent of alienation they felt from the system. They'd always been interested in my life and what I'd done, so I just had no idea. But I think they are alienated because they just don't understand how government works or the actual mechanics of the democratic process."

Within the year, granddaughter Paige, a law student hoping to work for the disadvantaged, visited Mary Ellen and Ken at their apartment, now in a university retirement community. During lunch, a new dialogue began.

"If I were to become more involved, Grandmother, how do I get started?"

"Whatever you feel passionate about in your community, Paige, that's where you start," said Mary Ellen. "That's what I did."

Can her path and accomplishment be duplicated in today's world? Mary Ellen will look anyone in the eye and say with unequivocal conviction: "Yes. With an understanding of the process, yes." Lesson 4.

In *Politics of the Possible* we retrace one journey inside our governmental process, providing an inside view of the inner workings of our representative democracy to demonstrate how the quality of governing — today, as always — depends upon us all.

— A.M.C.

The 42 capitol steps symbolize Washington's status as the 42nd American state admitted to the union.

CHAPTER ONE

THE GAVEL
CITIZEN PARTICIPATION IN A NEW BEGINNING

Every citizen must do his or her share

if our democratic form of government

is to survive

AT 12 NOON, THE GAVEL BANGS THE PODIUM and demands our silence as its portentous echo swells within the immense marbled walls of the chamber. All ninety-nine of us flinch into focus, surrounded by dignitaries, press corps, staff, and dozens of onlookers in two velvet-benched balconies, my husband and teen daughters among them.

Our capitol's best-kept political secret is about to be revealed — a move that could wrench our state from complacency, set it back on fair footing. Secrecy is key. So I've sworn to maintain a poker face and harbor my tightly held confidence — me, a 44-year-old mother of five in my first day of public office.

While I've jumped at the rap of the gavel, my hands remain properly folded upon my desk. I sit quietly, one row shy of the back in the formal chamber, right next to the marble-bowled water fountain. The next command is delivered by a human voice, that of Chief Clerk Si Holcomb who continues to clench the gavel as he speaks: "I hereby call to order, on this 14th day of January, 1963, the 38th Session of the Washington State House of Representatives."

At this, the sergeant at arms color guard delivers two flags to the rostrum — the stars and stripes of our United States and that of the state of Washington: George Washington leveling his classic gaze, encircled within a field of green.

The Chief Clerk addresses us again: "The opening prayer will be delivered by the Reverend Arthur A. Val-Spinosa of St. Thomas Episcopal Church of Medina."

The Clerk yields the rostrum to the reverend, who invites: "Let us pray."

I follow along, eyes closed, intent on absorbing each moment of this day.

"Ladies and gentlemen, at this opening of the 38th Legislature, I bid your prayer for these..."

United States, all of them, he says, and for the many legislatures convening this week as well as their governors, legislators, judges, and all the people they serve. He asks us each to pray for just deliberations, courage, wisdom and "guidance to distinguish party and self and party and people, and wisdom..." [1]

He warns against sinful passions and private interests, asks that our gracious God "be with us evermore, as Thou was with our fathers in their former days..." and offers a final plea for divine guidance in our work before we join in a collective "Amen." Then we sit.

"Our Secretary of State," says the Chief Clerk next, "has presented me with the following..."

Again, I take in every word, awed by the dignity of these proceedings.

"...Dear Sir: I, Victor A. Meyers, Secretary of State of the State of Washington, do hereby certify that the following is a full, true and correct list of the persons elected to the office of State Representative in the state general election held in the several voting precincts of the State of Washington on the 6th day of November, 1962," per the official election returns on file in his office, entitling us to these seats we occupy here in the House of our state legislature on this "fourteenth day of January, A.D., 1963" as this 38th biennial session commences.[2]

The roll call begins.

"Ackley."

"Here."

"Adams."

"Present."

"Ahlquist. Andersen, James. Anderson, Eric. Backstrom. Beck..."

No obvious sign of anything underfoot.

"Earley. Eberle. Eldridge. Evans... Gleason. Goldsworthy. Gorton. Grant..."

Outside, a bleak winter rain pummels the grounds of the capitol and dances on the skylights high above us while, inside this House and unbeknownst to most, our governmental machinery has been pre-set for a roiling boil.

"Mahaffey. Mast. May. McCaffree..."

I'm thrilled a hesitant second when I hear my name, but soon find my voice, albeit wobbly. From the very back I answer a giddy: "Here!"

Here. A housewife and mother, largely unschooled in legislative complexity. How did I come to sit at this formal desk that bears my name? What is it, exactly, I expect to accomplish? Can just one woman — one ordinary citizen — really make a difference? I believe I can, which is why I am seated amidst all this marble and pomp on this miserably rainy Monday in the middle of January.

I DIDN'T ALWAYS LIVE HERE. FOURTEEN YEARS AGO, in September 1949, I first rolled across this state's eastern border with my husband, Ken, our four small children and all our personal belongings strapped to our aging Dodge sedan.

Ken and I are native Kansans, born and raised on Kansas farms at the edge of the bluestem prairies of the Flint Hills — the heart of America's geographic heartland.

My great grandparents arrived in Kansas by covered wagon — pioneers — and my grandmother was born soon after in their hand-hewn log cabin. Grandma married a self-made horticulturist, and together they planted their acreage with trees: 15,000 apple trees to be exact. My mother grew up on the land of Kansas as well.

Both my parents were avid dairy farmers, college-educated Kansans dedicated to the farming communities surrounding our town of El Dorado, Kansas, a place where neighbors looked after one another, families gathered for potlucks and pies, and the townsfolk staged plays and music recitals — often as not featuring the town's children. As a child I always took part — in the family, in the community, and in all of our collective challenges and joys. Mine was a warm and satisfying childhood. I grew up within a family built on respect: Parents who respected not only each other, but each of us four children as well.

I loved my home state's vast horizons and her wind-swept bluestem prairies. I rode my horse for miles with a soft breeze blowing across my face while all around me wildflowers danced in delicate bloom.

Along with the rest of America, my family endured some excruciating years beginning in the late 1920's when the stock market crashed and steeped our nation in those twelve long years of the Great Depression. We lived through the mid-30's dust storms, when the winds and dust scorched crops and stirred angry nighttime auroras — every day, every night — for most of one long, hot miserable summer. My parents never complained. Instead, they methodically worked through each problem and managed to maintain a remarkably easy and companionable cheer.

The prevailing sense in my family was that problems could always be solved. This is my heritage.

I graduated from El Dorado High School, then from Kansas State Agriculture

College in Manhattan, Kansas (now Kansas State University — my parents' alma mater, too) with a degree in home economics. My parents placed a premium on college education.

Then I married my high school sweetheart, Kenneth McCaffree.

Our friendship had blossomed through years of school, 4-H activities and socials at the Methodist church. At the time we wed, Ken was completing his Master's Degree in economics at the University of Denver.

But just as we'd started our family, World War II intervened. Ken served four years in the U.S. Navy, about half of that on a minesweeper in the Mediterranean. Afterwards, we took advantage of the G.I. Bill and moved into student housing at the University of Chicago with our family of five (and then six), while Ken pursued his PhD in economics.

Which brings me back to that 1949 road trip.

We made that journey west to Seattle to accept a full time assistant professorship at the University of Washington. The fifth McCaffree child, our son David, was born at the Group Health Hospital — in the middle of an earthquake, with cribs and beds rolling — the following spring.

Now we live with our five children in the university district in the heart of Seattle. And although it's a mighty long slog from the flatlands of the Kansas prairies to this mountain-rimmed edge of the Pacific Ocean, Washington has become our true home.

For the first few years here, our young family fully occupied me and my outside activities centered on my kids — Little League, scouting, church functions, school. Eventually I joined the local PTA.

Ken's career, meanwhile, has taken some significant detours. During the first we spent a sabbatical stretch in eastern Washington, from 1953-54, while he worked in labor relations at the state's new Hanford Atomic Project. We got to know the more arid half of the state.

In 1954, we returned to Seattle in time for the new university year, and in 1955 Ken joined the board of trustees at Group Health Cooperative, the "radical" medical service based on monthly family membership payments rather than traditional fees-for-services paid to doctors. 'Socialist medicine' some called it, but for us it was reliably affordable. Group Health served our family well, so it was logical to us that Ken add this to his activities.

I still focused primarily on our family.

"You ought to come to my house next week," said my neighbor and good friend JoAnn Lampman, whose husband taught in the UW Economics Department with Ken. "I'm hosting the North Seattle unit meeting of the League of Women Voters. I have a hunch you'll like it, Mary Ellen."

My friend knew me well.

These women didn't just chit-chat over tea about their children or exchange favorite recipes, but studied. Serious issues. Their goal? To make government work more effectively. I was intrigued.

The League's agenda for this particular meeting focused on two major concerns. The first was the redistricting and reapportionment of Washington's legislative seats — a means of balancing all the state's legislative districts relative to population. The sensible goal: To assure one man, one vote.

The discussion leader, Lois North, made the introductory presentation. The problem: Our legislative districts were basically the same as those drawn when the state was founded the previous century.

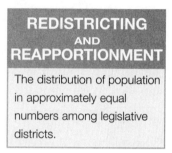

REDISTRICTING
AND
REAPPORTIONMENT

The distribution of population in approximately equal numbers among legislative districts.

"According to the principle of political equality," said Lois, "all legislators should represent approximately equal numbers of citizens."

But in the Washington State Legislature, she explained, the rural districts were over-represented relative to their scanty populations, while our urban centers — especially our populous metropolitan area of Seattle and Tacoma — were astonishingly underrepresented. 'Malapportionment' — not equally portioned out — was the official label for this malady.

"By reason of this under representation in the legislature," Lois continued, "we in the urban areas have less than an equal opportunity in Olympia to address our pressing concerns."

I tucked that away for further contemplation.

The second issue this League group was studying was our state tax base — more specifically, tax reform. Probably not everyone's cup of tea, but certainly mine. As a home economist, budgets were central.

I enjoyed these inquisitive women. I was stirred by this study of serious issues and drawn to this non-threatening arena where any of us could ask questions, explore alongside other women, learn more. One meeting, and I was hooked.

Meanwhile, my children were progressing through the Seattle public schools, and Ken and I were increasingly appalled at the crowded classroom conditions we found there. Funds were never sufficient to provide decent teacher salaries or to create reasonable class sizes. We became involved.

Only after a Herculean effort were some of us parents able to convince the school board to earmark monies specifically to reduce the size of such core classes as freshman English — to less than 40 students per teacher, whereas the typical class size before was forty-plus.

Our sons were soon to enter high school. Seattle's public schools were still struggling. As parents who valued education, we were both concerned and perplexed. How was it that such a thriving, educated community, complete with university families and Boeing engineers, faced such horrendous funding short-falls within its schools? What was wrong with the schools' priorities? What was wrong with our district budget? And why were our schools so dependent upon a special levy on local property taxes for operating funds every year?

Our state's public schools were financed almost exclusively from local prop-erty tax collections, based on a 14-mill rate set by law. However, in recent years, as the population boomed, state property values hadn't increased as rapidly. So this 14-mill regular property tax levy never produced enough, and we had to make up the difference locally, through special levies. Under this tax struc-ture, then, Washington's school funds were grossly inadequate, especially in our urban areas.

> ## MILL
>
> A 'mill' in tax terms is one one-thousandth of a dollar, or one-tenth of a cent. The 14-mill rate mentioned here equals 1.4 cents per dollar, or a tax of $14 per every $1,000 of property valuation.

This under-funding of our schools was not a matter of a few mere budget percentage points or a threatened elective or two. Some school districts relied on the special tax levies for as much as 40 percent of their budgets. In our state, the annual levies were absolutely crucial to running our schools.

Yet funding our schools by special levy was an iffy prospect at best: In order to pass, according to state law, special school levies needed a 60 percent "yes" vote, rather than a simple majority of fifty percent plus one. And not only that, a healthy voter turnout was mandatory as well: At least 40 percent of the number who voted in the most recent election, be it general or primary, must vote in the special levy election in order for the measure to validly pass.

The political uncertainty of this method — requiring not just a majority of "yes" votes, but a super-majority of 60 percent, along with a strict minimum voter requirement — seriously worked against stable funding for the expanding body of students filling our Seattle public schools. Any time this special levy did pass, it was only good for a year and then a new levy campaign had to start from scratch for the following school year. Understandably, property owners weren't thrilled about our schools asking them — yet again — to agree to another hike in their tax rate.

This method made no sense to me. It was almost as though our public schools were considered an afterthought or luxury, and if we wanted a good education for our kids, we'd have to scramble and beg for funds.

In the hours beyond my family duties, I began to puzzle this through with late night phone trees to other mothers and large stacks of reading pre-dawn. In the daytime, of course, we were all still moms.

I had worked hard on several of Seattle's annual special levy elections, and even served as campaign chairman of one. Yet no sooner did one effort end than planning for the next must begin. Exhausting. And the funding term was gone in a blink. Ridiculous!

Inspired by the model of the League of Women Voters, I began to study the ins and outs of budgeting within our school district and state, and then I took a more active step: I began to broach the problem with elected officials. Public school funding became my passion.

I joined a network of Seattle women working to tackle our school woes. We organized a babysitting pool so we could all take turns trekking to the state capitol, two hours away, to lobby our legislators. Many of the active League of Women Voters lobbyists were also PTA moms, doing dual duty, like me. We were voters, citizens, concerned and hard at work.

Each Monday morning of the 1955 legislative session, a carload or two of mostly women traveled to Olympia to talk with our legislators. I usually went with my friend, Kitty Prince, who voiced the League's concerns about the ongoing inequality between our rural and urban districts — the need for redistricting and reapportionment. I went specifically to address school funding.

As Kitty and I made our rounds, seeking out and talking to our Seattle legislators, we were always cordially received. We found them generally polite, extremely attentive, largely sympathetic. They seemed to share our concerns, and really, they couldn't be nicer.

"You gals are doing a tremendous job," was a common remark. Another being, "I couldn't agree with you more."

Once we left our legislators, however, nothing happened.

Agreement was all fine and well, but we wanted action.

Kitty and I spent time in the visitors' galleries overlooking the House and Senate — watching the action on the floor, studying how the system worked, learning key players. What happened in the caucus rooms, however — behind two doors off to the side of the floor, one for Democrats and one for Republicans — we would never know. What we did know was that those two issues Kitty and I cared about so deeply never seemed to materialize in any work on the floor of the Senate or House, despite our local legislators' genuine sympathy.

After a few weeks of this watching, it became crystal clear to me that when our representatives went into those side rooms and shut the doors, that was effectively the end of their conversation — or at least their ability to act — on

CAUCUS

A closed meeting of members of the same political party or faction during which they decide group strategy and policy positions.

the problems Kitty and I so carefully laid before them. I realized if I were to have a real influence in the legislative arena, I'd have to be on the inside, on the other side of those floor-to-ceiling doors to the party caucus rooms. And that would mean taking citizen participation — my participation — in our representative government to a whole new level.

Not long thereafter, as Kitty and I conversed with Representative Ed Munro from the 31st District in the south part of Seattle, we finally heard the truth: "If you ladies ever want to solve this problem of school funding, Mary Ellen, you'll have to tackle Kitty's issue first, and redistrict the seats of this legislature."

Therein lay the rub: Redistricting. By now I knew the term well — its definition as well as its consequence. Rural over-representation in our legislature meant the government of our state naturally focused more heavily on rural concerns. At that time, the rural vote placed lower precedence on funding for our schools. Our accelerating urban needs fell on deaf ears in the legislature or, more accurately, into the laps of a hamstrung minority. Our urban legislators cared but couldn't help. So redistricting and school funding were inseparably entwined, and until those district lines were redrawn, Seattle's schools were unlikely ever to garner more support.

Kitty and I reported Rep. Munro's advice to the League, and as a League we agreed to increase our lobbying of the legislature to redistrict our state.

When we did, the legislature just ignored us.

Our state's Senate majority leader, Robert Greive, personified the problem we were up against when he suggested we were just little ladies dabbling in politics for our amusement.

"It's their plaything," he said to others of the League's push for redistricting. "They're looking for an issue that will catapult them into the public eye, where they can be somebody." [3]

But this was no plaything. What we were doing was our duty. Our state constitution required us to redistrict every ten years, but redistricting hadn't been done on schedule. We were trying to address the delinquency.

Redistrict? Hmmph! Our legislative leaders showed no interest. This was confirmed in May of 1955 during our state convention of the League of Women Voters. Keynote speakers Ed Munro and William S. Howard (a former Chief Clerk in the House of Representatives) talked to us about "Political Realism and Redistricting." They said it would take a citizen mandate to get the state redistricted and reapportioned. The legislature would never do it. Why would the current leaders – those in power – want anything to change?

Accordingly, that weekend when the League proposed that we write our own initiative to the people to redistrict our state, I was fully for it. Redistricting became an all-new passion of mine, in support of my first: School funding, both sufficient and stable.

By the fall of 1956, the president of the Seattle PTA, Beverly Smith, asked me to join its board of directors, based on my school levy work and my lobbying efforts in Olympia.

"Only if I can be legislative chairman," I told Beverly.

Knowing my passion lay in tackling the problem of our pathetic school funding, Bev agreed.

As Seattle PTA legislative chairman I tracked school-related issues in both the legislature and city council, reported these monthly to the board and recommended action. The issue of school funding, for me, remained foremost. I traveled to Olympia when the legislature was in session every other year, to deliver an urgent message to our legislators from the Seattle PTA: *Our schools are in a funding crisis! This is affecting our children!* I told them we must eliminate the need for these annual special levy elections, rationally address state financing and remove the nonsensical restrictions on funding for our public schools.

I then focused on taxes. I studied some more and came to a conclusion: The Washington State tax structure simply isn't broad enough to support the expanding needs of our swelling urban population. More money for education was only part of the need. Also inadequately funded in my community were public services, roads and pollution controls. Urban issues were crying out, but responded to with neglect. And the property tax, our primary local revenue source with its myriad restrictions prescribed by state law, could never sufficiently support our urban needs.

In the absence of sufficient legislative concern for these problems, the state budget was never adjusted to address them. Therefore, every time a local government needed to better fund *anything*, it had to put another measure on the ballot, stage another campaign, and go back to property owners to beg for another property tax increase by special levy.

As Americans, we glibly tout the concept of 'one man, one vote', and we assume it's a given, without actually understanding what this means. Marking a ballot certainly doesn't guarantee it. In order for every ballot to carry equal weight, our legislative districts need to be divvied up equally – equal numbers of people in each, whether within a city, county or state.

In 1956, my state's legislative districts remained ludicrously out of balance.

District lines hadn't been fully redrawn since the dawn of our statehood in 1889 — when the state's population sparsely dotted the rural landscape. The districts had never been redrawn to accommodate the growth of the big cities — in the west, Seattle and Tacoma, and the new Tri-Cities in the east — nor did our districts account for the large influx of urban residents in general after World War II.[4]

The population of our original rural districts remained relatively sparse, even shrinking in some spots, and yet our rural legislators had the same political pull as urban legislators who represented thousands of voters more. One man, one vote? Not in Washington State. For many parts of our state, 'one man, half a vote' was common. For city residents, the disparity was diluted even more dramatically — in one notable district, to one man, one-seventh-of-a-vote![5,6,7] Conversely, in our least populated districts, a voter's single ballot mark could equate to as much as one man, seven votes. Seven times more powerful! No wonder our urban concerns were getting nowhere...

Hopefully I can help change all this from my seat in this state House.

ON THIS DRIZZLY JANUARY MORNING in 1963, I'd stepped out early from the home my daughters and I have rented in the capitol city of Olympia. Ken and our girls, Nancy and Mary, planned to leave the house later, in time to find seats in the balcony, to view the opening ceremony.

Ken helped the three of us move into our rental house on Saturday, attended the opening party with me last night, and he'll stay through the opening session today, then head back to our home in Seattle to hold down the family fort and be with our youngest, David, now 12. Our older boys are already off to college.

Alone in the early morning rain outside our imposing legislative building, I faced down its guardian pillars and its gorgeously illustrated cast bronze doors, conscious that with my next footsteps I would begin my inaugural legislative climb. I counted my way up the stairs: 42 steps on the outside representing our status as the 42nd state in the union, and dozens more inside — gorgeous marbled steps up to the rotunda beneath the magnificent chandelier, a 25-foot master-piece, ornately sculpted in brass which hangs above from a hundred-foot chain.[8]

Beneath the chandelier lies a five-foot round replica of our Washington State seal — a perfect circle of brass embedded within the marble platform. Respect-fully, I walked around the large brass likeness of George Washington, who eyed me somberly, though his prominent nose is worn snubby from repeated footfall. Just seventeen marbled steps more to the House chamber, where I immediately detoured to the wings and entered the doors to my party's private caucus room for the very first time. I had arrived in caucus before 9 a.m., as required.

I assumed we had all been asked to arrive here three hours early simply to meet and mingle and to receive a few last minute tips. The caucus room was small, with a small, worn oak desk in one corner, an easel and flags in another, and facing these, forty-eight steel folding chairs set classroom style — this was hardly the imposing conference and caucus room I'd imagined when Kitty and I watched legislators disappear here in sessions past. I took a seat near the back.

At 9 o'clock exactly, chairman Don Eldridge called the caucus to order. After all of us were accounted for, our floor leader, Dan Evans, ceremoniously locked us in — locked the door, dropped the key in his pocket, and began to recount a series of strategic events conducted in utter secrecy the previous evening.

"Some of you may have noticed we left the welcome party early last night," Dan ambled — a rather serious and awkward public speaker, for such a handsome young man.

DAN EVANS' PATH TO POLITICS was, if not direct, at least kindled early. His family was among our state's early pioneers, and his grandfather served as a state senator shortly after Washington achieved her statehood. Dan's mother was politically enthused, and he himself intrigued. Therein lay the Evans political legacy.

Dan, however, determined to become a civil engineer. He earned both a B.A. and M.A. in engineering from the University of Washington. But at age 21, his family doorbell set in motion a divergent course. Dan opened the door that day to an invitation to attend a precinct committee meeting at a neighbor's house. At that same meeting, a spontaneous second invitation materialized — to fill a vacant seat for the county convention, to which Dan casually answered, "Sure."

The political bug bit him hard from that commitment on — from the perspective of making a difference via politics — though he continued to work full time as a civil engineer.

Now serving his third legislative term at age 37, Dan Evans has slowly climbed the ranks of legislative leadership, having gained the esteem of many legislators of both political parties last session while serving as minority floor leader — well spoken and thoughtful. Although... at one time, he so angered reigning House Speaker John O'Brien — by opposing a certain bill during the time of the divisive debate over public versus private power — that O'Brien actually broke the head off the gavel as he hammered Dan to silence. Mr. O'Brien had admonished Mr. Evans to "keep the debate at a high level," to which Mr. Evans had replied, "Mr. Speaker, how can we keep the debate on a high level when it's such a low level bill?" Down came the gavel, and off came its head, spinning out onto the floor of the House.[9]

The "we" Dan referred to this morning, while admitting to an early exit from our party last night, were four from among our caucus: Slade Gorton, Tom Copeland, caucus chairman Don Eldridge and Dan. He described the previous evening's events — the groundwork for what lies ahead for us today.

In a darkened parking lot away from the party, these men gathered quietly and headed for a remote rustic cabin down a long dirt road outside of town. There they met up with a second group and a discussion ensued in the darkened cabin, lit only by the flickering of a fireplace…[10,11]

MY OWN POLITICAL INVOLVEMENT started on a street corner in Seattle in 1956, rallying the support and signatures of passersby. Others were doing the same across our state. *Please sign here! We need your signatures!* Over and over, I explained the need to support our League of Women Voters' ballot initiative. *We need to redistrict and reapportion Washington State!* We wryly shortened 'redistricting and reapportionment' to 'R and R' — though the marathon hours we invested in this campaign resembled neither relaxation nor rest!

Months before, just after our state convention, when we in the League realized the urgency of drawing new state political lines — knowing our legislature would never do it — we wrote Initiative 199 to redistrict and reapportion our state. This initiative was spearheaded by the League's state president, Julia Stuart, who had recently taken the state League helm from Myrtle Edwards, who left the presidency to become a Seattle city councilman. Under the guidance of initiative coordinators Bettina Bailey and Lorraine Goldberg, we enlisted a broad-based team to help draw up our proposal, a team that included both Democrat and Republican state representatives.

We needed 50,000 signatures from registered voters to validate Initiative 199 and earn it a spot on the general election ballot for November 1956. We sought at least 70,000, for security, since historically two of every seven signatures tended to be invalid. I was among the dozens who volunteered to take Initiative 199 to the streets. This was an all-volunteer effort. Not one of us was paid.

"Equal representation is essential in any legislative body in order for it to make good laws for the people," I said, paraphrasing Congress' 1787 Ordinance of the Northwest, which was based on the primer Thomas Jefferson wrote for all those territories bent on achieving statehood. I picked up the rallying cry: "The voice of every citizen must be heard equally."

I studied redistricting as ardently as I'd studied school funding and came across these Jefferson views in a valuable book by Gordon E. Baker: *Rural vs. Urban Political Power.* Then I carried this founding father's words to Seattle's streets: "Equal representation is so fundamental a principle in a true republic that no prejudices can justify its violation — because the prejudices themselves cannot be justified." [12]

Rural versus urban power has been a common struggle across American states throughout the course of our American history. I was simply fighting the battle on local terms, together with my neighbors and friends. My city's schools and roads and lakes were at risk.

When Washington became a state, it based its constitution largely upon the Jefferson-inspired 1787 Ordinance, as did most U.S. states at their inception. Among my state's constitutional mandates is the specific requirement that the legislature redistrict itself and reapportion the state's population based on each federal census — every ten years.

But when I first stumbled across the concept and problem of redistricting in 1955, that task had never been fully tackled in our state… in more than sixty years! True, through thirteen different lesser redistricting bills, several new counties had been added and a few select district boundaries shifted in the state's early years. However, other than one partial redistricting in 1930 (mostly to reorganize the number of seats, rather than to actually reapportion the districts — and even then by an initiative of the people, rather than by the legislature itself) our state's legislative districts remained grossly unequal in population. [13]

Today, in 1963, they still are.

In the twenty-five years since that partial redistricting in 1930, our state's population had nearly doubled — from 1.5 to 2.8 million. More than 60 percent of that growth was in Western Washington's four metropolitan counties, basically the Seattle-Tacoma region. [14] In 1955, a comprehensive overhaul was sorely overdue.

Initiative 199 wasn't the League's first attempt to fix this. For years before my arrival, the League tried to convince our legislators to comply with our state's mandate to redistrict, but always to no avail. The League had launched one previous redistricting initiative drive in 1953, but failed to collect enough signatures to place it on the ballot.

In 1956, however, with the participation of a large group of citizens led by the League, we gathered more than 80,000 signatures by spring. We fought off a legal challenge in late August when a group of status quo legislators filed a court action against us to keep Initiative 199 off the ballot. They lost. Initiative 199 was indeed on our November ballot that year — our carefully researched and newly drawn redistricting.

It passed by a large margin: Washington voters wanted equal voice. Our redistricting and reapportionment initiative became state law.

The legislative leaders hated it.

While the League had drawn a near-perfect redistricting — both equitable and legal — and succeeded in passing it by a citizen vote, we had not fully considered the political implications of ignoring the status quo, of disregarding all those seats securely held by our state's many long-term incumbents. By our new mapping, which was numerically and legally fair, several of these long-term incumbents ended up sharing the same district and would have to fight each other for their seats. In fact, under our plan, only one major incumbent remained untouched.

Thus, under the guidance of Senate majority leader Robert Greive of West Seattle — the one who'd been annoyed throughout by our redistricting campaign, who'd denigrated us as "little ladies playing at politics" and "cutting out paper dolls" — under Senator Greive, Democrats and Republicans alike, in both chambers of the 1957 legislature, proceeded to amend Initiative 199 to the point of effectively gutting it.[15,16] By the time they were done, their amendments returned most of our districts to their old boundaries, without reapportioning our population at all.

Their major bone of contention was that we had drawn the new districts based on census tracts rather than precinct maps — not a relevant complaint, from a legal stance, but a handy tool they used with success to whip up confusion and doubt among those who knew less.

We, the League, filed a State Supreme Court appeal, charging that the legislature had basically repealed the people's vote. Our complaint didn't yield us much. State law says the legislature may not repeal or set aside an initiative of the people, but it can certainly amend it, and this is what the legislature had done, said a slim majority of the court. Our legislature simply amended Initiative 199 to revert it to most of the old district boundaries, and the court ruled 5-4 that Initiative 199 would stand as amended. The decisive fifth vote was cast by Justice Robert T. Hunter, freshly appointed from Ephrata in Eastern Washington — a rural, status quo region.

By the close of the 1957 legislative session, then, our districts stood largely where they were in 1955. What a disappointment, not only to me and the rest who worked so hard on Initiative 199, but to the solid majority of citizens who voted our new redistricting into law. After all that, our state was back to square one.[17]

Nor did the legislature address redistricting in its 1959 session, nor in 1961, even after the 1960 census figures had arrived. State leaders continued to blithely disregard redistricting. To those of us in the underrepresented areas, our state government didn't feel much like 'ours'. Urban pressures and problems were getting worse.

As Baker wrote in *Rural vs. Urban,* "A legislature which is able to stymie the enactment of popularly endorsed programs is hardly in a position to inspire public confidence. And in states where rural-dominated legislatures have refused to obey constitutional mandates to reapportion, it would hardly be surprising to find a large degree of public cynicism, disillusionment and apathy." [18]

I refused apathy. This was my government. The quality of life in my community was at stake. I continued to work within the local League and the PTA on behalf of our schools, while Ken juggled university teaching with his volunteer work with Group Health to assure quality health care. And while Ken rose within Group Health leadership, I continued to keep my eye trained on our state — it certainly wasn't functioning as our founders designed.

My husband and I erected makeshift desks in our bedroom, crafted from a 4-by-8 plank of plywood sawn in half: My work on one desk, Ken's on the other, two separate phone lines and our bedroom window in between. Determined to maintain a solid focus on our children and our family life, we most often used these mom and pop desks in the wee hours.

In 1959, I was elected president of the Seattle League of Women Voters, and in 1961 to a second two-year term. School and state problems were still on my mind.

That spring of 1961 I persuaded my Seattle board to pass a resolution asking the state League to write a second redistricting initiative. By that time I'd become much better versed in the adverse impact of malapportionment: Our legislature's inaction, inattention and inequality specifically hurt us in the urban cores. As a result of Initiative 199, our state's voters were better educated on the issue. I felt it was time to try again.

I suggested this to a number of other local League presidents. We took our resolution to the state convention in Yakima a few months later. The state League adopted our resolution as an action item, and the state president appointed my friend, Lois North, to chair the committee that would write another initiative to redistrict our state's legislative seats. We set off on another campaign.

In the meantime, for the first time ever, the federal court system intervened in redistricting. In March of 1962, the United States Supreme Court ruled in *Baker v. Carr* that the 14th Amendment to the U.S. Constitution — with its second clause that deals specifically with apportionment — provides a basis for legal action on malapportionment if states fail to comply. [19] U.S. Supreme Court backing — what a powerful boost to our newest campaign!

As president of the Seattle league, I planned to attend our national LWV convention in Atlantic City, New Jersey in the spring of 1962. I would travel there with others from our local League boards.

Not long before leaving, my next door neighbor, George Bechtel, leaned across the shrubbery between our adjoining yards.

"Say, Mary Ellen, do you have any interest in running for the state legislature?"

George was a good Democrat and a good friend of our popular 32nd District state representative, Wes Uhlman — another good Democrat. My school levy work and League roles must have been noticed.

"At this moment, George? Not really," I answered frankly.

"Too bad," said George. "You'd make a great Democrat rep for our district."

About a week later, just before leaving for Atlantic City, I received an unexpected invitation to lunch with three current state legislators, this time members of the state Republican Campaign Committee: Dan Evans, Slade Gorton and Joel Pritchard. Was I interested in running for the vacant legislative seat in the 32nd District on the Republican ticket?

Both parties wooing me. How interesting.

"We're familiar with your work on redistricting and taxation," said Slade Gorton, the GOP consultant for Initiative 211, our League's newest redistricting effort now under way. "We could really use your expertise, Mrs. McCaffree."

Dan Evans confirmed this: "We tried to fight the legislative changes to Initiative 199 in the '57 session, but we were such a minority, we were totally wiped out by the smart older guys and all the farmers."

I was flattered by the attention of this trio, but needed time to think.

"Think about it," said Joel Pritchard, reading my mind.

"Our state needs a new direction," said Dan. "We know you understand this in terms of our schools. There's a lot about our state that's simply not working well. We're looking for smart young people to join us and help us change course. But we can't do anything as a minority."

Their emphasis on action and progress piqued my interest. Their focus on redistricting as a logical starting place impressed me even more.

"I'll get back to you when I return from the convention," I told them.

I talked this over with Ken and then I left for Atlantic City.

One night in New Jersey, after an evening League session, the Seattle delegates were relaxing in my hotel room. I asked the group what they thought of my running for the legislature. To my surprise, they quickly endorsed the idea. Several offered to resign from my Seattle League board right then and there, in order to help me if or when I decided to run.

Once I was home, Ken and I convened a McCaffree family council: Should Mother run for public office?

My husband felt the issues at stake were worth it. And while he wondered aloud about the time it would require of me, he was also proud of the prospect. My kids, by then, were used to a busy mom.

The League, meanwhile, launched Initiative 211. This time we were armed

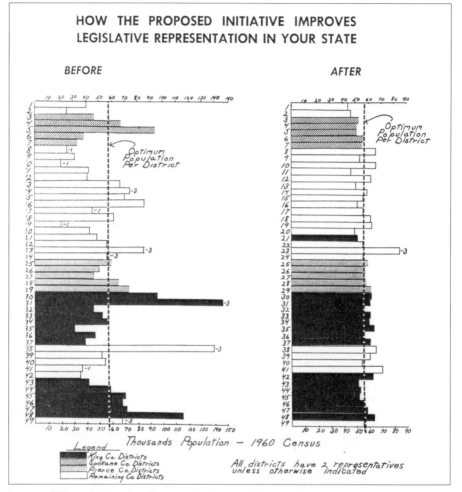

HOW THE PROPOSED INITIATIVE IMPROVES
LEGISLATIVE REPRESENTATION IN YOUR STATE

League of Women Voters chart illustrates how Initiative 211 would better balance legislative districts.

with hand-drawn 'before and after' charts to illustrate just how uneven our districts were at that time, and in contrast, how Initiative 211 would create greater voter balance.

On June 6, 1962, James Thigpen, a justice of the peace in the Seattle suburb of Auburn, privately filed a suit in the Federal District Court of Western Washington: *Thigpen v. Meyers* to enjoin our Secretary of State Victor Meyers from holding any further elections for legislators. Thigpen's charge? Our state's legislative districts were malapportioned, and according to the federal ruling in *Baker v. Carr*, this meant our legislature was violating the law.

Thigpen v. Meyers sought relief for this malapportionment, but the court took no action... yet. Aware that Initiative 211 was in the works, the court postponed a hearing on the matter until after the November election.[20]

On June 11, with the blessing of my family, and specifically my husband, Ken, I resigned as president of the Seattle League of Women Voters and immediately formed a McCaffree campaign committee. Operation Election.

Throughout the years, I've led many McCaffree family operations: Operation PhD, Operation Summer Canning, Operation Family's New Davenport Slipcover. When it came to projects, our family was a seasoned, effective team. This campaign was a most important project.

My campaign headquarters were housed in the daylight basement rec room of our home on 18th Avenue N.E. in Seattle's university district. Three among my League board — Virginia Bigelow, Elizabeth Harding and Myra Lupton — resigned, as promised, and started setting up downstairs, where we already had some office equipment courtesy of Ken's consulting practice.

The three Republicans who recruited me took some guff from our party's regulars:

"Are you guys crazy?"

"What do you mean you asked Mary Ellen McCaffree to run?"

"She's a Democrat, for heaven's sake!"

"If not a communist!"

"Isn't she head of that League of Women Voters?!"

This was a common misconception — that League members were all flaming liberals. I'm open-minded, to be certain, but hardly a commie!

The three who recruited me were admittedly progressive as far as Republicans went, with a steadfast focus on trying to set our state government to work on a big set of pressing problems. This Republican Party Campaign Committee of Dan Evans, Slade Gorton and Joel Pritchard didn't toe the conservative, right wing line of many of our state's mainstream Republicans. The trio defended me, stood up to the party regulars. There was work to do, they said simply, and I was just the sort of candidate they were looking for.

They asked a young Republican, Warren Guykema, to manage my campaign. Warren pulled in a long-time resident of the Wallingford neighborhood (in the heart of my district) to act as campaign chairman, which was terrific: Morrie Plummer was not only well-liked, but a home-based sales rep of stationers' goods who plied my campaign with all the pencils we needed. Together we recruited more committee members and set about our task.

With a mimeographed list of instructions on how to organize and run a campaign (authored by campaign veterans and brothers Joel and Frank Pritchard, who provided the same list to all the new candidates via the Republican Party Campaign Committee), we made homemade yard signs, developed homespun literature, and started doorbelling my 32nd District, house by house. This activity was optional for my children, but Ken and I doorbelled almost nightly. In the summer months we were occasionally joined by our college sons Jim and Chuck, plus Chuck's girlfriend Lee, and a wonderful crew of volunteers.

By the end of the summer, my family and friends and I had knocked on every door of the 105 precincts in the 32nd Legislative District, handing out my homemade brochure.

My knock on a door in Wallingford brought a gentleman with genuine concern.

"Hello," I said to him, "I'm Mary Ellen McCaffree and I'm running for the state legislature in your district."

"Mrs. McCaffree, why are you doing this?" he asked in all earnestness. "You should be home minding your children."

I told him why.

"Sir, I believe every citizen must do his or her share if our democratic form of government is to survive. I have studied our state government. I have some knowledge of our state's challenges and issues. I decided that it was my turn to serve."

Our eyes locked. He looked at me for a minute, then finally spoke.

"You really believe that, don't you?"

I looked right back at him.

"Yes, I do."

I not only knocked on doors, but attended coffee hours and district club meetings, always introducing myself as a Republican candidate for the legislature.

Incumbent Democrat Wes Uhlman was popular in our 32nd District. Wes was considered a shoo-in for one of the two House seats available. But the Democrats had no other "strong" candidate for the second seat — the vacant seat — and that's the one I sought.

The way this race worked, the two candidates who received the most votes in the general election would represent the district, filling its two seats. All nominees at this time essentially ran as a pack 'at large' — not specifically for Position 1 or Position 2 within a legislative district. A primary election determined the top two candidates from each party, both of whom would run in the general election. In the general election, however, if two from the same party garnered the most votes in the district, those are the two who would serve.

Among my Republican opponents in the primary election was Richard Ruoff, a four-term legislative veteran who had resigned his seat in 1959 when he moved outside the district boundaries (his property had been acquired for a new inter-state highway). Well known based on his previous eight years in the legislature, and therefore a formidable opponent, Mr. Ruoff beat me in the primary by 100 votes. And although my name would appear on the general ballot as one of two Republican nominees, that second place finish meant my road to capturing the second legislative seat was to be an uphill climb: I must compete with Richard Ruoff's name familiarity, while Wes Uhlman had one seat veritably locked up.

Fortunately for me, however, and unfortunately for Mr. Ruoff, these primary results were not the end of this matter.

Some Democrats (as well as some of my Republican colleagues, I suspect) successfully challenged Ruoff's certification to the general election ballot, based on the fact that he lived outside the district and had failed to re-establish residency here before he ran. This was in clear violation of the law. The court ordered his name removed from the general election ballot, to be replaced by the Republican candidate who'd polled third in the primary. Thus, my name moved to the top of the Republican ticket. This was a huge boost. My chance of election was increased immensely with the disqualification of Mr. Ruoff, for, except for Mr. Uhlman, I had beaten all of the remaining candidates in the primary election, Repubican and Democrat alike. Although I was in no way fully assured of that second seat, since I must come in no worse than second in the general election, I did indeed go on to win it rather handily in November, with the boost of that court decision and with a lot of hard work by my family and friends.

On the morning of her legislative victory, newly elected state representative Mary Ellen McCaffree is cheered by (from the left) her husband, Ken, and four of their five children: Mary, Chuck, Nancy and David. Jim sent best wishes from Wisconsin, from college.

Initiative 211, however, failed.

The League succeeded in collecting the signatures to get this second redistricting plan on the ballot, but the final vote on Initiative 211 was 441,085 against it and 396,419 for. This failure put redistricting back in the lap of the Federal District Court. Thus, on November 30, 1962, this U.S. District Court finally formally heard the case of *Thigpen v. Meyers*, with Mr. Thigpen as plaintiff, versus Secretary of State Victor Meyers and Attorney General John O'Connell. The League of Women Voters was listed as Intervener.

On December 13, the court filed its opinion: The legislative districts of our state of Washington are "invidiously discriminatory and hence unconstitutional" — consistent with the recent U.S. Supreme Court decision in *Baker vs. Carr.* However, rather than immediately righting the injustice, the court held back on a final decision, again: It would first give the 1963 legislature a chance to perform its constitutional duty and validly redistrict and reapportion our state's legislative seats.[21] This was the legislature to which I'd just been elected.

LOCKED INSIDE THE CAUCUS ROOM just after 9 a.m., I sat among the 48 newly elected Republicans, knowing we were still a House minority — by two votes — among the 99 seats.

Agreed, our position is more promising than last session, when the 1961 Republican legislators numbered only 41, or the session before that with only 33 from our party — the lowly number that both irked and spurred those moderate, progressive Republicans who recruited me. That 1959 number, a mere one-third of the House, first compelled them to build a better team.

Forty-eight is an improvement, but not enough. Democrats still control both our House and our Senate. And our two-term Governor Albert Rosellini is a solid Democrat as well.

We'll have to work miracles, or at least work hard to make any difference, I thought as I took a look at the legislators surrounding me in this caucus room.

Dan Evans resumed his narration of the events of the night before.

"It came to our attention that several Democrat legislators, six in fact, walked out of the statewide Democratic convention last spring, upset with their party's policies. You know the Democrat platform — the one we photocopied and highlighted during our campaigns."

"Half a million copies," interjected Joel, our campaign strategist. "Worked pretty brilliantly, I have to admit. We almost elected a majority here."

Slade Gorton picked up the narrative: "Bob Perry, one of those six dissidents who walked out on the Democrats last spring — he's a business agent with an electricians union in Seattle — well, Bob contacted me after the Democrat Caucus met in November and asked if we'd be interested in joining forces: Republicans and dissidents. This presented us with the possibility of building a different leadership team, even from our position of minority."

Joel jumped in again: "We figured with the half-dozen of them and the forty-eight of us, we'd have a majority if we agreed to work together. An odd group, to be sure, but it's amazing what you can accomplish if you don't care who gets the credit."

> **DISSIDENT**
>
> In politics, an individual who disagrees with the position or policies of the group to which he belongs.

"Politically," said Slade, "it's a coalition."

"Last night," said Dan, "we agreed — subject to your approval here in this caucus — to join forces with these six dissenting Democrats and form a coalition government."

Marjorie Lynch, another freshman legislator, leaned and whispered to me in her polite British voice, "What in the world is a coalition government?"

"A good idea," I whispered back. "They're proposing we team up with those dissident Democrats so we can assume the leadership of the House. I think we'd just carry on as if we're all from one party."

"Coalition... like coalescing?" Marjorie asked.

"Essentially," I replied.

Not everyone liked the idea.

Team with Democrats?

Why on earth should we do that?

Could we trust them? Did we have to?

I understood why, and asked a pointed question: "Is it your hope that by solidifying support from these six dissident Democrats — by forming this coalition and becoming the new House majority — it would give us the upper hand in creating a new redistricting?"

"Yes," several of our leaders said at once.

"We had a great election year," Joel said, "but we're still in the minority across the board — House, Senate, governor's mansion. This coalition is our best chance at a voice."

Republican candidates had received more actual votes this past election, but because of the way our districts are drawn, the Democrats still won the majority of the seats.

"If the Democrats draw our new districts this session, they'll likely gerrymander us all over again," Slade said. "It could sustain the imbalance in this state for years to come."

"Just as importantly," added Dan, "if we can gain the leadership of the House, it will allow us to finally set our government on a more moderate, progressive path. As we all know, this state's overdue for a new direction."

For the next three hours, the caucus members reviewed the ramifications, risks and gains of the strategic move. In the end, we nearly unanimously approved the coalition, with the exception of Dwight Hawley of King County who just couldn't stomach the thought.

"Then we're agreed. We will elect Representative William Day Speaker of the House."

Another outburst ensued:

"Big Daddy Day?"

"One of the Democrats?"

"Why not a Republican for heaven's sake?"

"Why not one of us?

The caucus leadership explained it to us: Dan Evans will serve as both the Republican floor leader and as our liaison to the dissident Democrats — the coalition leader, in effect — and those dissidents will basically conduct their own private caucus rather than working with the mainstream Democrats. Together with these six dissidents, we will drive House business. But it will only work if we elect the Speaker from within the coalition. If the mainstream Democrats have the Speaker's gavel, it would be enough to thwart us, even with the dissidents on our team.

"So, we will elect William Day Speaker of the House," Dan repeated, "but not right away. We need it to unfold like this..."

He then explained a carefully orchestrated series of votes, so as not to immediately tip off the regular Democrats. If they suspect anything in advance, they could throw any number of wrenches in the plan — procedural delays, arm-twisting of the dissidents, political 'cookies' from Governor Rosellini in exchange for votes for John O'Brien, the four-term Speaker considered a repeat shoe-in. We are reminded that the six dissident Democrats sit right now among their party in the

SPEAKER OF THE HOUSE

A House member elected to preside over sessions of the House, to serve as its chief administrative officer and as chairman of its Rules and Administration Committee.

Democratic caucus room across the way. Those dissenters are keeping this plan a secret, and we must too. It's imperative we keep everything under wraps until the designated moment.

"This is how it will work. Now listen carefully..."

WASHINGTON STATE HAS STRUGGLED for fair governance from the start. It took the people of Washington Territory thirty-six years to achieve statehood. By law, in order to convert a territory to a state, the U.S. Congress must pass enabling legislation. Territorial residents first petitioned Congress in 1852 to become the state of Columbia, which Congress rejected because the name might be confused with the District of Columbia. Among the requirements in 1878, when residents petitioned again to become the new state of Washington, was a minimum population of 125,000 territorial residents before Congress would even consider it. But in 1878 there were only 75,000 non-Native American residents in Washington territory. In the eyes of the United States government, the native population didn't count.

Thanks largely to some clever recruiting by successful Seattle pioneer Asa Mercer (the man who started the University of Washington in 1861, some 28 years before statehood), Washington Territory finally achieved the proper headcount. The determined Mercer toured eastern U.S. churches and towns to build Washington's citizen roster — to entice folks to Washington's jobs and husbands — and the territory's population gradually grew. On the heels of his recruiting tour, more than one hundred 'Mercer girls' arrived in Seattle, settling into marriages and jobs. By 1890, Washington Territory's non-Native American population reached 350,000. Congress passed the enabling legislation for statehood on February 22, 1889: George Washington's birthday.

Under this enabling legislation, our prospective state was required to hold a constitutional convention — to write a state constitution that would then be ratified by the eligible voters of the new state. Although the delegates to this convention had many disagreements, the group failed to resolve only two: First, should the sale of alcohol be prohibited here? And secondly, should women be allowed to vote? The delegates agreed to let the voters decide this final pair of sticking points during the election to ratify the new state constitution. And the voters (all male at that time) decided: Drinking in the new state should be legal, but they denied women the vote.

At that same special election on October 1, 1889, the voting citizens chose Olympia as the new state capitol and established the infrastructure for the fledgling government: A bicameral legislature with no more that 49 and no less than 33 members in the Upper House (the Senate) and no more than 99 members in the Lower House (House of Representatives). The elected representatives of each legislative district were to convene in January for 60 days every other year. Salary for those serving was set at $5 per month, with expenses paid during the actual time the legislators were in session in Olympia to do the people's business. This was a formula for a true citizen's legislature.[22]

In 1963, aside from a pay raise from $5 per month to $100, the structure of our legislature remains essentially the same — bicameral: Two houses that meet in 60-day sessions every other year, with 49 Senators and 99 Representatives.

Unfortunately, most of the original legislative district boundaries remain the same, too. We hope to add a new chapter to that saga.

AT TWO MINUTES PRIOR TO NOON, DAN EVANS unlocked our caucus door and we all filed out, lips sealed, through a throng of reporters who peppered us with questions. Remaining mum, we passed the columns of marble that separated the office hallway from the chamber, walked through the heavy velvet drapery and silently took our seats on the floor of the House, each of us committed to following our script.

We've maintained that same silent composure throughout this opening ceremony, as the roll call continues.

"Taylor."

"Present."

"Wang."

"Here."

"Wedekind. Wintler. Witherbee. Young."

All ninety-nine of us are present.

The Chief Clerk reads the final line from our Secretary of State: "In testimony whereof, I have hereunto set my hand, and affixed the Seal of the State of Washington at Olympia, this fourteenth day of January, A.D., 1963.[23]

"And now," announces the Chief Clerk, "the Honorable Robert T. Hunter, Justice of the Supreme Court of the State of Washington."

Justice Hunter approaches the podium, ironically the very justice who placed that final vote in the 5-4 decision in 1957 that allowed Initiative 199 to remain amended — and gutted — by the legislature. Such a devastating decision, after all our hard work.

"Please stand," says Justice Hunter.

We do.

"Raise your right hands."

We do.

"Please repeat the following oath, inserting your individual names, as appropriate."

I'm ready.

"I, Mary Ellen McCaffree, do hereby affirm that I will uphold the constitution and laws of the United States of America, the constitution and laws of the state of Washington, and that I will faithfully and impartially discharge the duties of the office of a Washington State Representative to the best of my ability."

My freshman term has begun.

While the sergeant at arms distributes our official certificates of election, I mentally survey those standing around me, and calculate the diversity of this legislative body that swears to carry out our shared work. We logically hail from every corner of the state, from Pend Oreille to Pacific County, from Walla Walla to Yakima to Bellingham. Ninety-nine citizen legislators from all walks of life: Two Spokane physicians — Dr. Al Adams, a well-respected orthopedic surgeon now retired, and the oversized chiropractor and dissident Democrat we hope to elect as Speaker, William 'Big Daddy' Day. Seattleite leaders Democrat John O'Brien, a certified public accountant, and on my side of the aisle, Republican Daniel J. Evans, the civil engineer. Don Moos, a wheat farmer and rancher from Edwall in the East; Charlie Moon, a veterinarian, and Jack Dootson, a former communist who engineers trains. An undertaker, a dentist, a commercial fisherman, several schoolteachers, an envelope manufacturer, and more than several attorneys — dozens, actually.

Of the eight women representatives, five of us call ourselves homemakers. The other three include public relations consultant Ann O'Donnell, Seattle research assistant Frances Swayze, and Ella Wintler, the popular retired schoolteacher from Clark County and a ten-year legislative veteran.

The King County Labor Council has two representatives here: One a staff member, the other an executive. Standing among us also are a real estate broker, a retail merchant, a man who'd spent more than a year in a Tokyo prison during World War II, and a war bride from England turned citizen of the U.S. — my charming desk mate Marjorie Lynch. Unfortunately, at this time in our state's history, there is almost no racial diversity. Sam Smith's is the sole black face. The rest of us are Caucasian.

How will this group of ninety-nine men and women reach consensus on anything? This is our challenge, and diversity will only strengthen it. Different ideas and discussion of issues by people from differing backgrounds — this, to me, is the backbone of a strong democratic, representative government.

After my swearing in, I am grateful to sit. But Bob Schaefer, the Democrat floor leader and an attorney, immediately rises from his desk in the front of the House.

"Mr. Chief Clerk," Schaefer says, requesting attention.

"The Chair recognizes Mr. Schaefer."

"I move that we adopt a resolution to make the Rules of the previous session the temporary Rules for the 38th Session."

Schaefer presents his formal resolution — a temporary measure generally voted in at the start of every session that allows the House to carry on business under old Rules until new House leadership is named, after which new business can proceed under newly formed Rules. This is routine, my colleagues instructed us this morning in caucus.

"All in favor say yea," the Chief Clerk directs us.

Aye! Yea! Yes! The standard variations of voiced assent.

"The motion passes," the Chief Clerk announces with a swift rap of the gavel.

Next, our party whip, Tom Copeland, stands to be recognized.

"Mr. Chief Clerk."

"The chair recognizes Mr. Copeland."

"I demand a Call of the House."

"All in favor say yea," the Chief Clerk directs.

We sustain the demand with our *Aye's*.

The sergeant at arms subtly nods, and his assistants close every single exit door surrounding us: Doors behind the rostrum, doors at the sides of the chamber, doors to the men's room, the cafeteria, offices, and finally the large heavy pair at the back. I knew in advance to expect this procedure, but was not prepared for the slight clutch in my chest as the massive bronze doors close all around us, followed by the finality of each audibly clicking lock. I tense.

As freshman, we've been schooled to expect these events, but schooling and their actual occurrence are two different matters. The Chief Clerk moves us along with yet another roll call, to determine whether anyone has left. Ninety-nine names later, we're all confirmed present.

> **WHIP**
>
> In a legislative caucus, the 'whip' enforces party discipline (i.e. proper votes on key bills) and assures party members are on the floor for key votes.

> **CALL OF THE HOUSE**
>
> A roll call of House members with all chamber doors locked, to determine who is present, who is excused. No House member may exit or enter the chamber under this 'Call'.

Tom Copeland, after being recognized again, moves that we proceed with House business under the Call of the House. We quickly approve his motion by a voice vote.

"So ordered," says the Chief Clerk with a bang of the gavel. "Nominations are now in order for Speaker of the House."

Representative Schaefer stands yet again, visibly assured.

"The Chair recognizes Mr. Schaefer."

"Mr. Chief Clerk, Honorable Judge Hunter, my distinguished colleagues, ladies and gentlemen: We are embarking today on the 38th Session of the Washington legislature…"

And then, wholly ignoring our delinquent redistricting, he tells us that our all-important business of providing services to the people within a balanced

1963 WASHINGTON STATE

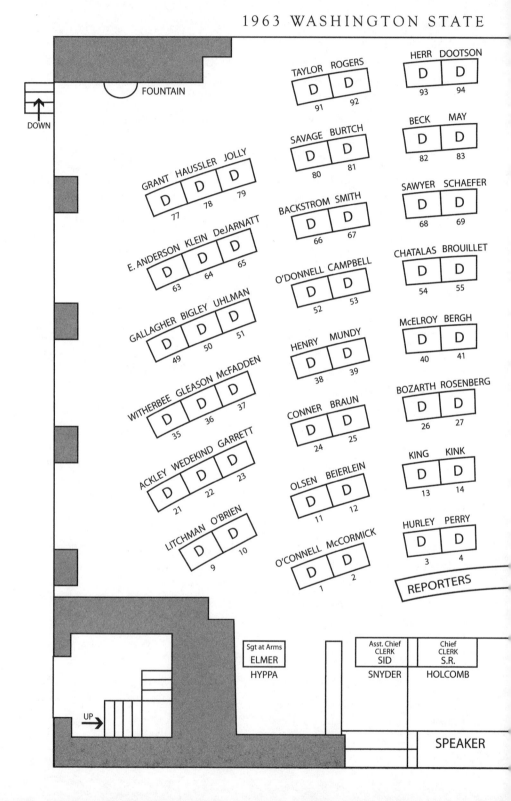

HOUSE OF REPRESENTATIVES

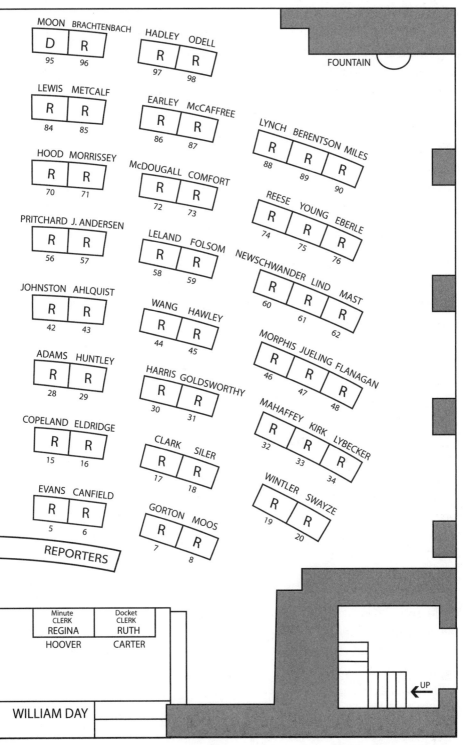

budget will require the strongest possible leadership, and reminds us the most important job in the House is that of Speaker.

"… I place in nomination the name of a man whom we have served under and respect, and who, you who have served with him know, has the qualifications to handle this position. He has served many years in this House. He has been elected Speaker four times. He has treated all of us with fairness and integrity…"

I focus, poker-faced, as requested.

"… At this time it gives me great pleasure to nominate, for the Speaker of this House for the thirty-eighth session of the legislature, Mr. John O'Brien. Thank you."

The Chief Clerk recognizes three more Democrats among those standing, all of whom add kudos on behalf of O'Brien.

Then Margaret Hurley, one of the six dissident Democrats, stands.

"The Chair recognizes Mrs. Hurley."

Mrs. Hurley greets the same honorable list of those present, then says:

"It is my privilege to take an important part today in the nominations for Speaker of the House. During the many sessions I have attended and participated in these elections, each has been exciting. Some have been tense. All have been important. But none has been more full of meaning for the people of our state than the choice we make today."

She notes that party affiliation is less important than doing the peoples' business with integrity and wisdom.

"I recommend to you a man whose wisdom, governmental principles, personal integrity, prudence and firmness of purpose qualify him to be selected as our presiding officer. He is congenial, fair in his dealings, and a man of his word. Let us recall for just one moment the oath of office we have just taken to serve the interests of the people of the state to the best of our ability. Your vote for a new Speaker will be your first opportunity to fulfill that oath.

"It is with every desire for what is best for the people of this state," she says, "that I place in nomination the name of William S. Day for Speaker of the House."

Bill Day, in his third term in the House, hails from a family of chiropractors in Spokane by way of Rockford, Illinois. This genial and respected WWII veteran weighs in at nearly three hundred pounds — hefty enough to give anyone's body an adjustment. Two more dissident Democrats add their accolades to the nomination of 'Big Daddy' Day.

Our party's assistant floor leader, Damon Canfield, stands for recognition.

"The Chair recognizes Mr. Canfield."

Again, we are all honorably greeted by Mr. Canfield who, with a less loquacious recounting of our legislative challenges, makes his nomination: "It is my privilege today to nominate a man for Speaker of this House who is eminently qualified and universally respected for his personal character, for his knowledge of political practices, for his leadership, for his dedication to responsible government. We are most confident that his actions will be guided by knowledge and not ignorance, with wisdom and not irresponsibility, with decisiveness and not weakness, always keeping in mind a program to promote the progress and the best interests of this great state of Washington. And so, ladies and gentlemen of this House, I give to you in nomination for Speaker the name of the honorable representative from King County, Daniel J. Evans." [24]

Representative Don Moos seconds the nomination: "He has the ability to lead this House of Representatives in the direction I believe this state wants to be led."

Once Mr. Moos completes his seconding remarks, Chief Clerk Holcomb surveys the floor of the House. No one else stands.

"There being no further nominations, the nominations for Speaker of the House are hereby closed," he says with a swift rap of the gavel upon the rostrum.

The roll is called, our votes tallied. In this House of ninety-nine representatives, fifty is the minimum majority vote required to elect a Speaker.

"The results of your voting are as follows," the Chief Clerk reports, "Representative O'Brien, 45. Representative Evans, 48. Representative Day, 6. The House of Representatives has failed to elect a Speaker. No one candidate has received a majority of votes."

But for the six dissident Democrats, our voting was straight down party lines.

The clerk calls the roll a second time. Again the House fails to elect a Speaker, with the votes distributed roughly the same, except that Day has picked up one vote from O'Brien. This was the movement we'd waited for.

As the clerk prepares for a third roll call, a subtle suspense builds on the floor among those of us in the know. I calmly eye my family members, who look on from the balcony without a clue. Also clueless are the O'Brien Democrats: They know those particular six among them are disgruntled and unsupportive, and are thus backing William Day. But the Democrat leadership never dreamed these six would seek collusion across the aisle.

I watch Dan Evans subtly signal Al 'Doc' Adams: *Now.*

This is it. The clerk begins the third roll call.

"Ackley."

And Ackley votes the same as he has twice before: "O'Brien."

"Adams."

But Adams doesn't. Doc Adams switches his vote from Evans to: "Day."

When they hear it, several members of the press in the press box up front whip around, as do a few puzzled Democrats.

This is our cue. When Doc Adams makes the switch, the rest of us — all the remaining 47 Republicans, or 46 rather, since Dwight Hawley still refuses to budge — have agreed to follow suit. We'll join the disaffected Democrats who have been voting to elect William Day all along. As the roll call continues and every Republican, except Dwight Hawley, now votes for Day, the press corps scrambles to keep track, the gallery squirms, and the regular Democrats stare gape-mouthed about the chamber, alarmed by each new Republican vote for: "Day."

So confident was John O'Brien of his re-election as Speaker, that he didn't assign himself a seat on the floor. He has been casually seated in an extra chair at the back of the House chamber throughout these proceedings, waiting to assume his 'given' House leadership post.

But halfway through this round of voting, the moment even Dan Evans changes his vote to William Day — O'Brien storms the center aisle and stops at Dan's desk, halfway down.

"I am sure we can work out a deal," O'Brien says to him.

From my desk I hear Dan reply: "School's out, John."

At the front of the House chamber, Democrat floor leader Schaefer catches on, and when it's his turn to vote, he abandons his vote for O'Brien and casts it instead for Day. How curious.

By the time the incensed O'Brien reaches the well of the House, the voting is done, signified by one more definitive rap of the gavel.

William Day has garnered 57 votes, a clear majority. He is thus elected our new House Speaker. A coalition government is born. Almost.

Representative Schaefer again stands for recognition.

"The Chair recognizes Mr. Schaefer."

"I move that the House do now reconsider the vote by which Mr. Day was elected Speaker of the House."

Tom Copeland rises. The Chief Clerk recognizes him.

"I would like to have a ruling of the Chair," says Mr. Copeland, "as to whether the motion to reconsider on this particular matter is a valid motion."

The Chair — in this case, the Chief Clerk, who will preside until the new Speaker takes over — responds:

"The authority of the Chief Clerk in presiding over this House of Representatives is limited to one thing. That is the election of a Speaker. A Speaker has been elected by your vote on the last ballot. Therefore, I do not consider that it is within the Chief Clerk's authority to consider any other business now that a Speaker has been elected. While the Chief Clerk is presiding, the motion to reconsider is declared out of order." [25]

The gavel comes down again. The matter is closed. The regular Democrats are stunned.

Chief Clerk Holcomb's rejection of this motion was written in advance, in anticipation of this very move. Si Holcomb was party to the previous evening's fire lit discussion that led to the formation of the coalition. He had also prepared a second speech — in case the election hadn't worked as planned.

> ## MOTION TO RECONSIDER
>
> This calls for the body to reconsider, at a time certain, the motion just voted on. It may only be requested by someone voting on the prevailing (winning) side.

The Chief Clerk now appoints Representatives Perry and Adams to escort Mr. Day to the rostrum, where the Honorable Robert T. Hunter stands again, this time to administer the oath of office to our newly elected Speaker.

John O'Brien, meanwhile, returns to his temporary seat. Defeated.

Speaker Day assumes the Chair to address us: "Mr. Chief Clerk, Honorable Judge Hunter and members of the House of Representatives: I am grateful as well as pleased with my election as Speaker of this great House. Grateful because of the honor which you have rendered to me and the confidence you have placed in me. Pleased because as Speaker of the House I shall preside during a period in which we must solve the all-important problems of living within our revenue and that of formulating a redistricting plan which has bipartisan acceptance of this legislative body and is responsive to the best interests of the people of this state."

It is music to many ears.

"Each of us, as a state representative, should serve the interests of his or her particular district as well as the interests of all the people of Washington. In addition, each has an additional responsibility to each member of this House to provide that member an opportunity to express his views, privately as well as publicly.

"To that end, let me now invite every member of this body, regardless of party, regardless of previous disagreements, to contact me and make his opinions known. While I am Speaker of the House, minority opinions and discussion will always be permitted; however, the ultimate decision on legislation must, as always, reside with the majority."

Many within our body understand his implications, relative to sessions past, and grasp his between-the-lines intent.

Speaker Day then calls for us to reexamine House Rules and procedures, to assure they're moving us forward, and that they promote effective legislation:

Progressive reforms, it sounds to me — of the nature Dan and Slade and more of us are promoting. The Speaker continues.

"Constitutionally, a legislative session is sixty days. In the past we have not always been able to abide by this constitutional requirement. I am asking that each of you assume a portion of the responsibility which will lead to our successfully accomplishing our work in the time allotted."

Each day we're in session costs state taxpayers.

The Speaker next addresses efficient committee work, laying the groundwork for the streamlined committee structure our leaders have in mind.

"The initial examination, rejection or passage of each measure introduced in the House is a task which of necessity must be performed by committee. It is essential to the orderly procedure of this body that bills without merit are rejected on the committee level, while important and necessary legislation be quickly passed upon and brought before the House for vote. This labor is of prime importance and requires the thoughtful consideration of each committee member. Because of the large number of committees which convene in this House, each representative must necessarily serve on more than one committee. However, considering the importance of committee action, it is obvious that committee assignments must be limited, in so far as practical, to permit each legislator sufficient time to devote to his respective committee assignments.

"In this brief acceptance speech, I have attempted to outline for your exam- ination several of the problems which, as state representatives, we must all consider. Each day of the session will bring before you issues of importance which will need your individual decision. It is for this reason that I am asking each of you to put aside any personal ambitions and partisan causes which you may have, and devote your time and efforts to a successful, responsible, and productive legislative session."

We applaud our new Speaker. At least most of us do.

As a component of his House leadership, the Speaker controls our individual voices on the floor — he has the sole ability to recognize, or ignore, any request to speak. He also has the power to shut off individual microphones, or never to turn them on at all.

Dan Evans stands: "Point of personal privilege, Mr. Speaker."

In his first act as Speaker, Bill Day acknowledges the man who helped put him there.

"The Chair recognizes Mr. Evans."

Mr. Evans begins: "I first would like to congratulate the new Speaker on his victory and on his speech, because I think it bodes well for the House of Representatives. I would like to address myself, however, more particularly to the members of this House and those in the galleries and those in the press, because we are embarking on a new era, a really new era.

"As most of you probably don't know, the Republican party during this last election for the House of Representatives polled over fifty-three percent of the popular vote in the state. Unfortunately, we elected only forty-eight out of ninety-nine Representatives, but I think it has been obvious since the last election, and certainly it's been obvious in the last few days, that the Democratic Party was split and could not by themselves elect a Speaker. Rather than sit here for many days, as we could have, in a deadlock, we felt that it was our responsibility to take some action that would organize this body and set it on its course."

I can detect John O'Brien's disposition.

Dan Evans continues, addressing Republicans and Democrats alike.

"The decision wasn't easy. We had three choices open to us: To sit still and hope we would have some support from the other side of the aisle to elect a Republican Speaker, or to vote for either of the two candidates on your side of the aisle as may have been presented here today. May I say clearly and most emphatically that the decision was not made on the basis of personality. John O'Brien has served this House long and well, and he is a good presiding officer, but the decision ultimately did not rest on personalities. The decision rested on a choice we had to make between two programs and two courses of action. We had to make our choice on the basis of the one we thought would help bring the principles and the ideals that we as Republicans have to the floor.

"In making this decision, we, as you know, voted for Mr. Day. Going back a little bit, maybe the Democratic convention this year was a pretty good deciding point. We had to make a choice between you who walked out of the convention, and those who adopted a platform we felt was radical and in the control of a radical element. We couldn't buy that kind of principle and that kind of idea. We had to go to those who had the courage to walk out of a convention like that, rather than those who either advocated or tolerated the type of platform that the Democrats adopted this spring."

The capitol press corps is scribbling madly. Mr. Evans continues.

"While this choice was difficult and has many thorns in it, our future course isn't very difficult. Our future course is to provide — and this goes for every member of this House — the best government we can and the best laws we can for the State of Washington. And we on this side of the aisle will advocate the principles that we hold dear — that individual liberty is the cornerstone of our democracy, that the local government which is closest to the people can best serve the people, that fiscal responsibility is not an end in itself but a means to an end, a means to give our children a government that is free from debt caused by the spending sprees of their fathers.

"These are the principles we believe in, that we will advocate, and that have a chance of being successful with the Speaker and the organization that we have just elected. To this end, we will devote our talent and resources, and we hope we will finish in sixty days."

Another round of House applause, with some more vigorous in expressing their approval. Speaker Day recognizes Mr. O'Brien, who rises to speak:

"Mr. Speaker, fellow colleagues, ladies and gentlemen: This is a very unusual position, for the presumably majority party to be in a minority position. We think it is a very bad mistake for the Republican Party to go to this low type of political maneuvering. In my opinion, it is absolutely politically dishonest and immoral. After all, we come here to Olympia to do a real job. There should be a code of ethics, even among legislators."

The Speaker interrupts him to admonish: "Mr. O'Brien, let's not impugn the motives of anyone."

House Rule 30, a few of my colleagues mumble quietly.

Mr. O'Brien continues: "I am not impugning anyone's motives. I am giving my viewpoint. First of all, I want to thank all the people on our side of the aisle who were so loyal. You have not only my admiration, but you have the admiration of all *thinking* Democrats in the State of Washington, and you can well be proud, because I think a price was paid here today and we are going to suffer by it."

The press just keeps on scribbling.

"There is no question about it in my opinion," says O'Brien. "Good government in the state of Washington has been hindered and handicapped, and the blame and the whole responsibility is going to be placed on the Republican Party. I, for one, will help in doing this. We could have had a very harmonious session. You people and I have in the past taken care of our differences.

"I feel very sorry for the people who have supported me and who were planning to take a very active part in this legislature. It was rightfully theirs to have important committee chairmanships, and now this isn't going to happen. For myself this doesn't mean too much. You people have been kind to me in the past and have given me all the honors any legislator could possibly have. I have been in the minority position in the past and I rather enjoyed it. When you are up on the rostrum you can't say very much. You have to be impartial and fair to everyone, but down here we can point out the deficiencies in your proposals.

"You talk about our political platform. Well we didn't like your platform either, and I can tell you people right now you are in for the most interesting sixty days you have ever had. We are going to do it on a high level. We are not vindictive about this. You have asked for the responsibility and you are going to have it.

"In closing I want to say to the people of our side, I am very sorry for what happened here today. We had our caucus. We had the contest for Speaker. We thought we had resolved it. However, during the last couple of sessions, we have had people on our side who just didn't feel they belonged to our party, even though they filed on the Democratic ticket. I believe there is one thing we should do here this session, Mr. Evans, and that is to get an oath of loyalty from each and every person who filed on a respective party position that they are going to abide by party principles and party caucuses. I think this is something that is most important. If you don't, it is going to destroy the two party system."

Now I am scribbling, too, rebutting John O'Brien on paper and in my head. Party loyalty? What about loyalty to all the citizens we represent? I, for one, consider myself an independent thinker. Both parties recruited me, after all. And my district is split with voters from each.

John O'Brien continues.

"We are going to have people file on the Democratic ticket who will do nothing but plan to destroy the party. One gentleman in particular has been planning for months that the Democratic party had to go. He ran on our ticket and he was successful here today, and I certainly think next time, Mr. Robert Perry should file on the Republican ticket. He doesn't belong on our ticket.

"I wish to thank each and every one of you who was so loyal not only to me but to our Democratic party. We are extremely sorry you people across the aisle saw fit to do this thing. Maybe you will regret it. Mr. Speaker, as minority leader, I will say let the chips fall where they may. Thank you very much." [26]

> **'THE AISLE'**
>
> In a legislative chamber, a center walkway that separates legislators by party affiliation.

Spoken like a spoiled child, in my estimation. I wanted to stand and address the members of the House, but didn't dare. By an unwritten rule, for the first three weeks of the session, freshman legislators are seen and not heard. My mental response to John O'Brien remains private:

Mr. O'Brien, there is nothing immoral or dishonest about forming a coalition government. It is a political strategy that is used often. Coalition governments are formed as a strategy of moving the governmental process forward so that the body politic will not remain in a deadlock over who is in control. Coalitions are not used by governments within the United States as often as in other countries. But this is a very legitimate political strategy, though I realize it is obviously a move that took most of your legislators by surprise.

Also, Mr. O'Brien, party loyalty is an honorable desire for any group. However, loyalty must be earned and the rights of the minority must be respected. No one can dictate loyalty in a free society. We may prefer party loyalty, but party leadership has to earn the loyalty of its individual members.

None of my thoughts travel beyond my own head.

We proceed to elect the veteran Ella Wintler as Speaker Pro Tem, then extend the term of S. R. Holcomb as Chief Clerk, and select Sid Snyder as our Assistant Chief Clerk. After approving some routine housekeeping resolutions, we recess for the day with one last resounding bang of the gavel. My colleagues and I immediately head for the caucus room.

I smile at my family before disappearing through the door.

"Congratulations, and thank you," Dan says to us, once we've taken our seats.

"Thank you for your cohesiveness out there on the floor," adds Tom Copeland. "Our coalition has passed its first test."

"Now what?" several ask at once.

Slade Gorton fields the question: "First and foremost, we must pass a fair and equitable redistricting."

I could deliver these exact words in my sleep, so familiar am I with this task.

"This means a redistricting that not only gives all citizens of our state an equal voice in the operation of this government, but also one that will feasibly give each party a chance to win a majority in either or both houses of the legislature."

"Sounds complicated," someone says.

Redistricting is the ultimate political task, I think to myself. It is honestly the only truly partisan issue of any state legislature. All other issues are the peoples' issues, but this one affects the parties. Done properly, it purposely tries to keep our two-party system balanced and strong.

"There is no more political undertaking," Slade continues, echoing my thoughts. "Fortunately, we have the moral high ground. Where the Democrats' incentive is to protect their districts, their seats, their majorities and to maintain the status quo, we just want a map that's fair — one that will provide us a break-even opportunity."

"What do you mean?" several ask at once.

"Ideally, a good redistricting and reapportionment law will create districts where elections can go 50-50… where either party stands a chance to win, and statewide, either party can feasibly capture a majority."

Several emit audible assent. Others silently nod. Some wonder aloud why we don't want to dominate.

Dan shifts to the issue of shaking up the status quo regarding a number of state policies that most of us find unacceptable. Our state needs a more moderate, progressive path, he repeats.

"I'm sure most of you have a list," he notes.

"School funding," I suggest as a start.

And the caucus list grows: Road repairs. Improved infrastructures — utilities and highways. Tax reform to help out our urban communities. Protection of our environment. The sewage spilling into Lake Washington. Better health care. Parity in pay for women…

"Do you think the coalition will work?"

"Do you think we can actually accomplish any of these?"

"How are we going to pull this off?"

We're ready to work, but we want to know how, within this new coalition.

Dan responds truthfully: "How will it work? We're not exactly sure, but we believe it's worth the risk. For one thing, the majority decides who will chair each committee. Under this coalition, we'll see to it Republicans occupy all those committee chairmanships important to our goals, starting with Constitution, Elections and Apportionment — the committee that handles redistricting. Slade Gorton has agreed to chair that committee. Mary Ellen McCaffree will help him out. Both are marvelously experienced and knowledgeable on the issue of redistricting and reapportionment."

I'm pleased my colleagues believe I can contribute immediately on something so key.

Tom Copeland explains some of the new House Rules he'll propose take effect immediately. These will provide a more organized and transparent daily agenda that should move House business forward much faster, and provide the public easier access to our deliberations. The lack of advanced scheduling for committee meetings and hearings, and the erratic planning rampant during the O'Brien years would no longer exist.

Our caucus finally adjourns and some of us head down to the dining room for a late lunch. As I wind my way down the narrow marble-cased stairway to our private cafeteria tucked away beneath the House floor, my head swims with the tasks that lie before me — all surrounding redistricting and reapportionment.

"You certainly are preoccupied," says Marjorie Lynch as I somberly scoop at my ice cream.

"I am," I apologize. "It's redistricting. I've been at it eight years. Hard to believe I'm still in the middle of it."

"It's a pressing problem, though, is it not?" she asks.

"It is." I take my last bite. "There's nothing else to do but roll up our sleeves and see if maybe this time we can make it happen."

Citizens have pushed for our state to redistrict and reapportion during the past eight years. It has been citizens, with the help of our legal system, who finally brought the Washington State Legislature to this brink, by confining our elected representatives within a 'box' where, before we can exit, we must comply with our state and U.S. constitutions and redistrict or face the judgment of the court. I'm boxed in with the rest, but at least I'm here with some compatible colleagues. I'm glad to have discovered such a like-minded team.

A representative democracy doesn't work effectively with the efforts of just one man — or even a few dedicated men and women. It depends on all of its citizens — and those who represent them — working together.

I've finally made it behind the caucus doors and into the center of legislative decision-making, only to find myself locked inside that 'box' I helped to create. The key out is redistricting... en route to my final destination, school funding.

My journey is off to a promising start: Our coalition holds the gavel.

CHAPTER TWO

COALITION
REACHING ACROSS PARTY LINES TO BREAK A DEADLOCK

‿

Risk-taking is part of the political process,
and the decision to form this coalition carries enormous risk...
Our leaders convinced us the risk is worth it.

Risk-taking is part of the political process, and the decision to form this coalition carries enormous risk for all of us within it. If we fail — if the six dissidents buckle, return to their caucus and return the gavel to the Democrats — then what little voice and clout we have as a minority party will likely be dashed by those across the aisle now licking their wounds. As for the dissidents, should this coalition dissolve they'll likely be shunned, their voices silenced within their party. If the coalition fails, all of us will fare far worse than if we'd never attempted this 'coup' in the first place.

Our leaders convinced us the risk was worth it, and I agree. My children's under-funded schools drew me inside the redistricting dilemma, which in turn led me to this legislative seat. I am willing to risk failure for the chance to work on our state's rusty gears — to set it into a more effective mode for my community and for my kids. But the first step has got to be redistricting.

My adrenaline has surged since the moment I woke. With yesterday's fireworks behind us, surely today we can now begin to legislate.

LAST NIGHT AT OUR FAMILY DINNER TABLE, conversation flowed, centered on my ceremonial first day that ended in a volley of bitter verbiage.

I know from experience that a view of legislative activity from the balcony doesn't deliver the whole story, even with the eagle-eye viewing I had done as a citizen lobbyist. Those faces yesterday — all those visitors packed snug in the balconies overlooking the floor, expressed perplexity and tension as yesterday's drama unfurled, my daughters and Ken among them. I know that much of what Ken and the girls witnessed publicly was the result of decisions we'd arrived at behind closed doors. Now, having been privy to yesterday's subplot behind those locked caucus doors, I am able to tell them with certainty how much more does transpire beyond what they saw. And while caucus deliberations are confidential, I was happy to explain to my family events on the floor — along with their consequences — as I understood them.

Ken consulted Webster's in response to a tumble of questions from the girls. *Coalition: When two or more political parties temporarily join together for a common goal or purpose.* In our case, our common goal is to first dislodge a leadership too often deaf to the majority of voters, and then to use our majority status to shape a new redistricting and some functional House reforms.

Defining 'coalition' is one thing. Making it work? Altogether another. How will this coalition function? More importantly, will it function at all? Considering those few frustrated, powerful Democrats, will this coalition endure? As a family, we had explored the possibilities.

Now, this morning, as we set off on our respective paths, these questions weigh heavier on my mind than on Ken's or the girls'.

Day two has dawned bright but bitterly cold, *mimicking our political climate*, I muse as Mary and I shiver across the frosty capitol campus. Brilliance and chill reflects the duality in our newly organized House: The sunny prospects of the coalition versus the icy backdrop of House Democrats as they turn a cold shoulder based on yesterday's events — a coldness borne of disappointment, frustration and shock.

Half-skipping along beside me, only partially to ward off the cold, Mary will begin her 'career' today as a legislative page.

"Excited, honey?"

She grins in reply. Her infectious smile ought to serve her well.

Meanwhile, Ken and Nancy are off to Olympia High, where our oldest daughter will brave a new school for this winter term her junior year. Then Ken will head back to Seattle — to the university and to David, who stayed the weekend with our friends Mark and Mildred Swoyer while our female branch of the family settled in at the capitol. For the next two months, our Seattle home on 18th Avenue will convert to a pad of bachelors.

The capitol dome glistens in the blinding winter sunshine. Mary and I round the corner to the legislative building back door, and run smack into Slade Gorton.

"Congratulations," he says to Mary. "You picked a lively session to be a page."
She dashes off to meet up with the dozens of other teens here to do the same.
"See you on the floor!" I call after her. She flashes one last smile.

"Warned you, didn't I?" Slade says as we enter the building.

"And how."

Yes, he had warned me fully in advance: My first day would be dramatic.

"Will it work, Slade? What happens next?"

The same questions flood as before. We enter the elevator. Slade is frank:
"It's a novel structure for all of us. To be honest, we had no idea whether we'd
pull this off—the coalition, Bill Day. It's an enormous risk, politically. No doubt
about it. But we agreed it was worth a go… now we'll just have to see if we
were right."

We join our Republican colleagues in caucus. For the balance of the session,
this room will be our private domain. The Democrats have theirs, as well. And
as for the dissidents—those six will caucus separately, in the office of Speaker
Day. Dan Evans, our go-between, will shuttle between the coalition groups.

While my colleagues share many of my same gnawing questions about the
odds of the coalition, combined with our daunting redistricting task—first
things first. And our first order of business is to get our House in order,
quite literally.

The initial task of this legislative body—this session and every session—is to
establish permanent House Rules: Procedures by which to operate the House.
The task of establishing these Rules traditionally falls to the majority party. Ordinarily the majority begins preliminary Rules work on the heels of the election,
several months before the session begins, by making amendments to the Rules
of the previous session which will then become permanent Rules. Ordinarily,
the House can get right down to business right from the start, with the Rules
already written and agreed. But 24 hours ago, our majority position was just a
daring uncertainty. Our coalition—the new majority—now has its hands full
with Rules to write. Our leaders must act fast.

Caucus chairman Don Eldridge welcomes us all to day two.

"We wanted a chance to steer this state in a new direction," he says. "Well,
this is it. Our job, my job, is to make sure you're all in the loop and up to speed.
Please—especially you freshmen—please feel free to voice your questions and
concerns in this room. OK? On the floor, most of the activity at the start will
be led by Dan, Tom and Slade from this caucus. And of the dissidents, Bob
Perry and Margaret Hurley will lead the way. All right. Time for today's nuts
and bolts. Dan?"

Dan explains some specific procedural improvements, beginning with

DAILY CALENDAR

A daily listing of bills to be considered in committee and on the floor, as well as the time and location of committee meetings and public hearings.

committee work: Under our new leadership, House committees will meet on a consistent schedule in consistent locations. We'll have a daily calendar of legislation so we can study proposals in advance, and we'll also receive advance notice on bills of particular constituent interest so folks from our home districts can plan to attend hearings or to otherwise play a role, have a voice.

From the nature of these proposals, it is easy to infer this body was previously less organized. I'd heard about the scrambling in sessions past—committee meetings and locations scribbled and posted in the House at the start of each workday, legislators clamoring to scan the postings, then frantically pulling together materials, rushing to find the right meeting spot, hoping their multiple committee assignments would somehow not overlap and that they'd know enough to be active in crucial decisions.

As for constituent participation, the public was welcomed to visit any time, but pre-planning for a particular action or concern? Nearly impossible, even for those who lived nearby. And out-of-towners were largely out of luck. I was familiar with this from having lobbied for money for schools.

"Beginning today," Dan says, "we hope to create a more effective, efficient House."

He spells out what to expect 'out on the floor' in the House chamber during today's session.

"After opening formalities, much like yesterday, we'll dispense with the Journal reading and consider amendments to the House Rules. At this point, our coalition colleague, Margaret Hurley…"

Several squirm.

"Problem?" Dan asks, taking note. Several pose questions at once.

"Do you think they'll stay with us, those six?"

"Do you think they'll fold?"

"Aren't the Democrats putting on the pressure?"

"Can we trust them?"

Dan laughs and assures us, "These are six of the toughest Democrats you'll ever meet. No one's going to talk any of them into anything they don't want to do."

He continues to describe the coming morning session: "Mrs. Hurley will introduce an amendment to Rule 59, proposing that we reduce the number of standing committees from 31 to 21. We're in the process of refining that new committee list right now."

Slade takes over.

"The number of committees from 1961 honestly stretched us all too thin. That committee number kept climbing under John O'Brien, possibly to mollify his many colleagues who sought out leadership perks. We've reviewed the old committee list, determined which seem redundant, combined others and feel we've arrived at an optimum structure for House committee work. True, there are fewer chairmanships to dole out, and that will disappoint any Democrats who came to this session with expectations. Nevertheless, we will propose that half the committee chairmanships do go to the Democrats…"

More squirming but no outright guffaws. The tone of the room seems classy, cooperative, conciliatory and earnest. I am comfortable in this midst.

"Being magnanimous across the aisle is not required of us," Joel said. "We don't have to offer those chairmanships, but it's a good faith gesture. It could lead to a more effective session, and that's our goal — to get to work on the challenges facing our state."

I watch Joel scan the room — the diplomat and team builder among us. Always sizing people up, calculating relationships, estimating where he can be of help.

On one hand, this caucus features a number of long-time legislators who profess less interest in reform, more complacency with the status quo. Their attitude is, *What's all the fuss?* They listen to all of this politely, but without much fire.

On the other hand, the thirteen freshmen among us lack familiarity with last session's mechanistic glitches. We're still getting our legislative bearings, and again, we're logically less on fire compared to the leadership group. Our role is primarily to listen, support and learn.

The definite heart and pulse of our caucus are the handful of determined young leaders bent on making a big difference and setting our legislative gears in productive motion. Dan, Slade, Joel, Don Eldridge, Tom Copeland. This is the team I've consciously joined.

"We're aiming for more transparency in what we do, and for more constituent access," Dan continues, "so we can govern on behalf of the entire state — bring the whole state into the process. Even those wheat farmers."

This he casts at Tom Copeland, born and raised on a Walla Walla wheat farm. Tom wrote the bill to create the Washington State Wheat Commission during his freshman session, six years back. Now he's our caucus 'whip'.

Dan continues: "Tom will distribute those bill calendars I mentioned. Once we get underway, look for them on your desks at the end of each day. Slade?"

Slade takes over to reiterate one of our primary jobs these next 59 days.

"If we're to have a chance to see to it Washington State is equitably redistricted, we need to work together, and hold together, until we finish. Forming this coalition was a risk, an undeniable challenge, but one we hope will be well worth it... for the future of our state. Remember, we formed this coalition in a large part because of redistricting."

Then he nods to me.

"Freshman Mary Ellen McCaffree will be my first-rate first lieutenant in this effort. As most of you know, this former president of the Seattle League of Women Voters is well versed in the complexities of redistricting—an eight-year veteran, in fact, with two redistricting initiatives under her belt. Don't let her quiet demeanor fool you. She's a hard worker and knows her maps! And Don Moos will oversee the rural areas.

"I encourage you to talk with any of us as this awesome undertaking unfolds. Our goal, as you know, is to craft a compromise redistricting bill."

"Compromise?" several ask. "Why?"

"By compromise, I mean that it be fair to Democrats, fair to Republicans, and fair as well in the more dispassionate eyes of our courts."

Joel adds: "It's simple. We want redistricting to reflect the vote. We're not trying to turn this state around to where it's to our advantage—we're just trying to reflect the vote. That's our pitch."

The room agrees. Dan draws us back to the current day's work.

"Bob Perry will lead much of what happens today on the floor, assisted by Mrs. Hurley. As many of you know, she and Bill Day have worked together a long time, both being from Spokane."

Joel chimes in again: "Those of you new to this, follow along as best you can. I'll come round to your desks when I can, especially to you freshmen — make sure you're keeping up. We're happy to answer your questions quietly on the floor, if possible, aren't we? Or else when we reconvene back in this room."

By 11 a.m., the new committee list isn't ready yet.

SHORTLY BEFORE 11, I'm at my House desk in the back of the chamber, back with Marjorie Lynch and that trusty marble-bowled water fountain. The morning caucus has inspired me. I've always preferred 'doing' to talking, and look forward to getting to work—for our state, my kids, our schools and my constituents.

Marjorie and I consult our little red books—our official "Legislative Manuals" personalized with our names stamped in gold on the front. Indispensable for any legislator, but particularly freshmen, this manual lists members, procedures, and most important to me today, the formal order in which House business proceeds on the floor. Chief Clerk Si Holcomb has written an introduction: *Parliamentary rules are designed solely for the uniform, orderly and expeditious conduct of deliberative bodies…* [1]

My League experience introduced me to the practice of parliamentary procedure and all the tidy pleasures inherent in a well-run group. We look orderly enough here, all the men in dark suits and white shirts — always white shirts, no stripes or colors — and a tie. And we women in suits or dresses, but never slacks and never pant suits. The dress code here is unwritten, but by history firm.

While Marjorie thumbs through her book and finally finds Rule 30 on 'Impugning of Motives', I consult Rule 10, 'Order of Business', and follow along:[2] At 11 precisely, Speaker Day gavels the House to order. The clerk calls the roll — all present. The flags come forth with the color guard. A local Methodist minister leads us in prayer. The First Order of Business is complete.

The Second: Reading of the Journal of the preceding day. As the clerk begins, Mrs. Hurley stands for recognition, is so recognized, and moves that the reading be dispensed with and the Journal ordered to stand approved. This is standard procedure, precisely as we've been tutored. By vote, we approve the Journal and skip the reading.

Mr. Witherbee demands a Call of the House. I'm better prepared this time for all the closing and clicking and shutting in. By the time the last of the doors is locked, we've all returned to the chamber but for three. Their absence is confirmed by this next roll call. Mr. Gorton — Slade — moves that the trio be excused. So agreed. We are now free to proceed with our business under the Call of the House.

The Third Order, Reports by Standing Committees, is quickly skipped. None have met.

However, one special group has jumped in early and in the Fourth Order of Business — Reports of Special Committees — the Committee on Claims, Auditing and Printing reports on the proper processing of our first three pieces of official legislative work: House Concurrent Resolution 1 (HCR 1, concurrent with the Senate) to notify the governor that the legislature is organized and ready for business (we've elected a House Speaker, at any rate); HCR 2 to provide for a Joint Session of the legislature to receive the governor's State of the State address tomorrow (another perfunctory task); and HCR 3, noting we'll meet jointly again to receive

> **LEGISLATIVE MANUAL**
>
> Official book of rules on the organization and procedures of the House and Senate. It lists current legislators and committee assignments, statewide elected officials, the state's federal and county elected officials, the capitol press corps, and copies of the U.S. and state constitutions.

> **CONCURRENT RESOLUTION**
>
> A measure by which the Senate and House conduct certain business together.

the governor's budget message Thursday at noon. All three concurrent resolutions are standard each session, but each formal resolution strikes me profoundly.

Fifth in the order of business: Messages from the Senate, Governor and Other Public Officials. The Senate sends one our way, via a page, which is read by the clerk: They've amended our HCR 3 to move the governor's Thursday budget message from noon to 5:30 p.m. We vote, concur, and adopt HCR 3 as amended, with little trace of the previous day's ill will.

At this point Slade — Mr. Gorton — moves that we dispense with further business under the Call of the House. We give it our *Ayes*. The doors open.

This second day into the session, we have little legislation to act upon. In the Sixth Order of Business, four small bills and one joint resolution are introduced and referred to committee. The 7th, 8th, 9th and 10th orders of business, designed for progressive activity on bills as they move toward passage, are again quickly skipped. Rather uneventful so far.

After Speaker Day announces his appointment of Mrs. Hurley to the interim Legislative Council (to replace a member whose legislative term has expired), he declares the House at ease. I already am. So far, my legislative floor work has not been the least bit taxing. I watch and listen and try to soak everything in.

Though our leaders remain busy — consulting among themselves, consulting the Rules, consulting with Speaker Day — there is little for the rest of us to do. I start a list on redistricting. I can think of plenty 'to do' in that respect.

Mrs. Hurley rises for recognition.

"Mrs. Hurley," says Speaker Day.

"I move that the House recess until 4 p.m."

We agree and that's that.

I join the line that winds its way down that slim marble stairway in the back of the chamber, down to our private House cafeteria tucked in rather cramped quarters beneath the House floor. On my tray: sliced turkey, potatoes and gravy, Jello salad. Joel finds me, and I assure him I'm enjoying it all so far. Despite the partisan split in the chamber, the dining room is jolly — a place of camaraderie, relationship building and small talk. I look forward to getting to better know these colleagues of mine, and this seems as good a spot for it as any.

Joel, in his element, amicably circulates among this bi-partisan crowd. I admire the fact that he's cultivated so many friendships, party ties aside.

Just after 4 p.m., when we've settled back in and are largely present, Mrs. Hurley stands yet again and is recognized.

Margaret Hurley is a seasoned legislator, elected six straight terms by her conservative district in Spokane — the major city in our state's far east. Petite and stylish, this spunky mother of four entered politics when her husband left his House post to devote more time to his work. She won a tough race to replace him, then caused a bit of a stir when she brought her babies to Olympia with a sitter. She's been active in the House ever since.

Staunchly defensive of her constituency — even when it means standing up to her caucus — Maggie Hurley doesn't find her role as a dissident daunting in the least.

"How can you do this to me, Maggie?" John O'Brien asked her yesterday.

"I didn't do it *to you,* John," she replied. "I did it for my voters."

I heard he then hinted she would pay at the next election, but she just laughed. Mrs. Hurley speaks with unapologetic assurance, flashes a frequent, flirtatious smile, or tosses her head back and lets loose a big, hearty laugh. She and I are night and day in demeanor. But I respect Mrs. Hurley's undeniable respect for her constituents, and for her devotion to serving her district.

"I hereby give notice that an amendment to House Rule No. 59 will be proposed to the House on the next working day," says Mrs. Hurley. "A copy of the proposed amendment to House Rule No. 59 will be on the desks of the members as soon as possible after adjournment today."

Rule 59 addresses House standing committees. John O'Brien queries his loyal Democrats on the floor: *Does anyone know what's going on? What's the coalition up to?* None of them know.

Mrs. Hurley moves for adjournment. We'll reconvene tomorrow at 11 a.m.

Shortly after 6 p.m., I arrive back "home" to my daughters, and we catch up as we cook a quick dinner and dine. Nancy's homesick for her friends and for Roosevelt High School.

"But I met a really nice girl in my chemistry class — Lynn Rosellini."

"As in Governor Rosellini?" asks Mary.

"Yep. That's her dad. How about the pages?"

"You should see the boys!" Mary reported. "Cute! But that Mrs. Hender-shot…"

"Who's she?" asks Nancy.

"Supervisor. Quite the taskmistress. Has to be, I guess."

"How did it go today?" I ask Mary. "I didn't see you on the floor."

"Oh, the work part!" she says with a smile. "Parliamentary procedure. We're supposed to memorize it. And they made sure we're doing our schoolwork, too."

"Glad to hear it!"

"How 'bout you, Mom?"

"Not as dramatic as yesterday," I report.

That being the case, Nancy quickly changes the subject.

"Can we go to the Brown Derby sometime, Mom? Or Wagner's Bakery?

Kids at school say their chocolate cake is to die for!"

Ah, a motivator.

"You girls keep up on your homework and it's a deal."

MY THIRD MORNING BEGINS PREDICTABLY. A call to order, the roll, the flags, the prayer, the Journal reading dispensed with. But the energy level is taut. All members have read "it" in advance – the resolution Mrs. Hurley now stands to introduce.

"Be it resolved…"

She formally proposes we amend Rule 59 of the temporary Rules to reduce the number of standing committees from 31 to 21. Included in the resolution is a list of the 21 committees.

John O'Brien is the first to respond. Pulling his distinguished frame erect, he addresses us with his dignified baritone: "Mr. Speaker, I rise to a point of order."

"State your point of order."

"Mr. Speaker, you have proposed a change in Rule 59. It appears to me that the rule change is incomplete in that you are reducing the number of committees but are not stipulating the number of members who are to serve on each…"

POINT OF ORDER

A claim that a floor action conflicts with the Rules of the House and requires a ruling by the chair (the Speaker).

He complains that this is confusing. He claims we can't vote intelligently. He sits.

Speaker Day disagrees: "I am going to rule that the resolution is the introduction of a complete amendment to the Rules of this House. After the reading of the resolution it will be open to amendment, and if you wish to suggest amendments, they will be considered."

Mr. O'Brien rises again.

"Mr. Speaker, further point of order. Then we are to believe that where a committee last session had twenty-one members, it will have twenty-one members this time? Do you want us to offer amendments stipulating the number of members on each committee?"

He sits.

"I think it is obvious," says Speaker Day, looking directly at his predecessor, "the way the membership of the different committees has been expanded over the last four sessions of this legislature, that the numbers designated for the committees has meant absolutely nothing to the previous Speaker. I am going to rule that your point is not well taken, Mr. O'Brien."

Mr. O'Brien stands again.

"Then, Mr. Speaker, I rise to another point of order. The Rules call for one day's notice before we can consider an amendment to the Rules. The notice was given to us last evening, about 4 o'clock. One full day hasn't elapsed since the notice. What is your ruling, please?"

He sits.

Speaker Day consults with Chief Clerk Si Holcomb, a procedural veteran who trained under the procedural master, John O'Brien. With the Chief Clerk at his elbow, our new Speaker is able to parry and thrust with the best of them, much to the growing chagrin of John O'Brien. Unfortunately for Mr. O'Brien, Chief Clerk Holcomb recalls several slights from sessions past, and now is only too glad to help Bill Day, who pronounces as Speaker:

"My ruling is that the notice was properly given."

Now rising is Mr. Beck — 'Red' Beck, a feisty, full-bodied redhead representative from Kitsap County.

"Mr. Speaker, point of information."

"State your point of information."

"We are talking about a change of Rules," says Mr. Beck. "I haven't seen a copy of the amendments. Have they been distributed?"

"Yes they have, Mr. Beck."

"I didn't receive a copy."

"Further copies are available at the desk. You may send up for one."

Mr. Beck hails a page, and here comes Mary, who has retrieved a copy and delivers it.

Mr. Ackley stands... one of the fifteen or so lawyers within our body.

"Mr. Speaker, another point of order. Rule 12 not only requires that one day's notice of the motion be given, but that the motion be presented in writing. This motion, it is my understanding, was not put on our desks until about 11 o'clock last night. I think that can hardly be one day's notice in writing. Therefore, we can't be in a position to consider this motion properly."

"Mr. Ackley, that specific rule applies to the desk here, not to each member's desk."

"I will read the rule, if I may, Mr. Speaker," Mr. Ackley continues. "It says: Any standing rule or order of the house may be rescinded or changed by a majority vote of the..."

Points of order. Points of information. Points of inquiry abound. Our very first coalition proposal is struggling in procedural quicksand.

Mr. Rogers moves to move consideration to 4 p.m. Mr. Perry speaks against it. Mr. Uhlman demands an oral roll call vote. Another immediately demands a Call of the House. *Slam! Click!*

"The question before the House," says Speaker Day, "is Mr. Rogers' motion that consideration of Mrs. Hurley's resolution be made a special order of business at 4 p.m. today."

Dan Evans speaks against this delay. Slade Gorton speaks against it as well. We have legislative business to conduct, they say, and this House must get underway. Should we postpone consideration until 4 o'clock? We vote: 43 ayes, 55 nays, one not voting: No delay. The coalition bloc wins.

"I rise to a point of inquiry, Mr. Speaker…"

For the balance of the morning Speaker Day moderates an interminable volley.

"Will Mr. Evans yield to a question?"

Over and over. Mr. Evans yields to each.

"Will Mr. Gorton yield to a question?"

"Yes."

"Is it your interpretation," Mr. Uhlman asks Slade, "that if we do not adopt specific numbers for the committees, it would be within the power of the Speaker to later appoint additional members to the committees?"

"Mr. Uhlman, the Speaker will appoint all the committee memberships at one time, and those will be the last appointments. I feel that the question is really frivolous because under any set of circumstances, as has happened previously, you can simply move that the rule be changed and one day later it is changed and the Speaker appoints another member anyway. As long as the Speaker has the majority of the House behind him, he can pretty well do what he wants in this regard, as has been evidenced by the career of the previous Speaker."

The proceedings teeter on the edge of civility.

I follow both sides as best I can.

Clarification is made by the Speaker himself that these Rules can be amended at any time — these are only temporary Rules we're discussing, and passage of this committee list does not preclude subsequent modifications. This doesn't seem to help.

The O'Brien Democrats continue to challenge the coalition: *Out of order! Illegal motion!* Allegations of ineptitude and delay. Mildred Henry from Clark County now rises.

"Mr. Speaker, will Mr. Evans yield to a question?"

"Will you yield, Mr. Evans?" asks Speaker Day.

"Certainly, lovely lady," Dan tells Mrs. Henry.

The wife of state Senator Al Henry, Mildred is politically sure, her movie star glamour aided by finely plucked brows, which she arches as she coolly addresses our Republican floor leader.

"Mr. Evans, we are now in the third day of our session and it is my belief we are far from being organized. Am I to believe that the committee on committees does not have any insight as to how many members there are going to be on the committees, and if so, when can we expect to organize this House?"

"If you adopt this rule," he replies, "you will give us the ability to go in and finish this job, and I am sure the Rules will be presented to this House as soon as or sooner than they were two years ago, which was on the fourth day."

Another arch of her eyebrows expresses her doubt.

Parrying on the floor continues. Mr. Schaefer repeats Mrs. Henry's question: "How long will it take to get the list?"

Mr. Evans replies: "It depends to a large extent on how long you want to delay the proceedings this morning..."

Mr. Schaefer bristles: "I don't know how you can say these are delaying tactics."

Wes Uhlman reads from Rule 43: Because of what just happened on the floor, the matter must be postponed until tomorrow.

But Dan Evans quickly notes that Mr. Uhlman left out several crucial words as he read to us from Rule 43 — that it actually applies only to "the final passage of bills," which is not the case with Mrs. Hurley's resolution. A resolution is before us, not a bill, so therefore, *No*, this matter does not require postponement. Check and checkmate.

Three times Mrs. Hurley presents her resolution for a vote. Each time the Democrats raise points of contention. We never vote. By late morning, we've made no progress. I sense some among us wondering whether the coalition can withstand the heat.

"The question is the adoption of the resolution before us," says our Speaker.

"It hasn't been read, Mr. Speaker," says Mr. Ackley.

"The resolution has been received...

"Point of order, Mr. Speaker," interrupts Mr. Ackley. "May I state my views on the point of order which I haven't yet expressed?"

"You will be ruled out of order, Mr. Ackley."

"My point of order is that there is no motion before us. All the other gentlemen were speaking on the motion which was before us."

"Mrs. Hurley," says the Speaker, "in order to satisfy Mr. Ackley, would you move again that the resolution be adopted?"

She so moves. Again.

"Point of order, Mr. Speaker."

It's Mr. Ackley yet again.

"State your point of order," says the patient Speaker.

"The resolution has not been read, Mr. Speaker. It is out of order to move its adoption until it has been read."

"You interrupted the reading before. If you wish it read, the clerk will read."

The clerk reads the resolution in full. Mrs. Hurley again moves that it be adopted.

"Mr. Speaker, point of order."

This time it's Mr. Litchman.

"State your point of order," says the Speaker.

"Am I right in my understanding that we are going to vote immediately on the resolution, without consideration of the ten or twelve amendments that are on the desk?"

"Certainly not."

We consider the dozen amendments. The debate drones on until time runs out. We break for lunch, then return to the floor for the governor.

"I'm nervous!" Marjorie says, though the dance in her eyes is all eagerness. She'll be one of five to escort the governor into our chamber to deliver his State of the State address.

At 1:15 p.m. the House is called to order, the roll called and we're immediately set 'at ease' until our guests arrive.

By tradition as well as practicality, Joint Sessions of our legislature are held in the House. It's a matter of space: Here we have 99 desks in place and must only seat 49 extras – the senators – among us when we meet as a legislative whole. The Senate chamber, while roughly the same square footage as here in the House, holds 49 larger desks, leaving little spare room for the 99 of us to join them there.

Once again, the House is called to order. Our guests arrive in traditional sequence. Senators first: They find seats in the folding chairs set up among our desks on the floor. Next, the President of the Senate – Lieutenant Governor John Cherberg – takes a seat at the rostrum, right next to Speaker Day, who calls this Joint Session to order. Another roll call is taken, Senate first and then the House, and then the lieutenant governor takes the gavel to preside.

He welcomes the balance of dignitaries, each escorted by his hand-selected committees of five – three representatives and two senators lead in the guests: Elected state officials, justices of the State Supreme Court, and finally, His Excellency the Governor Albert Rosellini and his wife, whose five-person escort includes my floor mate Mrs. Lynch.

A balking public address system has marred each gracious introduction and each welcome the lieutenant governor has attempted to extend. By the time Governor Rosellini takes the podium to speak, the microphone is grossly sporadic. It squawks offensively, cuts out, then blares back to life, fails, blares, screeches, until finally... the P.A. system is kaput. Lieutenant Governor Cherberg takes charge again, without benefit of amplification.

"Were this a football game," bellows this former head coach of the University of Washington football team, "the President would know how to stall out five minutes! But in lieu of that, the members of the Joint Session will please be at ease for approximately five minutes."

Testing. Testing. Nothing seems to work.

The lieutenant governor calls us to order again and recognizes Mrs. Hurley, who says, "I move that the Rules be suspended and that the Joint Session reconvene in the Senate chamber, because of the failure of the House public address system."

This time, Mrs. Hurley's motion carries easily.

Now we cram ourselves into the Senate chamber, all 99 of us, all 49 of them and all those dignitaries. The lieutenant governor speaks from the functional rostrum: "One consoling feature of this particular situation is that today we are all joined in the making of history in the state of Washington. This is the first time in our history a Joint Session has convened in the Senate chamber." [3]

The governor takes the podium: "What do I do for an encore?"

Albert Rosellini is the son of Italian immigrants. He was born in Tacoma in 1910, completed law school at age 23, entered the state Senate at age 28, and became the first Italian American Catholic governor west of the Mississippi when he was elected to the post in 1956. Now a father of five, and in his second term as governor, Rosellini enjoys both name familiarity and some solid kudos from his leadership career. But more recently, he is inspiring grumbling from an increasingly disgruntled state citizenry. He speaks.

"I will not be offended if you want to applaud in agreement that the address I made over there," he nods toward the House, "is the best I've ever made."

Unheard, interrupted, incomplete. I join in the laughter, but while our governor presents a glowing report on the state of our state – "We are on course and moving forward!" – I wonder how closely this leader is paying attention.

While I concur with the many hopes he expresses, I wonder, are those words sincere? If he honestly means it when he says, "Let us conduct our deliberations openly, honestly and realistically," then why has the House been allowed to conduct its business, especially its public hearings, so haphazardly in sessions past? And if he means it when he says, "Let us look at what we must do in this session to continue the progress which makes us proud to be a citizen of the state of Washington," [4] will he encourage both parties to work together on redistricting? That would certainly help.

When we return to the House, we agree to address the contentious Rule 59 the following day, and adjourn until Wednesday at noon.

"How'd it go today, Mom? Same ol' same ol'?"

I laugh. My goodness! Where to begin?

Day 4. On my desk is a shiny red apple and a small packaged confection. I look to Joel to explain. He raises an identical apple and identical sweet.

Once opening formalities finish, we're locked in for another Call of the House. After the roll call, Speaker Day announces that Mrs. Hurley's resolution will start us off. I hope we can settle the committee matter. I'm anxious to focus on the issues requiring legislative work. Mrs. Hurley reads the text in its entirety. Again.

"Point of personal privilege, Mr. Speaker."

The Speaker recognizes Avery Garrett.

"Mr. Speaker, ladies and gentlemen of the House. I have a statement here I would like to read into the journal."

He is invited to read.

Mr. Garrett's statement, entitled 'The Position of the Democratic Minority Caucus', lambastes the Republicans as "irresponsible," calls our formation of the coalition "a purely selfish partisan political maneuver," and claims the Republican House members "have made it impossible for the House of Representatives to function effectively this session." His statement further holds the Republicans solely responsible for this legislative session, and promises that the Democrats, by contrast, so he says, "pledge ourselves to do our utmost in carrying out the constructive and sound programs…" [5]

> **POINT OF PERSONAL PRIVILEGE**
>
> A request from the floor to make a personal statement for the official record.

When he finishes, Dan Evans rises on a point of personal privilege.

"The Speaker recognizes Mr. Evans."

Mr. Evans refuses to rebut Mr. Garrett's statement, emphasizing instead that actions will speak most articulately, and that the coalition is by no means afraid to accept responsibility for this session. He then asks all members to join together in the effective business of the House.

As one who came to the legislature to dedicate time to meaningful legislation, I find our proceedings, thus far, surprising. We have crucial lawmaking to do. Yes, partisan politics are part of the process, and these legislators have every right to engage in these battles of procedure and posturing, but this is not what I came to our capitol to do.

In earnest, and as a legitimate majority, our coalition has proposed a slate of committees that will consider and refine proposed legislation this session – our chief task as legislators. Yet objections to these committees, as proposed by the regular Democrats, are not to the substance or duties of each, but to their titles and to the numbers of legislators in each. Proposed changes to the committee names seem superfluous, or just silly. Yet each small proposed tweak requires a vote from the House. And each vote is inevitably preceded by speeches, debate, and what seems to me trite procedural nitpicking.

Comic relief arrives.

"The Speaker recognizes Mr. Haussler."

Joe Haussler, a crew-cut orchardist and businessman, begins: "Members of the House, ladies and gentlemen, Mr. Speaker: The apples which are on your desks this morning are distributed with compliments of Representative Bozarth and myself, the Cooperative Growers of Okanogan, and the Okanogan cattlemen. I would like to draw your attention to the beautiful red color of the Okanogan-grown apples, the enticing aroma of the Okanogan-grown apples, and the delicious taste of the Okanogan-grown apples. In no other place but the sun-kissed valleys of Okanogan can apples like these be grown."

"The Speaker recognizes Mr. Savage."

Mr. Savage stands, eyes twinkling beneath bushy brows. This Christmas tree farmer and former Congressman speaks: "Ladies and gentlemen, I would like to say that we are very appreciative of these apples and they certainly are evidence for themselves, but when it comes to cattlemen? We think *steaks* would have been better proof of what the cattle amount to in the Okanogan."

The ninth grade Washington history class from Sunset Junior High packs the south gallery, along with their teachers. Speaker Day welcomes them, asks that they stand and be recognized, and we applaud the adolescents. I wonder what these ninth graders will absorb from what they witness here today.

The O'Brien Democrats continue to pick apart Mrs. Hurley's resolution on Rule 59. They raise issues and complain about matters traditionally left to the discretion of the Speaker or to the majority — positions they lost to the coalition. In all, they introduce more than thirty amendments, and after each, following a motion for adoption, they systematically raise another umpteen related details. Procedural discussion. Procedural debate. Seven points of order, six points of personal privilege, four requests for a member to yield to a question, two points of information, a special point of inquiry… all endlessly elongating debate on our very first proposal. Many of the points raised require the Speaker to make a ruling. Many of the votes taken require a roll call. The ousted majority seems bent on breaking the coalition. Will day four also expire with nothing done?

The capitol press corps considers it great sport. Speculation among the reporters abounds. *Can the coalition go the distance?* Most predict not. *Will O'Brien and the O'Brien Democrats re-capture House leadership? Wear down the rebels? Force a procedural blunder?* Perhaps.

For once in legislative history, my more senior colleagues note, the Senate is not the media darling—the House has the spotlight. An editorialist in Spokane's *Daily Chronicle* writes: "The picture now awaits only the coming weeks to be painted. Whatever success the legislature achieves will be claimed by the Democrats; what failures there are going to the Republicans."[6]

John Komen of the Associated Press quotes a dramatic John O'Brien: "The scars left by the formation of the coalition will be long in healing."[7]

I jot a note and pass it to Marjorie: *Sick of all this wrangling and haranguing.* She scribbles back quickly: *Agreed!*

I begin to draft my first constituent newsletter: *Dear 32nd District...*

"Mr. Speaker, point of order."

"State your point of order, Mr. McCormick."

"Under Rule 35, no member may speak longer than ten minutes without the consent of the House. I am sure Mr. Litchman has spoken longer than that."

"Your point is well taken. Mr. Litchman, please take a minute to close your remarks."

"Mr. Speaker?" It's Ray Olsen, another Seattleite. "I yield my time to Mr. Litchman."

"Mr. Olsen, there is no provision for yielding time to a member," says Day.

John O'Brien calls for a point of order.

"State your point of order Mr. O'Brien."

"I didn't intend to get into this, but..."

He calls the Speaker's last ruling arbitrary and capricious and asks him to be so kind as to allow members to yield their time to others.

"It is true, Mr. O'Brien," says Speaker Day, "that when you were Speaker, you did allow this. However, it is not in the Rules. And I make the decision. Continue, Mr. Litchman."

No luck moving forward after Mr. Litchman finishes, for yet another point is raised. We are getting nowhere.

We recess until 5 p.m., a half hour before the prescribed Joint Session to receive Governor Rosellini's budget address. At precisely 5 p.m., we jump into floor activity again to consider Mrs. Hurley's amendment of Rule 59 of the temporary Rules of the House.

Mr. Litchman proposes an amendment. Mr. Perry moves that Mr. Litchman's amendment be tabled without taking the resolution with it. Mr. O'Brien rises and protests this tabling, citing a string of leading parliamentary authorities, to which Speaker Day replies: "Mr. O'Brien, there

TO TABLE

When an item is tabled, be it a bill or amendment, it is set aside -- removed from consideration.

is a precedent for this type of motion. Speaker Yantis, in 1933 on the 52nd day, page 550...."

Speaker Day allows the amendment to be tabled, without taking the resolution with it.

This sets off an explosive volley of precedents and technical citations, providing a fascinating education to this legislative freshman. Were it not all so frustrating, I'd be tempted to call these verbal interchanges dazzling — yes, dazzling: Technical maneuvering of the sort and sophistication you'd find in a Hollywood script. But this is happening right in front of me, and preventing us from doing our work. I open my little red manual and am struck by an irony therein: *The parliamentary system is necessary to avoid confusion and chaos — a system which will permit an assemblage to accomplish, in the best possible manner, the work for which it has been called.*

We're accomplishing nothing. We're stuck on our inaugural act.

Just prior to our 5:30 Joint Session for the governor's budget address, Mr. Perry withdraws his request that we table Mr. Litchman's amendment. Nothing gained... yet.

This time, when the senators join us in the House, the public address system behaves. This time, I've been chosen to escort the governor. I consider this a wonderful honor and feel a spring in my step center aisle, but I am less enamored as his message progresses: "Were it not for the needs of the schools, the growth between 1951 and 1961 in all other functions of state government — all other — could have been financed from the yield of taxes which were in effect in 1951... Schooling has been, and remains, the only function which cannot be financed from the normal growing yield of our present tax structure."

The link between our school funding woes and inadequate tax base has long been clear to me — property tax revenues are growing more slowly than the school population here. But other urban problems loom as well: Transportation, pollution, the many pressures of population growth. Yet the governor says schools are the sole culprit behind our state's prospective budget shortfall of $1.3 million. So I doubt he'll help tackle our school funding problems head-on.

He continues: "As the heart of our fiscal problem is education, so is the heart of the education problem one of numbers, compounded in recent years by our greater emphasis on quality as well as quantity."

I resent the way he frames this. Why *not* focus on quality?

Governor Rosellini lists our state's top three funding draws: Education, welfare and institutions cost us the most. He asserts a "no new taxes" stance and calls instead upon local governments to shoulder more expense. But what I've learned from studying our state's tax structure is that it is the state — the legislature and the governor — that determines *what* local governments can finance and tax, and *how*. Reforming our tax structure to take care of our education, welfare and our institutions for marginal citizens would require a shift in what we authorize and enable local governments to do.

He continues: "I know the legislature and I are of one mind in believing that constant, further progress and improvement are fundamental to the American spirit, yet I must express the devout wish that these next two breathing-spell years will bring a revitalization of the local levels of responsibility, without which the goals of progress may themselves become endangered."

Devout wish? Progress is not something to wish for, but to legislate and plan for, I silently assert. *And as for local control, the state must then shore up local authority.*

"The plan I propose for expending our state's monies," he says, "is a plan that can be lived with, but it is not one that can be enjoyed. It is designed for a period that requires soul-searching, re-evaluation and new approaches." [8]

By whom, I wonder. *As governor — our leader — will he lead this work?*

The speech ends, the Joint Session is dissolved and we return to House activity. On a motion from Mr. Perry, we immediately recess until 8 p.m.

We return at 8 and recess until 9.

We return at 9 and recess until 10.

Why?

Our caucus leaders level with us: They're just not sure how to combat the Democrats' protracted procedural maneuvering. Initially, the coalition leaders thought it prudent to allow the O'Brien Democrats to blow off steam. But the opposition has moved well beyond venting, and on into true obstruction. We must continue to hope the O'Brien Democrats will tire of it, give up this blockading, our leaders tell us. We need to move forward, so we can tackle all our critical legislative work.

When we return at 10 p.m., Mrs. Hurley moves that consideration of her resolution be deferred until the following morning — as a special order of business at 11:15. For the duration, the House performs routine tasks. Sixteen new bills are introduced and assigned to various committees — a minor accomplishment. Just before midnight, we recess until 11 a.m. the next day.

Day 5. Friday. A formal opening. A Call of the House. Messages from the Senate. Introduction of Bills. In other words — according to the Order of Business in Rule 10 in my little red book — a fairly normal day in the House of Representatives.

"Mr. Speaker, point of order."

"State your point of order, Mr. Ackley."

"It is now 11:15 a.m. and as I recall we moved to consider a special order of business at that time."

"Your point is well taken."

It is time to consider adoption of the resolution amending Rule 59 of the temporary Rules of the House. I can now recite this phrase by heart.

"The Speaker recognizes Mr. Perry."

"I move that consideration of the adoption of Mrs. Hurley's resolution be deferred, and that the matter be made a special order of business following the 8th Order of Business today."

This motion passes with 98 yeas and 1 nay, and we go on with our business.

Do I understand the significance of this? Not particularly. At this point I trust our leadership to call the strategic shots. If we're to adhere as a coalition and break this deadlock, we have to maneuver carefully. We want progress. We want a voice. We want to succeed.

Almost any organization engages in similar maneuvering, strategy, carefully timed action. Businesses, clubs, even the PTA! The legislature, however, is distinguished by more formality surrounding each step.

My League of Women Voters years instilled familiarity with much of the parliamentary procedure we use in the House. And I know, perhaps more than other freshman legislators, how this body functions on the floor, having spent several sessions in the capitol as a lobbyist. Even so, I am not abreast of every decision, nor aware of the precise function of every move. As a freshman I must go with the flow and assume our leaders have it figured out, have a plan. I just do what I am supposed to do. My job is to support our leadership.

By the afternoon, however, I have truly wearied of the lack of cooperation given our coalition majority. Floor speeches by the O'Brien Democrats are growing both in viciousness and in length. They present the House a signed resolution, once more decrying their relegation to minority... by surprise. To which Dan Evans responds that in his career as a Republican legislator he has always been in the minority political party, yet "our posture has not been one of delay and harassment such as we have seen in the last couple of days."

The concept of a loyal opposition is part and parcel of our system of government. Of course a minority may oppose what a majority proposes: This is the 'opposition' part. But the concept also includes the word 'loyal' — the opposing proposal should be a constructive alternative, one that perhaps better serves the public.

We recess until 5. We recess until 8. We recess until 9:30 p.m. We adjourn until the following day at 11 a.m. A Saturday. Rule 59 remains undone.

Day 6. I find this Saturday dreary, both inside the House and out. My inaugural week in office has not been what I expected. What will I write my constituents next week if this same stagnant bickering continues?

Speaker Day opens our session with great sobriety.

In our caucus meeting this morning, our leaders were frank: A day or two of delay allowed the coalition to organize, so the balking by the Democrats was not entirely detrimental. And to repeat, the coalition leadership thought that by allowing the O'Brien Democrats to blow off steam, it would clear the way for a more cooperative, productive session. But venting apparently hadn't diminished any of their resistance. Five days and we're no closer to beginning our legislative work. Due to relentless procedural roadblocks, the House of Representatives is not formally organized, and the clock on our legislative redistricting continues to tick.

We begin day six as usual: Open with fanfare. Close the doors. Call the roll. When Mrs. Hurley moves to dispense with the reading of the Journal of the proceedings of the previous day, Mr. Witherbee raises a technical objection, which the Speaker ultimately finds to be correct. Thus, the clerk must read the sprawling recap of Friday's contentious session. Enough of that, Mr. Witherbee decides shortly thereafter, and he moves to suspend further reading. The question again before the House is Mrs. Hurley's Rule 59 resolution – or rather, Mr. Litchman's amendment to it. Mr. Perry moves to delay this matter until after the 8th Order of Business again. We vote. So done. The question will be re-addressed at 2 p.m. At 2 p.m. it is moved until 3 p.m. When we convene at three, after formal pleasantries are extended to guests in the galleries, the House is declared at ease. Shortly after this, the Speaker again calls us to order.

"The question before the House is the adoption of the amendment by Mr. Litchman to the resolution amending Rule 59 of the temporary Rules of the House by Mrs. Hurley."

Slade Gorton stands to be recognized.

"The Speaker recognizes Mr. Gorton."

Speaker Day enables his microphone.

"Mr. Speaker, I have examined all the amendments on the desk to the resolution by Mrs. Hurley, and I find that they are frivolous, dilatory, and useless in nature, and impeding the organization of this House."

"The Speaker recognizes Mr. Perry."

Speaker Day enables Mr. Perry's microphone as well.

"I move that all amendments to the resolution by Mrs. Hurley in the possession of the Chief Clerk be tabled without taking the resolution with them."

Ah. Now I see. Mr. Perry established this precedent a while back, when he laid his amendment on the table without pulling the resolution along. That precedent is now put to work — to free Mrs. Hurley's resolution of its many amendments.

A half dozen Democrats jump to their feet. The Speaker refuses to recognize them, nor does he enable their microphones. As Speaker, that is his prerogative. Instead, he says: "All in favor of laying the amendments to the resolution on the table, say aye…"

I jump to my feet that instant, along with the rest of the coalition, and despite calls from several O'Brien Democrats for a roll call vote or demands for division, we shout our *'Ayes!'* at the tops of our lungs — in an unplanned outburst, a spontaneous spouting of frustration. We are all completely fed up. No one told us to do this in advance. No one planted a seed. This was simply a final straw and a bolt for daylight.

Bang! Speaker Day declares Mr. Perry's motion approved: All amendments are tabled. Now the Speaker declares that the question before the House is the adoption of the resolution by Mrs. Hurley, sans amendments. And in a split second we again shout our *'Ayes!'* over the gyrations, gestures and angry shouts of the O'Brien Democrats. In a chaotic 53 seconds of fast-action motions and deafening *'Ayes!'* the resolution is finally adopted, and the Rules are amended to establish our newly streamlined structuring of committees.

The Speaker recognizes Mr. Moos.

"I move the House adjourn until 12 noon on Monday January 21, 1963."

With another swift rap of the gavel it's done before anyone can lodge a protest. Speaker Day declares us adjourned. The O'Brien Democrats are outraged. The rest of us quietly prepare to leave. After five days of attacks and filibustering by the Democrats under John O'Brien, the coalition holds firm, and now the 38th Session can finally set sail.

The capitol press corps is clearly impressed.

Starting with this new committee structure, our progressive reforms can now begin. The coalition has just won a major victory.

No sooner has the coalition's gavel echoed to silence than Slade and Joel stop by my desk.

"Hey Mary Ellen," says Joel, "how 'bout a ride with us back to Seattle?"

"Thanks, gentlemen, but my family's already here for the weekend."

"In that case," says Slade, "remind Ken we could use his adding machine Sunday evening… redistricting, remember?"

"Hard to forget."

TONIGHT, KEN AND I HAVE BETTER PLANS. We join legislators from both parties and their spouses for dinner and dancing at the Olympia Elks Club, the only place in town for a real night out. During legislative sessions, the Elks Club gives legislators and their spouses complimentary memberships, the only price being to witness a 10-minute ceremony every night at 11 p.m. Some leave beforehand, but we don't mind. The Elks have hired a five-piece band and Ken and I dance to *Begin the Beguine, Chatanooga Choo Choo, Ol' Black Magic, Tonight We Love*. Ken is more the romantic and prefers the fox trot and plenty of cheek to cheek, where I'm the jitterbug type. Regardless, we thoroughly enjoy being together here on the dance floor.

Teetotalers for the time being, we sip coca colas and root beer. This is a decision we've made while we're raising our kids.

As we socialize, Ken hears various versions of the polarized week we had in the House, but not so much from me. I'm grateful for the chance to simply relax and be a couple. Our first legislative weekend together is truly lovely.

Meanwhile, back in Seattle, Chuck has abandoned his fraternity for the weekend in order to travel two blocks home to babysit his kid brother, David.

Our girls use the weekend to explore their temporary hometown.

Together, Ken and I read several Sunday newspapers over morning coffee. The capitol bureaus have reported on last week's legislative wrangling with all the gusto of sportswriters tracking a cross-town rivalry. From the *Tacoma News Tribune's* capitol bureau, C.E. Johns sums it up: "We could easily point with apprehension and conclude that all is going to the dogs. Actually, it appears that the coalition of dissident Democrats and the Republicans has the muscle to put over what they want, with up to 54 votes, and if they can stick together they can run the session." [9]

Sunday evening, having all said goodbye to Ken, my girls tackle their homework and Slade and I do some preliminary work on redistricting.

I arrive at work Monday morning refreshed and ready.

Day 8. After opening formalities and a motion by Mr. Perry to move the reading of the Journal until after the 8th Order of Business, Speaker Day welcomes seventy Cle Elum schoolchildren in the visitor's gallery, who stand and squirm while we applaud them. I'm happy so many students trek to our capitol to watch our legislative process at work. The first thing these children witness is a remonstrance: A lengthy written point-by-point complaint of the proceedings of Saturday presented by Representatives Ackley, Garrett and Burch.

"In short," their statement declares, "the entire Rule Book was thrown out the window, and mob rule prevailed within this legislative hall… The fact that these actions were planned and practiced in advance as a part of a secret conspiracy compounds the treachery." [10]

In truth, there was no planning or practicing. Our votes were spontaneous and heartfelt — individually voiced, collectively victorious.

Mr. Litchman asks that a statement he has written be included in the Journal as well. We will be privy to its contents the following day.

Thirteen bills are now introduced, authored by bipartisan teams and assigned to committees — those same contentious committees under fire last week. Finally. To work! The morning continues, less heated than the first six days.

When we reconvene in the afternoon, our first order of business is to read Saturday's Journal, and Mr. Garrett moves that we hear only the afternoon portion, when the final vote was made. Immediately, Speaker Day is answering points of inquiry, order and personal privilege regarding the events of Saturday afternoon. Then three representatives, Mr. Burtch, Mrs. Henry and Mr. Ackley, ask that their personal statements about those events be included in the Journal as well, joining Mr. Litchman's and the remonstrance. So granted.

Another protracted procedural debate erupts between the various floor leaders: Dan Evans and John O'Brien and Wes Uhlman and Speaker Day, all of them harkening back to Rule 59 of last week. Speaker Day refuses to reopen the discussion or to back down. He declares the House at ease, consults with the coalition leaders and Chief Clerk Si Holcomb, and when he next calls us to order, he speaks with particular emphasis.

"At this time the Speaker would like to explain his ruling. Under Reed's Rule 49, Duties of the Members, it states: *The duties of each member are based upon the considerations which arise from <u>his being a component part of the assembly</u>, which desires to act <u>together</u> and which, in order to act together, must come to some <u>agreement</u>.* And going down to the last paragraph of 49: *In short, as the object and purpose of an assembly is to enable men to act together as a body, <u>each member ought to so conduct himself as to facilitate the result, or at least so as not to hinder it.</u>* We all know how long we debated this particular issue. There are specific rules that apply to the organization of a body…"

He points us to Rule 52: *While it concerns certain kinds of assemblies to adopt a set of rules at once, yet it is not possible to make such a set of rules complete and perfect at once. After experience, modifications are almost always found to be necessary…The assembly can not deprive itself of power to direct its method of doing business. It is like a man promising himself that he will not change his own mind.*

More procedural rules are cited from the floor. I attempt to keep track. Mrs. Henry raises an issue that seems to make sense: "I would like to call your attention to House Rule 49. I see nowhere in the Journal where ayes and nays were counted. How, therefore, can you rule that a majority prevailed?"

"Would you repeat that point?" says Speaker Day, leaning to the Chief Clerk for advice.

"I said, I draw your attention to House Rule 49 which provides that the yeas and nays shall be recorded. We had a voice vote, if you recall, Mr. Speaker. How can you, without yeas and nays, say the majority prevailed and the amendment to House Rule 59 was adopted?"

He responds: "I believe that is the privilege of the Speaker on a voice vote."

Dear. Did our speaker overstep his authority? Dan Evans stands on a point of order.

"Mr. Evans."

"Mr. Speaker, just in order to clarify the answer to Mrs. Henry's inquiry, I remember very clearly last session, because I was involved in an identical situation, and the ruling from our previous Speaker was that this roll call was not necessary on a floor resolution but only on something similar to a House joint resolution or House joint memorial or a House bill that were subject to first, second and third reading. The Speaker did make that ruling last session. I remember it very clearly."

Checkmate. Giving John O'Brien some of his own. At this, the Democrats' stance perceptibly dissipates, and I wonder if perchance admiration is developing deep within the old leadership for the new.

We have finally come to a vote on the Journal of Saturday — an electric roll call vote, by request of Rep. Ann O'Donnell. I use my push-button board for the first time, and watch as a green dot alights by my name on the oversized roster up front in the chamber. We approve Saturday's Journal at last, roughly down the line of the coalition and O'Brien Democrats: 57 for, 41 against, one absent.

> **ELECTRIC ROLL CALL**
>
> Members' votes recorded on an electric panel at the front of the chamber, with two lights by each name: green for 'Yea' and red for 'Nay' -- lit by push buttons at each member's desk.

Within minutes, after a short at-ease, we're called back to order and Speaker Day begins to read his committee appointments, including the chairman and vice-chairman of each. After the second full committee is listed, Mr. Beierlein stands on a point of personal privilege.

"Mr. Beierlein, I am going to rule you are interrupting the reading. Let's complete the list first."

And the Speaker does. He reads all 21 committees and their leaders, with chairmanships divvied equally among party lines. Near the end of the listing, a commotion swells on the floor. The instant the Speaker finishes, Mr. Garrett stands and is recognized.

"Mr. Speaker, I cannot accept this appointment on the Rules and Order

Committee without first consulting the Democratic Caucus, and I am sure that many other members who received these appointments are in the same position. I now request that you grant us a recess to go into caucus so that the Democratic Party can discuss their approval of these various chairmanships and the membership on Rules and Order."

Speaker Day responds: "Mr. Garrett, you may discuss the appointments with anyone you please. The Speaker has just read his appointments."

We adjourn until the following day.

Day 9. When I reach my desk, I first read the printed Journal entry of the previous day, which has been distributed to each of our desks by the busy pages — a morning routine. I scan through for Mr. Litchman's personal entry, and shake my head at his comparisons of Saturday's floor activity to the dictatorships of Castro, Mussolini and Hitler.

Day nine begins with another explosion — after we welcome the Washington State Medical Association Auxiliary, that is. For after that welcome, Mr. Beierlein respectfully declines his appointment as vice-chairman of the Banking and Insurance committee, "believing in the importance of the two-party system for responsible government, and being of the belief that coalition government is not in the best interest of the state…"

Speaker Day reminds Mr. Beierlein of his oath to serve his state, notes that Rule 3 requires the Speaker to make such appointments, and explains that in making all committee assignments, he has tried to be both considerate of ability and also fair. He admonishes his old Democratic Caucus:

"As far as you ladies and gentlemen on the floor are concerned, the caucus action which is attempting to prevent you from serving either as chairmen or members of committees is forcing you to take a position that has never occurred in the House of Representatives before… It is the individual responsibility of each appointee to determine whether he or she is fit to accept his or her responsibility… It would be unfortunate to allow this caucus to deprive the House of the valued services of many of its distinguished members."

Mr. Beierlein continues: In committees, he says, the chairman wields all the power, "so why should I occupy a position where I, in the final analysis, do not have any influence?"

The Speaker has already noted: All his appointments will stand.

Mr. Klein rises on point of parliamentary inquiry, asks what other considerations the Speaker used to determine chairmanships in addition to Rule 3, since he couldn't find anywhere in Rule 3 language that says a Speaker appoints chairmanships.

Rule 3 requires him to appoint the committees, and committee membership logically includes chairmen, Speaker Day tells Mr. Klein, reminding him of his legislative oath to serve.

Mr. Klein then cites Reed's Rules on the selection of chairmen, which states that committees should select their own chairmen, and asks, "Does the Speaker care to rule on that?"

Yes he does: "It has been the precedent in this House, Mr. Klein, as long as I have known anything about this legislature and even before that, that the Speaker has named the chairmen and vice chairmen of the committees. I so rule, Mr. Klein."

Every time the Democrats raise what seems to me a valid complaint, it turns out they have acted exactly the same in years past — they've set the precedent for the particular action in question. And while procedural propriety certainly has its place here, I agree with Speaker Day's claim that our oath is to act as a body to serve our state. My overriding feeling is, 'Let's get going!'

Mr. Klein argues that the parties should select their own members to fill designated committee seats. He cites Reed 65 and 71. Speaker Day cites 52: A body can establish its organizational procedure under the rule of a majority, "and we have so proceeded, Mr. Klein, and this ruling is going to stand…"

Yet one by one, more Democrats decline their committee leadership appointments, including John O'Brien, who has been named to chair the Committee on State Government, Military Affairs and Civil Defense.

"…It just seems to me that in all fairness," says Mr. O'Brien, "since you people are willing to assume all of the responsibility — and there is absolutely nothing wrong with your doing that — you should take these chairmanships…"

"Mr. Speaker, point of personal privilege."

It's Dan Evans.

"I am not going to decline any committee chairmanships," says Mr. Evans, "or vice-chairmanships, because I don't have any. I think we have strayed a little under 'point of personal privilege'. I hope the House will allow me the privilege of speaking."

The Speaker nods.

"Mr. May made a reference this morning to the fact that he does not like to cross party lines or cross picket lines. It sounds to me like there may be a strike going on."

He says this with dismay.

"But party responsibility is subservient to the needs of the people of the state. I think every member of this House would agree we don't have Democratic highways or Republican highways. We don't have Democratic fish or Republican fish. We don't have Democratic schools or Republican schools. We don't even have Democratic banks or Republican banks. Most of our committees deal with the problems of the people of this state on a bipartisan or nonpartisan basis…

"For us Republicans, let me say that we realize we are here for serious business, and there certainly is no point in anyone acting like the little boy who wants to take his baseball and bat and go home if the game isn't played the way he wants… We are perfectly willing to chuck politics out the window and get down to the serious business of being lawmakers and — if the gentlemen across the aisle who are hugging to their bosoms their newfound weapon of 'minority status' will give us a chance — to legislate rather than vegetate."

Marjorie and I exchange a look.

Mr. Litchman rises on a point of personal privilege: "We cannot accept at any time a coalition form of government. Otherwise we will be playing musical chairs for years. This is a democracy…Therefore we must exclude ourselves from any participation in the coalition. We deplore the coalition type of government. We will never be a part of it. As I said before, the reason for this attempted boycott would be to preserve democracy in the House."

This is ridiculous. The concept of coalition is neither renegade nor new.

Dan Evans rises on a point of information.

"I see it is too late now," he says. "I wanted to remind Mr. Litchman that the television cameras had run out of film and if he wanted to wait a while, they would reload."

The debate continues, and the daily Journal reading remains in limbo.

Mr. Sawyer: "What bothers us on this side of the aisle is very simple. The Republican party has a program which is going to be crammed down our throats, and we want it to be known as a Republican party program, and not as a bipartisan program. In other words, if you are going to do it to us, at least accept the label and don't try to hide behind the label of bipartisanship."

Mr. Moon asks the Speaker to acknowledge the coalition's responsibility.

Mr. Ackley points out one committee in particular, Utilities and Transportation, in which a Democrat is named chairman, but only five of fifteen members are Democrats, a ratio that he says would force Democrats to take responsibility where they have no control. He turns to face our Republican side of the House and says, "You have the control. You take the responsibility."

Tom Copeland, our caucus whip, speaks for the first time in days: "I think it would be well to point out to Mr. Ackley and other members of the House that in the arrangement of a legislative body where we have a Senate and a House, oftentimes we build in checks and balances, and for your information, Mr. Ackley, I would like to point out that the Committee on Public Utilities in the Senate — where there are nineteen members — has only four who are Republicans."

In our caucus this morning we were each presented a statement written by our caucus attorney, Jim Dolliver. We had read our copies and signing was optional. We signed on. Dan Evans picks this moment to request that this statement be inserted into today's Journal. It recounts the first week of the session, cites the delays, and calls for us all to get on with our legislative business. We vote for its insertion.

When it appears on our desks in print tomorrow, the O'Brien Democrats can read it as well. I hope it will give them pause: "Legislatures are convened to legislate; to transmit the will of the people into the laws that will govern them," Dolliver wrote. No majority in any legislative body can long tolerate willful delay, dilatory tactics or continued obstructionism from any source. Otherwise the legislative process becomes a mockery and the will of the people thwarted... Reasonable and responsible men can tolerate unwarranted delay only so long."

It formally defends our leadership on Saturday, to counter Mr. Litchman's facism claims: "The procedures followed on Saturday evening to break the filibuster and end the tactics of obstruction were amply covered by precedent and fully in accord with the rules of this body and the constitution of this state. The rights of the minority have been and will continue to be scrupulously observed. But in our concern for the rights of the minority, we must not be blinded to the rights and duties of the majority. Politically motivated charges of violation of rules come with ill grace from those who by their actions have unconscionably delayed and obstructed the business of the House... It is now time for responsible men to be about the business of this House and the business of the state. We invite all members of the House to join together in this effort." [11]

As a freshman, I don't know what effect such a Journal statement may have. But I certainly don't want to waste more valuable legislative hours. I gladly signed on, along with the rest of our House Republicans... except for Dwight Hawley.

I HAVE VOWED TO WRITE MY CONSTITUENTS each week, and begin drafting my second Legislative Memo to mail to my voters back home. I pay for these from leftover funds from my election campaign, and personally type them up at my home typewriter: *In last week's edition, the bipartisan cooperation to elect William S. Day of Spokane Speaker of the House was reported.*

THIS WEEK. Immediately after the election, the routine temporary rules were introduced, embodying a long advocated reform — the streamlining of the committee structure from 31 to 21 to facilitate House business. The followers of former Speaker O'Brien attempted what one participant admitted was a filibuster over this issue, lasting from Wednesday through Saturday. Late last Saturday evening, after four days of patient negotiations, the coalition took firm action to end the delay and adopt temporary rules — all in a matter of 53 seconds. This is a "tough" parliamentary course to take, but it was necessary in order to overcome the delay caused by the O'Brien faction...

I write about the committee chairmanship refusals and about the pressure these balking Democrats face from their constituents, unhappy their elected leaders have shirked their chances to lead. And I express hope these Democrats will change their minds and behavior and participate in this function of the House.

I am pleased with my own committee assignments:

1: Constitution, Elections and Apportionment, chaired by Representative Slade Gorton of the 46th District. *This committee is particularly vital in light of the court's recent ruling that if the legislature does not fairly redistrict the state, the court will. One plan being discussed in the Senate would, in a masterpiece of gerrymandering, do away with the 32nd District entirely. Our committee will do everything possible to see that any redistricting plan which is passed will be fair to all areas and to both parties...*

Speaking of redistricting, I am co-sponsor of a proposed constitutional amendment which would set up a bipartisan commission to redistrict the state according to the constitutional requirement of once every ten years IF it is not accomplished by the legislature or initiative. The other sponsors are Frank B. Brouillett of Puyallup and Arlie DeJarnatt of Kelso, Democrats.

2: Education and Libraries, chaired by Audley Mahaffey of the 46th District as well. *Rep. Mahaffey stated at our first meeting that school programs would be judged by what we feel is best for our children, not by political considerations. Actually, this is true of most legislation. Roughly three-fourths of it is non-partisan.*

Education also has been in the news because of Governor Rosellini's conservative budget proposals, which were substantially below the amount requested by Superintendent Bruno...

3. Local Government. Which is sure to be stimulating, too.

I thank them for writing me their views on issues before the legislature. *We cannot effectively represent you unless we do know what you think, and are negligent in our duty if we do know your feelings, but fail to consider them strongly in weighing the information placed before us. I personally am delighted — not 'bothered' — to hear from you.*

I list my visitors from the 32nd District and sign off: *So much for now — more next week.* And type in parentheses at the end: *Not mailed at government expense.*[12]

Eventually, the coalition reorganizes the committees so that, per the druthers of the O'Brien Democrats, those members neither chair nor vice-chair a single one. And that is how, as a freshman legislator, I am able to report to my constituents during week three that I have become vice-chairman of the Committee on Constitution, Elections and Apportionment. Not surprisingly, I jump right into redistricting.

While the committee itself considers bills on topics ranging from campaign contributions to our state's open primaries, my main task is to spearhead the coalition's redistricting effort. We set up redistricting headquarters in an empty committee room upstairs from the House floor. Here I spend every spare hour of my workday — those times when I'm not in session or committee meetings or hearings.

I have done redistricting work twice before, with the League of Women Voters. We wrote complete redistricting measures with Initiatives 199 and 211, and this redistricting is really no different. However, whereas in the League I'd primarily campaigned on behalf of the issue — talking it up to the public in the streets — my job now is to actually help design and describe each newly proposed legislative district; more specifically, to oversee this work.

Do I work alongside my former League colleagues on this version of redistricting? Not really. While the League does continue to lobby the legislature on redistricting — League women attend all our hearings, and individual members lobby their representatives — they are not directly involved in my tasks. I am an elected public official now, aligned with a specific political party, and the League of Women Voters is strictly non-partisan.

PAPERWORK COVERS MY ENTIRE dining room table in the rental house, and Slade apologizes to my daughters as he and I embark on another long night of planning: "Sorry to invade your evening with your mother."

"That's OK. Mom's always busy."

"Doesn't bother us, as long as she doesn't forget the Brown Derby."

As my girls immerse themselves in their studies, Slade and I begin our methodical review and analysis of all 49 districts in our state. In each of these, we need to determine the current population, the political makeup as near as we can tell from public records on voting, and also the home address of each current representative and senator, along with their contact information and party affiliation, so that we can mark those legislators' homes with an "x" on the map. One thing I learned from my LWV campaign is that we must at least be aware of what any new district lines could do to incumbents.

Most elected officials know their districts inside out, so to flesh out our district studies, Slade and I also plan to draw on our House mates' knowledge.

For example, as a candidate, before I doorbelled my 32nd District, I made up 5 x 8 note cards with a map of each of the 105 precincts — one precinct per card. I also created a color-coded 32nd District map to illustrate the political complexion of my constituents: Which homes and which precincts were strongly

Republican or Democrat, which more mildly partisan. To gauge this political preference, my campaign team used the results of key races in the previous election. We marked precincts with a strong preference either deep blue or deep red, while milder party preferences had paler shades — these are precincts in which my district might swing in either direction, R or D. In my 32nd District and Slade's 46th, we have the details we need to start. Now we must gather similar information on the other 47.

In other states, this preliminary step in redistricting is made easier by the fact that voters register with one party or another in order to vote in primaries. But Washington State has an open primary. We don't register by party affiliation — we're all just voters and we can vote for whomever we please; we're not restricted to a certain party's primary ballot.

After we estimate the political complexion of all 49 existing districts, we'll do population counts in each. Using federal census tracts, like the League did for Initiative 199, we can arrive at fairly accurate district headcounts. If a census tract appears in its entirety within a single district, great! We can use that tract's official population total. But if a district line cuts through the middle of one of these tracts, each little black dot on the census must be tallied. This is not difficult work, but it is time consuming — hard on both the patience and the eyes. Hence the need for a team and a stockpile of adding machines. This is one part of the work I oversee.

From our prior collaboration on Initiative 211, Slade and I speak the same language and tend to think in synch. Rather than strategize or wax philosophic, we both just jump in and work.

We know, for example, that the current state population dictates that our optimum district size is 60,000 if we redraw our legislative districts into 49 equal parts.

The math, however, is simpler than the mapping.

Our state population has shifted dramatically since the last re-drawing. With reapportionment so horribly overdue, we'll upset the applecart all over the place as we create district equality. By law — by our state constitution — the number of districts is fixed at 49, so we must adhere to that, which will require us to delineate some wholly new districts and to completely eliminate others in order to keep districts equal in size, to make vote-weight as consistent as possible. In some rural areas here, populations are so sparse that a single new district might necessarily include several counties. Others districts might necessarily cross mountain ranges, or ecosystems or economies — not ideal, if you want representatives to represent a congruent constituency.

If it were just a matter of numbers, it would be easier. But it's not.

Partisan considerations play a role, too, and this calls for temperature-taking among our colleagues in the Senate and House. In the next few days, we'll pull together our district data and begin our interviews: *Do you plan to seek re-election? Do you have a strong stance on redistricting? Are you willing to run in a largely new district? If your district disappears, would a government job help ease your pain by saving your pension? Would you vote for our proposal if it looks like this? Or this? Or how about this?* Soon, we're continually canvassing our colleagues. And every response sends us back to the literal drawing boards.

To help with this painstaking delineation and re-lineation of new districts, Slade and I pull together a volunteer team — a fluctuating roster of spouses of legislators, state employees in their off-hours, anyone willing to occasionally or regularly chip in. With these hit-and-miss aides, whose presence may be inconsistent, but appreciated nevertheless, I must be tremendously organized. I set up a system of files, checklists and tasks that allows newcomers to walk in cold and immediately contribute. I divvy up the districts — one district per group of three volunteers.

"Hi, Mrs. McCaffree. How can we help?"

I know immediately: "Here, you three start on District 12."

A trio's first assignment is to find the most detailed road and street maps by which to determine a district's geographic bounds. We suggest Shell.

In 1963, "full service" at gas stations means the attendant will fill your tank and your tires, top your oil, wash your windows and hand out a free map if you'd like one. We take Shell up on their offer, having determined that among the various gas companies — Texaco, Standard, Conoco, Mobil — Shell's maps are most comprehensive, showing and labeling all the streets. Therefore, our volunteer teams begin by collecting dozen of maps from Shell service stations across Washington State. We end up with hundreds.

Once we have these detailed district maps in hand, we overlay population counts and precinct boundaries. Then, precinct-by-precinct, using data we've collected from colleagues and campaigns, we begin to estimate political preference, which will play a pivotal role as the new district boundaries shift. We also determine whether an existing district, as a whole, is basically Democrat, Republican or swing, again by tabulating previous election results by party for key races — for governor, for legislative seats, etc.

Our goal is fairly simple: We want the political complexion of the legislature to accurately reflect the statewide votes for the candidates of each party.

Our redistricting workroom has a couple of tables and one long bookshelf running along the back. On the tables, we can be working through several districts at a time. Once a district is finished with round one — a list of proposed boundaries, street by street — it goes into a file on the bookshelf in the back (after I've given it my personal stamp of approval, that is). Being responsible for the accuracy of my staff, I must carefully crosscheck each map with sets of figures, which I often do at home, well into the night.

Then the real redistricting work begins.

More difficult than the number game is the task of creating a new state map to balance the political complexion. We must craft some solid Democrat and some solid Republican districts to facilitate stable leadership, as well as a number capable of 'swinging' either way to assure an infusion of new energy and new ideas. This is the nature of the compromise bill we seek to author. Writing it will require our near round-the-clock dedication.

I spend most of my hours each day now working with other Republican House members drawing up endless redistricting plans, all used by Slade, Don Moos, Dan and Joel in their search for a combination that can garner enough votes for approval by both the Senate and House.

Whenever we change any single boundary line of any district, it affects the political makeup of two (or more) districts, thus affecting at least six legislators — two Representatives and one Senator in each. Finding the right combination of 49 districts that will attract the support of a majority of both House and Senate members is a tremendously complicated task. We need just the right mix.

Finding just the right combination of substances is Nancy's task in her chemistry class at Olympia High. Yet despite careful measurement and meticulous pouring and mixing, she and her lab partner really flub it.

"Guess what, Mom? We blew up the chemistry lab today."

"Who's we?"

"Me and Lynn Rosellini."

The governor's daughter and mine and the explosive consequence of an improper mix.

"BY THE WAY, MARY ELLEN," says Slade the next morning, "you're sponsoring this redistricting bill."

"Me?"

"You. You're not as well known yet, and that's what it needs. My name on it… I'm a lightning rod for the Democrats, needless to say, and for the press. Besides, Senate Democrats will never let our bill get anywhere, so no one else particularly wants their name on a failing proposition. We need a sponsor."

"But…"

I didn't want to sponsor a failing bill either, and I argued with my party's decision that I be the one — the sole sponsor. Then Dan also asked me privately.

And then so did Joel.

"Even if it goes nowhere," said Slade, "we have to demonstrate we're serious about redistricting, and show why this coalition was so necessary. And of course, there's the court."

"Yes."

"So it's settled. It's your bill."

"I… OK."

There was really no arguing.

Each time my volunteer redistricting crew completes another district baseline file, we stick it on the big bookshelf at the back of the room. Don or Slade will grab it, dash downstairs to the House, and conduct their interpersonal map reviews in the wings and hallways and byways surrounding the chamber.

One by one, they review each district with our colleagues — Slade with the urban representatives and Don with our rural contingent — to examine boundaries, barter precincts, negotiate miniscule shifts. Joel pitches in and patches up where needed: Our diplomatic maestro manages to maintain friendships with most of the 99 in the House. These three confer with colleagues from both sides of the aisle, show them our proposals, and district-by-district we begin to piece together a redistricting bill increasingly palatable to more members in both the Senate and the House.

Each time, however, the negotiators return with modifications: *Move these precincts. Can we move this over a block? Let's try this here. How about there?* Negotiate. Redraw. Recount. Recalculate. Adding machines *rat-a-tat-tat.* We count more dots. Sketch new outlines. New street boundary shifts make the list for another round.

Slade often leaves work earlier than me, begging fatigue. I begin to work very late into the nights. The capitol security force patrols 24 hours, so a guard escorts me on my walk back home in the wee hours. Warren Guykema, my campaign manager, has rented the basement room of our rental house here, so I'm comfortable my girls have an adult nearby when I'm absent so long.

"Hi Honey!" I'm always happy when Ken arrives for the weekends, though lately his visits tend to end up in redistricting work. He can read me like a book.

"What this time?" he asks when he sees me, resigned.

"The adding machine or counting dots," I offer.

"More long hours in the ol' redistricting room." He sighs. "Your workaholism surprises me, Mary Ellen."

"What was that, honey?..."

"I said, your workaholism…"

But I'm already distracted again.

Even when the girls and I travel home to Seattle on weekends, I often end up with redistricting work to do. My apology to my family comes in the form of dozens of fresh-baked cupcakes I leave behind — chocolate, vanilla and spice to suit several preferences, plus a couple of casseroles, spaghetti and meatballs, and several clean loads of laundry.

Our formal redistricting plan slowly comes together. As its only sponsor, I am receiving a first-hand tutorial in how a bill swims upstream toward becoming a law.

Day 34. On February 16, I file the Republican/coalition redistricting plan and it is assigned as House Bill 436.

"Mrs. McCaffree."

Speaker Day enables my microphone. I speak my very first formal words on the floor: "This bill represents a bi-partisan effort to legally redistrict the legislative seats in our state. I urge that the House approve this bill."

The bill is assigned to our committee — Constitution, Elections and Apportionment — and in our next meeting, we split it up regionally and form geographic subcommittees to work through regional details.

Daily conferring continues, even with Senator Greive, who is once again at the helm of the Senate's redistricting. We are making a serious, full-scale attempt to craft a plan that will work. We want to write a solid bill for our state.

Day 41. Redistricting isn't the only means of protecting our rights to vote. On February 23, the House passes a measure I've co-sponsored: A joint resolution to certify our state's ratification of the 24th Amendment to the U.S. Constitution — to abolish the poll tax, a discriminatory measure put in place after the Civil War to keep the less moneyed and many of our minority voters voiceless at the polls.

Day 52. March 6, eighteen days after I first introduced my redistricting bill on the floor of the House, Speaker Day calls us to order at 8:40 p.m. for a second evening session. Of this 60-day session, only eight remain.

The clerk calls the roll and all are present. Mrs. Henry demands a Call of the House and the sergeant at arms locks the doors. At the new roll call, Paul Connor is the only one absent. He has returned to his home in Port Angeles on our northern-most coast, critically ill. Mr. Connor is declared excused and we are declared at ease, then we're called to order again for the second reading of bills.

First up is a constitutional amendment regarding apportionment — Substitute House Joint Resolution 9. It proposes we increase the number of House districts to 53 to reduce the complications caused by our statewide population growth, though it would retain the Senate districts at 49. The resolution is read in full and sent to the Rules Committee for a third reading.

Next on the docket is House Bill 436, by Representative McCaffree: My redistricting bill. The clerk begins to read: "Mr. Speaker, We a majority of your Committee on Constitution, Elections and Apportionment, to whom was referred House Bill 436, reapportioning legislative districts, have had the same…"

Don Moos stands.

"Mr. Moos, state your point of order."

"If there be no objection, I suggest the last line only be read."

"Mr. Witherbee."

"I object to the reading of the last line only."

"Mr. Gorton."

"I move that the reading clerk read the committee amendment by sections."

We vote and approve this amendment by Mr. Gorton. The 'committee amendment' is basically the entire bill, as hammered out within our committee. Section one – District 1 – is read and the amendment adopted. The same with section two – District 2. Each section of the bill represents a district. Now, after a series of inquiries from the floor, the Speaker agrees that reading the final line of each section should suffice. This immediately meets with objection from those who worry we're trying to somehow finagle the districts.

Because each section of my bill equates to a legislative district, this reading would move us, one by one, through the detailed boundary descriptions of each proposed district. If the House is in general agreement with a district, the last line of the section is read, the section is approved, and we move on. If not…

"Mr. Speaker, will Mr. Moos yield to a question?"

Mr. Moos yields to Mr. O'Brien, who asks for the population of the new district presented in Section 8. This is Don Moos's sparse rural district in Eastern Washington.

"The new district will have roughly twenty-six thousand," Mr. Moos responds. "Let's see – the last time I counted it was twenty-five thousand nine hundred eighty-three. Now that my wife and I are over here, it is twenty-five thousand, nine hundred eighty-one."

"How many Democrats?" asks Mr. O'Brien.

"The last time I counted them? Let's see. My wife is over here…"

Mr. Witherbee stands on a point of personal privilege and claims we created the whole redistricting bill unfairly and in secrecy, using "tactics" of the League of Women Voters.

"I am protesting long and loud," says Mr. Witherbee. "But go ahead and push it out. Push out your gerrymander. You do it any way you want to, but I will be back! And a lot of the rest of us will be back anyway."

"The Speaker recognizes Mr. Gorton."

Slade defends our hard work: "Of course a lot of you will be back, Mr. Witherbee, because the bill as it is drawn will have a proportion of people coming back from each party which is equal to the proportion of the people who vote for the candidates of that party."

Then Slade addresses all of us: "In the fifty-some days we have been here, and in the approximately forty-five days I have been chairman of the Committee on Constitution, Elections and Apportionment, Mr. Witherbee has not so much as asked me one time about the boundaries of his district."

Mr. Gorton notes he is aware that Mr. Witherbee talked with Senator Greive about creating a preferable district to the one we've drawn, which would indicate Mr. Witherbee is familiar with both versions. Our committee chairman also defends in detail our committee's operation, singling out the intentional bi-partisanship of all our regional subcommittee work.

"I don't have any objection to Mr. Witherbee's voting against this bill," Mr. Gorton tells us all. "This is a very sensitive bill in a very sensitive area… Maybe the legislature isn't a good place to get redistricting bills through, but in no meaningful term of the word, either from the point of view of division according to population, or from the point of view of division along party lines, is this bill a gerrymander."

Speaker Day resumes presiding: "I have allowed Mr. Witherbee to explain his position under a point of personal privilege, and Mr. Gorton has answered. The subject properly before us is not a debate on this bill; that will properly take place when this bill is on third reading. There is an amendment before us to Section 8 at the moment."

Mr. Campbell moves that consideration of my bill be postponed, indefinitely. Mr. Olsen demands an oral roll call on the matter. Representatives Campbell, Uhlman and Henry speak in favor of postponement. Representatives Evans and Gorton speak against it. Debate rages on.

Mr. Garrett claims he's been kept in the dark.

Mr. Pritchard is asked to shed light, and Joel gladly obliges: "First of all," he says, "when the subcommittee was called for King County, Mr. Gorton personally told Mr. Garrett about this meeting. Secondly, I went to Mr. Garrett myself. I asked if he would come to the hearing two days ago. I said I would show him the entire King County map. *Oh,* he said, *does it make any difference?* I said, *Wouldn't you like to see what is happening to King County?* Not only was he invited to see it all, but the great Senator Greive two nights ago saw the entire bill and had an opportunity to have it all explained. So this hasn't been such a great secret. I resent the fact that Mr. Garrett did not come when I invited him. I told him any time he wanted to come, we would show him not only the King County map but the whole state map. I believe Mr. Garrett would bear me out."

And so goes the night: The coalition aiming for positive progress, the opposition digging in their heels in favor of an alternative plan. The O'Brien Democrats push to postpone indefinitely, we in the coalition push to proceed. Each vote splits, Democrat versus the coalition, with the coalition's majority vote winning each time.

"Mr. Speaker," says Mr. Witherbee, "I think my point of objection has been well made and I know this bill is going to go. I would like just to read the last line of the entire amendment to the bill and then we can debate the amendment as such. What sort of motion do I make?"

"The only thing you have to do, Mr. Witherbee, is stop objecting and we can take it section by section."

"I don't want to object on that basis," Mr. Witherbee says. "I wish to be able to read the last line of the entire amendment."

"We still have to adopt the amendment by sections," says Speaker Day. "It has been passed on by the body to do so."

We continue, setting aside several particularly contentious sections for the end. At midnight, we near the final sticky sections and work them through. Finally, House Bill 436 is ordered engrossed and passed to the Committee on Rules for third reading.

"The Speaker recognizes Mr. O'Brien."

"Mr. Speaker, I would like to have the privilege of inserting in the journal that the working day is now March 7, 1963. The time is 12:35 a.m."

"With the consent of the House, you may do so, Mr. O'Brien."

Day 53. The next morning, the Rules Committee sends HB 436 back to the floor, where it is placed on third reading and final passage in the regular order of House business. The House approves the bill by a vote of 55 yeas to 44 nays and we send it immediately to the Senate. The Senate sends it to its appropriate committee and does nothing else. For the balance of the session, my carefully crafted redistricting bill languishes there… and ultimately dies.

Day 60. By the final day of my first regular legislative session, redistricting remains undone, and so does the budget. Several rudimentary bills have passed, but we've accomplished little that's earthshaking. Governor Rosellini calls us into special session, to begin on March 15, after the weekend. My girls and I go home to Seattle, and I return to Olympia alone.

Extraordinary Session. On the morning of March 15, Don Eldridge welcomes us back to the caucus room, thanks our entire tired group, and our leaders deliver us a pep talk. Our job? Our job is two-fold: To prevent a gerrymandered Democrat redistricting, and to complete the state's two-year budget.

At 10 a.m. Speaker Day calls the House to order. The clerk calls the roll. Five are absent. Attendance tends to be worse in special sessions. The flag comes forth and the prayer is said, followed by a reading of the governor's proclamation: "Whereas, the 1963 Session of the Legislature, during the regular period of sixty days prescribed for said Session, failed to enact an appropriation measure; and whereas, the Legislature failed to enact a measure providing for redistricting of the state for purposes of representation in the Legislature as required by the State Constitution and as further directed by a Federal Court; and whereas, other measures important to the health, safety and welfare of the people of the State of Washington were not enacted…"

We hear the governor's list.

"And, Whereas, as a result of these conditions, an emergency exists, constituting an Extraordinary Session within the meaning of Article III, Section 7, of the Constitution of the State of Washington."

By the power vested in him, our governor thereby convenes this special session for the purpose of completing our specified work.

Mrs. Hurley presents a resolution: That the Rules of our regular session also govern this one. Without argument, her resolution is adopted. We officially notify the Senate to tell them we're organized, and they do likewise. The 38th Legislature is back in business. Several bills from the governor's list are immediately sent to committee, and I sense this atmosphere on the floor is more traditional.

"Yep," Joel confirms with a wink.

Our redistricting team is back to business, too. In this extra session, I sponsor House Bill 56 — to redistrict and reapportion our state — and it is assigned to our committee. In committee, we refine it per further negotiations with colleagues in both the Senate and House, and I continue to oversee each change in our workroom.

During this same stretch, under the leadership of Senator Greive, the Senate executes similar redistricting gymnastics, continually shuttling back and forth among members to craft a measure they hope will pass. In fact, Senator Greive spends a great deal of time in our vicinity, lobbying House members to support his Senate plan.

By the ninth day of our special session, my HB 56 is ready for second reading. The bill is read, section by section as before, but this time with much less balking. When we're done, Mr. Uhlman moves that it be re-referred to committee — not to the committee Slade and I lead, though, but to the Committee on State Government, Military and Veteran Affairs and Civil Defense, where, despite declining the chairmanship, John O'Brien plays a significant role. Representative Ann O'Donnell immediately demands a Call of the House, and *slam, click!* Sigh. We're confined. The clerk calls the roll: Six are absent.

Mr. Gorton speaks against the motion to send HB 56 to O'Brien's committee, whereas Mr. Uhlman and Mr. O'Brien back it as a splendid idea. Joel Pritchard also speaks against the motion, noting the amount of time Senator Greive has spent in the House conferring with Democratic leadership and legislators on behalf of his own measure. Contention erupts again.

Mr. O'Brien: "Senator Greive isn't a member of this House."

Mr. Pritchard: "Are you sure? He's been here almost more than you have this last week."

Mr. Sawyer: "In regard to these two districts, I was wondering what underlying principle you used. Was it cronyism?"

Mr. Gorton: "That wasn't a question, Mr. Sawyer. That was part of a speech. Why not go ahead and make the rest of it?"

Each proposal to amend the districts we've drawn in HB 56 is generally defeated by split vote. When Mr. Uhlman moves to strike our 32nd District from the state map entirely, and replace it with the 35th, he also asks if Mr. Gorton will yield to a question.

Mr. Gorton's answer is, "No, I will not."

District 32 — mine and Mr. Uhlman's — remains.

Finally, HB 56 is ordered engrossed and passed to the Rules Committee for third reading. Upon third reading, we send it to the Senate. Will it die again in committee? No. Nine days later, the Senate sends it back. In the second afternoon session, under a Call of the House, we are presented with the Senate's amended bill: "The Senate has passed Engrossed House Bill No. 56 with the following amendments…"

I know better than to hope they've left it largely as is. The clerk continues reading: "…strike everything after the enacting clause on line 8 of the bill and insert the following…"

The following being Senator Greive's redistricting bill. My bill has been 'scalped' — the meat of it carved out, scraped clean, and substituted with something entirely different. Only the title and number of my bill remains unchanged.

No, I'm not inconsolably disappointed. I suppose that because of my previous exposure to the political process, through the League and lobbying, I've entered this position less

> **SCALP**
>
> To remove the entire contents of a bill, except for its title and enacting clause, and replace it with an entirely different bill.

starry-eyed than new legislators whose sole background has been in business. I already have a fair amount of feeling for the process. I know the hot buttons inherent in redistricting. And I'm familiar with tactic of the scalp.

"Mr. Gorton," says the Speaker.

From his desk in the front, Mr. Gorton says: "I move that the House refuse to concur in the Senate amendments to Engrossed House Bill No. 56 and ask the Senate to recede therefrom."

"Mr. O'Brien," the Speaker says next.

And across the aisle from Mr. Gorton, Mr. O'Brien moves "that the House *do* concur in the Senate amendments to Engrossed House Bill No. 56."

Mr. Copeland demands an electric roll call, which is sustained. Rep. O'Donnell demands an oral roll call, which is denied. Speaker Day notes the electric roll call has already been approved, and returns us to the question before the House, which is Mr. O'Brien's motion that we concur in the Senate's amendments to my redistricting bill (their scalped version). Several members from both sides of the aisle speak their piece.

"Mr. Speaker," says Mr. Ackley, "I wonder if Mr. Evans would yield to a question?"

He will.

"Mr. Evans," says Mr. Ackley, "in order to help me make up my mind on how to vote on this motion, I wonder if you could reassure me, if there is a conference committee, that the O'Brien Democrats in the House would be represented on that committee?"

And our Mr. Evans explains to their Mr. Ackley that selecting members of a conference committee is the prerogative of the Speaker. Then he adds, "I think I would be more inclined to answer your question if I truly thought it would help make up your mind on how to vote."

The vote is taken. Mr. O'Brien's motion that we concur with the Senate amendment fails.

The House having rejected the Senate's amended version, Tom Copeland now rises on a point of parliamentary inquiry: "Now that the House has decided on Mr. O'Brien's motion in the negative, has the House now determined that we do not concur in the Senate amendments?"

"That is correct," the Speaker says.

"Would it be necessary to place another motion to ask the Senate to recede therefrom?"

Speaker Day explains: "Mr. Gorton's motion, which was placed before Mr. O'Brien's motion, is now before the House. We will now act on Mr. Gorton's motion."

When we vote, several of the O'Brien Democrats actually side with the coalition in asking the Senate to recede. I don't fully follow these technicalities. This second vote seems redundant. In caucus afterwards, the move is explained: When two motions are requested on the same piece of legislation, the positive action is considered first, then the negative. We voted on acceptance of the Senate's amended bill first, and then on the motion that the Senate recede.

Three days later, the Senate sends the House a message: *No, it will not recede!* It insists upon its amendments to House Bill 56, and requests a conference thereon.

Tom Copeland moves that we grant the Senate's request for a conference.

John O'Brien moves that we simply accept the Senate's amendments.

The Speaker rules Mr. O'Brien out of order per Reed's Rule 245.

Mr. O'Brien fights back, citing Reed 252.

The Speaker and the former four-time speaker enter into a debate over which is the originating house for this bill — the House or the Senate. I argue silently from my seat: *I sponsored this — this is a House bill.* The Speaker agrees with me, and again rules Mr. O'Brien's motion out of order, again per Reed's Rule 245.

Speaker Day then appoints three from our House to serve on a conference committee along with three Senators, purportedly to settle the matter of redistricting per my House Bill 56. Representing us are Republican Slade Gorton, dissident Democrat Robert Perry and an O'Brien Democrat — K.O. Rosenberg, and the Senate appoints three members as well. From this committee… none of us hear one word more. As far as I am aware, no further discussion or negotiation takes place. For this 38th Session, redistricting is truly dead.

ON APRIL 6, AT 11:45 P.M., the massive main doors to the House swing wide in concert with the equally magnificent doors to the chamber of the Senate. From our seats in the rear, Marjorie and I have one of the better views as we turn our attention behind us, across the marbled expanse of the rotunda, where George Washington smirks immobile in bronze beneath the chandelier, bearing silent witness throughout the decades to our legislative work. As a House we face the Senate, and they face us — the legislature working in tandem at last, if only to formally complete this hard-fought session.

Although we failed to approve a compromise redistricting in this 38th session, our coalition held steady throughout — with extraordinary results for our state.

- With the six-vote difference that delivered us the majority and the gavel, we succeeded in blocking a Democrat-gerrymandered redistricting bill.

- The dissident Democrats who joined us stemmed the leftward trend of their party, thus turning the Democrat tide to something more closely resembling a moderate middle and giving their party's more conservative bloc renewed voice.

- In truth, our Republican coalition leadership may well have done the same — nudged us more toward center as a whole, giving our moderate voice a megaphone.

- Not the least is our massive biennial budget — crafted, balanced and passed with bi-partisan support to finance the growing needs of our growing state, with no increased taxes.

Contrary to rampant January forecasts, the coalition survived indeed, shaking loose the deadlock in the governance of our state. Under our coalition, the legislature did not languish as feared. The House failed to fail. Our state did not fall on its face. We've done most of our job. We've set our state in gear for another two years.

From their respective posts across the marbled capitol foyer, Speaker Day and Lieutenant Governor Cherberg raise their gavels in unison, and then in unison these leaders gavel their rostrums to adjourn us *sine die*.

"Sine die," we say in a single voice that echoes through the marbled expanses. After 84 grueling days, we are done... with this session, but not with our responsibilities. We've promised to provide the citizens of this state equal representation. Our legislative districts remain to be redrawn.

SINE DIE

(Latin: 'without day')
The final adjournment of a legislative session without fixing a date and time to reconvene.

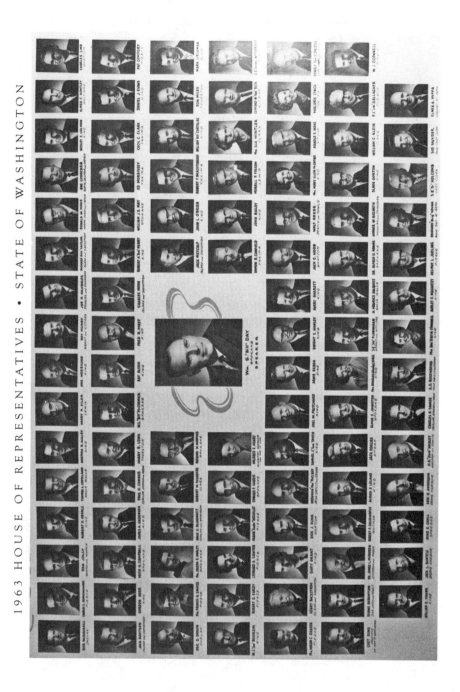

1963 HOUSE OF REPRESENTATIVES • STATE OF WASHINGTON

CHAPTER THREE

CHANGING TIMES
UNSEATING THE OUTDATED STATUS QUO

❦

Democracy is a delicate thing.
Our representative form of government must
be continually nurtured, continually tended —
the work is ongoing from inkling to inception,
to this very day and right on into the future.

As the pair of gavels echo to silence in the Senate and in the House, we depart our respective chambers at various speeds — some pack and exit immediately. I am among those who remain at my desk to reflect, but within moments my pensive introspection is burst.

"C'mon, Mary Ellen! C'mon Marjorie!" Joel invites. "You gals aren't finished yet — legislative tradition continues…"

He and Slade and Bob Goldsworthy usher us to a series of private "sine die" celebrations until, at 3 a.m., we drop in at Ben Moore's, the only all-night restaurant in Olympia. We place our orders for its famous country sausages and scrambled eggs. I discover I'm famished.

Afterwards, in the room in back, we chalk up cues for pool and shoot — both billiards and the breeze: *How are we going to redistrict now? The coalition was a start toward changing things here, but boy, now what?*

The General, as we all affectionately refer to Representative Goldsworthy, is handily wiping us all from the table. This six-term legislator/farmer from Rosalia in Eastern Washington developed some of his keen concentration the hard way. He served in our U.S. military twice – in World War II and again in Korea. During the first, his plane was gunned from the sky over Tokyo and plummeted in flames. The only survivor, he spent more than a year in a Japanese prison.

The night fades as we succumb to Bob's superior skill. By early morning, he banks his last shot, and we return to our individual Olympia homes in time for the morning papers.

"In spite of the frantic, frustrating, and sometimes bitter nature of its operation," writes Jack Pyle in the *Tacoma News-Tribune*, "the 38th Session wound up with best result for its time of any legislative session since World War II, even though it failed miserably to reapportion the state's legislative seats."

Pyle dubs Democrat Frank Foley, chairman of the Senate Ways and Means Committee, the best Senate member for managing to write and pass a biennial budget that is both balanced and avoids new taxes – "a remarkable feat for any legislator" – particularly in a session as contentious as this last. And he names Bill Day the best in the House for his role in the coalition: "The Democrat party was going too far out (to the left) and had to be held back before it destroyed itself. Right or wrong this was the theory… Under trying circumstances Day made the coalition work." [1]

Other newspapers commended us for a business-like session, despite the pressure of the court order to redistrict and despite our shaky start in the House.

But one paper reported that Governor Rosellini disagrees: "The 38th Legislature accomplished less than any session I've been in in 25 years. They devoted more time to bickering than to constructive legislation. This session has been full of controversy and rancor and bitterness right from the start." [2]

Yet we did do significant business. Of the 608 bills introduced in the House, 115 passed through the requisite steps to become new law. The governor signed 106 of these, allowed one to become law without his signature, and partially vetoed five others. Per tradition, the effective date for most of these is six months after we've adjourned.

The hallmark of our 38th Session, though, was the time we spent attempting to negotiate a successful legislative redistricting. Although my two bills are the only ones we ever formally considered on the floor of either house, leaders in both the House and Senate continually searched for a combination of districts that would satisfy a majority of our members. We failed, in large part because the Senate Democrats refused to negotiate on redistricting. Nor, in truth, were they particularly motivated to succeed.

Governor Rosellini, too, has maintained ambivalence toward any redistricting plan. He often expresses certainty that at the next election, because we drew no new lines this year, the Democrats will sweep the vote once again and thus recover full control of the legislature in 1965. He fully expects to win and serve a third term as our governor. The governor and Senate Democrats believe that in 1965, once the roadblock of our coalition is gone, they'll be squarely back in the saddle.

Though members of the legislature are thoroughly aware of the pending court action on redistricting, most decided they'd rather take their chances with the Federal District Court than vote for some compromise plan, whether by Senator Greive and the Democrats or by Representative Gorton and the Republicans. We worked so hard drafting districts, to no avail.

I am running on very little sleep, and try not to think of another round of redistricting. Not yet. For now my primary job is to pack my bags and head home. I'm back in the House chamber later in the morning, to pack the few items I'd kept at my desk, when again Joel approaches.

"Come to the caucus room, will you, Mary Ellen? Won't take long. I promise."

I join a handful of legislative colleagues and a few active Republicans — Slade, Joel, Montgomery "Gummie" Johnson, Dan's brother-in-law Bill Bell and Herb Hadley — for a quick meeting on a topic of some intrigue.

Herb — Representative Herbert Hadley from Longview, Washington — thinks Dan Evans ought to run for governor.

"Look what he did with this coalition," Herb says. "That ought to be worth some handsome political capital. I mean, really, just imagine what he could do for this state!"

Dan Evans did help glue a great divide in the 38th Session. The coalition held. Without it, the Democrats would have commanded both houses and the governor's seat, and we would likely now be facing all-new Democrat-drawn districts that would have cemented our state's lopsided Democrat majority until after the 1970 census — until the session in 1972. Yet without a new redistricting in place, our next election will follow old districts, perpetuate old disparities. No chance for us to overtake either house. Our best hope for a balanced state voice is to seat one from our party in the governor's mansion. Herb has a point.

But Dan Evans? The stiff elocutionist? The overly-serious, awkward engineer? As a candidate for governor? That would certainly take some work. Yet Dan Evans, the earnest, determined, attractive, fearless, problem solving engineer who helmed our coalition? Now that seems possible.

Dan has already departed Olympia to return to his pregnant young wife and young son and his engineering work. He has no inkling of this conversation here today. Perhaps he would protest, object. He would certainly laugh. But a Republican governor makes sense to us. We each toss a dollar bill on the table — tokens of our commitment to explore this prospect, this budding of a thought.

"Anyone ready to go home?" jokes Joel.

With weary laughter, we leave.

KEN ARRIVES FROM SEATTLE to drive me home. On this sunny Sunday, April 7, my husband helps me load my bags and boxes of paperwork into the trunk of our blue four-door Chevy Impala. We roll away from the capitol campus with its cherry trees fully in bloom to begin our slow trip back to Seattle on the old two-lane state Highway 99. The new interstate is still incomplete. When it is finished, it will cut this trip in half.

Inadequate transportation funding… budgets… I try not to think about it, but my head swims with the session behind me, then whirlpools toward the multiple tasks that loom: The end of the school year for Ken and the kids, summer vacations and camps and activities, constituent 'thank yous' and visits and speeches and interviews and, in the wake of our legislature's utter failure, the Federal District Court's new response to our failure to complete our redistricting. April 8 is the next scheduled hearing for *Thigpen v. Meyers.* Tomorrow — a Monday.

As my husband drives north, I settle into a sleepless quiet and my thoughts begin to drift. It occurs to me democracy is a delicate thing. Our representative form of government must continually be nurtured, continually tended. The work of maintaining a democratic government is ongoing – from inkling to inception to this day and straight into the future. Hence, my passionate work on our state's redistricting to keep our government working as designed. Hence, this afternoon reverie…

I recall eavesdropping, as a girl, on the adults who encircled my childhood family table: my mother, my father, Mother's sister Aunt Myrtle and her husband, my Uncle Claude Cunningham, a Kansas state legislator – avid readers, all of them, students of history, community activists. They were farmers, but they were also part and parcel of the fabric of my hometown.

As a young girl absorbing their conversation, their message rang clear – if your government isn't working to your satisfaction, you can always change it. That's the way our country is designed. But creating change is not so much an entitlement as a responsibility. My early role models recognized this and took part. Among these four, our American heritage and history was never taken for granted. Rather, our unique form of government was perpetually revered.

The history I picked up from them centered most on the women and men who came to America before there was any assembling or uniting of any states. Self-government began with the colonies, earliest among them being Plymouth in Massachusetts in 1620. Those English Pilgrims who actually survived the

Mayflower's Atlantic crossing set up a new community led by a group of 'separatists' whose names are now legend: William Bradford, William Brewster, John Alden, Miles Standish. First they'd broken with the Church of England – they believed it had not completely separated from the Catholic Church and Rome. Then they broke from England herself, fleeing first to Holland, and then to this new land in search of a place to practice their Puritan religious beliefs free from harassment, and worse, persecution.

Throughout the 1600's and early 1700's, those who journeyed to America from all parts of England and Europe were not substantially different from these Puritans. Various groups, for a variety of reasons, formed new colonies, set up self-governments, and were dedicated to the ideas, if not the practice, of individual liberty and equitable justice for all. They believed people could create their own governments to keep law and order, to provide certain services, and yet allow – not bind – an individual's freedoms.

This I learned by a Kansas kitchen stove.

"You all right, love?"

Ken is concerned by my silence as we hit the halfway mark driving home.

"Um-hmm."

"Memory lane?"

"Not what you think."

We share a quiet companionship at times.

I reflect back, not on the session but on the earliest immigrants to America, who set out to do what I have just attempted in Olympia – to make a government work better for us all. After 150 years of experimentation among those in this new land, America's founding fathers – authors of the constitution of the United States in 1787 – finally settled upon a form of government for us: A 'representative republic'. They recognized the weaknesses inherent in a true democracy – a government by each individual citizen, with its authority logically lodged in majority rule, subject to the sudden passions of the masses. Our founders wanted a government grounded in reason, discussion and compromise.

The word "democracy" comes from two Greek words – *demos and kratia* – joined to mean *the people's government*. The authors of our constitution, however, avoided the word 'democracy', much to my surprise when this was pointed out in American history class!

Our founding fathers emphasized that they'd specifically designed a representative republic. In a true democracy, every issue must be resolved by a meeting of the whole in a central community forum – a community hall, court house, capitol – with every person gathered, and each given a voice. Throughout history, true democracy has been tried many times, in many geographies, and it has failed because, more often than not, it eventually evolves into a monarchy or dissolves into chaos. Or perhaps it is just too unwieldy.

A republic is slightly different: The power still resides in the people (the electorate), but is exercised by representatives who are elected by, and responsible to, the people. Because those who are elected represent the rest, they must govern by a set of pre-agreed rules, rather than solely by a majority vote of the whole. These rules — these laws — guide their actions, rather than the simple majority sentiment within a room, or the passion of a moment, and this is the key distinction between the two systems.

'Democracy' and 'Republic' are often mistaken as one and the same, but there is a fundamental difference. For while the governing members in both are elected by the people, in a democracy the majority governs according to varying individual votes, while in a republic the government also governs according to its layer of laws.

Ours never fully was a people's government to begin with, in the sense that every single person took part. During George Washington's presidency only about one man in seven had the right to vote, and of course, no women — much to the chagrin of Abigail Adams and her gender. She complained loudly to her husband, John, via her pen, while he was away creating the framework of our country: "…All men would be tyrants if they could," she wrote him. "If particular care and attention is not paid the ladies, we are determined to foment a rebellion, and will not hold ourselves bound by laws in which we have no voice or representation." [3]

Her husband responded with wit, begging inferiority to women as a defense for excluding them from the right to vote: "We know better than to repeal our masculine systems… they are little more than theory… you know we are the subjects… We have only the name of masters, and rather than give this up, which would completely subject us to the despotism of the petticoat, I hope General Washington and all our brave heroes would fight." [4]

So only men got the vote. But not all men. A man's right to vote was tied either to his ownership of property, a certain quantity of education, membership in a state-sponsored church, or… some other test. There were many. As for a woman's rights at the poll booth, there were none. At that point, Thomas Jefferson's magnanimous words in our Declaration of Independence that "all men are created equal" were more idealistic than real — reserved for men, and certain men only.

Our redistricting battle today is just another in a long line of American demands for equality and equal voice at the voting booth — appropriate for a government built on individual freedoms and rights. In an ongoing spirit of independence, once we broke free from England's King George, more and more Americans came to demand the right to vote through the years. One by one, obstacles to the voting booth were leveled, both within the states and by amending our federal constitution.

One hundred and fifty years after the first of our colonies set down roots, the first set of federal voting rights were prescribed, predicated on property ownership and degree of community standing, as mentioned.

After another fifty years, most white men over the age of twenty-one could vote.

After the end of the Civil War, in February 1870, black men (but not women) were given the right to vote, too, when enough states ratified our U.S. Constitution's 15th Amendment: "The right of citizens of the United States to vote shall not be denied or abridged by race, color, or previous condition of servitude."

But it didn't mention gender. Women were still voiceless as voters: White, black and every woman between. Another fifty years again, in August of 1920, we amended our constitution once more to specifically give votes to women. The 19th Amendment provides that "neither the individual states of the United States nor its federal government may deny a citizen the right to vote because of the citizen's sex."

That still didn't cover us all. In the South, once the right to vote had been constitutionally granted the black man, some southern states set a hefty poll tax to prohibit the less-endowed from voting — not only blacks, but immigrants and minorities of all sorts, Native Americans, the poor white. Not until August of 1962 — seven months ago — did Congress pass a new amendment banning the poll tax, which awaits full ratification to this day. I'm happy to have played a role in the "yes" vote of Washington State, by co-sponsoring our confirmation of the 24th Amendment in this session that just came to an end.

Another voter discrepancy has been noted since World War II, when many Americans began to reason that if eighteen year olds were old enough to fight for their country, they should be old enough to vote. My collegiate constituents are arguing this, and we've begun to explore a campaign to lower the voting age.

My Midwest pioneer roots laid a clear groundwork for my community ethic. Knowing the history of our country and our community, anyone's community, is essential to....

"5014, honey," Ken says as he pulls our Chevy to the curb.

I'm home, and it is this home, this family, this neighborhood that compelled me to undertake such difficult legislative work.

I've learned so much about our governmental process this past year, particularly in the last two and half months. Yet I'm still a novice, and our schools are still woefully under-funded. Should I continue? Run for a second term?

"Hey, Mom!"

"Hi, Mom!"

Today my job is Mom.

My eyes snatch the local Sunday headline: "Members can't decide whether the legislative session was good or bad."

I just smile.

Monday, April 8, on my first morning home, the Federal District Court moves to continue (postpone) its decision on redistricting for three more weeks. A new hearing date is set: April 29.[5,6]

Of all my legislative colleagues, I am perhaps the best informed on this issue, thanks to the conduit of news on redistricting available to me through the League of Women Voters.

Tuesday, April 9, I get a call from my 32nd District Republican Club. Would I address them at their monthly meeting a few weeks away? They have a specific topic in mind: Was the 38th Session of the Legislature good or bad? The press and pundits and armchair politicians still can't decide. What do I think? I'd be happy to talk, I told them.

AFTER OUR POST-SESSION POWWOW in the Republican caucus room Sunday, Herb Hadley returned to his Longview legislative district, determined to organize a committee to "Draft Dan Evans for Governor."

This turned out to be a cinch — forming the committee, that is, not the actual drafting of the candidate! — for Evans had impressed many of Hadley's Cowlitz County constituents by successfully negotiating tough cross-party crossfire during the 38th Session. Herb's 18th District eventually passed a resolution suggesting Dan run for governor, so it was Herb who provided the spark that set the Evans for Governor notion on fire.

But would Dan Evans, could Dan Evans, be persuaded to run against our two-time incumbent Governor Rosellini? Those of us on the inside know how little Rosellini leads, but in general he is fairly well liked as governor and, I must acknowledge, a very likeable man. His fellow governors even elected him to chair the National Governors' Conference this year. [7]

Thinking Dan's candidacy is a good idea is one thing, but convincing him to run is entirely another. Yet if Republicans could win our state's governorship in 1964, we'd have a better voice in redistricting, and thus better odds of a political comeback — or more key, a better chance to reinvigorate our state's two-party system, and thereby to revitalize our state.

My mind circles two questions. *What will happen with this redistricting issue? And who will take the governor's office?* Both are of paramount importance to the future of our state. So though I'm largely enmeshed already in year-end school activities, seven family calendars and five children's lives, my professional thoughts bounce between the topics of statewide redistricting and the governor's race.

Joel calls: "So, Mary Ellen, what do you think?"

"I think it's a great idea."

"You do."

"Yes. Dan could be a great governor. Is he considering it?"

"He's hinting he's willing," Joel says. "You free next Sunday afternoon? I'm gathering a group to brainstorm this wild hare. Pros and cons. You know the drill. Frank and I have lined up a spot at the Ben Franklin."

The Pritchard brothers know the owner of this classic old hotel in the heart of downtown Seattle. The building is for sale, so our meeting space is free. On the second Sunday in May, I will join the small group.

MONDAY, APRIL 29, THE FEDERAL DISTRICT COURT now hears *Thigpen v. Meyers,* and after lengthy testimony, the hearing is continued again until May 3, effectively deferring any action on redistricting.[8] My phone rings that afternoon.

"Mom! *University District Herald!*"

I've already done my post-session interview. This must be about the court case.

"Mrs. McCaffree?"

"Yes."

"Congratulations!"

"Um... thank you. What for?"

"You've been named the University District's Ideal Mother for 1963."[9]

"I... oh my."

"Yes, you were nominated by Mrs. Mortimer H. Thomas and by Mr. E. Earl Richards..."

Having read about previous years' nominees, I knew what this entailed: Mother's Day breakfast with my family as guests of the Lions Club at The Wilsonian. The whole family treated to Mother's Day dinner at the Meany Hotel. But the meals mean less to me than the words of the two who suggested me. The reporter reads from their nomination letters:

"Her tremendous recognition of duty both to her family and her community has welded together what might well be described as an ideal family," Mr. Richards wrote. "The records of all of their children in accepting leadership responsibilities reflects the remarkable guidance given them in the family."

Mrs. Thomas (my neighbor Joan) is more effusive still.

"Her five children are the product of the highest obligations of motherhood, and the entire community has benefited from her inspiration and leadership… I have known the McCaffrees several years and I never cease to be amazed at their collective activities and accomplishments."

But even their words mean less than the privilege of parenting my five unique children. Jim has just completed his junior year studying dairy husbandry in the School of Agriculture at the University of Wisconsin at Madison. Chuck is concluding his sophomore year in chemistry at the University of Washington, where he fraternizes with the Delta Tau Deltas and competes on the Husky crew. Nancy is at Roosevelt High School, and Mary and David at John Marshall Junior High. Little League, Girl Scouts, youth groups, leadership. I lead a full life as a mother and, because they're good children, as a legislator as well. Of course, I can't deny the loving partnership of Ken.

Being part of such a family is the bigger honor, and I tell them all at the dinner table tonight, then place a spontaneous phone call to Wisconsin, to Jim. When I hang up, I rush out the door to address my 32nd District Republican Club at its monthly evening meeting—in the ballroom of the Meany Hotel. After a yummy slice of cake during the social half hour at 7:30, I take a seat for the business meeting and then I take the podium.

From here I can easily survey the diversity of my constituency—heavily populated with middle-aged working men and women, but an audience dotted as well with senior citizens and students from our two district universities. I tend to be much less conservative than most in this group, but I've come to know many among my 105 precincts. Having doorbelled my 32nd District twice last fall as I campaigned, many faces are familiar and most are friendly.

I set my notes within sight.

"I have been asked, do I think the 38th Legislative Session was good or bad?" I begin. "Let me tell you why I think the 38th Legislative session was a good one. For me the 84 days and nights I spent in Olympia representing you were filled with the exhilarating process of making our democracy work. It was exciting. It was fascinating. Sometimes disappointing and confusing. But on any account it is a stimulating challenge to be a participant in our governmental process.

"There are many reasons to label the 38th Legislative Session a success. Let me review the three I believe to be most important. I call these the three "R's": Reform, Revenue and Redistricting. In this session we successfully instigated some reforms in the daily proceedings of the legislature. We began with the formation of a coalition government. The minority of 48 Republicans and six disaffected Democrats voted for new leadership and a new focus for accomplishing the day-to-day operations of the House. No longer was the legislature controlled by a single party. This gave us Republicans, as your representatives, a fighting chance for reform and progress in the ideals dear to the heart of all of us: less government regulation, a balanced budget, and a consistent policy for taxation. As Dan Evans said on day one, 'We are embarked on a new era – a really new era.'

"Voting for a coalition is always risky, but it was our best alternative at the beginning of the 38th Session and it worked to our advantage, even though we were unable to achieve all of our desired goals.

"A second reason this was a good session was that we were able to vote approval of a balanced state budget. This budget was put together by our Senate colleague, Democrat Senator Frank Foley from Vancouver. This was accomplished without adding any new taxes, and we consider it a major step of cooperation among both political parties and a substantial improvement in our state government."

Some heads nod their agreement, others wag.

"The third reason I believe the 38th Session was successful is redistricting...."

Eyebrows raise: Redistricting remains undone.

"It is of course a disappointment that we were unable to reach a compromise solution to the redistricting issue during this session, but – we were able to keep a foot in the door for another session and to give the Republicans another chance at equal representation in our state legislature."

Scattered applause.

"We certainly developed some outstanding leaders in Dan Evans, Slade Gorton and William Day, to name three. As you may have already heard, Dan Evans says he is willing to run for governor at the next election. With all of us working together for the election of Dan as governor and the retirement of Governor Rosellini we will have an even better chance of reaching an acceptable redistricting plan in the next session. Equal representation of our legislative seats is the foundation of responsible government. One way or another we must achieve this result so that we can enact the kind of laws we all would like for our State.

"Yes it was a good 38th Session and I want to thank each and every one of you for your support, your suggestions, your encouraging phone calls to me during my time representing you in Olympia. It makes me feel good that we the people of this district and this state were working together to make our democracy a better, more productive process. Thank you for all your support."[10]

Friday, May 3, as promised, the Federal District Court continues to hear *Thigpen v. Meyers* and Judge Beeks issues an oral decision: As legislators we must complete the job of redistricting before the '64 election. Until we finish, he declares our existing legislative districts null and void and enjoins—prohibits, that is—our Secretary of State Victor Meyers from holding elections in our districts as they stand today. Judge Beeks does not, however, find circumstances so exceptional that he thinks the court should take over the task of redistricting.[11,12]

We are now at the mercy of Governor Rosellini, for the governor is the only one with the authority to call our legislature into special session. The governor, however, has no intention of doing so: Why tinker with a Democratic majority?

Donald Voorhees, a volunteer attorney for the League of Women Voters, had asked the court, during this hearing, to *please* take over redistricting. I heard later that midway through Voorhees' presentation, Federal District Judge Gilbert H. Jertberg interrupted him. If the court does this job, Judge Jertberg told Voorhees, the legislature will likely never redistrict itself again. Then the justice admitted he was leaning toward forcing an at-large statewide election—no districts, no constituencies. Everyone would run against everyone else: The top 99 vote-earners would win the 99 seats in the House, and the top 49 the 49 seats in the Senate, regardless of where the were from. Judge Jertberg's wildcard idea draws a major statewide outcry—from longtime incumbents, from political newcomers and from the general public alike.[13]

ON MOTHER'S DAY, SUNDAY, MAY 5, the newspaper takes my photograph with a plaque to which they've added my name. We enjoy our two complimentary family meals, then it's back to business and McCaffree busy-ness, as usual.

Jim is not coming home this summer. He'll spend his vacation in Colorado with his Uncle Dwight (my brother) and Aunt Bernice and his cousins Hull. Of all our children, Jim has remained a Midwesterner at heart. When Chuck completes his second year at UW, he'll start his summer job with the government of King County—as overseer of the county dump near the Sea-Tac airport just off the main highway. Nancy is preparing for summer at the Robinswold Girl Scout Camp on the Hood Canal on the Olympic Peninsula, where she'll be a counselor-in-training. Mary and David are booked in a series of hometown pursuits, and we all have our eyes on summer's end, when we'll uphold our family tradition of spending a long weekend on the Washington coast. Just before Labor Day weekend, we'll all clamber into the Impala and head for the Iron Springs Resort.

But first things first, and for now that means keeping one eye on an ambitious governor's race, and the other on the legal drama of our state's overdue redistricting.

Sunday, May 12, at the Ben Franklin Hotel, along with my increasingly familiar House colleagues, Joel, Slade, Dan and Don, we're joined by Dan and

Marilyn Ward, Helen Rasmussen, Jay Gilmour, our caucus attorney Jim Dolliver, and Ritajean Butterworth, a spunky mother of five — all boys — who has joined us at Slade's request. She is Slade's longtime top campaign organizer. Also in this small conference room are Dan's friend John Hayden (owner and editor of the *Marine Digest*), Dan's wife Nancy and her brother, Bill Bell, and Dan's younger brother, Roger Evans, a school teacher.

The question is simple: Should Dan challenge Governor Rosellini for the governorship in 1964? The answer is decidedly more complex. Dan questions whether this is the proper time for such a tremendous move, but he seems committed to exploring the notion, at the very least. Though I've not yet decided what my own political future might be, I gladly join the speculative talk surrounding the governor's race.

Dan thanks us first for sacrificing a Sunday afternoon with our families to join him, then begins: "This is an intriguing challenge and one I would like to explore more fully with all of you."

Still serious, still formal, still stiff, he recites a set of facts: 1. The Republican Party in the state of Washington has slowly been sinking into permanent minority status. 2. The coalition was successful this last legislative session, and most of us agree our success in blocking the Democrat-drawn redistricting gives Republicans a very slim foot in the door. 3. Winning the governorship in the 1964 election is the best way to take advantage of that slice of daylight. Without a statewide redistricting before the next election, there's honestly little chance Republicans will win majorities in either house.

"Nancy and I have talked it over..." he says, taking the hand of his wife, just 29. "I'm willing to give my best effort to a run for the governorship if the rest of you are willing to work alongside us to accomplish what seems almost... impossible."

He emphasizes that he has no financial base and is not willing, under any circumstance, to go into debt. Then he opens it up to the rest of us for pros and cons.

"I'm counting on you all to help me out with the heavy thinking," he says in all earnesty.

"Dan Evans' Group of Heavy Thinkers," Joel jokes, and writes on a board: D.E.G.O.H.T.[14] An acronym is born.

"On the negative side of the equation," I suggest, "we are looking at a long shot. But on the positive, we have a rising star in you, Dan."

Others agree. We are relatively young, and the challenge is mammoth, but as a group we're determined. We want a fair chance at helping our stalemated state.

I had witnessed firsthand, in my inaugural legislative session, how the policies of the present administration focus too fully on partisan and patronage concerns, whereas our particular group of Republicans (we're not the mainstream of the party, perhaps, but the most energetic component) wants to problem-solve for the people, particularly in our swelling urban cores. A successful governor's race would catapult our efforts and kick-start progress. After we toss around the possibilities and pitfalls, we conclude as a group: "Let's go for it!"

"OK. That's settled," Dan says. "Now, how?"

Joel has a ready answer: "What you do is you invite 200 of your best friends to a 7 o'clock breakfast. Tell them right up front, point blank, right in the invitation, Dan, you're going to ask them all for money. See if anybody shows up. That'll speak volumes about your support."

"I'll say," Dan says. "But 7, Joel? How about 7:30?"

"Nope. 7 a.m. Make it tough. You want to know who your real friends are."

We concur and set it in motion, drum up the guest list, volunteer for tasks. We'll ask each invitee to bring $50 to launch Dan's campaign. That agreed, we return to our family Sundays.

Monday, May 27, the Federal District Court issues its final formal order — in writing. Redistricting is a political act, Judge William Beeks explains, and judicial power to redistrict should be used rarely, and only under exceptional circumstances.[15] These are not exceptional circumstances, he says, but simply a failure of the legislature to do its constitutional job. I completely agree with him. Thus, the original court order remains in effect: the legislature must either complete a redistricting plan in the interim, or else. Or else what? Some speculate it's still possible all our state legislative candidates will have to run at-large, just as the district court threatened.

One part of me stands at the ready to redistrict, in the event we are called into special session. I know the maps. I know the drill. And I know Slade and Don are willing to work with me until a plan is in place. However, we can't do a thing without Governor Rosellini, and to date, our longtime governor is willing to simply let things lie — all the more reason to stay focused on electing Dan.

Wednesday, June 26: Bright and early — at 7 a.m. to be exact — we welcome a host of guests to the 'Dan Evans for Governor' breakfast. Ken is a table captain, having invited ten to attend. Mastermind Joel has set up the room full of tables *just so*, to make sure we're actually short of seating — a favorite ploy to suggest more arrived today to support Dan than we'd counted on. The breakfast raises nearly $10,000.[16] The campaign for 'Evans for Governor' is underway.

Where does Dan Evans stand in the minds of the citizens of Washington State? Is he really the best Republican prospect for governor? What are his chances of winning? The Republican State Central Committee is conducting its own statewide poll: who would make the strongest GOP candidate for governor against Albert Rosellini?

In the next DEGOHT meeting we review the likely competition.

At the top of the list is Dick Christensen, the evangelical Lutheran minister from Edmonds who rose to recent statewide prominence when he challenged our legendary U.S. Senator Warren Magnusson in the last campaign, and very nearly dealt the Senate icon a stunning upset. Passionate both in the pulpit and on the stump, and with a fierce fundamentalist following, it is fair to say that Christensen is one formidable figure. Not only is his name recognizable — it's household by now — but he's a seasoned orator, one phenomenal public speaker.

Then there's Joe Gandy, president of the 1962 Seattle World's Fair Commission. The overwhelmingly successful fair gave Seattle her landmark Space Needle plus a larger 'dot' on the global map. And it gave Joe Gandy a good public name.

Also on the list of possible candidates is retiring Seattle mayor Gordon Clinton — a youthful, popular and effective leader. And the two Republicans in congressional seats: Tom Pelly from Seattle, and Catherine May from Spokane. And then there's Dan, whose recent rise in the House is lesser known to the general public.

The pollsters are hard at it. We await their results.

WHEN WE HEAR THE POLLING IS COMPLETE and tabulated, we invite Kraft and Associates, a public relations firm, to join us at our next DEGOHT meeting at the Ben Franklin. Together, we'll review the results and plan Dan's campaign accordingly. Joel picks me up for the meeting, excited to examine the poll: "This oughtta tell us a lot."

He got that right.

Once we're seated in the conference room, a member of the Kraft team unveils the graphically attractive chart they've prepared of the polling results. Conducted statewide, the pollsters asked hundreds the question: "Who would make the strongest Republican candidate for governor?"[17] As we scan the results, the room sobers quickly, then deadens into absolute silence.

The Reverend Dick Christensen	37 percent
Congressman Tom Pelly	17 percent
Seattle Mayor Gordon Clinton	12 percent
Seattle World's Fair's Joe Gandy	6 percent
Congresswoman Catherine May	6 percent
Representative Dan Evans	5 percent

"What about the Republican split?" Joel asks. "Didn't they also calculate where everyone stood among just the Republicans they polled?"

The Kraft man produces a second chart[18] — a breakdown of the response to prospective candidates by those polled who identified themselves as Republicans:

The Reverend Dick Christensen	52 percent
Congressman Tom Pelly	19 percent
Seattle Mayor Gordon Clinton	7 percent
Seattle World's Fair's Joe Gandy	6 percent
Representative Dan Evans	6 percent
Congresswoman Catherine May	4 percent

In this summer of 1963, the notion of Dan as a candidate for governor occurred to only one in twenty of all those polled. He couldn't win a primary election if it happened any time soon, no doubt about it — especially with Dick Christensen the early pick of more than half from our party. With marks like these, Dan certainly hasn't muscle enough to oust the reasonably well-liked incumbent Governor Rosellini.

"Sorry, folks," the Kraft team tell us. "Based upon our experience and these figures, we really can't advise you to pursue this. Dan, perhaps you should consider a stepping stone position first, to build your reputation statewide. Lieutenant governor, perhaps."

"Governor," Dan says, resolute.

"No place to go but up!" chimes in Joel.

We have fourteen months until the primary election in 1964, and if Dan survives the primary, two months more until the general election for governor. As marketing managers, Kraft and Associates have their work cut out for them, and so do we.

"I'd say Jim and Dan oughtta hit the road," Joel suggests, "as of yesterday!"

Dan has named his campaign manager: Jim Dolliver, caucus attorney for our 1963 House Republicans. By the end of last session, these two had developed a deep, abiding friendship. The bond between them was founded in politics, of course, but permanently forged in our state's breathtaking wilderness areas. They share an affinity for scaling our challenging peaks and hiking our rugged mountain ranges — both the Olympics and Cascades. Last hiking season, prior to the '63 session, they hit the trails together, so that by the time they were working side-by-side in our caucus and coalition, they were splendidly in tandem.

During the 1963 session, Jim Dolliver not only dealt us sound legal advice, but also lent our caucus invaluable suggestions both strategic and political. A savvy navigator with a quiet presence, he's a smart choice to commandeer Dan's ambitious bid. Jim's inherent dignity and professional aura are exactly what our young underdog candidate needs. I think he lends just the right counterbalance to the fresh-faced 38-year-old.

Unlike native-born Dan, Dolliver became a Washingtonian in his teens, when he took a summer job during college as a ranger in the Olympic National Park. He fell in love with the state, moved here immediately upon graduation and stayed, eventually adding a law degree from the University of Washington to his Political Science B.A. from Swarthmore. He married a college classmate, Barbara Babcock, and together they're raising a large family. His two heroes? His father and George Washington. Jim Dolliver also admits to a weakness for Wagner.

Before coming to work for our caucus in 1963, Jim practiced law privately. More salient to this new position with Dan, he served three terms as administrative assistant to one of our congressmen in the 1950's. To our neophyte group, he brings a solid framework for political organization.

My own bond with Jim Dolliver derives from our membership in the Methodist church. However, though we share a mutual admiration, we've had little interaction other than our focus on this campaign. I do know him to be kind, gentle, intelligent and determined — more of a background personality… more like me.

After our initial silent intake of the statistics presented by Kraft and Associates, not one among us hints or infers that we ought to give this up. We "Heavy Thinkers" spend the balance of this Sunday afternoon calculating the best route from mostly unknown to public persona. We conclude that Daniel J. Evans, candidate for governor, must traverse our state to each cranny and nook — knock on doors, chat with the editors of local papers, and at each local radio station, make an attempt to get on the air. We basically want Dan's name and face and voice in front of as many of our state's citizens as possible.

With naïve optimism — our trademark as a group, and Dan most naïve of all — we all roll up our sleeves and plow full steam ahead. A swath of butcher paper goes up on the wall.

"Platform," Dolliver says simply, pen in hand.

As a team we begin to list our issues and concerns and goals — our ambitious and specific vision for our home state.

> **PLATFORM**
>
> The governmental policies and positions of a candidate or political party.

Over the weeks of DEGOHT meetings, these butcher paper brainstorms evolve into a five-category, multi-itemed 'to do' list for our state, which we eventually dub 'The Blueprint for Progress', partly in jest — to reflect Dan's systematic approach to every problem by viewing it from all angles and functions: He definitely thinks like an engineer.

Unfortunately, he also speaks and interacts like one. You wouldn't know this from hearing Dan Evans address the floor of the House, but he is absolutely timid when it comes to speaking to a group of strangers, and his timidity translates to a lifeless, leaden delivery. Those of us who know him know this, and as we begin to discuss his campaign trail, we agree. We'll need some version of speech patrol.

We're also familiar with Dan's tendency to drift to the corner in any crowded room and stay there in one conversation, listening at length, rather than circulate. Slade has taken to calling him 'Old Glue Foot'. And Dan's fascination with anything well engineered sometimes fuels his preference for studying this "thing" rather than greeting a crowd of well wishers – a structural support beam, for example, or a nifty gadget. Therefore, in addition to 'speech patrol' we organize 'corner patrol' as well. Ken often serves in this latter capacity.

Among those invited early to donate to Dan's campaign was Pat Goodfellow, an auto dealer, who asked if, in lieu of money, he could donate a used car to the candidate's cause. And that is how Dan and Jim ended up driving off in a used white Plymouth sedan to criss-cross our state throughout the summer of 1963, with the odometer immediately racking up the earliest of their tens of thousands of miles.

Of our DEGOHT group, Slade's campaign ace Ritajean Butterworth and I have the best innate knack for networking and mobilizing volunteers, so we jump right into it. I contact my newfound legislative friends across our state, and from Dan's campaign headquarters, Ritajean and I map out distant visits for our roaming duo. We also cull volunteers to make signs, stuff envelopes, and man a newly installed bank of telephones. The Evans for Governor team swells to dozens, then to scores, and over the months our number of volunteers mushrooms into the several hundreds.

Joel and Frank Pritchard serve as the campaign's chief strategists, in consultation with our core group: Gorton and Dolliver, Don Moos, Gummie Johnson, Roger Evans and Bill Bell, team Kraft, Ritajean and… me. I love the strategic nature of our work. I love the challenge. I am surprised to find myself so energized by this long-shot campaign. Each Sunday the DEGOHTs meet at the Ben Franklin and Jim and Dan report.

"That one day," Dan tells us, "we logged 550 miles on two-lane roads. Isn't that right?"

Jim nods and describes it: They departed Spokane early for a breakfast engagement in Colville, then drove across a slick, narrow road over Sherman Pass to Republic for a quick stop and handshakes at lunch, then down to Yakima for an organized afternoon coffee, and back over a Cascade mountain pass to an evening fundraiser in Tacoma. Oh, and with more stops in a handful of smaller towns along the way.

"But Wagner almost did us in," Dan shares, with a wink at Jim.

I suspect I know what they're talking about. I love opera, and being a young wife during Ken's grad school days, my one escape from motherhood and holding down our cramped campus household was to make an occasional trip to Chicago's opera house, where I allowed myself to be carried away by the operatic grandeur of Wagner.

As they drove that day, Jim had stumbled across a Wagnerian opera on the radio dial, and found it so inspiring that his normally leaden foot sat particularly heavy on the pedal. As we all have come to know, Jim Dolliver loves his Wagner.

"I guess it's sort of the seductive quality of his music, more than anything, that I like," he now confesses with a bashful grin. "He sure knows how to use French horns and violins! His politics were a little screwy, I'll grant you, but the music is... wonderful!" [19]

"Yeah," says Dan. "So wonderful that we were doing 80 miles an hour outside Moses Lake, and that's when we had that blowout..." [20]

THIS SAME WEEK, OUR SECRETARY OF STATE, Victor Meyers, goes public — or, more accurately, he goes straight to the U. S. Supreme Court — to air his ire at the Federal District Court and its stern stance on our state's redistricting. *How dare the court put a hold on legislative elections statewide! How dare it threaten to eliminate our legislative districts in one swift rap of the gavel! How dare it threaten a statewide election at large!* Thus, he appeals to our nation's highest court, in Washington, D.C.

After that, our secretary of state petitions the Federal District Court for a stay (a freeze) of their order, pending the Supreme Court's ruling on his appeal. *Don't do it*, his petition begs the district court justices. *Let the Supreme Court decide.*

In August, the Federal District Court officially denies Victor Meyers' request for a stay, so our secretary of state goes to the U.S. Supreme Court a second time: *Will you institute this stay instead?* [21]

Nearly two hundred years after we've declared our American independence, the battle and debate over the concept of one man, one vote persists, right here. For the balance of 1963, nothing more happens... with redistricting.

> **ELECTION AT LARGE**
>
> All candidates run as a group, and the top vote-recipients fill the contested positions.

OUR FAMILY TRIP TO THE COAST NEARS, and as the summer draws to its end, I split my time between Dan's campaign work and preparing to camp. Late in August we set off in the Impala, bound for the Iron Springs Resort, and I leave politicking behind in favor of the seashore. Then it's time for my McCaffree clan to return home to start the school year.

Autumn is a more marked beginning than New Years Day for me, with a university professor and five students in the family. This autumn of 1963 is as busy as the rest. Nancy begins her senior year at Roosevelt High, and Mary starts high school as a Roughrider — a sophomore. David will be top dog as a 9th grader at John Marshall Junior High. My, how the years zoom by!

"Hey, Mom, how do I look?" Mary asks me one day at the Evans for Governor campaign headquarters downtown. I'm there again, working with Ritajean. This is how my daughter looks: White skimmer hat rimmed with a red, white and blue bumper sticker — "Dan Evans for Governor" — in place of a hatband. She's wearing a white jumper, white blouse, white crew socks, white Keds, and hoists a big white sign on a stick with the words "Help Clean Up…" Mary's friend, dressed the same, arrives with another sign: "…the Mess in Olympia".

Mary is co-chairman of Teens for Dan Evans, and along with a trio of boys

Mary McCaffree, left, of Teens for Dan Evans (for Governor), campaigns in the streets of Seattle.

PHOTO: SEATTLE POST-INTELLIGENCER

in white coveralls, this group plans to take to the downtown Seattle streets to campaign. Armed with push brooms, matching skimmer hats, fresh faces and boundless enthusiasm, they deliver a singular message: Dan Evans and the Blueprint for Progress will set our state on a more progressive course. Their photo appears in the Seattle newspapers the following day, six giddy kids cleaning Seattle streets to plug Dan Evans' promise to clean up Olympia.

The other co-chairman of Teens for Dan Evans is Roosevelt High letterman and senior Tom LaPenske. If I read things correctly, my daughter has a bit of a crush. But she's also a bubbly campaigner, and she truly wants Dan to win. For her crush and for her candidate, therefore, she gladly helps Tom affix bumper stickers – Dan Evans for Governor – across the back of his cute little brand new bright white Volkswagen beetle.

With one year to go before the general election, the Evans campaign creates a fake newspaper to jostle the public's imagination. Why not plant a seed of success? Several of our campaign workers hand these out at bus stops in downtown Seattle and Tacoma during rush hour. *Extra! Special Edition!* The eight-page paper imagines an Evans win.

NEAR THE END OF EVERY NOVEMBER, our state caucuses gather, election or no. In these "off" years, with no elections in play, our Republican caucus gatherings are more social, less procedural. We coordinate this annual event with the annual Apple Cup football game: Husky versus Cougar, University of Washington against its cross-state rival Washington State U. Since I live just blocks from the UW campus and Husky Stadium, I've offered to host the group this year at my home.

On Friday, November 22, the day before the big game and our caucus gathering, I check my cupboards and fridge and jot a quick grocery list for our post-game potluck. Just as I'm heading out to shop, the phone rings. It's Slade.

"Mary Ellen? Have you heard?" His voice sounds strange. "President Kennedy has been shot. In Dallas. He's not expected to live. I think we should…"

"Cancel."

I hang up, sink to the nearest chair and succumb to grief.

Anguish. Anger. Fear. Remorse. A hundred emotions flood me at once, surely as they are surging through American hearts across the nation. *How could this happen?* I am home alone – alone with my thoughts and my heartache. Ken walks in. He dismissed his class when he heard the news. Mary and David return from school early as well.

Our caucus meeting, of course, is cancelled, and our entire country submerges in mourning. For America, the assassination of our president is a cultural tipping point, and we begin to take a closer look — at our lives, at our communities and at our country. In a subdued and serious state of mind, I redouble my commitment to working towards a healthier government in my adopted home state. In the wake of this violent, shattering loss, making a difference somehow makes the most sense to me.

IN EARLY JANUARY OF 1964, at a Sunday meeting of the DEGOHTs, Dan makes a sober announcement: His campaign is almost out of money. His campaigning for governor may have to halt. He reiterates his unwillingness to go into debt.

To date, we've managed to operate his campaign within that initial breakfast $10,000 we collected last June, plus a small monthly trickle of individual donations. Early on in this campaign, the business community put their money and mouths behind Dick Christensen — the polling frontrunner and the candidate they considered the better risk: 8.5 to 1 odds against Dan Evans. Yet the manpower we've managed to assemble is amazing, and support for Dan Evans for Governor continues to swell. We can't give up now, we agree. But what to do?

Two events turn the table.

Kraft and Associates agrees to stay aboard without collecting a fee; our marketing and our campaign materials can therefore continue. And towards the end of the following week, a well-known businessman makes a handsome $500 contribution to the campaign. This allows us to stay in business, however tenuously, and adds a welcome vote of confidence from the business sector.

A newer poll shows Dan Evans' name recognition and candidate status… improving. After eight months on the campaign trail, he's all the way up to ten percent.

THE FOLLOWING MONTH, TWO ITEMS of relevant national news hit home. The first arrives February 4, when the poll tax is officially abolished. The 24th Amendment to the U.S. Constitution is officially adopted, another step in our ongoing quest for equality within our voting booths and equal voice. The second, however, sets us on a less direct path toward voter equity: On February 17, U.S. Supreme Court Justice William O. Douglas grants a stay of the Federal District Court's order regarding our state's redistricting, pending the high court's decision on our secretary of state's appeal. Until that appeal hearing, our old district lines will remain intact for the coming election — those districts that have kept our state government so politically imbalanced, and Republicans here and urbanites disproportionately shushed. But the "pending appeal" component of Justice Douglas' response does acknowledge that this issue remains to be settled.[22]

If only Governor Rosellini would call a special legislative session so we can tackle this. No such luck.

As 1964 unfolds, the Evans campaign gains momentum and basks in broadening support, which prompts Joel to contact all the incumbent Republican legislators, including me: "Forget about Dan for now, team. Go out and get re-elected!" So while local 'Evans for Governor' campaign committees continue to sprout around the state, my family has another campaign to consider.

After I've helped to create the DEGOHT Blueprint for Progress and added my goals to our party's hopes for our state, I acknowledge I'd like to be a part of making it happen.

The Blueprint goes to press — on inexpensive newsprint, newspaper style — and then it goes to our volunteers, to local campaign groups and to all the small-town papers across the state, as well as to our major urban media. No slick publication, just plain truths on newsprint — positive solutions to real problems. This suited Dan's style.

I've developed a style that suits me as well in my district: Plain-spoken, home-spun, direct. Heartened by the homecoming reception my constituency gave me after the 38th Session, and heartily concerned about our state's redistricting dilemma and its consequence to a cascade of issues — including school funds — I weigh my candidacy, consult my husband and make my decision. I will seek re-election. Ken and I agree I should run for a second term to follow through on redistricting and my original aim to shore up funding for our schools.

Morrie Plummer, manager of my last campaign, offers to help for a second round, and brings me encouraging words, a legion of new supporters, and all the pencils we could possibly need. I consult my 1964 calendar and begin to sketch out a new campaign. The exercise holds less mystery now. I go about it with much more confidence than I remember two years back.

First, I consider my support.

Frankly, I don't have the wholehearted blessing of my district's Republicans. Though I've tried to be a part of the 32nd District Republican Club, I often sense a pervasive cold shoulder. Some members merely tolerate me, whereas some are out and out against me, and manage to say so in so many words. These particular conservatives have targeted Ken as well: The "liberal college professor" they've labeled him, which we both find ironic. He attends their Republican meetings with me, teaches Sunday school, for goodness sake, and tries to be a good neighbor to all, as do I. Getting along with the most conservative in my district continues to pose a real challenge. I am not one of them.

But neither am I the flaming liberal they would paint me to be. I choose to ignore the talk and jabs of these ultra-conservatives, and give thanks instead for those wonderful people in the 32nd who have been so supportive and helpful these past two years.

I'm a people person, and that certainly serves me well as a candidate, since the most important feature of any political campaign is its 'people power'. I start a list of those from my district who contacted me in Olympia last session. I add to it my friends and my acquaintances: Old campaign hands Dick and Palma McGowan; the school teacher Lillian Gibbs; neighbors Herb and Ann Angle and Mildred Cook; University District businessmen Ray Eckman and Don Lockwood. Can I list 100 people who might work for my re-election? That is Joel's yardstick. And looking at my list, yes indeed, I can measure up.

The second most important component of a political campaign is financial support. My finance committee chairman is essentially my fundraiser. This person must have plenty of personal, business and professional contacts, as well as the willingness to call people and ask outright for money to help re-elect Mary Ellen McCaffree. I prefer to find a business leader living in my district for this post, and I choose Don Lockwood, vice president of University Federal Savings and Loan, who says *Yes*. I estimate I will spend less than two thousand dollars.

Essential to serving as a state representative is maintaining close touch with my constituents. From my very first week in the 1963 legislature, and for as long as my funding held out, I sent home weekly newsletters to the households in my data bank, always with an invitation for my 32nd District residents to phone me, write me or visit me in Olympia any time. With this weekly update, I unknowingly generated a whole new generation of campaign workers for my re-election campaign. In addition, twice last year, I sent out a district-wide questionnaire on major issues to tap my constituents' sentiments. The return was a little more than two percent, yet this inquiry, and the fact that I acted upon their responses, is yielding results now as I venture into the neighborhoods of my district to seek renewed support.

And then there are the groups. Throughout the busy 38th Session, I did my best to stay in touch with those groups of constituents I'd networked with and served with in leading up to my first win. The schools, the PTA's, the church groups, neighborhood groups, business groups, political groups, service clubs. I'll reach out to each again.

My public speaking is improving as I make conscious rounds to all of these, asking them again for input and support. Yes, my enjoyment of people pays off.

My new campaign brochure is an improvement over the first, though with the same deep harvest orange-colored accents I selected the first time around. To me, red, white and blue is too predictable. The photo on the front page features me working from my desk on the floor of the House — I look thoughtful, facing considerable paperwork with my hefty legislative journals and bill books shelved

MIKE E. ODELL, Spokane, part

MARY ELLEN McCAFFREE, King, part

COLLECTION OF MARY ELLEN MCCAFFREE

Mary Ellen McCaffree's desk on the floor of the House of Representatives doubles as her official office.

behind, and the marble-bowed water fountain just out of view. The back-page brochure photo is the same we used before, for it hasn't been any easier to round up my family in one place at one time. I'm forced to use that same manipulated McCaffree clan photograph, with Mary's head carefully pasted in among us — she was gone when we snapped the shot. Inside the brochure, I am pictured conferring with a legislative group that includes Dan and Joel, two of my more constant capitol companions.

And of course, within these four pages, I deliver a message. It feels good to be able to list the measures I sponsored, supported and passed, to express my concerns about problems we've yet to address, to explain my stance on the economics of a fully functional state. As I pull together my campaign literature, it strikes me that in just two years I've grown immeasurably, both in confidence and capability, and this greatly inspires me to continue my public service.

My campaign gets a boost from the Seattle Municipal League, which gives me their highest rating: Superior Incumbent, Outstanding Performance. At Joel's suggestion, my campaign makes up a rubber stamp with these words — *Superior*

Incumbent, Outstanding Performance — and we stamp the endorsement in silver ink, right on the front of my new brochures.

Nearby, in District 46, Slade faces a more difficult re-election bid. Though we are both transplants to this state, having both arrived here in early adulthood, Slade is a particular target this year due to his highbrow education and East Coast pedigree.

In previous years, the very same suspicious, ultra-conservative Washington "natives" who are now fingering Slade had pointed their fingers at another well-educated transplant: John Goldmark. A New York Jew, Goldmark graduated from Harvard Law School, then moved to Washington's Okanogan with his wife to relax and settle into ranching. He also ran for the state legislature, as a Democrat.

The two Ivy League legal transplants, Goldmark and Gorton, developed a respect and fondness for each other as they elevated the level of debate in our state House with their skillfully waged verbal battles on the floor.

However, some years back, the John Birch Society leveled charges of communism at Goldmark, and though he sued them for libel and eventually won, the damage was done. His political career ended. Now those critical conservative eyes and pens are trained upon Slade. *What's a guy like him doing here? What's his motive in Washington politics?* That's what they'd like to know.

Yes, Slade Gorton is a product of the family that spawned Gorton's of Gloucester, the famous Massachusetts seafood line. But his family sold out of the company decades ago, and had relocated — not particularly solvent by then — to Chicago when Slade was quite young. Slade graduated first from Dartmouth, and then with a law degree from Columbia University, but for him, the prospect of becoming a Manhattan attorney held little appeal. He loved to ski. He loved to sail. He looked elsewhere. He first considered Colorado for its mountains, then San Diego for its surf, and then settled on Seattle, where he could both sail *and* ski.

Not long after he arrived, he met Dan Evans through a Republican group. Dan was serving his first term in the legislature and Slade said he'd love to become involved, too. But how? Dan passed on to Slade the same thing the Pritchard brothers had suggested to him: Get a Polk Directory — a 'reverse' directory which lists the names of residents, house by house and street by street, instead of alphabetically like a phone book. Then highlight everyone in your nearby neighborhoods you know.

Not long after this, Slade and Dan flipped through the pages of Polk, perusing Slade's new community, and between them identified about 200 names. Dan knew 194 of them, Slade only six. But the transplant Columbia lawyer wasn't daunted. Slade raised $200, doorbelled in quest of a legislative seat, was elected in 1958, and has since served his 46th District extremely well. His wife, Sally, is a UW journalism graduate, newspaper writer and native of our mid-state farming community of Selah. She helped to counter Slade's east-coast 'immigrant' image. However, there is no masking his considerable intellect.

Now, after serving three consecutive terms in the House, Slade is the new prime target of the ultra-conservatives, and not particularly happy with the distinction. Dedicated to Dan's election as governor, Slade is nevertheless working hard on his home district turf. As he must. We still face redistricting, and Slade is crucial to our work. We need him in the House, and he sincerely wants to be there.

The summer heats up, and so does our state's redistricting drama.

June 15: The U.S. Supreme Court delivers a blow to Secretary of State Victor Meyers and to Governor Albert Rosellini. Our nation's highest court rules that all houses of all state legislatures throughout the United States must be apportioned on the basis of population. *Now.* This renders the matter a federal mandate, rather than one defined and orchestrated state-by-state.[23]

June 22: Based on this new ruling, one week later the U.S. Supreme Court rejects our secretary of state's earlier appeal to preserve our old districts. Our state's legislative districts are therefore null and void. In *Thigpen v. Meyers*, Meyers has come up short. In its ruling, the high court upholds the ruling of the Federal District Court: The upcoming Washington state legislative elections may not be held in our ill-drawn 1957 legislative districts — districts the district court has deemed with distaste "invidiously discriminatory and hence unconstitutional."[24]

July 11: U.S. Supreme Court Justice William O. Douglas orders that the court's June 22 decision take immediate effect, rather than waiting for the full normal 25-day moratorium.[25] After all, the election filing period is upon us — we usually file as candidates in a one-week period at the end of July. Our state attorney general petitions the Federal District Court: *Will it please allow candidates to file for election under the old districts?* The district court says yes, candidates can go ahead and file in the old districts, but with no guarantee these are the districts in which any of us will ultimately run. Despite the turmoil in the courts and in our state, I am ready to launch my campaign. But to whom will I be campaigning? My old 32nd District? Or a district all new?

July 23: After hearing the matter yet again, the Federal District Court issues a decision it hopes will finally spur Governor Rosellini to act. Since the legislature failed to redistrict itself in 1963, the court gives the governor and us four alternatives: 1) a statewide at-large election for all the legislative seats, 2) a special session of the legislature to redraw the districts, 3) new district boundaries drawn by the district court justices, or 4) weighted voting — if you represent a district with fewer residents, your vote as a legislator will simply count less.[26]

District Judge William Beeks is perturbed with our state 'leaders' and his written opinion expresses it: "This is a narrative of frustration and failure," he writes in his finding on *Thigpen v. Meyers.* "This case was filed on June 6, 1962…"

He quickly narrates the path of Initiative 211, our second League-drawn redistricting, as it traveled toward the 1962 fall ballot, then failed.

Beeks recalls that in the aftermath of the failure, the court was persuaded to put its faith in the 1963 legislature: "On December 13, 1962," he writes, "we filed our opinion declaring the legislative districts of the State of Washington, established pursuant to Chapters 5 and 289, Washington Laws of 1957, invidiously discriminatory and hence unconstitutional. We took notice of the fact that a new legislature would convene on January 14, 1963, and after being assured that the legislature would perform its constitutional duty and validly reapportion itself if given the opportunity to do so, we continued the matter until April 8, 1963. The legislature thereafter met in general session, followed by a special session, but failed to reapportion itself… More than two years have now expired since the date of the original hearing without any accomplishment, and the woes of reapportionment are still upon us. Like an echo from the past, we are again assured that the 1965 legislature will lawfully reapportion itself if we will stay the effect of our decree of May 27, 1963, and permit matters to proceed as we did in December, 1962. This we refuse to do…"[27]

Judge Beeks spells out the four alternatives, assesses their flaws and improbabilities, and writes, "In hope that a special session of the legislature will be convened and will have performed its constitutional duty, we shall defer the entry of the decree carrying our views into effect through August 31, 1964."[28]

We have until summer's end.

Governor Rosellini must act quickly if we're to have a normal election on time. It is now late July and we must redistrict by the end of August — only weeks to do the complex work, but I'm ready.

The Justice adds: "…if at the expiration of the aforesaid period the hoped for solution has not materialized, this court will hold a hearing for the purpose of settling the terms of the final decree, and the adding of such parties as may be required to make the decree effective."[29]

In other words, if we don't do it, perhaps someone else will.

Election season bears down upon us without the matter being settled. Will there be a special session? A primary in September? A general election in November? What if Governor Rosellini doesn't call us into session before August 31?

The Democrats have been in control of our state for so long, and as a party they are now so splintered, that they really can't come to any solid agreement or confidently promise us anything. Our state voters are finally beginning to see this.

By contrast, our DEGOHT team is united behind a solid program and earning increasing respect among our state's voters — or at least a serious look. Despite chaotic circumstances, my legislative colleagues and I move ahead, determined to work towards a better state. *Progress!* Our campaign camps bustle.

On July 27, four days after the district court's blistering opinion, I mail a letter to my constituents:

"Dear Friends, I would like to announce personally to you my candidacy for re-election as one of your state representatives in the 32nd District…" And I explain why: "As vice-chairman of the House of Representatives Committee on Redistricting, it is my hope that Governor Rosellini will convene a special session to accomplish legislative reapportionment. The Federal District Court has declared that this be done. The state attorney general's office has asked the federal court to delay enforcement of the court order requiring legislative elections statewide. The court has in turn proposed a weighted vote scheme whereby each representative will have a vote in legislative matters weighted by the number of persons in his district. Either elections-at-large or the weighted vote system has many serious drawbacks, which make a special session of the legislature desirable now.

"If redistricting is not done prior to the 1964 election, this assignment to redistrict will be one of the most important items on the agenda for the 1965 legislature when it convenes…"

My constituents are all well aware I am unusually well-versed in redistricting.

In this re-election letter I include a self-addressed note card with a checklist on the back — boxes my constituents can mark: "I will help your campaign by…"

1. Placing a small sign in my yard
2. Holding a coffee hour
3. Doorbelling one night a week (or occasionally)
4. Signing postcards
5. Telephoning
6. Typing
7. Working at McCaffree headquarters — headquarters being my basement.[30]

And of course I'm always willing to accept contributions. Thanks to this little card, my campaign team continues to grow, and my 32nd District can't help but be aware that Mary Ellen McCaffree wants to serve them in the House in 1965.

Mary continues to do her part as a Teen for Evans, even at Girl Scout camp. During a boat trip up the Pend Oreille River, all the way to the Canadian border, Mary's straw campaign hat blows off and drifts away with the current. Though it takes a while to retrieve it, the girl scouts' giggling ruckus and Mary's wayward patriotic skimmer attract the attention of people all along the shoreline. *Dan Evans for Governor!* Mary shouts to them all.

Approaching 70,000 new miles on the loaner Plymouth sedan, Dan and Dolliver have hit nearly every state community at least once by now. In every small town, they climb out and greet the residents: Every Chamber of Commerce, every city hall, and I'd wager even a Little League game or two.

Each time they come upon a small radio tower, they stop and step inside: "Hello, I'm Dan Evans, and I'm running for governor. Could we talk?" When each disarmed disk jockey hesitates, the duo offers a quick set of questions and Dan's 'interview' sails the airwaves: A broadcast Blueprint.

My message is delivered less dramatically: On foot, with the push of a door-bell. With my 105 precincts mapped out on my 105 trusty 5 x 8 cards, my door-belling across the district begins in earnest, again with clear instructions. Always talk to a person if you can. If no one is home and you must leave literature, leave it in a place it will be found. Never place it in a mailbox — that's illegal. And I add a new national catchphrase: "Don't be a litterbug!"

Our state's political scene this year is sufficiently dramatic that I've paid little attention to the national campaigns. However, it appears that Barry Goldwater has the edge for the Republican presidential nod. Dan Evans is not an avid supporter of this conservative frontrunner in our party, but his opponent, Dick Christensen, is a vocal Goldwater fan, and Christensen's conservative backers form a formidable and vociferous pack that runs with the Republican mainstream. Regardless, Dan holds tight to his moderate stance and maintains focus on the governor's seat and on replacing 'Rosy' Rosellini.

Throughout the summer, we DEGOHTs continue to track Dan's progess, taking polls like mad. Dan's schoolteacher brother is particularly enthused. Roger Evans devises a poll that his school students help take and tabulate, and Roger is elated — literally jumping up and down — with each new set of returns: Dan is ahead in every single one of them. At the King County Republican Convention, those of us backing Dan Evans for governor all wave Dan fans, Mary perhaps most vivaciously. Printed on the front of this fan in bold red letters is, "I'm an Evans Fan." We consult lyrics on the fan's backside to belt out two cleverly adapted songs, "Take Me Out to the Poll Booth" and another to the tune of John Jacob Jingleheimer Schmidt:

> *Dan Evans, leading candidate — He's my man too*
> *Whenever Dan goes out, The people always shout*
> *There goes the leader of our State (and beat that Rosellini…)*

Thirty days before the primary, Dan Evans pulls ahead of Dick Christensen in the polls.

In my 32nd District, Wes Uhlman is running for re-election, too. And businessman Frank Perkins, another Democrat, is a solid contender. I'm no shoo-in in this Democratic-leaning swing district with only two seats. I must continue to convince my constituency I want to serve.

August 31 comes and goes with no special session convened by Governor Rosellini. Our state is not redistricted, but neither does the court abolish our districts — not for the primary.

In early September, I write my voters a letter printed on my official legislative stationery — a sheet topped with a watercolor of the capitol building, overlaid with the state seal, my name as representative, my home address, and a list of the legislative committees on which I served in the 38th Session.

> *Dear Friend: I want to thank you for your support during the past two years and to assure you of my interest in continuing to serve you as your representative in our state legislature in Olympia. My committee memberships indicate the areas of special activity in which I engaged in the 1963 legislative session. As your incumbent legislator, I was especially pleased to receive a "Superior" rating from the Seattle-King County Municipal League…*

I pledge to work for my district, for responsible state government, for essential governmental services and for the efficient use of tax dollars, then I ask for their vote for my re-election in the upcoming primary. I tuck in a self-mailing survey. *I want your opinion! Will you take 5 minutes and give me your opinions on these critical problems facing our state government? Sign it or not, as you please.* The questions range from Blue Laws to gambling, housing discrimination to unemployment, specific tax questions and a section on education — particularly community colleges. The returns begin immediately.

DAN EVANS' CHANCES FOR SUCCESS are a longer shot than mine, though throughout the summer he has zoomed upwards in each new poll. His newest slogan is "Experience Makes Him Effective" and the DEGOHTs hope the voting population will take this message to heart.

Because Dan must first weather a primary election against the better-known Dick Christensen, the DEGOHT team develops a series of promotional pieces to emphasize Dan's considerably greater political experience — as opposed to the fundamentalist Christensen's complete lack thereof. The new campaign theme is *57 days.* In a 60-day legislative session, a new governor has only 57 days to lead, due to the fact that his official swearing in doesn't take place until day three, according to state law. It's a crucial sprint, these 57 days, allowing little room for a learning curve. And with critical state issues at hand, this 57-day pitch makes a crystal clear point: Experience is essential.

The week before the primary, as Dan squares off against Dick Christensen for the Republican slot, the campaign releases another 'newspaper' that lauds Dan's candidacy with a series of bold headlines. *The state's biggest job demands leadership experienced in state government!!! Experience Makes Dan Evans Effective. The challenge: To change the course of Rosellini politics in the short span of 57 days! Dan Evans is most qualified for this important job!*

Autumn has returned. On cue this time each year, the gracious 50-year-old dogwood in my backyard bursts into bloom to remind me of nature's rhythms, in case I'm too distracted by other details — a political campaign, for instance. No matter how full my life may be, I always take a moment to note these blossoms, my lovely heralds of autumn. Yet after this annual communal moment with nature, I inevitably return to my task of the day. In this case, I drive our Impala downtown.

In a workshop on the first floor of a building at the corner of 3rd and Marion in Seattle, a media and marketing machine churns full steam ahead. At this Evans headquarters we mimeograph daily press releases, silk screen thousands of yard signs, paint scores of 4-by-8-foot plywood sheets: *Dan Evans for Governor.* From across the state of Washington, volunteer visitors have shown up at our Marion doorstep to pick up literature and signs, or just to help.

One day Gerri Reed, a woman with a big presence and a voluminous voice to match, walks into 830 Third Avenue with her two young sons in tow.

"This is Roger and this is Sam," she booms. "We're from Spokane. What can we do to help?"

By the time they leave, the Reed station wagon is loaded with yard signs and literature. Gerri Reed takes our message back to her hometown, seven hours cross-state, where for months she has run a bustling Dan Evans for Governor campaign in our eastern most city.

In a separate room at our headquarters, a beehive of workers stuffs and stamps campaign mailings — and personally addresses them. Per the Pritchard brothers, everything must be hand-addressed, personalized and inviting. Our fleet of volunteers cramps their fingers for Dan. Our bank of telephones stays busy at all hours with volunteer staffers rounding up workers, canvassing, fielding calls.

ON THE EVE OF THE PRIMARY, KEN AND I are at Slade's home for a meeting. At around 8 p.m. the Gorton family telephone rings. Sally answers, then hands it to her husband.

"For you, Slade. It's Ritajean."

"You'll never guess what I'm looking at," Slade's campaign manager tells him. "Right in my own front yard! It's the 7th Congressional all over again... the nerve!"

In the last congressional election – in 1962 in South King County – on the eve of the election, the John Birch Society had executed a midnight campaign stunt. In every yard in that district, they had planted a small stick with a little American flag attached and a placard supporting their candidate. They'd stuck thousands of homes. When the 7th District voters awoke Election Day, it looked as though every household was backing the Birch candidate. Two years later, with Slade up against an ultra-conservative in this primary, the John Birch Society appears to be at it again.

"Excuse me a moment," Slade tells us. "I need to make a phone call."

When he returns, Ken excuses himself. Our meeting continues without further discussion of the sticks.

Meanwhile, Dick Williams, an attorney with Perkins-Coie in Seattle, leads a stick-pulling crew to scavenge Slade's district on the tails of the Birchers – to uproot all those sticks with the placards and flags. In the dark of the night, my husband is stealthily uprooting sticks with this team, tossing these flag/placard sticks in the back of a station wagon. Hundreds and hundreds! Soon there's not enough cargo space for them all, so the men begin ripping off the cards with the flags and just taking the naked sticks. They deliver these to Slade's house to burn in the Gorton fireplace. It isn't long before Slade's fireplace can't keep up, so the crew discreetly begins to dump its carloads of sticks on darkened backstreets.

As Ken and crew are pulling sticks from yet another lawn, the flashing lights of a patrol car round the corner. The officers approach, all sternness and authority, but when the younger officer sees Ken, his eyes widen.

"Dr. McCaffree?! You were my Sunday school teacher! What are you..." He clears his throat, assumes a more authoritative tone: "Sir, you're molesting the peace!"

"Officers," Dick Williams says, with all due respect, "would you like it if someone stuck these in your yard without asking?"

"I… I suppose not, but… but Dr. McCaffree — this is private property."

"Our point exactly," Dick Williams responds.

The officers leave, apparently in agreement, and the men continue their raiding. But when a car full of the opponent's campaigners approaches, Dick Williams dives in the nearest bush. Ken doesn't. He holds his ground, confronts them with confidence, and agrees to return what he has in hand, which by this time isn't much. Though the stick pulling continues until somewhere near 5 a.m., Ken comes to get me at Slade's house around 11 and we go home and go to bed. When Election Day dawns in Slade's 46th District, in several backstreets it looks as though a kindling truck has crashed.

Despite confusing court rulings and a general election limbo, our state primary election proceeds on voting day, the second Tuesday in September. We go to the polls to vote in our old districts, with the possibility that by November, everything will change.

On the morning of this Election Day, I am sitting at a small display in my district, encouraging my 32nd citizens to remember to vote, when a group of my constituents storms up.

"Mrs. McCaffree, we can't vote for you!"

I know these people to be solid supporters.

"Why ever not?" I ask. "You know I'm always more than happy to answer any…"

"Your husband was disturbing the peace last night!"

I'm aghast a moment before I smile and offer to explain.

"I WAS SO ANGRY!" SLADE TELLS ME LATER. "My opponent probably wouldn't have beat me, but dismantling their stick campaign… that was a great psychological gain. I feel much better." [31]

In the final primary tally, I am assured a spot on the November ballot. Slade and Joel make it through, too. So do many more colleagues. And as for Dan Evans, he beats Dick Christensen by more than 100,000 votes and even garners more total primary votes than Albert Rosellini. The Christensen camp reluctantly throws their support behind Dan. He's not particularly their type of man, but he's preferable to the incumbent.

PRIMARY ELECTION

An election to select each political party's candidates for elected public office in a general election.

With the primary behind us, I meet again with our DEGOHT group. General election, here we come. We all move into highest gear.

I immediately draft a general thank you letter to my district voters, and more specific letters to specific constituencies: Housewives, teachers, church members, university staff, new voters, business people, Group Health and to fellow Republicans. Thanks to the devoted volunteer team in my basement, all these are sent hand-addressed. These volunteers efficiently address, stuff and stamp my mail daily and they're at it most evenings, too.

I plan six general election ads — three small and three large — to place in each of my community newspapers: *The Wallingford Outlook, University Herald,* and *Queen Anne News.*

October 5: Between the primary election and general, we hear anew from the Federal District Court on *Thigpen v. Meyers.* Ever since their July 23 ruling, the justices have been lobbied steadily by attorneys and political proponents peddling advice on how to handle our redistricting quandary. Now, after reconsidering the state's dilemma, the court decides to drop its four proposed alternatives. It rules instead that when the 1965 legislature convenes in January, it will not be allowed to take any action on any legislative measure until after we complete redistricting to the court's satisfaction. 'Housekeeping' bills to keep the legislature functioning will be the only exception.[32] Thus, when the 39th Legislature convenes, the hammer of the courts will drive home redistricting once and for all. At least, I hope so. The justices do, too.

In the meantime, there's a governor's chair to win and seats to gain in the House.

Doorbelling of my entire district resumes. We begin with the 40 precincts we missed the first round, then, beginning October 12, we hit all 105 of my precincts all over again. This time, the college students are back on campus. Chuck's fraternity jumps in to the doorbelling fray, returning afterwards to 18th Avenue to a big McCaffree spaghetti-feed.

The university remains a heartening source of support. And Ken remains devoted to helping me with my campaigning in addition to his full life in academia. This year he is teaching in both the Department of Economics and the School of Public Affairs, and has also been named to the UW Faculty Senate. His presence during doorbelling means the world to me. As for the dog bite he sustains on the job, I am truly sorry!

Mary continues to toot her horn for Dan Evans, and assures me she plugs her mother as well. Nancy and Jim are away at college. David simply tolerates all the hubbub. He's more interested in Roosevelt High's freshman football than Mom's political fate, and I believe that is exactly as it should be.

During our next DEGOHT meeting, Joel and Frank suggest we print sample ballots as a campaign handout, courtesy of individual candidates — as a public service. Voters can study these ahead of time, perhaps make their selections, and take them along as a reference into the voting booth. I print mine using my campaign colors, and highlight my name in Mary Ellen McCaffree-orange.

Someone else proposes we solicit absentee ballots from our servicemen and citizens overseas, and we do. Ritajean and I steer this effort in Dan's downtown campaign office. This generates a solid boost in votes for Dan Evans, as well as for many of the rest of us — a handsome dividend for our work.

Getting the elderly to the polls is yet another service we provide. I've taken out business card-sized ads in my local papers: *If you need a ride to the polls Tuesday, call Mary Ellen McCaffree, State Representative, 32nd District.* I offer two numbers that ring in my basement.

I develop my own mock 'newspaper' for my final week, similar to the one we've used in Dan's campaign. Joel coordinates the printing for several in our group. The front page simply announces my incumbency and my superior rating. A centerfold photo spread illustrates the diversity of my district outreach and work. The back page highlights my supporters, and includes a treasured letter from Dan dated May 5, 1963, after my freshman legislative session:

> *Dear Mary Ellen:*
>
> *Now that we have had a chance to rest a bit after the session, I would like to thank you for the terrific contribution you made to our team — and to the state — by your efforts in the House. Rarely have I seen a freshman legislator fill such an important role as quickly as you did. This is a tribute not only to your background of public service, but to your own obvious qualities of leadership and energy. Again, many thanks for your contribution. The people of the 32nd District are fortunate to have you as their representative. Dan* [33]

Lyndon Baines Johnson — who was sworn in as U.S. President on a plane back to Washington, D.C. after President Kennedy was shot down in Dallas — is now riding high, perched at the crest of a nationwide Democratic tidal wave in this new presidential election. So here in "the other Washington" Governor Rosellini taps into LBJ's clout in a new campaign ad: A photograph of President Johnson talking on the telephone, with a cartoon caption balloon at his mouth that shows LBJ asking: "Dan Who?" [34]

But here in Washington State, Dan Evans is also on the rise, and our job now is to keep his political ascent on track. When Senator Barry Goldwater comes to our state to stump for his presidential bid, Dan, as a high profile Republican candidate here, must make an appearance at the gathering as well. Don Moos has determined in advance he won't let the conservative Goldwater tarnish Dan's momentum, so when press photographers raise their cameras to snap Evans and Goldwater together, Moos jumps between the two, effectively interrupting an exclusive shot of the pair. I'm not certain I believe the report of Don Moos actually hitting a cameraman, but that's what I heard.

Not long afterwards, I receive a late night call.

"Mary Ellen? We need you at the Olympic Hotel. Heavy Thinker time."

"Now, Joel?"

"Now."

Though the Ben Franklin has long been Dan's official campaign headquarters, since early September, Gummie Johnson and Frank Pritchard have lived full time in a room at Seattle's Olympic Hotel, where they privately operate the actual nerve center of Dan's campaign. Here, daily polling results arrive and disperse, here each strategic new move is massaged. Now it is time for us to consider a big one.

"It's the polls," Gummie tells us. "The public's fed up with the negative campaigning."

The Evans and Rosellini face-off has spun down a vitriolic path of charges, counter claims and rebuttals to the point that one piece of Dan's campaign literature included specific detailed explanations to combat 56 different "lies, distortions and half-truths" leveled at him by Governor Rosellini. For his part, Rosellini has propelled much of his personal scandal all on his own, and we have simply reported it.

We want to hang on to public sentiment and votes now, so we readily agree: Dan's campaign must change course. Besides, we've promoted progress and positive action all along.

Dan is relieved: "Negative has never been my style, you know."

"Fortunately," Jim Dolliver reminds us, "We have our Blueprint."

We return our full focus to our Blueprint for Progress — our team's sweeping plan for our state — Exhibit A when it comes to positive and progressive. In the final week of Dan's campaign, and in all our respective campaigns, we look entirely to the future health of our state, via the five main paths of our carefully considered Blueprint: Economic growth. Efficiency in government. Equitable taxation. Educational opportunity. And most unique to Dan among the gubernatorial candidate pack: Energetic leadership. For if he manages to land in the governor's mansion, I have no doubt Dan Evans will lead and question and prod our state government. He'll be deeply involved. He will truly care.

With our change in tone, new life seeps into Washington's campaign season, and with it arrives a newly sensed optimism. The slung mud mostly evaporates.

Near the final week of campaigning, Trudy Wentworth writes me up in the *Wallingford Outlook*. She lists my history of service, my awards, and some of my specific measures from the 1963 session of the legislature: Expedited freeway construction, a children's center for research and training in mental retardation, equal pay for equal work for women, and of course a range of education issues and redistricting.

I'm fond of the photograph she's chosen, with Ken and me and our Seattle kids — Chuck, Mary and David — writing letters to Jim and Nancy out of town (while Jim and Nancy's two smiling faces float above us, framed in circles, as though near to us in thought... which they are). And I'm especially appreciative of the comment Trudy quotes, by the Reverend Lynn Hugh Carson from our University Methodist Temple: "I am one who has a vital concern that those who represent us in the state government shall be persons of unquestionable integrity, who can be depended upon in positions of public trust. I believe Mary Ellen McCaffree is such a person... We could have no finer person represent us." [35]

As November 3 approaches, our nation surges Democratic behind Lyndon Johnson.

As November 3 dawns, Albert Rosellini begins a comeback, riding the powerful wave of anti-Goldwater balloting at the polls.

And as twilight descends on this 1964 Election Day — as polls close across our state, and voting tallies unfold, it becomes clear: Daniel J. Evans has bucked our nation's political landslide. He has ousted Governor Albert Rosellini.

Slade, Joel and I will all return to the House of Representatives, minus many of our colleagues who were ousted in this Democratic rout. Our Republican House numbers have slipped as a result of this election, from 48 down to 40 of the 99. Among the defeated is Herb Hadley, the enthusiastic Longview legislator whose local committee kick-started the Dan Evans for Governor campaign.

Around 10 p.m., Ken and I celebrate my victory with our kids and my supporters in my McCaffree basement headquarters. Afterwards, we hit the town for a more public election night party — the traditional downtown bash of the Seattle/King County Municipal League in the Spanish Ballroom of the Olympic Hotel. We arrive mid-event, just as Dan is called to the podium, and I stretch on tiptoe, struggling to get a glimpse of him from the back of the crowded ballroom.

A deep, distinguished voice addresses me from behind, recognizable at once.

"Come with me, Mary Ellen," says John O'Brien, extending his arm. "You worked hard for this moment. You deserve to be up front."

The fabled leader of our state's House Democrats personally escorts me through the throng of well wishers until I find myself at the front, where I witness the welcome extended Governor Evans as the new leader of Washington State.

John O'Brien, meanwhile, slips anonymously back into the crowd.

CHAPTER FOUR

COMPROMISE
THE ART OF GETTING TO 'AYE'

Compromise is part and parcel of legislative work —

not a weakness.

It is not a buckling under or a sacrifice of values

so much as listening to multiple voices

to find a path that represents most.

I PONDER JOHN O'BRIEN'S ROLE in the wake of the national Democrat land-slide, and consider the opportunities now facing the party he leads and loves.

If ever a political party has been poised to capitalize on majority status, it would be these Democrats in our state legislature come January of 1965. When our session convenes, they will dominate our capitol with solid control of the House and the Senate, and — for the first two days — the governor's mansion, too. What a prime position from which to pass that most partisan of all legislative acts: Reapportionment and redistricting — without effective opposition. They have the court mandate. They have a majority across the board. All they must do is agree on it and vote.

Honestly, I can't think about this too deeply right now. Not yet.

Having spent much of my interim on Dan's campaign and mine, I now return my attention to my family. The holidays are near. First we clean up my campaign quarters in the basement and revert it to our family rec room — a hang out for our children — before they all descend upon us for Thanksgiving.

Thanksgiving Day always allows us to accentuate the positive, which comes second nature to me. At our McCaffree family table, I thank the good Lord and take stock of my many blessings, marred only by one solitary thorn.

Blessings first: Five thriving children, a loving husband engaged in important work, dear friends including the Swoyers who join us today at the table — Mark and Mildred and their daughters, Katie and Anne. And a second opportunity to serve in my state legislature. In January, I'll finally be able to tackle our state's budgeting issues and address the poor funding of our schools. And this time I'll have a governor on my side!

But the thorn? That two-day glitch.

Fifty-seven days is the phrase we campaigned on to position Dan Evans — with his superior resume of legislative leadership — against the Reverend Richard Christensen in the Republican primary. For 57 days of the upcoming 60-day session of the legislature, the newly elected governor will lead our state. But not for the session's first forty-eight hours. A hiccup in our state's constitution keeps Albert Rosellini in the governor's seat for the first two days.

Most years, on the heels of electing a new governor, this protocol poses little problem — just a small stutter before the ceremonial swearing-in, rather than a predicament critical to state law. In transitions past, these two days have allowed for a graceful handing over of keys — to the governor's office, to the governor's mansion — and for a gracious formal welcome and goodbye.

But this staggered start, with Dan not formally head of state for the first two days, combined with the court-ordered redistricting legislatively superseding all else? This staggered start swings wide a two-day window to Washington Democrats through which they may merrily ram a gerrymandered redistricting, unopposed. If they succeed, it will render Republicans disadvantaged for at least another decade to come. If they manage to gather their votes in those 48 hours, Governor Rosellini's pen can sign their Democrat-drawn districts into law, and that will be that. As a minority, we Republicans possess no viable roadblock. Our only hope for equity would be review by the Federal District Court.

Final election results have confirmed our party's losses: In synch with the national landslide that landed more Democrats in office across the U.S. — and soundly dumped the conservative presidential contender, Barry Goldwater — our Republican numbers slipped in both our state's legislative chambers. Yet here in this state, our party has done what it set out to do: Seat one from among us in the governor's chair.

In the entire United States, Dan Evans is the sole Republican to unseat an incumbent Democrat governor, a feat noted nationally and featured in *Time* magazine.[1] So we'll have a Republican governor when the new legislature convenes — but not until we've finished the first two days.

I tuck this fact away for the balance of 1964, and enjoy the holidays with my family. What else can I do?

As I did before my freshman session in 1963, I tell my children's schools I will be in Olympia full time through January and February. Other than my kids' teachers, however, few among our circle of friends give my political position much thought. To most I'm Mary Ellen, another university wife, another mom.

In December, Ken and I lead an all-day cookie bake with the Methodist Youth Fellowship, and help the kids deliver packages to the list of families in need. Then, with longtime university friends Doug and Lois North, we attend the annual UW Economics Department Christmas party. As a family we attend the church Christmas pageant, and throughout the month, I make dozens of trips to the local market for family meals and holiday baking, plus one quick trip to Olympia — to find a new place to rent. All in all, the balance of 1964 is wonderfully warm and homey.

ON THE MONDAY MORNING OF JANUARY 11, 1965, after swiftly inhaling this brisk salty breeze that blows off the South Puget Sound toward the capitol, I begin a fresh climb up the capitol steps, ready for opening day of my sophomore term. Before I push through the elegant bronze doors, though, I turn for a final look at the jagged snow-capped peaks of our Olympic mountains. What a gorgeous state I serve! With one last visible exhale, I enter the cavernous marbled expanse — now familiar — and give my respects to our bronzed George Washington, eternally entrapped beneath that spectacular chandelier.

Slade had telephoned first thing this morning: "Mary Ellen? I just heard. Greive's got every Democrat rounded up in the Transportation Committee room. House, Senate, everyone. Yeah, *that* big room."

Senator Greive single-handedly led the legislature in gutting our League redistricting in 1957. So powerful is Greive that he was able to convince his fellow legislators to toss out Initiative 199, though state citizens solidly approved it and voted it into law. Because our House coalition blocked Senator Greive's redistricting plan last term, he's determined to launch a redistricting blitz these first two days of the session — ram his plan through fast, before Dan Evans takes over as governor. If he does nothing else in his long Senate career, Bob Greive is bent on passing our state's legislative redistricting. His way.

"Do you think it's the plan he proposed last round?" I ask Slade. "If it's still 'invidiously discriminatory', certainly the court won't approve?"

"Unfortunately," Slade said, "from what I've seen, it probably is legal, but still not fair. See you in caucus, Mary Ellen."

Since Slade's early morning telephone call I've had some time to think. It isn't just Greive's gerrymandered map that bothers me, but his approach — his seeming belief that if he can simply secure a single vote beyond 50 percent, he will have his redistricting. And legally, he will. But this is a redistricting and reapportioning of our entire state. Wouldn't it be better to work through a plan that works for most, if not all our legislators and the people they represent, rather than simply please a simple majority?

This is the main distinction between what I have worked towards, in redistricting, relative to Senator Greive. Slade and I and our redistricting team have honestly tried to draft new districts that can swing our state either way, Republican or Democrat, but not by far. Under our plan, the resulting political complexion of each district would depend upon individual campaigns and candidates, not on any partisan gerrymander. The point is to maintain sufficient competition between parties to encourage new blood, new ideas, lively debate and to assure that if one party or the other obtains the majority of the vote statewide, that party would have a majority in the legislature.

I climb the interior flights of marble, find our new caucus room and take a seat among our subdued and smaller group. No coalition intrigue underfoot this year. But an undercurrent? Certainly.

Robert Goldsworthy is our new caucus leader. We admire him for more than his prowess at pool. Tom Copeland, last session's second in command behind Dan Evans, will step into Dan's shoes and lead us on the floor. Selah attorney Robert Brachtenbach, a Nebraska native whose Midwest devotion to community service parallels mine, will work as our caucus whip. He and Joel will tally our votes and rally support. And Gladys Kirk will be secretary, again. It feels a tad strange this morning without Dan.

"We have one goal in these next forty-eight hours," Slade tells us once we've all settled in and are accounted for. "And that is to block the Democrats' redistricting blitz. Our only hope, frankly, is if our House Democrat caucus splits — the dissidents are back in the fold, you know — or if the House and Senate Democrats split, which is much more likely. But these are mighty big 'if's. The Democrats have everything to gain by pulling together and pushing through their redistricting."

Adds Joel: "If it seems like the cards are stacked against us, ladies and gentlemen, they are."

Day 1. Just before noon, we enter the House chamber to begin our 60 days' work. A blitz is about to begin, and everyone knows it. I sit at my desk, fold my hands and wait while all around me apprehension throbs, intensity sizzles.

Chief Clerk Si Holcomb gavels to order the 39th Session of the Washington State House of Representatives, the color guard marches the flags down the aisle, a pastor calls us to prayer.

Our governor-elect must quietly bide his time elsewhere, hog-tied another two days while the Democrats rule the entire state roost.

At a desk several rows in front of me, I see the broad back of Big Daddy Day — William Day has returned to the House and rejoined the Democrat caucus. Despite the bitter threats by John O'Brien and other House Democrats last session, all the dissidents survived this recent election, victorious, and they've re-entered the Democrat fold.

I sit on our considerably slimmer side of the aisle — 40 Republicans now, compared with our 48 last term — 40 of us to the Democrats' 59. This session I will experience the stature, or lack thereof, of a true minority legislator. However, I have moved one desk more toward the center of the chamber, one desk further away from the marbled fountain.

"I, Victor A. Meyers…" Our Chief Clerk reads the statement from the secretary of state, certifying our election to office: 40 Republicans and 58 Democrats — the 59th Democrat, Paul Connor, is home in Port Angeles on the distant Olympic Peninsula, once again critically ill, but the Democrats have a healthy vote margin without him.

In addition to the new governor, the other Republican bright spot in the otherwise Democrat landslide in our state was the election of Ludlow "Lud" Kramer to the office of secretary of state, the post Victor Meyers held… holds. As with the governorship, Lud Kramer's swearing in, per protocol, is delayed until Wednesday — two days away. Aside from the ailing Paul Connor, all of us are accounted for and duly sworn in.

Next, we proceed to establish Temporary Rules amid several points of contention: Should a two-thirds vote be required to change the Rules? Or simply a simple majority? How long can someone speak on the floor — three minutes or ten? How will our committees fairly reflect our House partisan membership? The Democrat leaders tell us: "Any close fractional questions will be decided on behalf of the Democrats."

Our floor leader Tom Copeland extends a wry thanks: "I receive the message quite clearly." As a minority, we'll have no muscle in House committees.

With a blitz in the oven and the Democrats racing a 48-hour clock, Senator Greive has insisted that no permanent Rules be adopted by the House or Senate until his redistricting bill is approved. No time to waste on the committee process! No referring bills to committees for review. No regular floor leadership, no record of our proceedings, and no committee meetings, for goodness sake!

We'll just stay on the floors of the House and Senate and battle out redistricting here. Essentially we'll be operating as though we're a committee of the whole.

Floor debate on the temporary Rules proceeds, and members raise points and yield to inquiries until we arrive at a volley centered on a certain turn of phrase.

"Mr. Chief Clerk, I wonder if Mr. Moos would yield to a question?" asks Mr. Litchman, whose proposed change to the Rules has just been contested by Mr. Moos. Yes, Mr. Moos will.

"Mr. Moos, perhaps I have misunderstood," says Mr. Litchman, spelling out his misunderstanding: "Was it your purpose to eliminate this phrase of the rule as well?"

"Yes, Mr. Litchman," responds Mr. Moos, "on the advice of counsel, you are wrong."

But Mr. Litchman has sought counsel, too:

> **COMMITTEE of the WHOLE**
>
> A method to prevent long floor speeches or grandstanding, since the body acts as a committee rather than following formal floor protocol. No record is kept of individual floor remarks.

"Mr. Day, incidentally, is my chief counsel," says he, citing the authority of last session's capable Speaker, a chiropractor by profession, not an attorney.

"And Mr. Gorton is my chiropractor," retorts a dry Mr. Moos.

His acidic levity barely alleviates the tense undercurrent surging on the floor. The Democrats all hear a ticking clock and they're edgy.

We finally adopt our temporary Rules by a very slim margin: 50-48. The Democrats may rule this House, but their membership is not unanimous in its support. A rift continues within, we note, as the minutes of their 48-hour window slip by. We must now elect a Speaker.

"Mr. O'Brien," invites the Chief Clerk, and our esteemed veteran stands, clears his throat, and nominates another to the post he so desperately coveted last term: Robert Schaefer, his own 'yes' man in 1963.

After several speeches in support of Mr. Schaefer, Mr. Moos rises from our side of the aisle and nominates Thomas Copeland. The Speaker vote splits straight down party lines: 58 for Schaefer, 40 for Copeland, with 1 (the ill and absent Connor) not voting.

Mr. Schaefer — Speaker Schaefer — takes the rostrum and addresses us all:

"...I know you are all aware of the great problems that challenge us as members of this 39th Legislative Session. You are further acutely aware that prior to attacking and solving these problems we have an added burden. Our first order of business must be to redistrict the state's legislative boundaries in accordance with the 14th Amendment (to the U.S. Constitution), the recent decisions of the United States Supreme Court, and a direct order of the Federal District Court. The cooperation and selflessness of all of you is needed if we are to conquer this problem, and pass, without undue delay, a fair and equitable redistricting bill." [2]

When he concludes, Tom Copeland rises: "Mr. Speaker, ladies and gentlemen of the House, let me take this opportunity to offer you my sincere congratulations... I am not unmindful of the position I occupy here and its relationship to the gentleman who preceded me in this capacity..."

That gentleman being Daniel J. Evans, last session's floor and coalition leader and now our governor-elect. Tom continues.

"We are here on behalf of our constituents to work on behalf of the people of the state of Washington, and I am sure that the gentleman whose seat I now occupy feels the same responsibility to those same people. It will be my position and the position of my party to try to diligently carry his programs. We should all dedicate ourselves to working in the total interest of the state of Washington and not in the interest of petty partisanship."

He directs some final graceful remarks to our new Speaker, and then speaks to us all: "I bring to you, sir, our cooperation. Here is a gentleman who can disagree without being disagreeable. I think this should probably be the byword for all of us during this session. If I may be permitted to do so at this time, I would like to move that the records show that your election as Speaker is unanimous." [3]

We are under way, under a new Speaker, with much less vinegar in the mix than last term, but with no less at stake.

While floor formalities continue, I wonder how the Democrats plan to achieve redistricting in less than 48 hours, for the route from bill to law is a long one. First they must introduce a redistricting bill, then pass it out of either the House or Senate, and it must then be approved by the other, with time allowed for amendments by both bodies, and new rounds of voting, until at last it is ready to be engrossed — printed up with all changes in place before finally being sent to the governor for his signature into law. This is not an instantaneous proposition.

Careful coordination between all three — Senate, House and governor — is a must. These Democrats must gather their troops if they're to successfully launch this blitz, and hope that in the tightly-timed process, no one goes AWOL — hence, their rally this morning in the big legislative committee room. For a party that has bickered internally the last several years, this will be... well, I'll just watch.

John O'Brien has long been vocal about his displeasure at the Senate for ignoring the House — for leaving out House Democrats from state leadership in general, and more specifically, for leaving them out of Greive's Senate-drawn redistricting. Greive has largely crafted it to appease and protect their party's senators with little care about the fates of their Democrat counterparts in the

House. House Democrats feel left out, and it's no wonder. They are.

Within the Senate itself, there is a faction behind Greive, and then there are other senators from both sides of the aisle, either disenfranchised or disenchanted by Greive's redistricting effort, or outright dismayed at what this powerhouse has historically proposed.

And then there are our legislative newcomers. Here in the House alone we have 26 freshmen — 18 Democrat and 8 Republican — the newly elected who have come here to work for our state. They have less passion for party, more for the job to be done. A legacy of Democrat dominance impresses them less, and protecting that dominance isn't at their fore.

It is possible our Democrats ironed out their differences between Election Day and arrival in Olympia. If not, it is possible they smoothed things over this morning when Senator Greive assembled them en masse. But judging from our House Rules vote, with eight of them voting against the Democrat tide, the party's cohesiveness isn't a sure thing. I'll keep my eyes and ears open. It is still possible they have sufficiently rallied round.

"Our best hope," Slade says in our midday caucus, "is that the Democrats are as divided as ever."

And with that, our caucus leadership assigns us more to do than passively hope.

"Keep talking to your Democrat colleagues," says Joel. "Remind them they have an alternative. That we're willing to talk to them about redistricting, and to listen. We demonstrated that to 'em last term."

It's true. If we could convince Democrats in the House and Senate to reject Senator Greive's redistricting plan, our legislature could then work toward something prospectively better — for each of us and for the state. Redistricting should be more than a measure pushed through by force and favors, more than a protective mapping for specific incumbents, more than a measure passed by the difference of a single vote. It really should reflect the best for the whole state, and accomplishing that is going to require compromise.

I consider compromise part and parcel of legislative work, not a weakness. Compromise is not a buckling under or caving in. It is not a sacrifice of values so much as listening to multiple voices to find a pathway that best represents most. Marjorie Lynch and I do our best to keep our Democrat colleagues considering their options — to keep them open to contemplating compromise.

Our first day comes to a close with some rudimentary work on the floor, while behind the scenes the push for a Democrat redistricting pulsates throughout this capitol — and Senator Greive, in particular, seems to be everywhere. The House adjourns at a reasonable hour. We will reconvene Tuesday at 10:30 a.m. Not so the Senate: The senators are all still hard at it when we leave.

After a hasty dinner downstairs in the House dining room, I cross the foyer and take a seat in the Senate balcony. From this height the political undercurrent is made visible by the ceaselessly darting Senator Greive as he works his colleagues on the floor — lobbying for votes, perhaps striking deals, on behalf of his personally proffered redistricting. To me he appears neither relaxed nor confident. *What's wrong with you people?* his demeanor seems to say. *Don't you realize this is how it's always been done? Trust me!*

Democrats have held a majority in our state legislature for such a long time, and in the Senate even longer, that perhaps they've forgotten that compromise is a legitimate political art form, and that opposition has a legitimate role. These basic legislative skills — opposition and compromise — may have slipped into the background with such long-term dominance by a single party. As a guest in the balcony, I only speculate.

The evening unfolds in the Senate chamber without apparent progress. At midnight someone moves that they cover the clock, and the sergeant at arms covers the Senate clock accordingly — literally cloaking it with some fabric. This formally recognized procedure allows a legislative day to extend to the wee hours, beyond the

> **COVER THE CLOCK**
>
> To literally cover the clock in a legislative chamber so that the day's session may continue past midnight.

strike of 12, much like a toddler covers his eyes to be invisible. *You can't see me.*

Senator Greive tirelessly dashes about, trying to convince an adequate number of his colleagues of the absolute "rightness" of his plan. By 3 a.m. he and his team have finally mustered the votes. His blitz bill passes, 28-19, and is immediately sent to our darkened House.

I return home and slip into my bed.

Day 2. When I return to work in the morning, our staid state capitol is in a state of pandemonium. House and Senate Democrats are spreading the word: *Greive's redistricting plan is only one vote shy of passing in the House. Pass it on! Pass it on!*

I breathe easy. Slade and I and our redistricting team are familiar with these districts Senator Greive has drawn. We know which of our colleagues are disgruntled with the senator's design for our state, which of them Greive's plan grossly disfavors, and which legislators it would eliminate outright. Our morning caucus meets and Slade repeats our game plan: Tell your Democrat colleagues we can negotiate something far better if they're willing to let Greive's plan die. Tell them we can take the time to do this right — for our state and for all of us. But we won't have that chance if we vote in Greive's plan today.

The House convenes at 10:30 a.m. as scheduled, and we are now 34 hours into the Democrat-controlled first 48. A frenzied sensation continues to seep beneath the surface of our work on the floor. The Senate redistricting bill is not before us for a vote... not yet, even though the Senate sent it to our House at 3 a.m. – nearly eight hours ago.

Despite early rumors of its imminent passage, Senator Greive and several other senators circulate nearby, beyond the velvet curtains, in the House hallway just off the floor – desperately lobbying Democrat representatives to approve their district mapping and agree to back their bill.

We the minority, heartened by the apparent disarray, steadily attempt to dissuade our House colleagues from rushing into something wrong. As in 1963, Slade and Joel target the disgruntled from the Puget Sound urban core, while Don Moos reprises his role with our conservative rural contingent, along with the growing number of Eastern Washington independents.

Just before noon, with only twelve hours left now for a midnight signing, Speaker Schaefer and John O'Brien call the House Democrats into caucus. In fear of squandering this final chance to redistrict our state while they still have full control, these leaders set old House grudges aside and attempt to convince the undecided and the outright opposed to vote for Senator Greive's bill. Shortly thereafter, their group returns to the floor. But no one moves to bring Greive's bill to a vote. Word has it the bill is just too... wrong, somehow, for those holding out, who refuse to contribute their *Aye*. This rumor is confirmed by our House leadership's inaction.

Facing insufficient 'yes' votes in the House, and with fewer than ten hours left, Senator Greive and his staff rush back to the drawing board to take another look at their redistricting plan.

THREE HOURS NORTH, IN A POLITICAL SCIENCE classroom at Western Washington University in Bellingham, the Dean of Students interrupts a poli sci lecture.

"Is there a Dean Foster in here?"

Among the curious class full of students, one young man raises his hand. The dean then invites a state patrol officer into the classroom.

"Grab your things, son," says the officer. "We're taking you to the capitol."

"Right now?" asks Dean Foster.

"Right now."

So Dean Foster grabs his backpack, follows the trooper, and departs his college campus in the back of a state patrol car, leaving his professor and classmates gawking and intrigued.

Dean is a prominent student leader on the Bellingham campus. More applicable to this journey, the young man proved himself valuable during interim redistricting work under the guidance of... Senator Greive. And in fact Dean had taken this semester off to continue his work with the senator, but was back in Bellingham today so he could register for the upcoming term.

Today, however, Senator Greive can no longer do without Dean — he's in a pickle and needs his assistant, pronto.[4,5]

JUST AFTER LUNCH, WE'RE CALLED INTO Joint Session to receive the outgoing address of Governor Albert Rosellini. After the Senators and dignitaries find seats and the lieutenant governor calls us to order — with a fully functioning microphone this time — the governor takes the podium. And for the next 45 minutes, while Democrats from both chambers consult their watches and bounce nervous knees, Governor Rosellini ambles down memory lane. He reflects first upon his long political history, imagines our state's future and waxes philosophic. When he finally concludes, after eight years in the governor's office and a total of 26 years in elective service to our state, we applaud to salute the end of the era of the amicable, Honorable Albert Rosellini, and Mrs. Rosellini, too.

Until Dan Evans is sworn in at noon tomorrow, the Rosellinis remain our state's first couple. And feasibly, until that very same hour, the Democrats still have time to complete their redistricting. At least that's what most of us gathered here believe. But something's brewing.

"Here's the plan," Joel had divulged to a select few in an empty committee room just before we'd entered this Joint Session.

I wasn't among the insiders in the know. I wasn't aware of this plan... yet. But a handful of Republicans were preparing to hatch a surprise: By swearing in our new governor at midnight tonight, rather than noon tomorrow, they would chomp twelve hours off the deadline for redistricting our state on Democrat terms, unopposed.

Per tradition, the formal swearing in of our newly elected governors always takes place during the afternoon session on day three. However, after he thoroughly researched our state constitution and law books, Slade found nothing to prohibit a swearing in at one second past midnight tonight — day three, technically speaking. Thus, Dan Evans' gubernatorial term could officially begin tonight, at 12:01 a.m., thereby cutting short any last minute Democrat ditch to pass redistricting in the clock-covered hours past midnight, or even tomorrow morning — any time up until the normal afternoon swearing in.

It's all set, Joel had relayed to that inside group. *We've got a State Supreme Court justice ready to swear Dan in the moment our clocks strike twelve.*[6] The rest of us in this Joint Session remain clueless.

Following the Rosellini send-off in the early afternoon, while still in Joint

Session, our House clerk reads a resolution by Mr. O'Brien to recognize three more outgoing state officials. Two of these are retiring, while one was retired by voters in a November defeat: Secretary of State Victor Meyers, the defendant in redistricting's *Thigpen v. Meyers*. All three outgoing officers are sworn in as officers emeritus, then the lieutenant governor escorts Vic Meyers to the podium.

"By popular acclaim," says Lt. Gov. Cherberg, "and unanimous demand, I have been requested to ask if you would address this Joint Session."

Victor Meyers appreciates the honor.

"You know," he says, "I was thinking as I came down the aisle just now — I was trying to count back. That was the twenty-eighth trip I have made down that main aisle for twenty-eight consecutive times… I am wrong. There were twenty-eight times I presided over a Joint Session; it wasn't entirely consecutive. Something happened in 1952 that shocked the world. I was defeated! I think that was the year thousands of people promised to help me out, and they did, and I was out for four years."

Many laugh, but the Democrats in the legislature continue to check their watches. Their window is shrinking. This long, drawn-out ceremony to celebrate outgoing Democrats — in the face of a crucial party deadline — drives home the fact that the Democrats in our state are fractured and woefully out of synch.

Victor Meyers continues his farewell: "There is a lot of sentiment connected with this. I broke in Johnny as presiding officer over at the Senate, and he is doing a terrific job. And I don't mind telling you I have a very fine young man succeeding me as secretary of state."

Lud Kramer, his elected successor, smiles in the wings. Victor Meyers continues his good-bye, oblivious to the nerves of his colleagues on the floor.

"You can say what you want; this is an age of youth, and we old-timers, like the members of the supreme court and…" He cocks his head to Gov. Rosellini. "… and me, we've had it. You always make a mistake and run once too often. They finally got me."

He looks at the press corps, seated at their table between the rostrum and the floor.

"I'm talking about you newspaper guys up front there. But next to the real thing — I'd rather have a certificate of election, of course — but next to that, this is very good. The only thing I object to is that it doesn't carry any salary with it — no expense account, no credit card. That's murder!"

He knows we'll laugh.

"Well, I have enjoyed a terrific friendship with — most of you — over a period of thirty-seven years, and I am very humble and very proud to achieve this fine honor of being elected — what is this thing?" More laughter. "'Emeritus'.

I should know. I wrote it. We'll break up the dignity of this thing yet! Thank you very much, Mr. President. I appreciate this honor from the bottom of my heart… I knew it was a long trip coming down these aisles for twenty-eight years, but I don't mind telling you from the bottom of my heart…" a comic pause, "…it's going to be a long trip back!" [7]

Following the applause, the dignitaries are escorted out, the Joint Session disbands and the Democrats' redistricting clock just keeps on ticking. Speaker Schaefer immediately announces a recess until 3:30 p.m. and calls the Democrats into another caucus. When they emerge, the members are visibly discouraged, a sign they've achieved no change in redistricting votes.

Opposition to Greive's bill remains resolute.

When we reconvene at 3:30, a weak and weary Paul Connor is brought in by stretcher, carried up the aisle to the rostrum, and belatedly sworn into office for this 39th Session. Desperate for votes, the Democrats earlier in the day dispatched state troopers to fetch Rep. Connor from the Olympic Peninsula, several hours away, where he has continued to be critically ill. State patrol cars escorted the aid car that brought him here, and after the odd swearing in, Connor is immediately carried out again, and transported across the way to the committee room where Greive is at work on redistricting, and ready to show the sickly legislator his proposed new district.

"I'm too ill," Connor protests. "Please take me back to the hospital."

He departs by stretcher without donating a vote to their plan.

Democrat discouragement grows.

All afternoon on the floor, a flurry of bills is introduced on first reading, while behind the scenes the frantic Democrat scramble for votes continues. Rumors float, surge and sink on waves of a raging redistricting sea. By early evening, our caucus hears some hearsay: The Democratic leadership has supposedly called it all off. The rumor we'd heard this morning — that Greive's bill was only one vote shy in the House — was just rumor. The latest scoop now puts their vote shortage at three.

If only we could get those three votes from Eastern Washington, we hear. Indeed, Senator Greive and his team pull Representatives Haussler, Bozarth and Braun from the floor — the three Eastern Washington members whose districts his plan would merge into one. Greive is ready to deal. He and this trio disappear.

After a stretch, more rumors surface: Greive succeeded in bringing Haussler and Bozarth aboard. Just one more vote and they can pass his redistricting. This is our evening news.

Somewhere else in the capitol building, our Republican governor-elect is pacing. The plot to swear him in at midnight is still afoot — a definitive death knell to the Democrat redistricting if their battle for votes is still steaming along at that hour.

But will Greive's redistricting bill ever come to the floor of this House?

I am privy to the ongoing saga of votes via Slade. He tells me the Democrats are still massaging two votes from two particular members, neither of whom have suggested they're willing to budge. The first is Eric Braun, a Democrat from Cashmere and the holdout among the Eastern Washington trio Greive cornered earlier. Braun is holding firm to his preference for a compromise bill — per his personal beliefs, per his constituency, and per his wife Eunice. No matter what the Democrats dangle in front of him in terms of redrawing his district, there is no deal making in the cards for Representative Braun. He has made up his mind.

And then there is George Pierre, one of two representatives from Greive's own district in West Seattle. To be blunt, George Pierre thoroughly hates Robert Greive — a passionate hate born of the campaigns they waged leading up to the November election. More than a long shot, George Pierre's vote is a solid *Nay* and always will be. So for the Democrats, there is no apparent progress, no vote on the floor, no bill.

We recess until 8 p.m. and our House Democrats head back to caucus. At 8 we reconvene, call the roll and immediately recess until 9. At 9 we do the same. We're to be back here in session at 10 p.m. We're down to two hours remaining in day two.

At 10 p.m. we meet and vote on a bill that allows the state payroll to function — a housekeeping bill of the sort we're allowed to enact, despite the court's 'stop work' order until we redistrict. After all, we must keep our state afloat.

We then recess again until 10:45 p.m., and again the Democrats dash off the floor and disappear inside their caucus room. They must pass this bill soon, because whenever they do, it still has to travel back to the Senate and then to the governor's desk while Governor Albert Rosellini still sits there.

By now, with each recess, we Republicans simply remain on the floor, figuratively twiddling our thumbs. This plot doesn't seem to be changing. From what we gather, the Democrats continue to fail to rally the votes they need. Yet I can't relax. Our state is at the mercy of this vote. I fold my hands and hold my breath and wait, along with the rest of my party, while Dan Evans stands by for his potential midnight swearing in. The justice has gathered his robes and his seal, and stands by as well, just in case. Tom Copeland has written and rehearsed an introductory speech: *It is midnight now, Wednesday, and the governor is ready to be sworn in.*

At 10:45 p.m. the door to the Democratic caucus room cracks. Our Democrat colleagues return to their desks. Their body language betrays their verdict. On our side of the aisle, we collectively exhale enormous relief. We are called to order and formally gaveled adjourned until 10 a.m. on day three. Democrat redistricting has failed.

BACK HOME IN SEATTLE, at this very same hour, my younger daughter stands before our upstairs mirror to assess her new dress of watermelon-red satin, which she has chosen especially for her night at the governor's ball. She spreads the luscious fabric skirt to take a seat on her bed and debates whether she ought to disobey the words on the envelope beside her: "Don't open till Wednesday."

She decides she ought. Since Wednesday begins at midnight, and midnight is only an hour away, Mary opens it and extracts a handwritten poem from one of her girlfriends.[8]

I'll bet you're all scared and excited and such,
And you can't tell me, Mary, 'No, Chris, not much!'

The big day has come to go to Dan's ball,
And when you're all gussied, you'll look like a doll!

In your cute watermelon, you'll appear so divine,
It sounds simply darling — wish it were mine!

'Don't sweat the small stuff' — like being too tall.
I know that you'll be the real Belle of the Ball!

Now don't get all nervous and make a big fuss.
You'll have a cool time with Tom Babes, the old cuss
  (sorry, but it rhymes!)

Just one more short stanza and then I shall close,
I'll add a neat saying that everyone knows:

Have an absolute blast! And you know I'm true blue,
'Cuz there's no one deserves it more than YOU!

My very best wishes for a truly wonderful evening!
                                    Love always, Chris

Mary carefully hangs her dress within sight, wraps a pearl hatpin in a handkerchief, carefully tucks this parcel in her party bag, crawls into her bed and sweetly dreams.

Day 3. By morning, our capitol has a whole new feel—fresh start, clean slate. I mount the capitol steps. *Ah!* I can feel the proverbial spring in my practical pumps.

Our first two days were not a waste, by any means, even though as a minority member I had little role or voice. My eyes, you see, worked just fine, and by quietly observing my Democrat colleagues, I had just received an excellent lesson in what *not* to do if you want to effectively legislate. The Democrats had everything going for them, an absolutely perfect opportunity to pass a gerrymandered redistricting bill: One that could satisfy the courts based on numbers, while at the same time politically slant the districts out of Republican reach for years to come. They held all the cards. Our minority party had nothing. Nothing. No power at all.

There really was no reason they couldn't pull together as a party and set their own redistricting into our law books. But they didn't. They bickered instead. They fractured into factions. They scrambled and bent too late. I had just been a front-row witness to a golden opportunity, squandered.

"Senator Greive won't throw in the towel," Slade surmises when we caucus before our third day of floor work begins. "Even after we swear Dan in, Greive has majorities in both houses, you recall—if he's willing to work with them. But from today forward, he'll also have to convince our new governor."

We smile. We all know Dan's redistricting stance by memory, and most of us share it. Ideally this redistricting will balance the political complexion of our state — equal numbers of districts that bend towards one major party or the other, and a reasonable number of districts that can swing either way: An overall framework to provide party representation in the legislature that is tied directly to the statewide votes each party receives.

By contrast, Senator Greive's design specifically protects the specific Senate seats of specific members who back him. It's personal, and this is his number one aim. Number two is simply to pass it — by a fifty percent vote, plus one.

Not long after we convene, we enter into another Joint Session.

"The Washington State Senate has arrived at the bar of the House."

The Senators settle in among us. The Sergeants at Arms of both the House and Senate escort Lieutenant Governor Cherberg to the rostrum, and he calls us to order. Roll is taken, with every member of both the Senate and House present today, including the very frail Paul Conner. More dignitaries arrive, and then, from the back of the chamber our sergeant at arms announces: "His Excellency, Governor Daniel J. Evans."

I feel a welling of tears as I turn to pay my respects to my teammate and mentor. His formal escort includes two of his old capitol roommates: Representative Slade Gorton and now-Senator Chuck Moriarty. I can barely hear the lieutenant governor's welcome over the applause as Governor Evans makes his way down the aisle to the front.

Dr. Dale Turner, a clergyman adored for his warm, extemporaneous delivery (and not coincidentally, Dan's minister from the University Congregational Church in Seattle), delivers the inaugural prayer: "Almighty God, our Father, Who has given us this good land as our heritage, we humbly beseech Thee that we may always prove ourselves a people mindful of Thy favor and glad to do Thy will. May those whom we have chosen to lead us be concerned most of all in pleasing Thee.

"Especially now we pray Thy hand upon Daniel Evans. We thank Thee for all of the gracious influences in home and training that have prepared him for this high hour of leadership and responsibility. Deliver him from love of power and from motives of personal gain and from consideration of men and money in place of the demands of justice and truth. Guide him to an ever larger vision of the truth and an ever deeper sense of the demands of righteousness, that through his faithfulness the lives of our people may be guided through wise policies and lifted to higher ideals and nobler achievements.

"Deliver us all from every influence that would break down our reverence for law and corrupt our sense of corporate responsibility. Help us, oh God, to put right before self interest, the attainment of noble ends before the enjoyment of present pleasures, principle before selfish power, and to put Thee before all else, that we may know the truth, revealed to us through Jesus Christ, Who alone can set men free, for it is in His spirit of love for all that we offer this prayer. Amen." [9]

Paired one by one, a state Supreme Court justice administers the oath of office to an elected state official. Justice, official, justice, official, gradually leading up to our head of state. The lieutenant governor (and President of the Senate) steps to the podium.

"Ladies and Gentlemen and members of the legislature, before requesting the chief justice to administer the oath of office to Governor Daniel J. Evans, the President is sure that the members will grant him the privilege of presenting the very lovely, gracious and gentle wife of Governor Evans, Mrs. Nancy Evans. Would you please stand in order that you may be properly recognized?"

We applaud our new first lady.

"The President would also like to present Mrs. Evans' mother, Mrs. Bell. Mrs. Bell would you please stand in order that you may be properly recognized."

More applause.

"The President is sure that it will make everyone happy to learn that the beloved parents of Governor Evans are also present. It is with great pleasure and pride that the President presents Mr. and Mrs. Daniel L. Evans."

More applause still.

"On an occasion such as this, the best way to proceed is in the shortest possible manner. It is with great pride that the President requests of Governor Evans that he permit Chief Justice Rosellini to administer the oath of office. Ladies and gentlemen, His Excellency, Daniel J. Evans, Governor of the State of Washington."

Again my eyes are tempted to mist. I worked hard for this moment. So many did. With a quick oath, our new governor is installed.

"At this time," says Lieutenant Governor Cherberg, "the members of the Joint Session of the 39th Session of the Legislature will receive the inaugural address of His Excellency, Governor Evans."

I HAVE A PERFECT SEAT FROM WHICH TO OBSERVE this morning's proceedings, and in fact, all proceedings herein. The House slopes gradually downward, so from my desk near the back, my view sweeps the entire chamber. But for now, my eyes are riveted on the native son up front – the man who is fiercely in love with our state, and who has now been elected to lead us, who has just greeted us – justices, legislators, distinguished guests...

"... my fellow Washingtonians, and most particularly, my parents and my wife, Nancy: There were times during the last two days when I have felt like an outsider standing in the aisles and listening to the procedures of the legislature. I sometimes wished that I had a vote...

"But we are now beginning a new administration. This is a time of high purpose. A time when each of us must make our separate and collective decisions as to the kind of future this state is to enjoy in the years ahead.

"Washington is truly among the favored states. We have not suffered the silt and smog of over-industrialization. We have not felt the oppressive overcrowding of population; neither have our urban centers been blighted at the core. Our land is fertile, our water abundant, our cities clean, our people well-educated and our industry progressive...

"What then is our challenge? Our challenge is growth, growth through which the great resources of nature and the many talents of an educated people will effectively be harnessed for the benefit of all and to the detriment of none."

Political speeches can sound much the same. Politicians can promise anything.

But I have worked with Dan, brainstormed with Dan, and deliberated with Dan Evans' Group of Heavy Thinkers. I know the man behind these words, and know how earnestly he intends to work to improve our state – not by a sledgehammer, not by speeches, but by listening, looking, asking, conversing, by bringing together different viewpoints in an attempt to unearth the broad middle ground.

"...This administration brings to the office no commitment except to the people, no interest except the peoples'.

"...It does bring and shall retain the highest regard for the legislature. I shall never mistake deliberation for disinterest, or compromise for weakness.

"... We cannot solve the problems of the present with the outworn dogmas of the past. We must be bold in charting our course, resolute in our determination, compassionate in our assessment of human needs..."

Dan Evans is a loyal Republican, committed to the principles of Jefferson and Lincoln — that the most critical decision-making and responsibility ought to be pooled not in Washington, D.C. — not with Congress or the White House — but nearer our homes, within our communities, and by our states. He is not, however, a 'dyed in the wool' conservative.

A champion of the environment, of education and the less represented — women, children, minorities, our Native population — he believes that in every issue, even the most contentious ones, there is an element of compromise to be found. There is no such thing as a Democrat issue or a Republican issue, just the peoples' issues, he is known to say, perfectly articulating my belief in our government's obligation.

As he continues to list his goals for our state, I reflect upon the three "types" among us — the variety of elected colleagues who surround me here.

Some are here to champion a specific issue or cause. My ultimate goal, to shore up funding for our public schools, is but one of many examples.

Some are devoted to process — to seeing that our representative government works as it should, with a strong ear back toward our home districts and ongoing concern that our laws protect the freedoms our founders scribed. I have come to recognize this as my truest niche as a legislator — a fierce defender of the genius of our unique governmental process.

Still others are intrigued by the strategic — captivated by the ins and outs of rules on the legislative floor, and by creatively using these to create new law.

It takes all three working together — champions of issues, process and strategy — to make our state government, and indeed any representative democracy, work.

And then it takes a leader. I am proud to have helped place Dan Evans before us today and to have helped formulate his "blueprint" for our state.

"The Blueprint for Progress," Governor Evans continues, "which I outlined over the past six months and which I will now bring to the legislature, is founded on the needs of the state of Washington, not upon any political expediency."

In the time I have known and worked with this man who will govern us,

I have never heard him say to anyone, "This is the only way." He always says, "Together we will find a way."

He continues: "We now face the difficult task of turning words into deeds and proposals into accomplishments. We have not come to Olympia to perpetuate a conflict of parties; rather we have come here to undertake the important job of governing a great state… We have come here to exercise leadership, to bring the public and the private interest together; to witness the beginning, if not the final realization, of a great future…"

Our campaign polishing of Dan's oratory has paid off.

"I will not ask this legislature to lay aside the convictions of party," he tells us, "only that it support the needs of progress… For the success of the next two years will not be measured by how well we oppose one another but how successfully we unite to promote the common welfare of the people.

"This administration believes steadfastly in the future; that our promise lies not in the past, but before us. This administration will not shy away from new ideas, for as we begin our deliberations here we can never fail to reckon with the opportunities of responsible change, nor with the requirements of changing responsibility.

"This administration is not frightened by the word liberal, nor is it ashamed of the word conservative. It does not believe that the words 'fiscal responsibility' are old fashioned, nor will it ever fear to spend money if money needs to be spent.

"And finally, this administration is firmly committed to progress and to the principle that government — wisely and justly administered — can be an effective instrument of the people and for the public good…

"With an abiding faith in God and in this country, this state and its people, let us begin anew." [10]

The lieutenant governor extends the first public congratulation and promises that all will unite "so far as possible" to help our new governor work on behalf of our state. He appoints a committee to escort Governor Daniel J. Evans to the chambers of the governor, and all of us adjourn until noon the following day.

Governor Evans exits the House, enters his new office with his new chief of staff, Jim Dolliver, looks at the big blank governor's desk and says, "Now what?"

The answer is obvious: Plenty. But this afternoon, he must also move his young family into the governor's mansion, quickly! Television cameras are standing by for a mansion tour. And tonight he and Nancy will reign at his inaugural ball.

"How does it feel to be the state's youngest first lady at 32?" asks a KING-TV reporter while the camera rolls.

"I'm 31," Nancy Evans corrects him with a smile before she tugs her young sons inside the aging four-story mansion.

Mary missed school today to travel to Olympia with Tom LaPenske in his bright, white VW bug. The teens arrived in time to hear Governor Evans' inaugural address from the gallery of the House. Ken watched Dan's speech from the gallery seating, too.

After the speech, Mary met us back at the house carrying her watermelon-red dress, carefully pressed and hung, and a small, boxed boutonniere for Tom. After Ken and I welcome her with hugs, we all scatter to prepare for the evening ball. Ken fusses with his fancy new shirt from I. Magnin's, which he'll pair with his old tried and true tuxedo. The shirt has an attached white 'scarf tie' we call it, though I'm sure it has a more formal name a more formal person may know. The 'scarf tie' requires fastening down with a formal stickpin, an item Ken has never possessed. We've decided a hatpin will suffice.

"Mary, did you remember to bring…"

"This?" She pulls the pearl-headed pin from her bag and hands it to her dad.

Turned out in his old tux, Ken is dashing. He always has cut a fine figure, and I imagine this handsome husband of mine always will. I've picked a pink and white party dress, knee-length rather than a ball gown. It's the 1960's — anything goes, and a shorter style suits me better: Less fussy and frankly easier for dancing.

Our daughter has gone the most formal route possible, and who can blame her? As co-chairs of Teens for Dan Evans, she and Tom LaPenske were among the youngest to receive personal invitations to this ball, and they've dressed to the hilt for the swanky state affair: She with her dress and her dyed-to-match shoes, and Tom in a formal black tuxedo.

Ken and I revel in the celebration and in our time together, dancing and mixing with legislators old and new, from both parties, both houses, and also with the many well-wishers and townsfolk. The City of Olympia and its citizens host this affair each session, and everyone involved in state government tends to turn out. For the Evans team in 1965, the governor's ball is particularly jubilant, capping two years of relentless work toward the ambitious goal of seating this young man as head of our state. We join the toast to His Excellency, the Governor Daniel J. Evans and to his wife Nancy, the beau and belle of the ball.

Day 4. Speaker Schaefer calls us back into session at noon the next day. But for what? The Federal District Court has forbidden our work on any task but redistricting. We introduce a number of bills on first reading and assign them to committee, where — other than discussion — the bill activity will stop, by formal court order.

All is stymied, it seems, except within the Committee on Constitution,

Elections and Reapportionment. Slade Gorton, Don Moos and I sit on this key committee with our hands effectively tied by the Democrat majority. Of the committee's seventeen members, only six are Republican. Our chairman is Democrat Gary Grant, a second-term legislator like me, but with none of my years of experience with redistricting. The majority party members on this committee are not a seasoned bunch either; four of the Democrats are freshmen.

Slade, Don and I are each more expert on redistricting than any of them, yet we attend these meetings knowing our knowledgeable voices will likely never be heard, nor will our small block of votes ever prevail. So we focus instead on our own redistricting work, which we've just set up in the office of our new secretary of state, Lud Kramer. The committee room for the Committee on Constitutions, Elections and Reapportionment is not at our disposal.

For a week the House sputters along, our legislative activity harnessed by the courts. We ask for a ruling from our attorney general: *What are we legally permitted to do outside of redistricting?* We speculate in the dining room. *What's the latest on redistricting? What lines do you think will work?* We talk in the capitol hallways. *Who's got the best idea? What's the plan?*

Day 8. This is January 18, a Monday.

"Mary Ellen?"

"Lois!"

Lois Hauptli, an acquaintance from my League of Women Voter days, approaches my desk on the floor during a House recess. She is a working mother of three from West Seattle, and I haven't seen her since the accident.

"I heard your news," I tell her, "and I am so sorry. How is he?"

Lois' young son isn't the first to have smashed through a sliding glass door and collapsed on the other side, slashed and bleeding. In the mid-1960's, this has become much too common an accident. If Lois gets her way, her son will be among the last victims of these brittle walls of glass. She is here to lobby for better safety glass standards for sliding doors. I had heard from a mutual friend she was drafting a bill.

"I could really use some help," she said. "When will the House be in business again?"

"There's not much we can do until after redistricting."

We share a knowing look. As League women, we know what a battle *that* is.

"How long?" she asks me. "Any hints at all?"

"I wish I knew, Lois. I really do. Any luck down here? How are your legislators?"

"Well, Senator Greive's preoccupied, as I'm sure you know, and my representative, George Pierre, really hasn't been well."

She reports on her progress: She has found two sponsors for her bill but she will need much more support to help her measure stand out in our likely-to-be-frantic-later, unconventional session. Since redistricting is dominating our start, and all other matters on hold, we'll have a tremendous backlog of bills to consider and pass in a shortened time frame once our redistricting is done. I suggest some colleagues who might be sympathetic — Marjorie, for instance — and tell Lois to keep me apprised.

"Good luck."

"Thanks, Mary Ellen. Sounds like you'll need a dose of it, too!"

Day 10. At 2 p.m. Speaker Schaefer calls the House to order for an afternoon session. My glasses have broken, and I'm distracted. This lens won't stay put. If only this darned frame would hold together well enough to allow me to bend my head to read all this paperwork...

The clerk calls the roll. All members are present except for Rep. Pierre — Lois Hauptli's Rep. Pierre, and a Democrat redistricting holdout — who suffered what may have been a stroke some days earlier. He remains excused.

Mr. Sawyer demands a Call of the House. The motion is sustained, the doors locked. The Speaker then calls for the report of our Committee on Constitutions, Elections and Reapportionment. Rep. Grant rises to speak in support of Senator Greive's redistricting bill — roughly the same one that fell short of House approval in our session's first 48 hours.

"Mr. Speaker: We, a majority of your Committee on Constitutions, Elections and Reapportionment to whom was referred Engrossed Senate Bill No. 2, reapportioning the state legislature, have had the same under consideration, and we respectfully report the same back with the recommendation that it *do* pass as amended."

The committee chairman, vice-chairman and committee Democrats all concur, except for one: Democrat Jack Dootson, who considers the Republican redistricting strategy more fair. He left his name off this recommendation.

Mr. Gorton rises: "Mr. Speaker: We, a minority of your Committee on Constitutions, Elections and Reapportionment, to whom was referred Engrossed Senate Bill No. 2, reapportioning of the state legislature, have had the same under consideration, and we respectfully report the same back to the House with the recommendation that it do *not* pass."

We the minority are Slade Gorton, Ed Harris, Bob McDougal, Don Moos, Charles Newschwander and me. Jack Dootson, the lone wolf Democrat who tends to agree with our Republican redistricting aims, signed neither our minority report nor that of the majority.

Several hours of debate ensue as we work our way through Greive's Senate bill — through specific amendments to specific districts, with many of the blatant ones sparking controversy.

"Mr. Grant," Mr. Gorton says at one particularly flagrant partisan aspect, "I would like to know how you propose to keep the governor from vetoing that amendment?"

"I don't propose to keep the governor from vetoing anything," Mr. Grant responds. "I think we have here before us today a constitutional, valid reapportionment proposal. We would hope the governor would take that into consideration when this proposal reaches his desk."

The vote is taken. The amendment stands. The Democrats prevail. No surprise.

Mr. Moos proposes an amendment, a Republican amendment. When the vote is taken, the measure fails and the Democrats prevail again. No surprise. For the balance of the afternoon, the pattern repeats itself: Democrats win, Republicans lose. Majority status makes a measurable difference.

After another lengthy Democrat amendment passes, Mr. Gorton proposes one of his own, which scalps Senator Greive's bill and replaces it with our Republican-drawn redistricting. Mr. Brachtenbach asks if Mr. Gorton will yield to a question. He will.

"In view of your long standing and intimate knowledge of the redistricting problem, Mr. Gorton, do you consider Senate Bill No. 2 to be a completely fair redistricting measure?"

Slade cites several statistical analyses of Senator Greive's proposed bill, all of which indicate Democrats would win a majority of our legislative seats, regardless of which party wins the actual state vote count.

"On that basis," says Slade, "I don't think that this meets the standards of political fairness to any Republican or Independent or Democratic voter, other than one who believed that the Democrats should always be in control, no matter what the people thought."

Hear! Hear! I silently concur. *But, oh dear, there go my glasses again. That darn little screw. Where is it? Let's see, now, where did my lens go this time?* While I struggle with my rickety glasses and dip down to fetch my lens from the floor, another vote is taken — an electric roll call — and when I hear my name, I hurriedly press my button. Slade's amendment fails, no surprise, and the House passes SB 2 back to the Senate, replete with House Democrat amendments... but none of ours. The Senate will likely take this House-passed redistricting measure straight to the governor's desk for his signature.

We finish the session by introducing several more bills, as well as a House joint memorial to extend the Alaska Marine Highway to Interstate 5, a House resolution commemorating today's inauguration of Lyndon Baines Johnson to the U.S. presidency, and a word of appreciation for the Kelso Drum and Bugle Corps, which represented our state at the inaugural festivities in Washington, D.C. And then we adjourn.

In the House dining room afterwards, Jack Dootson takes a seat across from me, and digs in to his trademark nightly snack: Three scoops of ice cream — three different flavors — arranged triangularly on a generous bed of iceberg lettuce.

"Never thought I'd see the day," he says to me with a mischievous smile as he slowly scrapes a spoonful of some pistachio.

"What do you mean, Jack?"

"Mary Ellen McCaffree — you! — voting against Slade Gorton on redistricting… and siding with the Democrats. Astonishing."

I didn't get it.

"Today, Mary Ellen. That electric roll call. You voted Slade's amendment down. Which means you voted for Greive's SB 2."

"No I didn't… did I?"

Joel slides in beside me on the cafeteria bench.

"Dootson's right, Mary Ellen. You did. Voted as red as your face is right now."

Darned glasses! I excuse myself to these chuckling gents and rush downstairs to the bill room.

At this very same hour, this very same story is zipping across our nation by wire, spread by an amused staff writer with the Associated Press. Some of my Kansas relatives chuckle when they read this news in their local newspaper. They clip it and send it to our Seattle address, where it is chuckled at anew by Ken.

A written entry in our House Journal tomorrow, following the report of this evening's vote, will decidedly be an embarrassment to me, but it provides living proof that legislators are not infallible — they, too, can make some awfully stupid mistakes.

Day 11. When the pages distribute copies of the Journal record of the previous day's activity, the correction blares at me, as surely as it will shout out at every colleague who reads it through. My deep, hot blush of shame returns as I read it.

EXPLANATION OF VOTE

I voted 'nay' on the Gorton amendment by mistake. My glasses were broken just before the session convened. I intended to vote against SB No. 2 without the Gorton amendment.

MARY ELLEN McCAFFREE, 32nd District[11]

Fortunately for me, my vote didn't change the final outcome. After all my work on redistricting—I voted with the Democrats on their gerrymandered bill!

Day 12. The Senate finally passes Engrossed Senate Bill 2, as approved by both houses. Our state's redistricting is set in print and ready for the governor to sign. But rather than sending the bill along to the desk of Governor Evans, the Senate sits on it. They adjourn until Monday and the fate of our state's redistricting languishes. Why?

Whatever their strategy, the governor is incensed.

Some suggest the Democrats have decided to let it sit for the weekend to give the press time to let state voters know redistricting has been done—and that it is now up to the governor to sign it into law so the legislature can get on with the business of the state. In other words, they want to sway public sentiment against a veto, if that is what Governor Evans chooses to do.

But Governor Evans calls the Democrats' bluff—by calling a press conference this very afternoon. And because redistricting is the only issue at play these days in Olympia, the capitol press corps is hounding it every step of the way. They show up en masse.

During the conference, Governor Evans lambastes the Democrats for holding up the resolution to redistricting, and he also attacks Senate Bill 2 as partisan. He says the Senate's delay today has impeded the rapid settlement of the redistricting issue. Shame on them. The Republicans are ready to negotiate at any time, he tells the press, and he points out the Republican focus on compromise as the best way to redistrict our state. Then the newly elected governor says he will veto this bill and all others like it, no matter which party passes it, because the state of Washington needs a fair and equitable redistricting.

The press loves a battle and a hero. They gobble this up, and you can sense their glee in their written reports of Governor Evans' immediate and authoritative response. The Democrat delay strategy has backfired and Governor Evans earns an early edge with the media—at least on the issue of redistricting.

Day 15. On Monday morning, the President of the Senate signs Senate Bill 2 and sends it along to the Governor's desk.

Day 16. The governor replies:

To the Honorable Senate of the State of Washington
Lady and Gentlemen:

I am returning herewith, without my approval, Senate Bill No. 2 entitled "An Act relating to the legislature; providing for the redistricting and reapportionment thereof…"

In my inaugural message on January 13, 1965, I urged the legislature to pass promptly a constitutional redistricting bill which would insure that the party which wins a majority of votes would win a majority of the seats in the legislature. Senate Bill No. 2 totally fails to meet this goal. I have reached this conclusion after a great deal of thought and after meeting with the chief proponents of the bill in the House and the Senate.

After considering all of the facts I am convinced that this bill would thwart the will of the majority and guarantee perpetual control of the legislative process by one party.

As Governor, I have responsibility to all the people of the state, Republicans, Democrats and independents alike, to see that they have the right to choose, by majority vote, the party which will lead the legislature. This bill would deprive the people of that fundamental goal of the two-party system.

For these reasons I have vetoed Senate Bill No. 2.

Yesterday I called together the legislative leaders of both parties and urged them to lay aside partisan considerations and to negotiate in good faith a redistricting bill which will be fair to all of the people of the state. When such is presented to me, I will approve it promptly.

It is now the 16ᵗʰ day of the legislative session. The public business is pressing and demands immediate action.

> *Respectfully Submitted,*
> *Daniel J. Evans, governor* [12]

The governor's veto message infuriates Senate Democrats.
They call him an obstructionist.
They call him a partisan tyrant.
They call him… Danny Veto.

Day 17. I wake to a humorous twist on redistricting wars in this morning's newspaper, a perfect accompaniment to my morning coffee and buttered toast. *Seattle Post-Intelligencer* writer Charles Dunsire takes our redistricting battle an imaginary fifty years into the future.

OLYMPIA, Jan. 1, 2015 - Washington State will celebrate the golden anniversary of convening its 1965 Legislature this month, with high hopes that its dwindling body of lawmakers will at last pass a redistricting bill.

Gov. Daniel J. Evans, at 89 the nation's oldest governor, declared today: It is high time for the Legislature to settle down to business and solve the state's redistricting problem. We must cast aside partisan politics and come up with a bill that is fair and equitable.

Evans indicated that he will veto the latest bill because he regards it as a blatant attempt by the Democrats to gerrymander the state in their favor. This will mark his 109th veto of such measures since taking office in 1965...[13]

Dunsire's writing brings some jollity to an otherwise arduous task. But while the House votes to have the silly article read into today's Journal, the Senate stays on task with more sobriety: Senator McCutcheon presents Senate Joint Memorial 5, a proposed redistricting method that makes an end-run around the governor. SJM 5 asks the Federal District Court to simply enact Senate Bill 2 "as the apportionment plan for the state" so that the legislature can "conduct normal business." Thus, redistricting would circumvent the legislature, bypass any more floor votes, and bypass the governor's veto (or 'yes') as well. The legislature, Senator McCutcheon contends in this memorial, has done what the court has asked them to do by writing this specific redistricting bill, so why not go ahead and make it law?

The Senate passes the joint memorial and sends it to the House. House Democrats, however, do not agree that Greive's Senate Bill 2 has their interests at heart, so they refuse even to bring the joint memorial to the floor. Why would they ask the court to accept this?

McCutcheon's joint memorial is dead, but not the Democrat determination to author redistricting. On this very same day, after we formally greet our state's dairy princess, Representative Grant rolls out his own version of redistricting in House Bill 196, and the bill is assigned to our committee.

Day 18. The Speaker calls us into session at 10 a.m. and after opening ceremonials, he distributes us each a letter from state Attorney General John O'Connell: A ruling on how we may conduct our legislative business. The letter reviews for us the history of the Federal District Court case, then addresses the several questions posed by our membership. We follow as the attorney general's opinion is read aloud:

"In order to clarify the matter," O'Connell writes, "we contacted the court on an informal basis, both last fall and again earlier this week..."

He concluded that not only may we send bills into committee, but we can pass them out of committee and onto the floor, and from there to the Rules Committee, and then out of Rules and back to the floor of the House or Senate for second reading (for floor amendments). Our only restriction, he says, is that we may not put a bill up to vote on final passage (third reading) until after the state is finally redistricted.

While the opinion was being read, I've watched Slade scribble notes in his distinctive backhand, then pass them along to Joel and Tom Copeland, then I've watched Joel and Tom read them and nod in response.

MY YOUNGEST, DAVID, JOINED ME FULL TIME in Olympia the second week of this session to work here as a page, as Mary did during my last term. David's now a teenager through and through, judging from the stories he tells… and sings: "It's been a hard day's night, and I've been workin' like a dog!"

"Have you, David?"

"Probably not," he admits. "Being here with the pages is pretty cool, though. I wanna hold your ha-aa-and!"

"David?"

"I love The Beatles."

"Beetles? Bugs?"

"The Beatles, yeah. Yeah, yeah, yeah. We have a transistor radio in the page room. I mean, what else are we supposed to do down there, waiting for those little bells to ring so we can do something really important for someone, like 'Could you get me a cup of coffee?'"

"Coffee can be important."

"Yeah. Well one of my friends gets to run the elevator. 'What floor would you like, Sir?' Wish I could do that. Or the switchboard, maybe…"

My son keeps talking, but my mind has already drifted back to redistricting. I'm afraid it's a pattern in our life together. I am pretty preoccupied.

"Mom? Mom?…"

OUR COMMITTEE ON CONSTITUTION, Elections and Reapportionment is a tremendous disappointment to me. I've worked on the issue of redistricting a decade now, and it is difficult to watch our young chairman attempt to conceptually master it in a month. He has little regard for how difficult it is to accomplish a careful, balanced redistricting. The fact that he's quite cocky doesn't help.

Gary Grant is indubitably enthusiastic as our committee chairman, and he is set on authoring our state's redistricting bill… his own way. He has broken rank with Senate Democrats. He has broken rank with O'Brien and Schaefer in our House. As committee chairman, he wants to do this solo, though he's trying to pull the rest of us members aboard. His manner, however, is so condescending, so uninformed (in my eyes) and so outright obnoxious that I save my redistricting energy for our work in Lud Kramer's office.

My minority companions and I faithfully attend Grant's committee meetings, day after day. I usually sit between Slade and Don so I can easily (and quietly) take redistricting notes from them both. We try to make some productive use of our time here.

Day 19. Don Moos is a gentle giant of a man, adept at quietly listening to our rural legislators, securing their rural redistricting votes. But as we sit here in the committee room again today, listening to yet another bombastic speech by Gary Grant, the gentle giant rumbles to life and finally explodes: "Talk all you want," he shouts at Grant, "but don't kid yourself that you are writing the state's redistricting bill. The subject is too important to waste on a bunch of freshmen and third stringers. If this committee was going to do the actual writing of the bill, this committee would be made up of big boys."

He turns to some of our committee members and continues.

"And if you Democrat freshman think anybody is really looking after you, you've got another thing coming, because when this bill finally is written, it's going to be written by a lot of wheeling, dealing senators — not you. And they don't know you, either, so guess whose blood is going to come rolling out from under the conference door? Not theirs — yours!"

He's done.

Adele Ferguson, a sharp-witted, sharp-penned news reporter for a big daily, has covered our committee work all session, and I've watched her write down Don's every last word.[14]

Rep. Grant's House Bill 196 — his version of redistricting — comes to the floor this afternoon for second reading. Our six 'nay' votes in committee were a flimsy blockade. Someone asks how Grant's bill differs from the one I championed via Initiative 211. Someone else across the aisle glibly replies: *One district was too big and one too little and we fixed it.* But by and large, Gary Grant's HB 196 is not a balanced bill and would never meet approval by the court.

I know this. Slade knows this. Don knows this. And so does Senator Greive. *So what?* says Senator Greive and all the other Democrats, too. *Let the governor veto it.* Eventually, the Democrats believe, the public will turn against the governor based on his repeated redistricting vetoes. At least that's what they hope. Rep. Grant's bill is passed by the House and sent to the Senate.

We have Sunday off.

Day 22. When we return Monday morning, a barbershop quartet approaches the bar of the House and serenades us with *Heart of My Heart* to promote the Heart Association's annual fund drive. Then a visiting Canadian parliamentarian delivers a brief address. Then we recess until after lunch, after which the governor will address us in Joint Session. The topic: Our state budget.

Normally, the governor's budget address is scheduled for the session's first week, on day four, but due to our redistricting restriction, the governor has reserved it until now. Once the Senators join us and the dignitaries are duly escorted in, Governor Evans takes the podium.

"Mr. President, Mr. Speaker, my former colleagues, Ladies and Gentlemen of the Legislature: As we come to grips with the imminent matters of state — both to meet the Federal Court's demands to establish constitutional and equitable legislative representation, and to meet the peoples' legitimate needs for state services — this is, indeed, a time of high purpose.

"I regret that you have been as yet unable to resolve the vital matter of legislative redistricting within the three fundamental criteria I laid down on January 13. One-third of this legislative session has passed. I urge you, therefore, to broaden your perspectives to include, more completely, the representative interests of all citizens of the state, and to renew your faith that our distinctive representative form of American government only functions fairly when either political party whose candidates win a majority of the peoples' votes is assured a majority of the seats in the legislature....

"In order that you may legally and fully address yourselves to your budgetary and other important responsibilities, it is mandatory that redistricting be resolved promptly..."

I imagine that with our legislature locked into redistricting, and him locked out of the process, Dan has been working overtime analyzing the minutiae of our state budget.

"A new governor ordinarily has had neither adequate time nor fully comparable information from which to develop a detailed budget proposal," he continues. "Within such precedent, the acceptable course for me would be to say nothing about the printed budget placed before you by the past administration...

"But for me to remain silent would be to perpetrate an even greater act of irresponsibility than the one placed in printed form before you... Some among you have already uncovered some of the inadequacies of this fiscal sham..."

Heads nod, Democrat and Republican alike. Point by point, our governor outlines the Rosellini budget's over-dependence on federal programs, some of which have not yet even been enacted, much less funded.

"Some very risky assumptions don't you think?" he asks us all. "Responsible legislative leaders of both parties in each house have acknowledged, even upon initial review, that this budget is at least $40 million out of balance. In actuality, the past administration's budget is out of balance by more than twice that amount... To balance this budget, even when making substantial allowances for new federal assistance, and without reducing the General Fund deficit, would require a tax increase of at least $80 million. Neither you nor I would be fulfilling our responsibilities to the citizens of this state if we allowed such a budget to become reality...

"If we have not already reached the point where the federal tail is wagging the state dog – in the direction of programs, in actual services provided, in the determination of basic state policy – then, I submit, we are dangerously close to that point."

His engineering mindset emerges: "We must use all of the state machinery at hand to solve our problems at home. We must re-design the machinery of government, where it is inadequate, to enable the state and its political subdivisions to locally meet the legitimate demands of its citizens...

"Unquestionably, political courage is required... It is easier to dodge local and state problems and let someone else make the decisions – farther away, at some other time. But short-range delights have long-range consequences. In order to protect the integrity of our state and local government, and in order to retain control over our own future – as individuals as well as citizens of this state – we must face our local and state problems squarely."

So often we think of 'government' as the political scene in Washington, D.C. But truthfully, it is within our states and communities that we find the greatest opportunity to exercise our individual rights. The more local a government, the more relevant and less mysterious, at least from my perspective. Otherwise, as a housewife and mom, I doubt I'd have been able to insert myself here.

Following the butcher paper Blueprint we DEGOHTs scribbled and refined over the months of the campaign, the governor touches on key points he'll pursue this session, in his particular order of importance: Education, public assistance, institutions (mental health care and community health centers), highway safety, government efficiency and more logical revenue.

"The course I have charted is a challenging one. The decision to follow it will not come easily. Yet there is no low road to high purpose. I have a deep and abiding faith in the people's desire that we chart no expedient course – choose no easy road.

"The Legislature willing, we can attain together the objectives for which our government was created and to which all people aspire." [15]

Our new governor exits the House to bipartisan applause.

FOR THE NEXT TEN DAYS, I work nearly round the clock on redistricting in the office of our new secretary of state. I calculate each miniscule change proposed by Slade, Joel and Don as they negotiate tirelessly to craft a state plan that will muster support and fetch a collective *Aye*. At last count, we've created nearly fifty different redistricting plans, and all fifty variations sit atop Lud Kramer's file cabinet.

"Mary Ellen? Give me number seventeen," says Don. He takes it from me and hurries to the floor to try to work through a district with a legislator during a House recess. No luck. He's back. "No go. Give me twenty-three instead." And the big man dashes out again.

Redistricting first, revenue second, and then relieve our schools' reliance on those difficult annual levies. I never forget my purpose here.

I step outside for a bit of fresh air and notice something amiss: The capitol fountain is overflowing with a growing mountain of suds. I have left my son largely to his own devices this session, and when I hear the culprits were teen pages, I... just wonder. After that, I try to keep better tabs on my energetic 14-year-old, and I bring him with me to the next evening session, where we find him something reasonably 'cool' to do.

"Wow! Cool!"

He loved the switchboard at first sight, and so during after-hours in the capitol now, once the regular staff is gone, David is in charge of the switchboard with its panel of lights and all the little lines to be plugged in for phone calls accordingly.

"This is so cool!"

At mid-session, when we have to fire all the pages due to budget restraints, and can only re-hire a portion, David returns to Seattle.

As we're engaged in round-the-clock redistricting work, Slade challenges the attorney general's ruling on what we as a legislature can legitimately do pre-redistricting. I add my signature to the Journal statement Slade has authored: It cautions us that Attorney General O'Connell's recommendation is based not on a legal ruling but on a casual inquiry. Therefore, Slade contends, the focus in the House should remain on redistricting until we're done. Other work must wait — it's distracting. We can't lose traction now.

Senator Greive continues along his largely protectionist path, while we continue strict work towards a balanced redistricting. Our unswerving persistence really annoys him.

"Every time I try to talk to them about the actual people in specific seats," he complains, "they start talking philosophy."

'They' means us, our Republican team.

"I admit," he continues, "swing districts are a good strategy, and so on and so forth. It's a legitimate argument. It's one of those things you can talk about, you know, but you really don't want: *In every district but mine, Dear God. Make mine, Dear God, be a little Democrat or a little Republican — these other guys, they can run from the awful districts.*" [16]

I have been tapped to sponsor an executive request bill on behalf of Governor Evans — a redistricting bill to present to the legislature with the thought that if it's backed by the governor, it will logically avoid his veto. As with our 1963 redistricting measures, it was decided that my name would be more appealing as sponsor — by fact of being less inflammatory.

Don Moos shows a draft of this bill to Senator Greive as a starting point for working toward bicameral, bipartisan compromise. But rather than work with us, Senator Greive takes this draft straight to the press with a scathing criticism of our alleged 'deal-making'. The press bites, rips and gnashes the bill, and it dies a quick death. So do the multiple measures proposed by Rep. Grant. More than halfway through the 60-day session, we are nowhere with our redistricting. Those legislators not directly involved in the process are milling about with very little to do.

On the evening of one particularly long, dragging day, Maggie Hurley suggests we pep things up. She and our leadership arrange to have a piano rolled onto the floor of the House. She takes a seat, pounds out a string of old favorites, and a dozen or so harmonize in an old-fashioned song fest. *You Are My Sunshine. Home on the Range.* No particular talent among us, but as a diversion it's a hit. Our members sing until the Speaker calls us back to order.

Day 32. On this February 11, the House session opens with a spoof on Lincoln's Gettysburg address, written and delivered by Rep. Alan Thompson, a newspaperman and a Democrat: "Four weeks and seven days ago, our constituents brought forth into these chambers a new legislature, conceived in a landslide and dedicated by court order to the proposition of one man-one vote…" [17]

While humorous, Thompson's creative effort also irks me. We have a serious job to do and we aren't doing it. Our constituents who elected us to serve here are growing irate. Mr. Newman Clark, a distinguished, silver-haired Republican attorney, rises on a point of personal privilege.

"Mr. Speaker, with the consent of the House, I would like to read a letter from a Democratic constituent in the 43rd District — who incidentally voted against me."

Clark reads: "*I am disgusted with the behavior of the legislature in Olympia. I usually vote Democratic. This election I split, along with the majority of the state, and voted Democratic nationally and legislatively, and Republican gubernatorially. I thought you could choose a governor whose policy you admired and a legislature of your own political persuasion and expect them to work together for the betterment of the state. I thought that politicians were initially devoted to the public and secondly concerned with party. Why should this not be so? We sent Evans to you because we want what he wants. Why don't you let him give it to us?*" This is signed 'Disillusioned'. Her name is here, if you want to look at the letter." [18]

We legislators are obviously not the only ones tired of the deadlock. But we are tired. In both chambers — particularly in the Senate, where Senator Greive is pushing his plan from all angles — some sessions are running well into the night, and then on into the morning, sometimes for a full 24 hours.

Tonight, very late, Joel pokes his head into Lud Kramer's office, knowing full well he'll find me there, still hard at work.

"C'mon Mary Ellen — something's erupting in the Senate."

"At this hour?"

It is nearly 3 a.m.

"Redistricting season, y'know," he says. "Hurry!"

We rush across the marbled foyer and slide in beside Slade and Don on a leather bench in the wings, just off the Senate floor, where Senator Robert Charette, a Democrat from Aberdeen, is attempting to upset Senator Greive's redistricting cart. Slade brings us up to date: Charette is tired of the self-centered talk on the Senate floor and just said so. We've arrived in time to hear him accuse his Senate leaders: *You guys are motivated by nothing but your own personal district concerns.*

"If that's how this game is played," Charette continues, "I am presenting the one bill that best takes care of me."

He then moves to scalp Senator Greive's most recent redistricting bill — SB 237 — and replace it with the governor's executive request plan: My bill. In the wings we four exchange silent glances. Senator Charette continues: "Senator Greive has sold out for personal gain, and as long as the Democratic Party has been sold a bill of goods, we might as well go all the way with Dan."

Charette's speech infuriates Greive's supporters, not to mention Bob Greive. To shut him up quickly, Senator McCutcheon moves to lay Charette's motion on the table. The Senate votes on it. To everyone's surprise, McCutcheon's motion to quell the upstart Charette is defeated — by a vote of 27 to 21. Only 17 of these senators are Republicans, so ten Democrats contributed to this defeat. The Senate Democrats are still not united, and Charette's defiant move has exposed it — a gaping division endures in the Senate Democratic caucus.

A furious vocal barrage erupts right there on the Senate floor — Democrat versus Democrat waging vicious verbal warfare. The leadership is outraged over the 'turncoat' support for replacing Greive's bill with the one from the governor via me. Harsh accusations fly.

The Republican senators are visibly aghast, but refrain from entering the wee-hour squabble. When we leave the wings at 4 a.m., the Senate chamber is still roaring with rage.

Day 33. Less than 12 hours later, by our afternoon session, Senator Greive's

ESB 237 is presented to us on the floor of the House. Some of us are dismayed, not by the fact that his version eventually won Senate support, however, but by the way in which Gary Grant kept it under wraps when he first received it. He flashed it before our committee only momentarily while we Republican members were present, whereas earlier, the Democrat contingent had previewed the bill in detail, in private, to craft their amendments and work through the bill without us. When we complained in committee, chairman Grant just ignored us.

Therefore, on the House floor right now, after the majority bloc of our Committee on Constitution, Elections and Apportionment has recommended that we do pass Greive's bill, and after we the minority urge that it do *not* pass, Don Moos stands for recognition.

"Point of personal privilege."

"Proceed, Mr. Moos."

"Mr. Speaker, ladies and gentlemen of the House, I thought a brief explanation would possibly be in order after the reading of our minority report. We felt in the committee that the bill had not had proper exposure to us or to the people of this…"

"Mr. Speaker, point of order," John O'Brien interrupts.

Speaker Schaefer grants Mr. O'Brien the floor.

"It appears to me," says Mr. O'Brien, "that the remarks of Mr. Moos under personal privilege are not in order at this time. The bill has been read in from committee, and the action now would be to work on the committee report, not to discuss what happened to the minority in committee."

"You are right, Mr. O'Brien," Speaker Schaefer agrees. "Mr. Moos can make his remarks on final passage of the bill if it gets that far."

Having now been silenced on the floor regarding our treatment in committee, on top of being silenced within the committee itself, we make five floor amendments to this committee-amended Senate redistricting bill. All five fail. Senate Bill 237 passes the House by a vote of 53-43 and we send it back to the Senate with House amendments — none of them ours.

To pad his chances of redistricting success today, Senator Greive sends the House yet another measure: Engrossed Senate Bill 333. This is not a redistricting bill, however, but a referendum to the people of the state calling for a statewide vote on his redistricting proposal, and thereby again bypassing the governor. The bill is referred to our committee, where our disgruntled House leadership demands that it die — just like the proposed court rubber stamp measure before it. Again, they reason, why should they support Senator Greive's redistricting bill as is, when they haven't been allowed input? Among Democrats, a deep House/Senate fissure remains as well.

Later in the day, we receive another message from the Senate: It has passed Greive's ESB 237 as amended by the House. This redistricting bill is ready for the governor's desk and pen.

Day 34. On this February 13, a Saturday, Representative Sawyer reads us the valentine that arrived a day early from his wife: "Let me call you sweetheart — I can't remember your name."

It rings with truth. Some of us haven't made it home all session. We are stuck at the capitol this Valentine's Day weekend, too, most of us having left loving spouses back home. The long hours and lack of progress wears on us all — but probably more so on those not involved with redistricting.

Rep. Clark has a suggestion: Why doesn't the Legislature just recess except for the members involved in redistricting? It would save the state money, and we could resume our regular legislative work after our redistricting is finished.

Rep. Burtch has a reply: Fine. Those of you who want to leave? Leave. And leave the rest of us here to redistrict.

We stay in session. But we have tomorrow off. Sunday — Valentine's Day.

"Mary Ellen? Wish me luck."

"Good luck, Slade."

He'll need it. Not with his lovely wife Sally on Valentine's Day, but with the luncheon he's headed to now, across town, where he and Senator Greive have been invited to jointly address the state Chamber of Commerce. Their topic? What else but redistricting.

In the course of their joint appearance, Senator Greive slips in some situational satire, which generates laughs from the audience and breaks the ice between the two adversaries. Afterwards, this unlikely pair — Senator Greive and Representative Gorton, leaders of the two camps in redistricting — chat throughout their entire long walk home. They compare notes, swap stories and keep on talking another two hours... in the capitol office of Senator Greive. They agree: Their two young crackerjack assistants — Dean Foster and Howard McCurdy — should start working together on districts, at least to compare notes.

Slade telephones me, guardedly excited: "You know, Mary Ellen, I think we're closer than I'd imagined!"

He reports the same to the governor, who immediately asks us to meet, to review our maps and determine the sticking points based on what Slade learned from Senator Greive. Could it be the end is nigh?

Ken has come for Valentine's weekend, and here we are, the two of us on Saturday night in Lud Kramer's office, with my husband obligingly manning an adding machine yet again.

"Do we have to do this now?" he asks.

"Yes," I say, hard at work and not looking up.

"You, my dear," he says with more than a hint of irritation, "are the darnedest workaholic I've ever run onto."

"There's a lobbyist party we can go to later, honey," I tell him. "Does that help?"

"Some."

I love to socialize, but given my nature and the nature of this session, I squeeze in a bit of work, even at the party. Redistricting naturally enters into our small talk, anywhere we go in our capitol city, so if I hear or overhear anything helpful, I immediately report it to Slade, Joel or Don: "I just heard such-and-such. You might want to talk to so-and-so." And then I'm back to my Ken.

Valentine's Day, 1965. On the heels of yesterday's broken ice, Slade meets again with Senator Greive, then returns to our group in Lud Kramer's office with an entertaining report: "We decided to take turns drawing districts, and I said to him, 'Bob — you're senior. You draw first. Pick a district, any district. Then I'll draw up one. Sound fair?' He agreed."

In this little group, we've all worked at this so long we know the streets, the houses, the districts. In an instant, any of us can calculate the political implications of any proposed line shift on any map.

"So Bob went first and drew his own district, satisfied," Slade continued. "Then I picked the one just north of the ship canal, near yours, Mary Ellen — that Democrat stronghold. You know which one. I followed right along the current district lines, but then adjusted it right at that one boundary we've been looking at — to even it out, make it swing. Greive turned all red in the face. 'I knew you'd do that, you sunnava bitch' he yelled, and he threw his pencil at the wall and stomped out. Meeting over."

Day 36. My this Monday morning, two measures I am sponsoring have reached the floor of the House — both are house joint resolutions, and neither has to do with redistricting. One calls for a constitutional convention for our state to reorganize several elements outdated since statehood. The second would move the governor's inauguration to the day our legislative sessions start. The implications of this second one are certainly clear.

Day 37. The governor vetoes ESB 237 — Greive's redistricting, with a legal population count per district, but blatantly gerrymandered. It was common knowledge among all of us that the Democrats passed this poorly drafted bill specifically to solicit the governor's veto. They knew full well it wouldn't fly. That way they could lay all the blame for redistricting delay on His Excellency Dan Evans, rather than swallow it themselves. Inside the legislature, we know better.

"This bill does not represent a serious effort on the part of the legislature to solve the difficult problem of redistricting," the governor's veto message reprimands. He delineates in detail the numerous flaws in the bill.

"Clearly an apportionment plan which is only marginal and of doubtful validity should be avoided because of the possibilities of protracted litigation that could result in determining the constitutionality..." he writes the Senate. "Because the legislature will not be permitted to function in its normal manner until the court has approved its legislative apportionment plan, it is evident that a plan adopted and presented to the court must be one that is clearly acceptable." [19]

Back to our drawing boards.

Day 38. Lois Hauptli's sliding glass door bill arrives in the House for second reading and is returned to the Committee on Commerce and Economic Development for further work, where it will stay until we can act upon it as a House — along with hundreds of other bills. Until we complete redistricting, the rest of the state's business — the peoples' business — can only go so far, like Lois' bill, and then all must stop. And wait.

Behind the scenes, it's all still redistricting. The capitol's three-ring redistricting circus — Greive, Gorton and Grant — continues, with a few lesser acts on the side. I shuttle between my desk on the floor and Lud Kramer's office for my redistricting work. With so many new proposals coming to the fore, and the many subtle tweaks our team continues to negotiate, my line-drawing crew and I are working like demons to keep up, and then I must personally assess the effects of each small change. It's like a bowl full of billiard balls — move one a millimeter, all the rest move too.

Day 39 of this 39th Session. Mr. Backstrom rises on a point of personal privilege. At his request, the pages distribute copies of another silly speech, along with lapel pins courtesy of Avis Rental Car, printed with their company motto, *We Try Harder*. Rep. Backstrom reads us his handiwork: [20]

"We have, in a MC/CARE/FREE manner, drawn lines and curves and applied figures which ordinarily we would only see on the beaches in King County, or on Moos in Lincoln County or Big Daddy Day in Spokane. All this with the GREIVE/EOUS results that these GERRY/built districts have become decorations upon the walls of Room 8..."

Room 8 is our House barbershop, where some of Greive's district maps hang about. Mr. Backstrom concludes his speech with a hope that in ten more days, if we all try harder, all of us can finally say, "We did it!"

We'll see. To date more than 600 bills have been introduced in the House, and as a legislative body we have managed to vote on... almost none of them. Twenty-one days remain in this session. Twenty-one days to iron out two years of serious state business, if we can ever get past redistricting.

We convene each day with ceremony, then move into the reading of bills and resolutions, and our Speaker extends pleasant welcomes to an endless string of visitors in the balconies. If these groups have traveled to Olympia to hear stirring speeches as our drama of redistricting unfolds, they are out of luck. All our work is done behind the scenes by private negotiation or—to use less savory terminology—by striking deals.

In caucus, Slade rallies us: "We've been working long hours, every evening, every weekend, drawing districts we think will pass the court—we have dozens of versions, all of them valid," he tells us, and I can confirm this. "It's really a matter of getting the Senate to bend a bit."

"By the Senate, you mean Greive," says a freshman.

"Greive, yes, but he's not the only factor." Slade says. "Keep talking to your colleagues."

"We owe it to the people of this state to get this done," I chime in. "Our colleagues are going to suffer a bad reputation back home if they vote against a logical redistricting much longer. We can give them a way to make this work — through compromise. Remind them of that."

"Yeah, Don and I are happy to talk to anyone, right big guy?" Joel asks Don Moos.

The big guy smiles.

"Believe it or not," Slade says to us all, "we're close."

THE HOUSE MEETS IN SESSION THROUGHOUT the weekend and so does the Senate. After we adjourn on Sunday, Slade and his assitant, Howard McCurdy, and I meet again with Senator Greive and his assistant, Dean Foster—specifically to work through five districts in and around Tacoma.

As midnight nears, Slade says, "We want Lakewood."

"Fine," Greive agrees. "You can have Lakewood, as long as it looks like this."

The senator draws a relatively regular district, with one exception: A long, skinny finger up at the top, extending along one street that includes the residence of Senator A.L. "Slim" Rasmussen, one of Greive's Democrat enemies.

"Now there's a guy who's expendable," Greive says with a chuckle at this 'finger' that removes Senator Rasmussen from his long-time district and sticks him instead into one that leans Republican.

"Ah, the Rasmussen finger again," Slade jokes, having seen this very gerry-mander several times already. "I'm afraid that's not going to last, Bob." [21]

With a new negotiating web being knit between Governor Evans, Representative Gorton, Representative Grant and Senator Greive, our minority floor leader Tom Copeland feels left out. And so he assembles a coalition of his own. He arranges to meet — secretly and separately from other Republicans — with Senator Greive and the Senate Democrats to try to work something out. When the rest of us find out, Joel takes Tom to task.

"Play square," Joel tells him, "or our caucus will vote you out, and your leadership post here will be kaput! We're too close to getting this done, Tom. Shape up, or I'll send you in for an adjustment by Big Daddy Day."

Our chiropractor joke is alive and kicking. Tom is able to laugh.

Day 43. Monday, February 22. George Washington's Birthday. We are called into session at noon, but shortly thereafter recess until 1:50 p.m., when we'll reconvene in Joint Session for a memorial program — a state tradition on the birthday of our state's namesake. Once we've memorialized dozens of the deceased who formerly served in our seats, we recess until 4 p.m., convene, and recess again until 4:30. Our day's real work finally begins around dinnertime.

Following reports from several standing committees, we move on to the second reading of Engrossed Senate Bill 333 — Senator Greive's bill that would take his version of redistricting straight to state voters and bypass the governor. As we review ESB 333, the House erupts in a prolonged procedural tussle that produces a slam on the governor's interference, followed by a swift defense of the governor by Tom Copeland. Tom has not only realigned himself with our caucus, but now ferociously defends our minority voice in the House. The Democrats prevail, however. ESB 333 passes the House and is immediately returned to the Senate.

Day 44 passes uneventfully on the floor, while in the less public places, redistricting work proceeds full throttle. During this quiet floor session, Lois Hauptli's safety glass bill quietly passes to the Rules Committee, and the Rules Committee now has the power to send it back to us for a final vote, once we've finished redistricting. I watch Lois smile in the gallery when

CITIZEN LOBBYIST

A private citizen who presents and promotes an issue or piece of legislation to the legislature without the affiliation or support of any specific group.

we formally send her bill on its way. Lois Hauptli's relentless lobbying has paid off. Very few bills this session have journeyed as far. She joins me at my desk during the next floor recess.

"Thanks for your support, Mary Ellen."

"As a citizen lobbyist, Lois, you're Exhibit A."

Once the governor heard from his longtime friend Slade Gorton that Senator Greive had surprisingly little argument with most of our proposed district boundaries, the governor invited the state's two redistricting leaders into his office to present their respective plans. He then began to broker the grounds for a compromise.

"Rosellini never cared this much," Senator Greive grumbled during the initial meeting, half complaining, half in admiration. "Rosy was happy to leave it all up to me. Smart fella." [22]

But our new governor, before he was governor, had worked near the trenches of statewide redistricting. He knows that Slade and I know our state's districts forwards, backwards, inside out. He respects Senator Greive for knowing our state in the same detail, and has therefore determined that between the two sides, surely there is some means of compromise.

The governor reviewed Senator Greive's several plans. He reviewed Representative Gorton's plans (the ones with my name and my work). Then he called us all in — the key redistricting players — spread out both sets on the conference table, and pointed out weaknesses in each as well as what he saw as possibilities for compromise. We're stuck on five districts, he noted:

- New District 21 between Seattle and Everett, which would toss out Jack Dootson, the ice cream and lettuce munching Democrat who drives House leaders batty by preferring our Republican view on redistricting.

- District 5 in Spokane

- District 12 in Chelan and Douglas Counties

- District 16 in the Tri-cities area, and...

- District 32 in North Seattle (mine)

"Here they are," says the governor. "Five districts where the camps disagree. Now what are we going to do about it?"

Governor Evans is evolving a distinctive style of leadership: Identify a problem, articulate it, assemble the parties at stake, and together with them find a mutual solution. This is not the heavy-handed sledgehammer manner some assign him.

On this superficially quiet Tuesday, time is of extreme essence. The Federal District Court has scheduled a meeting Friday with the legislature to assess our progress on redistricting, and to decide whether to take on the task themselves. We have until the end of the week — a perfect prod for us to finish this compromise bill. The respective redistricting leaders are finally working from a comparable page, while I just keep tabulating.

With a successful end within sight, many others are now clamoring for public credit, among them our young Attorney General John O'Connell, who admits to an eye on the governorship. Without our knowing it, O'Connell persuades the Federal District Court to postpone Friday's meeting for ten days more — so he can get in on it, too, perhaps?

Governor Evans is incensed, and so are the parties hammering out the compromise. This delay could damage our tremendous bi-partisan momentum.

We discussed in caucus that John O'Brien may have masterminded the attorney general's request. O'Brien's brainchild was devised to derail the process that seemed to be chugging ahead successfully without him. Redistricting is the central issue in the state right now, and once again, this legislative veteran senses he is sidelined. So do many others. Do these colleagues not understand how hard we are working — for the benefit not just of some faction or individual, but for of all of us here and all the voters we all represent?

Fortunately, the court date delay doesn't derail us. Our compromise train is now on track and powering rapidly to its final destination.

Within our House, John O'Brien and Speaker Schaefer are demonstrably losing support. Despite outnumbering Republicans by 19, these Democrat leaders are down to no votes to spare, Joel reports to us in caucus.

Day 45. When we return to work on Wednesday, it is Rep. Grant's HB 196 that surfaces as the basis of our state's redistricting. The Senate wisely decided to use this bill as its basis, to placate the exuberant Grant. We've turned it into our compromise bill: The Senate scalped it and replaced it with the compromise we negotiated in the governor's office, where the two sides meticulously reviewed each neighborhood and every street throughout the state to craft a district boundary puzzle that promises to interlock and hold.

The intense negotiations in the governor's office this past week translated into a perpetual succession of rewriting, counting and comparing — for me and my volunteer staff. We double checked every single miniscule move proposed as it moved from idea to lines on paper and then into words, and finally as the text of the bill.

Because I provide the final set of eyes on these waves of change, I have entirely given up on a good night's sleep. I must assure an accurate transcription. The typists downstairs in the code reviser's office are accustomed to working night shifts. All night, these half-dozen clerks type up the proceedings of the day, be it our Journal, our bills, referendums, addendums and the like. A half-dozen attorneys are on staff here, too — legal wordsmiths on tap. Now I must stay with them, for in the middle of the night, who's to say who might slip in a change, slip a bribe, or simply err? Accuracy is crucial, the atmosphere charged. My responsibility in overseeing each new adjustment is enormous. Therefore, as redistricting steams toward completion, I dare not sleep.

After EHB 196 is introduced on the floor of the House, majority floor leader John O'Brien moves that the House do *not* concur with the Senate's massive amendment (the scalping of Grant's bill, replaced with our compromise). He asks that we ask the Senate to recede therefrom — in other words, to revert it to the version by Gary Grant.

Our minority floor leader Tom Copeland moves that the House do indeed concur in the Senate amendments to EHB 196 — the compromise.

The Speaker rules: Since Mr. Copeland's motion is affirmative — to accept the bill — the House will consider this first. Someone demands an oral roll call. After the clerk calls the roll to confirm our presence, Tom Copeland rises to speak and is granted the floor.

"Mr. Speaker, ladies and gentlemen of the House, there is no mystery as to what we are about to discuss and vote on today… this is an entirely different piece of legislation from what we have seen in these House chambers before, because this is a compromise to the extent where all parties involved are not happy, and this is the way a compromise ultimately results."

This is a somber chamber.

"Many people have come to me and asked me in all sincerity and honesty: What is going to happen to this bill in the event the House passes it? I want to remind each and every one of you of your position as legislators… There is no switch on your desk for 'Maybe' — *Maybe I will vote for the bill if the governor were to partially veto it, or veto it in full.* When I vote 'Aye' on a bill, I am sending with that bill my personal recommendation to the governor that he sign the bill as passed… If we kill this bill by our actions today, we have two further things to do: Number one, pass a concurrent resolution with the Senate requesting the courts to redistrict the state without consultation with the legislature, and number two, adjourn *sine die* until it is done…

"For 45 days we have labored over this and now comes the moment of truth. Do we put aside our own personal differences and get on with the business at hand, or do we hang tough and try desperately to see if we can gain some additional political ground one way or another? This is a tough decision for all of you to make… You are elected to come down here and take care of the state's business, and for 45 days we have been taking care of our own personal political business instead, and now it is time that the state should have your full time and attention... Give heed to the fact that all of your constituents at home sincerely hope this legislature will reach a mature point, act like a group of adults and get on with the business at hand."

When he finishes, Mr. Sawyer asks for the floor, contentious.

"What does this bill do?" he asks rhetorically. "Quite simply, it gives control of the Senate to one man, and it gives control of the House of Representatives to one man and his governor. Do you call this a compromise?... I think we should refuse to concur in the Senate amendments. This bill should go to conference. In conference a true compromise could be obtained."

With tension rising and words gaining heat, the young pages are dismissed from the chamber. Lengthy speeches ensue from both sides. Should we support this bill? Or send the matter into conference?

Mrs. Hurley rises.

"Mr. Speaker, ladies and gentlemen of the House, it has just occurred to me that somebody in this membership should address a few practical thoughts to the freshmen members, those who have never served a whole session yet, and have never had to go home to face their voters... I want to remind you that these voters are not as violently partisan as the people you will find on this floor... When you get home, ladies and gentlemen who are serving your first session, togetherness is gone. It has gone down the drain. All of the togetherness you feel in caucus, all the togetherness you feel with your friends you have made while here is gone, and you are all alone..."

Don't worry about what your leader will say, she tells the freshmen, or your caucus. Don't worry about who will like you.

"I have gone through this many, many times," she continues, "when nobody smiled on me, when nobody has wanted to be seen eating lunch with me here. But it pays dividends because the people at home like a fighter... You are going to have to decide whether you came over to Olympia for a big, round, fat zero or whether you came over here and did the one, great big tremendous job you knew was before you when you came. And when you meet your neighbors and friends back home at the grocery store, just like I am going to, and they say, 'For heaven's sake, when you had a chance to vote for that bill, why didn't you?' — you are going to have about one minute, and you are going to have to say, 'Well, gee, but — but' and that is all... I urge you, each of you, to be part of the solution today and join me in voting for this motion to concur in the Senate amendments."

Mr. Moos takes the floor and admits this proposed redistricting will destroy his district. He speaks directly to the Democrats: "I didn't know that after working some five weeks at loggerheads with Senator Greive, today I would be working shoulder to shoulder with him in attempting to pass this measure. What has happened?" he asks us. "In the process of legislation, in the process of give and take, there is a time when you reach what I would call the true compromise and the time to act. I think today is that day… This isn't show business, this is real business. We need some votes and I think, as Representative Hurley mentioned, you don't get too much applause in the local grange halls when you stand up and say, 'I voted straight caucus.'" [23]

He lists the Republican members who will likely not be back, because of this bill: Our caucus chair, Representative Goldsworthy, for one, and yet all of them plan to vote for this redistricting.

"Is this a good bill? Is it as close to being politically fair as we can arrive? I think it is… I think it can be a little more Republican. Possibly you think it can be slightly more Democratic. But when Senator Greive and Don Moos are lobbying for the same redistricting bill together, I would say it is getting pretty close to being a compromise."

We vote on Tom Copeland's motion. Do we concur with this bill as amended by the Senate? Yea 48, nay 51. It fails. We do not concur.

At the tail of our House alphabetically in any roll call vote, Mr. Wolf can easily see which side will prevail, and so he voted along with 'nays'. Now he moves that we reconsider: Do we *really* not want to concur with this compromise bill?

Mr. O'Brien quickly moves that we lay Mr. Wolf's motion to reconsider on the table.

An oral roll call is demanded and sustained. But before we vote, Mr. Copeland asks the Speaker to clarify: Does laying Mr. Wolf's motion on the table also table the bill as well? It does not, says the Speaker.

We vote again. Should we reconsider our earlier vote, in which we failed to concur with this redistricting bill, as amended by the Senate? Yes, we should reconsider our failure to concur: Our vote is 50-49. The chance to adopt this compromise bill is alive. We'll reconsider.

Again, Mr. O'Brien urges the House to vote down the bill as amended by the Senate, and he suggests we call instead for a conference committee to settle redistricting. This sets off another round of floor speeches and floor debate.

Mr. Brachtenbach says he is relieved about something: All session he has worried about personally costing his constituents his $40 per day — for 45 days now, with redistricting undone — and he's been wondering how that steep price tag will affect incumbents in the 1966 elections, both Republican and Democrat alike. But now he feels that yoke slipping from his neck and onto those who are voting against this bill in favor of sending the matter into conference. They're the guilty ones now, Mr. Brachtenbach implies.

"Those of you who think that a conference is going to settle this matter have been smoking something other than cigars and cigarettes!" he says.

"...On Friday we are all collectively going before that court. As a lawyer, I can assure you that the Federal District Court is going to be mad. It is going to be sick and tired of redistricting and of the 148 members of this legislature. More important, the people of this state are getting sick of us, too."

The court won't send us into conference, he concludes. The court will take over.

Well, retorts Mr. Litchman, don't blame us. Blame the governor. He has never promised us he'll support this bill as is. He has never guaranteed he won't veto it, or veto single lines.

Mr. Pritchard takes exception: "We are the legislative branch. We send down a bill we think is right and the governor studies it and signs it. That is the system we have and you all know it."

Joel then turns to reprimand Mark Litchman directly:

"Mark, surely you know that. I said when we arrived at this hall at noon we were on the courthouse stairs and we had an opportunity to get out of the courthouse. But right now we are going through the doors... Mark, this is it. You are going to court. Let's not kid anybody. We are going to court and this is the moment of truth... I am not afraid of going to court, but let's not have any talk about dumping this back into conference with the idea they can solve something we haven't been able to solve in 45 days. Who is going to be on the conference committee? I don't think you fellows over there..." — he turns to the Democrats — "...can decide on any two who are going to protect you. You know what I mean by that, don't you? Sure, you do! I have heard you talking in the corridors. To protect everybody in this House you are going to have to have a conference of 99 people."

And that's just the House. What about the Senate?

The final speech is delivered by Mr. Sawyer, a Tacoma attorney and assistant floor leader who earlier called for a conference on the bill, but now specifically addresses his fellow Democrats: "Mrs. Hurley is worrying about when we go back home. I think what we will hear is people saying we had a chance to do this in the first two days and it was ignored. I think, ladies and gentlemen, the burden rests with you. I wish it had been done a long time ago."

Mr. Olsen demands the previous question. The demand is sustained. This question is Mr. O'Brien's earlier motion that the House *not* concur with EHB 196 as amended by the Senate (our compromise bill) and that we request the Senate

DEMAND THE PREVIOUS QUESTION

A move that abruptly stops debate and requires an immediate vote on the matter before the body.

to withdraw its amended version, or 'recede therefrom'.

We vote: 51 yea, 48 nay. We send the bill back to the Senate, unapproved, and ask them to take back their scalping, just as John O'Brien proposed. Then we adjourn until noon on the following day.

Day 46. The quirky Jack Dootson has been a thorn in the sides of House Democrats all session long, and I would guess a prickly nuisance for most of his legislative career. Though he wasn't one of the six dissidents in last session's coalition, he did frequently vote with the Republicans and the coalition. Dootson doesn't care what people think of him. His campaign literature proclaims each election: "If you don't like what I have to say, vote for the other guy!"

A communist in the 1930's, Dootson holds four university degrees. He happens to believe the Republican approach to redistricting is the best, and we have drawn the 21st District to protect him. It's one of those five sticky districts we identified with the governor, one of the last we'd tussled through with Senator Greive.

This morning, Jack Dootson has a bone to pick.

"I just heard something disturbing," Dootson says, pulling Slade aside in the wings just as we're heading out to the floor. "I need to talk to the governor. Now. And bring Mrs. McCaffree with you."

Slade and I accompany Jack to the governor's office and we close the doors.

Dootson's tone is accusatory: "I understand you're holding up redistricting over me." He shakes his head slowly while, one by one, he looks us each in the eye. "You wonderful public servants — holding up the people's business over something like this. I'm disappointed in you. Give it up and get on with it."

We call Senator Greive into the governor's office and we agree to let Jack Dootson's district go. This final adjustment cements redistricting for all of us on the two sides. The Senate will make this single change before sending it back to our House. Senator Greive assures us we'll see the bill back on the House floor soon.

When we convene at noon, we move through an entire day of legislative work, none of it related to redistricting whatsoever. Our evening session is called to order at 8 p.m. We immediately recess until 8:45 and the Democrats march straight off the floor and into caucus. When we reconvene at 8:45, the redistricting bill still doesn't come to the floor, though those of us working on it are aware that the Senate already sent the bill back to us with the final amendment to District 21. Where is it?

Mr. Sawyer rises, quickly moves that we adjourn, and in that instant all hell breaks loose. *We can't adjourn! We have to vote! Redistricting is at stake and we have a compromise! We don't want another day of arm-twisting to send it sideways!*

Never have I seen or heard any thing like this — not during last session's battle for Speaker, nor on that Saturday of the 53 seconds when Bill Day assertively gaveled through our House Rules, not even the deafening Senate floor fight in the middle of the night last week. This beats all. My colleagues all around me are calling each other horrific names, waving arms, fists clenched, threats flying, both verbal and physical. Marjorie and I hunch low.

Beneath the furor, Mr. O'Brien calls for the vote on adjournment, but Mr. Andersen jumps right in with a point of parliamentary inquiry: "Mr. Speaker, is there no way under the Rules of this House that the minority party can ask that the redistricting bill be brought out here for a vote of the House of Representatives?"

"No," the Speaker says simply. "A motion to adjourn is before the House at this time. It is not debatable. It outranks all others…"

Mr. Brachtenbach rises.

"My point of personal privilege is only this, Mr. Speaker. Within the past 24 hours, we have had statements on this floor that we should pass this redistricting bill, and…"

"You are out of order, Mr. Brachtenbach," the Speaker interrupts. "We know that all kinds of statements have been made in this House. The clerk will call the roll."

We are to vote on adjournment.

If the House adjourns before we approve this bill, and it is returned to the Senate, under ordinary circumstances, the Senate would then ask the House to form a conference committee to try to work out differences. A conference committee, Mr. O'Brien has reasoned, is surely the best chance for him and for House Democrats to finally be involved — to at last have an equal voice with the Senators in writing the state's redistricting. Thus, Mr. O'Brien is pushing this abrupt adjournment.

But as Joel explained to us in our caucus gathering just ten minutes ago, John O'Brien needs enough votes to pull this off. At this heated hour, in this heated week, with the critical eyes of the press and the court and the public all upon us, this is a crucial vote. The man who quietly tallies our votes behind the scenes wears a non-committal grin.

The oral roll call on the vote to adjourn begins. We work our way through the alphabet. I keep track on a roster. It is going to be close. We're getting near the end. When the clerk reads the name of Ben Taplin, Ben Taplin very softly votes "Nay" and our House falls into an instant and absolute silence.

Did that freshman Democrat just vote 'Nay'?

The Democrat leaders charge to the back of the House and surround the desk of Ben Taplin from Asotin — farm country in the east — and that is when I see Don Moos, our gentle giant, quietly saunter away. I connect the dots: Moos has provided moral support for the fledgling legislator's courageous vote. When the pack of leaders surrounding him asks the freshman again, Taplin maintains a gentlemanly, unperturbed calm. He politely repeats his vote: *Nay.*

A cheer erupts in the visitors' galleries. Speaker Schaefer is exasperated. Can nothing go right for his party, under his leadership? He snaps at the visitors.

"We will NOT have any demonstrations from the galleries, or the galleries will be cleared!"

In our House of 99 members, 50 votes are required to prevail. Taplin's vote of 'Nay' was number 50. We will not adjourn. The compromise bill is alive.

The Democrats remain in full court press around the desk of Representative Taplin, and he is finally persuaded to vote to adjourn, but not until he has told his party leaders he is committed to the compromise bill, and he will vote for it tomorrow.

We vote again, Taplin with the Democrats. They win this vote, but know their numbers are lost. We adjourn just before midnight. The bill is still in the House.

By the way, it's my birthday.

Day 47. Two redistricting votes today are pending in the House: One to concur with the Senate amendments to the compromise redistricting bill (yesterday's adjustment to Jack Dootson's district), and a second vote on final passage. I assume our vote counter, Joel, is correct that we have the votes to approve both, with one or two votes to spare. I sure hope he's right.

The Speaker calls the House to order at 11:30 a.m. The clerk calls the roll and all of our members are present. I'm simultaneously tired and wide awake. The flag is escorted to the rostrum by the color guard. Reverend Arthur Anderson of the Gloria Del Lutheran Church of Olympia delivers the opening prayer. Reading of the Journal is dispensed with. The Speaker observes students from St. Patrick's School in Tacoma in the South Gallery and asks that they stand and be recognized. We applaud.

The next order of business is Standing Committee reports. We act on a single bill on mineral rights, and then, on a motion by Representative Sawyer, we vote to adjourn until 1:30 p.m.

As we head to the House dining room for lunch, I experience a rare lack of appetite. I worked again until 3 a.m., checking and rechecking the final draft of EHB 196. When we sent it back to the Senate, they had added a few adjustments based on our episode with Jack Dootson — changes to which our Republican leadership agreed. It must be recorded perfectly. Shortly after midnight, Representative Gorton had begged my pardon in the code reviser's office and left before the proofing was complete, completely exhausted. I was left alone to keep an eye on the typists and this momentous bill.

By the time we return from lunch, the House is packed. This capitol building has never been more abuzz. Some of our senators stand behind the back row of our freshmen desks. Even more of them hover in the wings. The press is alert. Many dignitaries stand nearby.

At 1:30 p.m. Speaker Schaefer calls the House to order. The clerk calls the roll. All our members are present.

Standing committees report on eight bills, and when they're done, Rep. Burtch demands a Call of the House. The call is sustained, our doors are locked, and the hundred plus of us are locked inside. Only our gallery guests have an ability to exit — through the gallery doors.

In the next order of business, the clerk reads a message from the Senate: "The Senate adheres to its position regarding its amendments to Engrossed House Bill 196, and asks the House to concur. Said bill, along with the amendments thereto, are herewith transmitted."

Rep. O'Brien moves that the House insist on its position — the non-concurrence he has been plugging — and suggests we ask the Senate for a conference thereon.

The Speaker asks for remarks, and selects Mr. O'Brien to deliver the first.

"Mr. Speaker, ladies and gentlemen of the House, today is a most critical one in the history of the state…"

John O'Brien draws upon his full six-foot height and his fullest Irish ire to launch barbs at Governor Evans — a 'power hungry gentleman' who considers the words 'governor' and 'dictator' synonymous, and whose vetoes have prolonged the state's process of redistricting. Voters gave a mandate that the GOP administer the state, O'Brien says, not legislate. He repeats his plea for a conference committee. Then he makes the same motion as before: That the House not concur with HB 196 as amended by the Senate, and that the Senate recede therefrom.

Tom Copeland again objects: "Mr. Speaker, ladies and gentlemen of the House, very briefly, you all know what this is about. It is about — excuse the expression — a lousy bill."

I don't care for his choice of words, but Tom's point is valid. This is a compromise bill, not a perfect one, and not exceedingly palatable to any one party.

We have a court mandate, Rep. Copeland reiterates, and we have state business to do. He encourages us to vote for HB 196.

Twenty-four more speeches are made on the floor before we do.

"I make no apology for our delay, for our soul-searching," says Rep. Burtch, who vows he will not change his mind. He is a Democrat through and through, he says, and will never vote for this bill.

"It is too late to go into conference," says Mark Litchman, the Democrat attorney who worked on the final stages of this plan, even though earlier he feared the governor's line item veto. He points out that 28 out of 32 Senate Democrats voted for this bill, as well as 90 percent of Senate Republicans. "The first two days of this session was the time for the Democratic party to do redistricting," he says. "The Senate did it, but the House failed... it is too late now."

Many state Democrats had clung to the assumption they would be able to lead this session unopposed, with commanding majorities in both the Senate and the House. I am sure some are still stunned by our tenacity, as a minority, regarding redistricting, and by the determination of our new governor to bring our two parties together to get this job done.

Mr. Litchman continues: "I first learned today that this bill, if it becomes law, may very well be the only redistricting law in the whole United States to have passed a Senate and House controlled by one party and signed into law by the opposite... The governor — I have heard his tape recording — has said explicitly he will accept this bill the way it is written, without any changes."

All in all, 26 legislators stand to speak — to register their comments in the Journal, in defense of their votes, providing a public record to prove where they stand. They must return home to their voters, after all, as Mrs. Hurley reminded them. For two hours, the speeches continue.

Representative Sam Smith complains that the bill dismembers his district: It strips away pockets of his Democrat votes — of voters who elected him — to improve the partisan complexion of neighboring districts, where some of the Democrat Senators needed shoring up.

"The people I represent don't like to be handled like that," he says. "...It just so happens that most of these people are Negroes and I feel kind of close to them... I hate to lose so many good friends in order to take care of my senator."

If this bill passes, says Rep. Savage, our 1967 House of Representatives will be Republican and therefore conservative... and that won't do.

"We are in an atomic age, an automated age," Mr. Savage continues, "and we have to make progress."

He must be locked in the Democrat mindset that every Republican is a pure conservative. Hasn't he listened to our new governor? Is he aware of our Blueprint for Progress? Does he realize the Republican party shunned me when I first ran for office because they said I was too progressive, too liberal? Scare tactics, Mr. Savage's speech sounds to me.

Rep. Brachtenbach attempts to summarize: We're tired. We're weary. No one is smiling. Redistricting was difficult, he says, but we did it, and not the court

"The essential thing," he concludes, "is that the people have won."

Rep. Gorton asks to be recognized.

"Mr. Speaker, it appears that this afternoon we may have reached the end of a long road... It seems to me that it was a long, long time ago that I stood on the floor of this House during the passage of Senate Bill 2, when this session started, and asked that a dialogue between the two parties begin in order that the problem could be properly solved. I suppose it was only four or five weeks ago, but it seems like almost that many years... That dialogue finally did begin and it involved a large number of the members of both parties in both houses."

He pays tribute to his chief opponent and eventual partner in this compromise: "I can only say of Senator Greive that he has been devoted to a solution of this problem for at least three years, that he has spent more hours on it than anyone else in either house, myself included, and that I have never noticed he was anxious to do in his own party. As a matter of fact, I hope I never have to deal with anyone who is tougher in working for his own party... It seems inconceivable to me that a proposal for redistricting approved by over two-thirds of the Democratic Senators could possibly do in that party... It is pretty difficult to see how a district in which, in Mr. Uhlman's terms "Saves our Senators" doesn't save our House members at the same time... So without being joyful and without being in the slightest bit triumphant, I do commend this bill to you... We have done what we swore an oath on the first day to do, and we have done what our state constitution tells us we should do. Maybe with practice we will be better the next time around, but there is always a first time and this will be the first brand new redistricting bill that this legislature has done since 1901. And to that extent, at least, I believe we can be proud of it."

I have no speeches in me. I am tired but also grateful we seem nearly done. Julia Stuart, our state president of the League of Women Voters during our redistricting campaigns and now the national League president for 1964-1968 (and the first from west of the Mississippi), found me before I came on the floor to say she had talked at length with her representative about the urgency of passing this today.

Mr. O'Brien rises on a point of personal privilege and is granted the floor.

"We could delay passage of this bill maybe four hours or four days," he says. "But we feel the time has come when we should act on it... The patience of everyone is at a low ebb... I want you people to realize that the leadership, primarily the Speaker, who is a compromising sort of fellow, a nice fellow, wants it to go to a vote. Because of this, we are going to let it go, but reluctantly."

As John O'Brien sits, Joel Pritchard stands and is recognized.

"Mr. Speaker, ladies and gentlemen of the house, Mr. Smith, and our very welcome line of Senators back here, I demand the previous question."

He sits.

"I want to compliment you Joel," says the Speaker. "That is one of the best speeches you have made all session."

The previous question is the final passage of Engrossed House Bill 196, as amended by the Senate. Our roll call vote begins. When we finish, our redistricting bill has passed with 56 yeas, 43 nays. The Speaker signs it and sends it right back to the Senate and we adjourn until Monday.

I cannot close this momentous chapter in the history of our state without paying tribute to the League of Women Voters. Our Washington state chapters and their cadre of families and friends voluntarily kept pressure on our legislature to do this redistricting — and to do it right — for more than ten years. They should be taking much of the credit here today. I am at the end of our decade-long fight, having been a key cog in our state's new redistricting. For our accomplishment here today, I give the League my deepest gratitude.

THE LEAGUE OF WOMEN VOTERS

The League of Women Voters is unique in politics in that it follows no agenda beyond good government, and promotes nothing more than active citizenship.

Preserving representative democracy is at its heart.

Founded in 1920 by the American suffragist Carrie Chapman Catt, just months before U.S. women won the constitutional right to vote, the League was an experiment designed to help these women use their newly won voting rights to the utmost.

Vibrant ever since, the League has spurred both activism and action. Our governments — local, state and national — have been beneficiaries, albeit reluctantly at times.

But as was the case with the state of Washington and its long neglected redistricting, the League's prodding and persistence nationwide has resulted in our democracy's ongoing health. I will always encourage American voters and citizens — men and women alike — to watch the League, to join the League, and to celebrate the integrity that the League of Women Voters brings to the often off-kilter politics we humans create.

By example, the League reinforces the stance that good citizenship requires not only knowledge and passion, but also a willingness to act. Before I knew anything about the League, I was an involved individual, but its focus on study and action provided me a perfect framework within which to jump in more deeply.

1965 HOUSE OF REPRESENTATIVES • STATE OF WASHINGTON

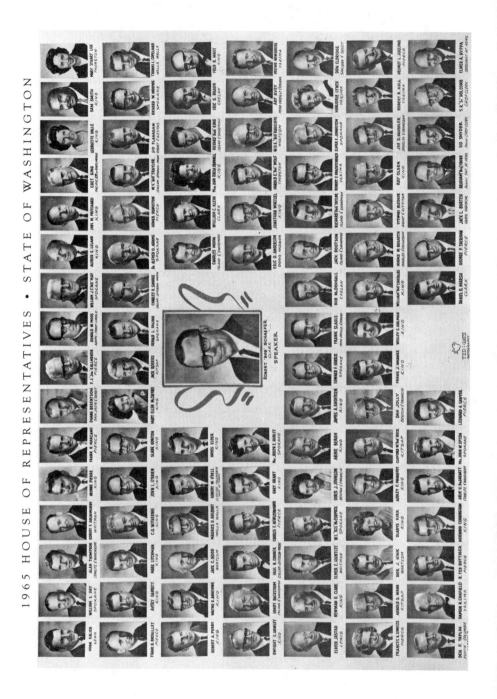

CHAPTER FIVE

PERSEVERANCE
LEGISLATING FOR GOVERNMENT REFORM

Writing a bill doesn't guarantee it will get anywhere.

It is the next steps — the education and negotiating,

the convincing and compromise,

the persistence and rewriting yet again —

that transform a good idea from possibility into law.

THANKS TO THE LEAGUE OF WOMEN VOTERS, I entered the legislature savvy about redistricting. I knew what it was, why we needed it and what made it so politically challenging. I knew how to actually reapportion our state, how to technically create new districts — the detailed nuts and bolts. I even knew how to author a legal redistricting bill: We'd done essentially that with our League initiatives. What I didn't know was how to convert a proposed redistricting from a bill into law.

Writing a bill, even a good bill, doesn't guarantee it will get anywhere. It is the next steps — the education and negotiating, the convincing and the compromise, the persistence and rewriting yet again — that transform a good idea from possibility into law.

The path and eventual success of our compromise redistricting bill — so complex and contentious, but with such crucial, far-reaching results — provided me a superb crash course in how to effectively legislate.

Day 50. By the time we reconvene on Monday, our calendars have flipped to March and only ten days remain in this 39th Session to process some six-hundred bills.

I've spent nearly every waking hour these past six weeks on redistricting, cloistered within the marbled confines of the capitol building from morning until... morning again. My exposure to daylight has been minimal, and I nearly missed our earliest heralds of spring. Now, rushing along on foot on this brisk Olympia morn, my eyes are drawn to the cherry buds — thousands upon thousands of them — plump, clenched and blushing. Will we finish before they bloom? Not likely.

As I travel this cross-campus path from my home to the House, I sense a subtle internal shift in my legislator's psyche. The legislative process no longer seems so mysterious, nor the setting nearly so daunting — not even the ostentatious office of the governor, where I've made a half dozen visits this session already.

Since January, our governor has chomped at his bit to charge ahead with our Blueprint. But the bridling *Whoa!* of redistricting may have been a blessing. For today, when I walk through the doors to the office of the Honorable Daniel J. Evans, Governor, I am welcomed by a well-oiled team. Quite a contrast to the stark, empty-desked office of the governor's first day, and his jest of "Now What?"

"Come on in, Mary Ellen," the gentlemanly Jim Dolliver invites.

In this inner sanctum, the first face encountered is most often that of Dan's campaign manager turned chief of staff. Not only is Jim Dolliver an exquisite strategist, he is a wonderfully insightful human being, a real gem with people. With his casual, dignified manner and his disarmingly gentle smile, he sets a splendid welcoming tone.

"Our fearless leader is... more than ready," he tells me. "As you may have guessed."

"Hi, Mary Ellen!" greets the governor's sunny receptionist, Ruthie Yoneyama.

"Good morning, Mrs. McCaffree," Esther Searing welcomes more formally.

"Missing those children?" I inquire of her. The governor wooed Esther from a post at Children's Hospital, not far from my Seattle home. Esther and I have known of each other since before our respective Olympia days. Ever since her husband's early passing some years back, she has worked full time and now has her hands full, charged with coordinating the governor's crowded calendar.

"Yes, I do miss the children!" she admits. "But Friday finally convinced me this move was worth it. Redistricting — done! Thank you for your hard work, Mary Ellen..."

She cuts me off as I start to demur.

"...and don't you dare tell me it was nothing."

My next attempt at deflecting praise is cut short as well by Joel as he bounds through the doorway. Slade trails him more sedately.

"Hey, Mary Ellen, finally catch some shut-eye?" he says, slapping my back.

"I slept half the weekend," Slade acknowledges. "Hope you did, too, Mary Ellen."

Both these DEGOHTs are bright-eyed this morning, however, behind their identical black-framed glasses. They're energized, knowing our redistricting will soon be signed into law. But we haven't come to the governor's office for that. Not yet. We've met to talk about finally enacting the Blueprint.

Elbow-to-elbow with my familiar team around this table, it occurs to me I have tutored under some doggedly determined legislative veterans. Collectively, these colleagues possess a sound political brilliance — an ability to envision and articulate, yes, but also a willingness to work and to listen, and perhaps most importantly, to bend a bit. This they demonstrated as we hammered out the compromise that became our redistricting. I've learned from them all immensely, first in the 1963 session, and again these past six weeks. Today, I suddenly feel less an apprentice, more a peer. But I'm still a bit weary.

"Well, this is it," says the governor. "Here we go!"

"Virgin territory," quips Joel, "Republican governor backing us and all. Pinch me!"

"Legislative work is still legislative work," Slade observes more prudently. "We all know the drill, though this deadline we're facing is crushing."

"Yeah," Joel agrees. "And we're still in the minority."

"If we're smart," Jim Dolliver notes, "we'll make the most of it — all of it. And we can be smart. We've proven that."

He tosses the topic back to his boss.

"We need to assess which issues have the strongest support in the houses," suggests the governor. "Take the pulse, then build consensus. That's how we'll start."

"Which issue first?" asks Slade.

The governor's reply is instant: "Whichever we can accomplish. We came down here to get a job done for this state. Not just redistricting. But we have to be realistic. Some items on our Blueprint are a natural for fostering support. Others are tougher to sell. We'll start with what we can finish first. It's as simple as that."

For the most part of two whole sessions — my entire legislative career so far — we have focused primarily on legislative redistricting. Now we must shift gears and leave that peculiarly partisan task behind to take up the rest of our lengthy agenda for this state.

"Sounds like a simple matter of getting down to work…" I add, and tack on an afterthought, "…and persevering."

"Budget?" asks Joel.

"We're working on it," the governor reports. "Jim, me, a small handful. Mary Ellen, you're sitting on Revenue in the House. We'll stay in touch, OK?"

A budget means nothing if you don't get the money to cover it.

But financing a state government isn't the same as running a household. Most family budgets begin with income — you calculate what's coming in, then determine how much you can spend. In contrast, the government draws up its budget by spelling out ongoing expenditures, pricing its programs, then it seeks the accompanying funds and works backwards from there. My job at this point is not to create the state budget, but to find ways to fund it from my position on our House Subcommittee on Revenue — part of our larger Committee on Ways and Means. But I sit in the minority and realistically will have little voice, if any. I expect to be largely ignored again. This doesn't mean I won't try.

"Hang tough," says Joel.

"I imagine it will be frustrating," I admit, having already acutely experienced minority committee status under Gary Grant. "But I know it's all part of the process. If you're in the minority, you're generally ignored. I learned that fact years ago, didn't I? When I came down here to talk to you all about school funding. Honestly, you couldn't have been more sympathetic or encouraging, but it became clear to me what kind of voice you *didn't* have!"

"Hence, her dedication to redistricting," says Slade.

"The operative word is perseverance," I repeat.

SPEAKER SCHAEFER CALLS OUR RELATIVELY QUIET House to order at noon. After the daily opening ceremonies — roll call, flag, prayer and Journal reading dispensed with, we hear a single report from a single standing committee: "We, a majority of your Committee on Medicine, Dentistry and Drugs, to whom was referred House Bill No. 360: *Requiring cigarette packages to contain labels stating the health hazards of smoking*, have had the same under consideration and we respectfully report the same back to the House with the recommendation that it do pass."

The minority concurs. We vote, and as a House we concur as well and send the bill to our Rules Committee, which will decide whether to send it back to us on the floor for a second reading on its way to warning smokers that cigarette smoking is hazardous to their health.

Next is a message from the Senate: House Bill 196 has been signed — our redistricting. Old news. We knew by Friday evening it had passed. Once the governor signs it (and I am certain as sunrise he will), our redistricting work is done, if the court approves.

We move on to the first reading of bills for assignment to committee, then proceed to bills on second reading.

Welcome, state Apple Blossom Queen and all your lovely princesses! Welcome, all you students and your teachers. Welcome, dignitaries of note! Our floor business proceeds swiftly, as if to underscore the heady task at hand: Bills, bills and more bills to consider, to refine and perhaps to pass. We peruse our bill books, consult calendars, jot notes. Legislative normalcy returns.

This is not to say that redistricting was not a normal part of our business. It is. And it should have been essential to our lawmaking every decade since the late 1800's. It was the delinquent nature of this duty that made our legislative redistricting work so unique this time around... and so uniquely difficult.

Redistricting is a major piece of legislation, and normally when a legislature is working its way through such a major bill, it is simultaneously processing other legislation as well. It is not uncommon for several large, contentious, complex issues to move through the process at once. However, with the unprecedented court-ordered moratorium on all our other work until we finished redistricting, I would guess — wager even — that never in the history of our state has a legislature had so much critical work on its plate with less than two weeks to go.

During today's second afternoon session (Day 50!), we finally adopt our permanent House Rules, and this finally makes our committee assignments permanent, too. In addition to sitting on the Committee on Constitutions, Elections and Apportionment, I am assigned to Higher Education, to Social Security & Public Assistance and to the Ways and Means Subcommittee on Revenue. I will work on each... as a minority member.

We recess and return for a third afternoon session. We recess again. After the fourth afternoon session we adjourn.

SLADE, JOEL, DON AND I QUICKLY CROSS THE FOYER to the governor's office, our footfall perceptibly energized as we clatter across the marble. My weariness of this morning has completely vanished.

Jim Dolliver welcomes us as part of a steady stream of arrivals. Ruthie helps move aside furniture, all the while greeting with her bright, sunny smile. Esther Searing, notebook in hand, stands quietly nearby. Wayne Jacobi, the governor's press secretary, directs us, positioning the room for the formal photograph.

"Governor Evans?" he says. "Yes, it's time to sit at your desk. And your pen. Yes. Good. Senator Greive?"

Jacobi invites redistricting's main negotiators and principal legislators — the men (and sole woman) who pushed and pulled, persuaded and demanded, wrote and rewrote so many sets of legislative district boundaries — to now join as one in a group just behind the governor. More of our colleagues flatten into rows at the back of the room, and we all watch as Governor Evans signs Engrossed House Bill 196 into law.

The pop and flash of cameras is quickly tailed by popped corks from champagne. *Hooray!* We are jubilant, Democrat and Republican alike, not because we adore the outcome of this compromise bill, but because we have tackled and wrestled and tamed a daunting legislative responsibility, and have emerged with enough mutual respect intact to now tackle this truncated session. Today's celebration is bipartisan, and thoroughly heartfelt. This one enormous job is… done.

Day 51. Once we convene, Speaker Schaefer shares a message from the governor: House Bill 196 is officially signed. The governor has written us congratulations, which the clerk reads aloud: "As the attorney general has observed, the plan is not perfect, but it probably represents the best yet produced by any state legislature in our nation. You can be justly proud of this accomplishment."

A page delivers me a note: *Congratulations, Mary Ellen. We've done it! Julia.*

From the visitor's gallery I receive the broad smile of Julia Stuart, still here from Spokane to witness this long-awaited feat. My return smile is flooded with admiration for her League leadership. I am bathed as well in a personal sense of accomplishment for my behind-the-scenes but consequential part.

With redistricting done, the House is now set in full motion, and we rapidly navigate the legislative process: Committee work, floor work, constituent liaising, back to the floor. I seem to be forever reading something, with occasional breaks to listen, speak or write. Communication skills are a legislative 'must'.

Day 52. On the third day after our redistricting passes, during our second morning session, Mr. Sawyer demands a Call of the House. The sergeant at arms locks us. The clerk calls the roll. We excuse the four absent and proceed.

Representative O'Brien proposes a House resolution: *Whereas Governor Daniel J. Evans has made budget requests which require new state revenue of over $140 million; and, Whereas Governor Evans has yet to introduce in the House of Representatives or the Senate of the State of Washington his recommended legislation to raise the necessary revenues…*

In four more paragraphs, Representative O'Brien lambastes the new governor for tardy work on the budget and demands specifics immediately, so we can prepare for our likely extra session. His criticism ignites another cross-aisle volley.

Mr. Moon speaks from the Democrat side, reminding Republicans that two sessions ago, when Governor Evans was still Representative Evans, he'd

Mary Ellen McCaffree watches the governor sign her state's new redistricting into law after she'd worked on the issue for nearly a decade. Among those in attendance, from front row left, Rep. Dootson, Rep. Copeland, Senator Greive in bow tie, Governor Evans, Rep. Gorton, Rep. McCaffree, and Rep. Moos.

forcefully demanded the same revenue figures from Governor Rosellini by Day 23, and here we are: thirty days further along.

Mr. Andersen rebuts this: "You had a governor who had been in office four to six years. He had all the facilities of state government behind him..."

Yes, I silently agree. *Governor Rosellini not only had years as governor under his belt, he also had Democratic state department heads across the board, as well as two friendly chambers.*

Mr. Andersen continues his defense of the governor:

"...When then Representative Evans, now Governor Evans, moved into the governor's mansion in January, I saw the vaults. There wasn't even any dust left in those vaults and files. There was absolutely nothing. It wasn't until very shortly before the session began on January 11 that he had access to any detailed information on which a budget is predicated. Governor Evans came in with a 595-page budget book and no staff for working on it. We have had to limp along, partly staffed, with inadequate funds, and try to put the whole show together in a matter of a few days, dealing all the while with this grievous problem of redistricting. The situation then was entirely — 180 degrees — opposite from today's situation."

We should not send this resolution to the governor, Mr. Andersen says. I fully agree. However, this debate continues, even after the demand for an oral roll call. Do we adopt John O'Brien's resolution and take the governor to task? We vote. It passes with 52 yeas and 43 nays. We send the scathing critique to Governor Evans.

This same evening, once we're back in session, we receive a brief reply from the governor in the form of a receipt: *Received, of John L. O'Brien: One bum political resolution full of political hogwash that wasted an hour of the taxpayers' time.*

After tonight, only eight days remain.

Though it's late, we keep on working. We consider bills on second reading: Should wine be taxed at wholesale or retail? Should we memorialize Congress to amend the Federal Sugar Act? Should we authorize the acquisition of ShiShi Beach for a county park? Raise motor vehicle fees? Increase the limit on the length of school buses? This one snags us, and we begin to debate the legality and safety of the measure, with many of our attorneys registering opinions as yet another long night plods along.

This school bus bill seems sloppy to me, which is always a hazard of quickly written bills. After considering one more bill on second reading — one to prohibit the use of lie detector tests to consider employment — we move on to bills on third reading and final passage, and unanimously approve the first one before us, to remove the toll and retire the bond debt on the Tacoma Narrows Bridge. Yeas 96. Nays 0. Not voting: the three who are excused. Other than the inherent divisiveness of legislative redistricting, many measures receive such unanimous support.

More bill work, and then it's on to the reports of our standing committees. It is after midnight when we adjourn, yet we vote to return at 10 a.m. the next day — to the floor, that is, for our work as legislators often begins much earlier. Before our daily session begins, and often afterwards, too, we must meet in our respective committees, find time to read up on bills or draft our own, discuss certain measures with our colleagues or respond to constituents, and hopefully share a quick word or two with our families.

Day 53. "Mary Ellen?" Lois Hauptli has relentlessly hounded our legislature on behalf of her safety glass bill, and seems concerned. "Should I be discouraged by all these other bills? Seems like literally hundreds."

"It is, Lois. Just keep your eye on yours. You're lobbying like the biggest and best of 'em, and so far, it seems to be working."

"Yes, well the League was my boot camp," she said. "And my family is behind me. But if I have to stay down here another sixty days…"

I admit to her an extra session's almost a certainty at this point.

"House Bill 476, remember the number, OK Mary Ellen? I just keep thinking about Gary."

Her eyes glisten but her emotions are composed. She has shared her story, one on one, with elected officials here in the House and across the way in the Senate. She can still see her 8-year-old son Gary, chasing that Frisbee that day — right through their family's sliding glass door. She remembers her bloodied child, vividly remembers that afternoon in the hospital, how she sat beside him and watched while those 68 stitches were sewn and knotted. She recounts to each legislator the difficult steps of slowly nursing Gary back to health. And then she shares the statistics: All those injured — some fatally — by similar accidents related to shattered sliding glass doors.

We need better safety glass standards, she says. Please support this bill.

Lois Hauptli came to Olympia with personal passion and conviction — but with no sponsor, no commitment from a committee, no funding for her efforts — just her own inner drive to fix a situation that wasn't working: A one-woman force. As I watch her make her way among my colleagues on the floor during this recess, I think, *What a beautiful example of our democracy at work*. One woman, one person, one voter making a difference.

Some of us are searching for additional sponsors for our measures as well, and we hope to begin laying down new laws per our DEGOHT Blueprint soon. Like Lois, we are pushing hard to get our existing bills through by Day 60. Understandably, considering the velocity of our House activity, many of the freshmen are struggling to follow along. With this frenzied level of legislating, it is virtually impossible to read and consider every line of every measure.

Each morning, the young pages deliver a new stack of redrafted and reprinted work to our desks. They pull out the outdated paperwork from our massive bill books and insert the new in the proper place — proposed amendments, bills as

PHOTO BY JESSICA MCCAFFREE MANS

Each legislator has at his or her desk an individual set of bill books in which to track each House and Senate bill and resolution introduced throughout the session, along with the amendments added to each.

This is Mary Ellen's set from a single session.

amended the previous day, bills to be introduced on second reading and third, bills passed. The paperwork is voluminous. Our multiple bill books stand eight to ten inches thick — each!

While the title of a bill may sound perfectly logical, the actual wording and clauses within become crucial as it heads toward becoming law. Considering a session's worth of legislation is thus a heady and weighty task — bills number in the hundreds, and very few legislators cultivate expertise across the board. My mentors — Slade, Dan and Joel — preached the buddy system my freshman term, and I continue to lean on it, determining who among my colleagues, regardless of party, has expertise or the proper background to grasp a topic and evaluate the merits or flaws of a particular bill.

Day 54. Our Republican leaders in the House have succeeded in bringing several Blueprint reforms to the floor. Among these is a legislative *per diem* pay raise the public is ready to pan. Many major state newspapers already have.

"I trust this will be of interest to you," says Representative Andersen, having risen on a point of personal privilege. He shares with us an editorial from his hometown paper, entitled "Living in the Lap of Luxury". After a big 'shame on you' to other newspapers that condemned our proposed *per diem* raise and derided our legislative lunchrooms, the editorialist crawls inside some legislative skin to take a look at the financial reality of serving in our state. With a monthly salary of $100 and another $40 per day to cover our expenses, we legislators hardly luxuriate, he writes, considering we must rent quarters during the session, eat meals out, communicate with constituents, and once in a while — if our marathon days and nights and weekends allow for it — we must pay to travel home. Plus, those of us (most among us) with jobs on the outside often give up pay to serve here. Luxurious it is not. Nor is it lucrative.

As my economist husband will attest, the legislator rolls in no surplus dough. Having been an at-home mother for years, just bringing my wardrobe up to snuff for legislative work was one way of waving good-bye to my pay before I arrived at the capitol.

Mr. Andersen continues to read: "Why, then, does a good man consent to beat himself to death financially to serve in the legislature and get insulted in the process? Well, you've got some pretty good people asking themselves that question right now. And when the next election rolls around there will be some who say: Not me, brother, not me again. And so democracy loses one more good public servant while the people make their big jokes about those overpaid 'clowns' in Olympia. You won't catch us joining in those jokes," the sympathetic writer concludes. "We don't think it's funny."

We recess for lunch, in our 'luxurious' House dining room, folding chairs and all.

I AM TOLD THE HOUSE DINING ROOM WAS CREATED in the interest of legislative efficiency. Before it existed, elected officials had to leave the capitol campus for meals, which necessarily extended the legislative day. And as we had no patrols against imbibing at lunchtime, the off-campus lunch or dinner could foster other delays. This aspect was recently underscored a few weeks back when we had to wait two hours for one of our colleagues to sober up before we could take an important vote on the floor. After pouring several cups of coffee down

him, after repeated soft pats to his face, and after much physical bracing to keep him upright, he was finally fit to rejoin us.

No, the dining room is no luxury — neither in menu nor in setting — but it does allow us to be more efficient in our work, and maybe to lobby colleagues with some good-natured banter.

For the balance of this Friday afternoon, we consider bill after bill and several resolutions — 64 measures in all so far — on roads, mining, ports, schools, floods, fruit trees, fire districts and sewer

PHOTO: WASHINGTON STATE ARCHIVES

Representatives Berentson (l.) Eldridge and Lynch converse with colleagues in the 'luxurious' House dining room, with its A-1 sauce, bottles of ketchup and all.

ones, too. Mental health, fishing rights, livestock fees, funeral services, rental cars, arson, handicapped privileges, human rights. Should our health care practitioners report suspected abuse or neglect? Should we pick some local roads to serve as emergency taxiways for troubled aircraft? Should fraudulent use of public assistance be treated as a crime? This is the stuff of state governance.

Late in this afternoon session, on the sixty-fifth matter before us since lunch, Representative Red Beck presents a mammoth, complex bill. It suggests the state acquire a hospital from his district to serve as a prototype public health center — a concept we targeted in our Blueprint to provide better health care for the less fortunate, a focus on community health. The title of the bill is read, then the long bill is read slowly, section by section. Then the Rules are suspended and, by majority vote, the House advances the bill to third reading, the second reading considered the third, which places Mr. Beck's complex measure on final passage. Right now.

Such a potentially significant measure. Such a weary House.

Mr. Uhlman asks if Mr. Beck will yield to a question. He will.

"Mr. Beck, this thing is moving so fast I haven't had a chance to read this measure. Is it permissive or mandatory as far as the department is concerned, and is there any money involved?"

Mr. Beck answers: "This is only permissive... only to authorize negotiations."

"Is there money in this bill?"

"There is no appropriation in this bill, no."

While the bill was debated at length, some of us took a closer look. Mr. Brachtenbach asks if Mr. Uhlman, who chairs our Committee on Ways and Means, will yield to a question.

"Yes," says Mr. Uhlman, "although I have not seen the bill. These things have moved too fast. That is why I asked the question I did."

Mr. Brachtenbach points to a certain clause: "Section 2 says the Department of Institutions is authorized to acquire this property and it specifies the manner in which it may be acquired, including purchase. Would not your interpretation be that there is no limitation as to dollar amount; in other words, we are giving the Department of Institutions a blank check as to the amount that could be spent?"

"Well," says Mr. Uhlman, "it would appear that there is no amount listed here in the bill. I imagine, however, that that amount would certainly be controlled by the amount of money we appropriate in committee. If we don't appropriate any money, they can't buy the property."

This bill needs more work, more clarification — yet here it is before us on final passage.

After some disparaging remarks are made about the actual building itself, the late House session unravels into a nasty procedural tennis match. Some members are increasingly irate as the session drones on into dinner time — our Speaker had promised the House this Friday night off.

Finally, the community health center bill is put on hold and placed on the next third reading calendar, whenever that occurs. We adjourn until 11 on Saturday morning.

Day 55. A visit by our U.S. Senator Warren Magnuson in Joint Session today inspires a dialogue on the division between federal and state funding.

Day 56. The Sunday session is another marathon, but with a bright spot, for within this long day of deliberation, Lois Hauptli's hard work gets a boost. *House Bill 476: Prohibiting the sale of certain sliding glass doors or sliding glass assemblies* *unless of stated quality* comes before us. We review, debate, then vote and pass Lois' bill with 91 yeas, no nays and 8 absent, and send it over to the Senate.

Day 58. Three days left in our regular session: The pace continues unbridled, the bill count is staggering. The Senate is moving through even more measures, sending us regular batches: "We have passed this, this, this and this…." by the dozens and scores. By evening we are tiring again, and the topic of capitol parking incites a petty flicking of barbs. John O'Brien fires a frustrated salvo.

"You people are running the state," the exasperated Democrat leader yells across the aisle. "You have the chief executive."

Indeed, despite being outnumbered in both the Senate and the House, we are advocating for our state agenda with the backing of our governor. We don't succeed in every instance, but we certainly persevere.

Day 59. Lois Hauptli is persevering, too. Her plate glass window bill returns to us from the Senate today, along with forty measures more. In the House, we enroll more than forty bills ourselves, and Speaker Schaefer soon announces he will sign another fifty-six, among them House Bill 476, championed by Lois. I've watched her watching intently from the gallery, following our work on the floor. As the Speaker signs her bill, she settles back with a small, wistful smile.

On the heels of my long redistricting labors, this staggering schedule of work is at once invigorating and a source of serious concern. How can we possibly make sage decisions at such a breakneck pace? We convened today at 11 a.m. It is not yet noon, yet we've taken formal action on nearly two-hundred bills.

"Mr. Speaker, I rise on a point of personal privilege," says Don Moos, wearily hoisting his broad frame from his desk. "I guess that is the only way I can bring the body's attention to the action on a bill just passed, in case anyone wants to change their mind or have a reconsideration. I think we are going kind of fast and have just passed something which has disturbed many people throughout the country…"

Ooops. More procedural volleying. More protracted discussion.

We recess at last for a very late lunch.

Early in our afternoon session, Mr. Slagle rises.

"Mr. Speaker, ladies and gentlemen of the House, as your local Rexall druggist, after noticing the tired, worn out looks on ninety-eight faces in this House, I thought vitamins were in order…"

He hoists high a bottle and rattles it.

"Maybe if you start taking them now, you will have a new look when we come back on Monday…"

Monday we will likely begin an Extraordinary Session. We take it for granted, now, that it will be called. The druggist continues to speak as he distributes vitamins to our desks.

"…I am giving one to everyone except for Representative Kalich, because after observing his operations, I don't think he needs them."

Tired chuckles ripple through the House.

By the end of the day, midnight to be exact, our session dissolves into another tired round of legal nitpicking centered on a time-certain cut-off for considering additional action on bills. We are at the tail end of a very long, serious deliberation – including a series of thoughtful amendments – on a bill on subsidized public transportation. It makes no sense to stop this very moment, right in the middle of our work. This is a Blueprint bill, but some are unimpressed by that fact, and with the clock hands reaching 12, a barrage of legalities are lobbed like grenades.

"Mr. Speaker," says Mr. Pritchard, "I am not an attorney, and I won't go into the legal aspects of this thing, but since everyone wants to settle this matter, why can't we just proceed with the consent of the House and vote? That is the intelligent, grown-up thing to do instead of playing games."

Mr. O'Brien objects. He addresses his protégé Speaker Schaefer, who wields the gavel.

"Mr. Speaker," he says, "you are bound by the Senate Concurrent Resolution on this matter. You have gone beyond your 12 o'clock limit and all action has to stop…"

On a party line vote, deliberation stops. Majority wins, minority loses. We were so close to settling this transit bill, but now must dispense with all further business and adjourn with just one day remaining.

Day 60. At the start of the final day of our regular session, our governor's proclamation arrives: "Whereas the 1965 Session of the Washington State Legislature, during the regular period of sixty days prescribed, failed to enact appropriation and revenue measures, and,

"Whereas, other measures important to the welfare of the people of the State of Washington were not enacted to deal with: Human needs (he gives us a detailed list), a clean and ethical government, education (he specifies school funding formulas and a higher education advisory council), modernization of our state government (another list), and reform of the state's constitution (he calls for a constitutional convention), and,

"Whereas, as a result of these conditions, an emergency exists…Now, therefore, I, Daniel J. Evans, governor of the State of Washington, by virtue of the authority vested in me by the Constitution, do hereby convene the Legislature of the State of Washington in Extraordinary Session in the Capitol at Olympia on the fifteenth day of March, A.D., 1965, at the hour of twelve o'clock noon..." [1]

After this, the governor tells us via his legal counsel that he has approved our House bill providing a facility for the mentally and physically deficient and mentally ill. Next we receive some messages from the Senate.

"Here goes," says Marjorie. "Must be nice to have only half the number deliberating."

The Senate, with only 49 members to our full 99, tells us today it has passed eighteen House measures and the President of the Senate has signed another sixty-two. By our afternoon session, it is announced that twenty-five House bills have been enrolled. The Senate sends us another thirty or so signed by their President. Our Speaker announces he is about to sign seventy-five. Another message from the Senate: The President has signed another twenty.

As the day proceeds, we receive another message from the Senate: They would like some forty bills back — those we likely won't finish today in the House. More bills enrolled. More Senate signed bills. Bill work explodes like a fireworks grand finale.

Before we adjourn, the Senate signs dozens more, and on a list of eighty, Lois Hauptli's safety glass bill appears. In this unusual legislative session, her bill has passed both houses of our legislature and will move to the governor's desk. She finds me, thanks me, and finally heads home to Seattle and to her family. Lois is a legislative success story. Meanwhile, the Senate returns us the incomplete House measures we've requested.

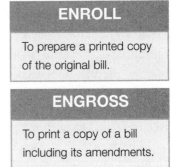

ENROLL

To prepare a printed copy of the original bill.

ENGROSS

To print a copy of a bill including its amendments.

"Mr. Speaker, how many of these bills did you say were returned to the House?" asks Mr. Canfield.

"I think there are over one hundred," Speaker Shaefer estimates. "We sent more than two hundred over there."

All this in the thirteen days since we finished our redistricting.

"Mr. Speaker, is that all our bills they're returning, or just the bills that were in the Rules Committee over there?" asks Mr. Hawley.

"This would be all House bills that were in the possession of the Senate, whether they were in the Rules Committee or somewhere else."

The Speaker explains further: If we have these House bills back in our possession before our sixty-day session expires, we can place them on instant third reading here when the special session begins. If we left these in the Senate, they could die there.

"The bills are all alive?" asks Mr. Hawley.

Says the Speaker: "They certainly are."

Several House employees present our Chief Clerk with a thank you gift. The timbre of this session finally softens as our legislative activity winds down.

Mr. Kalich — the sole House member our resident druggist deemed didn't need vitamins — leaps for recognition on a point of personal privilege and is recognized.

"Mr. Speaker, ladies and gentlemen of the House, as you know, this is my first term down here," says Mr. Kalich with gung ho enthusiasm and all due respect. "I have been in the Army, I have traveled all over the world — in eight different countries and 38 different states — and I don't think I have ever enjoyed anything more than the people on both sides of this aisle, the 99 people I have served with. I think it has been tremendous. And I want to tell you if this was an ordinary session, I am certainly looking forward to that Extraordinary Session!"

Not all share his outlook.

The Speaker appoints a special committee to notify our governor that the House is about to adjourn *sine die*. The committee delivers our report and returns with the governor's approval. A committee from the Senate delivers us a message: They're ready to wrap up as well. We send a committee their way to say the same, then the doors to our two chambers swing wide, and across the marbled expanse, in a single unanimous action, we adjourn ourselves: *Sine die!*

SINCE MY ARRIVAL IN OLYMPIA early in January, I have not returned home. Now Ken has come to fetch me for the long weekend before I return for round two.

"That it, love?"

He's surprised by my tiny satchel.

"I'll only be home four days," I remind him.

My husband sighs. But always the gentleman, he holds the umbrella over me, gently settles me into the passenger seat, gives me one of his sweet kisses, closes my door and considerately locks me in. When he scoots behind the wheel of our Impala, I automatically curl beside him, close as I can snuggle without jeopardizing his ability to safely drive. My voice emerges lazy and muffled: "What's new at 5014?"

"Oh, not too much," he says, before reporting our family version of 'not too much'. "Jim called from Ithaca. He's trying to figure out the best way to get to Independence for his wedding."

"I'd better call him." I make a sleepy mental note. Our eldest is now doing graduate work at Cornell and will marry in August.

"Haven't seen much of Chuck," Ken continues. "He and Lee are tied up with finals... and with tying the knot."

Son number two will wed in July. Two summer weddings on tap.

"Nancy?" I nearly whisper, sorely tempted to drift to sleep.

"Tough math problem last week. She telephoned me and we talked it through for quite some time, and I think we finally... Oh, I forgot to tell you Ritajean called. Asked if you needed any help — shopping or anything."

"Mmm. She and Fred are great friends, aren't they, honey?"

"Mary and David sure are anxious to have you home, Mom. Don't be surprised if they're in the front window when we... You're awfully tired, aren't you love? Why don't you take a little nap? I need to pay attention. Traffic seems worse every visit, and this rain..."

My eyes have closed. I've missed the comfort of Ken.

What a wonderful partner I have.

I slip into a stretch of reflection before fully dozing off. Ken and I have learned to accommodate each other, to help each other with our brood of five, to laugh. We seem to have worked as a team from the start.

I first noticed Ken in my Methodist youth group, when I was a Kansas farm girl. In our small community, our paths couldn't help but intersect. During our college courtship, while he studied at one college (Southwestern) and I at Kansas State, we began to plan out our life together, though our parents convinced us not to marry before I'd earned my degree. Nevertheless, we planned: Ken would teach at the college level, we hoped, and his graduate work would be our first team project. We wed after I graduated with my degree in home economics, and I set about setting up house with the plan that Ken would earn his master's degree at Denver University while he continued to teach at Colorado Women's College, and then he'd go on for his doctorate during the summers.

Soon after we settled into our two-room apartment on Vine Street in Denver, the news arrived: The Japanese had just attacked Pearl Harbor. In that instant we knew our plans couldn't hold. Ken would have to serve in the war, even though our first child was about to be born. My husband enlisted in the Navy, went to officer's training school and then to a minesweeper in the middle of the Mediterranean Sea. By the time he went abroad, I was pregnant with our second.

We endured long separations, and the war years were hard for both of us — the being apart, the danger, and not knowing what the future held. Communication between us was scant and infrequent while he was gone. Fortunately, for most of his last two years of military duty Ken served as an instructor on the mine warfare base near Norfolk, Virginia. We were able to be together as a family.

A second son and a daughter were born while Ken was still a Navy man. During the war our life seemed to be on hold, except for the arrival of our babies. After VJ-Day, we set up shop in cramped quarters — in barracks converted to married student housing at the University of Chicago while Ken pursued his PhD in economics. He taught, studied and wrote nearly around the clock for two solid years, and while I knew this was the right course for us, I was largely alone in charge of our growing family. I often felt left out, occasionally resentful, and shouldered the bulk of responsibility of raising the family while he studied and progressed. Mary arrived in Chicago, joining Jim, Chuck and Nancy.

What saved us, as a couple, from sinking too deep into resentment or separation, was our ability to talk — to express without anger or fear our honest disappointments, hard feelings and any concerns. Over the years, we developed our conversational ability with each other, and worked out our differences without involving the children. This is not to say we never argued.

It wasn't until we arrived in Seattle that we began to feel comfortable and settled, to feel like a real family.

Once all five children were in school, I was asked to serve on the board of our Seattle League of Women Voters. Ken was concerned about the time this would take from the family. But I knew that one day all our children would fly the home coop and I would be left alone without an outside interest or activity. Ken has always been deeply involved in his work, and in a couple of outside professional pursuits as well. Reluctantly, he agreed to my League work. He knew me all too well. He knew that whenever I made up my mind to do something, I pursued it with all my heart.

I assured him our family would not be neglected, and that it might actually be good for our children to have a mom with some interests outside the home.

By that point, we'd become quite skilled at talking through our differences, seeing each other's point of view and then finding a way to accommodate. Pragmatically, we agreed that if I were busy outside the home, it would make sense to spend some family resources on extra household help. We didn't need elaborate furnishings or fancy vacations or trendy clothes, but we did want time with our children. If we were both busy outside the home, we wanted our home hours devoted to our family.

First we hired a wonderful babysitter — Mrs. Bergseth. She was great with our children and they certainly loved her. She stayed with them the rare occasions both Ken and I needed to be away. Then we hired Mabel and Mae, sisters who came to our house twice a week to do the washing and ironing and cleaning. So, when Ken and I were home together, we actually had time to converse and relate, and time for our kids and their projects and their many activities.

I tried to schedule my "work" during the early morning hours or late at night, so to be there for my children in the hours they were home. For Ken's part, when he traveled our region for consulting work, he made it a point to fly home by nighttime, so he could wake up with the rest of us, and not miss our family's school morning routine.

When I was asked to run for the legislature, however, Ken's misgivings were stronger than usual. I would have to be gone for these legislative sessions — two months, mostly gone from our family and home. Yet he had had his years of various absences, during the war and grad school, when I'd carried the greater weight. In some ways I felt this was fair.

He is now involved on the Board of Trustees for Group Health Cooperative — a joint decision between us. We considered this a family activity, as work on behalf of our family. Serving in the legislature would be the same, I had argued: A family activity. I wouldn't have been invited to run for this seat if, as a mother, I hadn't started to seek better funding for our children's schools.

As we pull to a stop at an intersection near home, Ken slips his arm around me a moment and gives me an affectionate hug.

Our love for each other has grown over the years, with freedom to constantly express to each other our individual needs, with a shared respect for our respective requirements and unique concerns. We have never let a sun disappear before working out knots in our marriage. This car ride at the end of this long session, with my husband dearly holding me, is testament our teamwork has paid off.

AT NOON ON MONDAY, MARCH 15 — THE IDES OF MARCH, my legislative colleagues and I return to the cherry blossomed capitol to open the Extraordinary Session of our 39th Legislature, convened by our enthusiastic governor. But while only the governor can convene a special session, his control ends there, for the legislature controls the adjournment. And when the legislative leaders are at partisan odds with the governor, as today, there is no guarantee we will stay in session long enough to make headway on the governor's ambitious agenda.

"Whereas…" The governor's proclamation is read aloud again, describing our failure to set a biennial budget or to deal with his other priority issues: human rights and needs, government ethics and reform, education, our economic climate, our environment. We quickly organize in both the Senate and House, adopt Rules from the session just ended, and get to work.

The Speaker recognizes seven Daffodil Princesses from Puyallup. Once they leave, Representative Smith rises on a point of personal privilege.

Sam Smith is a Boeing employee, father of six and a graduate of both Seattle University and the University of Washington. He is still our legislature's only black man.

"State your point of personal privilege," says the Speaker.

"Now that we are through with this fine occasion, I feel it appropriate for me to say a few words seriously to the members of the House and, particularly, to the members of the Rules Committee. I don't believe it is necessary for me to call attention to this august body what is happening in the Southern part of these United States and Alabama..."

Bloody Sunday in Selma was eight days ago. Some 600 protestors had taken to the highway in Selma, Alabama, bound for their capitol in Montgomery to ask Governor Wallace to act against the intimidating tactics white leaders were using to prevent black citizens — half the city's citizens — from registering to vote. Instead, the governor called their march a threat to public safety. With TV cameras running, police brutalized the group using billy clubs, tear gas and bullwhips.

Sam Smith continues: "I'd like to call to the attention of the members of the House and the Rules Committee that in the Extraordinary Session of 1961, I rose and made a motion to suspend the Rules and asked the House at that time to take a vote on a civil rights housing bill that was pending before us... I stressed the fact that the demonstrations then taking place in the South had not reached our northern areas and I urged us to take preventive action."

Six days ago in Selma, the head of the Southern Christian Leadership Conference — a charismatic young minister, Dr. Martin Luther King, Jr. — helped organize a second march, soliciting both permission and protection from the courts. But when the court refused to protect the marchers, Dr. King instead turned the gathering of 2,500 into a 'ceremonial'. They peaceably stopped on a bridge just outside Selma, rather than continuing on to the capitol. One of the white participants, a Unitarian minister, was attacked afterwards and seriously injured, but the local hospital refused to treat him. *Black sympathizer.* Yet the next nearest hospital was two hours away. The day after our *sine die*, that minister died from his injuries. That was four days ago.

Again, Mr. Smith continues: "When I read in the newspapers what is taking place in Selma, I am almost in tears. I believe, because of the seriousness of the situation, it is necessary that the state of Washington take some positive action now to show that it does not believe in the things that are going on, and assure the rest of the country of its stand in the field of human rights... We should take action in testimony that they have not died in vain, and that we in the state of Washington will lead our people not to a path of violence, but into a path of brotherhood for all men. Thank you."

Representative Elmer Johnston responds: "I want to say to my dear brother, Sam Smith, that we fully appreciate the problems that confront his race in this country..."

As 'proof' of his appreciation, Johnston cites one Civil War battle in which

27,000 white men died in a single afternoon to free the slaves.

"Now Sam, in all your life, don't you ever forget the fact that we all have the same sympathetic feeling toward other races. We have been a little careless over the years, we white people, and we are ashamed of that. But, Sam, we will have to take our time on this. It takes culture, education, love of God... Certain legislation tends to inflame people — tends to create animosities. I'm thinking about Berkeley. I can't understand why they had to have a big riot... You have a problem, I admit, but I don't think it is one where we can disturb the peace. Mr. Speaker, I think the whole community, our whole nation, is too emotionally disturbed; I think we have made too much ado about these things. I think we should be patient and get along and not let this get out of hand..."

Mr. Smith responds: "...I'd like to call attention to the fact that the governor of our state, being a Republican, has seen fit to mention open housing as the first item listed in his call for a special session. That would mean support from across the aisle; and Democrats have had that philosophy for years and years, so there is absolutely no reason why the House can't act... I think we should act now when we can act calmly and in good judgment." [2]

Mr. Savage changes the subject to complain about the governor calling this special session, and the issue of civil rights abruptly drops from discussion. Yet it is true, civil rights ranks high on our Blueprint agenda. Less so for our House leadership, though — Mr. Smith is basically ignored. He must sit.

WE ADOPT THE RULES OF THE 39TH SESSION, and reintroduce the previous session's measures. We'll pick up right where we left off on each of these bills in the House. Those returned to us by the Senate are back in play, too, but with the Senate's amendments removed.

We consider a single bill and then we adjourn.

For the first several days, I meet with the DEGOHTs to assess our Extraordinary Session strategy. Have we found any promising measures to promote? Our community colleges idea seems to have bipartisan backing. We'll start there.

On Thursday, on the other side of the country, a federal judge rules in favor of Dr. King's request for permission to march in Alabama: *The law is clear that the right to petition one's government for the redress of grievances may be exercised in large groups . . . and these rights may be exercised by marching, even along public highways.* It has been a week since the Unitarian minister died. The group marches Friday and keeps on marching, five days and four nights, in harsh wind and pelting rain. By the time they reach Montgomery their ranks have swelled to 25,000. Dr. King delivers a speech outside the capitol building in a resonant voice: *How long? Not long!*

From a philosophical distance — a theoretical stance, geographically removed — many of my constituents are sympathetic to this battle for civil rights. But the general response *here* to the events of this week *there* illustrates one of my frustrations as a legislator. While we face major issues, as a state and as a citizenry, my constituents are often more passionate about picky little ones. And I must represent them.

THE MOST EMOTIONALLY CHARGED AND DIVISIVE ISSUE this session centers on our Blue Laws — enacted in 1909 to restrict business on Sunday, and still in effect. Should the Blue Laws be repealed? *Save Sunday for the family!* Its proponents emotionally rally, although family life and our society at large has changed considerably here since 1909. Our state's Blue Laws make it a statutory misdemeanor on Sunday to:

- Promote any noisy or boisterous sport or amusement

- Disturb the peace of the day

- Conduct, perform or employ any labor incident to trade or manufacture, except for livery stables, garages and works of necessary charity conducted in an orderly manner

- Open any drinking salon, or sell, offer or expose for sale any personal property, except for meals without either intoxicating liquor or tobacco

- Open a barbershop or permit the sale of uncooked meats, groceries, clothing, boots or shoes.

The law does permit the sale of milk, fruit, confectionaries, newspapers, magazines and medical and surgical appliances… but only if sold in a quiet and orderly manner.

In 1965, a legislative proposal urges that these laws be repealed. Over the years, all attempts to revise or abolish our Blue Laws have failed.

My 32nd District swings both ways, from the ultra-conservative and religiously strict to the intellectual, the liberal, the laborer. It swings both Republican and Democrat. It swings progressive and not. If an issue has two strong sides, you can be sure that it will have a lively audience in my District 32.

When an all-day hearing on the Blue Law repeal was set in early February, five busloads of voters from my district converged on our state capitol: The committee hearing room was packed. But after hours of testimony and animated discussion, it was clear there was no consensus — not only among my constituents, but across the state. I had no clear mandate for how to represent them, and in such an instance, I must rely on my own good conscience and clear head.

In this case, I have chosen to ignore the matter entirely. I believe not every matter must be settled by legislation. I come from a church-going family, but a busy family, too, and sometimes it's easier for us to shop for our groceries on a Sunday. I have broken this law.

In practice, the Blue Laws are erratically enforced, with more establishments closed Sundays in our larger city areas, but choosing to be open on Sundays out in the suburbs. Some areas levy fines. In others, authorities turn a blind eye. Sometimes, sporadic surveillance is used to discriminate or play favors: One business is fined, the next is not. It's a messy situation and a social tug of war, with most of the vehemence centered on the Sunday sale of liquor.

Because I had taken the time to listen to all of my constituents, made the effort to let them know about the February hearing, encouraged them to attend and to express their views, and helped arrange their bus rides to the capitol, they were happy with me. I had included them in the legislative process.

However, without consensus, the committee couldn't act, so there the bill died.

Consideration of the Blue Laws faded from view, and to me that is precisely as it should be. When people say, "There oughtta be a law," I don't necessarily agree, though I'm a lawmaker. There is simply no way a legislature can solve all the problems of the world by passing laws, nor should they. Many people's problems can be solved in other ways. I would never scoff at a constituent concern — I always try to listen carefully. But often as not, I suggest how they might solve it themselves... rather than me taking it to the legislature to solve by law.

But I do believe in our Blueprint. These critical issues must be addressed by us here, and I am happy to be part of the inside team attempting to lay its foundation in law.

Governor Evans and Jim Dolliver and their staff are methodically dissecting the state's top issues and reconstructing them in a series of proposed legislation. These are the governor's executive request bills — 35 in all — and our job as a team is to continually evaluate which we think can pass. I admire our new governor for the level of his concern, and his willingness to team with the legislature to improve our state.

Our DEGOHT 'team' meets frequently in the governor's office to discuss the most prominent issues. Jim Dolliver tends to sit off to the side and listen, saying nothing, but then he'll deliver a perfect summary. We work as a team — we each have our roles. I can't imagine much prospect for progress if, instead, we each worked alone.

As our House works through the details of our proposed state budget — now being authored primarily by Senate Democrats, but with input from the rest of us — it is increasingly clear that as elected representatives serving this state, we really have more in common than not.

I am beginning to relax into my work, and my desk on the floor reflects this now that the bill crunch of the regular session has passed.

Our desks in the House are quite small, compared to those on the floor of the Senate, with only one small drawer under the desktop for storage, and that's it. There I keep my little red legislative manual, my phone directory of the capitol campus, a pad of blank paper and a few sharpened pencils. On top of my desk are my phone and my microphone, plus the red and green lights for registering my electric roll call votes. Also at my desk are my bill books, which the pages continue to update each morning: Out with the old, insert the new. Some legislators keep a file box beneath their desks, but I don't like the clutter. I keep all my background paperwork at home, study there, and bring to the capitol only what's necessary. My briefcase does the shuttling.

Food is not allowed on the floor, except for occasional gifts from our farmers, or from a bill's prime sponsor when the governor signs it into law. Celebratory chocolates and cigars are the norm, though one among us once suggested toothbrushes would serve us better — this was a colleague with dental ties. Should we receive a bouquet of flowers, they may stay on our desk for the day but no longer. We must maintain decorum. These desks are our offices — we have no other. We do have a secretarial pool to do our typing.

ON DAY 10 OF OUR EXTRAORDINARY SESSION, it is announced in the House that the governor has signed another 68 of our session bills. Halfway down that list is Lois Hauptli's. Her safety glass measure will take effect on January 1, 1966.

At the end of today, as I often do, I remain at my desk to study the bills on tomorrow's docket. Then I retire to our dining room for a late ham sandwich or bowl of ice cream. The chef prepares only breakfast and lunch, but he puts out leftovers for the evenings. And ice cream is available any time, much to Jack Dootson's delight, and to mine. What a great place to unwind and socialize with my colleagues from both sides of the aisle.

Not wanting our Extraordinary Session to last another sixty days, we're working hard and fast through the most rudimentary legislation: Those house-keeping bills that keep our state and local governments going (departments, employees, salaries, utility bills), and all the bills slated for sunset. A sunset clause is put in place when a bill first becomes law. It designates how long the measure will be in effect and when it will expire — when the sun will set on it. So one

SUNSET

A sunset clause specifies when a measure will no longer be in effect -- when the sun will set on it.

part of our housekeeping is to decide upon which of these the sun should keep shining; conversely, which of them should simply fade to black.

Day 45. A month and a half into this extra session, we've dealt with many of our reforms and most housekeeping bills, and now it's time to fine-tune the state's biennial budget. I'm back to working late nights, analyzing this vast Senate budget bill: Do their projected revenues match their proposed expenditures? I propose to the governor's staff how to rectify imbalances — or rather, how I think the House Budget Committee should do so.

Between redistricting and my revenue research to help finance the governor's agenda, I've been involved in the two most laborious issues of this session. But our budget is close — I would guess within days — so I'm motivated to work hard a few days more. Today, when I finally crawl into bed, it is well past 2 a.m.

I am still sound asleep at 8:29 a.m. when my bed begins to roll from side to side across my room. I toss off my covers and run to the window in time to see brick chimneys on the houses surrounding me crash to the ground. The earth is visibly rolling, the light poles swaying. *Earthquake!* I make my shaky way to my TV and turn it on to an amazing sight — a wide-eyed breakfast crowd huddling in the Space Needle restaurant, 520-feet in the air, where they're tossed first to one side of the gigantic landmark, then to the other as it sways like some wild, gigantic carnival ride, sans a driver.[3]

Just as suddenly as it started, the violent shaking stops. Ken telephones from his office at the university.

"Mary Ellen! Are you all right?!"

"I'm OK, honey. I'm fine. The kids?"

"OK as far as I know. They're at school."

I quickly pick up the broken dishes that flew from my kitchen cupboard, throw on some clothes, and run outside, bound for the capitol. I run the steps of the legislative building and dash inside before the capitol guards close it off — perhaps an unwise maneuver on my part. Inside the dome, the big brass and glass chandelier is still swinging like a pendulum.

The doors to the House stand open and I am shocked by what I see inside: All the skylights have shattered and our desks are buried under broken glass. Sam Smith is nervously laughing at the center of a small group of colleagues. In his hands he holds his most current bill book — one-foot thick and pierced clear through with a deadly shard!

"What were you doing here so early, Sam?" someone asks.

"Catching up on my reading," he says, the bill book in hand. "Dashed to the wings, quick as I could when the shaking started. First time you ever saw a black man turn pure white."

Across the way, the Senate chamber has fared just as badly.

The governor is standing at the side of George Washington-the-bronzed, surveying the damage, examining the massive dome. He is, after all, a structural engineer. 160We must evacuate.

Outside on this lovely spring morning, hundreds of shaken and curious gather in the sunshine, and as I join them a funny thought threads through the crowd: "It took an earthquake to the get this legislature to leave!" [4]

We can't return to the House until the glass is gone and the damage repaired.

A rumor spreads: The cleanup will take a week. Perhaps even longer. The ballroom at the Tyee Hotel becomes our backup chamber, but because we're down to just the budget to prepare, some legislators leave. All we need is a quorum — in the House, in the Senate, in our respective budget committees. Everyone else can go home.

By now the cherry blossoms have fallen, brown and decomposing on the capitol grounds. One last hard rainfall washes away the final remnants as we finish the last of our legislative work. On May 9, we gavel a second *sine die.*

The 39th Session of the Washington State Legislature lasted 114 days — the longest in state history; longer, even, than the session to establish our statehood in 1889.

More than 700 bills were introduced by our House throughout the session, and nearly another 600 by the Senate. About one-third of these passed both chambers, including 13 of the governor's 35 executive request bills (despite the Democrat majorities). Governor Evans signed nearly all of these measures into law, including, at long last, our state's new redistricting.

Our state, under fresh leadership, is beginning to hit a new stride. Deadlock and stagnation have dissipated, and with the battle of redistricting behind us, our legislature seems as though it's beginning to coalesce.

Some of us will leave, never to return: Too harrowing — all those decisions. Too demanding of intellect, emotion and time. This... is political winnowing.

But many will remain in the game and return to make the hard choices at critical junctures, and those are the few who gradually grow into legislative leaders.

CHAPTER SIX

THE CHALLENGE
RACE FOR THE MAJORITY ON A LEVEL PLAYFIELD

It is imperative we maintain two strong political parties if our government is to function as a representative democracy. The two-party system is not about one party winning or dominating, but about our government working as it was designed — it thrives on the vigorous competition of ideas.

EXHAUSTED AND EXHILARATED BOTH, I help Ken toss my bags in the trunk then bid Olympia adieu, buoyed immensely by the newest blossoms splashing our picturesque capitol. Though our astonishing variety of cherry trees have long dropped their varied pink blossoms, western Washington's springtime parade of blooms continues its vivid display — we're now onto azaleas and rhododendrons. No, I'm not in Kansas any more. In the early May of my childhood, the vast expanse of green grasses danced in the breeze and the prairies burst into bloom with a profusion of wildflowers. Recalling it calms me down.

I can't yet mentally package the momentum and thrill of these past four months. Perhaps once I'm home, these events will eventually sink in and I'll have absorbed all that we completed. But for now, I am ready to be "Mother" again: Mary Ellen rather than Representative McCaffree. The slow drive north to Seattle allows this transition. When we pull up in front at 5014, I find myself blinking back tears. After months of legislative absence, I am now home to stay.

With Ken's setting of the parking brake, I shift into organizational gear, counting down the upcoming highlights of our flurried McCaffree summer. In a few weeks Chuck will graduate from the University of Washington, then head directly to El Segundo, California for his new job with Chevron Chemical. His fiancée, Lee Bracken, will don graduation garb for that very same ceremony, then exchange her dark gown for a white wedding one in July.

Because of these two special graduates, the economics department hasn't had to scrounge for faculty to represent it at this year's commencement ceremony. Ken has volunteered. This prompts my immediate concern for his attire. Is that social science hood of his from his University of Chicago days in decent condition for the faculty march? It's been mothballed nearly fifteen years! From our family seats way up top at 'Hec Ed' — UW's Hec Edmundson Pavilion — we may not notice if the garment is rumpled, but others will have a more intimate view. I really must check into this right away.

Our oldest son Jim has wedding plans, too, after he completes his first year of graduate work at Cornell. We'll attend this second family marriage in August, in Iowa.

Nancy is to arrive home mid-June from Pullman, when she finishes her freshman year at Washington State University. Our youngest two are still home — Mary at the tail end of her junior year at Roosevelt High School, and David a junior high schooler at John Marshall.

Though I'm done with my 'outside' work, now that the session is over, Ken isn't. His university classes are still under way, after which he'll have finals to grade. Then he'll work all summer again as a labor consultant for the West Coast insulation and asbestos contractors: Extra college tuition funds for our kids. My $100 a month of legislative pay hasn't helped the family budget at all — it doesn't even cover my costs of holding office, of which Ken will occasionally remind me.

I walk through our front door and into the midst of a full-fledged family life. I know my husband, for one, is grateful for my return.

Yes, I face serious decisions about my legislative career and the DEGOHT team. But not yet. First there's a family of seven to orchestrate. I dive into our summer and couldn't be happier, but within weeks — the second week of June — my home telephone brings a disruption.

"Mary Ellen? Joel. You rejuvenated yet?"

"Well, I certainly am enjoying my…"

"We've been summoned to the governor's mansion Saturday morning. Around 10."

"Well I…"

"If you'd like to ride down with me, I'll pick you up at 8. Let me know."

Click. Just like Joel. No chance to reply. No good bye. No explanation.

So much for the leisurely contemplation of my ongoing role.

The reality is, we have just pulled off redistricting at long last. Our state has a fighting chance of renewed political balance, renewed vigor. If we — this Republican team I've wound up on — manage to win a legislative majority for the coming session, we could really break loose those logjammed gears of our government. But in between here and fulfilling that potential lays a whole new round of elections. How can I quit now? I've labored nearly a decade plugging "the fair and equitable redistricting and reapportionment" of our state. My personal sense of accomplishment at its completion is incredible. But am I done? To the point, is secure school funding in place? Not yet. Not yet.

On the other hand, there looms a huge political battle in the coming election year. Partisan politics is not my fancy — I never intended to become so entwined. I feel a need to clear the cobwebs, to weigh my family priorities against my political goals. As I tackle my household tasks these next days, pros and cons do a little dance within my head.

We convene a McCaffree family council and those of us at home discuss my concerns. Ken and the kids — just Mary and David now — assure

> **PARTISAN POLITICS**
>
> The interplay of political parties stemming from their different ideas about the direction of government.

me they're able and willing to fend for themselves if I decide to leave our home again for the House. It's a tough decision. I'm not yet ready to make it.

When Joel calls next, however, I do accept his offer of a ride, and together we head to the governor's mansion early on Saturday. I instantly pry: "What's the agenda?"

"Oh you know, Mary Ellen. Just that little matter of winning control of our legislature next election."

Joel is nonchalant with the wheel as we head south towards the capitol.

"Is there a plan?" I pry further.

"There's a need," he says. "That's our starting point."

We roll along. After a quiet stretch, he talks again: "If we're going to get our Blueprint for Progress moving ahead in high gear, the governor needs a legislature he can work with. Personally? I doubt we can win both the House and the Senate. But I think… I think we have a chance in the House."

"With hard work."

"Yep. That's why we're in this car a whole year and a half before voters hit the ballot booth. Hard work, Mary Ellen? You bet."

As the door to the governor's mansion swings wide, Joel and I are accosted by the governor's gargantuan Irish wolfhound, Peggy, who has become an honorary team mascot.

"Peggy! Here girl! Thatta girl," says the governor.

Peggy abandons us, rears on her strong hind legs and slumps her huge paws on the governor's shoulders to stare her master in the eye, despite his six-plus feet. Joel and I have seen this dance before — it's no longer startling. We just laugh and join the rest of our DEGOHT team, and the governor thanks us all for giving up our Saturday.[1]

"And thank your families, too, for allowing you back to Olympia so soon."

Then he gets down to business, concisely summarizing the situation and possibilities, beginning with Attorney General John O'Connell's review of the state's new — and court-approved — redistricting.

The attorney general estimates that in the upcoming elections in 1966, either party can hypothetically capture a majority in the House with a minimum of 47.7% of the popular vote. This is a big improvement over 1964, pre-redistricting, when the old lines heavily favored old headcounts (and in many cases, favored Democrat incumbents). Pre-redistricting, it was possible for Democrats to elect a House majority with a popular vote of only 38 percent. In the Senate, the new, improved balance is equally marked. Our new districts allow for either party to secure a majority with at least 47.2% percent of the vote, a notable rectification of the maps of old, which allowed Senate Democrats to sustain their majority with a popular vote of only 35.6 percent… a little more than one-third and they were in.[2,3]

With the odds now evened, the governor suggests we can feasibly overtake both bodies. Then, in his typical leadership style, he hands off deliberation to us.

"What do the rest of you think? Gummie?"

Gummie, short for C. Montgomery Johnson, is one earnest bundle of political enthusiasm — an erstwhile optimist and, as of January, chairman of the Central Committee of the State Republican Party.

"We have a fighting chance to gain the majority," Gummie says, "so what are the risks and what are the gains? Either we become a majority in one house or both, or we continue in the minority. I say we roll up our sleeves and challenge the Democrats."

We're all in agreement. But Jim Dolliver, the deepest thinker among the Heavy Thinkers here, is more guarded.

"We're talking about a tremendous amount of people power," he cautions. "Do we really have the cadre of men and women — and financial supporters — to carry off this kind of challenge?"

Ritajean responds: "The people support is out there, Jim. I know plenty of volunteers eager to support the governor's reforms. We just have to get them all organized."

Which is what Ritajean does best. Joel reminds us of the amazing number of volunteers we amassed for Dan's election. But then he posits another hurdle: "Do we have enough of the financial community behind the governor's proposals?"

"Good question," Gummie concedes.

Dolliver modifies it: "Tough question."

Our governor enters the discussion to note that from his viewpoint, if we're going to be able to implement the new directions we proposed in our Blueprint — which, he acknowledges, are not just his goals but all of ours — we'll need a majority in at least one house of the legislature.

Slade has sat by silently until now.

"Getting to where we are today wasn't easy," he says. "But we did it."

Indeed we did, and we did it from the minority disadvantage. I smile at this satisfying thought.

"Mary Ellen and I worked extremely hard on this, as you all know, and as a result we have some swing districts out there for the taking. If we work those districts intelligently, it is possible to win them, and those seats could make all the difference."

"Majority," Gummie says.

"Has a nice ring," adds Joel.

Slade returns to the topic of the upcoming election: "The crucial thing is to convince good candidates to run."

Joel reviews for us his tried and true trio of campaign mandates we've come to know and respect: "Number one, good candidates. Number two, good campaign strategy. And number three, a lot of hours of tough work from a lot of dedicated people. If you ask me…"

"Take it away," jokes Gummie, knowing there's little stopping Joel now.

"…I think we should take a poll," Joel says, and we react, recalling the early polls in the governor's last race last interim. "Seriously. Figure out the characteristics of these swing districts, then recruit our candidates tailored to who will really represent the district."

A great strategy, we all agree.

"The State Committee's got funds," Gummie says. "A poll like that is something we could pay for."

I'm feeling inspired, and speak up: "We've all worked so hard to make this possible, I think we owe it to ourselves to bring two strong political parties back into play in this state."

To me the two-party system is not so much about one or the other party winning or dominating, but about our government working as it was designed — it thrives on the vigorous competition of ideas.

"When there's no competition," I continue, "that's when we run into problems... complacency, corruption, inequalities, deaf ears turned to the people. I witnessed it firsthand with school funding."

"And with redistricting, too, I dare say," says Slade. "Or lack, thereof."

"Oh yes, that."

We've all been witness to various versions of our home state's ills, born of the lengthy dominance by a single party. I complete my thought before surrendering my soapbox.

"It is imperative that we maintain two strong political parties here if our state is going to work as a representative democracy. I agree wholeheartedly: We have to fight for these seats."

Gummie reconfirms that the state committee will finance polls and we continue to brainstorm, scribbling on notepads we've spread across the governor's expansive coffee table. Suddenly, Peggy bounds in, paws flying, and with a single, powerful swoop of her tail, all our paperwork flies off the table and onto the Persian carpet.

"Nancy!" the governor calls, and his wife retrieves the exuberant Peggy.

We laugh — *I guess that does it!* — and agree to adjourn. Jim Dolliver will call our next meeting once the polling of our new districts is done.

A short time later, in between Chuck and Lee's graduation date and their wedding, I make my post-session rounds to my local newspapers.

Ever since I've been in office, I stay in regular touch with all three and have come to know their editors and reporters well. We talk about the recently adjourned 39th Session, and the success — at last — of redistricting. *Will you run again?* each asks. But I haven't yet decided. My telephone rings within days.

"Mary Ellen? Jim Dolliver. The governor has a request."

"Oh?"

"You know that Advisory Council for Higher Education we set up during the session? He'd like you to serve on it."

"This summer, Jim? Didn't we decide that council should meet every two weeks?"

"We did. I know it's summertime, Mary Ellen, and you're busy with your family, and I'm sorry. But he wants you on it. You know the universities, you care about education, you know the state budget."

If it were anything else, I'd decline. But education?

"All right."

Another task to add to my to-do list in this summer of '65. I'll have to tell Ken.

The impetus for this council came in 1964, when the presidents of Washington's five state colleges and universities told us their student populations were growing too fast. They recommended we establish a new four-year college somewhere in the western part of the state. As a result, during our last legislative session, every Chamber of Commerce west of the Cascade Mountains, it seemed, came to Olympia to pitch us their cities and bergs.[4]

> **ADVISORY COUNCIL**
>
> A group of citizens authorized by the legislature and appointed by the governor to study and report on a specific complex public policy issue.

But how could we as legislators honestly represent our statewide voters on a whole new decision of this scale, and this expense? Especially since, with redistricting running overtime, we barely had time to go home mid-session and talk with them? We discussed this in the House Committee on Higher Education. Rather than make this big decision during that frantic session, it seemed more prudent to do our homework first. Thus, this Advisory Council was formed, to be made up of 23 members in all: Ten legislators, the five college presidents, one community college head and seven other citizens. Little did I know, when I agreed this Council was a good idea, that I'd be spending my interim hours sitting on it — for $25 *per diem*.

Since educational issues fall within our McCaffree guideline of 'good for the family', and with two more children yet to enter college, Ken supports my decision to serve.

At our initial meeting as a Council, we pick Senator Gordon Sandison of Port Angeles as chairman, with me as vice-chairman and Dr. Rodney Berg, president of Everett Community College, as our secretary. Our first job is to formally document the need for a new four-year college. If the need is substantiated, we're to locate a specific site. Finally, we're to report to the governor on all of the above on or before October 1, 1966, so he can prepare a presentation to the Legislature when the 40th Session convenes at the start of 1967. We have slightly more than a year.

I send Mary off to Olympia. She and Don Moos' daughter, Mary Kay, have decided to work as tour guides at the capitol campus this summer. They've found an apartment to share, and Mary has been boning up on the capitol's colorful history: It's audacious multi-building campus design, selected in the early 1920's by America's preeminent architectural scholar from among competing submissions from across the nation, its 278-foot self-supporting dome — fourth largest in the world, its tons of Alaskan marble, the controversial placement of George Washington in the center of the floor... *And incidentally*, she plans to tell the tourists, *this is the part-time workplace of my mom.*

Ken, too, takes to the road at the start of summer, a traveling diplomat of sorts as he helps his contractor group navigate union negotiations.

Throughout the summer my mind mulls the problem of whether it's possible to simultaneously maintain a legislative career, a family and my energy! The juggle requires careful planning and meticulous scheduling. Fortunately, I've done both all my life.

In July, Chuck and Lee are joined together in a lovely ceremony at the University Methodist Temple across from the campus, after which they head off to begin married life in California.

In late August, the girls join Ken and me on a road trip to Independence, Iowa, to attend the wedding of Jim and Konnie, while David stays behind to attend Camp Orkila in the San Juan Islands. On our drive home from Iowa, we stop in Kansas to visit relatives and friends and admire the blue stem prairie of my girlhood. It's been so many years…

Once back home, I am quickly immersed in Advisory Council meetings, but it's not just the meetings that take my time — it is preparing for them as well. Fortunately, we generally meet close to my Seattle home. Some of our other members must travel many hours.

As the new school year looms — for Ken and for our kids — I have plenty of work cut out for me, beyond being Mother. Included are some potentially heady challenges — one in particular has worked its way forefront.

AT THE START OF THIS SEPTEMBER OF 1965, the Republican Party in Washington State faces a crippling predicament — one more critical, even, than our upcoming races against long-entrenched Democrats. For some years now, and even more so since Barry Goldwater's defeat last fall — which set off a Republican nosedive nationwide — our party has been subject to infiltration by extremists. Republicans in Washington State are no exception. Throughout this past spring and all summer long, Gummie Johnson has fielded increasing complaints from one county Republican chairman after another: *Can you help us? These guys are killing our party!*

'These guys' are members of the John Birch Society, a group whose membership is sworn to secrecy: *No one's to know who we are. Join us, but stay incognito.* Their strategy is to silently infiltrate existing organizations — PTAs, church groups, and… political parties — through which they spread the extremist Birch doctrine: A platform centered on conspiracy, suspicion, outright paranoia and dislike, even hate. They label any who don't toe their line "communists": The likes of Governor Evans, for instance, or Gummie Johnson. Of the 39 counties in Washington State, 18 are battling Birch infiltration, including mine. Surprisingly, the populous Seattle and King County are particular Birch bastions.

When John Rousselot, the John Birch Society's national director of public relations, visited Seattle at the end of July, he boasted their membership has tripled in western Washington in little more than a year.[5] And frankly, I don't doubt it.

At the end of August, at a Republican teen leadership camp — the Young Republican Federation, another group now largely driven by Birch membership — when Gummie announced that Governor Evans would be coming to speak, the junior and senior high schoolers hissed and booed.

All year, the Birchers have been causing tremendous infighting in our party, as well as stirring up suspicion — with hate letters, name-calling, racism, changing of locks. Formally, they oppose the Civil Rights Act, the United Nations, U.S. Supreme Court Chief Justice Earl Warren ("a communist!"), and they've even suggested we abolish our national park here at Mount Rainier.[6,7]

And yet, they won't disclose their membership. They hide. They sneak. They are driving away our party's moderate voters, moderate party members and moderate potential candidates.

With such an important statewide election ahead of us, this "Birch" issue looms large.

I'M GRATEFUL TODAY, SEPTEMBER 4, for the reminder of a more generous, positive, universal outlook on life, though with some sadness. Albert Schweitzer has passed away. He was my hero.

From his most recent work against nuclear proliferation to his doctrine of 'Reverence for Life' that extends beyond humanitarian care to respect for all living things — laboratory animals, farm animals, the smallest insect, the field of green — Albert Schweitzer looked for connection, rather than division or hate. He had abandoned a successful career as a university professor in philosophy and theology to do medical work in Africa, a choice made specifically to atone for white man's mistreatment of the black. He paid for his medical schooling and training by writing books, giving lectures, and performing recitals on the organ. It was the organ that personally led me to Albert Schweitzer.

Across the street from our married student housing at the University of Chicago was the Rockefeller Chapel, complete with a beautiful organ. I could sit on our lawn and listen to students practicing, or hear recitals without paying admission. Albert Schweitzer was coming tp the chapel, I heard, to lecture and to perform. On the day he did, I sat my small children on the curb across the street and, thanks to outdoor loudspeakers wired from inside the chapel, we listened to him speak and play. What a thrill!

Afterwards, we watched the crowd spill from the chapel in the noonday sun, and then, from a back door opening slowly, there he was: Albert Schweitzer. The Nobel Laureate, the global pacifist, the man I revered — was walking right past us on the other side of the street. A man of peace, not violence. Respect, not enmity. Nurture, not injury. He urged us to dismiss prejudice and embrace the good we all share.

My home phone rings September 5.

"Mary Ellen? Team meeting tomorrow. I'll pick you up."

Guess who.

We arrive at the governor's mansion to discuss a single topic: The John Birch Society. Should we continue our policy of tolerance and try to ignore the radical group? Should we keep our inner-party battle under wraps? Or should we publicly confront them?

Jim Dolliver, Gummie and the governor are all of one mind: It is time for us to risk public confrontation. Already, one Republican county chair has publicly renounced the John Birch Society, and she told Gummie her party membership has jumped dramatically as a result.

THE JOHN BIRCH SOCIETY IS POISONING OUR PARTY and jeopardizing our potential for a good performance in the elections next fall. That, in turn, means our chance to bring meaningful change to our flagging state government is in jeopardy as well. After all our long, hard work on redistricting to level our political playfield, what a shame! The situation has us hopping mad.

Joel expresses it best: "If we can't make a difference now — if we can't recruit and elect top flight people to our legislature this round, and have an honest chance of governing and getting our Blueprint in gear, then my guess is, most of us here today will finally turn our energies elsewhere."

We agree. Confrontation is worth the risk. Now.

The Republican Party State Central Committee meets quarterly, and the next meeting is set for next weekend — Saturday, September 11, in the town of Port Angeles in the far northwest corner of this northwest American state. Jim Dolliver and Gummie propose a detailed strategy for the weekend meeting, and the rest of us give it our blessing. This is a make or break deal. If it works, we'll have a fighting chance of gaining seats in the House. If not, our party will suffer in the grip of John Birchers, and we can all kiss our Blueprint goodbye.

I return to Seattle. I'll have to hear second-hand what ensues in Port Angeles.

On Friday evening, September 10, at the banquet preceding the next day's Central Committee meeting, Governor Evans takes the podium to deliver a heart-felt plea.

"We have had the winter of our discontent," he begins, "and we have had our long, hot summer. We have suffered through our own private little Hell, our agonizing reappraisal — and it is now time to discard hyphenated Republicanism and the 'splinterism' which seems to have captivated the political physicians who are conducting post mortems on our party, and return to the business of winning elections."

Among the guests are several party leaders and supporters, numerous John Birchers perhaps (who knows?), and many of the 78 members of the statewide committee — two representatives from each of our 39 counties.

So far, this audience is listening.

"No one here has to be reminded of the opportunity and the challenge which lies ahead of the party in our own state of Washington in 1966..." the governor continues. "Not every state — and there were literally dozens of them where the Republican victims of the most thorough political housecleaning of this century — not every state was so fortunate as Washington in passing a redistricting bill which guarantees a great opportunity to the Republican Party..."

So far, still so good. The governor then raises the promise of youth and the young peoples' vote, emphasizing the need to be in touch with crucial contemporary issues and to offer real solutions.

"Ideas and imagination and a little intestinal fortitude in the field of government are not the exclusive property of the Democratic Party — in fact, historically these have more often and more effectively been Republican tools."

The dinner crowd seems to agree.

"It will come as no surprise to you, I'm sure, that I believe responsibility on issues can begin only after we have achieved a degree of responsibility within the party..."

A few squirm.

"The Republican Party is not narrow in scope, nor is it confined to one point of view. But those who seek to rally under its banner must be builders of success, not architects of disaster; responsible citizens, not character assassins."

More detectable squirming. He proceeds.

"I am committed to the position that the modern history of the Republican Party should be written in the forum of responsible debate and constructive dissent — and not in the foxholes of irresponsible and irrational extremism..."

The governor then lists the qualities of any extraneous group that wishes to attach itself to the GOP — qualities that determine whether a particular group will ultimately help or hurt the party:

Is their business conducted in public or in secret? Do they motivate by faith and hope, or by fear? Do they use the tools of truth or of lies? Engender trust or distrust? Follow democratic procedures or militant authoritarianism? Embrace the art of compromise or deal in absolutisms? Further, does the group help the party attract candidates, voters, funding, and volunteers? Does it clarify the party's message, or distort it?

So far, the governor has spoken with theoretical conjecture.

Now he gets specific.

"The John Birch Society and its frightened satellites…" That does it. A host of chairs are shoved away from the tables as members storm out, but the governor continues, "…as shown by their methods, their leadership and their rash policies, meets none of the traditions of the Republican Party. They care not for the Party's victory, but for its defeat; they work not to strengthen it but to weaken it; they do not promote conservative principles, they pervert them.

"I do not intend to watch silently the destruction of our great Party — and with it the destruction of the American political system. The false prophets, the phony philosophers, the professional bigots, the destroyers, have no place in our Party. Let them leave!

"For our part, let us be on with the job at hand. We must be as we have always been, the Party composed of people alert to the menace of communism at home and abroad and concerned over the erosion of our constitutional guarantees; the Party responsive and responsible to the needs of the people; the Party that believes in local self-government and is willing to take the risks and endure the sacrifices to make it work.

"It must be a party that is color blind, which has no exclusions of race, geography, status or creed. A party which welcomes a diversity of opinions within the broad American political tradition, but which refuses to become the captive of the narrow demands of the fanatic few. A Party of and for people, not of pronouncements, propaganda and promises…"

The governor next rails against state Democrats as a group in "leaderless disarray," led by those who have "substituted the whine and the whimper for statesmanship, and the petty complaint for imaginative leadership. They stand prisoners of their past, unwilling to face the problems of the present and inadequate to meet the challenges of the future."

The governor challenges the Republican Party to grow and win and lead — to not only confront pressing issues but also to answer them.[8,9,10]

With several rallying phrases, the speech is done. No cheering. No standing ovation. From some corners, robust applause. From scattered others, discernible confusion. Some outright sit on their hands. Our Republican Party is teetering tonight; a bold risk taken to save it.

The executive committee confers late into the night, weighing the issue, weighing the delivery of their new materials tomorrow, and weighing the mode of their subsequent deliberation. They'd adjourned after 3 a.m., and felt prepared.

On Saturday, September 11, Gummie Johnson hands out to committee members a pamphlet created and mimeographed just for the occasion: *The Challenge for Responsible Conservatives*. On page three, directed dead aim at the John Birch Society, is a 'Bill of Particulars':

1. They weaken Party councils, setting Republican against Republican. Their criterion is, "If you are not as conservative as I, or if you disagree with me, then you are a communist or a communist sympathizer."

2. They are using the Republican Party framework to gain respectability for their radical causes, such as the impeachment of the Chief Justice of the United States Supreme Court.

3. They are driving away regular, previously dependable financial support for the legitimate party efforts in the traditional political arenas.

4. They are saddling the Republican Party with an image of radicalism painted by an infinitesimally insignificant group, numerically.

5. They have caused, directly or indirectly, a number of seats normally held by Republicans to go to Democrats in the state legislature and in Congress.

6. They have driven responsible citizens — both voters and workers — away from the Republican Party by their irrational statements and approaches to politics and government.

7. And perhaps the greatest disservice of all, they have made it almost impossible for a conservative to publicly espouse legitimate conservative views without being labeled "kook", "extremist" or "Bircher." [11]

Based on the previous evening's speech, several members refused to show up for this Saturday meeting. Once this pamphlet appears, several more walk out.

A resolution is introduced: A repudiation of the methods, leadership and policies of extremist groups on both the left and the right, and specifically the John Birch Society.

In a surprisingly civilized proceeding, the membership slowly debates the resolution, registering dozens of questions, scores of considerations, and one final quiet observation regarding whether to adopt it as a policy of the party in our state: "When we get right down to it, all the guidelines we've talked about focus back to one question: Will this group, the John Birch Society, help elect Republicans?"

The final vote is 43 to 15, with one abstention from Yakima: "You're damned if you do and damned if you don't," said the delegate with a sigh.

The margin of victory seems solid, but Gummie, Governor Evans and Jim Dolliver agreed in advance they wouldn't consider this resolution passed without a committee majority. The full committee membership is 78, so they needed more than half those votes — at least forty — for legitimate approval. Only 43 yes votes is a narrow win for moderate Republicans.[12,13]

The next morning Ken reads to me from our Sunday *Seattle Times*.

"Hey honey, listen to Herb Robinson."

I offer an educated guess on the columnist's topic: "Port Angeles?"

"Yes dear, Port Angeles. Here's Herb: 'Even non-partisan observers are saying that Governor Dan Evans' action urging the state Republican high command to repudiate the John Birch Society and its 'frightened satellites' was a singular demonstration of political courage.'"[14]

This victory against the Birchers presents one more factor for me to weigh as I contemplate my future.

Running as a Republican has never been easy in my Democrat-leaning district. The extremists in the King County GOP have certainly never supported my candidacy. However, the governor and moderate Republicans are winning growing admiration throughout the state, particularly on the heels of this Port Angeles stand. Perhaps the tide is turning our way. Should I seek re-election? My decision remains.

Full bloom of the giant dogwood that dominates our backyard tells me, *Hey, it's October!* My family has been back in school several weeks — professor and students alike. Both sets of newlyweds are lovingly launched. I am home alone, my full-time duties as mother are dwindling and for the first time in a very long time, I feel I have some space to breathe.

But then Gummie calls Jim Dolliver. And Jim Dolliver calls the governor. And the governor calls a meeting, and Joel calls me: "Poll's in."

He honks curbside a few days later.

"Ken? Honey? I'll…"

"I know. See you later, dear."

My political ambitions have never centered on party success. They're driven more by my desire to see our political process function as our founders envisioned it during that long, muggy summer of 1787, when they hammered out our U.S. constitution. My goal is to be part of that representative government Abraham Lincoln so masterfully described during his presidency: "Of the people, by the people, for the people." I still consider myself an ordinary citizen, so it is heartening now to feel I play a substantial role in making our state more efficient, more effective. I am living Lincoln's vision — "of the people, by the people, for the people" — and wonder how it is that our various levels of government so often stray so far from this simple premise.

"I believe you'll find this enlightening," says Dolliver as he hands us each copies of the statewide poll. "These new districts have distinct personalities. Younger. Young families, better educated, focused on education, and for the most part — not politically active."

"You've got that right," says Gummie. "No strong political leanings. Pretty independent, in fact. Lots of uncommitted voters who could easily go either way."

Just as I had been when I first ran for office.

"Swingers in a swing district," quips Joel. "Means they're more likely to vote for the candidate than the party, so… we all know what we've got to do, right?"

We do. Our job is to come up with candidates who fit the population profile of each new legislative district, and then to persuade them to run on the Republican ticket. We agree to focus specifically on the swing districts.

"The 21st is one big key," says Slade. "Mary Ellen? How about it?"

Slade and I know this district inside out — southern Snohomish County, just north of Seattle: Jack Dootson's territory, redrawn to his demise. A bedroom community if ever there was one — no commercial business to speak of, no industry — the 21st is just homes and schools and families and lots of Little League. This was the district where I'd inadvertently folded one precinct into extinction in the redistricting bill by earmarking a corner of a map and forgetting to unfold it. I corrected it later. I tell Slade I'll help.

"Me too," adds Joel.

We three agree we'll canvass our contacts in the new 21st and compare notes in a couple of weeks. We adjourn with a brand new campaign under way, and with groups of us bent on building new candidacies in these brand new districts.

KEN AND I HAVE GRADUATED from our twin plywood desks in our bedroom. He's moved his study to the small bedroom vacated a few years back by Jim, while I've set up permanent 'camp' in our basement, where I juggle party politics, legislative duties and motherhood.

Most stimulating and enjoyable of my work to date this interim is my membership on the Advisory Council for Higher Education. As a groups we spent the summer crisscrossing the state to confer with various communities — about educational trends, student needs, the interrelationship between colleges and towns. These discussions, driven in particular by the five college presidents on our Council, have drawn our focus to new possibilities. I explain these to my University District Rotary Club, where I've been invited to speak.

Rather than just duplicate the academic offerings we have in place in this state, the college presidents are suggesting we aim for a whole different type of school, with an alternative curriculum focused on emerging issues — the environment, for example, or new energies or new technologies. We've added a professional component to this process: Nelson Associates, a respected consulting firm from New York, will help us analyze and forecast state population growth. Thus, my study of issues continues and I relish it.

In the mean time, I also continue to scour the 21st District for a suitable candidate. I talk with local acquaintances, call on local Republicans, venture into local grocery stores when all else fails. So far, no real luck.

Slade has news, though. He has come across a self-starter who plans to run for one of the two district seats — Bill Kiskaddon, a Boeing engineer. Slade likes Kiskaddon and deems him a credible candidate in the 21st District. Now we just need one more. Who will that be?

GOT A PROBLEM, JOEL SAYS IN HIS NEXT phone call. "Gotta meet. With everyone."

So Slade, Joel and I travel back to Olympia to confer with Gummie, Jim Dolliver and the governor. We're concerned. A right-wing extremist has just declared his candidacy for the second position in the 21st District — as a Republican. This gentleman could win the Republican primary for this seat, unopposed, but considering the moderate makeup of the district, he'd never be able to defeat a Democrat in the general election. We could lose this swing district seat.

"So what do we do?" I ask.

"It's a tricky business, opposing our own party in the primary," Gummie agrees with us, shaking his head. "Regardless of the guy's political philosophy, it's risky."

"This is not a terrific time to arouse the ire of party regulars," Slade notes. "Particularly after Port Angeles."

"But this is exactly why we risked Port Angeles," notes Joel.

The three of us return to Seattle, focused on winning a House majority, but aware our strategy for a second candidate in the 21st must be thought through responsibly. We don't want to thoroughly alienate our party regulars.

Not long afterwards, on another trip through the 21st District, someone suggests I talk to Dale Hoggins. Dale is the popular principal of a local elementary school, and a winning Little League coach to boot — an ideal match for the district! I telephone.

"Dale? This is Mary Ellen McCaffree. I'm a state representative from Seattle and I'd like to talk with you."

When we meet, I discover Dale Hoggins is very much like I was at my political start — neither a Democrat nor a Republican, really, and never actively involved in elective politics. I talk to him about school issues, about my start in Olympia, about campaigning.

"You sound like a veteran," he says.

I scoff at the thought, but then realize the truth in it and laugh: "I guess I am."

Gummie visits Dale next and promises financial help if Dale decides to run for the 21ˢᵗ District seat as a Republican. Governor Evans telephones to personally invite Dale to join our progressive team. I assure Dale I'll help his campaign, and dispense many lessons learned from Joel through the years and from Gummie Johnson's campaign school. Step one: Draw up a list of 100 people you know will help you campaign. When Dale produces this easily, I know we have our candidate. Slade and Joel offer to help as well. We promise to invite him to our upcoming Campaign Training School.

My year ends with another phone call, not from Joel but from Dolliver again.

"Happy holidays, Mary Ellen."

"Same to you, Jim."

"Brace yourself," he says.

"What's wrong? Not Barbara, I hope. Your new kids?"

Jim and Barbara have just adopted two black children, added to the four of their own, to create a racially mixed family as living testament to their support of civil rights.

"The family's fine, but… the governor has decided to resurrect Rosellini's Tax Advisory Council. We've been puzzling our way through the school funding issue and, as you know, it is really a revenue problem. He wants a thorough study of our tax base."

I can guess Jim's next words. I can also guess my husband's reaction.

"You're his first choice, Mary Ellen," Dolliver says. "I know you're already doing yeoman work between the campaign and Higher Ed, but will you serve on this council?"

"Give me the details, Jim. I'll need to discuss it with Ken."

Jim explained: The council of fifteen members, hand-picked by the governor, will have one year to study our state's existing tax structure, weigh it against our state's mushrooming revenue needs and present a proposal to the governor before the start of the '67 session. I hang up the phone.

"Ken?"

Within a week, I am seated around a conference table with the new Tax Advisory Council of fifteen: Two from the legislature — one Republican (me) and one Democrat (Senator Frank Foley of Vancouver, an attorney and the lauded architect of our state's 1963 budget), the Dean of Arts and Sciences from the University of Washington, a county assessor, a labor union official, two more lawyers (one each from Seattle and Spokane), an official of the state cattlemen's association, a public school superintendent, the League of Women Voters' chairman of the fiscal issues committee, and from the business community — representatives of the timber giant Weyerhauser, West Coast Grocery, Seattle First National Bank, a technology company and, in a category all his own, a Methodist minister from Spokane. We're a remarkably balanced group. Also seated with us is Don Burrows, a quiet tax expert who worked as a consultant with Rosellini's group as well. Don will be our executive secretary.[15]

We quickly discuss our marching orders and divide into study groups — I'll study our property tax structure relative to revenue and levies — then we lay a course for the coming months, and finally wish each other Happy New Year.

AT THE START OF 1966, JUST AS I'M READY to turn some of my energy and hours toward considering a re-election campaign, my husband pulls my focus in a whole new direction.

"Guess who I heard from today?" Ken asks when the two of us are alone after dinner. "Dick Lefwitch, from college. Remember him?"

"Sure I do. How's Dick?"

"Chairman of the Department of Economics at Oklahoma State."

"Good for him!"

"He offered me a job."

I fall silent.

Not only has Dick offered my husband a tenured full professorship, which Ken has long awaited here, but a handsome salary, and even more — directorship of the university's new Industrial Relations Center, a perfect home for Ken's longstanding love of labor relations.

I finally dare ask: "What did you tell him?"

"That I'd discuss it with my family."

My mind begins to race. What about the rest of the family? What about my legislative career? But this is a perfect professional opportunity for Ken.

"Investigate," I tell him.

"To the limit!" Ken agrees.

"I'm going to keep this quiet."

And I do. I carry on with this secret, my mind traveling two paths at once. I want what's best for Ken and for his academic career. I can build another career for myself wherever I live, can't I? Community is community. Government is government. Public service can transfer, though public office is trickier. We've talked many times of moving back to our Midwest roots. Perhaps this is the time. An inner dialogue debates the dual possibilities as I continue my work.

MY PARTY COLLEAGUES HAVE MADE ME CHAIRMAN of our Campaign School, so I am tutoring not only newcomer Dale Hoggins for the coming election, but also shepherding potential new candidates statewide. Joel is our real educator, but I've agreed to help coordinate the program, pull together the faculty, and to invite all possible candidates who have said they may run. I set up a two-day event in Seattle for early March with two guest speakers: Governor Dan Evans and Governor Mark Hatfield of Oregon. On February 18, I mail out the word.

Dear Mr. Hewett (of Richland, one of 82 new legislative prospects I'm sending this to):

Good campaigns — more importantly, successful campaigns — are those that start early and start right. Because 1966 is a critical year for all elections, and especially critical for Republicans, the Republican State Central Committee has undertaken PROJECT: GET SMART — which is simply another name of a Statewide Candidates School.

We believe that you, as a prospective Republican candidate for office, will benefit substantially from the GET SMART program scheduled for Friday and Saturday, March 4-5 at the Olympic Hotel and Seattle Center. The Statewide Candidates School program is designed to give you information and assistance in two important areas of your prospective campaign:

• Building Your Campaign Organization

• Campaign Techniques and Materials

At the sessions on Saturday morning and afternoon, you will participate with experts in each phase of organizing and running a successful campaign for political office. What's more, you'll have the opportunity to talk to successful incumbents at all levels of government — Congress, state legislature, the county courthouse — and to discuss your own ideas and problems with a variety of people who have had a successful campaign experience.

We invite you, and your husband or wife, to join with Governor Dan Evans, Governor Mark Hatfield of Oregon, and incumbent Republican legislators and office-holders in getting a good start on your "Victory in '66" campaign. Please read the attached information sheet and then mail the enclosed post card.

Sincerely yours,

Representative Mary Ellen McCaffree, Campaign School Chairman[16]

Joel suggested our 'Get Smart' theme as a play on the new TV show that entered our cultural mainstream last fall.

"Guess that makes you Agent 99," Joel says to me in jest, "...one of the 99 in our House of Representatives."

I dash off a note to Tom Copeland across the state in Walla Walla – our Campaign Committee chairman – to let him know I've sent this letter to: 39 county chairmen, 82 possible legislative candidates, 56 incumbent legislators, 163 county incumbents and 2 incumbent Congressmen. I'm missing a few names – does he happen to have those? And let's see, we must still assign faculty, but I can be in charge of that. We're going to do phone calling at Joel's office on February 28 at 2:30 – can he come for that? I suggest a faculty meeting before we start on March 4th, add a few more details and express my hope I haven't forgotten anything. I enclose sample R.S.V.P. postcards with reservation details. The return address is my home at 5014. That should suffice. My mind is full.

> **CAMPAIGN SCHOOL**
>
> A political party-sponsored 'school' to provide candidates with the best tactics and practices for running a successful campaign.

SO IS KEN'S. HE TRAVELS TO STILLWATER, OKLAHOMA for an interview, followed by meetings with the faculty and a full facility tour. Soon after he returns, a formal invitation arrives: The full professorship Dick promised, as well as the promised tenure, pay and directorship of the new center. We talk.

"What about asking the University here if they'll match the offer?" I suggest.

"Ask them to make me a professor or good-bye?"

"Full professor or we're off to Oklahoma."

We agree, Ken will ask the Economics Department for both the promotion and a salary increase. If they say no? We'll move.

At the University of Washington, promotion approval is a four-step process. We know we'll be on hold a while more. Our final decision will depend on whether the UW Economics Department agrees to up their ante to keep Ken on.

Competition comes into play in all walks of life, and universities are certainly no exception. Ken's reputation as a teacher is solid. And with his new interest in health economics, his reputation is growing among the University of Washington Medical School as well.

We wait, knowing Ken's request will first pass through his department's senior faculty and that his promotion must be recommended by a majority of this staff. An affirmative vote would then require the blessing of the department chair, and if that comes about Ken's request will move on to the College Council, followed by review by the Dean of the College of Arts and Sciences, all of whom must also approve. But even after all that, it's still not a done deal. If Ken's request survives those four passages, it will then be sent to the President of the University, who could veto it then and there, but if he doesn't, it passes on to the Board of Regents, and they make the actual promotion in the end. Quite a series of hurdles for Ken and for our future. We hold modest hope it will work.

Meanwhile, I go about my work without a word of it.

IN MAY, NELSON ASSOCIATES submits to our Higher Education Advisory Council its population forecast and recommendations: The state of Washington needs a new four-year university, and soon. Within 10 years, the state's college-level student bodies will likely exceed current college space by thousands — 4,900 too many upper level students, to be exact, and 12,600 extra freshmen and sophomores.

The consultant's impressively detailed analysis presents us several options that range from absorbing these increases within our existing colleges, community colleges and universities, to building a college level campus entirely new. The report ends with solid, specific advice: Build new, and build a school for 9,800. Design it for 4,900 upper level students, and 4,900 lower.

One appendix in their report provides us detailed statistics on projected state growth, and we use this to examine likely locations for a new facility. The report identifies two potential growth spots in particular. The first is east of Seattle, east of Lake Washington, near the city of Redmond; the second, an area in south Puget Sound, somewhere between Tacoma and Olympia.[17]

When monetary benefits to a community stand in the balance, predictions of this nature can be a little dicey — especially when the projected project expenditures total millions of dollars. A new college could be a windfall in more ways than one to some lucky community.

We next retain a real estate consultant to explore available acreage — large parcels in these two regions; we'll need between 700 and 1,000 acres.

Some Council members begin to talk about the advantages of locating a college near the capitol, the seat of state government. Not surprisingly, our capitol city of Olympia heartily supports this idea. I'm not sure I do. We have a lot to consider.

SO DOES KEN. IN JUNE, THE NEWS ARRIVES. Dr. Kenneth M. McCaffree has been approved for promotion to full professor at the University of Washington, effective in the fall of 1967. I'm so grateful, I feel almost guilty.

Now my husband will have to choose. Ken assures me that any differences in opportunity between the two universities are undoubtedly offset by my own greater opportunities in Washington state government. Bless him. I have a true partner. We remain in Washington. I've never told my colleagues, and never do. Few people know what we've just been through.

For the better part of six months, now, my decision has been on hold, but in mid-July, when candidates file in our state, I formally announce my candidacy for re-election.

"Mrs. McCaffree?"

"No, this is her daughter Mary. Just a minute, please."

Mary covers the receiver and shouts, "Mom! Phone call!"

It's a constituent. An electrician.

"Mrs. McCaffree? I've never voted for a woman or a Republican, but I'm going to give you my vote. Even if I don't agree with everything you say, you say it very straightforward. And I know if we're ever going to get this levy thing straightened out it will be because people like you, who studied the situation and know what they're doing, are working on it."

The next time I visit the *Wallingford Outlook,* I relay the electrician's nod of confidence. His words soon appear in print, along with writer Trudy Weckworth's commendation: "Mary Ellen McCaffree has a close relationship with her constituents. She considers their desires and beliefs most important." [18] I'm grateful she recognizes it.

It's time to organize my newest McCaffree campaign. As a result of redistricting, my district has changed both in name and configuration: 32A. It's only half as big as my old district and it's more of a swing district now, with a larger percentage of independents and pretty equal odds either a Democrat or Republican can win. I set up my new campaign and pass along all my strategies to newcomer Dale Hoggins, who has formally agreed to run in the 21st.

"First of all," I tell Dale, "take just two sentences to set out your basic campaign positions, and then just keep repeating them, over and over again. That's campaigning! It's the same strategy we use in doorbelling. The idea is that anyone who doorbells for you mentions *your* name as many times as possible in two minutes."

My veteran doorbellers have this system down pat: The words, the drill, no conversation, no talking about issues, no mention of their own names. Every evening, six to eight volunteers come to my basement and pick up the 5 x 8 precinct maps I've picked for that particular evening. They pair up, each choose a side of the street, and begin. Most nights, Ken and I doorbell, too.

"Hi, I am a friend of Mary Ellen McCaffree, who is running for the state legislature," my doorbeller will say. "Here's something for you to read about Mary Ellen McCaffree. I hope you vote for Mary Ellen McCaffree for the Washington State legislature. If you have any specific questions I'll have Mary Ellen McCaffree call you..." or... "Mary Ellen McCaffree is right over there. I'll have her come over and talk to you."

And many times, that's exactly what I do: Cross the street, introduce myself, and ask what questions I can answer for them. Invariably, the first is, "Are you a Republican or a Democrat?"

"I'm a Republican."

Inquisitive voters will want to know my position on a particular issue: "What's your position now on special levies?"

"One of my major goals for the next legislative session is to find a permanent solution to funding Seattle's public schools... without the need for annual special levies."

"Can it really be done?"

I address frequent skepticism with a plain truth: "It will require comprehensive tax reform. I welcome your specific thoughts or suggestions."

I usually get their name and address to forward them further materials, and suggest voters talk to my opponents, too, so they can make an informed vote.

Personal campaigning is hard to beat. There is no better way for voters to learn about a candidate and what they stand for than to ask directly – in his or her office, in a coffee hour, at campaign meetings or a campaign event – at any venue that allows for direct conversation. Conversely, for the candidate, it's the best way to get to know the constituents you're asking to represent.

"HI MARY ELLEN! I THOUGHT YOU'D LIKE TO KNOW my mother just published a new book about the constitutional convention. I know you're a history buff."

"I am, Kitty. Thanks."

Kitty Prince, my lobbying partner from my days in the League of Women Voters, is the daughter of Catherine Drinker Bowen, a noted historian and scholar. This interim isn't the time for me to read for recreation, but I'm interested in this book, especially since it deals with our founding and founders.

"What's the title, Kitty? I'll look for it."

"*Miracle at Philadelphia*," she says. "Sort of like 'Miracle in Olympia' maybe – finally getting redistricting done."

IN THE MIDDLE OF CAMPAIGN SEASON, with my own seat to stump for and a flock of fledgling candidates to tend, I also continue my work on the two advisory councils. Our deadlines for the governor loom: October 1 for Higher Education, and the Tax Advisory report due on his desk December 10.

The idea of locating a new college near our state capitol gains momentum, and an Olympia landowner comes forward with a 900-acre waterfront parcel on Puget Sound, directly across from the capitol campus. The price is extremely reasonable. Our council discussions begin to tilt that way.

In the Tax Advisory Council, based on our studies, we're beginning to shape a brand new format for a state tax base — a groundbreaking rearrangement of our state tax structure that would give our revenue stream the flexibility to fluctuate with the economy. If we put it in place, we wouldn't have to keep adjusting (raising) tax rates with each new session of the legislature, or rely on special levies to help finance our schools. And this plan would distribute the tax burden much more equitably — putting less strain on those of lower income, one of the main goals assigned to our group. We continue to study and refine this promising proposal.

The governor telephones one afternoon: "Mary Ellen? Dan. How's it going with the Tax Advisory Council?"

When I describe the novel tax system we're exploring, he is thrilled.

"What a great idea! That really takes the pressure off. Anyone else doing this?"

No state we know of, I share. It's a brand new system as far as we're aware.

"I'll look forward to the December report," he says. "Thanks, Mary Ellen."

As the only elected Republican on the council, I feel a huge obligation to get this task right so that we can put it to work when... *if*... come January, I'm back in the House.

DOWN IN THE BASEMENT, my campaign headquarters has hit full stride. My children refer to this as "buzzing." A crew addresses thousands of envelopes by hand, while others stuff them and lay them out, staggered assembly-line style, their gummy flaps opened all in a row, awaiting a long swipe of wet cloth efficiently administered by one of my campaign veterans.

Not all my new volunteers know about my separate basement entrance, so my son David, now a lanky 16-year-old, answers the front door to strangers who often brush right past him and walk right on in.

"Where's the basement?" they'll ask as an afterthought.

My teenage son wordlessly points the way. Annoyed.

OUR TEAM IS SPREADING ITS ELECTION EFFORTS throughout the state.

"Mary Ellen? How about we carpool?" says Slade. "This time, bring Ken."

Ken prefers to drive. We agree to join five carloads of Republicans and independents both, converging one weekend on the Tri-Cities area, six hours east, across state. We spend the weekend doorbelling this boom region in the long-awaited new districts created by our redistricting.

Our rallying cry: *Leave not one stone unturned, nor one home un-doorbelled! We want a majority in the House!*

One day, early on in the fall election crush, a group of us spends the entire day preparing another round of absentee ballots to mail overseas.

Closer to home, Slade and I repeatedly doorbell the 21st, both for Bill Kiskaddon and Dale Hoggins, but we have to be sly. Supporting a second Republican against the declared right-winger here has drawn some bile.

Statewide, we are trying to run a positive, optimistic campaign. Our strategies pay off. In the primary election, most of our progressive Republican candidates make it through. Now for the general election push.

But first? An October report to the governor.

After extensive study, many interviews, and careful reflection upon the independent recommendation by the professionals from back east, our Higher Education Advisory Council recommends to the governor the following: That a new four-year college, with a novel curriculum centered on emerging social and environmental issues, be located near the City of Olympia, near the seat of state government. The governor will present this to the legislature come January.[19]

Now back to the race. My Democratic opponent in the general election is a part-time student at the University of Washington, a pleasant guy without much heart in the process. From his candidacy, I take it the Democrats have decided not to challenge me.

As election night nears, our basement hubbub swells. Around the state, all our candidates have the three McCaffree telephone numbers which make my basement communication central.

On election night, these telephones begin to bring us early election returns. Ken volunteers to keep a careful tally.

The early news is almost all good news for Republican candidates. As the night progresses and results pour in, I begin to sense something approaching glee. We're down to just two districts now — both of them in Spokane. We wait. And wait. But those phone calls don't arrive. What's going on? We call around and

Mary Ellen and Ken at work in the McCaffree family's U-district basement campaign headquarters. Mary Ellen's basement eventually became a major state campaign hub.

COLLECTION OF MARY ELLEN MCCAFFREE

finally track down our errant 'reporters' in a local tavern, celebrating their good news, too. We consider the wait well worth it.

By morning the final statewide count is confirmed. In the 1967 legislature, there will be 55 Republican representatives in the House and 44 Democrats. For the first time in years, Republicans have won the majority.

And when we convene in January, 35 of our 99 in the House will be freshmen – more than one-third! This new lifeblood – 28 Republican and 7 Democrat freshmen – gives us the largest number of new legislators since 1889, the year our state government began. Thanks to redistricting, our state has returned representation to the hands of all the people. We've come as close to one man, one vote as possible. We have a fresh start.

Hugh Bone, a professor of political science at the University of Washington, has watched our Republican revival with interest: "The extent of the Republican gains in 1966 cannot be credited to redistricting alone. Republicans concentrated on the House, sought new attractive candidates to run, conducted a campaign school for them and, in the aggregate, waged more vigorous campaigns than the Democrats." [20]

My efforts in the 21st District and elsewhere are recognized by Gummie, who tells the *Daily Olympian*, "Mary Ellen is the best organizer and effective political worker I have ever known." [21]

The final tally of state legislative races in this 1966 election closely resembles the predictions of Gorton and Greive, the primary architects of our compromise redistricting bill. Republicans won five of the six districts where the newly drawn boundaries were predicted to tilt Republican, and also won several of the swing seats, some by a squeaker. Also of note, we achieved our House majority with just fewer than 52% of the popular vote. From every angle, we earned this victory.

DOES THIS UNITE US? NOT NECESSARILY. Politicking doesn't end on election night. In November, after the election, positioning begins within our Republican caucus as we contemplate who among us should become our House Speaker. We caucus on the morning after the Apple Cup game, and in the annual home team flip-flop, this year's game and caucus is in Spokane – Pullman, more specifically – home of the Washington State Cougars.

Prior to this caucus meeting, the DEGOHTs met in Seattle and we agreed to try to elect Don Eldridge from Mount Vernon as Speaker of the House. We prefer seating someone from the west side of the state as Speaker for our new majority; eastern Washington Republicans have controlled our caucus too long. But we're also aware that Tom Copeland, from across the mountains east, has been working hard to collect Speaker votes of his own. Our party victories may have been widespread, but they haven't assured us unanimity. We head to Spokane.

After the Democrats' divisive disaster last session regarding redistricting, we are well aware of the problems that can plague even a majority. Therefore, we vow to avert any dissension before the legislative session begins. We meet after Saturday's Husky/Cougar football game, and when the confidential caucus ballots are counted Sunday morning at the Hill Top Motel, Don Eldridge emerges as our Speaker designate, Tom Copeland our Speaker Pro Tem. When the session begins in January, with our new majority vote in the House, these two men in these positions are virtually assured. And as the majority in the House of Representatives, we will set the House agenda for the 40th Legislative Session. I can't wait.

On this Sunday morning, before we disband as a caucus, we unanimously pledge to cooperate with Governor Evans to complete our Blueprint for Progress. At last, our state is set full sail in a whole new direction — to complete our journey toward progress and reform.

KEN HAS THE WHEEL AGAIN DURING OUR LONG DRIVE back home across the state. With us are Slade and Sally Gorton and Jonathan Whetzel, the new representative from Dan's old District 43. As we approach Snoqualmie Pass, a terrific snowstorm shrouds us in white, and a long line of traffic skids to a halt behind an accident. Our Impala slips to a standstill. As we wait, then inch along… then wait, and inch some more, our automobile is finally rear-ended in chain reaction to a more serious pile-up three cars back. No one is hurt.

The state patrol is duly impressed by the three state legislators in our car, but they don't exempt us from our citizen duty to stop in North Bend — like the rest of the fender bent travelers — to file a report with the police. Once we're on the road again, navigating the wintry interstate, Slade relentlessly back seat drives: "Keep moving, Ken, don't stop!"

Ken returns us safely to Seattle shortly after midnight.

When we pull onto 18th Avenue, I feel much as I did the moment my last legislative session came to a close — exhausted yet thrilled. This time, I have someone to share it with.

"It's been a good weekend," I say to my husband.

"I'd say it's been a good year," he replies.

"I feel like I contributed my share."

He chuckles and takes my hand.

"Yes love, you certainly did."

Republicans now hold both the state House and the governorship, and this gives our Blueprint for Progress a fighting chance. I have one more report to help assemble — from the Tax Advisory Council, due in mid-December — then my interim work comes to an end.

When the 40th Session of the Washington State Legislature convenes on January 9, I'll be there.

Washington State House of Representatives legislative chamber, including visitor galleries, electronic voting board and velvet-draped wings.

PHOTO BY JESSICA MCCAFFREE MANS

CHAPTER SEVEN

LEADERSHIP
TACKLING THE CHALLENGING AND COMPLEX

Serving as chairman of a major committee

requires a distinctive combination of leadership skills —

in-depth knowledge of a particular subject,

the ability to referee negotiations and compromise, and to keep the

process moving forward to accomplish legislative goals.

EN ROUTE TO OUR CAPITOL CITY I DO MY BEST to maintain an outward calm, though in actuality, excitement is bubbling within me. Just after noonday, I sidle my little Ford to the curb at my rental home, quickly unpack a few items, then head off to work. It is Sunday, January 8, 1967 — the day before it all begins. Already this 40th Session feels different.

My third term will definitely not be more of the same. For the first time I will serve in the majority. For the first time I will chair a committee — and a major one at that. I will have my own office and part-time secretary — we all will this 40th Session, thanks to a last-minute measure we passed in the 39th. We decided state legislators should have better support for the volume of critical work we shoulder.

I park outside the Public Health Building, find room 403 and take a moment to appreciate all this office space that now is mine. I put away a few files, pull out a family photo, and consult my wristwatch as I time my walk to the legislative building. My new commute? Desk to desk in five minutes, says my Timex.

My desk assignment on the floor this year is another row forward and nearer center aisle, evidence of my escalating seniority. Happy with my placement, I now wend my way down the narrow marbled stairway at the back of the chamber to the dining room, where I dish myself a big bowl of ice cream — strawberry — and slowly spoon meditative bites of pink, my mind adrift. A clatter of footfall echoing broadly in the stairwell quickly returns me to the here and now. The duo who emerge — Slade and Joel.

"Greetings to you both!" I wave with my spoon, delighted.

Slade heads straight for the ice cream counter and returns with a trio of flavors — three enormous orbs heaped in his bowl, which is quintessential Slade. Joel ventures to the fridge for a heartier snack: Two slices of rye he piles high with pickles and cold cuts. He swaps a few words with us not bothering to take a seat, and then with a trademark maneuver of his own — a fake of a phone call, invisible receiver to ear — he informs us: "Senate calling," and departs for his new home across the foyer and beyond the chandelier. Senator Pritchard. The title will take some getting used to.

"Ready, Mary Ellen?" Slade asks.

"Excited. But ready? I'm not sure."

More footsteps.

Tom Copeland arrives and boldly declares: "We're ready to roll!"

Before I take another spoonful of pink, I ask our Speaker Pro Tem, "Are we?" Tom's spirits drop like a hurt little kid.

I quickly make amends: "You've done a terrific job getting us organized." I mean it. "But I'm not sure we all can claim we're ready to roll, Tom. Get your ice cream, come grab a seat and tell me how to get my committee organized."

Slade sputters, chokes and whispers: "Are you kidding me, Mary Ellen? You know more about organizing than…"

"Tom knows that," I smile. "Campaign School. But I can always use hints."

The next set of footsteps delivers two hungry House Democrats.

"Buster! John!" I wave a melting spoonful. "Welcome to the inner sanctum."

'Buster' Brouillet is the Democrats' caucus chair this session and John Rosellini a freshman. They dish up their ice cream and join us and some playful jousting begins. These Democrat colleagues remind us that we Republicans haven't been in power for ages here in the House. It's been fourteen years — 1953 is the last time we had a majority. And in the two entire decades prior to that, we had House control only one other year, in '47. For more than three decades, then ever since 1933, other than those two aberrant sessions, our state's House of Representatives has been Democrat-controlled.

"However," says Slade, "this state's natural state is Republican. For its first four decades, for its first 22 sessions straight, we..."

"Except the Populist year," interrupts Buster, a history buff. "Anyway, Slade, this session we plan to just sit back and enjoy ourselves on our side of the aisle and finally let you Republicans do all the work for a change."

"Hear that, Mary Ellen?" Slade says. "We've been lazing around enjoying ourselves these past four years."

Both of us know better. Redistricting was no slouch job. The congenial chatting continues but I excuse myself, aware of my duties ahead.

"See you gentlemen in the morning."

I step out into Washington's late afternoon dusk. Winter days are short here. The steady breeze off the Puget Sound is whipping towards something more blustery, and I pull my coat tight at my neck for the walk to my car.

A sharp, playful whistle precedes a shout: "Mary Ellen, wait up!"

The whistler swiftly beelines toward me.

"Hi, Gummie," I greet.

"Nice holiday with your family, Mary Ellen? Ready for the session? Got a plan for eliminating those pesky ol' school levies?"

I reply to Gummie's question number three.

"Not an easy one." I shiver, hunched against the cold. "We still can't solve school funding until we solve some other issues first, and priority number one is revising the state tax structure."

"That all?" he jokes, followed by another whistle — the 'sounds tough' sort. "You're in charge, I suppose."

"Yes."

He walks me to my Ford — a loaner for the session.

"See you tomorrow," he says as he closes my door, thumps the hood and waves me off.

Gummie has been infected with that particularly virulent strain of political bug that will keep him swimming amid these capitol circles for years. He was a Weyerhaeuser lobbyist before he became chairman of our state party.

LOBBYIST

Any person who conducts activities to influence legislators and public officials. A lobbyist can be paid, professional or volunteer, and may represent more than one issue, client or cause.

I'm less a political creature than he, but I do have a mission — that elusive reliable source of funding for our children's schools, via tax reform. Redistricting first, tax base second, then some day soon, I can finally say 'Mission Accomplished' — I hope. By the time I turn the key in the ignition, my mind is racing backwards down my long road in search of... something, anything... to fix our state's incredibly ill funded schools. I'm a decade into this quest. Ken and I raised our first concerns ten years ago. It's hard to believe this is taking so long to achieve. Public school funding is critical, so why can't we find a solution we can all agree on? Now? It remains a mystery.

No one back home is finding the annual levy campaigns any easier — neither my constituents (parents and teachers alike), nor their counterparts in communities throughout the state. And property owners are tired of shouldering the costs: School levies are beginning to fail.

I'm trying. I know what it will take to lay the best financial foundation for our schools, and that is a better-built revenue base in this state. But many colleagues remain unconvinced. *More money for schools? Why? They already receive the bulk of the budget in this state.* I've heard their repeated arguments, and I mentally rebut each one as I shift the Ford into gear for my short drive home.

MONDAY, JANUARY 9 ARRIVES, frigid but brilliant with the next morning sun. Shortly before noon our Democrat members settle into their seats on the floor of the House. Then the door to our Republican caucus room swings wide, and as we exit, we fail to suppress our broad smiles. What the numbers on election night rendered unto our party is about to become palpably real. We will choose our Speaker, we will chair our committees, and we will set the agenda for this 40th Session. We're the leaders of this House.

Just before I enter the floor, Don Eldridge taps my shoulder.

"Will you be willing to second my nomination, Mary Ellen?"

"It will be my privilege, your Honor."

Don Eldridge remains at the back of the chamber, takes a spare seat to await his election, and I continue on to my seat and my seatmate, Marjorie Lynch.

"Welcome back, Marjorie. How go things in Yakima?"

"Brilliant!" she says, her clipped British accent undiminished. "Prepared to make history, Mary Ellen?"

I assure her I am. For the first time in our state's legislative history, two women will chair major committees in a single session: Marjorie as head of the House Committee on Higher Education, and me at the helm of our Committee on Revenue and Taxation.

"Busy interim," she remarks.

"I'll say."

Marjorie has no idea! While she and I both sat on the interim Higher Education Advisory Council, that was only a fraction of my interim House work.

Ken's support has been ever crucial, and I look to the visitors' gallery to locate him and Mary, both of whom made the trip from Seattle this morning to attend yet another opening ceremony.

By now, all our members are seated. *Bang!* The 40th Session of the Washington State House of Representatives is formally gaveled to order. Acting Chief Clerk Sid Snyder leads us through the formalities. After the opening prayer and flags and roll call, our House elections are certified and we're duly sworn in – nothing amiss. No leadership coup, no 48-hour blitz. For once, a normal opening day. Our next order of business: Nominations for Speaker of the House.

The Acting Chief Clerk recognizes Stu Bledsoe, an Eastern Washington rancher who drawls, "I now take pride in placing before you in nomination as Speaker of the House for the 40th Session of the Washington State Legislature, the Honorable Don Eldridge."

The clerk then recognizes Mr. Newman Clark who seconds the nomination. Then he calls on me. Freshman jitters long gone, I firmly clasp my hand held microphone and make my first remarks on the floor for this 40th Session:

"Mr. Chief Clerk, Justice Hill, ladies and gentlemen of the House of Representatives, I also rise to second the nomination of Representative Don Eldridge for Speaker of the House. It is indeed an honor for me to do this…"

When we speak on the floor, we can look straight at the Speaker or down at our desks or survey the chamber. We can gesticulate or not. I prefer a straightforward delivery.

"…Representative Eldridge has served the people of this state of Washington most capably and expertly for many years in this House of Representatives. He has been a dedicated legislator with integrity and honesty. He is a man with a keen sense of responsibility and obligation, with fairness to all. He will give his best for a successful session of this legislature and for the welfare of the people of the state of Washington. I believe that Representative Don Eldridge is the best qualified to serve as Speaker of the House for the 40th Session of the Legislature. I would urge that you support him for this position." [1]

I'VE COME A LONG WAY IN FOUR YEARS, with an assurance on the floor born of practice. And I seem to have earned respect within this political body – from both sides of the aisle.

The Acting Chief Clerk now recognizes Representative Sawyer, who nominates John O'Brien for Speaker. Again.

After two seconding speeches for Mr. O'Brien, Mr. Gorton (Slade, our majority floor leader) moves that the nominations be closed.

The clerk calls the roll for the election of the Speaker of the House. We vote straight down party lines: Don Eldridge 55, John O'Brien 43, and one absent and not voting – a Democrat colleague scheduled to arrive tomorrow.

Representatives Berentson, Goldsworthy and Garrett escort Mr. Eldridge from his spare seat in the back of the House to the front. The Honorable Matthew Hill, justice of the State Supreme Court, administers the oath of office, after which our new Speaker takes the rostrum: "I may be Speaker of the House here," says Don Eldridge, "but back home I am considered by my family as chairman of the entertainment committee. This is the highest honor and also the greatest responsibility that has ever come to me."

He recounts the pre-session work we did as a caucus, describes the "new look" of our facilities, our new procedures for processing bills, and preemptively thanks John O'Brien for his cooperation as minority leader in getting us off to a speedy start. Smart move.

"In conclusion," says Speaker Eldridge, "with your help we can meet and solve the tremendous problems facing us during this 40th Session of the Washington State Legislature. Thank You."

Our House is swiftly organized and ready to proceed with legislative business. With little ado, we recess for lunch with plans to reconvene at 3:45 p.m.

"Excuse me, Mrs. McCaffree?" A reporter approaches in the velvet-draped wings. "I'm Bobbi McCallum from the *Seattle Post-Intelligencer*. May I talk to you?"

"Certainly." I've heard majority status brings added attention from the press.

"I'm planning to interview all the women of the House, you see…" Apparently, so does minority gender. I'll be Bobbi McCallum's first interview for her story. We converse on a nearby bench and I explain my responsibilities this term, including my major chairmanship of the Committee on Revenue and Taxation.

"Oh," she says. "I… I wasn't expecting so much, Mrs. McCaffree. I mean, I just want to know what it's like being a woman in office. Can we hold the tax talk for another time?"

My silent response is, *Being in office is being in office, regardless of gender. Our tax structure is far more critical.* What I say aloud is, "Yes, Bobbi, of course."

"Thank you, Mrs. McCaffree," she says. "Look for my story in another week or so."

She flags down the next representative wearing a skirt.

Marjorie and I compare notes over lunch downstairs in the House dining room. The reporter wasn't eager to discuss Marjorie's committee chairmanship either, despite the fact that her Higher Education Committee has charge of two enormous Blueprint issues — the creation of a brand new statewide system of community colleges, and contemplation of our proposal for a new four-year college. Whether our groundbreaking roles will feature in Bobbi McCallum's story remains to be seen.

The Speaker approaches: "Excuse me, Mary Ellen, a word with you?"

"Yes, Mr. Speaker."

The word is this: The House is unexpectedly short a docket clerk.

"Do you think your daughter Mary would be interested?" he asks. "Slade suggested her. She's a college student now, isn't she?"

"Yes, at the University. She's here today. I can ask her."

Ken and Mary and I converse in the foyer before the session resumes, and Mary agrees. We'll arrange to get her things to Olympia when Ken returns to attend the ball.

When the House re-assembles at 3:45 p.m., a trio of Senators approaches the bar of the chamber — two of them former House colleagues. Senators Joel Pritchard, Wes Uhlman and Frances Haddon Morgan let us know the

DOCKET

The official written record of the daily status of each bill introduced.

Senate is also organized and ready to proceed with business. This opening day continues to unfold calmly in comparison to my previous two: The coup, the blitz. Slade assures me the pace today is more the norm.

The Mayor of Olympia extends the annual invitation to the Legislative Ball at the Tyee Motel to take place, as always, on Wednesday night, and the sergeant at arms gives us each a guest card to place on our windshields for parking and a guest pass for admission.

After this, we process a handful of joint resolutions, three of which I present on the floor, being a more senior member this year. Then Speaker Eldridge announces our new committees, and this step is remarkable, because he announces not only the names of the committees themselves, but every committee member and chairman — all of them pre-agreed by both parties — in astonishing contrast to my freshman term when our coalition struggled the entire first week just to set up committees, then wrestled another week more with the regular Democrats over membership and chairmen.

After the Speaker reads this entire list of committees and members, he reads two certificates which really make me smile: Both party caucus chairmen have certified not only the sixteen committees themselves, but also each individual committee chairman and member. No dickering. No time wasted. I'm proud of this feat on the afternoon of day one.

The role of majority is new to nearly all of us in our caucus, yet we're determined to lead, and to lead our House well. We spent the last stretch of the interim whittling the number of standing committees to just sixteen. With fewer committees on which to serve, we legislators will not be spread so inordinately thin within the pressured clock of a 60-day legislative session. And because I had worked so closely with all our candidates and their campaigns, and hence knew our newest members better than most, I agreed to one final task this past interim: Committee assignments — matching representatives to committees. I compiled a thorough list.

Between November's election victory and today — for two full months — our caucus has devoted long hours to laying sound groundwork for this session we've begun, which is what the incoming majority will normally do: Plan ahead. In the coup year we didn't have that luxury. Such advanced preparation this year, however, has been no small feat for us, with 27 freshmen requiring legislative tutelage by our 28 returnees.

Temporary Rules have already been hammered out and are now accepted. Some Democrats complained they were gagged in this process. In actuality, they were not. But being a minority is new to them and they're not used to it. They've lost control of this chamber. They've lost their majority vote and voice. House Democrats are mourning their loss of status.

GAGGED

Allegation by a minority that its speech or actions have been limited or prohibited by the majority.

PRE-FILED BILL

A written bill given to the Chief Clerk of a legislative body prior to the convening of a legislative session.

On this opening day, with our committees in place and some legislation pre-filed during the pre-session stretch, we are truly off at a sprint. We assign the 113 pre-filed bills to our new committees, wrap up tidily, and adjourn until tomorrow at 10 a.m.

"Hi Mom! Wow, is this a step up!"

After her tutoring session with the Speaker and Chief Clerk to review her duties as docket clerk, Mary pops in to inspect my new office, a step up indeed, and a welcomed Blueprint reform. We agreed at the end of last session to fund modest office space for each legislator somewhere within the capitol grounds.

We're a bit spread out, and the lobbyists are grumbling loudly. We no longer spend our 'down' time on the floor or in the wings, where the lobbyists hovered and frequently bent our ears — a captive bunch we were then. Now the capitol lobbying corps, the 'Third House' they're commonly called, is forced to seek us out individually — 99 House members and 49 Senators, scattered in offices throughout the capitol campus. I don't think it will hurt our lobbyists any to make specific trips to speak with specific members on specific issues.

"Come on in, honey." I continue to unpack my Rolodex and reports. "I sure was proud to see you up there today."

Today Mary just observed, but my daughter will fill the docket job admirably. She's a hard worker... who also happens to possess a broad capacity for fun.

"Wasn't that camera man cute, Mom?"

"Can't say I noticed, Mary."

"You didn't see him? From KIRO-TV? Well I did."

I change the subject.

AT 8 A.M. ON THE SECOND DAY, I welcome the twenty members of my Committee on Revenue and Taxation to this second largest committee room of the House. I'd arrived an hour beforehand to rearrange the four large rectangular tables into a perimeter square around a central opening – the closest I could manage in order to approximate a roundtable.

"The House Committee on Revenue and Taxation is now called to order." I rap my gavel. "Thank you all for being punctual."

Lining the room are additional chairs for onlookers – the public, the lobbyists, the press – and this morning I note quite a few of these are filled.

"As chairman I would like to welcome you to this most important committee, and to introduce my vice-chairman, Fran Holman. Fran is new to the legislature this year, but not a newcomer to law or to lawmaking. As most of you know, Mr. Holman represents the 1st District in King County."

There are varying breeds of legislative freshmen; Fran Holman would never be labeled green. He holds degrees from Stanford, Oxford and Harvard, is a current mayor, and serves on his local school board as well as the Metro Council in Seattle.

In addition to Fran and me, my committee of twenty includes ten more Republicans (Slade among them) and eight Democrats, including former coalition members Bill Day and Margaret Hurley, plus Gary Grant, last session's heavy-handed chairman of our House redistricting committee, along with the longtime Democrat activist Ed Heavey from a district near me in Seattle. Eight of our twenty are freshmen, five are attorneys, two are women.

"We have a monumental task before us this session, beginning with the bills pre-filed since November 20. I have listed these here. Please take a look. We always welcome more sponsors. I have also designated areas of concentration on this sheet here. You may choose your assignments."

I came ready. I hand out the lists and pass around sponsor sign-up sheets.

"No one should lack for work."

The members of this committee represent all reaches of our state, as well as various occupations and enterprises. We're guaranteed to hear differing viewpoints on the tax and revenue issues at hand, which is ideal – any solution we reach as a committee will have a broad basis and some solid elements of compromise, and that in turn spells a better chance for the acceptance of our measures by the House as a whole.

As chairman my duties include sorting through the bills assigned to this committee, assigning them priority, determining which we will consider in depth, which are redundant, which are less crucial, which make no sense to address at all. I do have the option to outright ignore some. If no one 'chooses' to take on a certain bill, I must match it up with a member of my committee, or sponsor it myself. I must also find sponsors for measures proposed by the governor – his executive request bills. And I must track each piece of this committee's legislation as it travels through the lengthy legislative process. *Which are in committee? Which in Rules? Which are bound for the floor of the Senate or the House? Which have been amended, and how?* I must actively promote those that need a boost. I must make certain the most urgent measures remain alive.

Organizationally, I'm in charge. I single-handedly set our committee's agenda, convene the meetings and run them. If any measures warrant a public hearing, I'll set that up, too.

I am also the committee's conduit to the media, to lobbyists, to fellow legislators (each with their distinctive district concerns), to our leadership in the House and Senate, to the governor and his aides, and to the people of the state – our public. This is an enormous step up from simply interacting with my own constituency. All of us chairing committees this term will experience this same broadened interactive scope – we've become more than simply one district's representative.

This session, I must also champion tax reform.

Being a woman in the House doesn't faze me, nor does chairing this committee. My comfort with leadership and ease following formal rules (Reed's Parliamentary Rules here, versus Robert's, which I've used elsewhere) were both formed within the League of Women Voters.

However, being the primary legislative leader for the governor's platform on tax reform is decidedly a bigger challenge.

On my way to the House chamber, I pass Jim Dolliver outside the governor's office, where inside the governor is reviewing his State of the State address – the first he'll deliver to a legislature half friendly to his Blueprint for Progress now that we've attained a House majority. I missed the rehearsal, due to my committee.

"We're counting on you to lead tax reform, you know," Dolliver reminds me. "We haven't found a suitable counterpart in the Senate. Are you ready?"

"Ready as I can be. I know the Tax Advisory Council recommendations."

"Yes," he chuckles. "You do."

In the afternoon of day three, we gather in Joint Session for the governor's

State of the State address during which he'll lay out his agenda for the coming two years.

Our DEGOHT Blueprint had a tough battle last summer at the statewide Republican gathering, when our party's most conservative arm struck two key points from our platform — our civil rights stand for equal employment and fair housing, and our push for statewide strengthening of the arts. Party backing or no, however, the governor will delete neither of these from his agenda. He is determined to move our state forward, as are all of us DEGOHTs.

"…My fellow Washingtonians: With a faith in the traditions of this House and with the traditional homily that life, indeed, begins at 40, I welcome you — the 40th Session of the Washington State Legislature — to the renewed and continuing task of government as the freely elected representatives of a free and responsible people."

Interesting words — perhaps urging us to think and vote freely, regardless of party affiliation. Clever.

The governor cites the great strides we've made as a state during the first two years of his tenure: Thriving employment, climbing per capita income, healthy state revenues that built a handsome budgetary surplus. We are the fastest growing state in all of America.

"From these figures," he says, "I wish it were now possible to declare that progress has been fully achieved; that we could now view the accomplishments of our government with satisfaction."

But the governor, and those of us who understand how government works, know better than to bask in one bright set of statistics during one unusually bright year.

"Instead," he says, "we have before us an agenda of work unequalled in the history of this state legislature. For in creating prosperity, we have also created new problems."

He asks us to confront what he calls the most compelling questions of our time:

"Can we have our growth and live with it too?

"Can we become urbanized and remain civilized at the same time?

"Can we achieve continuing economic growth without relentlessly exploiting our resources of natural beauty?

"Can we devise an education system which provides both equal opportunity and unlimited individual attainment?

"Can we preserve an effective structure of local government and at the same time recognize the urgency of regional and metropolitan need?"

Substantive questions, all.

"And can we both reorganize and refinance the foundations of state government in a manner which preserves the best of past principle yet prepares us for the changing tasks of the future?"

Here he references tax reform. This is my (no small) task.

As the governor continues, Senator Martin Durkan, chairman of the Senate Ways and Means Committee (who admits to eyes on the governor's seat), listens intently and gnaws the stem of his pipe. John O'Brien, from his desk front and center, also studies his former House adversary. Every so often O'Brien fervently scribbles on his yellow pad, either nodding agreement or irascibly shaking his head.

Our governor urges us to consider the whole of the legislative program — *his* program, he means — as well as each individual part. Yes, he has pet issues as do many of us here, but his overarching concern is that our government function superbly, both now and into the future. His staff is at work full time, he tells us, crafting bills to propel his visionary agenda.

"During the next few days," he says, "we will submit for your consideration in excess of sixty executive requests."

Sixty! Both sides of the aisle react. The governor lists five central issues underlying his pending requests:

- The pressures and conflict inherent in urban growth

- The need to protect our environment and set aside open space

- The need to reorganize state government to address our modern needs

- Acknowledgment of growing transportation demands…

- And "Fifth and finally, and perhaps most important, an intelligent recognition of human needs — ranging from welfare programs and our institutions of care to the requirements of vocational rehabilitation, and from the primary resource of education to the fundamental principle of human rights."

I am proud to be so closely aligned with this leader. As the governor describes in dizzying detail those legislative elements he imagines within each arena, I realize how actively I've been involved in conceiving this wide, articulate vision — our collective Blueprint for Progress, our butcher paper list on the campaign office wall.

EXECUTIVE REQUEST BILL

A bill introduced by a legislator at the request of the governor.

When the governor tells us these myriad goals are obtainable, I agree. It will simply take hard work. And teamwork. And that is exactly what I am here for.

"The constitution of this state," he says,

"makes us not rivals for power, but partners in the unfolding tasks of government."

He pauses to look at us all: At the partners, the team — "not rivals for power," he has expressed so wishfully.

"I ask no miracles…" This comment elicits several coughs from the press corps. "…only common dedication to the future of Washington, and a common commitment to its great needs.

"To accomplish the things that must be done for the future will require vision as well as maturity, courage as well as conviction, leadership as well as understanding. I have every confidence that the 40th Legislature possesses these qualities." [2]

He sends us off with marching orders: Tend to the business of the people.

"LOOK, LOVE," SAYS KEN AS HE DEMONSTRATES deft expertise with the flouncy tie attached to the I. Magnin shirt — the one that caused him such considerable exasperation two years back. With a quick flip and flourish, he is finished and proudly adds the hatpin, ready for another formal legislative ball.

"Impressive," I acknowledge. "Shall we?"

We leave behind us on the kitchen table the evening *Daily Olympian*. The big news in this capitol town — the banner headline of this local paper — is the speech the governor delivered this afternoon. Before departing tonight, we had read reporter Mike Layton's story that while the governor asked for no miracles, he "nevertheless seemed to be seeking some miraculous cures for the state's ailments from a Legislature that has already indicated that politics as usual will take up a lot of its time." [3]

Politics as usual. That phrase never has thrilled me. But it is true, partisan positioning threatens to divert our focus — from what we aim to accomplish this session, to a political scramble for who will get the credit. The governor's term is set to expire and a new gubernatorial election in the coming interim. That means jockeying for state leadership is already in play, and it will undoubtedly affect our session. This jockeying is ubiquitous to the process, but we're elected to serve the public, and public service should take precedence over our political careers.

Perhaps it is good that we traditionally dine and dance together each session on the heels of the governor's State of the State address: Democrats and Republicans tossed together in formal attire forces a civilized prelude to our collaborative state chores.

At the ball, Ken and I study the mounds of fresh Olympia oysters and enormous piles of cracked Dungeness crab over ice — local staples, and succulent reminders of the ample bounties of this state that belongs to us all, the state we must tend as elected leaders.

Tonight our first lady's mother, 'Grandmother' Bell, must pass on the oysters and crab. She is back in the governor's mansion babysitting the first family's sons — three of them now. The youngest Evans boy was born this past interim.

The next morning, while I make coffee, Ken reads aloud from the *Seattle Post-Intelligencer,* or as Seattleites call our morning paper, the *P-I.*

"Front page headline's pretty good, love," he says. "*Evans' Blueprint for State Applauded by Both Sides.* Let's see what Shelby Scates has to say. *Gov. Dan Evans' 'long and demanding' legislative agenda, spelled out Wednesday in his first major address to the 40th Session, faces a bright future in the House, some major question marks in the Senate.*" [4]

Ken keeps reading while I quickly eat breakfast and gather my files.

"And here's Bob Greive," Ken reads from further down on the page: "'*Finally,' said Senate majority leader R.R. Greive, 'he has revealed his Blueprint for Progress. We were going to do these things anyway.*'"

I can just imagine Bob Greive's droll delivery; the Senate majority leader seems ready to arm-wrestle us for credit for any success. All the power to him, I say, if he actually collaborates. He came round to compromise last term. I suppose he can do it again. From what Ken reads, Democrats in the House are carving a role for themselves as well: "'*It's a very liberal program,' said Representative Alan Thompson. 'He's going to need our help to pass it.*'"

Well," Ken says, "Dan's not averse to asking for help now, is he? He's already proven he'll work with just about anyone on the Blueprint."

"And I have proven I'm willing to work, period."

"Yes, dear, to my consternation and delight."

"I'm off to the governor's office."

"Case in point, love," he says.

"Mary?" I holler down the hall to the bathroom. "I'm leaving now, honey. See you in the House."

"Bye, Mom!"

I kiss my husband — he'll return to Seattle today — and add: "Tell David I miss him."

I leave father and daughter to say their good-byes and rush off to work.

WHEN I ARRIVE AT THE GOVERNOR'S OFFICE, Dan is adding the finishing touches to his budget address. Again, Jim Dolliver greets me.

"Thanks for coming, Mary Ellen. We need something from you… for Friday."

"What's that?"

"The governor's budget…" He nods toward Dan, hard at work on his speech. "We've got to balance it. We'll need a revenue measure in the works right away. Ray Haman and I have done the math with the governor, and here's our draft bill. It's a sales tax rate increase. Look it over. Let us know what you think. We need to finish it up so you can add it to the hopper on Friday. Feel free to add as many co-sponsors as you like."

It's a joke. No one is ever eager to sponsor a tax hike.

"Easier said than done," I note as I take the draft and proceed to the floor of the House.

Our busy morning session ends with a dispute over Engrossed Senate Bill 1, the Senate's measure to increase the salaries of state employees. Representative Grant — Gary Grant — moves that our House Appropriations Committee "be relieved of the bill," a move that would effectively bypass the bill's review by our Republican-controlled committee and automatically place it on second reading for amendments from the floor.

Both political parties in both houses support this salary increase for state employees. That is not in dispute. What *is* in dispute is the amount and the methodology — and even more significant, *Who will get credit for writing it?* Our legislative power struggles formally begin. House leadership doesn't want this important measure to bypass the committee process, where it can be duly heard, discussed and refined. Besides — and not insignificantly — the governor plans to propose a similar pay increase in his budget address today, under different terms. So we are not interested in Grant's motion to consider this Senate bill here and now on the floor, in lieu of committee review, and as a majority we have the votes to have it our way. We vote, reject Grant's motion, and send ESB 1 to the Appropriations Committee for review. Then we recess until 1:20 p.m.

When we reconvene, we gather once more in Joint Session for a second major address from our governor: The traditional budget address, traditionally delivered on the first Thursday of a session, Day Four.

The governor deems our robust economy a double-edged sword: Yes, we've seen our revenue jump as the fastest growing state in the nation, but with this growth came a burgeoning population and growing demands for state services. We can't assume a surplus will continue beyond this year, he warns.

"This budget satisfies two critical requirements," he tells us: Resources to catch up with present demands, and also enough to address future challenges posed by growth. "It faces our responsibilities squarely — both present and future — and chooses the demanding road instead of the convenient one."

Demanding in dollars, yes. His range of proposals is staggering, but all are derived from our Blueprint and refined by research.

"The budget I have outlined in this message totals nearly $3 billion… This is an increase of 36.7 percent over the present biennium," he acknowledges. "Some may call this increase ambitious — and indeed it is. It must be, if our state government is to meet the serious responsibilities created by our dynamic economy and the legitimate needs of our people."

Current and recurring expenses exceed our expected revenue, he says. We must bridge this gap with revenue that is "assured and continuing" — exactly the type of revenue I have sought so long for our schools. Yes, he acknowledges, today we have an $80 million budget surplus, but no, he doesn't recommend we use it to make up the budget shortfall. For that he proposes a sales tax increase — from 4.2 to 4.5 percent: The bill Dolliver handed me this morning.

"This is not a recommendation I relish," the governor admits. "It is, however, the logical answer to balancing the state's budget for the next two years. The appropriate long-range answer lies in comprehensive tax reform, rather than repeated increases in the sales tax."

This is my homework — my House work, rather: To reform our state's tax structure, to stabilize revenue.

The governor dangles before us the tempting suggestion that we could balance his budget without a tax increase by "two deceptively simple methods" — spend our surplus, which he has already dismissed, or cut the requests. He favors neither, and explains.

To spend the surplus to balance this budget would be totally irresponsible. Why set a spending precedent based on a one-time income spike? A portion of the surplus would be better spent on one-time capital outlays, he suggests — for institutions, higher education, parks and recreation, our many overcrowded, inadequate facilities — and then we should save the rest for a rainy day.

He also dashes the prospect of cutting back. More than 90 percent of our state budget goes to schools, to our cities and to the many services related to institutions, all of which logically cost more as our population grows. These spending increases are all justifiable, he says — minimum levels of services we're obligated to fund. Leaving them in is a matter of fiscal integrity.

"The budget and revenue program I have proposed to you is not based on expediency. Its major guideline is a demand for excellence..." [5]

After the applause, and after the governor leaves, our majority leader Slade Gorton moves that our Joint Session be dissolved.

As I watch Joel Pritchard exit with the rest of the Senate, it occurs to me that the trio who first encouraged me to run for office has made good on their intention to work toward progress in this state: One is now our governor, one the majority leader of our House, and one serving in the Senate. And then there's me, both saddled and challenged with tax reform. We are separated, now, but our aim is the same and we're all still a team.

WHEN I ARRIVE HOME AT DINNERTIME, I turn on the stove, tie on an apron, open the fridge and begin to assemble dinner for Mary and me. Ken has left me a note: *I made it into your story.* I hadn't had time this morning to read the paper before I left. Bobbi McCallum's article about women in the legislature ran in today's *P-I* with the headline "Kitchen Kicked for Caucus." [6]

"Kicked the kitchen?!" I laugh as I chop vegetables for a soup. "Says who?"

Ken has underlined one sentence: *Kenneth McCaffree even takes over his representative's Sunday school classes during her biennial trips to Olympia.*

I telephone my husband: "I didn't tell her that."

"I did," he replies.

Bobbi McCallum did mention that Marjorie and I chair major committees.

I wake the next morning to a new edition of the *P-I* on my doorstep, pour a cup of coffee and sit down to read. Page one features a photograph of the 6-year-old Danny Evans, the governor's eldest, dribbling a basketball on the shiny wood ballroom floor of the governor's mansion, right beneath a dazzling chandelier. The caption reads: "*When company comes, the 'court' is off limits for young Danny.*" The major headline alongside the cute photo is considerably less endearing: "Democrats Stiff-Arm Evans' Budget."

Democrats gladly went on record after the governor's address.

"We intend to determine the needs," Senator Durkan told the reporter, using the royal 'we'. "Where there is a need, we will support the governor's program."

Durkan, chairman of Senate Ways and Means, gave no sign of rubber-stamping the governor's budget — he wants to keep positive press away from Dan Evans, because he wants Dan's seat and mansion in the next election.

Several Democrats ask of the surplus: *Why not put it straight into this year's budget?* Maggie Hurley, never shy, sneers at the goals of her former coalition teammate: " He appears to be one of the greatest spenders of all time. And we used to think he was a conservative!"

Others oppose the proposed sales tax increase: "He raises it to 4.5 percent now, what about next session — 5 percent?"

This is a fair question. It is also exactly the point. Our DEGOHT drive for tax reform aims for a state tax structure that won't require us to raise this tax rate every legislative session. We specifically addressed this ridiculous cycle in our Tax Advisory Council study.

Senate majority leader Bob Greive makes a political concession in the same article: "If more money is needed, I'd prefer getting it from sources other than the sales tax. But face it, the sales tax is the easiest one to pass." [7]

I fold the newspaper, take one last sip of coffee, and head to the legislative building for Day 5. It's Friday, the deadline for introducing revenue bills. Just before the session begins, Slade stops at my desk on the floor.

"You'll need to do it today," he says, meaning introducing the governor's bill to increase the tax rate to cover the budget.

"I got it from Dolliver, yesterday," I assure him. "It's ready to go, but I haven't had luck getting anyone else to help sponsor it."

"No doubt," Slade acknowledges.

Though he sits on my committee, he too has declined.

"Just sponsor it for now and get it in the hopper," he says. "We can work on adding sponsors as we go along."

Sponsoring a tax increase is not popular with my colleagues, and never will be. Writing tax legislation is always a tricky business, especially if you want to be reelected. Voters continually look to us to provide more government services, but seem eternally unwilling to pay for these out of their tax bills. In political campaigns, an incumbent's challengers and opponents often exploit this irony: They use the support of any tax increase as a 'negative' to defeat an incumbent, even if the increase has funded a popular public improvement.

SPONSOR

A legislator who places his or her name on a bill, usually prior to it being read into the record.

But I am chairman of our Revenue and Taxation Committee, and it is therefore my duty to support the governor's budget. So today, under the Sixth Order of Business, my name is read aloud as the sole sponsor of a bill "relating to revenue and taxation ... and declaring an emergency." It would raise the sales tax from 4.2 to 4.5 percent, exactly as the governor described in yesterday's address. The bill is assigned Number 205 and referred to my committee.

By midday, during a caucus meeting before the afternoon session, our caucus publicity team hands out sample news copy — pre-written items we can send back home to our constituents or our hometown papers. I quickly scan the handy tool. Not this week, I decide. *No time!* The governor's budget calls for millions of dollars in additional revenue, and he is counting on my committee and on me to find it. We disband our caucus with ten minutes to spare before the afternoon gavel slams us to order.

"Mrs. McCaffree?" I recognize Betty Hopper of the Associated Press. "May I have a moment with you?" she asks, pen and notepad in hand.

I tell her I have ten minutes. We find a quiet pair of chairs in the wings, and she begins: "Slade Gorton says you're one of the most valuable members both inside and outside the legislature."

I shrug at his claim as exaggerated and explain: "What I do, Betty, is leg work — I do what needs to be done."

She doesn't ask for details, so I don't disclose to her the long hours I've devoted — to redistricting, to the campaigns, to my interim committee and council work, and now to spearheading tax reform. Everybody should contribute to community, I believe. I tell Betty I'm just doing my part.

"Tell me again about your start," she says, "how it was you got involved in politics."

I recount my path, and add a realization: This is a terrific job for women.

"Women have the time and the energy to devote to politics," I tell her. "So if you have a strong belief, a strong cause, you'd better find a way to be in a position to work for it."

We talk about the effect of our redistricted state, about how the Republicans recruited and trained specific candidates to run for specific districts, and then we discuss the fact that so many of these new candidates actually won in November, giving the Republican Party its rare majority in the House.

"Gummie Johnson really sings your praises," Betty says.

"I knew the potential of all the districts," I explain to her — the result of my detailed work on redistricting. "I was a logical choice to help recruit our candidates."

We talk about the two advisory councils — on higher education and taxes. And then she asks how my committee will come up with financing for the governor's massive budget. Until we fix our tax structure, I tell her, finding increased revenue will usually require a tax rate increase, and we agree, raising taxes is not a popular task for anyone.

"But honestly, Betty, I don't think there will be too much furor," I say with genuine assurance. "The people know the cost of bread and housing has gone up. Why wouldn't government costs increase, too?"

For the record, I don't like being photographed, but a photographer shoots me anyway — Betty insists — as I leave for my desk on the floor. By the following Wednesday morning Betty's story has traveled the wires, courtesy of the Associated Press. It appears in its entirety in newspapers all around the state under various headlines.

Mrs. McCaffree Sets Busy Pace for Solons, one headline blares, followed by Betty's story: "Ask on any street and you may get a blank stare at the mention of the name Mary Ellen McCaffree," she writes, "but knock on any door of a Republican Party worker and you're apt to get a different story. And ask her colleagues in the Washington State legislature and the party and you get an inkling why." [8]

SOLON

A legislator...

As I read along, I discover Betty has talked to Gary Grant about me, and to other Democrats as well. I approve. Balanced reporting, freedom of the press.

Most have called me competent, Gary Grant in his partisan fashion: "She did an excellent job on redistricting — for her side."

I finish Betty's article, then rush to the bathroom to ready for the day. The photograph they used is just horrible! Do I really look that tired? All the papers carried it. My colleagues will likely have seen it, and will have read this. I don't normally give my looks much thought, but after seeing my weary face in print, I want to at least feel fresh.

"Mom? Mom! Have you read this yet?"

Mary reads Betty's story at the breakfast table while I work on my hair. I tease it first, then twist it up high in the beehive style women wear these days, and pin it into place, while daughter reads aloud, with occasional emphasis.

"... *an attractive, dark-haired mother of five whose quietly intensive drive shows through when she talks about the ingredients of good government.* Heard that lecture, haven't I, Mom?"

"Yes, honey."

After a quiet minute, I hear from Mary again.

"... *Hard as it was, her work on the Tax Advisory Committee will be nothing compared with the job she now faces...* Is that true, Mom?"

"Read on."

"...*For Mrs. McCaffree is head of the House Revenue and Taxation Committee that will have to find ways to finance the governor's $2.93 billion program.* Huh. So that's what you're doing this session?"

"Part of what I'm doing, honey."

Mary finishes aloud: "*It will be difficult to get taxes increased... she knows the people will have to be sold the program. And one gets the feeling that when it comes to selling the people on a program she feels will result in better government, Mary Ellen McCaffree is the best pitch man in the world.* Cool! So Mom?"

"Almost ready, honey."

"Remember that TV cameraman? He asked me skiing next weekend."

REP. O'BRIEN HASN'T PARTICULARLY ENJOYED his first days in the minority. In fact, he has been exceptionally crotchety. On the tenth day of the session, he stands at his desk on the floor.

"The Speaker recognizes Mr. O'Brien on the point of personal privilege."

"Mr. Speaker," says the Irish baritone, "something has been disturbing me all day. There is a sign prominently displayed in the majority caucus room which says, 'When you are in the minority talk; when you are in the majority vote.' I don't know whether it means anything or what the significance of it is, but I don't think it adds to the decorum of the House. It is put in the position where the minority can plainly see it when the door is ajar, and I wonder if there is any chance you could put it some place else. It isn't a material matter, but I wonder if you could put it some place else so we don't have to look at it."

"If it intrigues you so much," responds Speaker Eldridge, "I am sure we can have a similar sign made for your caucus room." [9]

Mr. O'Brien sits.

FRIDAY MORNING, JANUARY 20, MARKS THE END of week two, and I arrive to find on my desk on the floor a third major message from the governor — a letter laying out his goals for preserving our state's natural environment.

Dear Representative, Senator, Ladies and Gentlemen...

He tells us our state's natural beauty is "more than just a fact of geography." It is an economic asset, and contributes to a satisfied life and peace of mind. It is something we owe our future generations as well. I agree. The governor writes in detail about the major environmental clauses of our Blueprint — what we hope to accomplish legislatively: Protecting open spaces, scenic views, the quality of our water and air, our shorelines, rivers, state parks, trails. He suggests the nature of several executive request bills he will send our way, measures that strike a balance between economic affluence and natural wealth.

"No citizen of Washington, nor any visitor to these borders, can fail to recognize the wealth of beauty we possess," he writes. "Neither, then, should they fail to recognize that in a time of swift development, even a great natural heritage can be placed in jeopardy... We have relatively little time to protect our beauty, and to preserve a portion of our great open spaces. But if there is little time, there is at least enough time; and if we begin now, I am confident future generations will look upon their luxury of natural beauty as a legacy from this 40th Legislative Session." [10]

I agree with the governor: The time to protect our natural resources is now.

At the end of the day, after the close of our second Friday session, I finally take a moment to assemble some news to send my constituents back home. I sort through the latest pre-fab copy from our publicity staff, weigh my own thoughts, and settle upon five topics:

1. We're off to a fast start: 353 bills introduced so far. We've averaged only two hours a day in session, and spend the balance of long days in committee meetings and hearings, wading through the legislation. (This reminds me: I've found it a bit surreal to see Mary, our docket clerk, formally seated on the elevated platform at the front of the House, officially recording the progress of each of these hundreds of bills.)

2. Health and Welfare legislation — particularly the package of five executive request bills. I concur with the governor: It is our duty to protect our least protected, our most vulnerable.

3. Changes in House Rules: Specifically, a change to prevent filibusters, and another to strike the secret vote in Rules Committee. The result of this latter is that all Rules Committee actions are now transparent. Individual Rules Committee members are now publicly accountable, on par with members of all our other standing committees.

4. Our two major proposed changes to higher education: A new statewide community college system, and a brand new and novel four-year college.

5. Governor Evans' trio of formal challenges: His State of the State and Budget addresses, and this morning's letter on preserving our natural resources and creating natural playgrounds.

I make a final note to my secretary: Use the publicity group's language about how I appreciate and encourage constituent letters. She finishes typing it on my letterhead, I add my signature, show her my Rolodex, explain my system for annotating constituents, and for the first time in years I don't have to individually hand address my newsletters home.

MY LEGISLATIVE WEEK MAY HAVE COME TO AN END, but another challenge beckons. My daughter won't let me forget my promise to teach her to master a manual transmission. There she sits in the driver's seat, parked outside my office building. She breaks into an enormous smile when she sees me. I'm grateful to Pat Goodfellow for loaning me one of his dealership's cars, this little dark blue two-door Ford. Mary can drive, but she's never used a stick shift.

I signal her to slide to the passenger side.

"Mom!" she complains, but I insist.

"I'll drive downhill, honey, and give you some pointers. Then you can drive back up. Uphill is the best way to learn."

In about 30 seconds, we reach the bottom of the hill. Along the way, I've explained my footwork and my shifting. I put the car in neutral, set the brake and Mary and I trade seats. The five-block return trip, bottom to top, takes her 45 minutes. I don't gloat.

"OK," she concedes, "maybe I'm not ready to drive to the ski slopes... yet!"

On that we agree.

EARLY TUESDAY MORNING, I GAVEL TO ORDER the House Committee on Revenue and Taxation, lead us through the opening agenda items, and then introduce today's top topic: Tax reform.

I begin by explaining the origins of Washington's state tax base. Our earliest tax structure relied on a single source of government revenue: The property tax. Land was the only thing available to tax in this state — at the start. People came here to homestead, to claim a piece of real estate and work the land. Few pioneers derived outside income. No paychecks meant there was no tax on income to be had. It made sense at the time. A property tax would best fund our state, so in our state constitution, this is how our state founders structured our tax base.

When our state economy sank in the 1930's during the Great Depression, our state laws were changed to institute a sales tax as well. Too many here were falling in arrears on their property taxes or losing their properties outright. Our state revenue stream dried to a meager dribble. But people still had to buy things — food, for instance — so the sales tax helped our state stay afloat during that long twelve years of economic depression. The sales tax has remained a revenue source ever since.

In the ensuing decades, our cities have grown, businesses have proliferated, incomes have diversified. Our state now bears little economic resemblance to those pioneer days, yet we've never reorganized our revenue base accordingly, other than that one emergency patch job mid-depression. [11,12]

These days, if our state revenues fall short of state needs, the legislature simply adds another small tax, or more often, raises the rate of an existing tax. But no one likes to raise taxes, especially every single legislative term, and especially since the 99 members of the House must run for re-election every interim. Because the state legislature is a body of elected officials, and because we must defend our tax votes to voters during each new campaign, as a state we've tended to tax those items that voters find easiest to swallow: Taxes on gasoline to fix our roads, taxes on cigarettes, taxes on liquor. Luxury taxes, sin taxes — band-aids, all. We've never created a logical, stable system of revenue.

Just as illogically, our state constitution restricts the revenue-raising ability of our local governments. If a local government needs more funds, it must turn to the only tax our constitution allows: The property tax. Or it must ask the state for more money.

Over the years, rather than revise our tax structure in step with societal change (which is admittedly a gargantuan job, both fiscally and politically complex), our legislature has just added monetary patches here and there. Thus, nearly every single legislative session requires a tax hike.

I sense my committee has followed this history so far.

"I hope you've all read this."

I raise my copy of *Proposals for Changes in Washington's Tax Structure* — the

130-page report the Tax Advisory Council sent the governor and each legislator in December.[13]

"What the Tax Advisory Council proposes, here in this report, is a new revenue system designed to bend and flex with the economy. It's an ingenious system — unlike any used in any other state. It is responsive, and measurably more stable than what we have now. And it's more fair."

I look to Don Burrows, seated among the public and lobbyists. This executive secretary of our Tax Advisory Council knows our state tax data inside out. Per a quick conversation we had beforehand, I now ask Don to stand and he obliges, saying, "I have volumes of data to support this proposal, if anyone…" but noting little interest among my committee, he sits again.

I continue: "This proposal is elastic — to use an economic term — so that revenue needs, whether they increase or decrease, will be met automatically based on this new design, without continually adjusting our tax rates."

"Wouldn't that be nice," quips Maggie Hurley. "Never defend another tax vote again!"

"No more Mr. Bad Guy in the legislature," says Stu Bledsoe. "I could handle that."

"But we're staring at a huge budget surplus this year," argues Ed Heavey. "I don't get it. If we're the fastest growing state, and we're bringing in extra money, what's the big deal?"

"A faulty revenue base," I reply.

"But why inflict the taxpayer with new taxes now?" Ed Heavey continues.

I explain.

"This is not a proposed tax increase, Ed, it's a proposed shift in our state tax structure. There's a big difference. The net result of this council proposal is no significant tax increase overall — a decrease in fact, for the taxpayer at the low end of the income scale."

Gary Grant speaks before I grant him the floor: "Did Dan Evans dictate this plan? Sounds like one of his dreamy-eyed Blueprint for Progress deals."

I decide not to reprimand Gary for speaking out of turn, opting instead to explain: "The governor was not involved in this council study, Representative Grant, nor in the specifics of its recommendation. He did hand-select the council membership, and his office explained the parameters of our study, but from that point on, the governor entrusted the Council to devise a better revenue system for our state. He did not dictate, by any means, but deferred to our results."

"Then how do you explain why this 'plan' sounds so much like the rumblings coming out of the governor's office?" Grant asks.

"Because the governor has based his tax reform program on these recommendations."

"I thought so," Grant says. "I suppose he bought the single rate tax baloney, too. Well, the Democrats won't go for it, I promise you that."

The Democrats have repeatedly advocated for a graduated rate income tax, period.

I explain again that this plan effectively works as a graduated rate tax via exemptions and deductions that reduce the tax burden on lower income groups relative to higher income households. The graduated feature of the tax burden of our proposal becomes even more pronounced when the steeply graduated federal income tax is taken into consideration.

"Our proposed single rate net income tax, as part of the entire proposed structure…"

But Gary Grant and Ed Heavey stand, shove their chairs, and exit in a huff.

> **SINGLE RATE TAX**
>
> A tax with a single rate that remains the same as income increases.

> **GRADUATED RATE TAX**
>
> A tax with multiple rates that increase as income increases.

THE FOLLOWING DAY, WEDNESDAY, January 25, our governor stands before us again — House and Senate together in our chamber — to address us as a whole body yet again. Whereas the State of the State and the Budget addresses are delivered by each governor each session, today's third Joint Session address is something new.

"Mr. President, Mr. Speaker, Ladies and Gentlemen of the Legislature," says the governor, "I have asked for the privilege of addressing this legislature in Joint Session today because I believe that the subject for consideration is of the highest importance. Because it is important, it is therefore fitting that we come together, where we are not only visible to each other, but to the people as well."

Accountability, the governor is looking for — shouldering responsibility, owning up. The press is out in full force, the galleries full, the wings swollen with lobbyists. Before this public crowd, the governor continues.

"Harry Truman once remarked that 'if you can't stand the heat, stay out of the kitchen.' I am suggesting now that we — as duly constituted executive and legislature — step into the kitchen, acknowledge the heat, and proceed with the long overdue business of tax reform here in the state of Washington."

I must rally my assistants — diverse though their palates may be — to concoct and deliver an amenable tax base for our state. A tall order, but I am glad and honored to be part of the solution *for the sake of our schools and our schoolchildren.*

The governor spells out our state's tax history — one of reaction and patching, not policy. He and I have discussed this at length, and also with everyone who will listen. I hope my committee members find his narrative familiar.

"…The day of reckoning has come," says the governor. "I am convinced if we do not succeed in achieving some basic reform in our tax structure now, the degree of the problem will become too great to respond to the remedy.

"It is not this decade that will suffer, but the next; not ourselves, but those who succeed us," he says, looking forward, taking the lead, taking responsibility. "And I would rather institute reform at the risk of defeat, than accomplish victory at the price of disaster."

Do the right thing for our state today, he's saying, versus worrying about personal re-election a year from now: My sentiments exactly. We're here to serve the people, not ourselves.

"In order to assure that the state of Washington can obtain revenues consistent with growth, that we can place tax emphasis where it belongs, and that we can both reduce the degree of unfairness and improve the degree of uniformity, this administration is now prepared to make five tax reform recommendations to the legislature: First, that a constitutional amendment be placed on the 1967 election ballot to create a single rate state income tax on net taxable income; and…"

He suggests we establish an income tax rate of 3.5 percent on both individuals and corporations. Judging from a shuffling in many seats, all are listening – some with discomfort.

"Next, that a second constitutional amendment appear on the same ballot to establish the property tax rate at forty mills based on an assessment level of twenty-five percent of true and fair value; but that this amendment be so written that should the income tax fail, then the property tax rate would increase to a constitutional limit of fifty mills."

Many brows furrow at the complexity, though I know these clauses inside out. It's easy to gauge from this chamber today how much more detailed explaining remains to be done.

"Third, that with the passage of the income tax measure, the legislature reduce the sales tax rate from its present level to 3.5 percent of sales (the same rate as the income tax), and that food and drugs be specifically exempted from the sales tax.

"Fourth, that with passage, the basic rate of the business and occupation tax be reduced to two-tenths of one percent.

"Finally, that a new Department of Revenue, requested by this administration, be directed to enforce the uniform application of rates and uniform standards of assessment to all property, both real and personal."

The governor then proposes the same thing we on the Advisory Council determined: That the three taxes — income, sales and property — become the three legs essential to the stability of the state's three-legged revenue stool, an image we used as we attempted to balance our revenue base. Until all three legs are firmly in place, the stool will wobble and fail... just as our revenue structure is failing us now. The two legs it stands on at present — property taxes and excise taxes — provide us neither stable revenue nor sufficient funding, and these taxes certainly aren't equitable. It's obvious: Our state needs a better-built stool.

Most state taxpayers wouldn't feel these reforms in their pocketbooks, contrary to common fears and rampant fear mongering. These reforms to our tax structure the governor is describing are total revenue neutral. Over time, however, they will generate increased revenues without a commensurate increase in tax rates, simply because the proposed system is better designed. As a whole, the package will reduce those taxes paid by low-income families, while slightly increasing taxes paid by households with higher income. It is very fair, contrary to some loud oppositional grumbling.

The governor continues. He promotes the administrative improvements our Council suggested: Eliminate the Tax Commission and replace it with a Department of Revenue, accountable to the governor, and then add a separate board for Tax Appeals.

"There is no question that these recommendations constitute a major reform of our present tax system," the governor admits. "But... their accomplishment will provide for the first time in our state a sound, reasonable, equitable and responsive tax policy. We will have a system in which the demands created by population and urban growth will be equaled by the revenues available to meet them."

He emphasizes schools in particular. When it comes to public schooling funds, the governor is my best ally in state government. I hope we can pull this off. It takes rare leadership to shift the errant course of such a big ship, but the governor doesn't flinch at the challenge, and neither do I.

"In the history of every state and its people, the truly significant acts of government are few in number and rare in nature," he tells us. "Because they are significant, they are seldom easy, and their accomplishment requires not only wisdom but courage."

Amen.

"I believe this is one of those significant times... No bill or measure — past or present — is more important to the future of the state of Washington than tax reform." [14]

When the Joint Session disbands, we complete our day's House business and adjourn.

I spend part of the next two days in the office of the governor with Jim Dolliver and Ray Haman, the governor's special legal counsel on tax reform, crafting the governor's executive request tax reform legislation. All of it will come through my committee:

- A House joint resolution: The constitutional amendment to authorize a single rate net income tax and a property tax lid.

- A House bill: The enabling counterpart to the resolution, to establish the single rate income tax at 3.5 percent, reduce the sales tax to 3.5 percent, eliminate the sales tax on food and drugs, cut the Business and Occupations (B & O) tax in half, and adjust how we administer our property tax.

- Another House bill: The major administrative overhaul to establish the Department of Revenue, eliminate the Tax Commission and create a new state Board of Tax Appeals. This would give the governor – our executive – an administrative voice in state revenue decisions, since the governor would appoint the new department director who would then report back to the head of our state.

Throughout this session, I'll report to Jim and Ray and the governor on my committee's progress on this trio of tax and revenue measures. They'll give me legal and moral support in return.

COLLECTIVELY, THE GOVERNOR'S OFFICE AND HOUSE Republicans have set an ambitious agenda, and the days of this 40th Session are quickly ticking by. We're determined to move our state forward, to lead. It isn't easy, but we never asked for 'easy' – we asked for the chance to solve our state's problems and to bring about change.

We don't stop on Saturday. By this 20th day of this 60-day session, the legislative pace is astonishing, although most of it is confined within our committees. We've sent hundreds of bills to our sixteen House committees. Very few of them have returned to the floor. Yet.

Speaker Eldridge calls us to order at 11 a.m. The clerk calls the roll. Seven are absent and excused – it's the weekend. After the flag and the prayer, and the daily reading of the Journal dispensed with, we move on to standing committee reports. The labors of our committee deliberations are beginning to bear fruit. This keeps Mary busy up front, recording each new step in the docket. Seven measures are brought to the floor by the chairmen of various committees. All seven arrive with unanimous recommendations that they do pass: Full bi-partisan support! The committee chairs have ably guided good compromise.

We hear messages from the Senate: They too have passed another seven bills, plus two joint measures.

Now new bills are introduced and assigned to committees: Thirty in all, plus two resolutions. We are up to House Bill Number 518 for the session — each new bill assigned its number in order.

More Senate bills. More House bills. Mary is earning her pay.

We arrive at the third reading of bills — those ready for our vote on final passage. Each of these bills has been refined through the committee process, and all eight pass quickly: Seven by a unanimous House vote, and one nearly unanimous, with 90 yeas out of the 93 present. This incredible consensus is a strong indication of the thorough work we're all doing off the floor, within our committees.

Speaker Eldridge recognizes our floor leader, Mr. Gorton, who says, "I move that the House revert to the third order of business for the purpose of receiving reports of standing committees."

That approved, I stand and the Speaker grants me the floor.

"Mrs. McCaffree."

Tax reform is not my only leadership task this session. I am also our House leader on open space lands and have two measures to report.

"Mr. Speaker, we a majority of your Committee on Revenue and Taxation, to whom was referred House Bill Number 121 providing for open space land, have had the same under consideration, and we respectfully report the same back to the House with the recommendation that Substitute House Bill 121 be substituted therefore and that the substitute bill do pass."

The majority includes all of my committee but two. Representative Gary Grant rises and is recognized.

"Mr. Speaker, we a minority of your Committee on Revenue and Taxation, to whom was referred House Bill Number 121, have had the same under consideration, and we respectfully report the same back to the House with the recommendation that it do *not* pass."

Rep. Frank Marzano joined him in the rejection. The bill passes to the Rules Committee nevertheless.

I rise again: "Mr. Speaker."

"Mrs. McCaffree, you have the floor."

This time my entire committee has concurred in recommending the passage of House Joint Resolution 1, "Amending the Constitution to allow the assessment of agricultural, timber and open space lands on the basis of use rather than value."

I am excited about these measures. The concept of protecting our open spaces, natural lands and large sweeping parcels is relatively new to America. In its vastness, do we really need to worry? But having closely witnessed Seattle's population explosion and urban sprawl, the DEGOHT team and I believe now is the best time to protect these lands for the future. Throughout the recent interim, I regularly discussed open space with my constituents – in coffee hours, as I doorbelled the community, throughout much of my campaign. My 32nd District Republican group asked the same questions many others do, and raised the same objections the DEGOHTs hear everywhere we speak.

"Why should they get a tax break?" – 'they' being property owners with enormous parcels of land. "...And why should we have to pay for it?"

People find it difficult to understand the value of preserving open space, and it is particularly unpopular with city residents. This will be a long educational process, but development pressure is increasingly clear here in Washington State. I imagine I'll be stumping for open space for years.

Why are these open space measures traveling through my committee? Because they have a tax consequence: They remove property tax dollars from our tax base. If we pass these open space measures, the state won't be able to assess (and tax) these lands according to the value of their highest potential use – at a high per-acre or square-footage rate, for example, if they lie near a region of rapid development and thus have high commercial appeal. Rather, we will assess them at their current use – for farming or as undeveloped terrain – to allow farmers to affordably continue to farm their acreage, for example, rather than buckle to development pressure and sell it off. If we assessed these lands at their 'highest use' value, we would value the acres according to how many homes could be built there, or factories, or business centers, and then raise the property tax accordingly – to a rate too steep for a farmer to afford. So by setting aside open space, the state will feasibly lose tax dollars, but it gains, or rather, it retains open spaces: Agricultural land, natural habitat, greenery.

While these two pieces of legislation curb a revenue source, they protect a natural resource. It's a conscious balancing act, a conscious choice. The discussions in my committee have been lively.

After two more committee reports, our day's business is nearly complete except for a vaudevillian "yield to a question" exchange between our caucus chairman and Republican whip, whereby they gracefully denounce our Senate leadership.

Mr. Bledsoe, our whip – a feisty rancher and chairman of our state's most popular rodeo – sets up the exchange by asking whether Mr. Goldsworthy has perchance had time to ascertain what's going on today in the Senate regarding all the House legislation we've sent them to consider.

"It is interesting that you should ask..." Rep. Goldsworthy replies, and he casually reports that he did indeed pay a visit to the Senate today, only to find that, alas, the Senate was not in session. They'd gone home for the weekend, "except for quite a few Republican senators still around." Our caucus chair frames his conclusion in the gentlest of terms, but his message bites: "While the state is waiting for this important legislation, the senators again have had a vacation."

I will not go home for the weekend.

In addition to chairing the House Committee on Revenue and Taxation, I sit on two others: Higher Education and Labor and Employment Security. I am not deeply involved with the latter, but having been part of the interim college study, my role on Higher Ed is more substantial. All our House committees are proceeding full steam ahead, and I must spend my "off" hours reading piles of proposed legislation.

FROM THE VERY START of this session, I've heard regularly from unhappy educators — first from my district, then gradually from other towns around the state. PTA officers, too, who have handled the ongoing levy campaigns, are complaining loudly, as are many parents. They've called me. They've written me. They've flooded my office by phone, by mail, in person. Because I've campaigned from the start of my legislative career on the issue of securing school funding, everyone now wants me to answer: *What's happening? When will the job be done?* Tax reform has to come first, I tell them, and it needs their support.

PHOTO: WASHINGTON STATE ARCHIVES

"Call your legislator," I urge those who live outside my district. "Complain!"

"Telephone the governor," I suggest to them all. It appears they've been calling each other as well.

From what I can piece together with the governor's

From their desks on the House floor, Representatives Mary Ellen McCaffree and Marjorie Lynch continue to take care of business during a session recess.

staff, a sizeable swarm will materialize here Monday afternoon. Monday morning, before the session starts, Dale Hoggins stops by my desk on the floor.

"What do you know about this?" the freshman legislator and school principal asks. "My phone's been ringing off the hook."

"Mine, too," I tell him. "The last one said, *We're going to demonstrate! We're going to picket the legislature!* And I tell you, that teacher's voice was full of glee."

"Are you going?" Dale asks me.

"We'll see."

Not long after Speaker Eldridge gavels our session to order at 11 a.m., the noise outside our chamber doors is difficult to ignore. We can hear a crowd in the rotunda, their numbers audibly swelling. Their chants are made more magnificent by collision with the marbled expanse. Curious, Dale and I slip out for a look.

Hundreds of citizens, some with children in tow, crowd our rotunda beneath the capitol dome, spilling onto the steps, chanting and waving placards — a relatively wholesome gathering. This is our first demonstration of the session.

The doors to the governor's office swing wide on the second level, and the governor steps to the railing. He awaits their hush, then speaks: "I fully support the idea of eliminating annual special levies for regular school operating costs."

A rowdy cheer rises and reverberates. Placards dance.

"We've been working towards this for many years," he says. "And now we have a solution, but first we must convince our legislators and all of you to support it. If the tax reform package I've proposed is adopted this session, and you follow through at the polls, we have a chance to eliminate our schools' dependence on unreliable levy results from here on out."

More cheering. The governor waits again for the noise to subside.

"We want the same thing you do," he says. "But we need your support on tax reform." [15]

The range of the protesters' expressions in response to the governor's tax reform plea is a sobering reminder: Educators need tax reform education, too.

TUESDAY MARKS THE SESSION DEBUT of some major elements of our Blueprint for Progress. When a bill or resolution makes its 'first appearance' it is usually hand-delivered to the clerk of the House at the start of the day by one of its sponsors. During the Sixth Order of Business, the Speaker introduces new bills by title or brief description, reads its list of sponsors, assigns it a House Bill number, then assigns it to a specific committee for review. Thus, it actively joins our legislative 'to-do' list for the session.

Today, the community college bill leads the way. This would create a brand new state-funded system of community colleges in two-dozen new community college districts located throughout the state. These colleges would offer two-year post-high school programs through which students earn college credit – either for transfer to a four-year college or for a two-year higher education degree. In our state at present, the only post-high school public education we offer is tied to the K-12 system and funded subject to those same iffy levy funds, and these offer only a small-scale curriculum past the 12th grade. The new system would stand alone, and would be funded directly by the state – a popular concept. The bill has thirty-five sponsors including me and Marjorie Lynch. But since nearly everyone wants a community college in his district, a geographic battle looms. Agreeing on a final form for the bill will be tricky, with everyone lobbying to locate one of these new colleges in their hometowns.

Wednesday, the first major tax reform measure arrives: The constitutional amendment I've worked through with the governor's team, to set a lower lid on property taxes and add a new single rate income tax. As the primary sponsor, I hand it to the clerk, after which it formally becomes House Joint Resolution 29 and is assigned to my committee. I continue my frequent trips to the governor's office to fine-tune this measure as my committee weighs in.

On Friday, Mrs. Lynch and I each deliver another major measure to the clerk. When the House arrives at the Sixth Order of Business, these two bills surface, and I take note of my colleagues as the Speaker reads mine: "By executive request: An Act relating to state government…" This is the bill that overhauls our tax administration creating the new Department of Revenue and new Board of Tax Appeals. The clerk continues: "…by Representatives Holman, Backstrom and McCaffree. This House Bill Number 576 is ordered printed and referred to the Committee on Revenue and Taxation."

Next is the bill to establish a new state college. I am listed among these sponsors, too, among colleagues from both sides of the aisle. Per our Temporary Advisory Council on Higher Education, the bill spells out guidelines for a new four-year college explicitly located near the state capitol, in Olympia. As with the community college bill, location will likely spark the biggest controversy. Most colleagues agree we need the college, but they don't agree where. This House Bill 596 is assigned to the House Committee on Higher Education, where as a committee member I will certainly add to the discussion.

Upon adjournment, I return to my office. On my desk, the February 3 caucus publicity report reminds me I face a torrid schedule in week five: Not only my committee work, floor work and work with the governor's team, but two out-of-town public hearings on two evenings in two different cities on the topic of tax reform, hosted by the House committee I chair.

NOT ALL MY WORK THIS SESSION is as pervasively statewide as tax reform. I do represent a specific district, after all. I am responsible for tackling issues unique to District 32A, and in the case of one particular issue, a bill that affects just a few city blocks. But this little bill is stirring some mighty strong sentiment.

In the heart of my legislative district, at the intersection of 45th Street and Brooklyn Avenue, is the lovely Meany Hotel named for an early University of Washington history professor, Edmund Meany. (Meany Hall on the campus is named for Professor Meany as well, but it was condemned after our big quake in 1965, and has yet to be rebuilt.)

For decades the Meany Hotel has been the favored gathering place for many affiliated with the University of Washington — faculty and administrators, visiting dignitaries and professors, for out-of-town guests, for families visiting their university students. It is also central to the U-District's businesses and citizens.

But as the years have passed, this dear old hotel has suffered an increasing handicap due to a legal prohibition against serving alcoholic beverages to its guests. No other hotel in our city — or in our entire state, for that matter — is legally bound by the same. A 72-year-old law restricts the sale of liquor within one mile of the University of Washington campus, and the popular Meany Hotel sits within this boundary. So the Meany cannot compete with other hotels and motels that have sprung up nearby, carefully sited outside the mile mark and therefore replete with cocktail lounges, and able to serve their guests alcohol. Because of this decades-old prohibition, and its increasingly deleterious effect, the owners of the Meany recently made a difficult decision. They will put the beloved hotel up for sale — as a retirement community.

"Help save the Meany Hotel!" many businessmen and university staff within my constituency are pleading. Legislators from nearby districts are hearing the same. Conversely, many churches and other constituents are equally adamant, if not more so, that the one-mile liquor ban should remain in place, though no other state college is bound by the same. Not only is this a local issue, very specific to my district, but it also has two vocal factions, both lobbying me fiercely from opposite sides. I must weigh this matter carefully.

Senators from two adjacent districts — in the 46th John Ryder, and Walt Williams in the 43rd — also have constituencies within the one-mile boundary, so we agree: These two senators should originate a bill in the Senate to repeal the 1895 law and help save the Meany Hotel.

On February 6, Monday of week five in the House, tucked inconspicuously within a list of fourteen Senate bills ready for assignment to House committee, is Senate Bill 138: "An act deleting certain territorial restrictions on the sale of intoxicating liquor near the University of Washington campus." It goes to the

Committee on Businesses and Professions.

BACK TO TAXES. On Wednesday, February 8 — the exact halfway mark of this 40th Session — another landmark executive request bill makes its debut in the House: The large omnibus bill that would implement our tax reform proposals, *if* the tax reform constitutional amendment is approved by a vote of the people.

"By Representative McCaffree, by executive request," the Speaker reads. "An Act relating to revenue and taxation; establishing a single rate net income tax; amending the state business and occupation tax; amending the state retail sales and use taxes; and…" a very long list of changes to our state code. Not surprisingly, this House Bill 639 is assigned to my committee.

The moment today's session adjourns, I join the governor's staff aboard the state's prop plane, bound for Spokane — for a public hearing on tax reform.

I buckle in, and immediately Esther Searing shows me some beautifully bound copies of the governor's Joint Session address on tax reform, plus a new brochure they've designed and titled with powerful suggestion: "Why the people of Washington should choose Tax Reform." In very small print is a very large amount of information: Commonly asked questions (and answers) about the governor's tax reform program, plus a graph that shows how taxes would fall for lower income families, a chart of its impact on ten sample families, more graphs, an explanation of each specific reform, and of what each will do specifically for our state. On the cover, just below a photocopied 1965 quarter coin (George Washington with "Liberty" above him and "In God We Trust" at his jaw), is a personal note from the governor requesting "long overdue reform in Washington's antiquated tax structure." I scan the brochure, agree it is complete, but it seems too complex for the layman. This last observation I keep to myself. The governor's staff loves it.

We're taking tax reform on the road. Taking it to the people.

We land in time for the 8 p.m. hearing at Spokane's Ridpath Hotel, and I'm floored not only by the size of the crowd but also by the depth of their interest and concern. The governor's staff articulately presents our package, and I help field questions. It's a lively evening. Not everyone who signs up has time to testify before time runs out. Late at night, we all fly back to the capitol, and I'm back in my seat in the House for our 11 a.m. opening of Thursday's session.

Earlier this morning, a different public hearing drew another large crowd right here at the capitol, in House Hearing Room 2. The topic was LSD.

Caucus leadership encouraged us to invite our younger constituents to attend the hearing, particularly student body presidents and student newspaper editors from high schools and colleges around the state. With the University of Washington in my district and a large urban high school adjacent, my young people were well represented in Hearing Room 2. They added their views: Should we add LSD and other hallucinogenic drugs to the state's existing Dangerous Drug Act?

Early in the afternoon, several students drop by my office. We talk a bit about the drug issue, but among these students, another matter matters more. Our conversation quickly drifts to the voting age: It is legally 21, and these young people want it lowered to age 18.

"Did you hear, Mrs. McCaffree? The Senate's going to hear it this afternoon!"

I've had a busy week, and frankly I wasn't aware of it, but I'm delighted and say so.

"Well, they're not going to hear it, really," says Sam Reed, a college student with political savvy. It's hard to believe this is little Sam Reed, whose mom Gerri dragged him across the state from Spokane in her station wagon to work on Dan Evans' campaign.

"But at least we got sponsors and a bill," Sam continues. "And they've agreed to age 18!"

"What do you mean they won't hear it?" another student asks Sam.

Sam explains: "Today they just announce it. They'll give it a number and assign it to a committee."

I don't tell them this bill could very well die in that committee. Why squash their enthusiasm? Instead I promise to support their right to vote.

"Do you think it will pass, Mrs. McCaffree? Some senators seem pretty supportive."

"That's great!" I mean it. "You deserve a voice. Good luck! Stop by any time you're in town."

This evening, the House dining room conversation over ice cream is enlightening, or "mind-expanding" to borrow a phrase from this morning's hearing. Between hallucinogens and the 18-year-old vote, we're reminded of a whole different demographic — newer newcomers to the political process. I almost feel old.

When I return home, I place a call to my youngest son in Seattle.

"David?"

"Hi, Mom."

"Lots of homework tonight?"

"Tests tomorrow. You know."

"I have a question for you."

"Fire away, Mom."

"Do you think we should legalize marijuana?"

Mary's eyes widen from across our Olympia kitchen table: "Mom!"

"I'm serious," I say to them both. "David, I want your opinion."

After a long, long silence on the other end of the line, David says only, "Wow."

FRIDAY, ON THE HEELS OF ADJOURNMENT, I head out of town once more, this time to Seattle for another public hearing on tax reform at the Olympic Hotel. We travel by car.

This hearing is equally crowded and equally energized by people with more questions than time allows answers. The testimony sign-up list is miles long. We make the same presentation, answer the same range of questions, and I find it interesting how little difference there seems to be among the people on either side of our state, largely a rural/urban divide.

Bobbi McCallum catches up with me, flashing her press badge from the *Seattle P-I.*

"Can I cash in my rain check on that tax reform interview, Mrs. McCaffree?"

Her timing couldn't be better. We find two chairs in the hotel lobby.

I explain to her that I need 66 'yes' votes in the House — two-thirds rather than a simple majority of fifty — to place the constitutional amendment part of our tax reform package on the general election ballot. I explain the political math of my challenge: In our House of 99 members, 55 are Republicans, so in order to pass this constitutional amendment out of the House — with two-thirds voting 'yes' — I'll need eleven Democrat votes as well, assuming all the Republicans vote for it. I'm frank: This tax reform package isn't an easy sell — on either side of the aisle. The fact is, what we are proposing is entirely new.

"New for Washington State?" Bobbi asks.

"This proportional tax is brand new, period," I explain, "and that means it is easily misunderstood."

"A giant step," the reporter says, quoting the governor's tax talk.

"Yes, that's what he calls it, and it's my job to help people understand — my colleagues, business people, lobbyists, voters, the press."

"So basically, tax reform has been dumped in your lap," she says.

"Not entirely, but legislatively, yes." I sigh, but hadn't meant to. "It's always a big order, getting 66 House votes on something this controversial."

After the interview, I spend a rare night at home with my husband and David, and then bright and early, I drive back to Olympia in time for our Saturday session in the House.

PROPORTIONAL TAX

A tax that remains the same proportion of income as income increases. Term frequently used in lieu of 'single rate' tax.

EARLY THE NEXT WEEK, ON VALENTINE'S DAY, Bobbi McCallum's story appears with the headline: *Tax Reform is Left in Lady Legislator's Lap* — along with another particularly unflattering photograph in which I seem, accurately enough, to be hard at very difficult work.[16]

We are now 40 days into this 60-day session. We'd started with a bang, with our hyper-organized committees and agenda, but at the two-thirds mark, our agenda has a long way to go.

Gathering support for the governor's tax reform package is tough. The math really isn't that complex, and the statistics needn't be confusing. The Tax Advisory Council researched and computed long and hard and arrived at an excellent system — an altogether new way to securely fund a vibrant government and to spread the tax burden fairly. But resistance is high.

Nearly everyone is leery of adding an income tax in this state when we've never had one. Emotional resistance to and prejudice against change keeps support for tax reform… lukewarm at best. A distaste for taxation in general doesn't help.

While I've been working on tax reform measures, my House colleagues have been hard at work drafting the budget bill. A handful, including Bob Goldsworthy (chairman of the House Appropriations Committee, in addition to chairing our caucus) are making daily trips to the governor's office, like me, to work with the governor and his staff.

On February 16, the governor invites the capitol press corps to his office to present them his fiscal programs: State finance, the budget, reforms to our revenue base. The governor's ready with a large display and handouts — statistics, charts, graphs — his earnest engineer side in full view.

Afterwards, Shelby Scates tracks me down.

"Hey, Mrs. McCaffree, you know what your governor just said?"

"Our governor," I correct the errant reporter.

"Fine. Our governor said it would have been politically wiser to just use the budget surplus this session to balance the budget, and skip the push for tax reform."

"Yes, he's said that before."

"You know what he said next? That it wouldn't have been responsible. So he's going to keep pushing for tax reform. You know a thing or two about this. Can you explain to me why the Democrats are so hot about a graduated income tax versus the single rate?"

"It's partly a traditional Democrat position, Shelby — they consider the graduated tax more fair for the little guy, though our proposal is fair, too," I tell him. "And it's partly purely political. The basic issue, really, is between those who want an income tax and those who don't."

"Well, your governor said…"

"Our governor."

I'm surprised he's bothering to talk to me. Shelby does most of his reporting via the Senate. He flips through the scribbled pages of his reporter's pad and finds what he's looking for.

"Here. The governor explained the different ways it could go. Add a tax. Reject another. Offer combinations. Or, and I quote: 'Or voters may approve the two constitutional amendments, which would virtually eliminate the need for special school levies and broaden the tax base.' Is that really true, Mrs. McCaffree? I know you're a pro on this school levy thing."

"It's true, Shelby. It's going to take tax reform to get rid of the endless levies." [17]

I hope I can convince my legislative colleagues of this, and then convince the voters. It's been a long haul from my PTA days to here, and I'd like to shore up school funding once and for all.

"Thanks, Mrs. McCaffree."

He's off to the senators again. The Senate Democrats are dead set against our package — for one of two reasons, or both: Either because they demand a graduated income tax and no other form, or because they don't want Republicans to get credit for actually fixing the system.

The next day, February 18, and already well into Friday evening, Bob Goldsworthy is finally ready to unveil the House budget bill on the floor. We must review this bill thoroughly — item by item, line by line. Every session, this is a long and tedious task, and we're just beginning it after dinner.

As majority floor leader, Slade Gorton moves that we operate as a Committee of the Whole during deliberation of this budget bill, rather than follow floor protocol. The Democrats object, verbally and viscerally outraged. *No formal record of the proceedings?! No formal votes on each item?!* But we vote on it, the Republican majority holds sway, and Speaker Eldridge holds firm. We will consider the budget as a Committee of the Whole.

Prior to this evening session, Slade explained this decision to our caucus.

"This is a pragmatic strategy," he said. "As the House majority, we have a responsibility to efficiently carry out the business of the state — to lead the process along. As those of you who have sat through previous budget bill deliberations on the floor can confirm, this process can drag on for days while individuals grandstand — basically campaigning for their next elections."

Many heads nod. Slade continues: "A Committee of the Whole allows for the circumvention of such picayune elocutionary hindrance."

"Plain English," someone requests with a laugh.

I translate: "We'll avoid lengthy nit-picking. The Democrats can still nit-pick.

We're not denying them that — the Committee of the Whole allows everyone to say everything that's on their mind — but they won't grandstand if it's not being recorded in the Journal. We can avoid their posturing and focus on the actual bill."

"This way, the minority can't stall the budget," Bob Goldworthy explains further. "We're taking our leadership seriously. The people elected us to get this state on its feet. So we're hoping to cut out the 'campaign' speeches tonight and just get down to business."

Even operating as a Committee of the Whole, it is daylight before the budget bill passes the House. Early Saturday morning, we send it to the Senate.

AS FOR TAX REFORM, before any tax reform measure can come to the floor for House debate, it must be passed out of my Committee on Revenue and Taxation.

The committee meets early Tuesday, as usual, and I announce that we will focus on the income tax/property tax constitutional amendment: HJR 29. Each legislator in this committee received the Tax Advisory Council's detailed report in December; each was present at the Joint Session when the governor addressed us on the specifics of his tax reform package; each legislator has a copy of the governor's brochure to the people of Washington on his tax reform plan, yet their questions continue to abound. And despite our attempt to thoroughly inform them about our proposal, these questions continue to run remarkably parallel with those from the public, beginning with: "Is tax reform really necessary?"

I follow the script I now know by heart: "Yes, for four reasons. First, this state needs a tax structure that responds to growth. You're aware how fast we're growing. We need a structure that produces enough revenue for our state to support the services our citizens demand — as quickly as the demands appear — without a tax rate increase every single session. Secondly, we need a tax structure that reduces the disproportionately large tax burden on our lower…"

"If you cared about the low income folk," interrupts Gary Grant, "you and your governor would give up your inane single rate income tax and…"

"Mr. Grant, please do not interrupt."

I continue: "We need a structure that substantially reduces the tax burden on our lower income families. Third, we need to set realistic constitutional limits on property taxes, instead of repeatedly saddling property owners with the brunt of funding our local governments. And tied in with that is reason number four — we need to end our increasing reliance on special levies to finance our public schools."

This ignites a volley of remarks on schools. *Why are school costs so high and climbing? Do we really need to spend so much? It's just school kids.*

I'm always surprised by how many among my peers here don't consider school funding critical – or rather, they don't understand that a good education creates solid citizens, a solid foundation for our communities. Thank goodness, at least the governor agrees with me.

"Do we really need an income tax?" asks a Republican. "Scares the daylights out of the businessmen in my district, a whole new tax on income."

"Yes we do," I answer. "Income tax revenues are the only tax revenues that respond proportionately to state growth. It's the only tax that can increase our revenue at the same approximate pace the economy grows – without having to adjust the tax rate."

"How do you know?"

Skepticism abounds. I refer my committee to the relevant section of the Advisory Council report. Ignoring this, Ed Heavey jumps in, contentious.

"Doesn't mean it has to be single rate," he says. "Wouldn't a graduated income tax do the same?"

"Yes, a graduated income tax would flex with our economy in a similar way," I acknowledge, and he looks vindicated. "But our concern, Mr. Heavey, is our lower income families. We're trying to create a balance between the state's revenue needs and our lesser earning families. We don't need to rake in more money than we…"

"Hogwash," Gary Grant interrupts again. "A graduated tax works better for low income…"

"Mr. Grant, I have asked you kindly not to interrupt. That is simply not true. Our Tax Advisory Council study indicates that when taken collectively, the several components of our tax reform proposal actually better reduce the tax burden on the low…"

Gary Grant interrupts a third time, jumping to his feet: "The Democrats have…"

I've had it. I slam my gavel.

"Representative Grant, shut up and sit down!"

At which he angrily slams his hefty bill book on the table in my direction – so hard that it crashes to the floor and slides to a stop at my feet. The room is dead silent. I set down my gavel.

Slade has been a relatively quiet member of my committee. At Gary Grant's outburst he suppresses a smile. He and I well recall last session when, during redistricting, Gary ran the Elections Committee with such a heavy gavel that Slade and I were rarely allowed to speak.

"Are there any other questions?" I ask.

Margaret Hurley has one: "What guarantee can you provide, Mrs. McCaffree, that the income and property taxes won't go the way of the sales tax—escalating to the moon, with new increases every year? My voters have a right to know, and so do I."

I answer, patient, trying to find the right words to make this clear.

"The tax structure we are proposing is elastic, Mrs. Hurley. Income tax receipts, in particular, grow as the economy grows. By adding the income tax to help balance our state's revenue stream, we won't have to continually raise other tax rates as we have in the past. Again, the amount of state revenue from the combined taxes, in the combination we propose, will increase comparably to our increased need for services, without changing the tax rate to cover increased costs."

"How much money are we talking about?" asks Ed Heavey. "If we actually pass this thing?"

"*If* the legislature agrees to place the constitutional amendment on ballot in the fall, and *if* the voters then pass it and we've adopted the accompanying implementing measures this session, we estimate the new tax structure will bring in an additional $100 million each biennium, without any tax rate increase for our citizens."

The committee room has been filling throughout the morning and now holds not only our 20 members around the table, but labor lobbyists, tax groups and several educators. They've waited all session for my committee to reach this day.

From early January, lobbyists and myriad groups have continually hounded me. *When is your committee going to vote on tax reform?* They've bent my ear, my committee members' ears, my colleagues' ears. They keep close tabs on the calendar and in close communication with me. That's their job.

And my job is to make sure that anyone who has an interest in any measure before my committee — tax reform, and all others — is aware of which day their "bills of interest" are coming up on the calendar. It's not unusual for me to spend two hours on the telephone after a session in the House, letting my constituents know what's slated for the next day's calendar — in committee and on the floor — and suggesting they make a trip to Olympia if they want to speak up or even just listen. This goes for every committee: I keep track of all the committee calendars' bills and also note my constituents' specific legislative pets. I am a firm believer in allowing people to have a voice.

I also firmly believe in healthy differences of opinion as the best crucible for creating the best legislation. And I know, beyond believing, that if a measure is to gain the support it needs to successfully pass out of a committee and into the House and then to the Senate and on to our governor, it must represent the voices of our state — we must be willing to compromise and find common ground. And so I invite my committee 'guests' to testify, beginning with the chairman of the United Labor Lobby, Joe Davis.

"It's not an income tax we object to," Davis says, "and it's not a constitutional amendment we oppose, but the language that limits the constitutional amendment to a single rate income tax. But hey, we can compromise if your bill has language that says it's up to the legislature to determine whether the income tax is single rate or graduated."

But if we leave this in the legislature's hands, as Davis proposes, who can predict the future political complexion of the legislature? Wouldn't it be better to establish the system now, while we've so much good study behind our proposal? And while the need is so great? The governor and I agree: Now is the time and this plan is solid.

Stu Bledsoe raises a hand, and though I enjoy this colleague immensely, I hesitate a moment before granting this committee member the floor. Stu is a bonafide cowboy, and the coarse language he brought to our capitol is really — well, it's a barnyard vernacular peppered with a vocabulary you can't believe! We've all reprimanded him, from both sides of the aisle, and I've pulled him aside more than once for being uncouth. Stu is the first to admit he needs to scrape the manure off his boots and clean up his act now that he is a member of the legislature, but it hasn't been an easy disinfection.

"Go ahead Mr. Bledsoe," I say, hoping he'll keep it clean.

He stands to address us, then turns and squares off with the labor leader: "Glad to hear *you're* willing to compromise, Joe. We've already made a substantial compromise, you can bet your sweet... uh... we've compromised, you bet, from a position of no income tax at all to a single-rate tax. Do you realize the tensions within the Republican Party over this?"

Davis laughs: "I imagine you Republicans are experiencing tension over quite a few of these issues plugged by your 'Republican' governor. They don't come much more liberal than him."

Hugh Mitchell, chairman of the Committee for Washington Tax Reform, is more strident than Joe Davis in his insistence on a graduated income tax: "A single rate tax is regressive and unfair."

This isn't true. I direct him to our Tax Advisory Council report, which shows that our proposal actually is progressive. He is neither thrilled nor convinced.

Ray Haman regularly attends my committee meetings on behalf of the governor's office, normally just to take note, but not today.

"May I say something, Mrs. McCaffree?"

"Yes, Mr. Haman."

"Governor Evans' tax package is not remotely regressive, as Mr. Mitchell suggests. It is progressive. It would relieve the burden on lower-income families relative to those in higher income brackets, and it takes most of the pressure off special school levies, too, to meet the educational needs of schoolchildren and their families."

Representatives from the League of Women Voters, the Association of American University Women, and the statewide PTA all tell us they agree with labor's notion of a constitutional amendment that allows the legislature to debate the form of income tax — single or graduated. However, the Washington Education Association adds its support to the governor's tax package.

"Our first choice was a graduated income tax," admits WEA spokeswoman Gladys Perry, "but after further study of your proposal, we have determined that your single rate tax, as part of the entire reform package, includes many features endorsed by the WEA. If the legislature chooses to give the people an opportunity to vote on the single-rate income tax, the WEA pledges its support."

> **PROGRESSIVE TAX**
>
> A tax that increases as a proportion of income as income increases: as income increases, so does the tax rate.

> **REGRESSIVE TAX**
>
> A tax that decreases as a proportion of income -- as income increases, the tax rate decreases.

I call next on Larry Robinson, active in Yakima Republican politics.

"Thank you, Mrs. McCaffree. I am speaking on behalf of Let's Be Heard."

"I am all for hearing the public voice, Mr. Robinson," I say. "Can you explain to this committee the nature of Let's Be Heard?"

"Anti-income tax, plain and simple," he says. "We don't like it. We don't want it. And our membership is 20,000 strong."

"Thank you, Mr. Robinson. We will take this into consideration."

"I sincerely hope so, Mrs. McCaffree. There'll be serious consequences come next election for anyone neglecting or not listening to the people."

"How do you suggest we resolve our ongoing revenue shortfall?" I ask.

"Sales tax," he says, "because it taxes everyone, including the welfare recipients."

Several gasp at this. Mr. Robinson sits. No one else asks to testify. Slade motions me.

"Yes, Mr. Gorton?"

He summarizes the public input: "So our proposal is too soft on our low income citizens for your tastes, Mr. Robinson, and not soft enough for Mr. Davis and labor." [18]

At this point, I ask for a motion on the constitutional amendment as we've amended it here today. A do pass motion is made and we vote. HJR 29, including a single rate income tax and a lower lid on property taxes, passes divisively 12 to 8. All the committee Democrats say nay but our Republican majority prevails. Consideration of HB 639, the omnibus bill with its many sections to implement the proposed changes to our tax code, must wait for another day. I adjourn this morning meeting and we head upstairs to the House.

In our afternoon House session, I present our report: "We, a majority of your Committee on Revenue and Taxation, to whom was referred HJR 29, amending the 40-mill limitation, and to permit an income tax, report the same back to the House with the recommendation that the attached substitute resolution be substituted therefore, and that the substitute resolution do pass."

The Democrats make their minority report, recommending that HJR 29 do not pass. Our tax reform resolution is referred to Rules.

EARLY THURSDAY MORNING I POUR MY FIRST CUP of coffee and sit down at the kitchen table to read my *P-I*, a routine spawned at home in Seattle, transplanted to Olympia, and generally the source of a peaceful start to my day. But today peace is fleeting.

Sprawled across the entire top of page two is a big bold headline: TAX REFORM BILL TO TRIGGER BIG ACTION. The full-page story features a photo of Bob Greive. The reporter writes, "Selecting the 'big action' this session might take an agent and a grant from the Central Intelligence Agency. Potentially there are half a dozen such issues. But by general consensus, the big one is the tax reform package proposed by Gov. Dan Evans."

I've had my nose to my personal grindstone, and this claim surprises me. As a majority leadership team we're promoting many crucial issues all at once. From our beginning in 1963, our DEGOHT team has never been one to talk endless strategy. We share similar goals — making our state the best it can be — so we all work from a similar page, but once we've identified the issues, we gravitate to our individual areas of strength and get to work. That's what I've been doing with tax reform. And Slade with civil rights and mental health care. And Joel with his team-building strength in the Senate.

Is tax reform really tops? I continue to read, sip my coffee.

"No one in the legislature agrees 100 percent with this proposal," Joel says of our tax reform package. "Since we have to get a two-thirds vote to get the issue to the people, it has to be a compromise. We can't get it with a flat non-progressive income tax on the one extreme, or an all-out graduated net income tax on the other."

"Get this straight," Senator Greive tells the reporter, "I'm for a graduated net income tax. Have been all my political career. But you don't get everything you want in politics and a hard position isn't called for at this time. If we don't get some kind of tax reform we'll eventually wind up with a 10 percent sales tax."

The reporter explains the 'sides' to our tax reform issue, explains that the plan is complex, and I bless him for getting to the crux of it: "A basic fact of tax life lies behind it: In the past two years, special levies, mostly for school operations, have increased from $60 million to $120 million. This means a couple of things. A) Property taxes are coming to share an inordinate slice of the tax burden. And B) Schools are perilously dependent on expensive, risky special levy elections." [19]

And who stands to lose from this perilous dependence? School children.

I head to work.

The House is called to order. At the appropriate time, I make another report from my committee: "Mr. Speaker, we, a majority of your Committee on Revenue and Taxation, to whom was referred House Bill Number 639…"

This is the omnibus tax bill, with all the specific tax reforms. I attach our committee's substitute bill, and recommend that it do pass. The minority report recommends against it. We send the bill to Rules for review.

OMNIBUS BILL

A bill that relates to or provides many elements of a general subject.

Two weeks remain in our regular 60-day session and everyone in the Republican caucus keenly feels the pressure — the responsibility of being the majority party, in charge of leading the way. We are trying to complete our state business, doing it well and finishing on time.

The governor is pushing us hard on his executive request bills. We're working diligently in our committees to move these along, build consensus, refine them and herd them through the complex legislative process. We have already sent several Blueprint measures to the Senate. But so far, there they sit.

The press and the public are watching us — watching for the progress and momentum long promised by our Republican team, now the majority. They're comparing our actual work to the promise of our campaigns and our Blueprint.

We wanted to lead. We asked for it. We got it.

1967 HOUSE OF REPRESENTATIVES • STATE OF WASHINGTON

CHAPTER EIGHT

BLUEPRINT FOR PROGRESS
LEGISLATING FOR A NEW DIRECTION

As we work through our differences
on this enormous proposed change for our state, the
House is fully engaged. Everyone is here, everyone is voting.
This is how our legislative process is supposed to unfold.
This is how bills should take shape.

KEN HAS DRIVEN DOWN FOR THE WEEKEND, stopping at Wagner's Bakery in downtown Olympia to pick up a chocolate cake. On Saturday night he convinces me to take a small break so that he and Mary and I can indulge in cake and ice cream — the least I can do for my birthday.

Then it's right back to business. For the first time this session, our House will work on through Sunday, foregoing a weekend respite. There is simply too much we must do. If we work straight through to the end of this 60-day session, we'll work eighteen days straight — workdays, incidentally, not bound by 9 to 5. I am willing to face this pace, and I'm not alone: As a leadership team, we're determined to get things done.

On Monday, Day 50, Marjorie Lynch takes the floor of the House to announce that her Higher Education Committee has discussed House Bill 596 — the new state college — and recommends that it do pass. The bill is then placed on second reading, open to our amendments. The sergeant at arms locks us in under a Call of the House, and two Clark County legislators immediately jump into action. Rep. O'Dell, a Republican, asks if his Democrat counterpart from the area, Rep. Marsh, will yield to a question. Yes, Mr. Marsh will. Mr. O'Dell then asks Mr. Marsh if he was able in committee to suggest Clark County as a location for this future college. Mr. Marsh replies: He was not. Nor, he says, were others allowed to suggest any alternate locations.

"The committee chairman said that she would only recognize a motion to move the bill out of the Higher Education Committee," Mr. Marsh said. "She stated, 'We are not here for the purpose of making amendments.'"

Marjorie is incensed, then visibly flustered at this charge. She jumps to standing. The Speaker recognizes her on a point of personal privilege.

"Mr. Speaker," she says, "I think Mr. Marsh has, has... impinged on my immunity... or whatever it is."

I wish she'd asked me. 'Impugned my motives' she meant.

"Whatever it is, Mrs. Lynch," Speaker Eldridge replies, "I think you are right."

Mr. Charette, the Aberdeen Democrat who was a senator last term (and stood up to Greive on the Senate floor on redistricting), has been working closely with us on this new college bill. He asks if Mr. O'Dell will yield to a question. O'Dell will.

"Mr. O'Dell, on what just took place between you and Mr. Marsh — if I brought some musicians in here, would you dance to it?"

"Yes, if it is necessary," says Mr. O'Dell without a blink, "in order to get the bill referred back to committee...There has been some discussion whether this has been properly considered in committee... We thought this should be re-referred... All we want is fair consideration." [1]

Every committee chairman has a distinctive style of leadership. Some manage from the top down, stern hand on the gavel, strictly limiting discussion and debate. I tend to be more flexible and encourage all my members to speak to the issue at hand. Through the League I developed this style of building consensus. I believe a true leader respects his colleagues' opinions and holds the door open to compromise. However, regardless of style, the committee chairman's job is to steer the committee in line with caucus policies and to bring along all legislation the leadership has identified as key. Sometimes that requires a heavy hand, whether due to the specific issue, or in order to meet the ticking 60-day clock.

The House debates at length — should the college bill be re-referred to committee for further consideration? (Beneath this question lies a silent second one: Has Mrs. Lynch been unfair?) Someone moves that it be re-referred. Mrs. Lynch speaks against the motion, setting off more debate.

Mr. Gorton moves to lay the motion on the table. Mr. Grant demands an electric roll call. We vote. By 56-42 we table the re-referral to committee and continue to consider the actual bill. After another squabble over parliamentary procedure — *Was laying the motion on the table just then legitimate?* — we vote again, and again vote to table the re-referral: 57-41. Thus, the re-referral to committee remains on the table, while the college bill remains alive on the floor.

Our debate on HB 596 now swings to finance. *What are the costs of this new college? Shouldn't they be specified?* We conclude that the legislature must first approve the college — its nature, its location and size — before we estimate a price tag, before an appropriation is asked.

We then return to the true bone of contention. *Who gets the new college town?* And for the next four hours, legislators propose amendments to HB 596, each suggesting the new college be built in his district. Every single time, the majority tables the amendment and cites the Interim Council's recommendation that we site the college here in our capitol city of Olympia.

Hal Wolf, an Olympia Republican and a member of the Higher Education Committee, says, "We have been successful in keeping this discussion of a new site for the college out of politics." To which Representative Taylor objects: How can Mr. Wolf say such a thing straight faced, given today's hours of contentious testimony? Could he please elaborate?

"I have not been able to keep it out of politics on the floor today," Mr. Wolf admits, eliciting grunts of agreement. "My reference was to the advisory committee. With the assistance of Senator Gissberg from the Senate, we placed the responsibility with the seven college presidents and the lay members of high stature from each of the congressional districts. This was a great start toward having blue ribbon committees make those decisions that in the past might have been political 'pork barrels'."

Yet amendments suggesting new locations continue.

Each district's representatives want to deliver their voters this plum of access to higher education — a college with an easy commute for the students, and college town revenues for their communities. Finally, when tempers and tolerance on this topic have deteriorated to a brittle frazzle, Representative Avery rises for recognition.

"Mr. Avery, you have the floor."

"I move that we amend House Bill 596 as follows: In the clause specifying the location for the new four-year college, in the place of Olympia, substitute Kettle Falls."

The laughter is mildly hilarious at first, but then it swells among our terribly tired House into outright delirium, until our entire formal chamber has completely come undone, rocking with raw, aching belly laughs, and many of us wiping wet eyes. For all of us know that Kettle Falls, population 300 and plopped in the dusty middle of nowhere — a blink along a straggly road near the

Idaho border that meanders northwest into Canada — is a perfectly preposterous spot for a college town.

At this moment, however, little Kettle Falls has performed a noble deed, having delivered our House some sorely needed humor. Kettle Falls brings our debate to an end.[2]

We vote and pass HB 596 with the Olympia location intact. It is ordered engrossed and passed back to Rules for third reading. The next day, this four-year college bill comes before us on third reading and final passage. We vote: 80 yeas, 17 nays, 2 absent and not voting, and send it straight to the Senate.

Now the community college bill is before us, and protracted debate returns. Very few argue the merits of the bill — they argue only location. At long last, we pass it out of second reading and move that it be engrossed. But Mr. Gorton moves that we suspend the Rules and place HB 548 on final passage, the second reading being considered the third. We agree, and we pass this community college bill 88-4 (with 7 absent and not voting) and send it along to the Senate as well. Our Blueprint's two major education measures are now on their way.

And now it's my turn. I report that the majority of my committee recommends that we pass House Bill 576 — the proposed administrative changes to our tax and revenue system that would give our state a new Department of Revenue. We send it along to Rules for second reading.

FEBRUARY COMES TO A CLOSE and March brings with it a welcome change of pace. On this first day of the month, on this 52nd day of our 60-day session, the Senate presents us a bill of a different stripe: A stadium commission to develop a stadium for professional sports. This is the darling of a large group of business owners and sports fans in King County, the seat of Seattle, and it is backed by a big bi-partisan group of state senators from districts in and around the city.

"If we build it, they will come," these senators have been telling us, lobbying the House in advance of the bill's arrival. "Just think, we'll be able to attract not only major sports teams — football, baseball, who knows? — but also a big infusion of funding into our local economy from all the fans!"

Senate Bill 505 suggests that two cents of every 4.5 cents of retail sales tax collected on hotel and motel rooms in King County be diverted into a special state account established specifically to fund the construction of this professional-league sports stadium — The Kingdome, its authors are calling it. This plan would bypass the fact that local governments are not authorized to levy a sales tax, nor does our lid on property tax levies allow fundraising of this scale. Our House Committee on Business and Professions will consider it.

Not to be outdone by Seattle, five Pierce County representatives introduce a House 'Tacoma Dome' bill the very next day, and it swiftly reappears on the floor, recommended "do pass" by a majority of the House Committee on Local Government. House Bill 730 would authorize Pierce County to acquire, construct and operate or maintain a multi-purpose domed sports stadium, including the authority to acquire or condemn property to create it, and an ability to issue revenue bonds. We send this to Rules and it reappears the following day on second reading, which becomes the third, and we vote on final passage: 82 yeas, 9 nays, 8 not voting. Next stop for the 'Tacoma Dome' bill: The Senate.

These stadium bills are neither earth shattering nor a part of our Blueprint, but at a time when all our more major bills still face a tough uphill struggle, they have injected some life and liveliness into this late hour in our legislative session.

Again, we work straight through the weekend. We process less contentious matters and attempt to find consensus on the big ones: Tax reform, the budget, the new four-year college. All three of these major reforms are now in the Senate, but with luck we'll have them back before the end of the week — the end of the session — and as leaders, we want to make sure we're ready for the trio. We talk with our House colleagues. We talk with our Senate friends and foes. We confer, re-tool and chart our course for the regular session's final week.

To our disappointment, but not our surprise, an extra session needs to be called. We had hoped to stave it off with our efficient January start, teamed with the fact that we'd presented such a clear agenda at the outset. But ours is a two-party system, and we must work with and within it. The loyal opposition is alive and well this session, as is their role and their right.

TOM COPELAND TELLS ME FIRST, and then Slade Gorton and finally Don Eldridge, who pulls me aside to let me know: The Senate's Meany Hotel bill will hit our House floor on Monday for final passage. I appreciate the advance warning. This gives me the weekend to do what I must.

All session long I have fielded constituent phone calls, scores of letters, and have even been visited in person by a few anxious groups — all centered on the fate of the Meany Hotel. This is a hot-button issue in District 32A (and in the 46th and 43rd too), but as for the rest of the state, it is completely inconsequential — of no concern to my other colleagues, whatsoever. In this fantastically busy session, with so many critical measures at stake, who cares about the Meany Hotel bill? Not enough to pass it, that's sure.

That is why, one-by-one this weekend, I talk with my friends in the legislature — to rural legislators, urban, suburban, Democrats, Republicans, Senators, members of the House. I talk to everyone I know, and even to some I don't. Only by talking up this tiny bill, face-to-face, will it stand a chance. By nature, when legislators aren't familiar with a bill, their most common response (and the safest, politically) is to vote it down, unless... someone they know and trust recommends they do otherwise. Since the Meany Hotel bill is important only in my district and in two others, but extremely important to me as a legislator who is devoted to serving her constituents, each House member's vote on it Monday will fall into one of three categories: 1) Those who actually have a position on this bill and will vote yea or nay based on that, 2) Those who are supportive of me as a legislator and will thus follow my recommendation to vote for it, or 3) Those who oppose me, and know this matters to me as an elected official of the 32nd District, and will thus purposely vote the crucial bill down.

All weekend long, I tell each person I talk to, "I'd like you to vote for Senate Bill 138 when it comes to the floor on Monday. It's important only in the environs of my district, so you're not likely to be familiar with it. But I have studied the text of the bill, conferred with my constituents, and given it considerable thought, and I believe a yes vote is the right one to make."

I field their questions, and answer in all honesty.

"Yes, it will authorize the sale of liquor within a mile of a major university campus."

"Yes, I realize the old law was written with concern for the college students. I understand your concerns."

"Yes, it's true there is no similar restriction near the Washington State campus in Pullman."

"No, I'm not a big fan of drinking."

"Yes, I am a Methodist. No, I am not a Free Methodist, but I respect the fact that you as a church do not drink."

"Yes, it is the only hotel in the state that has such a prohibition in place."

"Yes, it is a prestigious and historic setting for university visitors."

"No, I don't think alcohol will add to the prestige of a visit, *per se*, but I do respect the hotel's right to operate on a par with our other hotels."

During my weekend rounds, it dawns on me how many good relationships I've established in three legislative terms in these past five years. My lobbying effort for this tiny bill, salient only to my constituency, makes a clear point: My tendency not to judge, not to strike a strident partisan stance, my willingness to reach across the aisle for the sake of legislative momentum, my preference for work rather than partying, and my true enjoyment of so many diverse colleagues — all of this is now bearing fruit. I've developed and accrued some good legislative equity. Because of who I am and what I've done in this House, over this weekend I'm able to gather the necessary votes.

On Monday, late in our evening session, SB 138, the Meany Hotel bill, finally comes to the floor for our vote on final passage. After listening to months of passionate lobbying, pro and con, I must now make public my stance. I must vote and take whatever heat my constituents toss me. Some of them will inevitably be displeased.

John O'Brien speaks first, delivering reasoned support for SB 138.

Big Daddy Day speaks second, also in favor.

Slade Gorton urges our support.

Audley Mahaffey does not.

Mr. Mahaffey delivers a heartfelt statement against passage, a plea that exhibits his sincere concern for youth and families and quality of life.

Because of the 'morals' attached to it, this little bill has the potential to carry big consequence. There is a sense that many here today are weighing their votes with utmost care. The clerk calls a roll-call vote, and when the alphabet is complete the final tally is 56 for, 38 against and 5 absent and not voting. We pass the Senate's Meany Hotel bill and send it to the governor to sign into law.

Audley Mahaffey holds his head a long while, and then he begins to write. The next morning, his written statement is added to the Journal: *The following is an explanation of why I voted against Senate Bill No. 138 on the evening of March 6, 1967. I am opposed to removing the one-mile boundary around the University where the selling of alcoholic beverages has been prevented. With the removal of this boundary there will be at least two cocktail lounges and two taverns opened in this area where the ban is removed—a liberalization of the liquor laws.*

These new outlets for the selling of liquor will make for more drinking, with its consequent incidents on the highways, and increases in our institutional care and in our family disintegration. In fact, a great deal of our moral and social degeneration of our society can be traced to the use of alcohol. In having this line around the University there is no discrimination, as liquor is sold closer to the University campus than it is to many other campuses, including Washington State.

We cannot legislate morals, true, but we can help our young people by not giving them more temptations than they already have. We are our brother's keeper—for his good and for the good of society. To quote Bishop Fulton J. Sheen, "Liberty is not an heirloom. It requires the daily bread of self-denial, the salt of law and above all the backbone of acknowledging responsibility for our deeds."

The University District has been my home for nearly 50 years. It is a good place to live and I would hope it would continue to be that way. I appreciate the opportunity of explaining my 'no' vote on SB No. 138, Audley F. Mahaffey, 46th District. [3]

I'll have some explaining to do when I return home to 32A.

TONIGHT WE RECEIVE FROM THE SENATE OUR BUDGET BILL, scalped and replaced with a budget written by Senate Democrats under the leadership of Martin Durkan, chairman of Senate Ways and Means. John O'Brien immediately defends Durkan's budget bill, suggesting that if we accept and pass this bill — as is — then perhaps we can avoid a special session and all go home.

But Slade Gorton and Bob Goldsworthy both discourage our 'yes' vote, and move that we refuse the Senate amendments. We vote. The majority and majority party wins, 54 - 42. We refuse the Senate's version of the budget bill and send it back, sans their scalp, retaining the House-drawn budget we sent them the first time. Not surprisingly, the Senate refuses to agree.

Without agreement, a conference committee is formed. The Speaker names Mr. Goldsworthy, Mr. Saling and Mr. DeJarnatt, two Republicans and a Democrat, to negotiate for the House.

On Tuesday, Day 58 of the session, while as a House we're working our way through the two stadium bills, the Senate enters into a floor debate on a constitutional amendment: To lower the voting age from 21 to 18. A page delivers me a message. It's from an excited young Sam Reed: *Senate debating 18-year-old vote bill right now!*

A short House recess allows me to peek in on the Senate debate, where a half dozen

> ## CONFERENCE COMMITTEE
>
> Authorized by the House and Senate when the two fail to reach agreement on a bill as amended. Three members appointed from each body confer and report only on the specific contentious amendment(s).

senators champion the case of the young people. Among the common 'pro' comments a steady refrain: If they're old enough to fight, these kids should be old enough to vote.

"They already face tough decisions out there in those mud paddies of Vietnam," says Senator Kupka of Tacoma.

And Senator Greive likes the idea of adding younger voters: "They'd be more liberal and more progressive."

Other Senators, though, argue that our voting age is just fine as is.

Constitutional amendments require approval by two-thirds of a body to pass — or 33 Senate votes out of the 49 members here. The final vote brings 25 ayes — a simple majority, but in this case not enough. In the Senate gallery, rows of eager young shoulders sink with this defeat.

TWO DAYS REMAIN in our regular 40th Session. What can we accomplish in only two days that will demonstrate significant progress? Our voters will want to know, to see. We've promised dynamic leadership and action, yet we have no desire to pass mini-measures just to appear busy—what we want to do is to catalyze our meaningful reforms.

The Senate sends us HB 596—the new four-year college bill—with several small amendments including a good suggestion, I think, that the name of this new college be decided by its new trustees.

"Mr. Speaker," says Mrs. Lynch, "I move that the House concur with Engrossed House Bill 596 as amended by the Senate."

We vote: 85 yeas, 9 nays, 5 absent and not voting. The state of Washington has a new college coming its way—to the vicinity of Olympia. This is a huge success for the governor and for our team, and an exciting educational piece now in place from our Blueprint.

On the final day, one more major bill returns from the Senate: SHB 548—the community colleges. The Senate has substantially amended this bill. We refuse to concur. We send it back, and ask them to recede therefrom.

In the meantime, both the House and Senate are trying to reach agreement on the state's biennial budget, a central task of every legislature, every session.

From the start, we've aimed to complete our budget within these first sixty days. But now, on day sixty, the clocks reach midnight before we reach agreement. Neither body is ready to vote, nor ready to give up. So we cover said clocks and artificially extend midnight.

In these wee hours a proclamation arrives from the governor. Speaker Eldridge reads it aloud to his weary House: While we have enacted more significant measures than any legislature in recent history, we have failed to complete the business of this state. The governor bluntly lists our failures—his list is both scathing and long—and he calls us into an Extraordinary Session, beginning at 10 a.m.... just a few hours away.

SHORTLY BEFORE SUNRISE FRIDAY MORNING—without a funded budget in place—we finally adjourn *sine die*. Most of us rush home for a shower, a quick bite, maybe a catnap. Mary and I are exhausted. I try to sleep for an hour or two, but mostly toss. Just as I'm finally dozing off, my alarm clangs to life, I rouse myself, dress, and we hop into our Ford and dash to the capitol—Mary now quite capable with the gearshift and clutch.

While legislators flock back to the chambers of our Senate and our House, the capitol press corps flocks to the office of the governor, who has called a morning a press conference.

At 10 a.m. on the dot, the House comes to order. The Speaker re-reads the governor's admonishing proclamation.

Meanwhile, in the governor's office, the press gets an even harsher ear full.

The governor blasts Senate Democrats for holding up the 40th Session. He tells the reporters and TV crews in no gentle terms that the Senate is sitting on eighteen different House-passed executive request bills. The Senate sent these bills to committee weeks ago, where they've languished since, neither seen nor heard. The governor lists these neglected measures – including the two in his tax reform package – and says the people of Washington deserve this chance to choose a tax structure that responds to their needs and, incidentally, impacts taxpayers much more equitably. He sends the media off with hot ears and a furious list for them to pass on to the public over the weekend.[4]

The only major House work today for our sleepy ninety-nine is the community college bill, SHB 548. Yesterday, our final regular day, we'd returned it to the Senate, asking them to recede from their multiple amendments. They sent it back, refusing to change the bill, their amendments intact. Today we vote again, and again we reject their amendments and ask them to please recede therefrom. They will not, and call for a conference committee. Marjorie Lynch stands.

"I move that the House grant the request of the Senate for a conference on Engrossed Substitute House Bill 548."

We vote it so. The Speaker appoints three members to the committee: Marjorie Lynch, Buster Brouillet and Charles Newschwander, a dentist from Tacoma.

We recess for the weekend, having failed to finish our business on time, chastised by the governor, critiqued in the press, and all of us incredibly tired. Many colleagues go home this

TO CONCUR
A motion to agree with an amendment attached by the other legislative body (House or Senate).

TO RECEDE
A motion requesting that the other body withdraw its amendment from a bill.

afternoon, but I stay behind to meet with the governor, his staff and a handful of legislative leaders. We review our Blueprint agenda, review the status of each bill, review the opposition and reluctantly conclude that we still face a long, steep, strenuous climb.

On Sunday mornings, I regularly read two newspapers: *The Seattle P-I* and *The Seattle Times*. The *Times* is Seattle's evening daily – delivered evenings except on Sundays – and is considered more stodgy than its a.m. rival. *Times* political reporter Lyle Burt is much less colorful as well, both on the page and in person, than the *P-I's* Shelby Scates. This morning I appreciate Lyle Burt's straightforward approach. I came to Olympia for the work, not the drama.

This past week's haggling and stonewalling and partisan positioning – integral to the legislative process to be sure – has thoroughly sapped me. I much prefer to just get to work, get to the compromise, get our lawmaking done. With so much before us still, it won't be easy.

WHILE I'VE LABORED LONG HOURS on behalf of state government, my husband has made huge strides in another direction: Toward the national fore of health-care economics.

Dr. Kenneth M. McCaffree is now considered one of the top health economists in the nation. Ken is simultaneously serving as an economics consultant to the National Institute of Mental Health (NIMH), to the Health Economics branch of the U.S. Public Health Service, and to our state Department of Public Health. Plus, he's been elected a member of the University of Washington Faculty Senate and is thus active in university budget and salary decisions. And he's teaching economics across disciplines — both in medicine and public affairs.

We're an active pair, reflecting our Kansas community activist roots.

I receive little sympathy from Ken about the demands of my work in the legislature. But since he's the same breed of "doer" as I am, he does give me plenty of genuine understanding.

During my first legislative session, and my second, too, Ken and I navigated through some personal resentments and hard feelings, not to mention the difficulty of living and working in separate cities. But we're problem solvers — we argued and discussed our way through, and this has allowed us to lead two full, valuable lives.

ON MONDAY, MARCH 10, we begin the real work of this Extraordinary Session of this 40th Session of the Washington State Legislature, and the dozens of freshmen have the same question I did my first year: *What happens now? Do we have to start over? What about all those bills we sent to the Senate?*

Fortunately, we have an articulate floor leader in Slade. The Speaker recognizes Mr. Gorton, who is happy to fill us in.

"Mr. Speaker, members of the House. There have been a number of members who have asked about the status of the bills which passed in the regular session or which did not pass all the way through to the governor's desk, and I think this might be as good a place as any to try to explain..."

Even those of us familiar with the process are grateful for the clarity of this review.

"Any House bill which did not pass the House at all is in the same status as it was at the end of the regular session. That is, if it was in a committee such as Business and Professions, that is where it is now, and it is open to discussion in that particular committee, *if* the committee wishes to take it up."

Of nearly fifty bills in my committee, we will discuss only a few. The major measures first, and then if there's time, those with less full-scale impact, such as the bill to exempt chick hatcheries from the B & O tax, for example, or one to exempt fruit tree spray from the retail sales tax.

Slade continues: "If it was in Rules Two or Rules Three at the end of the session, it is still in Rules Two or Three."

Now it gets tricky.

"Any bill that passed the House and went to the Senate but failed to pass the Senate, or passed the Senate in a different form and was sent to a conference committee which didn't complete its work, reverts to House Rules Three. It will have on it the same amendments the House placed on it during the second reading of the regular session, but will not have on it any Senate amendments which may have been agreed upon. When our Rules Committee places it on the calendar, it will be on third reading and final passage here, *unless* it is brought back to second reading for the purpose of amendments."

Over the weekend, this is what we as leaders reviewed in the governor's office — which bills sit where, which have lost their Senate amendments, which should be moved back to second reading from third for a bit more work...

"The same is true of any Senate bill which passed that body and arrived here but didn't pass the House — it is back in Senate Rules Three, stripped of any amendments we may have added," Slade tells us, and I can see some colleagues losing concentration, or perhaps they are just plain lost. "We made quite a few such amendments, and I suggest you look at these Senate bills with great care if you were interested in any amendments that the House put on those bills, because now they're gone." [5]

"What about committee meetings? What's the schedule?" Rep. Humiston asks.

Speaker Eldridge tells us Tom Copeland is working on that right now, hence his absence. He'll distribute new committee calendars shortly. And yes, our committees will remain the same.

"Can the Senate change the Senate bills they send back to us?" asks Rep. Adams. "How will we know what's been changed?"

Yes, the Senate can amend its own bills if they move them back to second reading, the Speaker explains. As of now, he says, any Senate bills acted upon by the House and sent back to them would be in Senate Rules Three, and would remain unchanged (with our House amendments intact) *unless* the Senate sends them back to second reading. We'll have to keep track in our bill books — these several books upon our desks which now stand about ten inches thick... each!

The competition here is tough. With a ticking clock and hundreds of bills in play, each sponsor will have to fight to see his measures through the lengthy legislative process. And that includes me.

A trio of legislators escorts a trio of lovelies to the rostrum, and Speaker Eldridge introduces the state Apple Queen and her two-princess court. Another session, another Apple Queen or Daffodil Princess, another perennial parcel of this process. The queen addresses us.

"As ambassador of the State of Washington, home of the apple capitol of the world, I would like to take this opportunity to thank you for asking us here today, and in return I would like to extend a royal invitation to each and every one of you to meet with us on the first weekend of May when we will all take part in the state Apple Blossom Festival!"

Marjorie scribbles: *If we're home by then.* The queen proceeds.

"During these springtime festivities, we pay honor to King Apple – as old as Adam, yet ever new," says the bubbly monarch, her smile unfailing, "especially when it is apple harvest time in the Wenatchee Valley. I am sure if you will come to Wenatchee you will see and agree with us that harvest time is good news for the whole apple-loving world!" [6]

The Apple Court sashays out, smiles intact, and we adjourn until tomorrow, Tuesday, at 1 p.m. We scatter to our committees, find some time to eat and sleep, and convene at 1 as scheduled on Day 5 of this Extraordinary Session.

In the afternoon, we hear from the Senate: The conference committee on the community college bill has failed to reach agreement. It therefore requests a free conference committee, 'Free' meaning they no longer have to limit their bill work to the original proposal and amendments, but can start from scratch on the topic and arrive at something altogether new.

Mrs. Lynch moves that we grant the Senate request for a free conference committee. We vote: Be free.

"What's up?" I ask Marjorie.

"I'll explain in committee," she says.

Speaker Eldridge now moves HJR 1 – the Open Space Act limiting property valuations, which I strongly support – out from Rules and onto the floor on third reading, where it passes

> **FREE CONFERENCE COMMITTEE**
>
> A conference committee, authorized by the House and Senate, which is free to confer and report on the entire subject matter embraced by a bill.

by a solid margin: 84-9 with 6 not voting. It's off to the Senate for open space.

The new Department of Revenue Bill (now SHB 576) is also slated for action – on second reading. Rep. Ted Bottiger and I both speak in favor of a small committee amendment, which is easily adopted along with several more small refinements proposed on the floor. We suspend the Rules, move it from second reading to third for final passage, and the clerk calls the roll. To my surprise, Tom Copeland votes against it, and Dwight Hawley too, though it passes easily,

84-10 with 5 not voting. We send it to the Senate.

Tom finds me in the dining room afterwards.

"I'm so sorry, Mary Ellen. I'm so embarrassed! Dwight and I were talking about a glitch in the committee schedule when your bill came up for a final vote, and I just plain voted wrong."

"These things happen, Tom."

I recall my broken glasses. Of course, if the vote had been a squeaker, the mistake could have done some damage.

Our Extraordinary Session begins to move more smoothly, at a more productive pace. We spend the bulk of our time in committees, many more hours conferring with each other, and hold out hope we can wrap up this session soon and go home.

My main focus now is gaining the votes for tax reform. I confer with our leadership daily to update our vote counts. Though it has been several weeks since my committee approved the two tax reform measures, we wait for the perfect time to bring this critical package to the House floor.

On Day 7, the time has come. Slade, Don and Tom let me know to expect the tax reform package on the floor today for second reading. At the appropriate instant I stand and Speaker Eldridge enables my microphone.

"Mrs. McCaffree."

"Mr. Speaker, I move that Substitute House Joint Resolution 29, as amended by the House Committee on Revenue and Taxation, be substituted for HJR 29, amending the constitution as to the 40 mill limitation and to permit an income tax, and that the substitute be placed on today's calendar for second reading. Please refer to your mimeographed copies of the substitute resolution in your bill book. The copies were distributed to each of you this morning."

Democrats Buster Brouillet and Arlie DeJarnatt propose an amendment: To extend our school levy period to two years rather than one. This would cut down considerably on levy campaign hours. I approve. Buster and Stu Bledsoe speak in favor of adopting the amendment. Someone demands a Call of the House. Sergeant at Arms Eugene Prince has recruited a young supply clerk, Ralph Munro, and two other young men from some downstairs offices, to act as unofficial assistant sergeants at arms — to keep close watch on our doors during our critical debate on tax reform.

We're locked in before we go any further.

Gary Grant is recognized. He proposes that the phrase "single uniform" regarding the income tax rate be replaced with the word "graduated". This debate will not die. This measure is on second reading, and this is what the second reading is for — to allow any member of the House to propose amendments from the floor. In this case, an amendment to an amendment. With this recurring income tax argument before us — single rate versus graduated, Rep. Chatalas demands an electric roll call, the quickest way to provide a permanent record of everyone present for this debate. All ninety-nine are here. All must participate. The citizen galleries are packed with onlookers, the atmospheric tension thick.

Five legislators speak in favor of changing the language (and structure) to a graduated tax, as proposed by Rep. Grant. Five speak against it, including me. We vote. Grant's change fails, 44-55, straight down party lines. The single uniform income tax rate remains a component of SHJR 29.

Mr. Moon proposes another amendment: Change the phrase "single uniform rate" to "rate or rates" — which would open the door to a graduated rate. We discuss. We vote. This, too, fails.

A third amendment, by four Democrats, echoes the labor lobby suggestion that rather than specify the tax rate, we should leave the specifics of rate and structure up to the next legislature, but should allow the sales tax elements of the bill to move forward: Reduce the sales tax and eliminate the sales tax on groceries and drugs (but not on restaurant food or alcohol). Not surprisingly, this amendment to separate the two taxes draws prolonged debate, and I allow Slade to take up the mantle of our uniform single rate income tax. Back and forth the arguments fly. We eventually vote: This newest proposed amendment to the amendment by Brouillet and DeJarnatt fails as well, 44 to 55. Majority rules.

The next proposed amendment is extremely complex: It formally links the rates of each tax — income, property and excise — each 'leg' of the three-legged revenue stool. This is a well-crafted amendment, much like the governor's twin 3.5 percent rates on both the income tax and sales tax, and it is articulately presented by Representative Day. After a series of clarifications — *Where we are in the process?* — we approve the Day amendment by a voice vote.

As we work through our differences on this enormous proposed change for our state, our House is fully engaged. Everyone is here, and everyone voting. This is how the legislative process is supposed to unfold. This is how bills should take shape. I find it absolutely exhilarating!

The Speaker calls for a final vote on the Brouillet/DeJarnatt amendment, as amended by Day. It passes with a bi-partisan mix: 68-31. I am thrilled with these 68 'Yeas' — a promising indicator we may have the sixty-six votes we'll need to the pass the resolution in full.

With this final amendment approved, SHJR 29 is ordered engrossed and passed to the Rules Committee for third reading. Its biggest test lies ahead. On second reading, we voted only on the resolution's amendments — and amendments require only a simple majority vote to pass. Once the resolution returns on third reading, we'll need at least 66 votes to keep it alive.

Now the omnibus implementing bill comes before us, by executive request: To establish a single rate net income tax, to amend both the B & O tax and the state retail sales and use tax, and to make a number of administrative changes as well.

"Mr. Speaker," I say, "I move that Substitute House Bill 639 be substituted for House Bill 639, and that the substitute bill be placed on the calendar for second reading."

Again, the bill has undergone significant change since first introduced, a result of my ongoing consultation with legislative colleagues, with legal revisions approved by the governor's staff, and with all the work we did in committee.

With the floor open for amendments, five legislators — three from Eastern Washington and two from Tacoma — propose two small amendments... relating to candy. The Eastern Washington trio speaks for their region's sugar beet industry, whereas the Tacoma pair champions the local confectioner Brown & Haley of Almond Roca fame. We adopt the pair of candy amendments without debate, and that's it. House Bill 639 is ordered engrossed and passed to Rules for third reading, wrapping up a successful day for tax reform — and a long one.

Mr. Gorton moves that the House defer further consideration of the bills on today's calendar until tomorrow. We adjourn until 10 a.m., Friday, March 17.

I SPEND MY NEXT WAKING HOURS talking with my colleagues, answering their questions about the tax reform measures, trying to convince 66 of them to support the constitutional amendment — an essential precursor for the rest of the package to work. We need that two-thirds majority. I continue to lobby.

By the time I enter the House chamber on Day 8, I am aware of 61 confirmed favorable votes on our tax reform package, and am moderately hopeful of the five more we need to pass it.

St. Patrick's Day and the wearin' o' the green is appropriate, perhaps, for this day on which we'll be dealing with dollars and a steadier flow of state funds — if we can pass this tax package. I take my seat at my desk on the floor and continue to review my vote count all morning, and continue to lobby accordingly. Roughly a dozen colleagues are wavering — from both sides of the aisle. Hopefully I can persuade five of these to shift 'yea' before we vote. We aren't confined to our seats. Any of us can move about to confer on the floor as long as we don't disturb the proceedings, and of course I am free to talk with colleagues during the break. The only time we're required to be in our seats is when we vote.

A message arrives from the governor's office: The governor has signed eight House bills into law. Small steps forward, but progress nevertheless.

We are locked in under a Call of the House before we proceed to third reading of bills. First is the constitutional foundation for tax reform: Engrossed Substitute House Joint Resolution 29, or ESHJR 29 (for short!) is before us on final passage. The inevitable verbosity begins.

Slade leads off the speeches in support of this gateway for restructuring our state's defective tax system: "Whatever its immediate genesis, this proposal is an effort to work toward the middle ground between Republicans, who have opposed any income tax in the past, and Democrats who want a graduated tax."

Eight others also speak in favor.

John O'Brien leads the opposition: "Tax reform is a misnomer for the governor's proposal," he says. "If we're going to be honest, we should call it what it is: A $150 million tax increase."

It is hard to hold my tongue at inaccuracies, including this by Mr. O'Brien. I've no idea where he got that figure or how he arrived at that conclusion. With our restructuring, there is no increase in the total taxes paid. Slade continues to explain and defend our reforms, while others sing O'Brien's tune, ending with Gary Grant in his typical fashion.

The clerk calls the roll on final passage, and one by one we register our votes, *Yea* or *Nay*. We need those 66. When the voting is complete, the tally delivers the verdict: 58 yea, 40 nay, 1 absent and not voting. It fails. I wear a poker face as well as anyone, but this is an immense disappointment. What happened to the 61 votes? Why only 58? We did not attract even one of those 'on the fence'.

Next, SHB 639 (the omnibus implementing tax bill) comes before us on third reading and final passage. This is not a constitutional amendment; it requires only a majority vote to pass, and it does, 52 to 46 with 1 absent and not voting. We immediately transfer the bill to the Senate, but this bill alone is useless — it needs the underlying constitutional amendment to authorize an income tax before its many provisions can take effect.

Maple nut ice cream — my favorite flavor of this '67 session — provides me the smallest consolation on this disappointing day. I scoop at my bowl full in the House dining room Friday evening, my presence here on a Friday night living proof I am no political party animal. Several colleagues join me.

"Eight votes," says Chuck Newschwander, the soft-spoken Tacoma dentist who always urges us to brush after eating our ice cream. "Surely we can find another eight votes this weekend…"

"You voted against it Chuck," I remind him.

"Prevailing side, Mary Ellen," he says with a wink. "So I can resurrect it."

That explains one of the three lost votes. I was sure I had 61. Maybe the other fallout votes were trying to salvage this too.

"Any new leads?" asks Slade.

I suspend my spoonful, look him straight in the eye.

"Believe me, Slade, I'm trying."

I will spend my weekend talking tax reform again, attempting to get our number of votes in the House to the magic 66. This is a process of education — I must educate them all. Though it's a complex proposal, if I can help people truly to understand how it works, I still believe we'll get the support we need to repair our state's rickety revenue base.

HOUSE TURNS DOWN EVANS' TAX PACKAGE blares the Saturday headline. Ouch. If readers don't read beyond it, they'll think not even the Republican-controlled House supports the governor's tax reform plan. This is just not true. But not everyone reads the small print, especially on Saturdays. I read the entire story and re-live the disappointing defeat.

"This is what we hoped to do," a gloating labor lobbyist has told the reporter. "I'm very gratified that enough people saw it our way and killed the proposal."

The lobbyist says labor will wait until Democrats control the legislature again, then push through a graduated tax. They assume this will be next term — a bold assumption, I note with some comfort. He did compliment the governor for drawing attention to the sore need for tax reform.[7]

I close the paper. I have weekend work. I continue to seek at least one co-sponsor for the budget-balancing sales tax rate increase. No luck. Old-timers, newcomers — no one wants to link their name with a tax increase. But as chairman of the Revenue and Taxation Committee, I must link mine. I don't bother putting this bill on my committee agenda. Even with a Republican majority, I don't have the votes to pass a sales tax hike out of committee, but I must find some way to get this bill in front of the House.

In the meantime, I still need 66 tax reform votes.

On Monday, March 20, part way into Day 11 of the Extraordinary Session, Mr. Gorton moves that we defer the balance of our third reading calendar until tomorrow. We agree. He then moves that we revert to the 8th order of business. We agree again — at least a majority of us do. At each House vote, I am grateful I now sit with the majority — that we have the ability to lead so much of our floor work along as we've planned it.

Mr. Newschwander stands and the Speaker recognizes the dentist, who says to us, "Having voted on the prevailing side, I move that the House do now reconsider the vote by which the House failed to pass Engrossed Substitute House Joint Resolution 29 by the constitutional two-thirds majority."

Tax reform. Slade immediately stands and moves that we defer this reconsideration until tomorrow.

John O'Brien stands: "Point of order."

"State your point of order, Mr. O'Brien."

"It appears to me, Mr. Speaker, that the motion to reconsider has to be acted upon now, not tomorrow. Probably the procedure would be to vote on the motion to reconsider. If it is carried, then you have the right to defer action on this House joint resolution until tomorrow, but first you should determine whether or not the motion is going to be carried or defeated."

The Speaker recognizes Mr. Gorton, who acknowledges, "Mr. Speaker, Rule 71 governs this and it seems to me that Mr. O'Brien is right." [8]

Mr. O'Brien enjoys the small win.

Should we reconsider our vote on SHJR 29, to amend our state constitution as to the 40 mill limitation and to permit an income tax? We vote and agree: Yes we should reconsider. That agreed, Slade now moves that we defer further consideration, and the resolution is placed at the end of tomorrow's third reading calendar. We have another chance, and another day, to collect support for this constitutional reform.

We adjourn until 1 p.m. Tuesday, and I set out in search of votes.

On Wednesday on the floor, we again debate SHJR 29, with little progress. The constitutional amendment is eventually referred back to Rules… again.

Among the measures being considered right now in the Senate are two other notable resolutions. SJR 13, a constitutional amendment to adjust the property tax lid, is similar to that one element of our HJR 29, but theirs mentions nothing of adding a state income tax. And a second, SJR 23, is similar to the Brouillet/ DeJarnatt amendment to HJR 29 — a proposal that school levies cover two school years versus one, and that we relax the stringent voter requirements for these levies. Both Senate measures arrive in the House on Thursday, March 23, and both are referred to my Committee on Revenue and Taxation, where we may consider them or not. As committee chairman, it's up to me.

DURING THE NEXT LEADERSHIP GATHERING in the governor's office, Governor Evans is upbeat: "We're getting closer," he says. "You should see the mail coming in. It gets better and better as time goes on."

"How much better?" Joel asks.

"More people are realizing something has to be done or we'll just keep increasing the tax rates every session. They're recognizing this is actually a terrific chance to deal with the school levy problem. They're figuring out we really care about the tax burden on the lower income class. They're finally starting to put two and two together. Mary Ellen? Comments?"

"Yes. When you go home for Easter, talk to your constituents and encourage all your colleagues to do the same. I can't get around to everyone in the House and Senate in the next 24 hours, but I think if people would talk honestly with their constituents, they'd find support for our reforms."

"Mary Ellen's right," the governor says. "We've had good success at our public hearings."

"Press conference tomorrow afternoon," Esther Searing reminds us all.

The following afternoon, Jim Dolliver welcomes reporters into the governor's office. I slip in later, sit quietly out of sight and listen to the governor plug our tax reform program to the press, aimed at Easter weekend readers and viewers.

"What we are trying to do," he repeats for the umpteenth time, "is to broaden the tax base to ease the burden on those packing a larger burden as time goes on, and to have that burden shared more equally by all the people throughout the state."

"Governor Evans," says *The Times'* Lyle Burt, "Senator Durkan said on the Senate floor that you are deliberately holding up adjournment of the legislature by not bringing Mrs. McCaffree's tax reform resolution back onto the floor of the House until you have the 66 votes lined up, and he says the delay is costing taxpayers money. Who do you blame for the delay?"

"I am not in the business of trying to lay blame," says the governor. "This state has a serious fiscal problem. I wish our legislators would spend more time trying to address that honestly and reasonably, and I would hope their response to the fiscal dilemma would include tax reform."

"Governor, do you agree with Senator Ryder that Senator Durkan is to blame for the delays?" asks someone else. "Ryder said every time you have enough votes lined up in the House to pass your reform package, Durkan goes over to the House, talks to his colleagues, and peels off a few votes to sabotage it." [9]

The governor refers to his previous comment on blame.

AS WE HEAD INTO EASTER WEEKEND, tax reform is finally attracting the public's attention. Newspapers around the state do indeed give readers something to think about as they celebrate a resurrection and dye their hard-boiled eggs. I'm heartened — some of the press is on our side.

"Those who want restrictions on property taxes should recognize by this time the utter futility of their efforts, unless they also support an adequate alternative source of revenue," writes economics lecturer Paul Ellis in Easter Sunday's *Seattle P-I* in the column called 'Voice of the People'. "If we are to have a progressive system of state governmental services, we cannot also have more restrictions on property taxes, lower sales taxes, exemptions on food and drugs and lower business and occupation taxes without also having some kind of an income tax…" [10]

Dreamers and schemers, a *Vancouver Columbian* editorial writer calls those opposing the governor's tax reforms: "The governor proposes a 3.5 percent rate on income tax AFTER all federal deductions and exemptions have been subtracted (on the graduated federal scale). Legislators who hold out for a more progressive tax than this should know that, for the present at least, they are holding out for the impossible. If the dreamers don't know this, the schemers do. Some oppose the proportional tax because they don't want Evans to get credit for basic tax reform. He's up for re-election next year, you know." [11]

I'm home Easter weekend, and after church I spread the various headlines in front of me on the floor.

"Why can't I get the support to pass this?" I ask Ken.

"You're in politics, love."

"Yes, with some healthy opposition."

MONDAY MORNING I'M BACK IN OLYMPIA, peddling our tax reform package to wavering colleagues and gingerly cradling our state's financial future.

On the floor, the House hears the report of the Free Conference Committee on the community college bill. We deem this new proposal acceptable and launch a new state community college system by a vote of 85-10 with four absent, and send it to the Senate, where, even after all the conference committee work, it meets with some more major fireworks. The senators from Tacoma, in particular, argue that technical and vocational training falls short. The Tacoma school board has ferociously lobbied these senators to bolster voc/tech. But the Senate passes the bill as is: 40-7. Once it is signed all around, SHB 548 will become law, and on July 1 a new state community college system will begin. Buster Brouillet is ecstatic. So is Marjorie Lynch. So am I. So are all of us DEGOHTs who first envisioned these new schools in our Blueprint for Progress.

By Thursday, the House receives EHB 576 — the new Department of Revenue bill — back from the Senate. The Senate amendments seem fine, so we place the bill on final passage. The clerk calls the roll, and we vote in favor, 80-3 with 16 absent and not voting. Another Blueprint victory: Administrative reform for tax and revenue.

We adjourn in the early evening, but across the way — beyond bronzed George and the chandelier — the Senate roils at full boil in a heated debate. I make a hasty sandwich in the House dining room, down it with a cup of tea, and accompany Slade to the Senate chamber where energized Senate Democrats face off against equally insistent Senate Republicans on HB 639 — our omnibus tax bill.

"It's going to be a long one," Slade predicts. It is. I remain in the gallery to the end of their bitter debate, watch the final vote, and leave well after midnight, thoroughly drained.

On Friday, the final day of March, Speaker Eldridge signs our Department of Revenue bill and sends it to the Senate for the final signature there. Our Extraordinary Session is picking up steam. But every step forward seems paired with another setback. We arrive at the Third Order of Business, Messages from the Senate. Don Eldridge takes the Speaker's microphone to read the formal report: "Senate Chamber, Olympia, Washington, March 30, 1967, Mr. Speaker: The Senate has failed to pass Engrossed Substitute House Bill Number 639 (the omnibus tax bill), and the same is herewith transmitted." [12]

With my very own eyes last night, I'd witnessed this voting and watched our hopes for reforming our tax base wither, perhaps irreparably.

But not until these words are read aloud, in front of my colleagues here in the House, do a few frustrated tears begin to form. I am deeply disappointed. Our tax system is failing us, and this single rate tax on net income is the best solution. Enough Senate members may yet be convinced of it. More Democrats may yet let it happen on this governor's watch. Only time will tell.

March ends, April begins, and we enter week four of this extra session with no biennial budget in place — no funds specifically appropriated, no revenues paired with state needs.

We convene again Monday at 1 p.m. for the 25th day of the Extraordinary Session, and today's Senate message brings better news: The President of the Senate signed the Department of Revenue bill and sent it to the governor. Bit by bit, our Blueprint is becoming reality.

IN THE EVENING, OVER ICE CREAM, Slade relays a quiet report from Tom Copeland: A Senate bill on tomorrow's House calendar could help me out with the sales tax impasse. Together we hatch a plan.

Tuesday, Engrossed SB 255 arrives on the floor of the House, a departmental request bill "relating to changes in the excise laws" — a topic sufficiently salient to allow me to scalp in my sales tax rate increase at the governor's executive request. The Senate bill is read into the House record. *Here's my chance.* But before I can introduce my amendment to scalp it, as we'd discussed last night over ice cream, Slade moves to defer further consideration of this bill until the end of today's second reading calendar, and the House agrees.

"…to make sure we have our votes lined up," Slade explains to me during a break. "This is our best chance to get this revenue bill through, Mary Ellen."

"Agreed," I reply. "And you're going to co-sponsor it, right?"

I'm still kidding. We've discussed this from the beginning. I'm the committee chairman — the one who must risk sponsoring this tax hike, solo, if no one else politically dares to sign on.

In the meantime, the Senate Democrats' version of a constitutional amendment for tax reform, SJR 13 — the proposed lid on the property tax, but without adding an income tax — has been sitting in my Committee on Revenue and Taxation. The Democrats want it out. They're pressuring me to act, to bring some version of tax reform before the House, arguing that partial tax reform is better than none. They're eager to end this long session. What they don't acknowledge, however, is that while a property tax lid is indeed a reform, if we don't add the income tax in tandem to counterbalance a revenue slide, the reform won't help our state tax structure — could worsen it, in fact.

House leadership calls a break. I quickly confer with the governor's office and then with our caucus. We agree to release this SJR 13 from Rules when Rep. Litchman returns from Seattle. Among the several Democrats supportive of the governor's tax reform package, Mark Litchman has been most vocal. We need his vote.

Evening arrives, then plods interminably. Tempers are fused incredibly short. Everyone is tired and hungry, but we must remain in session long enough to act on tax reform, and late enough to ascertain every crucial vote. Finally we bring the matter onto the floor. I stand and am recognized.

"Mr. Speaker, we a majority of your Committee on Revenue and Taxation, to whom was referred Engrossed Senate Joint Resolution 13, requiring the assessment of property at 25% of true value, have had the same under consideration, and we respectfully report the same back to the House with the recommendation that it do pass — with the following amendment…"

At their desks on the floor, my House colleagues follow along, reading the printed bill, pens in hand. I continue: "Strike all of the Senate and House amendments to the printed and engrossed resolution, thus restoring the resolution to its original form. And on page 1, line 3 of the printed resolution, after the comma following 'THAT' strike the remainder of the resolution and insert "At the next general election…" [13]

I scalp the Senate version and substitute the governor's plan — HJR 29, including the single rate income tax — with renewed and realistic hopes that this evening the requisite 66 votes are with us. Impassioned speeches ensue from both sides. In the midst, Rep. Litchman, the absent Democrat, finally arrives and makes a quick speech on the floor: "The governor's proposed tax package is a tax break for lower income groups, and a far better alternative to our state's financial imbalance than an increased sales tax."

Rep. O'Brien's unimpressed eyebrows speak volumes. Rep. Litchman continues, impassioned: "This is as close as this body will come to a graduated net income tax in 20 years."

We bring the resolution to a vote, with sixty-six votes now promised.

Speaker Eldridge presides: "The motion before us is Mrs. McCaffree's amendment to Engrossed Senate Joint Resolution 13."

More floor debate, during which a series of amendments to my amendment are proposed and each is defeated. I move to lay one final amendment on the table, which means the matter before us is my proposal that we amend the Senate tax reform resolution by scalping it and replacing it with ours. Mr. Chatalas asks if I will yield to a question, and I agree.

"Mrs. McCaffree, did I understand you to say that this amendment before us now is exactly identical to House Joint Resolution 29?"

"As Mr. Gorton said," I explain, "it is House Joint Resolution 29 with the amendments which were put on on the floor of the House when we had HJR 29 before us."

"So it is identical?" he asks again.

"As far as I know."

Mr. Chatalas then asks to speak on a point of order and is granted the floor.

"Mr. Speaker, since this is an identical resolution to HJR 29, which is still in Rules Committee, I don't know how we can really consider this resolution at the present time."

Speaker Eldridge explains, over the course of Mr. Chatalas' next several questions, that we can legitimately address this Senate resolution as amended and proposed, even though an identical version, HJR 29, still sits in Rules.

"Mr. Speaker," Mr. Chatalas continues, "for clarification, when we vote on this amendment, even if it is not the whole resolution, we will still have another chance to vote on final passage, will we not?"

"This is not final passage," our Speaker confirms.

Mr. Chatalas wants to be perfectly clear: "We will vote on the amendment first, and then again on final passage?" [14]

That is correct, the Speaker affirms. We will take two separate votes.

The clerk calls the roll and the amendment passes — my scalp is approved, 64-32. The 64 vote figure makes me nervous. But since this is an amendment to the measure, and not the constitutional amendment itself, this vote allows the amendment to pass. We only needed fifty. Now we must vote on final passage — and this time we'll need all 66 votes. It is conceivable someone voted against the amendment this past round, to express support of the Senate version, but will then vote in favor on final passage — to put tax reform on the ballot.

Mr. Gorton moves to suspend Rules and to move the resolution from second reading to third for final passage. But we don't vote yet. More debate, first, and then we're finally ready for the final vote to be taken — by roll call. Alphabetically, we register our votes. Some Democrats vote in favor of the governor's tax reform measure. Some Republicans vote against it. I keep careful tally — with a sinking heart. In the time span in which we waited for Mr. Litchman to return from Seattle, many House Democrats may have been sufficiently irked by the delay (or perhaps persuaded by Senator Durkan or Representative O'Brien, or any number of others during that stretch) to withdraw their support. I know the final result before the Speaker formally announces it: We failed to meet the two-thirds majority. The measure loses, 59-39, with two absent and not voting.

No constitutional vote will go to the people.

Tax reform in this 40th Session is dead.

LEGISLATIVE LEADERSHIP IS A HUGE RESPONSIBILITY, and while I feel I have done my duty here, I have suffered some real defeats. Defeat is part of the process, I know, but that doesn't make it easy. This tax reform loss hurts. But I've been around long enough to know these complex reforms can take time. We've made progress. I'm not giving up. I'm just a bit bruised.

Mr. Gorton moves that the House defer consideration of the remainder of bills on second reading, and that these bills be placed on tomorrow's calendar. We adjourn until 10 a.m. Wednesday, April 5.

I RISE EARLY AND HEAD TO THE HOUSE dining room at daybreak, in need of comfort from my colleagues. I am grateful to find a dozen others there, poring over the morning papers and actually laughing. One front-page headline bellows EVANS' TAX REFORM PLAN KILLED IN HOUSE.[15]

"You find this funny?" I ask. I have already read every word.

"No, Mary Ellen," says Joel, who continues to hang out here as a regular. "We are. While we've been fighting for our Blueprint for Progress, there's a whole new world... *mushrooming* out there."

Another burst of giddy male laughter.

"Going bananas, you mean," says Stu Bledsoe.

Again, they all crack up.

"It's in the *P-I*," says Tom Copeland, quoting the newspaper's slogan. "Your *P-I*, Mrs. McCaffree of District 32A, I may add."

"Check it out," says Stu. "Damned if I..."

I give him a look before looking at the source of their chuckling. I've been immersed in my legislative work, and whenever I do raise my head, it's to check in on my husband and children. I haven't had time for much else.

"Whole new g. d. world out there, Mary Ellen," Stu says, trying to appease me.

Upon closer look, these guys have a point. In a highlighted box on page one of the paper, right next to the dismal death knell on tax reform, is a tiny item picked up from the *New York Times*: "Banana Peel Smoking Probed."[16] A federal investigation, assigned to the FDA, is exploring the possible hallucinogenic effects of banana peels — the latest craze among collegians.

"Pro-Hippie Petition in U-District" is the story right beneath it — the aim of the petition being to end the harassment of hippies in my university locale.[17]

"Flip the page," Tom says.

"House Kills Evans' Tax Plan," I read. "Gee thanks."

"Not that, Mary Ellen. This."

Stu grabs the paper and reads aloud: "...Seattle's first *Love-Arts* Festival will be held in the lower level of the Pike Place Market Thursday, Friday and Saturday... The sponsor is the Seattle Committee to End the War in Vietnam."[18]

I'm quiet.

"What's wrong, Mem?"

'Mem' — Joel has coined me a new nickname from my initials. I gather my thoughts and explain.

"Here we are at the capitol, trying to change Washington State, and we're oblivious to all this change being chanted in the streets. We're actually on some kind of parallel track with these activist students — except in some sense, we're actually way out front."

I ran for public office in the early 1960's in order to battle the status quo, and I'm still in the trenches, fighting hard to make a difference and bring about change. Now, in the later 1960's change seems to be 'in', the establishment 'out', and citizens decidedly more aware. Joel's right. This bodes well for our aims here.

> **EXCISE TAX**
>
> Tax on the manufacture, sale or consumption of a commodity, or on a privilege, usually assessed in the form of a license or fee.

AT 10 A.M. ON DAY 28, OUR HOUSE session convenes. Again, I'm in the thick of things when Senate Bill 255 — the Senate's excise tax bill, the one I'll use to scalp in the tax rate hike — comes before us on second reading. I waste no time, grab my microphone and jump to my feet. The Speaker recognizes me.

"Mrs. McCaffree."

"I move the adoption of the following amendment: 'Strike all the matter following the enacting clause and substitute the following."

The substitution, of course, is my House bill that proposes an increase in the sales tax rate from 4.2 to 4.5 percent, by request of the governor, to cover his biennial budget shortfall. I read the final sentence: "This act is necessary for the immediate preservation of the public peace, health and safety, the support of the state government and its existing public institutions, and shall take effect July 1, 1967." [19]

Midway through the debate over my scalping, the Speaker interrupts us to welcome Mr. Tatsuo Miyazaki, deputy mayor of Seattle's sister city of Kobe, Japan, along with the large group of Japanese mountain climbers at his side. These interruptions are frustrating, but it is not uncommon for the Speaker to interrupt our floor proceedings to welcome guests. In the case of these mountaineers, timing is of the essence: Climbing season has a window, and a team of Japanese and American climbers is headed for unclimbed peaks in Alaska and the Yukon. After their polite reception here, they head for the hills and our legislative business resumes.

"The question before the House," the Speaker says, "is the adoption of Mrs. McCaffree's amendment to Senate Bill 255."

More debate. More amendments to my amendment. Some are adopted, some not.

"The question before the House is again the adoption of Mrs. McCaffree's amendment to Senate Bill 255 as amended."

We vote. We adopt my amended amendment — my scalp, in effect. I stand: "I move to adopt an amendment to the title of the bill…"

We approve this as well and the bill is advanced to third reading. The clerk calls the roll on the final passage of Engrossed Senate Bill 255 as amended by the House. Our vote is 82 yeas, 11 nays and 6 absent and not voting. My tax rate increase from 4.2 to 4.5 percent is immediately transmitted to the Senate. The Senate sends it right back. They refuse our amended bill and ask for a conference committee thereon. We agree and the Speaker appoints Representatives McCaffree, Gorton and Sawyer to represent the House.

By Saturday, we finally conference with the Senate on SB 255/HB 205, and for four days our joint committee haggles over the sales tax rate increase, to no avail. Therefore, on Tuesday, April 11 — Day 33 of the special session — we ask the Senate for a free conference committee. The Senate approves. On the matter of a sales tax rate increase, we have now returned to the drawing board.

Meanwhile, turf wars continue in the battle over the state's biennial budget. For nearly three weeks, a budgetary tug-of-war has transpired behind the scenes, first within a conference committee and then in free conference committee.

Publicly, we continue to pass other measures to the governor.

But the budget fails to arrive in the Senate or House.

In a partisan skirmish, the Democrats are pressuring me to release from my committee SJR 23, the other Senate resolution on tax reform — to constitutionally relax school levy voting requirements. On the face of it this is a great idea, but if it is passed it would work as a disincentive for dealing with the underlying problem of school funding, and that is reforming the state's revenue base. I hold tight under their pressure. With the support of House leadership and the governor, I continue to sit on this resolution in my committee.

As a leadership team, we finally decide to revamp SJR 23, with a special look at the clause about relaxing the voting requirements for special levies, which could cause an uproar that would lose us crucial votes. We bring our version to the floor on April 25, the 47th day of the Extraordinary Session. A series of proposed changes to SJR 23 are withdrawn when I argue against them, and the resolution is finally assigned to Rules. It returns to the floor again a couple of days later, when we amend it substantially: To provide for two-year special levy periods instead of one, but abandoning the more liberalized voting requirements for lack of support in the House. As amended, this resolution is subsequently approved by the Senate, too, and it is on its way to a vote of the people in the 1968 general election. Although this does nothing to resolve the underlying problems of special school levies, it will marginally improve the stability of school funding, if the voters approve.

Day 51 of the Extraordinary Session is called to order. On the House agenda is the report of the free conference committee on ESB 255, the one I scalped and replaced with my sales tax rate increase. I present the new bill with a recommendation that it do pass.

Slade Gorton speaks in favor.

John O'Brien speaks against.

Someone calls for an oral roll call to determine who is present.

Two more speak in favor, four more against. We vote. It fails, 39-53 with seven absent and not voting. *Who wants to vote for a tax increase?* Seeing the numbers going awry, Rep. Joe McGavick from my nextdoor district, 32B, votes on the prevailing side and asks that we reconsider. His motion carries. Speaker Eldridge immediately gavels the House at ease.

We flock to the lobbies to talk among ourselves. This session can't go on forever. We have to fund state services. Surely our voters will understand — the state of Washington has bills to pay... on their behalf! Until we achieve tax reform, the only way we can sufficiently cover our growing state costs is to raise the rate of our sales tax.

The Speaker calls us back to order and declares the question before us to be a reconsideration of the failed vote on ESB 255, as presented by the free conference committee. The leadership has applied some pressure, including a reminder that this long special session needs to end, which seems to have had some effect. Representatives O'Brien, Kalich and Sawyer explain the House minority's position on the bill. We vote again. This time it passes: 52-41 with 6 absent and not voting. We send it immediately to the Senate.

The Senate sends us a message, not relative to this tax hike, but to HJR 1, the very first measure introduced in this 40th Legislative Session — our resolution on Open Space. They have passed it, a month and a half after we first sent it over there. The Speaker signs HJR 1 and returns it to the Senate where the President of the Senate signs it, too. Another Blueprint item, done.

No word from the Senate, however, on my scalped excise tax bill.

But a flood of other bills and conference committee reports receive our attention. We approve a referendum on an outdoor recreational bond issue, authorize capitol improvement bonds, establish a traffic safety commission, create a new correctional institution for women, adopt a capital budget, note the appointment of interim committees...

The following day, Day 52, is a Sunday. We're determined to wrap up and go home. The free conference report on the budget arrives from the Senate, approved, and after full House debate and discussion, we approve this budget as well. We pass several other major reforms, and during the course of the day, the House and Senate trade smaller pieces of legislation for final approval, many of which one or the other of us had passed already way back during the regular session. Each counterpart swiftly considers the others' legislative handiwork, and passes them through. We send a long list of bills along to the governor.

BUT BY MIDNIGHT, WE'RE NOT DONE. Each chamber tosses a cover over its clock to bring time once more to a man-made standstill.

In our final act, the Senate finally adopts the 4.5 percent sales tax proposed in my original bill and as confirmed by the free conference committee. It is signed all around — by the Speaker of the House and the President of the Senate — and we deliver it to the governor's office for his signature. The session thus ends by covering our growing state's expanding costs with an increase in the rate of our sales tax.

After we pass a few routine housekeeping resolutions, and our special and interim committees are announced, our majority leader Mr. Gorton moves that the House of Representatives of the Extraordinary Session of the 40th Legislature adjourn *sine die*. We end the marathon session — 112 days in all, only two shy of our record-breaking 114 days of two years ago, despite this year's speedy, optimistic start.

FOR ME THESE 112 DAYS CULMINATE IN IMMENSE personal growth — they've delivered me both excitement and exhaustion, disappointment and success.

I am learning to lead, as a team leader in a majority caucus and as the head of a crucial committee. Serving as chairman of a major committee is perhaps the most challenging part of the legislative process. It requires a distinctive combination of leadership skills, in-depth knowledge of a particular subject, the ability to referee negotiations and compromise between opposing and competing interests, and to still keep the process moving forward to accomplish legislative goals.

I contemplate my legislative future. My colleagues and I just achieved some major governmental and policy reforms — a sizeable number of these defined by our Blueprint for Progress which we've been building upon legislatively beginning in 1965. But many reforms remain undone, not the least of which is restructuring our revenue base... to stabilize school funding.

Would a second legislative effort on my part for tax reform be effective? Do I have the enthusiasm and resolve to tackle it again? We shall see.

CHAPTER NINE

COMMUNITY VOICE
REPRESENTING A CONSTITUENCY

*I am a firm believer
in allowing people to have a voice.
I also believe in differences of opinion as the best crucible
for creating the best laws.*

From the wintry frigidity of January ninth to the springtime warmth of late April, I have endured a tension-filled stretch of four months, and I've reached *sine die* exhausted. Yet the interim is only minutes old when I head downstairs for a committee room.

The Legislative Council is about to convene.

Speaker Eldridge, who chairs this council, has asked me to sit amidst its thirty-one members: Sixteen from the House, by his appointment, and fifteen from the Senate appointed by Lieutenant Governor Cherberg. By law, we're a bipartisan group with no more than seventeen from any one party. And by law, each of our appointments had to be approved by the full legislature — Senate and House — before we disbanded. This we did just hours ago.

Throughout the state, throughout the interim, this council will carry on our legislative work in between formal legislative sessions with a research staff, a modest operating budget and a steady calendar of meetings. Our job is to research the most complex pending issues, assess our state's administration, consult with the balance of our legislative colleagues as needed, and take care of some of the legislature's less dramatic matters — correcting errors, closing overlooked loopholes, removing exemptions or adding them. Then, ten days before the new session begins, we will present our next legislature a comprehensive interim report which will include a package of Legislative Council request bills we'll have hammered out by then. In the session just adjourned, we passed 48 of 67 of the last Legislative Council's bills into law.

Today, the thirty-one of us cross-reference our calendars, agree on an initial meeting date and time, and divide up subcommittee tasks. When Don Eldridge asks me to chair the Revenue and Regulatory Agencies Subcommittee, I accept.

"Thanks, Mary Ellen. Thanks one and all," he says. "And thank you all for all your work this session."

My colleagues and I enacted nearly one-third of the reforms from our Blueprint for Progress — the college bills, rules for clean water, clean air, community health care, construction guidelines for the handicapped and elderly, several complex voting and municipal reforms, mandatory driver's ed in public schools, but as for school funding... I admit, our considerable successes don't fully counter my disappointment that we have failed to resolve the deficiencies of our revenue base.

My third legislative session is gone, and I've not yet managed to secure our school funding.

I knew my journey would entail some difficult steps — redistricting, trying to win a majority voice in the legislature, reforming our state's revenue base to find more secure dollars for schools.

What I didn't factor in was how much time each gigantic step would swallow. Major reforms and real change done well, however, frequently demand a long journey — in this case, epic. The process requires deliberation, constructive argument, works towards a firm consensus, and plenty of my personal forté: Study.

My legislative career is threatening to veer full time. This interim, not only do I sit on the Legislative Council and chair its Subcommittee on Revenue, I've also agreed to serve a second term on the Tax Advisory Council. With the failure of our full tax reform package, Governor Evans asked the same team of fifteen to reconvene, review our research and findings, and present a new proposal for 1969. And, if I plan to be in the legislature in '69 to continue my tax reform quest, another re-election campaign will lie ahead.

I accept the hearty handshakes of Council colleagues when our organizing is done, say my goodbyes, descend the dozens of marble steps and return to my rental home to pack.

Ken arrives the next day with a lovely nosegay.

"I've made an executive decision," he tells me. "I'm absconding with you to the coast."

"Just the two of us?"

What a wonderful idea!

"Yes, love," he says. "Thought you could use a few days off."

"And how."

Ken helps me gather my belongings from my office and small home, and we head to the Iron Springs Resort on the Pacific coast. For the next three days, my husband and I walk Washington's vast, sandy coastline, encountering very few souls along the misty, monochrome beach. We rejuvenate our relationship with laughter and talk in the salt-spray breeze. And with solitude.

My tension slips away.

When we return to the University District, we immediately convene a McCaffree family council in anticipation of summer. My legislative career is a given now, and we fold it in to all else on the family calendar for the coming months.

David wants to spend another summer at Camp Orkila, a YMCA camp on Orcas Island among that cluster of islands we call the San Juans — one of the most gorgeous settings in our picturesque state, a collection of lushly studded evergreen oases in the wind-swept waters between the Pacific Ocean and our Puget Sound. Half of these tiny islands are ours, the other half Canada's, distinguished only by a dotted line printed on a paper map.

Mary says she and Nancy are hatching a plan to visit New York City. Ken has business in Montreal, and I'd like to visit Washington, D.C. We set our summer sights on all three.

Within days of returning home from the session, my speaking engagements begin to mount. At the end of May, I deliver my third post-session report to the 32nd District Republican Club. The club president, my own husband Ken, calls the evening meeting to order. (These Republicans have decided we're not the dangerous, flaming liberals they once feared.) I do detect a few suspicious souls, however, as I launch into a particular section of my talk.

"One of the social issues which I know is of great concern to you here in the district is the Meany Hotel bill."

This topic is never benign.

"Because it is so close to us, and because I received a great deal of mail concerning this particular bill, I would like to discuss my reasons for voting as I did."

Several rearrange themselves in their seats. I move right along.

"There is never complete agreement among a legislator's constituents as to the desirability of any one bill. I realize some people in the 32nd District — that some of you here this evening — are opposed to this bill, and I respect your reasons for opposing it. I received many letters from those who were in favor of Senate Bill 138. These people were concerned that we might lose this fine hotel in the University District. So tonight I would like to give you my reasons for voting *for* this particular piece of legislation."

Voters deserve a detailed explanation of their legislators' votes, I've always felt — especially on an issue like this that eventually proved so divisive.

"I did not believe Senate Bill 138 to be a wet-dry issue, nor did I think it a moral issue. However, because drunkenness and the effects of drinking affect the entire community, some regulations may be required. It is my sincere belief that prohibition did not work in the 1920's. Neither do I believe drawing a restrictive line in one isolated location in our state will solve the problem of drinking. I believe that the moral issue of drinking and drunkenness should be and must be resolved in our homes and in our churches. I think that the Meany Hotel should be allowed to compete with the other west coast hotels without this restriction, which has been the only one of its kind in our state. Thus my 'yes' vote on Senate Bill 138." [1]

The Meany Hotel may now begin serving liquor June 7, in a little more than a week. I don't assume everyone feels better or agrees after I explained my vote. However, we do move on to other topics — my sole sponsorship of the sales tax increase, for instance. Again I explain, fully expecting their questions. And since this Republican Club represents only a small portion of my constituency, I map out other public visits as well. Right away, I am invited to talk with a handful of groups. After serving three terms, I'm in demand.

The school year comes to a close for the summer, and Ken shifts gears, devoting less time to professorial work and more to his consulting. He also serves on the board of directors of an international foundation for employee benefit plans — the group that beckons him to that meeting in Montreal in July.

I ready my youngest son for camp and enlist my daughters to help embroider his initials — DKM — on every single item of his clothing. Nancy has now returned from Washington State University. Mary has moved home from the Chi Omega house at 'The U', where she'd rejoined her sorority sisters after her winter stint as docket clerk. As they sew — DKM — the girls begin to plot our trip east, with a focus on the prospect of shopping along Fifth Avenue.

Together with our family's map master, Ken, they devise our summer trip with the same meticulous efficiency my husband used to transport our young family west in that loaded-down Dodge many years ago. Ken and the girls pore over maps of New York, D.C. and Montreal — the site of this year's World's Fair. They study, compare, research, reserve us hotels and tickets to New York shows, and assemble a stack of brochures on historical sights, tours, galleries and museums.

WHILE THEY PLOT, I SINK INTO TAXATION. I meet with both the Tax Advisory Council and the Legislative Council, and lead the latter's Revenue and Regulatory Agencies Committee. I am aware our state's tax system is complex and flawed, and as a result of my work last interim, I'd seen the best path to shoring it up. This interim, however, what is clear as I dig in deeper is just how confused the public remains about the issue of taxes and government budgets and how, within our state, there is little public understanding of how both interrelate.

It's not the question of *how* to structure our taxes that poses our biggest challenge. We have figured out an incredibly responsive solution. Our challenge, as amply demonstrated during the legislative session just past, is to explain this 'incredibly responsive solution' to our state and to convince our voters it is actually good for them.

David walks into the room, transistor radio plastered to his ear.
If you drive a car, I'll tax the street;
If you try to sit, I'll tax your seat;
If you get too cold, I'll tax the heat;
If you take a walk, I'll tax your feet.
"What are you listening to now David?"
"Taxman!" he sings in synch. "Beatles, Mom."
"I should have guessed."

We deliver David and his initial-embroidered gear to the local YMCA four blocks from our home. The campers will board a Y bus to Anacortes, then this bus will drive aboard a ferryboat, and after a bit of island hopping via ferry, they'll finally reach Orcas Island. We wish him happy camping.

In July, while the girls and Ken and I fly east, other American youth are migrating west. In San Francisco, a hundred thousand 'hippies' are basking in the Summer of Love. It kicked off in June at the Monterey Pop Festival where, according to David (my personal resource on all things rebellious or hip), the lead singer of a band called The Doors said, "We want the world and we want it now," and Seattle's own Jimi Hendrix blew minds and eardrums.

By mid-summer, however, *Time* magazine and others are reporting that some of the love-fest 'trips' are traveling in a dangerous direction, particularly in San Francisco's drug-riddled district of Haight-Ashbury.[2]

I AM GRATEFUL FOR A DIFFERENT TRIP. Our first stop is Washington, D.C., where we have rooms in the Marriott in Alexandria, Virginia, near the airport and across the Potomac from the nation's capitol.

First on our agenda is a tour of the White House, graciously maintained by the first lady, Lady Bird Johnson, and courtesy of tour tickets arranged by our congressman, Tom Pelly. The White House rooms are splendid, the atmosphere here awesome and staid. Only a handful of protesters hover nearby. From this iconic vantage point, it's hard to believe our cities are in such uproar. Yet dozens of American cities this very moment are embroiled in bitter racial battles as angry black populations lash out in pent-up rage.

As we tour the seat of our nation — where as a people we've pledged to defend individual liberties and to view all as equals — I contemplate today's unrest in our land. America was born of unrest, by those seeking equality, justice and a voice. Although our nation has yet to fully achieve these three, it is difficult for me to know how to view this violence.

My overriding emotion at being here is easier to name: I am thrilled to return to the sites of so much of our American history. And I am sobered — we all have a role to play in sustaining this remarkable nation, launched by revolution to serve us all.

The sixty-nine square miles that make up Washington, D.C. — neither state nor city, but a neutral ground — were purchased at the suggestion of Alexander Hamilton. Our earliest Congress delineated this unique plot of land during the administration of George Washington, who appointed the commission that eventually tipped him their hat by naming the area Washington, District of Columbia.

President Washington tapped Pierre l'Enfant to design the capitol city. It wasn't until 1800, however, that our federal government actually made the move from Philadelphia to Washington, D.C. Our leaders moved in while the capitol building was still mid-construction. A dozen years later, all was destroyed. In the war of 1812, English troops set fire to our capitol — not only the capitol building, but to the White House and other federal buildings as well. Reconstruction began when the bullets subsided, and was completed in 1819.

A century and a half later, Ken and the girls and I explore the nooks and books of the impressive Library of Congress, one of the earliest buildings built here. We tour the trio of memorials erected to presidents Washington, Jefferson and Lincoln, and spend half a day at the National Gallery perusing its exquisite collection of art, then attend an evening outdoor concert by the American Marine Band. This seat of our nation is a world unto itself.

Congress is in session, and though all four of us watch the formal proceedings, first in the Senate and then in the House, I imagine I'm ingesting the activity differently than the rest of my group. I could stay for days. My family feels otherwise. During a recess, we track down Congressman Pelly.

"Can't thank you enough, Tom," Ken says after the congressman has led us through some of the more historic corners of the capitol. "Chuck still talks about your hospitality."

Chuck visited when the Roosevelt High School crew traveled east to compete.

"I'd forgotten about that!" Pelly said. "'61 was it? Always glad to welcome a McCaffree here. And happy to meet your lovely daughters."

"Congratulations to yours," I reply. "Though I sure miss Joel in the House."

Tom Pelly's daughter married our state Senator Chuck Moriarty, the former Olympia roommate of Slade, Dan and Joel when all four first served in the House. Once Chuck Moriarty was a married man, he decided to give up politics, so Joel ran for the vacant Senate seat and won.

Next stop: New York City.

AGAIN WE STAY AT A MARRIOTT, this time in the midst of Manhattan's theater district. The girls and I immediately choose a bus tour. Ken's not big on such things. He occupies himself otherwise while Mary and Nancy and I take in the city — all five boroughs and the majestic Statue of Liberty at our immigrant port. In the evening we take in a different historic struggle — the displacement of Russian Jews in Broadway's *Fiddler on the Roof*, and afterwards we dine among the theatergoing throng.

The following day we walk Fifth Avenue. Both Mary and Nancy find just the perfect dress shop, and Ken purchases them each the dress of their choice — the one thing we'd promised our daughters. We visit the United Nations, attend a session of the UN Security Council and buy a few small mementos at the gift shop plus a lovely fruit bowl that caught my eye, from France.

The next day we explore the Metropolitan Museum of Art. To our dismay, we've scheduled poorly. One day is not nearly time enough to absorb its bounty, and we're sorry we slated this on our final day in New York. But it's time to leave for Canada, and perhaps that's just as well: New York has now joined the many American cities erupting in violence.

While Ken attends several days of meetings in Montreal, the girls and I explore the World's Fair. Jim drives north from Ithaca to join us, on break from his doctoral studies at Cornell. I can still remember his phone call nearly two years ago.

"Mom, I'm going to grad school."

"Really, Jim? You've never mentioned grad school before."

Jim had his Bachelor's Degree in dairy husbandry and seemed happy in dairy work. When Ken overheard, he picked up our other phone.

"I am not going to go to Vietnam," Jim told us. "It's either grad school, Mom and Dad, or I'm joining the Peace Corps."

As a World War II couple, Ken and I were surprised to hear our son so bent on bypassing military service. This was our first personal brush with the changes America's young people would voice more and more. We talked it through with Jim, listened, and ultimately supported his decision to pursue his PhD.

At the fair, the girls and Jim and I dissolve into the crowd of 50 million who eventually visit this exposition: "The World of Man." My kids compare it to our 1962 World's Fair in Seattle. With fifty-nine nations from every continent, this one is grander by far. We end this week and our three-week trip with a lovely dinner out. The next morning, four of us return to Seattle and Jim to Ithaca — relatively peaceful destinations, both. During the month of July, while my family was exploring our American heritage, America was writing a tough new chapter in her history.

This week alone, forty different American cities are engulfed in chaos and flames: Atlanta, Boston, Philadelphia, Birmingham, Cincinnati. The worst is Detroit, where black leaders are urging "guerilla war on the honky white man." By the end of the week, Detroit is shattered. A full week of terrible and terrifying riots, looting, firebombs and enraged clashes between the disgruntled and the law renders the city a veritable war zone. Detroit's mayor likens it to Berlin in 1945. Damages are estimated at $500 million.[3]

In total, 70 different cities experienced a version of this violence, but not Seattle. We've experienced no major eruption in our state to date. I'm knocking on wood.

OUR STATE GOVERNMENT DOES FACE A CRITICAL CHALLENGE, though, and that is our revenue base. The dilemma calls to mind a similar dysfunction during my days as a Kansas farm girl. Among my morning chores was milking Ormsby, our family cow. This I did while seated on a small three-legged stool. I'd become quite adept: I could empty Ormsby in no time. Until, that is, one of the stool legs broke. That morning, try as I might, I couldn't keep my balance with the two that remained, and that day — with that defective stool — I lost our family both milk and time.

Our state revenue structure is doing the same silly balancing act — attempting to accomplish secure government financing from an ill-constructed base that's missing a leg. Hence our focus on adding a state income tax — the best design for the funds we need, and also best for the taxpayer.

Upon our return from our family vacation, I am immediately swept up in my tasks on taxation. Both Councils demand my time and energy. We meet throughout the state, holding public hearings and open sessions. This allows our more distant citizens — those who live far from the capitol — a chance to register their ideas in person, to engage in discussion first-hand. We want everyone involved.

I am still amazed at the numbers who show up to participate and stay all day, like the crowds last session at our hearings in Seattle and Spokane. Each time I witness so many citizens eager to participate in the process, I wish we could take our entire state legislature on the road, occasionally meet elsewhere in our state. What would it do to the dynamics of our legislative work, I wonder? What it would do to the dynamics of our state?

IN EARLY AUGUST, THE GOVERNOR APPOINTS ME as a founding member of the Board of Trustees for our state's new four-year college. I am truly both honored and thrilled to have been named a founding Trustee, and my college professor Ken is incredibly proud. The founding board members' names are engraved on a plaque to be placed on the college grounds, once the college construction is complete.

Our initial trustee meeting is August 26, and I agree to serve as board secretary. Our planning begins for this 'distinctive' college aimed at a progressive curriculum focused on environmental and social needs – the many modern challenges of the day. To address this inaugural gathering, we've invited state Senator Gordon Sandison, who chaired the Advisory Council on Higher Education that proposed this school. He hails the new college as "a unique opportunity to meet the needs of the students of today and into the future," and tells us, "Your planning is not bound by any rigid structure of tradition." [4]

We're excited to explore a new type of higher education whose framework is entirely modern, entirely new.

Governor Evans reviews for us our budget: $905,000 for the site, $500,000 for start-up expenses and, arriving on the 1968 ballot, a Phase I construction bond of $15 million.

Within days of this first trustee meeting, storm clouds gather.

My appointment to the board is challenged by two legislators from Thurston County, who are irritated at being passed over for the post. After all, the college sits in their district. They cite a long-standing clause in our state constitution, Article II, Section 13: "No member of the legislature, during the term for which he is elected, shall be appointed or elected to any civil office in the state which shall have been created ... during the term for which he was elected." [5]

Governor Evans and I were aware of this constitutional provision – one that had been ignored by administrations for decades. We were aware of many examples of earlier appointments to boards and commissions under similar circumstance. We'd discussed this in advance, looked at the lengthy state precedents, and the governor continued to express his wish that I sit on this founding board to help lay the groundwork for this new and novel college.

I had been both a member of the Advisory Council that recommended it, and a sponsor of its formational bill. I know the state budget, know our revenue needs, and having spent years connected with our state's premiere university, via Ken, I am well versed in both the politics and administration of higher education. The governor was confident I was an excellent choice, and I felt well suited to serve.

But with the opposition of these legislators, whose threats and complaints are casting negative attention, the governor and I change our minds. Neither of us wants a public showdown to mar the birth of this college. And the constitutional provision is clear. I submit my resignation with considerable heartbreak.

But leaving the board does not leave me at a loss for work, for chairing the Legislative Council's Revenue Committee is, excuse the pun, taxing. Our large hearing calendar delivers us a steady stream of diverse input to cull. As for the Tax Advisory Council — in which we again focus strictly on analyzing our state tax structure with an eye toward improving it — I am encouraged by what we begin to uncover as we meticulously review last interim's findings and study our existing structure in even greater depth.

Before long, my disappointment (literally) over the college board begins to fade.

The school year begins. Ken returns full time to teaching, Mary joins him on campus for her sophomore year, Nancy leaves for her senior year at WSU across state, and David is now a senior as well — the fifth and final McCaffree Roughrider enrolled at Roosevelt High.

WHEN THE COLLEGE STUDENTS RETURN to the UW campus, they also begin to knock at my door. These young people are disconsolate their voting age campaign fizzled last session in Olympia.

"What can we do, Mrs. McCaffree?"

"Yeah, what else can we do? We talked ourselves blue to all you guys down there at the capitol."

"Look where it got us. Nowhere!"

"You know," I respond, having just now drawn a mental comparison, "it took women seven decades of active campaigning to earn the right to vote."

"Seven decades?!"

"We'll be dead!"

"Or at least ancient!"

"You're young," I say. "You can win this voting right if you're smart — and if you're willing to look at your forebears in petticoats."

I remind them that when women sought the right to vote, they campaigned and stumped for years, but finally had to swallow some of their fervent pride and enlist the men in their lives — those who already had the vote — to provide their message the urgency it needed to succeed with the decision-making body: Congress.

"The truth is," I tell these kids, "women didn't have anyone inside the all-male government pulling for their proposal."

"But we have you," one student argued. "You're inside the government."

"You need more than me. Many more. Changing our voting age is going to require a constitutional amendment, and as you know from last year, that requires a two-thirds majority vote to pass. That's 66 votes in the House and another 33 in the Senate. And that's just to put it on the ballot, where state voters will decide."

Silence hangs as the students consider this.

"No need to be down," I tell them. "I suggest you follow the women's lead: They got their spouses, their fathers and brothers, their male friends — anyone who had access inside the government's decision-making process — to carry the day for them."

A few of the young women shake their heads. I continue.

"Yes, the law needed to change — to give every adult the vote, regardless of gender — but changing the constitution requires that we follow a process. These women did just that. Their job was to persuade enough males in power in the government to approve their right to vote. Your job is to persuade enough adults here in this state to advocate for these same rights for you."

In an era in which the term "generation gap" is rightfully gaining momentum, the idea of enlisting their elders holds little appeal.

"You could learn from the suffrage experience," I say. I am absolutely serious. "The suffragettes' problem was that their votes didn't count. And unfortunately, neither do yours. Those women could campaign and stump and lecture and protest all they wanted. And they did, just like many of you did with your legislators last session in Olympia."

"Of course we did. They're the lawmakers," one student noted. "Isn't that who we have to convince?"

"Yes, and many of us agree with you. But the reality is, you're not voters. As a lobbying block you really don't have enough clout."

I sense discouragement. But one young woman gets it.

"You mean we can't just tell some senator who disagrees with us that we'll vote for someone else next time."

"That's exactly right," I say. "That's no threat at all!"

"So what can we do?" asks another.

"You need a strategy that will work."

Since these university students come from hometowns all over the state, I suggest they begin to enlist important adults in each of their home legislative districts.

"If," I tell them, "…and this is a big if, and it's just my suggestion — if you each organize a sponsoring committee of businessmen and women, church members, presidents of influential organizations, say, or your teachers, plus your parents and grandparents and aunts and uncles and any adult you know who votes for your local legislators in the Senate and House, and then you get that committee to work with you on a plan for lobbying your legislators in Olympia next session, you might convince enough of us to approve that constitutional amendment you need to give yourselves — 18 and up — the right to vote."

They're not particularly enamored.

"Ask our parents?!"

"We want to do it ourselves."

"Yeah. It's our issue. We should be the ones lobbying our legislators, not our grandmas."

"But," I remind them, "you talked to me and to my colleagues last session. You conducted yourselves admirably. You presented a wonderful case. It didn't work. I'm suggesting a different route."

This is not the campaign they wanted to rally around, but by the end of our meeting, most agree that what I've proposed makes sense. They begin to organize adult support 'back home'.

THIS SAME AUTUMN, THE VIETNAM WAR is rapidly losing support on the home front. In October, tens of thousands of war protestors converge in Washington, D.C. to march on the Pentagon. In other cities, other protests net a series of arrests, and some of those incarcerated are celebrities. Doctor Benjamin Spock is jailed, and the novelist Norman Mailer. Anti-war protests have quickly become regular front-page news. In November, our U.S. Secretary of Defense, Robert McNamara, resigns. He disagrees with the administration's decision to keep at this battle.[6]

Before I know it, it's Christmas. My second grandchild, Leslie, was born last week to Chuck and Lee. Mary just left to spend her holidays helping out with her two sweet little nieces, while the rest of the family gathers here on 18th Avenue.

Interacting with a growing, grown-up set of children is deeply satisfying. I'd easily envisioned my role as a mother, raising children, but this new phase is an unexpected delight. Our five children are each extremely different — different goals, different activities and passions. It is sometimes amazing to realize they derive from the very same stock. Yet they like each other and we continue to enfold an expanding family at our gatherings. When they're with us, Ken and I take pleasure in every minute. And then they scatter and are gone.

David is our only child home now days, his best companion here being his big dog "Teddy" — a beautiful black standard poodle, a breed heartily recommended to us by Slade. Teddy is one of the most loveable, family-friendly dogs our McCaffree family has ever owned, and over the years we've nuzzled our fair share. To our teenaged son, perched just the other side of our generation gap, Teddy provides immense creature comfort: No arguments, no parental prodding, no unrelenting requests to cut his hair.

No sooner has the glow of Christmas subsided than news overseas darkens again. As 1968 dawns, our U.S. military, previously the aggressor in this protracted foreign conflict, is now under siege in South Vietnam: The North Vietnamese and Viet Cong have launched the massive Tet offensive.[7]

In these turbulent times I must launch something else — another campaign for re-election. By now I'm considered a seasoned incumbent, but I certainly can't rest on any laurels. Even if redistricting rendered my district slightly more Republican than before, the truth is it can still swing very easily either way. I am not guaranteed an automatic win by any imaginative stretch. Besides, the name Mary Ellen McCaffree is now inextricably linked with taxes.

In most people's lexicon, 'tax' is a dirty word. Politically, working with taxes is equated with professional suicide (unless you're cutting them), but I have chosen to tackle taxes deliberately. It is essential we shore up our tax base. This is a millstone I willingly bear, but I must help my constituents understand why. I need to remain in touch and accessible. It is to my distinct advantage that I enjoy this.

IN A LOVELY LIVING ROOM IN DISTRICT 32A, a silver coffee service sits on the sideboard, next to cups and saucers, artfully arranged, and two trays of lemon bars. In ten minutes a dozen guests will arrive. The hostess suggests I make myself comfortable, and offers to take my coat.

"Is there anything else I can get you, Mrs. McCaffree?"

Coffee hours are a staple of political life, and among my favorite obligations.

"Welcome," I begin, once the small group has served themselves. "Our hostess has asked me to speak with you today about neighborhood safety."

I hear their concerns. I hear their suggestions. I listen as their topics stray — to school levies, logjammed bridges, someone's wish for a park. There is never a lack of services my constituents would like me to champion. Yet with each good suggestion, I say the same: "That's a good idea. How do we pay for it?"

This simple question is inevitably met with silence, blank stares and more silence. *Pay?*

"Would you be willing to fund it with a tax increase?" I can predict the answer.

Their responses range from, 'No, I will not pay more taxes!' to arguments that if we'd just cut government waste we could find the money. I find it so frustrating that so few voters tie government services to costs — costs that must be funded… by taxes.

One woman then reminds the group I sponsored our state's latest sales tax rate increase. I explain: "I worked on tax reform this past legislative session specifically because I care about most of these very same things you do. We have very real needs, as you have pointed out, but each service, each improvement, comes with a price tag. And I believe the best way our state can continue to cover the costs of serving us all is to reform our tax and revenue base so that it can adequately keep up with our demands."

This is rarely an enticing topic, but I must keep at this message. We continue our coffee hour conversation, and at the end of our time together I always ask my hostess to hand out cards.

"If you would like to volunteer for my campaign for re-election, please fill out a card," I tell them. "During election season we always need help addressing envelopes, doorbelling, putting up signs… any number of tasks."

At home, in a drawer in my desk downstairs is collection of blank thank you cards. When I return from this coffee hour, I send the hostess a sincere thanks. Personal interaction is the best tool to help effectively represent my constituents.

A NEW CAMPAIGN DOESN'T DISMISS ME from other legislative duties. I continue my active role on the Tax Advisory Council, where our task remains the same: Study our tax structure and propose improvements. When the fifteen of us first met two years ago, in the previous interim, we agreed upon four basic principles to guide our work, and listed them at the front of our final report:[8]

- A tax should equitably distribute its burden among those taxpayers upon whom it falls. *It should be fair.*

- A tax must be susceptible to efficient administration and uniform application and enforcement, and its cost of administration must not represent a significant percentage of the revenue it will yield. *It should be cost-effective and easy to administer.*

- A tax must be consistent with major governmental policies. *It must serve state needs.*

- A tax must be reasonably responsive to the revenue requirements of the governmental agency that imposes it. *It must give us a steady, dependable revenue stream.*

Fair. Easy to administer. Reflecting government policies. Responsive to our needs. We know the guidelines, and while we did make some progress during the last legislative session — by creating the new Department of Revenue and Tax Appeals Board — we still haven't adequately transformed our state's revenue base to successfully pair money coming in with demanding state expenses.

This interim, after reviewing our Council report of 1966, and after adding the input of additional experts, more citizens, more business interests, more comparisons from other states, and then, after weighing our actual economic realities and meticulously doing the math, we arrive at a firm conclusion: Our original proposal was sound. Is sound. It meets the four criteria. It meets our state needs. It is the best solution available now.

So once again, we will recommend to the governor and our colleagues a complete overhaul of our state's tax structure, and our proposed restructuring remains the same: Add a single rate income tax, lower the B & O tax, lower the sales tax, lower the property tax limit. The net result of all these changes? Also the same: Not only no net gain in total taxes for state taxpayers, but also a smart new tax base that will fluctuate with revenue needs. What this translates to is that we shouldn't have to run repetitive levy campaigns year after year, or repetitively raise state tax rates on our taxpayers. And most importantly, our proposed structure of taxation is eminently more fair. In contrast to our current tax structure, it doesn't place the biggest tax burden on the poorest — those least able to pay. In fact, it substantially reduces the overall regressive nature of our state tax system of today.

The problem is not this proposal, we again conclude after we review each of its features against our failure to secure full support from the 1967 legislature.

The problem is education. We must help our legislators and voters understand the logic and brilliance of this new design.

As THE NEW ELECTION SEASON GAINS MOMENTUM, my incumbency does come in handy. I'm able to assemble a new campaign team with relative speed, and we agree to meet every other Monday in my basement, which Ken and I have cleared again to make way for the latest rendition of Operation Elect Mom to Office. We also re-activate our second phone line.

This year, using the delegation skills I honed last session, I enlist a part time secretary to help with my correspondence and typing. And I have more university students interested in working than ever before. One is Dallas Salisbury, politically active at the University of Washington. Dallas serves with Ken on the University Book Store governing board: My husband as faculty representative, Dallas representing UW students. Also joining us is a political science intern, Robert Doherty, who will study my campaign as the basis for his senior thesis.[9]

My veteran McCaffree campaign team knows the drill: Mailing lists, precinct maps, a master calendar, campaign literature, my major messages, and... a gimmick.

In years past, Joel and Gummie have contrived candidate gimmicks — a dishrag to clean up government, potholders to handle the heat. Tonight in my basement, we toss about ideas for a gimmick to attract the attention of voters this year.

"Something comtemporary."

"Peace, taxes and lovebeads?"

"Very funny."

One team member is more serious:

"With all the protest and violence, it seems like people could use a nice warm batch of cookies."

This gives me an idea: "I do have this recipe..."

"Recipe for an outstanding candidate?"

I've been interrupted. My brainstormers are in high gear.

I continue. "...a recipe for an upside down chocolate cake. Eggless."

"No bad eggs?"

"Farm girl turns tax system upside down?"

"It has a noble history," I explain. "It came from the Kansas State College Department of Home Economics for the women of the Kansas State Farm Bureau during World War II, when you couldn't buy eggs at the market — they were all shipped overseas to the military. My mother made this cake often during war time, and I've used it for my family."

"OK, Dr. McCaffree, be honest. Is this recipe good enough for your wife's campaign?"

"You bet," says Ken.

"Let's do it," says Ann Angle, my campaign manager. "Cake recipe on side one, recipe for a great candidate on the other."

We vote and it's agreed. I find the recipe, someone makes a quick sketch, and my latest campaign gimmick is hatched: A handy little piece of campaign literature — a recipe card.

I'm grateful for a swift start. It's only January.

AT THE BEGINNING OF FEBRUARY, GENERAL WESTMORELAND makes a request to President Johnson and to Congress that we move 206,000 more troops into Vietnam. The war protesters roar in response, and my university students redouble their local efforts to seek the right to vote.

In March, in an evening television broadcast, Walter Cronkite abandons his neutral journalist's stance and uses his position as a venerated news anchor to speak against what he calls a "futile and immoral war."

A new presidential campaign season is upon us, and this war is fast becoming a central issue. In the Democrat Party, in the early New Hampshire primary, the pacifist candidate Eugene McCarthy garners a startling 42 percent of the vote against President Lyndon Baines Johnson.[10]

On the final day of March, President Johnson is scheduled to address the nation on Vietnam in a televised broadcast. We ask David to join us for this in the living room. He and Ken have had words over the war, and over the concept of war in general. David doesn't understand how anyone could support war — any war, ever. Ken tries to explain his own commitment to serving our country. The twain do not meet. But we want to keep this conversation going with our son. We are a family that discusses issues and respects each member's right to articulate an opinion. In this case, we want to discuss the Vietnam war from the same set of facts, so tonight we gather around our family television set.

Ken turns on the TV and he and I settle onto the couch while David slouches barefoot on the carpet. LBJ's deeply lined face comes into focus as he prepares to address the American people. But instead of discussing the war, Johnson immediately announces that he is withdrawing from the presidential race. He will not seek another term. This is stunning, sobering news. The leader of our seething country is walking away. Giving up.

"This war has created division in the American house," he says to us, speaking straight to the television camera and to American households. My husband and son, divided, don't blink. "I will not permit the presidency to become involved in the partisan divisions..." [11]

DAN EVANS HAS NO INTENTION of abandoning his leadership of Washington State. He plans to run for a second term as governor, and I am requested to join in his campaign strategy team. The DEGOHTs reconvene in the governor's mansion.

"How about 'Design for Washington?'" Joel suggests as we discuss a new message to build upon the last campaign's Blueprint for Progress.

"We haven't finished the Blueprint yet," someone argues.

"My point exactly," Joel says. "We keep the Blueprint in play, but now we're working toward the design."

"What's the difference?"

"Semantics?"

The governor has been silent until now.

"We need to look further down the road," he says. "I'd like to add greater emphasis on environmental protection and overseas trade."

The Heavy Thinkers develop the newest campaign — still driven by our Blueprint, but more forward-looking. Dan will be running against John O'Connell, our popular young attorney general who has decided to step down in order to challenge Dan for the governor's spot.

Late in the last legislative session, Slade confessed to me in private that he's tired of the House after serving five terms, though he's ascended to become an effective majority leader.

"Why don't you run for attorney general?" I'd suggested to him at the time.

"You're kidding me," he said.

Apparently, it had never crossed his mind.

"You'd be great," I told him. "Excellent, in fact."

We dedicate the second half of this DEGOHT meeting at the mansion to developing a Republican slate for statewide offices. At the end of the day, everyone agrees Slade should enter the attorney general race. For lieutenant governor, we have a new candidate for these times: Art Fletcher, an African-American city council member in Pasco, in the newer Tri-Cities area in the state's far east. Governor Evans is thrilled that Art will join him at the top of the ticket, and we're determined to help our state break the color barrier with

Art in the number two spot. It won't be easy. In fact, it will be some sort of miracle. Our work toward improved civil rights for our state's minorities has met with mixed success. Art's election would certainly help deliver our DEGOHT message: Everyone deserves a voice.

LESS THAN A WEEK AFTER PRESIDENT JOHNSON announced he won't seek another term, and days after we add Art Fletcher to our party's state ticket, Dr. Martin Luther King, Jr., travels to Tennessee to support a sanitation worker's strike, just in advance of a Poor People's March he'll lead on Washington, D.C. After the striker's rally, as Dr. King chats on the balcony of his Memphis hotel room, an assassin's bullet guns him down, and whatever racial tension had remained tempered now explodes with collective shock at Dr. King's brutal, senseless killing.[12]

Our political season is suddenly infused with fresh waves of outrage.

National campaign rhetoric swells to passionate heights.

Our own far corner of the country works through civil rights strife more quietly. In Seattle's East Madison neighborhood — a "black ghetto" according to many here, including the press — our governor meets in person with several groups of disenfranchised black youth. Their discussions lead to a decision to establish a local resource center there, where all the state's social services will be conveniently consolidated under a single roof, to better serve these youth and their neighbors and families.[13]

DOWNSTAIRS AT 5014 18TH AVENUE, MY BASEMENT is also serving multiple functions under one roof. Because our home is so centrally located, and because my basement is so well equipped, we've attracted several other candidates seeking support for their campaigns. I am running our party's campaign schools from here again, too. My basement has also become an office away from 'home' for our Republican state party chairman, Gummie Johnson, since state headquarters is in Olympia, more than an hour south, and the King County Republican office is not an option. Our local party machinery is still dominated by the far right — if not John Birchers — and still has little affection for the state party as headed by Gummie.

By June the campaign season is fully in swing, both nationally and here in Washington State. Added to the Vietnam conflict and its ongoing protests, political races are now top topics on our nightly TV news. Tonight, for instance, we learn that presidential candidate Robert Kennedy has just won the California Democrat primary, a win that pushes him into the lead in his party's three-way tussle — with Hubert Humphrey and Eugene McCarthy also running strong. On the Republican side, Richard Nixon is leading hands down.

The next day, after Bobby Kennedy wraps up his California victory speech to a luncheon crowd at the L.A. Ambassador Hotel, he and Ethel head back to the campaign trail, taking a back route through the hotel kitchen, where he is gunned down, point blank. His wife drops to his side, clears breathing space for her husband, but within 25 hours Bobby Kennedy is dead.[14]

For a second time in months, we reel with this news and mourn another violent high-profile death right here in our homeland. A nagging sensation of national chaos and fear begins to seep in.

These are changing times indeed. Sobering and unsettling.

WITHIN THE WEEK, NANCY WILL GRADUATE from Washington State University on the same day David is to graduate from Roosevelt High. So while Ken drives cross-state to Pullman to attend to Nancy's commencement ceremony, Mary and I climb the steps at Hec Ed on the UW campus to witness David in his cap and gown, his brown hair tumbling well below his mortarboard. He will enter the University of Washington in the fall.

By the end of June, taxes hit our national headline news when Congress passes a controversial measure: A ten percent 'war surcharge' this year on Americans' personal income tax to help foot the bill for the long, ongoing conflict in Vietnam. This arrives right after the administration dismissed a proposed 'excessive earnings tax' on corporations whose profits swelled as a result of supplying the U.S. military for this war. Our elected leaders in Washington, D.C. were persuaded that the tax on excess profits was unfair. Thus, the nation's demand for more revenue fell to individuals.[15]

Taxes have never been popular among Americans, ever since our founders rallied against 'Taxation without Representation' and angrily dumped tea overboard in Boston Harbor. But in the wake of this new surcharge specifically levied to bear the costs of an increasingly unpopular war, the emotional charge to the word "tax" hits high voltage.

I am not unaware of this as I lead the Legislative Council's Committee on Revenue and Regulatory Agencies. My committee members are attuned to public sentiment, too, and this emotional climate tells us our proposed new tax — the flat rate income tax — and a major overhaul of our tax system will be no easier to sell to the legislature in the coming term than it was in 1967. More difficult, perhaps.

As for our Tax Advisory Council study, we remain convinced our original plan is best for our state, both in the near term and far into our future.

Yet even this proposal is losing support from a critical sector. Originally, the powerful Weyerhaeuser Corporation strongly favored this proposed tax reform, and was thus a credible business ally in our effort to reform our tax base. Weyerhaeuser would have derived substantial long-term benefit from exchanging the heftier B & O tax for the proposed flat tax rate on income. But when we passed the Open Space Act last session, it changed Weyerhaeuser's tune, or rather, its urgency. With some of their forested property values reduced by our Open Space Act, their tax burden was lessened without our larger tax reform. Thus, our state's timber companies have less incentive to rally on behalf of the governor's tax reform policy. Good government involves such a delicate balancing act.

In addition to the lessened support by corporate giant Weyerhaeuser, for a second time, one of our fifteen Tax Advisory Council members remains outspoken in her dissent: Eleanor Brand doesn't approve our proposal, and insists her two-page minority view remain in the report we submit to the legislature. Her main objection centers on the single rate income tax we recommend, versus a steeply graduated rate of income taxation. Though she was appointed to this Council because of her position within the League, this is Eleanor Brand's personal view — The League of Women Voters does not have consensus on this subject at this time. But rather than represent the League's position, she has chosen to express her own. We include Mrs. Brand's dissent — again — in the report we will send Governor Evans in December.[16]

KEN RETURNS FROM CAMPUS ONE AFTERNOON with a grin and a handout: "For you, dear," he says, "from one of my economics grad students."

My opponent in the primary race is also a grad student — in chemistry — and active in our local Young Republicans: Ray Hendrickson. This brochure is his. WHAT'S HAPPENING TO THE UNIVERSITY DISTRICT? the young Mr. Hendrickson's brochure screams in large, bold type. The photo on front is from the *Seattle P-I*: Barefoot, long-haired students lounging in the sun on the UW campus lawn.

Ken's student has scribbled me a note. *Mrs. McCaffree: After receiving this scare literature, I was pleased to note in your folder that your son's hair is just a little bit on the longish side! Judd Hammach, Grad Student, Economics.*

Opening the young Mr. Hendrickson's brochure, I read in even larger print: THE SHOCKING FACTS!!! The three he mentions are crime, business losses and high taxes — this last with a photocopy of House Bill 205, which is the sales tax rate increase with Representative McCaffree listed as sole sponsor, which he has positioned alongside pictures of bearded university students wearing dark glasses and strumming their guitars. *Ray Hendrickson, a man with answers*, says his brochure. I welcome a discussion with Mr. Hendrickson any time.

The campaign phone line rings.

"Mrs. McCaffree?" says a voice on the line, "are you aware…"

"Yes, the eggs," I say.

With so many serious issues on tap this year, I'm surprised at the number of my constituents concerned about my recipe. They think I've forgotten the eggs. For the umpteenth time, I explain the recipe and its history during the egg shortage of World War II, always happy to chat with one of my voters.

"Is there anything else I can help you with?" I always ask.

"Not today. Thanks, Mrs. McCaffree, and good luck."

One of my local grocers tells me the sale of baking chocolate in District 32A is on the rise. He is continually re-stocking, and believes it is due to my recipe.

Throughout 32A, Ken and I continue to doorbell as often as possible, but I am grateful I can turn much of this over to volunteers. I am traveling constantly to serve on my councils and various committees, and often arrive home quite late. Mid-summer, the McCaffrees experience something remarkable — all five children home at once — a wonderful family reunion. My kids say they're here to help Mom campaign.

As August approaches, every campaign is running full tilt. Slade has his hands full against a feisty prosecutor, John McCutcheon, for the attorney general spot. Art Fletcher's battle for lieutenant governor is all uphill against incumbent Lieutenant Governor John Cherberg, but Art is determined and classy and takes the hard work in stride. Wes Uhlman, once in the House with me, then serving last term in the Senate, is now running for mayor of Seattle.

We all carry on our campaigning as summertime temperatures rise, in parallel with a steady inflammation of our national temperament.

IN THE FIRST WEEK OF AUGUST 1968, the Republican National Convention takes place in Miami. Among the names speculatively floated for vice-president is that of our very own Governor Daniel J. Evans. Dan has been tapped to deliver the convention's keynote address, appears on the *Today Show* before that prominent speech,[17,18] and afterwards makes the cover of *Time* magazine — as a party up and comer.[19] Dan is backing Nelson Rockefeller for president, but the nomination goes to Richard Nixon. Nevertheless, thanks to Dan and the strides our team is making here in Washington, our state is gaining in national prominence.

So are the anti-establishment voices of the young. The Beatles' 'Revolution' hits the airwaves. *You say you want a revolution? Well, heyyy, we all want to change the world...*

The Democratic National Convention takes place at the end of the month in Chicago, a sweltering city in any August, but especially oppressive in this tension-fraught year. Protestors amass as the delegates and candidates arrive, and the four days of political positioning inside the convention hall take a back seat to the brutal clashes outside – between the protestors and some 20,000 National Guardsmen and police.

"The whole world is watching. The whole world is watching," the protesters chant as they are clubbed and charged and bloodied and restrained. Due to television coverage, they're right. We are watching, and what we see is startling and horrible: More violence in our American streets, more war between factions of Americans. Security officers report that eighty of their ranks are injured, while the reported number of wounded protesters tops seven-hundred. Among the 650 arrested is a handful of accused ringleaders – 'The Chicago Seven' – including Tom Hayden, Jerry Rubin and Abbie Hoffman.

Vice President Hubert Humphrey emerges from the chaotic convention as the Democrat's presidential nominee, though he didn't run in a single state primary. By Democrat Party standards of the day, all that is necessary to win the party's nomination is to capture enough convention delegate votes. Humphrey negotiated delegate support without spending one day or one dollar on a primary campaign.[20]

We've spent many days and some dollars campaigning in Washington State. My basement is "buzzing" again, a regular hive of campaign life. I easily defeat Ray Hendrickson in the primary, 2460 votes to 706, and all the candidates I've supported survive the September vote, too. Now it's on to the general election, where I face a well-known, well-liked University District Democrat, Jack Harvey. Thus, I set out to doorbell each of my precincts again – every household in 32A – before the general election.

Slade's campaign against John McCutcheon seems to be in a dead heat, the two running neck and neck. McCutcheon is a bulldog of a prosecutor, with a high profile political name thanks to his state senator father. My close colleague is struggling in this race, and Gummie calls me shortly after the primary: "We've got to do something, Mary Ellen."

Slade has been campaigning hard, but he sometimes talks over peoples' heads. He's so bright, so articulate, so abundantly vocabularied, and he knows the governmental process inside out, but he doesn't always connect. In his brainy enthusiasm, he sometimes misses the mark when he talks to a gathering of ordinary folk.

"What do you suggest?" I ask Gummie.

"Something statewide," he says. "Something with your name on it."

We put together a mailing and post it a few days before November 5.

According to hearsay and polls, our incumbent governor Dan Evans and our attorney general, John O'Connell, are also running a close contest. All of us are campaigning like we've never campaigned before. With so many Americans angry, and so many voices and placards calling for change, politics this year are in tight, critical focus.

Not even the Olympic Games, normally a wholesome distraction, can divert us from our fracturing national woes. On the medal stand on the Olympic track in Mexico City, after placing first and third in the 200 meter race, Americans Tommy Smith and John Carlos raise black-gloved fists during America's national anthem: Black pride, black power. The vivid image strikes a bulls' eye and sails around the world. We know what these black fists represent back home.[21]

AS THE SCHOOL YEAR SETTLES IN, university campuses fail to settle down, teeming with protests, sit-ins, marches, occasional outbursts of violence. Our large campus here, thank goodness, remains relatively tame.

David is a wide-eyed freshman, still willfully avoiding short hair.

"Can't you do something with it?" I ask him as it drapes his handsome face.

"What do you want me to do, Mom? Put it in curlers?"

One day, he did. The fabled 'generation gap' is on full display in the McCaffree household. I have confidence we'll weather it.

Raising a family in a democratic society whose philosophy is based on the dignity of man and the inalienable rights of each individual, our children learned at a very early age that their wants and desires are listened to and considered. Without fear they were able to say, for example, "But Mom, I don't like cottage cheese!" Hence, my son's freedom to grow his hair. And to put it in curlers.

Three blocks north of the University of Washington, my well-worn basement headquarters harbors a robust political community, increasing in number and intensity by the week, having become a home-away-from home for huddles of politically minded college students, as well as growing numbers of young singles and young marrieds. They gather here regularly, chipping in as typists, folders, stuffers, hand-addressing envelopes or heading out to my district to doorbell and distribute yard signs.

But this is no hip coffeehouse hangout, no place to loll and talk political shop. This is a place of action. I have always focused on action, and I expect the people around me to do the same.

In preparation for the general election, we add three more phone lines for a total of five. Now, gearing up for election night, we are taking a basement poll: *Who can spare a set of rabbit ears? Anyone have an extra TV?* We need four, for our three local networks and our local PBS.

I've done my campaign legwork, having spoken to the University District Rotary Club, the Business and Professional Women's Club, the U-District Chamber of Commerce, my local Republican Club, the League of Women

Voters, a Ravenna neighborhood citizen's group, and I can't recall how many living room coffee hours I've attended, nor how many interviews I've given my local press.

ON HALLOWEEN, PRESIDENT JOHNSON announces American bombing in Vietnam has come to an end.[22]

In less than a week, Americans will cast votes in our general election.

November 5, 1968 dawns surprisingly sunny in Seattle — a spectacular autumn day in the Pacific Northwest. I head to my favorite beauty shop to have my hair done and receive a rare manicure, an Election Day routine I've adopted to prevent me from biting my nails.

My campaign committee is busy driving constituents to the polls and answering the telephone. I never answer my phone on Election Day. Every time an election rolls around, people telephone to ask me how to vote. But I never tell anyone how to vote — not even my children.

I report to my local polling booth and exercise my citizen right, grateful for so many who fought to make my one voice count — our founding fathers, the suffragettes, more recently all those who worked in this state on redistricting. I think of my young constituents as I pull the levers to record my votes. If their lobbying succeeds, next election their votes will count, too.

By 6 p.m. my basement is beginning to rumble.

The borrowed television sets are ready. One TV, on the table we've used for collating, is set to Channel 4, KOMO, our Seattle network affiliate of ABC. The second sits atop my battered metal filing cabinet, tuned to KING-TV Channel 5 (NBC). The third TV, on its wobbly perch on our tired hand-crank mimeograph machines, is tuned to CBS's local Channel 7, known in this town as KIRO. And the last features KCTS Channel 9, publicly broadcast from the University of Washington campus.

Ironically, much of tonight's statewide election news on these stations will originate from the results we gather right here.

On a big piece of butcher paper, Ken is setting up a grid to tally results as they arrive from across the state. He has lined up a couple of adding machines, quiet for the moment; once polls close, these 10-keys will rapidly tat to life. My husband has also verified the pens have ink, the pencils are sharpened. McCaffrees are nothing, if not organized and prepared.

Already, a handful of those gathered in my basement have transistor radios plastered to their ears to catch the national election news trickling in from more easterly time zones. On occasion, a familiar face from our local media will pop in — for a look around or a chat, hoping to glean a feel for the day, a sense of the trends. Mary Ellen McCaffree's basement has developed a reputation as the place to be.[23] It really amuses me.

Gummie has masterminded a network of correspondents to deliver us results. They all have the phone numbers of these five lines, with orders to call in results right away, as soon as they arrive. These 'reporters' have been assigned to track the races in our legislature and Congress, plus races in the county court-houses, other state offices, and the Nixon campaign. Tonight, C. Montgomery Johnson plans to track each Republican campaign in Washington State, and he has assigned my husband the task of meticulous tallying.

The phones are lively.

"Mary Ellen's basement," a volunteer answers.

The voice on the other end is relieved.

"I was hoping I wrote the right number. This is Shelby Scates from the *Seattle P-I.*"

"Mary Ellen's basement."

"Mary Ellen's basement."

Another line rings, then another. As the early evening transitions toward the closing of our local polls, all five phone lines begin to transmit us voting projections, non-stop.

Every hour on the hour, Lyle Burt has been phoning here from the *Seattle Times* until he and his *P.I.* counterpart Shelby Scates make the same decision — to drive the 10 minutes here from downtown Seattle, amble down my base-ment stairs, and gather results directly instead of by phone. They join the gaggle of reporters already here: From the Associated Press and U.P.I. (United Press International), KING-TV's political commentator gathering notes for an election night broadcast, KOMO-TV's Brian Johnson making the rounds of the room. Mary Ellen's basement is media central.

When the polls formally close at 8, the speculative milling about turns serious. The trickling of early results swiftly swells to a deluge. Ken is busy at his butcher paper chart. Those with radios maneuver their dials to pick up distant reports, zipping through static to find an intelligible voice. All five phone lines continue to ring.

Clark County reports in first. This year they've used experimental punch-card ballots — their votes are quickly tabulated by machine. Our bigger cities use voting machines, like the levered one I used this morning, while smaller municipalities still use hand marked paper ballots. The big city votes are the next to arrive.

Shortly before 8 p.m. my campaign committee scatters to various local polling places — *See ya! Back in a flash!* — to pick up results as polling place volun-teers work their way through the hand counts or post machine tabulations. Our messengers are grabbing results, not just for my campaign, but for the statewide races: Gorton and Evans and Fletcher. Crews from the other campaigns with which I've worked send out their 'fetchers' as well, then call in their numbers. Ken remains at the ready, pen in hand. From telephone booths around the state, results arrive here first before anywhere else.

As the evening progresses, trends are taking shape.

Dan Evans pulls ahead early in the governor's race and seems to be holding steady — some 80,000 votes ahead in King County alone with more than a third of those ballots accounted for. Statewide, his numbers are consistent, too, at the 54-55 percent mark. That's a relief.

Art Fletcher's numbers for lieutenant governor are not quite as commanding, but John Cherberg is sure to be perspiring if he's following this race as closely as we are.

The attorney general race between Slade and John McCutcheon continues to run at dead heat as we tally the returns. Cheers rise from our crowd every time Ken adds an advantage to Gorton, followed by an emotional sag as another set of results come in, then a cheer again. Neither candidate ever pulls ahead by much.

In three previous campaigns, I've never managed to win my seat by much beyond a simple majority. Tonight I wind up with a tally near 54 percent.

"A landslide," says Gummie.

"Hardly."

Within an hour after polls close, my district count is confirmed, at least by our calculations. Shortly after 9 p.m. friends begin dropping by to help celebrate.

But the night is young. And as in years past, some of our distant correspondents are less... urgent... about this process. And in fact, some counties and districts and precincts won't have final numbers in place until at least tomorrow night. Hand counting election ballots is never speedy.

By midnight, however, most results are clear, and for the first time in forty years in our state, for two consecutive elections, our party will have won control of the House of Representatives. Eight of the campaigns I've helped appear to be headed for victory.

In the Senate, during my first two terms, Republicans held only seventeen of forty-nine seats, then last session climbed to a more respectable twenty to their twenty-nine. We hope to close that gap even more, if not win Senate control. At this hour, though, it appears another several seats is the best we can hope for.

The attorney general race continues apace, too close to call. Slade is understandably tense. He sacrificed his House seat and majority leader post to pursue this office. Art Fletcher is in a photo finish, too, it appears — both races are still undecided.

Tonight's other tight race is the U.S. presidency. By midnight we're still waiting to learn: Is it Humphrey or Nixon? With 95 percent of our national vote tallied, fewer than 50,000 votes separate the two. Nixon has just over 29.7 million votes, Humphrey just under. Independent candidate George Wallace is nearing the ten million mark – votes the two frontrunners likely wish they could tap.[24]

Sometime before daylight, Ken and I finally retire for a few hours' sleep. At 11:35 a.m. the next morning, Richard Nixon delivers his victory speech, promising to bring together the American people.

LESS THAN THREE WEEKS LATER, Ken and I head to Spokane for Apple Cup weekend and another statewide caucus. This same weekend, in this same eastern town, the Legislative Council meets as well for the very last time this interim: On November 22 we take a final accounting of the 95 Council request bills we've drafted for the upcoming session. We vote to send them all along for the entire legislature to consider in January.

After the Husky/Cougar grid match, our caucus meets Sunday morning to vote on a slate of leaders. Don Eldridge and Tom Copeland will repeat as Speaker and Speaker Pro Tem, but we must replace our majority floor leader. Slade was ultimately victorious as our new attorney general, whereas Art Fletcher lost his lieutenant governor bid by a squeaker. In Slade's place, we elect Stu Bledsoe to lead us on the floor, having witnessed the rancher's effectiveness last session as our whip. Jonathan Whetzel and Irv Newhouse will back Stu as assistant floor leaders, and Gladys Kirk, who has been our caucus secretary forever, will assume that post at least once more. Bob Goldsworthy, however, declines to serve another term as caucus chairman, opting to simply chair Appropriations. Norwood Cunningham is the man we elect to replace him.

Only one legislative task remains for me in this calendar year: The formal report of our Tax Advisory Council. We send our conclusions to the Capitol Print Shop to be bound in a book, complete with an introduction from our chairman dated December 10, right on time: "We remain convinced that the basic tax structure of Washington should be substantially changed."

It will be my job, yet again, to see this through. If Eleanor Brand's dissent is any indication, I don't forecast clear sailing for tax reform, but I am ready to fight for it.

MY YOUNG CONSTITUENTS ARE READY TO WAGE their voting campaign as well, and my youngest son, in his own unique way, will join them. Although my rebellious youngest is not particularly enamored with my work – inside the 'system' and part of 'the establishment' – he nevertheless considers it 'groovy' that I'm working with students to lower the voting age. It is to my great surprise, however, when he responds to my morning request with, "Sure, Mom!"

Sure, he'll maneuver his lanky form into a cumbersome metallic knight's armor costume for the newspaper. The story runs on December 22 with a bold caption beneath David's photo that proclaims: "Today's 18-year-old Knight in Shining Armor — Voteless" and in smaller print beneath that: "David McCaffree's mother will spearhead youth drive."

The accompanying story details the students' upcoming battle for the vote in the '69 session. The headline? *A fighting chance to vote.*[25]

Just one of my battles.

I've agreed to repeat as chairman of the House Committee on Revenue and Taxation. The aim is clear. We must succeed this time in stabilizing our state's financial footing. It matters not that my children are no longer public school kids. I must secure that stable funding for other schoolchildren, for other families, because I believe in the importance of education. It is educated citizens who grasp the importance of our founding principles, who understand our government's unique mechanics. Through education, people are equipped to make our country work, to make sure our representative democracy continues to thrive, and if it is failing, to step in and fix it.

Students like those at Columbia University and UC Berkeley are raising their rebellious voices loud and clear in protest against our government and societal norms. But complaining is only a first step toward change. If these young people really want to 'change the world' as they say they do, they need to determine how, and then get involved. Right now, their guiding emotion seems to be outrage, rather than a resolve to make things better.

I look at the newspaper photograph of David, the symbolic warrior, and smile at our local university's much gentler campaign for voice and rights.

PHOTO - SEATTLE POST-INTELLIGENCER

—(P-I Photo by Tom Brownell. Costume compliments of Brookline

TODAY'S 18-YEAR-OLD KNIGHT IN SHINING ARMOR—VOTELESS
David McCaffree's mother will spearhead youth drive

David McCaffree is among the voteless.

ON CHRISTMAS EVE, near the end of this interim's tumultuous two years, Apollo 8 astronauts transmit a television message to earth's millions. This morning they became the first men to orbit the moon, our nearest heavenly body, which Colonel Frank Borman describes from the spacecraft: "A vast, lonely and forbidding sight." Captain James Lovell marvels at our earth by comparison: "A grand oasis in the big vastness of space." After they take turns reading from Genesis, Colonel Borman signs off: "Merry Christmas. God bless all of you. All of you on the Good Earth." [26]

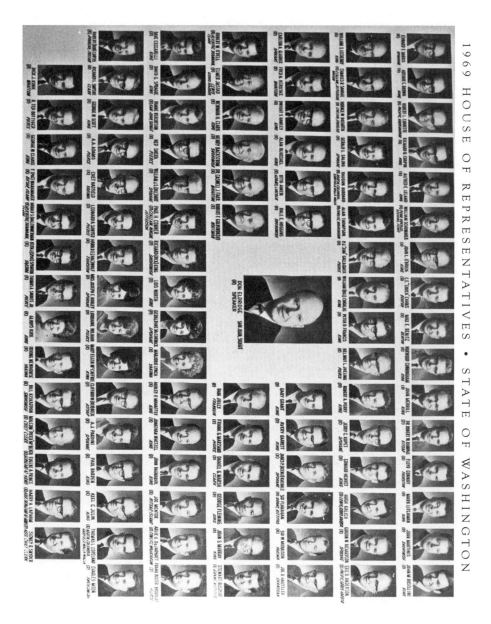

CHAPTER TEN

TAX REFORM
STABILIZING A LOPSIDED REVENUE BASE

Mr. Speaker, I would like to have the record show that this House is indeed indebted to a very fine public servant... As this young lady stood on the floor today and explained this most complex measure in its entirety, I could not help but salute her.

I POUR MYSELF A MUG OF BLACK COFFEE on the first Monday morning of January and venture outdoors to our small back deck, bundled warmly to watch the winter birds. Sparrows, juncos, finches — an occasional fat robin — all scavenge and forage the ground beneath our dogwood, its branches now bare.

One week from today I will return to the House of Representatives of Washington State to serve a fourth term — the sole remaining member of the team I joined at this decade's start. Everyone is still active, of course, and still at work in the capitol: Joel in the Senate, Slade our attorney general, Dan our governor entering a second term. I'm our only remnant in the House, and some loneliness admittedly accompanies this prospect. Yet I have a job to see through: orchestrating tax reform.

I study these industrious birds and contemplate, *How do I feel?* — a thing I rarely ask of myself. By nature, I prefer to simply tackle the task at hand, like these tiny birds so intent on their wintertime harvest. But if I were asked to put into words how I feel at this moment, I feel… good. I face an enormous responsibility, but feel capable of the work. I have the explicit confidence of our governor, who bases it on my work ethic, which he has experienced first hand throughout our seven years of teamwork. I carry beneath my belt a session of solid legislative leadership, having chaired our Revenue and Taxation Committee and led considerable progress in our campaign for tax reform. I will enter this term with another session of seniority to my McCaffree name, accompanied by a no-nonsense reputation and an inside track to our governor. And, despite all my work on our Republican campaigns, I bring a substantial history of working across the aisle per my belief in bi-partisanship. Once I'm in Olympia, I work for the people of this state and partisan labels become much less consequential.

So I believe I'm well positioned for the challenges that face me. Getting here has been a process, a progression — I've grown.

For the first time, this coming session, I will have a legislative roommate. Lois North was elected to a freshman House term. We were colleagues in the Seattle League of Women Voters (via redistricting), and are also linked by our husbands' roles in the Department of Economics at UW. We've rented a place off of Sleater-Kinney Road — a waterfront home on Johnson Point, which juts into Budd Inlet in the Puget Sound. We'll be joined by my daughter Mary, who is adding another legislative post to her young resume this session: Serving as a House committee clerk for Local Government. I don't envision much socializing among this trio. We three are confirmed worker-types… like these foraging birds.

Sunday, the day before the 41st Session is gaveled to order, Peggy the wolfhound welcomes me to the governor's mansion with 3-year-old Bruce Evans astride.

"Come on in Mary Ellen," says Nancy Evans with her ready, warm smile. "Great to see you. Boys! Put away those nerf balls — your father has a meeting. Bruce, be gentle with Peggy or she'll buck you off. Coffee? Black, isn't it?"

Our team continues to meet regularly at the governor's mansion to assess our Blueprint for Progress and our strategy to complete it. The core team remains: Jim Dolliver, Slade, Joel, Gummie and me. We're occasionally joined by Ritajean, Jim Ellis, several others. Today the gang's all here.

The governor begins: "I know this isn't a favorite of anyone except for me and Mary Ellen, but our focus — right from the start — must be tax reform. If you haven't read the Tax Advisory Council's newest report, do. Or at least be aware: Their recommendations from the '67 session hold firm. Isn't that right Mary Ellen?"

"Yes, governor," I confirm as the sole DEGOHT voice on the Council. "We reviewed our tax structure from every angle, reconsidered our goals, held more hearings. I'm sure you can appreciate how hard we all studied this, or at least most of us. What we found was that our original recommendations really do make the most sense."

Jim Dolliver delivers the quick version, ticking off the items on his fingers: "First we authorize it by asking for a constitutional amendment for a single rate income tax and a lower lid on the property tax. Number two, the imple-menting bill, will set the single rate income tax and specifically adjust the tax rates for the B & O and sales taxes to balance our revenue stream."

"How are we set on votes?" asks Slade. "Gummie?"

"Seventy-seven returning from last term, and Representative Savage is back after skipping a term, so twenty-one total newcomers. Not completely from scratch, to start, but it's still a steep uphill. You ready, Mary Ellen?"

"Ready."

"As for the balance of the Blueprint," says the governor, "we've got the environmental concerns, the 18-year-old vote, unemployment compensation…"

AUTHORIZING BILL

A bill that establishes the legal basis for action on, or relative to, a specific subject.

IMPLEMENTING BILL

A bill that provides for carrying out those legislative items legally authorized by an authorizing bill.

Conversation and strategy begin. State Democrats have a similar group. Most well organized parties do. These think-tank teams are an essential cog in the political process — a combination of elected officials, business people, community leaders and volunteers who help shape and focus a party's positions and strategies and goals. I'm grateful to belong to this exceptional team gathered at the governor's coffee table.

"Here's to the 41st Session!" says Joel.

We raise our cups of coffee and clink to that.

Ken drove with me down to the capitol yesterday, and as our 41st Legislature prepares to convene this morning, he has found a familiar seat in the House balcony overlooking the chamber. My husband continues to support me to the nth degree, and I him. Many marriages suffer in the realm of political life, but I believe those that fail were under stress to begin with. I am grateful for a solid marriage and such a committed partner. It allows me the freedom to work as long and hard as my nature demands.

AT NOON, PRECISELY, ON MONDAY, JANUARY 13, 1969, Chief Clerk Malcolm 'Dutch' McBeath gavels our House to order. The color guard brings forth our flags. A Baptist minister delivers our opening prayer. This morning, certain phrases seem attuned to my duties on tax reform — my hope of delivering a restructured state tax base that is more reliable, more balanced and much more fair to those of lower income. "…And above all," prays the Reverend Willholland Williams, "a spirit of service which will abolish pride of place and inequality of opportunity… May not the web of outgrown precedents veil their moral vision. Grant them a penetrating eye for the rights and wrongs of today and a quick human sympathy... Grant them wisdom so to refashion all law that it may become the true expression of the fairer ideals of freedom and brotherhood which are seeking their incarnation in a new age…"

We sit in newly refurbished chambers, the Chief Clerk notes as he welcomes us next. I barely notice. My attention is on my tax reform tasks.

We vote in the leadership we selected Apple Cup weekend: Don Eldridge as House Speaker, Tom Copeland as Speaker Pro Tem. And two more we don't formally vote in on the floor today: Stu Bledsoe now steps into Slade's old shoes as majority leader — I suspect Stu will do a terrific job, cowboy boots and all; and our new caucus chairman Norwood Cunningham, a capable school administrator from Kent, seems ready to keep us in focus and on task.

By the time we adjourn on this wind-whipped afternoon, a light flurry of snow dapples the early darkness. Ken agrees to warm up the car while I check in quickly at the governor's office. As I reach the big door, Slade exits.

"Mister attorney general!" I greet him. "Enjoying your new work?"

"Most assuredly," he says with a genuine smile. "I can't thank you enough for encouraging me, Mary Ellen, even if election night was a cliffhanger. The position suits me."

"I knew it would," I said. "I was looking out for our state, too, you know."

"Sally said to be sure to invite you and Ken to dinner if I ran into you."

"We'd love to, Slade, but not tonight. Too much on my mind."

"Mine, too." He holds the door for me. "I'll get back to you about dinner. And Mary Ellen? Good luck with tax reform."

He knows as well as anyone what I face. Jim Dolliver and I confer quickly — we've remained in touch throughout the interim. By the time I exit the legislative building, Olympia is thinly blanketed in white and Ken and I drive home in a building snowstorm. We skid down the driveway, just off the main road, and slide to a disconcerting halt at my beachfront home. By early morning Lois and Ken and I agree, the cars will not make it out.

"What do we do?" asks Lois, not wanting to miss her second day.

I know just what to do: "Call the sergeant at arms."

Our sergeant at arms handles House transportation — usually for off-campus committee meetings or to fetch an errant legislator. This snowy morning, he sends us a Jeep and staff driver, and Lois and I climb in with our briefcases, grateful to be capitol bound. My husband, at the wheel of a brand new Oldsmobile Cutlass (his first new car ever in our family history), follows the Jeep tracks up the driveway — his only hope of making it up and out and back to Seattle in time to teach today's classes.

OVER MY YEARS AS A LEGISLATOR, my campus day routinely begins with breakfast in the House dining room. This helps me gauge the pulse of my colleagues, and I appreciate the freshly brewed coffee and custom-made omelettes. Today, with new faces to learn, I begin to mentally log friendships and alliances — it's good to know who knows whom as I work my way through the roster of ninety-nine to secure new votes for tax reform. Sixty-six is still the magic number for the constitutional amendment half of our two-part package.

After breakfast, I generally stop by my desk on the floor, even if the House won't convene until later. Tom Copeland has seen to it we all have daily copies of the daily schedule — one of the best innovations we introduced as a majority in '67. These arrive on our desks in the chamber early each morning. In the middle of this legal-sized sheet is a chart of our House session hours: Morning session, lunch break, afternoon session, pre-scheduled recesses, caucus meetings, and a slot for an evening session, if necessary. The top of the sheet lists committee meetings: Committee name, chairman, meeting hour, location and a list of measures scheduled to be discussed on this particular day. The bottom portion of the sheet is for public committee hearings, and again includes a whole list: The name of the committee conducting the hearing, the chairman, location, hour and measures to be heard. It's difficult to imagine our House ever ran without this 'day at a glance' with its useful detail.

Also on my desk each morning is a pre-printed 'Status of House Bills' created each night — usually in the middle of the night — by those worker bees downstairs. The daily list is organized by bill number (or resolution number as the case may be), and tells the title of the bill, where it sits in the legislative process, how it originated — by executive request or proposed by an interim committee or a department, by the Legislative Council or Budget Committee — and then whether it has been amended or substituted. Every day on our desk is a brand new list. As the session progresses, this bill list swells both in length and complexity. Today's Status of Bills is rather spare with only the 95 pre-filed by the Legislative Council.

Every workday morning we meet in caucus just before the session begins, sometimes for an hour or two, depending on the day's agenda. It is essential that our caucus work as a team and work out our questions and differences within the confines of the caucus room — the better to lead cohesively on the floor, and to make our majority count.

Clipboard in hand this morning, I begin to make notes. I begin with a blank slate: An alphabetic roster of the ninety-nine members of the House. Our legislative printing office produces a big stack of these rosters, and they come in handy for any number of tasks, but most often we use them to track support for our bills. One such list is attached today to my clipboard. At the top, I've created three columns: Y, N and U — yes, no and undecided. Task number one, then, is to tally how many of last term's 'friendly' votes on the more controversial element of our tax reform plan survived our interim break... the constitutional amendment to add an income tax.

Here in our caucus, as in the dining room, I discreetly note friendships, note newcomers, and recall colleagues' opinions from my tax reform campaign past.

Last session, when we voted on both tax reform measures, I had finally garnered fifty-nine yes votes from my colleagues — shy of the sixty-six we needed for the constitutional amendment, but a solid start. Today, though, I'll largely start over.

Although I made tremendous strides last session in generating support for our tax reform proposals, I no longer face the same combination of representatives. Our House runs through an election cycle every two years — between each session — which means each session, the legislator mix here is new.

ELECTION CYCLE

The period between the election and re-election of an elected public official.

I begin in 1969 with 39 Republicans who voted for tax reform the session before, and 7 returning supportive Democrats for a total of 46 'Y' votes if, that is, none have changed their minds between then and now, which is certainly not guaranteed. At very best, each of these votes has indeed remained intact over the interim. This still puts me twenty votes short of that requisite 66.

By the end of this second day, I've begun to fill in the blanks: Y, N, U. By the end of the first week, the scale of my duty is clear — I must convert a couple dozen undecideds into Y's, and in addition, change the minds of some N's. Which column has the most votes? The U's by a long shot — the undecided.

As with the previous session, I don't approach this work solo. A handful of colleagues from both sides of the aisle will help me build support for our tax reforms.

Marshalling the clipboard is just one component of my tax reform work, alongside chairing the House Committee on Revenue and Taxation another term.

On the second Tuesday of the session, our first committee meeting will begin at 8 a.m. I'm an early bird and prefer this hour for committee work.

My committee this year is a blend of old faces and new, veteran legislators and freshmen, representatives both rural and urban. Again, they reflect our state's contemporary complexion, and remind me anew how well redistricting aligned our districts with today's population. Less than one-fourth on my committee (six in all) hail from the less populous eastern part of our state, two come from the central region, and eighteen from the urbanized west. These colleagues comprise a mix of favorability and opposition to tax reform. My committee seems a perfect microcosm of our House at large, a feature that will help us hash out an acceptable path to revenue reform, at least among those in the House.

Among the returning committee Democrats who opposed this tax package last session are Margaret Hurley, Gary Grant and Ed Heavey. But we've also added Democrat Bob Charette, who joined our House from the Senate last term and has long championed the governor's policies, tax reform included. Bob and I spoke last week, and I've unofficially deputized him to work with me on the Democrat votes, along with his fellow Democrat, Buster Brouillet, who champions tax reform by way of his support of our public schools.

Seattle freshmen Lois North and George Scott, Republicans both, will be committee allies. I've worked with them before: Lois through the League, of course, and George on my political campaigns. He and his wife Carol also babysat David my freshman term.

My vice-chairman, Bill Kiskaddon, joined the House when Republicans turned the tide last session — from the new Snohomish County District 21 created by our redistricting, where Dale Hoggins holds seat two. Stu Bledsoe returns to my committee this term as well, this time elevated in status as our majority floor leader. Stu and I are already in synch on a strategy for passing the tax package.

As my committee members file into my committee room and take their seats, it again occurs to me I've been at this long enough to have developed some real allies and friends, which is precisely how legislators build successful careers and develop the ability to lead and legislate effectively. Legislating is not a solitary activity, nor is it a task for a maverick. It requires teamwork, skill in the art of compromise, an ability to listen.

That sense of preparedness I felt as I watched the winter birds from my chilly Seattle deck — returns. I have laid the groundwork to have real hope of improving our state's unreliable and floundering tax structure.

"Good morning, all. This meeting will now come to order."

Down comes my gavel.

Although tax reform is the overarching highlight of what this committee will process this term, I don't begin with this issue the first day out. Until the governor's staff and I work through some specifics, I'll hold the tax reform measures aside for now. Today, we've several other measures to address, courtesy of the Legislative Council.

After the meeting, on the way to the House, Jim Dolliver flags me down.

"How did it go?"

"Good, Jim." I'm energized. "Another sharp committee. I don't expect clear sailing, but I sense we'll engage in some fairly vigorous discussion."

"Perfect."

"Yes. I'm looking forward to it. When do you want to meet?"

"Could you drop by tomorrow, Mary Ellen? The governor's working on his address."

Our governor has improved his oratory considerably since his early wooden delivery, but he continues the practice of an occasional trial run with a mock audience, and I'm glad to add my two cents worth.

THURSDAY, JANUARY 23, ONE WEEK AFTER HIS BUDGET ADDRESS, a week and a day after his State of the State, the governor addresses us in Joint Session once more — on one precise topic.

"The need for tax reform is now," he tells the crowd assembled on the floor of the House. "The task before us is not to do as little as possible; it is to do what is right as soon as possible, and to take that solution to the people for their approval."

This is a pointed challenge from a confident leader.

"For too long, now, we have swept tax reform under the rug; we have added new burdens to old taxes, and taxed what was convenient. We have spent our time protecting ourselves against excessive taxation, instead of looking for a system which is more productive, more equitable, more reasonable and more responsible. In short, we have worried so long about pleasing the people, we have ended up failing to serve them instead."

I'm grateful the governor and I share such a strong commitment to getting this done. He's more comfortable in the limelight than I. Thus, we're a complementary team: I am in charge of the trenches here in the House, while he leads the entire brigade. He concludes: "I am prepared to compromise where compromise is dictated by the choice between two equal alternatives. But this administration will not compromise in the name of political expediency at the sacrifice of the citizens of Washington." [1]

I add my hearty applause. The governor is escorted from the chamber and back to his office, one floor down, by the appointed committee of three, including my housemate Lois North.

Outside, the snow continues to fall.

FOR THE NEXT TWO WEEKS, I DO STOP BY the governor's office from time to time as my clipboard numbers begin to shift and I begin to understand what tax reform 'should' look like in the eyes of others. My goal is to garner not only the votes we need, but to create a tax package that has strong bi-partisan support and genuinely serves our state. So with each new comment from colleagues (those I deem additive, anyway), I return to the governor's office, where Ray Haman and I adjust the two proposed measures.

"How goes the battle of tax reform?" the governor asks as he passes through.

"Slow," I respond in all honesty. "But I think we're making progress."

"Anything I can do?" he asks.

"As a matter of fact, yes. I have an idea."

I'd thought of it last night while spooning ice cream. The governor is well respected in our state among the business community, among community leaders and among many local governments.

"How about I give you a list of VIPs?" I suggest, "so you can drum up some support?"

I explain: If he would use his clout to contact some of these leaders throughout the state, it could trickle back to our legislators — perhaps add to my column of Y's.

"What do you need?" I ask. "Should I draft a letter?"

"No, I'll telephone," he said. "Names, titles, phone numbers. I'd rather talk."

"That's great! Thank you."

Once I'm home for the evening, staring at the quiet moonlit waves on Budd Inlet, I draft the list from memory — major "Who's Who" state leaders I encountered during my two interim stints on the Tax Advisory Council.

First my Council mates: Keith Grim, council chairman and a practicing Seattle attorney; Les Bona, council vice-chairman, and assistant to the president of West Coast Grocery; Harold Heath, president of Heath-Tecna Company; William Jenkins, chairman of Seattle First National Bank; Dr. Philip Cartwright, Dean of the College of Arts and Sciences at the University of Washington; Dave Foster, secretary/treasurer of the Washington Cattlemen's Association; Dave Swenson, assistant comptroller and tax manager of Weyerhaeuser; Charles McNurlen, superintendent of schools in Selah; Rev. James Albertson, senior pastor of Spokane's Central Methodist Church; and Mrs. Eleanor Brand, chairman of the fiscal issues committee of the state League of Women Voters.[2]

To this Council list, I add more VIPs — those our Council spoke with over two interims, and those who spoke to us. Among them are Reed Hanson, a professor of economics and business at Washington State University; T. Wilson, president of the Boeing Company; Malcolm McLaren, secretary of the Metal

Traces Council in Seattle; and Baker Ferguson, president of Baker-Boyer National Bank in Walla Walla. Several days later I deliver my list to Esther Searing: Names, titles, phone numbers.

"What's this?" she asks.

"The governor's request—a VIP contact list for tax reform."

"Phone numbers, Mary Ellen? Are you sure? He never calls anyone. The governor hates to talk on the phone."

"I'm sure. He asked specifically. Tax reform is near and dear to his heart, as you know, Esther, so maybe…"

Later in the day, Jim Dolliver stops me outside the House to report, "The governor's been making those calls."

A MONTH INTO THE SESSION, MY CLIPBOARD DATA—on both the constitutional amendment and implementing bill—are beginning to take promising shape. During a recess on the floor, the House empties, but I remain at my desk to make a few more notes. Speaker Eldridge, I notice, is doing the same up front. When I stand to leave, he calls to me.

"Representative McCaffree—a word with you."

A 'word' is an understatement. The Speaker has several: "Blankety blank, Mary Ellen, when are you going to get this blankety blank tax reform out here on the floor?"

I am totally taken aback, but he's not finished.

"It's a sixty-day session, lest you forget. We've only got so many days to get to work on it. So get it out here!"

I try to explain myself: My method of building support, my clipboard, my tweaking the two measures accordingly to assure a positive vote.

"Well speed it up," he says.

I depart in a bit of a shock. But our speaker is absolutely right. Perhaps I've been dilly-dallying a tad too much. At my next committee meeting I jump in with both feet.

"For those of you new this session, please review the December report of the Tax Advisory Council—it lays the clear groundwork for the basic elements of our tax reform package, and shows how we derived the specifics of these two proposed measures. For those of you returning, you may have noted that our original recommendation stands."

Once again, for the newcomers, I review our state's tax history: Just a property tax at the outset, the sales tax added in the Great Depression—because one of the biggest hurdles I face is that natural resistance to change. If I can help these colleagues understand why our state's tax structure was initially built as it was, why it substantially changed once before in response to societal change, and why, as our state has changed, it is again out of date and not serving us — I stand a much better chance of securing their support.

Emphatic letters from the public begin to arrive, some of them underlined.

"To the Honorable Mary Ellen McCaffree, Thank you for your yellow news-letters keeping us informed on progress in the 41st Legislature. Also, I send a personal plea and a plea from my Bryant School PTA on tax reform this session. As PTA President this year I found out personally how hard it was to get people to work as 'Room Mothers' if they had to work on yet another school levy. We accepted, finally, quite a few who refused to work again for a levy but would do the other work we needed. Please....... And thank you for your help in this very urgent matter. Mrs. Leonard G. Wells." [3]

Another, from an elementary school principal outside my district, includes a copy of the pro-tax reform message he sent to every family from his school. It spells out five features of our package: balance, fairness, the elimination of special levies, a reduced dependence on the regressive tax structure, and, there-fore, relief for those of limited income.

"As a citizen, parent and taxpayer," he writes, "I feel the above should be taken care of this session by my legislators — and taken care of in an aggressive and positive way. Yours truly, Bert Billdt, Principal." [4]

A Bellingham teacher sends me a desperate letter addressed to my desk on the floor: "Dear Representative McCaffree, I most fervently urge you to use your position of leadership to help our legislature bear fully upon the problem of school finance in our state. As both a teacher and taxpayer I find it increasingly difficult each year to envision a stable educational climate for our state in light of financial crises that have befallen many school districts...."

She describes the morale among fellow teachers when programs are intro-duced then cut, and class sizes fluctuate wildly with the 'temperamental tide' of special levies.

"It is an imposition on taxpayers to go to them year after year with the unceasing cry of 'More money — we need more money!' Soon, we have misun-derstandings between the citizens and the schools. Hard feelings develop, and those who really matter, the children, are the injured parties in these confronta-tions. We depend on your sage foresight to choose the best way, but please, let us find another way to finance our schools!" [5]

Speaker Eldridge doesn't have to say another word. His facial expression each day says it all: *Where is it, Mary Ellen? We need those tax measures on the floor.*

On Monday, February 17, I comply.

The clerk reads into the record House Joint Resolution 42 (the constitutional amendment to provide for an income tax and lower the lid on the property tax—the major reforms) and also the accompanying House Bill 582, another omnibus bill to implement the income tax, further adjust our property tax administration, and change a host of provisions in our state's excise tax and sales tax laws. The measures are assigned to my Committee on Revenue and Taxation.

Ken telephones Tuesday evening, February 25th, after I've spent a long day in committee, in caucus, in several floor sessions, and then a quick stop at a lobbyist party before I finally return home.

"Mary Ellen? Happy birthday, love!"

My husband telephones again on Friday evening, February 28, after yet another marathon day in session, in caucus, in the governor's office, and in marshalling tax reform votes.

"I heard the news," he says. "Everything OK down there?"

"What are you talking about, honey?"

"The Black Panthers," he says. "I just saw it on TV."

"Again? Mary, Lois — turn on the TV."

And there they stand on the steps of our state capitol, black leather jackets, black berets over Afros, menacing rifles aimed skyward.

"Ken? I didn't hear a word about it today. Honest."

And it's true. Whatever the Black Panthers were doing today on the capitol steps, it wasn't dramatic enough to travel to me. Yesterday, however, was a different story. The governor was out of state yesterday to attend the national

Black Panthers on the steps of the Washington State capitol in Olympia in the spring of 1969.

PHOTO: WASHINGTON STATE ARCHIVES

governor's conference in Washington, D.C. In his absence, Lieutenant Governor Cherberg had panicked.

Yesterday, dozens of Black Panthers had arrived on our capitol campus, and when they similarly stationed themselves on the capitol steps, word of an "invasion" quickly spread. In response, the lieutenant governor called in the state patrol, who arrived en masse in riot gear — an impressive and aggressive display.

The governor was furious when he heard. He has long been a proponent of listening to minority voices, and spent several occasions during heightened black uprisings last year personally talking through dissatisfactions — to great success, and without the aid of police.

Today, with the governor back in charge, the Black Panthers came and went, having been given a full audience with the Senate Ways and Means Committee and free reign to vent, which they did: *Give us safe streets. Give us a real black history curriculum. Give us respect.* [6,7,8,9]

"So," says Ken, "it's safe to make the trip?"

"Come on down, honey. All clear."

KEN TRAVELS TO OLYMPIA NEARLY EVERY WEEKEND, and though I continue to spend more than my share of hours working, we usually manage a dinner out or we pop in as guests at a lobbyist bash. Once in a while, we harvest oysters and clams from the beach here and just dine in.

Unfortunately, even at social gatherings, I can't escape tax reform. At lobbyist parties I eavesdrop or listen directly to my colleagues' pointed comments, and occasionally attempt to persuade someone to change his mind. I collect tidbits and pass them along to my team: "It sounds like you should talk to so-and-so." Or I gather feedback for the governor's staff: "I think if we adjust this part of the bill a bit…"

Ken is patient.

Fortunately for me, because we have dual careers, he is equally wrapped up in his university work and his consultancy with the various government health agencies. And with his post on the Faculty Senate, he also devotes time as a calming, authoritative presence while our neighborhood campus of 30,000 occasionally floods into UW's central quadrangle.

I spend part of this Saturday afternoon, after our session adjourns, catching up with constituent correspondence, writing several more letters on tax reform.

"Dear Mrs. Wells, Thank you for your letter. I understand only too well the fury of room mothers who have for so many years worked on special school levies. We are working here to put together a bi-partisan tax reform package… This is very badly needed legislation, as you realize, and it is important that people at home understand that. Sincerely, Mary Ellen McCaffree." [10]

We send it out, even though my secretary typed over a couple of errors. Better to send an imperfect letter than none at all.

BY MID-MARCH I'VE RECEIVED HUNDREDS of letters and postcards on tax reform — not just from educators, but from growing segments of the general population. Because of the volume, I finally and reluctantly draft a form letter for my secretary to send. I prefer to be more personal, but the letters are mounting, while my available hours to gather votes for our tax package wane.

"Dear Mr./Mrs. _____, I want you to know that your letter was received and read by me. Although I don't have enough time to answer each of you individually, I do want you to know how much I appreciate your comments regarding tax reform. I received over 200 letters last week alone from you who live in all parts of our state. The central message was clear: That you want the legislature to pass a tax reform package, and that I have your support in my efforts to get this accomplished..." [11]

I encourage them to contact their own district's senators and representatives, and then I give them my warmest regards.

Once I finally introduced our tax reform measures in the House (to the wry delight of our Speaker), even more correspondence poured in and the incoming mail has begun to flood the whole capitol — not just the office of Mary Ellen McCaffree.

My committee receives mail, some of it delivered straight to our committee room, addressed both to me and to my members, urging us to stabilize our state tax base: "... Education of the leaders and workers of tomorrow's world should not be left up to the whim of the levy voter — it must be placed in a more stable position, which tax reform would definitely accomplish. I urge you each to consider seriously tax reform in the best interest of our future adults." [12]

Many voters send letters to every member of the Senate and House. One such typed letter has an added hand-written P.S.: "It is urgent that a <u>compromise</u> is reached quickly on the type of income tax. It would be an inexcusable shame if partisan politics on this issue were to prevent or further delay the critically needed total reform." [13]

By the end of March, I modify my form letter: "I have received hundreds of letters and many petitions... and these letters, written so very individually by each of you, and the petitions, gave me a determination to redouble my own efforts, if that is possible, on your behalf..." [14]

By my clipboard calculations, even if I convince every 'undecided' member to vote yes, I'm still going to need a good half dozen of those 'no' votes, too. On the Senate side, the governor is working directly with senators from both sides of the aisle. Part of our strategy is to keep the Senate apprised of each adjustment we make to our legislative package, and to update them on the growing support in the House, so that by the time the measures reach them, they'll be familiar with the content, perhaps even supportive.

STATEWIDE, THE GOVERNOR KEEPS TAX REFORM at the forefront of every public conversation and address. And so do I.

On March 13, our sixty session days are up. The 41st regular session of the legislature must end, but we have not yet completed our tax reform. While I readjust my course for the Extraordinary Session, Mary heads home in time to ready for her spring term… in London. The next day, March 14, we move swiftly into Extraordinary Session. In his proclamation, the governor spells out our legislative 'to do' list: First and foremost, tax reform:

"It is imperative that our citizens be given the opportunity to vote on a thorough and complete tax reform program."

He lists the specifics and reminds us this is a top priority of his administration.

My committee argues the merits of the two tax measures along familiar lines. First the constitutional amendment: *Should the income tax be single rate or set at graduated rates? Should our tax policy ideally be regressive or progressive?* A new issue has surfaced in the Senate: *Should we allow the people to change our tax structure by citizen initiative?* I firmly believe not.

Secondly, we debate the omnibus implementing bill — specific exemptions, specific taxes. *Is restaurant food still considered 'food' — is it tax exempt? Prescription drugs — where should they fall? What about the B & O tax — how do we calculate inventory? Should senior citizens get a special break?* Debatable details abound.

I continue to work with the governor's legal staff to fine-tune our package. My role is mostly behind-the-scenes, a specialty I developed during redistricting. I assess each point raised or questioned, then I fold each nit-picky little detail we deem additive into the broader package. Each change is the result of careful listening, compromise, and my willingness to do the laborious shifting and math. I'm trying to make each of these tax reform measures work for everyone.

I meet regularly with Stu Bledsoe in his majority leader's office, just off the House floor in the legislative building's northwest corner with windows that overlook the Olympic mountains and Puget Sound. Every several days, Stu and I consult my clipboard and talk strategy. As the 'yes' votes build, we begin to discuss timing, too. When should we bring each of these two tax legislation matters to the floor for a vote?

In the legislative corridors I talk with colleagues whenever I have a chance, in the dining room, during the occasional recess, and again as we socialize at various gatherings at the end of the day — at the Tyee Motel in Tumwater, for example, or at private homes rented out by legislators and lobbyists during the session along the shores of the spectacular Sound.

IN POLITICAL LORE, COCKTAIL PARTIES are a stereotypic feature — a place where bargains are struck, deals made. There's a potent element of truth to this mythology. I find most legislators to be more measured in a formal setting. And I would be the first to admit: I'm the same. Legislators are often loathe to talk frankly with a lot of other people around. They have constituent interests to protect, partisan allegiances to honor. And in the House, where we serve single two-year terms, there's always another election to win. To have a real conversation, therefore — true back and forth, real argument — it's often best to track down someone socially, and chat within the buzz of a lively room.

T. Wilson, the well-known head of the Boeing Company, gives me a boost one evening when our paths cross at one such party.

"What can I do to help your tax package pass, Mary Ellen?"

"Spread the word, T.!"

I ask him to spread it among our other top state employers. And then, since T. Wilson is the biggest employer of all, I decide to level with him.

"T., I'm afraid your Boeing lobbyists aren't doing their job. The story they're telling my committee doesn't match what you've shared before on Boeing's tax reform stance. When they spelled out your company's position, I didn't recognize it, from what you said in our Tax Council meetings. It seems you and your lobbyists aren't working from the same page."

"Really, Mary Ellen?"

When I explain the gist of their message, he just shakes his head.

"Glad you told me, but sorry to hear it," he says. "Let's have lunch. I'd like to talk more."

When we meet several days later, he's upset his Boeing lobbyists are so off the mark. He asks how I think a lobbyist ought to work and communicate. I never do hear from T. on the lobbying matter after that, nor do I ever see those two lobbyists thereafter in my committee meetings.

It's surprising how seldom major legislative decisions come about as a result of sober discussion around a table or in a committee room. The banter outside organized session work is a valuable part of the political process, and though this type of wheeling and dealing carries with it a certain stigma, I believe it should be accepted for what it is — a chance for human legislators to express their very human ideas.

Fortunately, I don't have to conduct ninety-nine one-on-ones on behalf of tax reform. My team of assistants is tireless. Buster Brouillet and Bob Charette steadily converse with their Democrat colleagues. Republicans Sid Morrison and Gerry Saling rally our legislators from the eastern side of the state. They're a balanced duo: Gerry is more liberal than a lot of our Spokane legislators. Sid, most definitely, is not. In fact, Sid remains firmly opposed to the principle of a single rate income tax, but he's helping build support for our package anyway, just as he did last session — based on the fact that he does agree that tax reform should be left to the people to choose. Largely due to the efforts of my team, my clipboard columns are edging closer to passage.

NOT ALL THE GENTLEMEN OF THE HOUSE, however, are as comfortable with my leadership as my tax reform team. Because I am one of the first women in our legislature to play a significant leadership role, many old-timers are ill at ease — the amount of control I wield doesn't fit with their image of a bona fide legislator in suit and tie, nor their image of the demure and modest woman. John O'Brien, in particular, has been uncomfortable acknowledging my position as the leader of tax reform in the House.

Despite ongoing chauvinism, one reason I've been able to be so successful within our legislature is that the team who recruited me — Slade, Joel and Dan — have become not only good friends, but serious working colleagues. They brought me aboard for my abilities. They knew I could do this job, and their confidence in me has played a huge role in my acceptance into this legislative fraternity. I've since developed good working relationships with colleagues across the aisle, as well, and all of this has allowed me to lead effectively.

But as we hit week three of this Extraordinary Session, our Speaker again questions my performance: "Where is it, Mary Ellen?"

This time I'm prepared: "Give me one week."

"One week it is."

STU AND I HAVE TRIPLE CHECKED OUR NUMBERS — we know the sentiments of the ninety-nine. We know who may support these measures here and now, even if they personally plan to vote 'No' at the ballot box at the next general election. We know which legislators will likely vote everything down on a first round of voting, either 'for show' for their voters back home, or to demonstrate party loyalty or party cohesiveness, regardless of their personal stand — but may then change that vote if we bring it back for a second consideration.

On Monday, April 14, the thirty-second day of our Extraordinary Session, during reports of the standing committees, I address HB 582 on the floor of the

House, "providing for certain changes in revenue and taxation statutes." This is the omnibus bill I've refined as we gathered our tax reform votes, changing it bit by bit, clause by clause, shaping it into a piece of legislation that works for the people in general, but also for these specific legislators from specific districts who must cast their votes on behalf of constituencies. We send the bill to the Rules Committee on second reading and adjourn for the day.

On Tuesday, April 15, we take no further action on this omnibus tax bill.

On Wednesday, April 16, we re-convene for the afternoon at 2 p.m., and

Stu Bledsoe (l.), Don Eldridge and Tom Copeland among bill books in the House Rules Committee.

after an opening roll call and standard formalities, our majority leader moves that we advance to the ninth order of business for the second reading of bills – opening them to amendments from the floor. Stu looks to me, and I stand, prepared to defend HB 582, our version of tax reform, against any crippling or emasculating amendments lobbed my way by vocal opponents.

This bill has been hammered out substantially, even forcefully, within my committee by the intelligent, articulate and extremely diverse membership there. I've done my best to consider their suggestions, to work with them all. I've worked with voters and constituents, harking their concerns, too. I've worked with lobbyists, educators and business interests and tabulated their input. I've worked hard to craft a bill that will hold. I have basically re-worked an entire substitute bill with literally dozens of modifications to the version I first introduced in February. And therefore, rather than explain each miniscule amendment today on the floor of the House, I have written a whole new bill, with the help of the tax and legal experts on the governor's staff. Now, I urge the House to accept it.

"I move that Substitute House Bill 582 be substituted for House Bill 582, and that it be placed on second reading."

I can defend and explain each element. I am confident it's as good a compromise as anyone could have crafted. My goal today is to prevent the addition of any amendments that could unravel my two solid months of thoughtful, laborious weaving of this draft.

For an hour, and then a second hour, and then a third and then more, legislators stand one by one to propose pet amendments to this omnibus bill. And one by one I speak against each with specific argument, and with a broad appeal to leave this bill as is so that it stands a chance of representing us all — and passing. Over the hours, sixteen amendments are each brought to a vote, and after lengthy argument and my defense of the bill as written, each is voted down.

Now Representative Grant offers an amendment that would scalp my bill and replace it with his — with a graduated income tax clause instead of the single rate. We vote. This one fails as well, 40 to 55.

Having listened carefully to each of the concerns and arguments presented on the floor, I propose one clarifying amendment. It passes on a voice vote: The *Ayes* have it. Substitute House Bill 582 is finally ordered engrossed. The Speaker puts our House at ease.

DINNERTIME HAS COME AND GONE and stomachs are rumbling. *Should we take a break?* House leadership confers: Not with this momentum. We'll proceed.

Representative Newhouse moves that the Rules be suspended, that the second reading be considered the third, and that we place the omnibus bill on final passage. Representative Wolf demands a roll call vote. The demand is sustained.

Representative O'Brien stands for recognition and speaks against passing this bill. I stand next, and briefly urge its passage. The clerk calls the roll and the final tally is 43 yeas, 53 nays. Our tax reform bill has failed.

Sid Morrison has placed his vote on the prevailing side — the nays — and immediately after the vote, he serves notice that he will move for reconsideration of this bill on our next working day. Tom Copeland also voted on the prevailing side, for the very same purpose as well as a piece of the action, but with Sid's support already clear, Tom doesn't need to say a thing. We adjourn until 10 a.m. the following day.

Tonight I stay late at the capitol to analyze the votes. Just as Stu and I guessed, several nays came from Democrats I am confident support this package, but who felt pressure — from voters or party peers — and registered these 'Nays' to appease them. The same could be said of several of the Republicans who also voted against it. Constituents want to see their representatives actually represent them, and by voting against this proposal during this round, some of these Republicans can tell the tax-wary folks back home, "At least I tried."

I have some confidence, however, that if — when — we bring this to the floor for reconsideration, I may have had time to swing enough of these votes.

The next day, Sid Morrison makes good on his promise to me to move for reconsideration of our vote on ESHB 582. On a voice vote, we agree to reconsider it. Stu Bledsoe moves that we send the bill back to Rules, and we vote it so.

Afterwards, I confer with Stu. I confer with Jim Dolliver. I confer with the governor. We confer with the Speaker of the House. *What message can I give these nay-sayers to share with their voters back home? What will allow these legislators to support this, and to still save face in their districts? How can we get this on the ballot?*

"Voter choice," suggests Stu. "That way no one has to say they agree or disagree — they're just supporting the voter's right to choose how to change how we're taxed."

This is an emphasis and argument I've used many times: The people's voice must be heard. It certainly suits our tax reform scenario.

We agree. We've talked ourselves blue on the actual logic and merit of our proposed reforms — fair, equitable, balanced, flexible, responsive, responsible taxation — but what voters might actually grasp is the chance for a choice.

We spread the word: If you vote to support our package of tax reform, including the constitutional amendment that will put it to a statewide vote, you are giving your constituents a chance to voice their individual opinions on tax reform — you'll be allowing them the all-American right to choose.

Buster and Bob spread the word among Democrat colleagues. Sid and Gerry spread the word east. Stu and I talk to as many members as we can. Ever since late Thursday, we've been spreading this perspective: *Support our voters' right to choose!*

At 9 a.m. on Saturday, April 19, the Speaker calls us to order. The clerk calls the roll and all of us are present except for Representative Litchman, whom we excuse. After the flag and the prayer, the Speaker declares our House in session and Mr. Bledsoe demands a Call of the House. Our exits are emphatically locked. Another roll call: Only Mr. Litchman is gone.

We move straight into reports from the standing committees, and first on the docket, on first reading is House Joint Resolution 42, "Amending Article VII of the Constitution relating to taxation" — which we've withheld from the House until an opportune time, and that time is now. Thirteen of us recommend that it do pass. Nearly as many recommend that it do not, led off by Margaret Hurley. My clipboard tells me that despite our valiant push for voter choice, we do not quite have the sixty-six votes to send this constitutional change to a vote of the people.

Stu Bledsoe moves that HJR 42 be placed on second reading. We vote to place this tax reform resolution on second reading, but our leaders hold it for action later in the day.

Now we move on to Engrossed Substitute House Bill 582. Stu Bledsoe moves that the Rules Committee be relieved of this bill — it has been sitting in Rules since Thursday when, after our vote to reconsider the bill, we voted to send it there. This is the detailed implementing bill designed to accompany the constitutional change — the omnibus bill we failed to pass as a House on Wednesday night. As in 1967, the two are inseparable — resolution and bill — both equally crucial to the tax reform package. If the constitutional amendment measure fails, the bill is automatically invalid. But so far, all is still alive. The omnibus bill returns to the floor of the House on second reading.

Representatives Marsh, Adams, Rosellini and Ceccarelli propose several small clarifying amendments to make the bill "more understandable" to their constituents. We approve each by a voice vote. I propose several more clarifications. These, too, are approved. Tom Copeland proposes another — to clarify a section of the bill relative to the Federal Tax Code. Again, we adopt this by voice vote. Each of these amendments is aimed at the absolute clarity of this bill. This second reading is running smoothly.

Rep. Red Beck, however, proposes the first substantial alteration — a major increase in the proposed personal income tax exemption. This could kick the bill back to the drawing board, so the majority leader moves that we lay Mr. Beck's amendment on the table. We vote — we agree.

No more amendments lie in waiting, according to a look around the chamber and a final call by the Speaker, so he orders Engrossed Substitute House Bill 582 to be re-engrossed, with the new amendments added. Then, majority whip Hal Wolf moves that our Rules be suspended and we place this bill on final passage, the second reading being considered the third. Our majority leader demands an oral roll call, our Speaker sustains the demand.

Under a Call of the House, the clerk calls the roll. Our tax reform implementing bill is finally on final passage. We move through the House roster, the ninety-nine votes (minus one) each voicing 'Yea' or 'Nay' in our alphabetical order. I follow along on my clipboard, several pages

RE-ENGROSSED BILL

A bill printed to incorporate new amendments to a previously engrossed bill (one previously printed with previous amendments).

CONSTITUTIONAL MAJORITY

A majority of members elected to a legislative body who are recorded as voting 'yea' on a bill.

thick now with rosters to track my progress with the Ys, Ns and Us, including one that lists the vote on this bill two days ago, and a new page to mark each vote today. As the alphabet progresses, I begin to feel hope. Several of the early alphabet 'Nays' from Wednesday night have switched to 'Ayes'.

"McCaffree."

"Aye."

Midway through the roster, it is still too close to call, but looking good. We need fifty yeas for this bill. We get sixty-three. After failing 43-53 Wednesday night, our omnibus tax reform bill passes the House, 63-35. My heart races. I hardly know what to feel.

The Speaker announces: "Re-engrossed Substitute House Bill 582, having received a constitutional majority is declared passed. There being no objections, the title of the bill is ordered to stand as the title of the act."

I look at my clipboard: 45 Republicans and 18 Democrats voted to support this dramatic change to our state's antiquated tax base.

Stu Bledsoe stands: "I move that RESHB 582 be immediately transmitted to the Senate."

We vote our agreement, and off it goes.

I must stand again, for the Speaker has now called forth our accompanying resolution – the constitutional amendment, sponsored by Bill Kiskaddon and me. I propose a correcting amendment, carefully explaining it to my colleagues. This amendment passes. Rep. Barden proposes a second amendment. It fails. Mr. Bledsoe moves that the resolution now be placed on third reading and final passage. Without further ado, Mr. Newhouse demands an oral roll call and the constitutional amendment measure is now before us for our final vote.

I flip to my clipboard page entitled HJR 42 and review the roster. In all our campaigning, we've never secured the sixty-six votes. Even with the omnibus bill we just passed, we only hit sixty-three. I'm still jittery from that win, but here goes.

The clerk begins the roll call. I tick off each vote, next to each name. By the time I say 'Aye' mid-alphabet, the trend is clear. After Harold A. 'Hal' Zimmerman registers the final vote, the House clerk announces the final result: "By a vote of 84 yeas, 14 nays, and one absent and not voting, House Joint Resolution 42, having received a constitutional majority, is declared passed."

Stu Bledsoe jumps to his feet, bursting with energy, and moves – with the most enthusiasm I've ever seen from this most enthusiastic man – that we immediately send HJR 42 to the Senate. He remains standing.

"Point of personal privilege," our majority leader requests. It is granted.

Meanwhile, I begin to review the voting roster, to examine the 'Ayes', and I pay little attention as Stu Bledsoe drawls out commentary from the floor.

"Mr. Speaker," says Mr. Bledsoe, "I would like to have the record show that this House is indeed indebted to a very fine and loyal public servant. The chairman of the Committee on Revenue and Taxation..."

He pauses for effect. But I am busy at study.

"...though just a *mere woman*..."

The House erupts in laughter and I decide perhaps I should listen.

"...is a *giant* as a legislator. As this young lady stood on the floor today and explained this most complex measure in its entirety, I could not help but salute her. I am most proud she is one of ours on this side of the aisle. But at this point, she is not just a Republican — she is... a *legislator*. I can't tell you how proud this legislative body is to claim her as one of its own. Mrs. McCaffree, we are in your debt."

The House applauds and then applauds some more, and as the applause begins to swell, to my surprise, my colleagues begin to rise, one by one, in something I've never seen in four terms. For my work on these tax reform measures, they are giving me a standing ovation. I am at once honored and astonished.

When our chamber quiets, the Speaker calls on me, and I experience a rare surge of strong emotion and must force a response.

"Thank you, Mr. Speaker," I manage. "Thank you, Mr. Bledsoe. Thank all of you for the opportunity to serve as a legislator in this session." [15]

I'm walking on air.

Not for the accolades, but because of the number of votes!

And then I remember the Senate. Reality returns.

WHILE I WAS IN THE THROES of this final House push toward tax reform, my husband has fought other battles one hour north. University students across the nation are in revolt, and the University of Washington's tens of thousands are no different, staging sit-ins, walkouts and protests that vary in volume and in form. Ken is one of several faculty volunteers who willingly monitor and appear in the midst of many of these student "riots" and assemblies.

Five days after my standing ovation, Ken stands outside the student center — the Husky Union Building or The Hub — with a megaphone to address a rowdy crowd. As he sees it, his role as an authority figure is not to threaten the students so much as to calm them. He and other faculty leaders agree — they'd rather encourage respect, pre-empt any violence.

Today, hundreds of students have amassed in a writhing, riled-up coil of humanity, clogging the roadway that runs between The Hub and the engineering building, Lowe Hall. Protestors shout outrage against the corporate and military recruiting taking place right now inside Lowe, while the students inside Lowe — potential recruits — are trying to lock Lowe's doors against the protest, with much shoving and tussling as the protestors aggressively attempt to break in. Both the protestors and the curious are surrounding both buildings, and the swelling mass continues to block the roadway in between. Among the outer crowd is a young man with wavy brown hair tumbling part way down his back.

As Ken tells it to me on the telephone this evening, he repeated through his megaphone, over and over: "Will you please disperse! Will you please disperse!" To which the teeming students responded: "It's the heat! It's the heat!" and probably some other choice remarks, my husband was quick to point out, but polite enough not to specify.

(In a later phone call, the young man with the wavy brown hair told me that at that point in the UW afternoon, he'd dropped his jaw in astonishment: "It's not the heat — it's my dad!")

Ken, however, is only midway through his tale. I feel a tinge of concern. Elsewhere, student protests have turned violent, and I worry about my husband's safety. But Ken laughs, and some of my apprehension departs.

"All of a sudden," he says, "along the roadway past Lowe comes this flatbed truck, stacked with a dozen hives of bees, trying to maneuver its way through the mob. And I couldn't quite tell how it happened from where I was standing, but in the melee, some of those hives got overturned, and before I knew it those bees were flying everywhere!"

"Did you get stung?"

"Several times," he said. "I wasn't the only one. The bees were crawling down shirts, up necks. Well, that was the end of the protest. The bees ended the rioting, that's all I know."

The beekeepers were looking for the Department of Biology where the research staff had agreed to conduct a study — the bees were diseased.

I'm grateful Ken is safe. I'm grateful our UW is trying to keep things peaceable.

And I'm reminded of my students — the young people lobbying to lower the voting age here at the capitol, actively pursuing a constitutional amendment of their own.

ON FRIDAY MORNING, WITH THE HOUSE VOTE on tax reform behind me — though the Senate vote looms — I take a break. Not a vacation, but a switch to a long neglected task: Compiling another constituent newsletter "From the Desk of Mary Ellen McCaffree, State Representative, Olympia, Washington, April 25, 1969."

I'm thrilled to be able to lead with such wonderful news: "CITIZENS OF

WASHINGTON TO DECIDE TAX REFORM MEASURE: House Joint Resolution 42 and House Bill 582 have just passed the House and are now in the Senate. This constitutional amendment, combined with this House bill, provides the vehicle for the restructuring and revamping of our tax system. The need for tax reform is crucial at this point, and this tax reform package represents a genuine effort by responsible legislators to resolve their political differences and reach a compromise." [16]

I describe the two measures and remind my readers that none of it will come to be unless they — the voters — approve the constitutional amendment at the polls.

I have space for four more items, and choose: My mass transit bill — one I'm sponsoring that would give local governments a percentage of our vehicle excise tax to plan and construct local mass transit alternatives; the 18-year-old vote amendment, which I note is lagging in legislative support — not enough adults have contacted their legislators; my stance against another Lake Washington bridge — any increased traffic capacity should include light rail, I believe, not just more lanes for cars; and lastly, a note about our budget and fiscal pragmatism — how we'll continue to vote down any measure that doesn't have accompanying funds guaranteed.

Back in the Senate, our tax reform measures are stalled in the Ways and Means Committee while the senators battle them out, beginning with the implementing bill.

Mrs. Mortimer H. Thomas — Joan — the new state president of the League of Women Voters (and my Seattle neighbor), asks to address this Senate committee on Monday, April 28.

"Thank you for giving us this opportunity to appear before you today to comment on Re-engrossed Substitute House Bill 582," says Joan, the long title of the bill rolling right off the tongue of this seasoned League lobbyist. "It is hard at this late date to suggest improvements in this specific bill because it seems so unlikely that both houses will be able to agree if any changes are made. Instead, it is a temptation — to which I shall yield at least slightly — to lecture you on the need to agree on <u>something</u> so that the voters of this state will not again be denied the opportunity to vote on meaningful changes in our tax structure…"

Joan delivered the Senate committee some rather pointed critiques, which made me nervous as I read the transcript she dropped by my desk today right after she testified. But her concluding remarks give me hope she may have some effect: "League members throughout the state have come to accept the realization that we aren't going to like everything in a tax reform package that passes the legislature, but we are convinced that it is absolutely essential that we get on with the job — another two years under our present tax structure is intolerable." [17]

Another week passes. Still, the Senate fails to act. We enter the month of May. Another seven days pass. No tax reform action arises in the Senate.

Intrepid political reporter Adele Ferguson, from the *Bremerton Sun*, asks me what I think about the rumors now floating from across the rotunda — that the Senate is adding a clause to the ballot measure that would give voters a right to change our tax structure by citizen initiative, rather than by legislative process.

"I am very lukewarm toward the initiative," I tell her plainly, and explain why. "The legislative process is deliberative. It involves reason and argument." [18]

By contrast, the citizen initiative process invites decision-making based on catchy mottos, a sweep of voter enthusiasm, scant information. I worry about the ability of the initiative process to circumvent the legislative process, particularly regarding amending our constitution. Complex issues are best left to the legislature, which as a deliberative body may take several sessions and weigh many viewpoints to write the best law. (To clarify: The League's initiatives on redistricting were pursued only after the legislature refused to do its work.)

I've gone to the governor with my concerns about this initiative idea, and I tell Adele the same: "When you start tampering with initiatives on constitutional amendments, you can get in deep trouble."

My words appear in print the next day, the same day the Senate finally returns our measures on tax reform, both amended.

We agree to their changes to the House bill. Our ongoing communication with the Senate throughout this session has paid off in their support, for these are minor changes, in line with our goals for reform. But we cannot accept their amended resolution (with the added dread initiative clause), so instead we convene a conference committee, and when the conference committee can't agree, we agree to a free conference committee, on which I sit along with Bob Charette and Sid Morrison, two of my go-to tax reform point guards in the House. On the Senate side are Senators Greive, McCormick and Ryder.

At this point, tax reform teeters on a precipice. Tilted one direction, it could move ahead, but on the other lies a deep, divisive crevasse from which it would be... irretrievable.

THE GOVERNOR CAN NO LONGER STAND TO STAND BY and just watch. He calls together leaders from both the Senate and the House: Senate Democrat heavyweights Martin Durkan, William Gissburg, Robert Bailey and Augie Mardesich. Senate Republicans Charles Elicker, John Ryder, Joel Pritchard and Frank Atwood. The governor does not invite Senator Greive — whose advocacy of the initiative clause is well known but not particularly well liked. From the House, the governor calls in Democrats John O'Brien, Bob Charette and Buster Brouillet, and Republican leaders Stu Bledsoe, Tom Copeland and me.

For two full days, we gather in the governor's office while he listens to arguments from every side, then to counter arguments from each. After all his listening, he identifies the sole sticking point: The initiative clause in the constitutional amendment.

As the resolution is written now, the public does have an option. The single rate income tax element of the constitutional amendment is slated to go to a re-vote of the people in 1975 — six years from now — at which time voters can retain the single rate tax on income or change it to graduated rates. This is much more practical than the initiative clause. It gives our proposal some time to take effect, and it gives us all time to assess it.

The late hour add-on of this initiative idea has the governor as perturbed as the rest of us.

"We have been elected to govern," he reminds us.

He then reviews our work as elected leaders on tax reform: We studied in depth our state tax structure via the citizen-based Tax Advisory Council. We proposed reforms weighing the needs of all our state's citizens against inequities and inadequacies in the present system. And we've spent two full sessions working through details with the legislature. The initiative option ignores these deliberative legislative steps, many of us agree.

The governor reviews our concerns: The people could approve a single rate income tax one year, and right behind it, on the very next ballot, an initiative by special interest groups could change the people's plan completely. This is not an acceptable alternative to the work we've done as a legislature. It is not an acceptable alternative to the exceedingly equitable and flexible tax reform package before us right now. And it is certainly not a formula for stable state revenue.

From the start, the governor has advocated strongly for tax reform — not a tax increase, but tax reform — and he feels as powerfully as I do that it must happen now, for the good of our state, and that it will serve us best in the well-studied format proposed by the House.

Bespectacled Bob Bailey, a retired newspaperman from blue collar Grays Harbor County and chairman of the Senate Democratic caucus, speaks for us all: "It would be a tragedy to get this close and then lose it." [19]

As a group we determine a final structure for HJR 42 — the proposed constitutional amendment — which largely resembles the reforms to our tax structure we first designed in the House. We take this revised resolution back to the House, where we pass it by a vote of 84-12, give it back to the Senate, and they proceed to pass it this very same day.

On Friday, May 9, both our Speaker and the president of the Senate sign this tax reform resolution and send it straight to the office of the secretary of state, asking Lud Kramer to place it on the ballot in the next general election. Tax reform is up to the voters now.

On Saturday, May 10, with the constitutional amendment resolution passed, the House formally considers the implementing bill, HB 582, with the Senate amendments. We agree their changes are fine and pass it. Sunday, Speaker Eldridge signs it, Monday, the President of the Senate adds his signature, and finally our satisfied governor signs RESHB 582 into law to accomplish tax reform — pending, of course, the vote of the people. If state citizens agree to amend our constitution to allow for that steadying 'third leg' of an income tax, our tax reform package will finally become law. I eagerly await the day.

In the past four days, while we'd put the finishing touches on tax reform, Bob Goldsworthy had guided another disciplined drawing of our biennial budget, so that now on this very same Monday, May 12, we pass our budget and prepare to adjourn.

Many of us, however, are perceptibly dissatisfied.

Senate and House, we face each other across the marbled expanse and collectively face the fact that despite this longest legislative session in state history we failed to finish our work. So many major reforms — patiently negotiated, carefully crafted — now lie dead on the table, nearly complete but not quite.

Our House leadership team feels the frustration most profoundly. We launched this session at a productive pace with our clearly delineated goals and tasks, and we thought that within sixty days — and then another fifty-seven — we'd have completed our agenda. Not once in these 117 days did we ever let up. Could we have worked any harder? I doubt it.

In the two sessions we've held the reins, we've made remarkable progress — in what we've accomplished for the citizens of this state, and in working as an effective legislative body. This session, tax reform in particular forced our entire legislature into a serious, selfless relationship. Senate and House, Democrat and Republican had coalesced for the good of the state. We'd matured. As a legislative team we had just hit our stride. What a shame the session had to end now.

As the gavels sound and we add our "*sine die,*" uncertainly lingers.

Now what?

CHAPTER ELEVEN

INCOMPLETE
DISAPPOINTMENT AT AN UNFINISHED AGENDA

It's amazing how much you can accomplish

as long as you don't care who gets the credit.

IN THE WEE HOURS BETWEEN SEVERAL SINE DIE celebrations and dawn, Stu drops me off in his trusty pickup, which has bounced us along to celebrations all night.

"Well Mary Ellen, what do you think?"

I know exactly what he's asking — the same thing everyone asked me all night.

"We left a lot undone," is all I reply, not venturing to mind-read the governor.

"Got that right for damned... sorry."

And with that he's off. I return down the moonlit path to my rental home. Moonlight shimmers on the gently rippling bay, a view that inevitably inspires in me deeper thought. I curl on the couch, watch the waves and wonder.

"Will the governor call another Extraordinary Session?" Colleagues hounded me all night. "You're good friends with him, Mary Ellen. What's the word?"

To each I answered honestly, "I don't know."

Our intent had been to finish the progressive renovation of our state, and that is exactly where we were headed with measurable progress in every vein, when time ran out. Do we give up now? Wait for another election, another session, an all-new legislator mix?

In 1964, we captivated the public with our Blueprint for Progress, attracting unprecedented attention to our capitol with our long list of progressive reforms.

Ever since, state voters have watched more, participated more, expected more. We promised our state government would serve them better, so our citizens have been naturally more engaged. They've had high hopes we'd put progressive promise into practice, to keep apace of our growing state's pressing needs.

Progressive. What does that actually mean in terms of a state? To me it means allowing for progress, prepared to confront any challenge, poised to respond to change. Governments need the ability and flexibility to deal with change because times change, situations change — status quo won't suffice forever.

The turbulence and dissonance of the 1960's have made this clear: Our government 'as is' hasn't worked for all the people, and as a result 'the people' are demanding change. We need a progressive government.

How close we'd come. In our committees we'd worked through the balance of our Blueprint nearly to completion — administrative overhauls, a sounder fiscal and revenue frame, better programs to serve the voiceless and vulnerable, better measures for business, too, and many first-time protections for our wilderness, water and air. Close, but imcomplete.

I will finish out the remaining three-fourths of my two-year term in the House, but my ability to help legislate additional change is gone. Our session is done, our agenda on hold. Come sunrise, we will all head home to constituents.

Among mine is my friend and neighbor Joan Thomas who, like others, has maintained a tenacious focus on our legislative failures and feats.

Joan is active on several community fronts. As the League of Women Voters' state president, she made that powerful plea to Senate Ways and Means to push for the passage of tax reform, and now she's following through by rallying public support for the coming ballot vote.

This past year, she also helped organize dozens of environmental activist groups into a single voice to fight for protections: The new Washington Environmental Council, or WEC, vehemently bent the ear of our governor as our 41st Session was winding down and our environment bills remained largely on hold. *If you're so committed to the environment, then why has so little been done these last five years? Were your campaign promises empty? Your public addresses all eloquence and no execution?* The WEC had organized specifically to lobby the legislature, so while the governor was first to hear from them, quite quickly we'd all had a blistering ear full. Their concerns traveled straight to my heart.

I WAS MID-CAMPAIGN IN MY FIRST ELECTION BACK IN 1962 when Rachel Carson's *Silent Spring* debuted in print on September 27. I devoured it. Her exposé of America's chemical industry condemned the harmful effects of chemicals on both human health and the balance of nature, something I'd already experienced first-hand, with sorrow: My young father had passed away just two weeks before Carson's book came out — a likely victim, along with my mother, who some years before had expired in my arms.

After World War II American farmers eagerly spread their fields with a brand new miracle pesticide and weed killer — the chemical DDT.

My parents were among the many Kansan farmers fully exposed. No one knew then what we know now: DDT is a carcinogen. Developed by military laboratories for biological warfare, DDT served multiple military roles. In powdered form it was not easily absorbed into human skin, so they dusted it on soldiers to fight lice; the weapon version was obviously more potent. At war's end, America's agricultural community adopted DDT for crop use. Dissolved in oil, it was easier to spray, we discovered, but this also allowed it to more easily enter the human blood stream.

My dad and I used a mixture of DDT and oil — it was black, like oil, I remember clearly — to battle chinch bugs. We spread it around the edges of our fields of all our corn-like grains — sorghum and kafir. Perhaps my mother did the actual mixing. I don't recall. But within a few years, my healthy, vibrant mother fell ill, victim to cancers of the bone and breast. I was a young mother myself when I traveled home to Kansas one difficult summer, kids in tow, to nurse my mother through incredible pain until at last the cancers killed her. She knew, or at least she sensed, it was the DDT.

As lovers of the earth and of nature, my parents had a profound respect for the rhythms and reasons of biological life. Their un-natural deaths were incongruent and heartbreaking.

Early in 1963, while I was a House freshman learning legislative ropes, President Kennedy was learning, too, from his Science Advisory Committee about the effects of pesticide use. Just after *sine die* my freshman session, I watched Ms. Carson's famous television interview on *CBS Reports*, after which the U.S. Senate, spurred by this troubling broadcast, immediately organized hearings on pesticide use, newspapers reported nationwide the next day.[1]

But here we are in 1969, and America has done very little in response.

During our butcher paper Blueprint brainstorming I was vocal on environmental issues, based not only on my family's exposure to DDT, but on my kids' more recent brush with pollution. *No swimming! Water unsafe!* Several summers back and for several summers on end, to the disappointment of many families young and old, public swimming beaches on the shores of Lake Washington had signs that screamed these warnings. Seattle's largest, residentially ringed lake — a natural beauty with stunning views of Mount Rainier — was sewage-sullied, algae-choked and disgusting, trashed by an absence of regulation. Public outcry led to a cleanup, with a big public price tag and revised local law. Yet in these subsequent six years since the emergence of *Silent Spring*, and despite our legislative intentions, too many environmental items from our Blueprint dangle.

No wonder I feel uncertain, even down.

I RETURN HOME TO A FAMILY THAT NO LONGER needs me daily, except for Ken, who is one of the least needy humans one could adjoin. He is a wonderful listener, though, and I need a sounding board.

"Ken, I'd like to talk." We've just finished dinner my first night home.

"You have the floor, Mrs. McCaffree," he jokes, but I'm serious.

"It's time for me to make a change. I need to find something else to do."

We review the goals I set when I took office, and then we retrace my political path. I'm grateful to have been able to serve my constituency, to have served as a legislative leader and to have led a major reform. In those respects, I am content.

But then I recount what I left nearly complete but incomplete on the table: Administrative overhauls to our departments of social services, transportation and environmental protection, not to mention the many specific ecological protections in and of themselves; a sorely overdue revamping of our state's system of compensating the unemployed — a thorny measure on which we'd made remarkable strides before we had to quit; a lowered voting age; a better tax base for local governments. My frustration is clear.

"Well, love, do you think the governor will call a special session?" he asks, having no idea how many colleagues had asked me the same last night.

"I have no idea," I tell Ken, too.

"Another special session would be another chance to finish up," he says. "Would that make a difference to you? To your decision?"

I honestly couldn't say, and tell him so.

On the heels of this grueling session, I am tired.

By law we can only legislate during formal legislative sessions, defined in length and scope by our state's constitution: 60 days every two years. This may have sufficed at statehood last century when we were a small, rural Washington, but not now. Now, these biennial sessions are woefully inadequate for running our vibrant state — a formula for staggering workloads, intense pressure, and basically insufficient for completing our time-critical work. As a governing body, we need more time. But our sessions are constitutionally limited. What can I do?

Nancy dashes in after work at the Department of Social Services, her first full-time job as a college graduate. She's living at home for a stretch.

"Oh, Mom! Thank goodness you're home! You don't know how happy I am to see you!"

Ken and I exchange an amused look.

"Your father has filled me in."

My oldest daughter is engaged, and her wedding just six weeks away. I would naturally love to have been involved in her wedding plans — I'm a planner at heart — but my head was entirely buried in legislation. Ken and Nancy did their best to plan without me.

It hasn't always been easy juggling parenting and public service. I've had to sacrifice. This is a perfect illustration, and a perfect occasion to allow me to ponder what life could be like post-legislature. I dish up some dinner for Nancy and we chat. When she's finished and gone, I drop Ken a new tidbit.

"Gummie's been putting a bug in my ear," I divulge.

"What species?" he asks.

"The Senate."

Ken is silent a stretch before he quietly repeats, "The Senate."

More silence ensues before he asks me, "How does that strike you?"

"It doesn't. I haven't given Gummie a response."

Ken waits for more. I'm sure he can tell I'm fatigued.

"Right now," I tell him, "my modest goal is to follow through on this term. I did my job getting tax reform onto the ballot."

"Yes, dear, you did. You needn't decide today." My husband is right. "And about the Senate, love? You know my sentiments: It's your life. It's up to you."

In late June, our Nancy Jane wed Aubrey Richardson Carter, Jr., newly graduated from Washington State University and heading east to dental school in the fall. We gathered for this happy occasion at the Everett Yacht Club one county north. The only smudge was the absence of Mary, who was in Paris for another term abroad. When she telephoned from overseas, mid-reception as planned, to wish the newlyweds "Bon chance!" I couldn't speak to her: A lump filled my throat. That moment I realized how much I've missed my family.

THIS SUMMER OF 1969, LIKE THE SUMMER BEFORE, is another national carnival ride, with news that alternatively plunges then soars, zipping lickety-split from splendor to disaster to disgust. It begins with hope when President Nixon announces his "Vietnamization" plan to begin withdrawing troops and to return local governance to the Vietnamese. But hope is swiftly followed by a disturbing political scandal in the sleepy eastern town of Chappaquiddick. Next, we're glued to our TVs as Neil Armstrong places a tentative boot on the moon, followed by a grisly cult-crazed murder. The week after that, as summer draws to an end, thousands of youth amass on a New York farm for the weekend of Woodstock, where David joins the crowds, vicariously, via the pages of *Time* and *Life*.

Though you won't find me in *Time* and *Life*, my profile in our urban community has expanded to the extent that even casual conversations these days venture into issues, especially tax reform.

To everyone who asks I explain: "Yes, it is crucial that you support this in the coming election. Well, yes, it does add an income tax, but it also lowers some of your other tax rates. No, it will not raise your taxes. Why? Because it restructures our tax base. It's a great system — it will fluctuate with the economy. What does that mean? It means we won't have to keep on increasing the sales tax. We're lowering some tax rates. Yes, lowering them. Yes. Yes, it's a ballot measure, so you get to decide. Will it work? Yes, I firmly believe it will."

I'm a broken record.

I have to be to get the message through and make it stick. I can only hope my colleagues are doing the same. I can't assume voters will warm to tax reform any more readily than the Senate and House. It's a long year and more before the general election.

A new citizen-led Tax Reform Committee — neither partisan, nor governmental — is taking this to the streets. The League of Women Voters surveyed 600 voters on tax reform. The Committee will use the results to shape a strategic statewide campaign for this crucial ballot vote.

Meanwhile, I remain on the Legislative Council, where our House leadership team stays in touch and in step in the interim, since our hometowns are scattered across the state. After today's Council meeting, I step out for coffee with Don Eldridge, Stu Bledsoe and Tom Copeland.

"What do you think, Mary Ellen? Will he do it?"

The special session question lingers. And we agree that if the governor does call us back into session, it will be up to us, the House leadership team, to drive the agenda. We can't count on the Senate to lead — Senate Democrats remain fractured, Senate Republicans remain a minority. And as for our House minority members, many are still quite unhappy.

While we don't know for certain whether the governor will summon us back to the capitol, nor under what conditions — a strict environmental session, perhaps, or to singularly address our crisis-bound economy? — we're aware of what we left undone, and again, are equally aware it would be up to us to lead. For while the governor can submit all the executive requests he likes, only the legislature can write and re-write state law. Those of us in leadership roles must determine exactly how.

AS SUMMER DRIFTS TOWARD AUTUMN, AND AMERICA'S role in Vietnam is on the ebb, a new issue ignites Americans' passion — the environment — so that now, not only is the Washington Environmental Council bearing down upon those of us in elective office in Washington State, but suddenly our entire nation is embracing the earth.

In early September, a quick layover stop in Seattle by U.S. Senator Gaylord Nelson of Wisconsin brings this home. Speaking at a WEC event, Nelson announces a thought that popped to mind mid-air on his journey west: Why not channel the young energy that launched all the war protests, civil rights marches, sit-ins… and put it to work for the planet? By the time he'd landed at Sea-Tac, he'd decided what to do: Stage a nationwide environmental teach-in.[2,3]

Nelson departs the WEC podium to take his teach-in notion to his next tour stop in San Francisco, and Governor Evans takes his place to tell the WEC the legislature is wrestling with how best to protect our surroundings. He lists the measures we have in the works: Creating a single administrative roof for a diversity of environmental issues — air pollution, water pollution, noise pollution, pesticide use, oil spills, thermonuclear waste, waste management and strip mining — each now scattered throughout state government. Transportation, he notes, is an environmental issue too (to perplexed response, though 'smog' is becoming a household word). Another environmental issue is open space.[4]

Tomorrow, the governor's environmental retreat begins, a multi-day event for which he has gathered state department heads, legislative leaders, and citizen leaders in the field. I am not invited, nor is Joan Thomas. All men, we hear later But within days we both learn about what transpired.

NOT LONG AFTERWARD, JOEL PICKS ME UP for another trip south to the mansion where the governor greets us with his unique combination of energy, earnestness and — on this particular day — grass-stained knees.

"Touch football," he explains as his two eldest sons scamper off. He gets down to business: "You're aware of the conference."

Joan had filled me in on some details by phone. The governor tells us today that he mainly listened, as usual, during the two-day event he hosted at the lodge at the Crystal Mountain Ski Resort on Mount Rainier.

"And?" asks Joel.

"Well, we didn't do anything sophisticated," says the governor. "Just talked and I jotted notes on a blackboard. The environmentalists came up with a long list of, oh, fifty issues, I'd say — good issues, but an impossible list for this state to pull off overnight. So I told each person in the room — activists, legislators, state employees, me included — to each pick three, their three most important issues, and to raise their hands as we went down the list of fifty. I kept a tally.

By the end, six items stood out as significant to us all. So I told the environmental crowd if they would agree to focus on only those six, and drop the rest for now, I'd consider calling a special session of the legislature." [5,6]

Internally, I gasp. In talking to my constituents, I've come to realize a special session could open a big can of tax reform worms.

"They agreed they'd keep it to these six…" the governor continues, but I've momentarily lost focus, intent on tax reform worries. I snap to in time to hear: "…if I could assure them the legislature would give priority to these six."

He shows us the list: Guard the Puget Sound against oil spills and our shorelines against development, regulate strip mining, expedite pollution control cases through our courts, finish all the logistical pieces involved in setting aside open space — trail systems included, and above all, establish a department dedicated exclusively to environmental protection.

"And?" Joel asks again.

The governor is wry: "I told them I can't guarantee a thing from our legislature. But I did suggest I might carry a little weight with the Republican House. I told them if I called a special session, they'd be in charge of swaying the Senate and the public at large, and working with the business community. Then I turned to my department heads, who do happen to work for me, knitted my brow and said with the sternest voice I could muster, 'You will give these measures support.' It got a good laugh, but they know I meant it."

By this time, we all want to know: "And?"

"And so I'm considering calling a special session in January."

"Isn't that risky, Governor?" I ask. "I mean, murder for some of us, politically. It could open our hard-earned tax reform package to new…"

We all know the risks. A governor can call a special session of the legislature, but then the legislature is in the driver's seat, determining where the session goes, when it ends. What if the session's a failure? What if it lasts too long and costs too much? What if there's bitter politicking? A poor performance legislatively? If this proposed session goes either sideways or interminably forward, combined with the tax reform measure on the upcoming ballot, which everyone knows was headed by House Republicans — it could deal us disaster at the polls come election time. Taxes — even sensible taxes — remain politically poisonous, a reality that is sad, and in this case nonsensical, but altogether true.

"I agree, Mary Ellen," says the governor. "Calling a special session would require that we all spend a lot of our hard-earned political capital. I am weighing this very carefully."

Yet we agree we have a problem: Too much of our original Blueprint remains conceptual rather than concrete. Another session has come and gone — my fourth, Slade's sixth, Dan's seventh at work for the state — and yet the fully functioning government we envisioned in our 1964 Blueprint isn't finished.

"What's the temperature out there in your districts?" the governor asks.

Plenty of citizen unrest remains — centered not so much on war and peace in our corner of the country, but on escalating challenges in each community. School levies are failing like never before. Traffic bottlenecks are worsening, pollution worries real. Local governments are overwhelmed and precariously short on funds. And young people won't let me forget they want to vote.

STUDENT UNREST AT THE UNIVERSITY OF WASHINGTON, Ken has written atop the legal pad sitting on our kitchen table. While I sip coffee and he takes tea, we plan another meeting of our 32nd District Republican Club, where he still presides and I still represent us. *Newsletter, September 24, 1969.*

We brainstorm the contents. By that night, we're running off copies on our basement mimeograph machine.

Ken invited as guest speaker Dr. Robert 'Bob' Aldrich, former chairman of the UW Faculty Senate, who was replaced in July by my husband (Faculty Senate vice-chairman until then). Bob and Ken marshaled all the major incidents on campus last year — the day the administration building was bombed, the grape boycotts to support immigrant farm labor, the ROTC recruiting protest (the bees!), protests by the Black Student Union when the UW Husky men's basketball team scheduled games against BYU — no blacks allowed at Brigham Young.

"Clear communication will keep our community calm," Ken notes.

He and Bob will share with our Republican group the brainchild they hatched: A forum for student voices — a quarterly campus event that will let the students pick a hot topic in advance, then freely voice their concerns, speak their minds.

Of the three-page newsletter, president Ken wrote the first three paragraphs and Representative McCaffree the rest: About a potential special session and two key bills I'll present if it happens. *Our meeting will begin at 8 p.m. in the University Towers Hotel, on Tuesday, September 30.*[7]

We add address labels and stamps and stick them into the next day's mail.

RUMORS OF A SPECIAL SESSION ARE SO RAMPANT by now that my colleagues and I are largely proceeding 'as though' it will happen — and so is the public.

My pile of mail mounts.

"Dear Mrs. McCaffree, I am deeply concerned about taxation. My husband, and a growing number of others who feel the same, are consistently voting 'no' on the special school levies. They are saying 'no' to the method of financing schools; they are not against education. During the special session in January, tax reform is an absolute necessity, but we are rapidly reaching the tax saturation point and small business is wondering how long it will be able to survive… Very Truly Yours, Mrs. Dale A. McDonald." [8]

"Dear Sir…" begins a form letter sent to me from the Episcopal Diocese in Olympia — a safe salutation considering it applies to more than 95 percent of those in our legislative seats. "… The convention has asked me to send you a copy of the enclosed resolution."

The enclosed Episcopalian resolution is on abortion. Its three 'whereas' clauses spell out problems with our state's current abortion law, followed by, "Be it resolved that this convention urges the governor, the legislature and the people of the State of Washington to legalize therapeutic abortion after medical consultation approves the abortion as beneficial to the mother, and especially when a mother's physical or mental health is endangered, when pregnancy is the result of rape or incest, when a fetus may be deformed and when socio-economic factors would seriously inhibit the atmosphere of love into which all children should be born and raised." [9]

And another: "Dear Mrs. McCaffree, The Political Action Committee at the University of Washington is part of a statewide student lobby organization which attempts to represent a variety of student interests on a non-partisan basis. During last year's legislative session, a bill was introduced in the House, designed to adjust some of the inequities with regard to 18-year-old legal responsibilities. That bill asked that 18-year-olds be allowed to marry without parental consent, execute a will, enter a legal contract, serve on a jury and last but not least, to vote."

The author asks for my feedback and some tips for the upcoming session. "Sincerely, John Britt," posted from his P.O. Box in the HUB on the UW campus. [10]

I've collected stacks of constituent letters ever since *sine die*. If the governor calls the session, I'll take this mail with me to Olympia, where my secretary can help me type and send many dozens of personal replies. If we don't go into another session, I'll have plenty of time to handle these all by myself.

AS I WEIGH MY FUTURE, VOTER PRESSURES and state pressures both bear down. Our state's robust economy has squealed into an sudden u-turn: The boom that delivered our state a handsome surplus has dramatically slowed, and as a result, our city and county governments are gasping desperate monetary breaths. Mayors and county officials from throughout the state have begun to steadily bend my ear, as I am now our state's recognized legislative leader on revenue. Their plight has my sympathy. It stems from an incomplete Blueprint item I champion more than many of my colleagues — empowering our local governments, assuring they have the tools to function both autonomously and well.

My activist start — that very local challenge of keeping my neighborhood schools fully funded and functioning — taught me that the most important 'government' to each of us is the government closest to our homes. Local governments, our cities and counties, are the most accessible in the midst of our daily lives. This is where we can best exert influence on decisions that touch us daily, and where I believe quality of life decisions are most appropriately made.

I care that our local governments are strong. Not everyone in Olympia shares my view. Some believe the state should manage most. Some favor the federal government. My commitment to the premise that our nearest governments are also our dearest, combined with studying our state's tax and revenue flaws in great detail, has led me to conclude that in this state, right now, our cities and counties are fiscally wrist-bound.

While no special session has yet been called, and our governor continues to weigh the risks, we continue to lay the groundwork for our dangling Blueprint measures — whether for another special session a few months from now, or for the next regular session in another year.

The governor phones me: "Hi, Mary Ellen. How goes it with the cities?"

I deliver Dan the latest: "Governor, they are lobbying me like mad."

I've agreed to field interim pleas from our cities and counties for more dollars, and I have now personally visited with our state's six biggest cities — each city hall and every mayor.

For the first time in state history, we're considering giving our local governments the authority to charge an add-on to the state sales tax — as much as .5 percent, or half a cent per dollar, on top of our regular state sales tax rate. To me, and to our leadership team, this makes sense.

We'd like to hold the ceiling at half a cent — the highest rate we figure will attract the legislative votes to enact it, or at least not repel too many. Of our state's six major cities, four of them agree: Tacoma, Yakima, Pasco and Spokane all consider the half-cent measure sufficient, given their local needs.

"But Vancouver is balking," I report, which surprises neither of us.

Our cities along the Oregon border have always struggled with revenue shortfalls. Oregon has no sales tax, so Washington residents gladly take the bridge across the Columbia River to make their purchases there, out of state and tax-free. Towns that border Canada similarly "bleed" shopping dollars north whenever the exchange rate is favorable — which is often. Both bleeding borders illustrate how our tax reform package could stabilize our state revenue base. As our local economies expand and contract, the third leg of an income tax would calm the fluctuation of money-out, money-in.

"And Seattle?" asks the governor.

"One percent, says Wes. Minimum. Period. End of discussion."

Wes Uhlman, once my 32nd District mate in the House, and then a state senator and now Seattle's mayor-elect, insists that Seattle's revenue woes are so dire, nothing less than a full one percent sales taxing authority for the city will dig them out in this economic downturn. The city's revenue is plummeting, yet its operating costs are on the rise.[11]

"One percent would kill the whole thing," said the governor.

"I know. I've talked myself blue. So far, Wes isn't budging."

"Keep at him."

"I will."

"Thanks, Mary Ellen. I know I can count on you."

Even if this is my final term, it's no time to slither to the sidelines, inactive or unseen. I can't ignore today's problems, letting them fester for a successor. I asked, and agreed, to serve and swore an oath to do so.

THROUGHOUT THIS INTERIM, AS IN INTERIMS PAST, my legislative work has continued nearly full time. I continue to chair the Committee on Revenue and Regulatory Agencies of the Legislative Council. In this particular year, I thank goodness for the interim tradition of this group, which provides us an instant framework for our staggering preparatory work to launch another extra session, if need be. Each committee of the Council includes both senators and representatives, which will allow us to work out agreement on certain matters and measures beforehand, rather than wrangling between chambers once the session begins. If it begins.

After our next Legislative Council meeting Stu, Don, Tom and I begin some speculative brainstorming: Which issues would we emphasize? Which specific bills? How can we finish our ambitious agenda at the least expense to taxpayers — in other words, fast?

Tom maps out possible committee schedules.

Don suggests a tight deadline to move things along.

I list our outstanding bills and issues.

And Stu proposes something uncomfortably genius: "We get the Senate on board right away. No joke. Let them pick their issues, maybe take credit for the highest profile bills. Whatever it takes. We've got a state to serve and you know what Joel says."

We do, and recite it verbatim: "It's amazing how much you can accomplish as long as you don't care who gets the credit."

BY THE WEEK BEFORE THANKSGIVING, my professor husband and student son have settled into an increasingly chilly standoff at our U-District home. David

Representative Mary Ellen McCaffree and Governor Dan Evans confer regularly on revenue matters.

is in sympathy with the quarter million anti-war protestors who marched on Washington, D.C., last week while Ken, a military veteran, has greater compassion for the challenges of President Nixon. Nixon is having no inaugural-year honeymoon with the public nor the press, a reality that recently spurred his defensive vice-president to lash out memorably.

Our nation has real problems. So does our state. And so do our cities and counties, which is why I've regularly touched base with the governor's office throughout the fall. Today I deliver the governor's staff a section-by-section analysis of the two tax and revenue measures we negotiated in my Legislative Council committee — one on open space, the other on local taxing authority — both ready to go, *if* we go into session.

TEN DAYS AFTER THANKSGIVING, the Sunday *New York Times* features an article that perhaps seals the deal on the governor's decision to convene an historic mid-term session. The environment, writes Gladwin Hill, is on its way to eclipsing the Vietnam war as the top issue on America's college campuses.

"The deterioration of the nation's 'quality of life' is a pervasive, here-and-now, long-term problem that students of all political shadings can sink their teeth and energies into," Hill writes, "and they're doing it!" [12]

Picked up in Sunday papers across the U.S., the article excerpts dozens of interviews from American campuses. Our University of Washington features prominently: A 'learn-in' staged by the student Committee on the Environmental Crisis; an 80-page report on Puget Sound ecological woes compiled outside class by UW graduate students just because they cared.

"This is not just a social movement for Biafra or Vietnam," said UW Crisis Committee president Terry Cornelius, "but one for everybody and for our closed system, Earth."

Gladwin Hill also reported that Gaylord Nelson, who stumped here just two months ago, succeeded in garnering enthusiasm for a nationwide 'teach-in' next spring, including Congressional backing for what they're thinking of calling 'Earth Day'. Denis Hayes, 25, the former Stanford student body president and a Washington State native, will be at the helm of the Earth Day event.

In addition, several environmental crises, very recent and real, have pushed our nation into readiness to fight for the environment: The spontaneous combustion of a pollution-choked river near the Erie Canal, dead fish belly up in the Great Lakes, the Santa Barbara oil spill last spring.

Environmental protection is an issue many in Washington State will gladly rally round, and in fact, Senate leaders Durkan and Gissberg have begun to lean on the governor about a special session centered just on that.

Jim Dolliver is no doubt wielding great influence on the governor as well. He and Dan continue to climb another of Washington's peaks each summer, and while Dan originally envisioned himself as an 'education governor', Dolliver likely envisions an 'environmental governor' too. Escalating ecological concerns nationwide mean this state and its governor could carve a valuable and prominent leadership path. As a ceaselessly sage advisor who keeps the bigger picture in mind, Dolliver steadily asks himself, how best can this popular young governor make a difference? Having our Senate aboard would be a giant plus.

ON MONDAY, I'M AMONG THE HANDFUL of leaders summoned to the governor's mansion, where he tells us he's made his decision. We suspected as much.

"I'm calling a special session," he said. "But I'd like to make it quick. Something like thirty days."

We all enjoy a good laugh, except for the governor: "I'm serious," he tells us. So are we.

We still need to restructure several major departments of state government, deal with transportation snags, restructure our municipal revenue streams, bolster certain retirement funds, detangle a ludicrous system of compensation for unemployment, lessen the tax burden on the elderly, stem the effects of this economic downturn, lower the state voting age to 18, and safeguard our environment in the six arenas the governor promised the WEC.

In thirty days?

This unusual mid-term special session is at once an opportunity and enticing challenge. For if we truly manage to legislatively construct the balance of our Blueprint reforms, and to do it swiftly, we will demonstrate how a perfectly functioning representative democracy can and should work. In theory, our forefathers' brilliant design of our government is a thing of genius and beauty. In real life, however, if improperly construed or poorly applied, our government is also capable of ugly political implosion and quagmire. My goal, therefore, with this second-chance session — and that of my colleagues — is to align our state with our founders' ingenious vision.

And so we argue. We discuss, we strategize. We question, and then we argue some more.

The governor listens, thanks us, and says he'll take it from here and he'll take all the heat.

As much as I'm waffling about my political future, very little excites me more than this prospect of buckling down and getting things done. Luckily, the House leadership feels the same.

ON DECEMBER 9, THE GOVERNOR ISSUES HIS FORMAL proclamation: The 41st Legislature will convene for a third time on January 12, 1970, making state history. In calling us back to Olympia, the governor lauds our work of last spring — specifically the success of our tax reform package and its constitutional amendment now headed for a statewide vote.

"However, other critical issues remain," his proclamation continues, "issues which cannot be held over for yet another year, but which demand action now."

Pervasive fiscal problems. Our local government financing crunch. Administrative illogic. Voteless 18-year-olds. An environment at risk.

"These issues demand action now, and to resolve them we cannot afford the luxury of a leisurely approach."

He declares the requisite state of emergency and spells out our six major areas of concern: 1) The environment and its protection, 2) unemployment compensation reform, 3) our transportation infrastructure, 4) better revenue streams for our counties and cities, 5) quality housing for the low income, elderly and everyone in between, along with services to care for our state's most vulnerable, and 6) more rights for our youth.

Then he mentions the nonsense of trying to conduct our state's business within the constitutional restraint of sessions every other year.[13] More and more, I agree with him.

The Extraordinary Session is no longer speculative — no more "Mary Ellen, what do you think?" On January 12, another session will convene — the third formal gathering of our state's 41st Legislature.

We have one month to prepare.

CHAPTER TWELVE

EXTRAORDINARY
THE GOVERNMENT OUR FOREFATHERS DESIGNED

This is why our founding fathers

crafted our government as they did — so that

We the People can problem solve for ourselves.

WITHOUT THE ENVIRONMENTAL BLOC knocking down our doors last spring, this special session would never have come to be, I have no doubt. The issues we left dangling at *sine die* were excuse enough for another try — from our legislative perspective, but not likely in the eyes of the public. Thanks to the impetus of the environmental voice, we now have a legitimate opportunity to tackle both.

It's largely up to our House leadership team to drive the agenda.

The five of us, including our caucus chairman, Norwood Cunningham, spend the remaining weeks of 1969 fine-tuning the framework for our work: A careful weaving of Senate and House, Republican and Democrat, the balance of our Blueprint and the environmental six. Joel's mantra remains forefront: *It's amazing how much you can accomplish as long as you don't care who gets the credit.*

While each of us ninety-nine in the House have potential re-elections at stake, we can't think of that now. Selfless public service will be key to this session's success.

At midnight on December 31, Ken and I toast a brand new decade and bid adieu to both the 1960's and our years as full time parents. David has staked his independence, despite continued free rent on 18th Avenue. Mary is off on another term abroad. Nancy and Aubrey have left for Virginia. Chuck and Lee have a third child 'in the oven'. And Jim is now Dr. James McCaffree, with his doctorate in animal husbandry from Cornell.

By early January – midterm in a normal interim – a state representative is either gearing up for re-election or winding down public duties. Not this year. This new decade brings with it a new chance to complete our journey, to complete the reforms and restructuring of our state, to complete laying those paths for progress we promised.

TWO WEEKENDS AFTER NEW YEAR'S DAY, late on a Saturday afternoon, Ken and I load my files in the Oldsmobile Cutlass and we drive once again to Olympia. It feels like I never left. I move into my new rental, then back into my old office, and spend Saturday evening attending to long-overdue correspondence to constituents who have penned their concerns:

"Dear Mrs. McDonald: Thank you for your letter of December 3. With regard to the increasing problem of special levies in this state, the last session of the legislature did pass a tax reform package which provides a more equitable tax system and gives us a better way to finance our schools. It will allow us to support public education at the state level and relieve the necessity for special levies at the local level. You will have the opportunity to express your support for tax reform next fall when the tax reform package is submitted to voters for their approval in the form of a constitutional amendment authorizing a state income tax…" [1] – a relentless campaign, but necessary: The public vote on tax reform is still another ten months away.

On Sunday morning, January 11, in the small loft I'm renting in a private home, Ken and I read our Sunday *Seattle Times* and our *Post-Intelligencer* with all the skeptical presaging of another long, drawn-out session. I hope to prove these journalists wrong.

Ken drops me off mid-day at the capitol, and while he prepares for his Monday classes, I prepare for my Monday start. Early evening, we drive to the lovely Falls Terrace Restaurant on the Deschutes River across from the Olympia Brewery. The slogan of this local beer is, "It's the water" – the water of the lively Deschutes.

"Dr. and Mrs. McCaffree!" Our regular waiter greets us as we settle into our favorite booth. "How wonderful to have you back for another few months!"

"Thirty days," I correct him.

"Oh?" He's confused. "You won't be with us the entire session?"

Ken explains: "Representative McCaffree believes the session will end in thirty days."

"Thirty days?!" says the waiter, brushing it off with the flick of a napkin.

"Preposterous."

"Extraordinary," Ken replies, pleased with his play on words.

But I am all business: Dinner, then cake, then home to the loft to prepare while my husband turns our Oldsmobile north on the interstate back to Seattle.

FIRST THING THIS OPENING MONDAY MORN, hours before we formally convene, I walk straight up the aisle to the Speaker's podium, place my hands on the rostrum, survey the empty chamber, clasp the gavel and practice a swift authoritative rap. I try the microphone next. Testing, testing. From here I will lead our first joint hearing this afternoon, after our opening session.

Next stop: The caucus room.

This initial caucus meeting is brief, in line with the peppy pace we anticipate. Norwood Cunningham is appropriately succinct: "Stick to the agenda. Stick to our main measures. No pet bills. No bogging down. Any questions?"

Yes. Dozens, centered on why and how. We on the leadership team explain.

The governor has been very clear about why we're all here, Tom Copeland reminds us. As for how, in order to tackle this session as swiftly as possible, with the straightest route to results, we'll do a few things unconventionally. We begin with much of our major legislation already well along, he says, per our previous session and interim refinements by the Legislative Council, which includes members from both chambers and both parties. Now, during this opening week, we will hold joint House/Senate hearings on the most critical of these. Tom looks to me to explain.

"The purpose of these joint hearings," I say, "is to get every voice on an issue into play at once. This should help us identify any glitches or tripping points in these bills right off the bat. With both House and Senate committee members attending the same hearing, we can all work at an issue from the same set of emotions and facts. I'll chair the first of these hearings today, this afternoon… right after our opening session adjourns. You're welcome to attend."

"And the environment?" someone asks.

"Don't worry," says Stu, still our majority leader. "The Senate is already pushing. And the governor's never shy about his requests."

> **JOINT HEARING**
>
> A public hearing on a specific bill or issue hosted by two or more legislative standing committees, usually one each from the Senate and House.

Mid-morning, Speaker Eldridge gavels into motion the familiar ceremonial cadence of opening day. But unlike our regular opening days — since this is yet another special session of the 41st Legislature and an extension of the legislative work we left mid-deliberation last spring — we immediately read sixty-some measures into the record, assign them straight to our pre-formed committees, promptly segue into Joint Session, welcome the Senate, welcome the court and dignitaries, and welcome the governor to deliver another State of the State now, rather than three days in.

GOVERNOR EVANS HAS TAKEN TREMENDOUS HEAT for calling this session — from the public, from his legislature, from the press. He doesn't sweat. We have agreed — we being the original DEGOHT team now in leadership posts throughout state government — that our state needs us now, not twelve months hence. He steps to the podium.

"This is, if not a popular session, then at least an extraordinary one... But if it is an Extraordinary Session, then I would remind you... that these are extraordinary times... Not in the history of all mankind have those of us who represent the people been faced with such awesome challenges. Nor have those of us in state government been so vulnerable to the demands of a single genera-tion — both old and young — which finds much in the past to deplore and little in the present to commend."

The public outcry of the 1960's didn't catch us by surprise here in this state, for unlike in most other states and strata of our government, we had identi-fied problems early and teamed up to solve them earlier than most, which has placed our state at the nation's leading edge. But we must combat this trend of public distrust.

At this beginning of my eighth year in public office, in search of steadying our state, I am determined to see our slate of reforms through to comple-tion. I'm not alone. From my seat center aisle in the midst of the chamber, I see Senator Durkan gnawing his pipe with attentive demeanor refreshingly new. Representative O'Brien's yellow pad remains nearly empty. He, too, is listening intently. Senator Greive is visibly itching to get things under way. Stu Bledsoe, Buster Brouillet, Bob Goldsworthy, Bob Charette — I'm surrounded by a bi-partisan team prepared to play as one.

The governor continues: "We must now share in the responsibility to deal with the overwhelming impact of change. This Extraordinary Session was not conceived by whim, nor was it shaped by politics. It was called because in the judgment of this administration there are compelling needs which must be answered now — not in 1971."

The downturn of the nation's economy these past twelve months, and a similar slide the last six here at home, is wreaking havoc on the biennial budget we crafted just last April, when our state's finances were ample and our economy robust. Today, people have stopped buying, and for a state financed largely by its sales tax (secondarily by a property tax), this 'buying freeze' puts state revenues terribly behind projections. In a domino effect, state services are threatened accordingly. In addition, unemployment here is rapidly on the rise: Unemployment compensation and welfare payments are draining our state coffers.

It is tough to imagine the mindset behind this legislature's unwillingness to propose that we change our constitution to allow for annual sessions. We're a big state now, with a very big budget, and it seems ridiculous to chart the course of a billion dollar enterprise within only sixty days in alternative years. Each time a new legislature meets, every two years, we're a new mix of players — with the newly elected among us tossed a steep curve of learning. No corporation would operate this way — bind its hands and strip itself of an ongoing ability and flexibility to respond to change. We are elected to tend to the business of the people of this state. Our mandate is clear, our responsibility enormous. Perhaps someday annual sessions will be the norm.

"I ask you these questions," the governor continues. "What price must the people pay for 12 more months of…"

His six questions spell out the six policy areas we'll tackle this session, after which he notes, "I have heard it said, more in anger than in sorrow, that the people are unhappy with this Extraordinary Session of the Legislature. I do not believe this… People of this state are aware of change. They are aware that government must operate differently today than it did yesterday… And I think they are aware — because of this — that money spent in prompt and proper legislation is not a waste of the taxpayer's dollar; it is an investment in the taxpayer's future."

He pauses to assure we're attentive for this next:

"It is not the price of progress that the average citizen deplores; it is the price of politics. It is the debate without purpose, the delay without conscience and the unreasonable exercise of privilege and power that causes him to rise up in protest… We are all here to advance the cause of representative government — to demonstrate in full view of the people that this administration and this legislature can address themselves to the timely problems of the state.

"We have at this moment the opportunity to deal with legislation of high priority and to do so in a manner which all of the people will commend. We have the opportunity in the first month of a new decade to reaffirm the role of the citizen legislator and to reassure the people that in times of great stress and grave challenge, our system can function with an efficiency and a sense of purpose which transcends ordinary politics."

Our House leadership team has tried to organize this session entirely outside politics, with our eyes on the optimal functioning of our government — the ideal focus of any session, to be sure, although political considerations inevitably enter the fray. This special session, with its specific topics and targeted length, allows us to hone in on those few items that will steady our state and complete our Blueprint for Progress — not drafted per partisan ideology, but tied to the specific contemporary needs of our state.

How good it feels to be able to deliberately articulate, *Here's a real problem, here's a real crisis* — and to finally be poised to tackle it with every tool our representative government enjoys by design. This is why our founders crafted our government as they did. So that we the people can problem solve for our selves — respond to our pressing community issues on any day. They didn't establish our unique forum solely for argument, political positioning or debate. They created a self-government that would allow us to debate and discuss, yes, but then to accomplish things, to solve problems, to progress.

Admittedly, I've participated in the political as a means to arrive here today, via the necessary partisan tasks of redistricting and election campaigns, but now I can function purely as a servant of the people. This is why I ran for office, why I chose to serve.

This Extraordinary Session, under the specific challenges we face today as a state, may allow us to live up to this imagined promise of self-government — if we're true to our task. Better yet, perhaps we can create a sterling model for those who follow. The governor is aware of this opportunity. And so am I. And frankly, so are Washington's citizens.

The governor speaks on: "If there is a danger in action, so there is a greater danger in delay. For while this state may be salvageable, it is by no means secure. And not one of us here today wants to be known as part of that body of men who played it safe and authored a disaster."

He reviews his list of six key reasons he called us back into session — the six issues he expects us to address, ending with the youth vote.

"This sixth and final priority strikes deeply at the heart of the emerging America of the 1970's. Events of the past few years — from our campuses to the battlefields of Vietnam — have left no doubt about the deep involvement of youth in our national life and security."

He urges us to lower the voting age to 18, and to pair youth rights with more youth responsibility. In response, several of 'my kids' who line the front row in the balcony gallery now raise their crossed fingers.

Having absorbed my suggestion that their best hope lay in enlisting those who had the power to help them, these 'kids' formed an 'Eighteen Year Old Vote Committee of Washington State' and came to Olympia early last session to meet with three legislators — Representatives Ceccarelli, King and me — to brainstorm how best to pass their bill.[2,3] With a list of resultant techniques and committees, they set about their work: Fact sheets, phone calls, editorials, endorsements, press releases, petitions, meetings with student leaders and news editors, and lots of talking 'man to man'. But rallies? No. I managed to convince them otherwise. The generation gap is alive and festering and in this day and age, adults automatically label youth 'rebels' whenever they raise a collective voice — an unfair link that could nevertheless work against them.

The governor brings to a close his State of the State: "If we are to be judged harshly by those who follow us, then let it be for what we did and not what we failed to do. For that is the test of true commitment and the price of true progress."

When the applause softens, the governor has two final words for us: "Thank you."[4]

By the end of this session, I hope he can thank us as well.

BY 2 P.M. I AM READY TO PRESIDE OVER A JOINT HEARING of complementary committees from the Senate and House: Twenty-odd from my Committee on Revenue and Taxation and more than a dozen from the Senate Committee on Ways and Means. My joint hearing this afternoon will serve as a prototype for the subsequent seven we've planned this initial week. Today, twenty local government heads have signed up to testify on the new local sales tax proposal.

Several advance feature articles in the state's major dailies, plus a quick scan of the floor, tells me we publicized this well. In addition to mayors and county leaders, I see members of the media, government watchdogs, several lobbyists and a surprising number of colleagues who may be interested in the issue, or simply curious about how this super-committee process will work. By week's end, each of us will be involved in at least one of these large joint hearings. I am happy to pave the way, and enjoy the autonomy I have to strike the right tone.

Washington's state legislature is unique in the power it vests in committee chairmen. The legislatures of America's western states, as a rule, disperse their power more broadly than our counterparts east. Here, we give greater voice to members of caucuses, committees and committee chairmen in particular. As a result, as chairman of this committee, I'm no pawn of an executive dictate. I've been given the issues to address, and have taken part in selecting them. It is up to me to examine each, to hear the sides, propose a route to completion, and then to guide the compromise that will eventually lead to new law.

Back East, where states formed earlier — less distant in history from monarchs and strata of class — state power tends to be more concentrated at the top. This formula in Washington State suits me better as a person willing to lead, and it allows for a broader citizen voice.

I arrive at this afternoon's hearing with several distinct advantages.

To begin with, this legislature is not new: No newly elected members, no newly configured committees, no new committee heads and no new leadership. We're a practiced team. Within each committee room, within each chamber and between them, too, our allegiances, positions and personalities are all largely known. There is no dance to be done to gauge any of these, no necessary prelude. We can get right down to work. And because I worked so intimately last spring with such a large swath of legislators on tax reform, I am well equipped to work with this entire class of colleagues.

Every step of my legislative career has led me to today, where I comfortably preside over this chamber full of traditional adversaries, and over each voice invested in this testy new tax proposition for our local governments.

"The joint hearing on House Bill 21, authorizing cities and counties to impose a local sales tax, is now called to order." I bring down the Speaker's gavel. "Welcome."

I quickly review the bill for the crowd, then read aloud a letter from the governor that spells out his preference for a half-cent ceiling on this tax, but with additional help for those cities and counties bordering Oregon.[5]

First to testify is Jack Rogers, executive secretary of the Washington Association of Counties. In our state, the taxing authority of each county is limited solely to the property tax.

"We must find a new source of revenue," Rogers says. "Kitsap, King, Pierce and Snohomish have all assured me they'll take advantage of this the minute the legislature puts it in place."[6]

He has just listed the four big urban core counties surrounding the Puget Sound. Next up is Kitsap County Commission Chairman Frank Randall.

"We had our heads in the sand about this," Randall says, "but we finally got wise, and we're just about broke. Where do you start reducing costs? In the sheriff's department where you haven't added deputies for 15 years? Reduce planning? Or the treasurer's office, the auditor, the clerk? They're barely able to do the job now with what they have. And to reduce the assessor's staff would just be suicide."

He lists more county woes: Their jail is uninhabitable, the fairgrounds grandstand is falling down. They can't wait another ten months for our general election vote on tax reform, and certainly not another twelve for the next legislature to convene. They need more revenue now.

"It's go the emergency route, or we close up shop," Randall tells us. "We support tax reform, but frankly, we can't wait. Give us the authority to tax, and we'll take the heat. But please, in the name of common justice, give us that right."

We all hear him, plain and clear.

In a normal session, my House committee may have heard this testimony first, discussed the bill and modified it, brought it to the House as a whole for more discussion, then sent it to the Senate, where the process would start all over again: The Senate would send it to their own committee, and these same parties would testify all over again — perhaps using different words and definitely speaking to different ears. Our decision to hold joint hearings all week should expedite our legislating immensely by providing us all an identical factual foundation as we deliberate.

Next, James Swinyerd, president of the Association of Washington Cities and a local mayor himself, assures us: "We are all firmly behind this legislation."

Seattle's new mayor, Wes Uhlman, asks to speak, and though I'm fully familiar with his viewpoint, I welcome him to present Seattle's plight: A $12 million revenue drop this year against the city's need for $8 million more than last year for law enforcement and firemen, for transit and annual increases in salaries and operating costs for a total deficit this year of $20 million.

"It is disturbingly obvious," he says, "that Seattle is on its way to becoming another New York City with its slums. We are not coming to Olympia for handouts of any kind. We are simply asking for the right to levy our own taxes. One percent is what we need. Nothing less will do the job for us. If it is not given to us, you share the responsibility of sentencing our cities to the slums."

I've argued with Wes all interim — that I do understand his one percent need, but we have to balance it against an amount that will earn this new measure sufficient statewide support. If we don't pass some version of this bill this month, if his insistence on one percent ruins everything, then the percentage of authorized local taxation available to the City of Seattle will be zero.

"Thank you, Mr. Uhlman," I say, sincere.

Spokane's mayor David Rogers also raises concerns about the onset of slum conditions, and Everett's mayor Robert Anderson underlines the dilemma each city here seems to face: "We are not practicing mere economy in the City of Everett, Mrs. McCaffree. We've been practicing poverty."

Next, city officials whose towns border Oregon describe fiscal hemorrhaging. Their tax dollars disappear across the Columbia River to Oregon, where there is no sales tax. Nor are there tolls on the bridge crossings — nothing to keep their shoppers local. These cities stand to benefit nothing from this measure — no amount of additional sales tax will help, so why should they back this bill?

"This is a bum tax."

"This is a serious situation."

"All we do is lose business to Oregon."

"Even gas in Oregon is two cents a gallon cheaper!"

James Ellis of Forward Thrust (the same Jim Ellis who led Lake Washington's anti-pollution and cleanup campaign) steps to the microphone and attempts to reconcile the border city problem with the bigger one: "This is local officials asking for one thing — a chance to perform and then stand on their own performance. I don't see how we can give them less. An objection of border counties may mean we require some form of enabling legislation, which would be a valuable tool in the arsenal of any of our counties."

The Oregon border towns have everyone's sympathy. And on occasion, our northern border with Canada poses a problem as well, depending upon the exchange rate. For the time being, all is quiet along this front.

Our tourist towns have a different problem: Their only source of local revenue comes from property owners, via the property tax, since sales tax revenues now legally all go to the state. When these tourist communities swell during high season — winters in our ski resort towns, for example, or summers along the coast — the cost of providing basic local services swells too (services that the waves of outsiders enjoy). And this added expense is shouldered disproportionately by property-owning locals. The increased sales tax revenues tourists bring with their local spending has not been available to these tourist towns to offset the costs of the tourists' presence. The imbalance is clear.

The coastal salmon fishing mecca of Westport is a prime example.

"We are taxing 1,400 local residents to provide services for the 20,000 people who come down and fish each summer," says Westport's Mayor Ralph Boohm. "Give us this half cent of the sales tax, Mrs. McCaffree, and we can tax the 20,000 while they're in town."

One cent, a half cent. Opinions differ as to amount, but everyone agrees this is a tax we need.

Today we also hear from union officials, urban affairs groups, advocates for good government. The need is urgent and unanimous, the answer imperfect.

Sunnyside Mayor Jerry Taylor sums things up: "Just give us the authority to go home and levy taxes and take care of our own problems."

When everyone who registered to testify has spoken, and no one else stands or raises a hand, I gavel the meeting's end.

"Thank you all," I tell the crowd. "Our two committees here will take into consideration your comments, and we hope for action on this bill by Saturday."

Saturday!

Faces register skepticism, and more than one person mutters, "We'll see."

After the hearing, I confer with the governor's staff. We review the major measures slated for this special session, discuss an optimum timetable and assign priority to specific bills. I stop by the House dining room for a quick evening meal, and then it's off to the Speaker's office, where Don, Stu, Norwood, Tom and I and a few other leaders review our session strategy.

"Do you really think we can do this?" asks Stu.

"If we're disciplined," I answer.

During our Tuesday morning session on Day 2, the Senate sends us a concurrent resolution to limit this special session to 21 days. The press corps laughs.

Ignoring them, we discuss this on the floor, modify the resolution to 30 days, return it to the Senate, and they agree. Thirty days it is.

The press enjoys a veritable heyday in print, calling our timetable various versions of ridiculous, or the more generous 'overly ambitious'. Before we convened yesterday, all our major media had predicted this special session would last a full sixty days — at the very least. They peppered their stories of our capitol return with words like "drudgery" and "pessimism" and "reluctance" and called our prospects for progress "dismal".

UNDAUNTED BY THEIR DOUBT, THEN AND NOW, we go about our first week's business, continuing with our big joint hearings and steadily processing bills. And in fact, I bring the local sales tax measure to the floor of the House on Thursday, two days ahead of my 'bold' prediction, with a committee recommendation that it do pass. Pass it we do, and send this first of six major 'extraordinary' session issue elements to the Senate for their review.

House Republicans are not, as a group, very thrilled with this local sales tax measure. It adversely affects business, and most Republicans champion business as the cornerstone of community prosperity. But it is something our state needs.

As a leadership team, we have worked hard to keep our session agenda (and our Blueprint agenda) non-partisan — not party based, but people based, tailored to needs of the people of this state. So we will take on our own House Republicans if need be, or at least try to figure out a fiscal compromise they can swallow. If the local sales tax measure doesn't pass, our cities and counties will still need help. The $10 million we appropriated for them in April under our funding formula of last spring is… no longer there. We need to address our state's ailing economy from a few different routes.

"How else can we help?" Jim Dolliver asks our small gathering in the governor's office.

"Ideas?" asks the governor.

We toss about several and decide we should levy the state B & O (Business and Occupations) tax on the banks. Until now, all financial institutions here have been exempt from the B & O tax, based on the fact that prior to 1960, national banks could not be taxed by state governments. To keep the banking playfield level, our state has always opted to exempt our state banks and other out-of-state banks from the B & O as well. Last year, however, this federal limitation came to an end. It seems an appropriate time, then, to end this exemption. By levying the B & O tax on financial institutions, we could bring in another $4.2 million annually.[7]

"Mary Ellen?" says Jim Dolliver.

I immediately understand.

"Yes, Jim, I'll sponsor it. And yes, I'll get it in on time."

Another prod to hasten this special session is a Friday deadline for introducing new bills. The governor's staff and I work late tonight to draft this one. When I arrive home sometime near midnight, my telephone rings.

"There you are!" says Ken. "Getting any sleep?"

"A little."

WITHIN THIS FIRST WEEK, A DIFFERENT BILL I'm shepherding this session emerges from committee: The comprehensive open space implementing bill to add to our formal statutes the several open space practices we authorized three years back. Because a designation of 'open space' removes dollars from state revenue rolls (via lower property values and lower taxes), this has been under lengthy discussion in my committee two sessions already.

As with many of these major bills, the bulk of our difficult work was done long before we returned to the capitol on Monday. In 1967, the first year we held a House majority, we introduced many of these seminal measures. We've refined them since and continue to build support. This Open Space Bill is just one. We treated it to a joint hearing Tuesday, during which another long list of citizens testified. As the bill's chief legislative architect (aided by the governor's staff), I fielded questions throughout the afternoon about its tax consequences and its necessity. Since Tuesday, I've been working with individual committee members to accommodate their various voices in refining this bill. Now, Friday during committee reports on the floor, I report that the Revenue and Taxation Committee recommends that it do pass. We send it to Rules for review.

Also this past week we held a joint Natural Resources Committee hearing on several of our key environmental measures, among them an oil spill bill to levy large penalties on any tanker accidents in the Puget Sound. The opponent? Small oil carriers, who complained the liability could run them out of business. The bill's proponents? Other than the oil industry, basically everyone else.

Testifying on the oil spill bill's behalf were oceanographers from the

University of Washington, a respected legal expert who provides local television commentary on pollution controls, and the owner of Foss Tug and Barge, which runs the biggest fleet on the Puget Sound. Most agree, if we were to suffer a spill in the Puget Sound — a harbor-like saltwater inlet of the Pacific Ocean ringed by Seattle and Tacoma and many of the most populous communities in our state — the monetary cleanup costs could be horrendous (in the hundreds of millions of dollars), and the price paid biologically even worse.

The lobbyist who spoke on behalf of the ten major oil companies was incensed. He called the bill's philosophy lousy, his clients' potential liability outrageous, and said he'd like to kill the bill outright.[8] His outburst aside, I am happy with how the hearing unfolded. As one of the sponsors, I am hopeful for this bill. We all want to prevent disastrous destruction, like the spill that blackened Santa Barbara's beaches just last April. It must not happen here.

Fortunately for this legislative session, for this issue, and for our state, many of our Senate leaders (Democrats all) happen to champion the environment, too, though few as fervently as our governor, nor perhaps as adamantly as those of us leading the way in the House. We aren't likely to disagree with the Senate over the content of these environmental bills, but rather over who among us will ultimately get credit. Daily, in caucus, we repeat our mantra: What matters is what we accomplish, not who gets the biggest pat on the back.

Today, Friday, marks the deadline for introducing new measures. I slipped in the B & O bank tax bill on time.

RIGHT AFTER ADJOURNMENT, OUR LEADERSHIP TEAM congregates in the Speaker's office to examine the list. I'm thrilled. We all are. We telephone the governor: So is he. In just five days, we've managed to put every item into play — all the major reforms and major programs the governor identified at this session's start. We've brought forth the entire environmental package, plus the balance of progressive reforms we began in '67, along with some complex economic stop-gaps we quickly drafted to address the urgencies that arose in the state in recent weeks. One by one we must usher them through the process. What a wonderful challenge! Our House dining room is the most energized ever, I note as I spoon at my ice cream.

With three weeks remaining, we obviously won't follow through on all 669 bills in the hopper, and that is just as well. Some are redundant, some nonessential this session. The important point is that, thanks to careful prior planning last autumn, and to our persistence over a number of years, we are now well positioned to move all our main measures into law.

When I return to my office, my secretary hands me a stack of letters. The first is from 45th Street, Apartment F — a student, judging from the address.[9] He has two concerns.

Dear Representative McCaffree,

I really don't know what your proper title is, and I hope that 'Representative' will do. As a voting age student at the U of W, I get a good chance to see a lot of students younger than myself who feel completely cut off from the political world, no way to let themselves be heard about issues that affect them directly (Vietnam, welfare cuts, etc.) except to demonstrate or some other counterproductive method of getting someone to listen. If you could do everything in your power to help 18 year olds get the right to vote then we will probably have fewer students turning to SDS with frustration. Good God, these people are being told by the political leaders to go and fight a war that they can't legally say anything about with their vote! You can help change this.

The one other area I feel very strongly about is abortion reform... There is no question about it, that this is a problem that hits the needy the worst. Those with $285 can go to a house in the outskirts of Vancouver, B.C. and get an abortion. I know, because my wife and I helped an unmarried friend of ours get one. Every doctor and lawyer knows someone who can either help or recommend someone else who can... Unwanted children stand a good chance of ending up on the public welfare system. So in short, please do everything you can to support abortion reform and the 18 year old vote. Sincerely yours...

Measures on both issues made our deadline: Abortion reform in both the Senate and House, and several on expanded rights and responsibilities for our state's youth. The numbers of letters I've received on both indicate how publicly urgent these two issues remain.

By Saturday, Day 6, the Open Space Bill returns to the House on second reading. In front of each of us ninety-nine is the long list of amendments – ten entirely new sections and a half-dozen line item changes as well, some of them worked through after the joint hearing earlier this week, others hashed out during the interim and in sessions past. The Speaker grants me the floor.

"Mrs. McCaffree."

"I move the adoption of the committee amendment to page 5, section 7, line 12..."

And so we begin. After more than an hour, we are still working our way through the lengthy bill, amending amendments, accepting them or voting them down. I rarely sit. Shortly after 3 p.m., the Speaker interrupts.

"The Speaker would like to advise those of you in the gallery, who I am sure are here for the 3 o'clock hearing, that we are going to be in session until 3:30. I hope you will bear with us in the delay on that important hearing."

We continue to debate the Open Space Bill until everyone has had his say, then take the necessary steps to place this bill on final passage. My colleagues largely agree — by a vote of 75-22 — on this specific implementing bill that will allow us to manage the legally protected open spaces we defined in 1967. Six days in, and we've passed our first major bill with commanding consensus.

My first session remains my benchmark — the year of the coalition and coup. By Saturday of that year, on day six, we were still arguing over how to structure our committees.

After today's session, we hold our final joint hearing of the week: On whether to give eighteen year olds the right to vote. The youth in the gallery had indeed been perfectly happy to hang around for the delayed start.

Just last week, rather than holding a protest rally, they'd organized a 'Committee 18' event on the University of Washington campus, with the governor delivering the opening speech, and a long list of powerhouse support: Our top state legislative leaders, our entire Congressional delegation minus one, and a clipboard list to track their legislative support (Y, N, U).[3,10] The name at the top of their clipboard is Mary Ellen McCaffree, with a solid 'x' in the Y column. During today's joint hearing, they hope to add many more.

This evening I go out to dinner with Ken, who arrived last night.

"Exhausted, love?" he asks.

"Exhilarated, honey." I really am. "This is what it's all about."

WEEK TWO BEGINS WITH AN EARLY PHONE CALL from Stu Bledsoe, who calls me into his majority leader's office, pronto.

"Mary Ellen McCaffree," he drawls, his head wagging in disappointment as I walk through the door. "And here I thought you were a lady."

I'm perplexed. What does he mean? His eyes make their way down my legs and stay there.

"What are you wearing those for?" I am wearing knee-high leather boots. "That's no look for a lady."

"If you men can grow your sideburns, Stu, I should be able to wear boots."

He bursts out laughing: "Just kidding you, Mary Ellen. Hell, if I can wear these dung-kickers, you can wear those. But dang, if I didn't overhear Bill having another hissy fit this weekend."

William 'Bill' Schumaker, a gunsmith, outdoor writer and photographer from Colville in Pend Oreille County, and obviously one of our conservative own, is uncomfortable with those of us 'city slickers'. Doesn't Bill know I come from a Kansas farm, for goodness sake? Bill gave me a personal lecture on my boots last spring. Apparently these boots are still bugging him.

I laugh it off—I've more important matters to deal with—and my boots and I march to the floor of the House, where another of my measures is introduced.

Though I am the prime sponsor of this next bill, and sit on the State Government Committee, our committee chairman Tom Swayze duly introduces House Joint Resolution 6, a constitutional amendment to lower the voting age to eighteen, and he tells us the committee majority recommends that it do pass.

The youth in the gallery mime silent cheers as we send HJR 6 on to Rules.

Working with these young people, I feel perfectly justified wearing my youthful boots. Nor does my attire prevent me from now leading more serious deliberation on the floor—on a bill that clarifies the ability of our state's municipalities to tap into a new federal program: Federal Metro Development Dollars designed to help finance transportation infrastructure. It passes handily, by 88-2 with 9 not voting.

On Tuesday of week two, January 20, the first Senate bill finally arrives: For safe pedestrian walkways approaching our public schools. This is important, but not a major policy measure.

WEDNESDAY, JANUARY 21, BOTH THE NORTH AND SOUTH galleries brim with youth—high schoolers, collegians, schoolchildren too, who are welcomed by Speaker once our opening formalities are complete: From Mountain View School in Lacey, Yakima High School, Mount Vernon High, Yelm Elementary and the Seattle YMCA. In the first order of business, a bill on voluntary commitment for drug addiction is reassigned to a different committee, and then it's time for today's big attraction: House Joint Resolution 6, sponsored by thirteen House members, including me, by executive request and by a request of the secretary of state: "Proposing a Constitutional Amendment to lower the voting age to eighteen years."

Eager rustling animates the balconies.

Immediately, Representative Amen, a Republican, proposes an amendment sponsored by him and Representative Litchman, a Democrat: That we change the age from eighteen to nineteen. In the midst of the ensuing debate, Representative O'Brien rises on a point of personal inquiry. Will Representative Bledsoe yield to a question? Stu will.

"Mr. Bledsoe," says Mr. O'Brien with all due sobriety, "as I understand it the governor has come out in favor of eighteen-year-old voting. Have you cleared this amendment with the governor of the state of Washington? We would like to have the policy of the Republican party clearly specified." He then adds very gravely: "We don't like to see this confusion."

We had discussed this in our morning caucus, right before we came to the floor, and agreed the main purpose of this measure is to lower the voting age. Because a majority of our caucus felt more comfortable with age nineteen, we were willing to put this element of the resolution to the entire House for a vote. So when minority leader John O'Brien chastises us with feigned worry over a party split, our majority leader is unapologetic in reply.

"Your concern, Mr. O'Brien, has touched my heart," drawls Stu. "But I suggest you worry about your troops and we'll worry about ours. Fair enough?"

Debate continues.

And I wonder if it is because the gallery is packed with youth that the Speaker is being unusually tolerant of action on the floor. Right now, for example, Representative Gladder suggests tying together military service, age and voting rights — not a bad notion. But first he wants to revert the age in the amendment to twenty-one, which would effectively wipe out the previous amendment entirely, and thus revert the resolution to existing law that sets the voting age at twenty-one. Regarding the Amen/Litchman age amendment, then, Mr. Gladder might as well just vote plain 'Nay'.

Following each of Rep. Gladder's proposals, the Speaker patiently explains proper process until Tom Copeland, Speaker Pro Tem and master of our extremely tight thirty-day work schedule, finally loses a little cool.

"Mr. Speaker," Tom says, his due respect wavering, "I know that you are being exceptionally kind this morning, but please, sir, I think that because of the gravity of this situation, we have to point out that this is inconsistent with our rules on amendments on amendments. What has been done is that Mr. Amen's amendment is stricken completely. There is nothing left of Mr. Amen's amendment that Mr. Gladder can even append anything to... I appreciate the fact that you are giving Mr. Gladder a great deal of latitude, but I suggest his amendment at this point is out of order and inconsistent with our rules covering the ability to amend." [11]

The Speaker takes a deep breath. Tom doesn't, so the Speaker bends a bit.

"I wouldn't agree with you entirely, Mr. Copeland. I think if Mr. Gladder can conclude his remarks and we can get a vote on this, that it will be taken care of."

Mr. Gladder concludes his remarks. We vote. His age amendment fails, so he withdraws his proposed military service tie-in, and that is that.

We now vote on the amendment to change the age from eighteen to nineteen, and the final result is 53 yea, 44 nay and 2 not voting. The Speaker orders HJR 6 engrossed to include the change to age nineteen. I am disappointed, but not crushed. This is a step in the right direction. We recess until 1 p.m. and I am instantly swarmed by 'my kids'. We move off the floor of the House to talk, and I explain as best I can, answering as rapidly as they fire off their questions and complaints.

"I know you're disappointed," I tell them. "But remember, you have good support in the Senate. It is entirely possible the final resolution will end up being an 18-year-old vote. No, that wasn't the final House vote — just a vote on the amended age. Yes, certainly the Senate can agree to age eighteen. Yes, the House could still re-vote. Yes, I understand your disappointment, but you should feel good about this."

After lunch, the House begins with a related bill on expanded 18-year-old rights and responsibilities. We discussed this at length as a House on a previous day. I speak in favor of it, along with two others. Four speak against it. We vote. It passes.

We return its sister measure to the floor, EHJR 6, hear five impassioned pleas on both sides, then pass by a vote of 73-24 this resolution to place on the 1970 general election ballot a constitutional change to the legal state voting age, reducing it from twenty-one to nineteen. It's off to the Senate.

When I arrive home tonight, I write a summary of the kids' campaign and address it to the *University Herald.* I am terribly proud of them.

By Friday, January 23, Day 12 of the special session, the House passes another major measure from our agenda: A more secure retirement plan for our state's law enforcement officers and firefighters.

AND THEN WE DIG IN TO ONE OF THE THORNIEST, sloppiest, most neglected issues on record: unemployment compensation, or UC — an issue that has nagged our state for years. Its political hot-buttons are so volatile, no majority has dared touch it… until now. Because the issue pits labor against business, and because most legislative districts in our state serve both, legislators and legislative leaders have historically turned a blind eye to UC, to avoid the crossfire, and to avoid alienating either big voting bloc — politically prudent, perhaps, but the result of this historic avoidance is that the people have paid a price.

By neglecting the matter, we now have one of the worst unemployment compensation systems in America. Our state ranks near the bottom of the U.S. in terms of quality, effectiveness, and actual dollars of compensation we pay, yet it ranks number four in the amount the program costs us! This is due to A) its myriad loopholes, B) the ability to easily double dip the system, and C) an unwarranted inequity between seasonal labor industries and steady employers — with both contributing to the system in the same amount. [12,13]

Our UC hearing in the initial week brought forth each familiar, long-standing complaint: The business side notes that stable industries and businesses pay into the system at the same rate as seasonal industries (a set dollar amount per man hours worked), which means that full-time, year-round employers essentially foot a major portion of the unemployment pay collected by seasonal workers — fishermen, loggers, canners, packers and agricultural workers during lengthy off-seasons, whereas the employers in those seasonal industries contribute much less.

Business's second complaint is that our state law requires a worker to earn only $800 in a calendar year in order to qualify for unemployment pay. As a result, our UC payrolls are disproportionately flooded with people who work a few weeks a year — for example, a person could work a month or two in a seasonal industry, or earn up to $800 in any job, after which, following a layoff, he or she could immediately begin to collect unemployment for the rest of the year. Ken has college students who work summers fishing in Alaska, are laid off at season's end, file for UC benefits, and use their unemployment comp to pay for their next year at school.

As for the double-dip, the way our current system works, certain employees can feasibly draw UC benefits for two consecutive calendar years without any intervening employment. Other loopholes that invite abuse include a lack of accounting for any pension pay received (when calculating the UC amount), and no waiting period after losing a job before state UC pay begins. That sums up the basic business complaints.

From labor's viewpoint, the dollar amount of our state's unemployment pay is far too low. The rate hasn't changed through the 1950's or 1960's, ever since the legislature began to turn a blind eye.

In summary, our system is completely inefficient.

This is not a sexy issue, nor is it politically appetizing, but it is a very real problem in our state and it needs resolution. We added it to our Blueprint back in 1963, and we've kept at it ever since. This legislative round, we're determined to finally right it.

On the heels of our UC joint hearing during week one, we are working hard to plug the loopholes, stem the abuses, raise the pay rate to a level reasonable for 1970, and reconfigure business contributions to the system on an 'earned credit' scale, something like this: Stable and/or year-round businesses (who send fewer employees into the system to collect UC pay) would pay into state UC coffers at a lesser rate than seasonal industries whose workers regularly fluctuate in and out of employment, and thus more frequently collect state UC pay. This graduated pay-in idea is a novel approach. It's also sensible.

Aerospace giant Boeing's recent addition to our state's unemployed helped bring this dialogue front and center. After decades of neglect, the revision of our state's illogical system of unemployment compensation is finally taking practical shape.

And so is another matter, one that did not appear on our original Blueprint but has increasingly captured the public eye and struck the public nerve center.

TWO YEARS AGO, AT OUR DINING ROOM TABLE, Ken and I were involved in an amiable after-dinner conversation with the three couples in our Great Books discussion group. This gathering is an extension of the Great Books program of study Ken and I joined at the University of Chicago during our grad school days — when dollars were scarce but intellect in good supply. When we moved to the University of Washington to accept his first faculty post as Dr. McCaffree, we soon found new University of Chicago friends among the faculty — the McIntyres, the Hognesses, and the Storers — and the tradition of reading and discussing (and dining) endured.

As hosts that particular month, Ken and I had invited one more couple — a practice the group had followed for years. Therefore, at the table with us that evening were Joel and Joan Pritchard.

As it happens, Don McIntyre is a physician and the head of Planned Parenthood in Seattle, and Ed Storer and John Hogness are both on the faculty at the UW Medical School. With this trio of physicians around the table, our conversation that evening ended up drifting to the topic of abortion.

Don shared ghastly cases that had come through his office — tragic patching he and colleagues regularly attempted on young women who'd had crude black market procedures, or worse, had tried to do it themselves. He talked to us at length about the medical community's concern. Abortion is illegal, here and throughout the U.S. for the most part. Physicians who use their medical training to do these procedures properly, or to help women whose non-medical abortions threaten their health or lives — these medical professionals risk losing their license to practice. For physicians, abortion posed a professional and ethical quandary.

Joel was taken with the issue — the plight of physician and patient both — and as a result of that dinner party,[14] he led a strong campaign in the Senate last year to legalize abortion, which drew both popular steam and fervent dissent.

On the day this Extraordinary Session began, a hundred or so picketers parked on our capitol steps, some urging us to revise our state's abortion laws, others urging us to keep abortion illegal.[15]

Joel has resumed his Senate campaign, Lois North is leading abortion reform in the House, and during this second Saturday we take it up formally on the floor. Not surprisingly, convictions run high. The divide is primarily religious. The many Catholics among us are against abortion reform, while others claim our current law is class discrimination, codified — that only wealthy women can afford the trips abroad to obtain abortions in the countries where it is legal.[16]

As it stands, our state law allows abortion only if the mother's life is in danger. We are now discussing changes to this law that we will present as a referendum to the people for their approval or rejection. We want our abortion law to reflect the statewide voice.

Democrat Dick Kink, a strong opponent of abortion, tells us he'll vote for the bill because he believes state voters should have the right to decide (echoes of our tax reform stance).

"I wish everybody felt the way I do about abortion," Dick said, "but they don't. I'll vote to pass this bill out of the legislature. But I'll vote against it at the polls."

After a long floor discussion, the House abortion rights referendum passes 60-36. And while there were certainly some emotionally charged moments on the floor, Speaker Eldridge thanks us for our high level of debate. And then he thanks us for our hard work in these first two weeks. We're behaving as a mature legislative body, it seems to me. Two weeks down, less than three to go.

MONDAY MORNING OF WEEK THREE, I ARRIVE AT MY OFFICE early, anticipating my secretary will have fielded a flood of calls on my 'yes' vote on abortion reform. A Western Union telegram is taped to my door: "Your vote for abortion was a vote against the ten commandments. Your vote favors killing of innocent human life. How can you reconcile this with your promises before your last election? Please do what you can to rectify this error in judgment." [17]

I take the telegram to my desk, and at the bottom of it write my secretary a note: *Please send the same letter we sent to all the other such persons.*

For more than a year now, I have received passionate words on both sides of this issue. And as with any divisive issue, I've given the matter of abortion both deep study and my equally deep thought. Ever since that dinner table discussion, I have read every abortion article that happens to cross my path. Our household subscribes to local and national newspapers, professional journals, newsmagazines, and we tune in regularly to public radio and public TV. My 'abortion' file contains dozens of clippings — editorials, an essay from *Time*, a *Christian Science Monitor* column called 'Let's Think', a research pamphlet from the Committee for the Protection of the Value of Human Life, the testimony transcript from when the president of the Washington State Medical Association spoke to our Senate Judiciary Committee and House Committee on Public Health and Welfare last spring, and of course… scores of constituent letters.

Those of my constituents who favor the right to an abortion have generally had personal exposure to the traumatic or tragic results of illegal procedures, or exposure to rape and incest victims who are doubly victimized by abortion's dangers – both physical and legal, have concerns about unwanted children or population growth. The medical community, as I first learned at my dinner table, is extremely supportive of legalizing abortion. They are loathe to break the law, but equally loathe to ignore the medical needs of the many endangered women who cross their professional paths. They've sworn a Hippocratic oath.

Those who oppose abortion, to be fair, hold thoroughly earnest convictions on the sanctity of human life, the sanctity of marriage and the sanctity of sex. As one constituent wrote me, "God doesn't change his commandments to suit man's immorality." [18]

When the issue entered our state legislative realm, I developed two formal responses, one to those who oppose legalized abortion, and another to those who favor this right.

For those who urge me to support reforming our state's abortion law, I thank them for understanding the need for this very important revision: "If passed, House Bill 116 will go a long way to assuring that necessary abortions are performed under professional circumstances, and eliminate many of the tragic situations which have resulted from our present laws."

Conversely, the author of this morning's telegram – like others who oppose abortion and lobby me – will receive a letter I have developed with real care:

"Thank you for your telegram expressing your views on House Bill 116…" (placing abortion reform on November's ballot). "I am pleased that all the people of Washington will have a chance to vote on this issue, for there are few things which arouse so much emotional response as the subject of abortion. It is an area of discussion which seems to have no absolutes, and people who are equally good, wise, trustworthy and honorable hold directly opposite views.

"My own conclusion to support this very controversial legislation was not lightly arrived at, and I understand very well the intensity of your feelings on this matter. The heartbreak of a violated mother, or worse, the terrible agony of the life ahead for the totally unwanted child, the real victim of this tragedy, has moved me to feel that this is good legislation and should become law. If this decision costs me your possible support, I feel that it is the price I must pay, for my conscience will not permit me to do less.

"I want you to know that I do respect you for having such a well-defined position on this very controversial issue, and I hope very much that even though we disagree, you can respect me for having mine." [19]

I place the annotated telegram on my secretary's desk and head to the House.

THE CLOCK ON WEEK THREE CONTINUES TO TICK. Today is day fifteen – the session's midpoint if we can keep it on track.

We are now primarily waiting on a pokey Senate.

They send us Senate Bill 2, which allows our courts to expedite cases on pollution control. This is one of the 'Crystal Mountain' six. But nothing else arrives. No more Senate measures. No Senate approval of House bills. By contrast, we've sent them dozens. Before this session began, House Republicans agreed we would keep things moving. So did the Senate, Democrats and Republicans alike. The governor is perturbed by their sluggishness. So are we.

WHILE WE AS A STATE LEGISLATURE ARE DEALING WITH state business, the Boeing Company continues to ask us to help them out with theirs. Struggling financially, they want a special exception via easement of their inventory tax. Because our tax structure here is premised on the property tax, inventory (early on) was defined as property, too, and subject to the property tax. However, our state budget is having a tough enough time as it is without also pardoning taxes.

"Sorry," says Senator Durkan, who still chairs Senate Ways and Means. "If there's going to be a reduction in the inventory tax, it has to be for all industries."

"What do you think about the Boeing request, Mrs. McCaffree?" asks Dick Larsen of the *Seattle Times*, balancing his report by asking the Revenue Committee chairman from the House as well.

"Well, Dick, even though we're sympathetic with their problem," I tell him, "there is simply no money to replace the lost revenue if we allowed it. If we get tax reform in the fall, however, we'll be on the road toward relieving this problem of the inventory tax." [20]

I emphasize our tax reform ballot vote at every possible turn.

Several mayors and county leaders swarm my office this afternoon.

"Mary Ellen, where's our local sales tax bill?"

"Do you realize how much red ink we're staring at, Mrs. McCaffree?"

"I am sympathetic," I tell them. I am. "But we're still trying to line up votes."

Until we're sure we can pass it, Stu and I agree we can't bring this bill out to floor of the House.

AFTER A QUICK START, OUR SESSION ACTIVITY SEEMS STALLED in every sector, an ominous echo of our disappointing finish in 1969. What was promoted as a dynamic session — one built around a slate of protections for the environment, one that had our citizens excited and full of hope — is now unfolding as more of the same: Ensnared in the political and stymied by the Senate.

Wednesday morning Shelby Scates of the *Seattle P-I*, ever sarcastic, ever cynical, pokes fun at our lost momentum, particularly on our heralded environmental bills: "This was supposed to be the session of the birdwatcher, the politics of Aquarius, where legislators were more concerned with environmental quality than economic royalty. You came down here looking for a Sierra Club pin on Senator Martin Durkan or seeing Senator Bob Greive in lederhosen with alpenstock. And 'after hours' might mean a nature walk through Tumwater Park... Two weeks of the process have elapsed and you begin to think of Ernest Hemingway's old fisherman. He has landed the magnificent giant marlin and is hauling it back to port, when sharks close in to strip it clean of all its flesh." [21]

I can't assess the accuracy of the hyperbolic Shelby Scates, who intimates that the business community is diluting our environmental protections or stripping them clean. We won't know if the flesh has really been stripped until the Senate sends these bills back to the House. But I am concerned. Our House leadership team is concerned. And so are Jim Dolliver and the governor.

By the end of the week, while the House continues to process major bills in our committees, to send them out to our floor for debate, to pass them and pass them along to the Senate, the imbalance remains: Very little is traveling in our direction from over there.

I don't know what else I can do to expedite legislation. I have personally seen to it that every bill the governor asked me to champion has safely traveled into its assigned committee for refinement and revision and out again — negotiated and ready for voting. It's a big workload for a legislator, but I have carried it.

By contrast, and by its nature, the Senate is slow.

On Friday, January 30, a single Senate measure arrives: Senate Bill 1, by executive request, to create a Department of Environmental Protection.

Before the session began, Senator Durkan asked for this bill. We agreed. Though the House had worked for two full sessions to define and delineate the scope of this new department, we agreed the bill could now originate and take shape in the Senate, since Senator Durkan was so enthused. The governor, too, was happy to oblige him.

Yet the Senate version delivered today contains a glaring glitch: A major administrative restructuring of the version we wrote. Part of our progressive agenda has aimed at restructuring our state government to function more efficiently. Central to this is the idea that the governor, as executive, should 'execute' or administer what the legislature designs, and this is key to many of our proposed administrative reforms. But the Senate has altered the leadership of this new department, from a director appointed by the governor and over whom the governor would have administrative control, to oversight by a community board, outside of executive reach. This the governor adamantly opposes.

Thus, by Friday of week three, we've received a whopping total of one major bill from our colleagues in the Senate, and this one major bill very likely won't work.

On Saturday, three more Senate measures arrive — one to create the Department of Social and Health Services (also by executive request, and also relinquished by the House to the Senate after all our previous sessions of detailed work), Joel's Senate version of abortion reform, and a Senate version of another of mine: An adjustment of property tax mills and assessed value.

Ten days remain and this session's agenda is enormously incomplete.

He's not happy, the governor tells the small group of us gathered today in his office. Despite all our pre-session planning, despite the fact that we've thoroughly worked through many of these measures two sessions already and in the Legislative Council, too, and despite the considerable support from the governor's staff (in writing and research), not a single bill has yet reached his desk.

"Most of these were executive request bills to begin with!" The governor's exasperation is clear. "We're two-thirds of the way through this session and nothing has moved."

He looks at Jim Dolliver. He looks at Joel. He looks at me. He looks at Esther Searing. And he spawns an idea. We refine it in a House leadership meeting, and in caucus early Monday morning, Norwood Cunningham introduces it in the form of a pep talk.

"You've worked hard, you're doing a terrific job, and each of you deserves credit for that, but here's the deal, Republicans. Mary Ellen?"

I've agreed to explain.

"Our number one focus, as leaders of this 41st Legislature, is to set this state on steady footing and set a solid future path. We've done a great job, putting all these major measures into play. Now we have to put them into law. We really need to wrap up this session.

"We've spoken with the governor. We've spoken among ourselves. And we've agreed on the following course of action, which may not sit well with all of you, but bear with me: Those of us who are committee chairmen need to stop holding up Senate bills in our committees. If they duplicate a House bill, set the House version aside and get that Senate version out on the floor. We'll be able to move things through faster."

I respond to my colleagues' groans.

"I know this is disappointing, especially to you who have worked so hard on your bills, but we're here to get a job done."

"Sacrifice. Straight up," says Stu. "From now on, when the Senate sends us their bills, buck up. We've gotta pass every Senate bill that's acceptable. Head 'em up, move 'em out. Yep, you're going to have to swallow your pride of authorship, and explain it later to the folks back home. But believe me, you guys and gals will be real heroes if we can finish in 30 days and finish this job. I'm sure your hometown voters will understand."

Pep talk complete, we take our seats on the floor, and our committee chairmen begin to bring forth a handful of measures from the Senate. The Senate bill to create a new Department of Social and Health Services: Recommended do pass. The Senate's more stringent bill on abortion: Recommended do pass. Two more of theirs from the environmental six: Thermonuclear power plant guidelines, and liberalized local bond financing for outdoor recreation. Do pass. Do pass. We send them all back to the Senate, approved. This should grease the legislative skids.

But forty-eight hours more go by. Nothing.

By Wednesday morning, the governor's desk remains empty. Seven days remain, and not one of the requested environmental bills is ready for his signature, so right after lunch, the governor hops in a car and drives to Seattle.

ON THE EVENING NEWS, ON KING-TV, THE GOVERNOR spends a full fifteen minutes on air, leveling his steady gaze at the camera and delivering viewers a public appeal: Wire your legislators — wire, not write, because time is short — and ask them, please, to save the state's environmental quality bills![22]

"It is time the public interests prevailed over private interests," he says, his remark shot dead aim at the business lobbyists putting pressure on the legislature to dilute or dash our protective measures.

From the start, our six environmental bills have been trapped in a standoff between the Washington Environmental Council and Washington Association of Business — WEC versus WAB. The Environmental Council followed through on its promise to work with our senators and to limit its legislative aim to the Crystal Mountain six. They've also been actively negotiating with the Washington Association of Business, but a balance between protection and profit has not yet been struck. The better-funded WAB still appears to be winning.

While the governor was driving Highway 5 north today to the studios of KING-TV, I was standing on the floor of the House, scalping the Senate's Department of Ecology Bill. I replaced it with the one we authored previously, per the governor's request. Our House version retains the Senate's department new moniker — 'Ecology' instead of 'Environmental Quality' — and preserves the Senate's bill number and sponsors: They'll get credit for this bill, if they accept it, along with their chosen department name. But we've reverted the department leadership structure, standing firm on the governor's original request for executive appointment and oversight.

Next on the day's agenda? The Senate's bill on abortion reform. A Call of the House locks us in. Lois North leads the debate. She favors the House's more liberal measure, whereas Maggie Hurley calls for even more restraint than that in the Senate bill. After many amendments and many votes, the bill is on final passage. For many, this is the most ethically-wrenching, personally agonizing vote they've ever cast. This is the first time I have ever seen male colleagues in tears on the floor. For so many, this is a choice between personal principle and the principle of allowing all voters their constitutional voice. In a sobering roll call, we vote 64-31 to send abortion reform to a vote of the people in November.

The next morning, Thursday, I arrive at my office early to find my desk buried beneath a sea of yellow telegrams, courtesy of Western Union. All down the hallway, I can hear my colleagues, incredulous at the same — we've all been walloped by a telegram tidal wave, and it's not about abortion.

The governor, it appears, was a sensation on prime time TV.

The public pressure is on to protect our planet, now.

I put in an early appearance on the floor, but must miss part of the action today due to yet another luncheon speaking engagement. With our state's economy so shaky, this governor's lead revenue legislator has been in demand: I have turned down many invitations to speak in these past several weeks, but accepted a few and today is one of those.

Today I'll miss placing votes on two of our major new departments: Ecology and Social and Health Services. But as Stu and Norwood reminded us, this session is all about getting the job done, not about whose name is where. I feel confident both measures have sufficient votes to pass, and I know that my constituents will understand. This will be a working lunch, to keep the business community up to date, and to put in one more plug for support for tax reform.

I do return in time to hear that an estimated 5,000 telegrams flooded the capitol today on the heels of the governor's televised plea. With this public pressure, our legislative floodgates have finally opened wide. But only a few days remain.

We've spent this entire week, Monday through Saturday — days 22 through 27 of 30 total — rigorously processing bills, passing them back and forth between chambers, into our committees and out again, subjecting them to thoughtful, detailed debate. Each measure is major, each crucial, but we're aware of the ticking clock. Therefore, whenever a bill begins to bog down on the floor, we defer it until later — later in the day or onto the next day's calendar — and instead take up one that is ready to readily pass.

One of my complex bills is thus deferred four days running, not that it is an impossible measure to pass, nor ill-crafted, but it will require more explanation than most. Therefore, each day when it comes before us, we move on to another bill we know we can pass more quickly.

The pace here is frantic... and sublime!

BY SATURDAY, FEBRUARY 7, A WEEK AFTER OUR GOVERNOR IMPATIENTLY tapped his pen on an empty desk, we have sent him approximately half of our major measures. Today, we hear that the Senate has passed two more: Our bill on Federal Metro Dollars for cities, and a new Washington State Trails System Act — another of the Crystal Mountain six.

In advance of this afternoon's session, I notify one of my special constituencies about a very special signing today, and they've packed the galleries, north and south, to witness it. The clerk reads: "House Joint Resolution 6, proposing a constitutional amendment to lower the state voting age to nineteen years, has been signed by the President of the Senate and returned herewith." He then hands it to the Speaker. Don Eldridge adds his signature, then leans to his microphone: "Will the sergeant at arms please deliver this to the office of the secretary of state?"

The gallery erupts in cheering, and I salute them, not noticing that behind me a trio of my Committee 18 has approached center aisle.

"Mrs. McCaffree?" Three beaming collegians hand me a giant bouquet of yellow roses. "We couldn't have done it without you!"

Two major constitutional measures now head to the 1970 general election ballot for a statewide vote: This voting age change, and the framework for tax reform, alongside our referendum on a liberalized abortion law — it's shaping up as an emotion-packed ballot-to-be.

SUNDAY IS AN OFFICIAL DAY OFF, BUT I FIRST SPEND TIME at the governor's mansion with our party's leadership team, reviewing the remaining bills and setting new strategy, followed by two hours more in the governor's office with leaders from both parties and both houses, again to take thorough stock of where we stand and where we still must go. If we are to finish this session in thirty days, as resolved, we have two days in which to do it.

We focus, House and Senate both, all wanting this session to end on time, but not without success — we aim to complete our entire agenda. While we work on our respective floors and within our respective committees, the governor and his staff circulate among us, promoting their supplemental budget, taking our pulse, gathering feedback, negotiating and redrafting in response. The governor's budget team faces a tough analytical task: State revenue forecasts are fluctuating wildly, and the trend indicates a definite trajectory south. State unemployment has escalated to double digits, state revenues continue to drop and companies from the behemoth Boeing on down are struggling. The governor incessantly calculates. What will it take to get us through?

On Day 29, a Monday, the House addresses the Senate-amended oil spill bill. We accept their changes and pass it: 69-29, ready for signatures all around. Another vote of relative consensus.

Our earlier near-unanimous votes, though, which had signaled solid team-work, seem to be disappearing. I suspect I know why. As this session has progressed, more and more of my colleagues are having trouble making up their minds — politically fearful of taking a solid stand. They know the public is watching us. They realize their re-elections loom. They're weighing their votes for political reasons — *If I vote in this way, which constituent bloc do I stand to gain or lose? Who else is voting for this bill? Will it pass without my vote?* I frankly find their hesitation disappointing. We came here to do a job for our state, not for our personal political futures. What they should be asking is, *Is this best for the most?*

Today the Senate sends us those major bills they passed to us earlier, on the Trails System Act and Federal Metro Development Dollars, both unmodified, both signed by the Senate president, both ready for our Speaker to sign and send to the governor for his signature into law. Later, the leaders of both houses sign another two major bills all around: One on county open space and recreation, the other liberalizing the process for outdoor recreation bond issues. We send these to the governor, too. We've completed debate on four of the six environmental bills now, plus one major revenue measure, but... on Tuesday, Day 30 and theoretically our last, the pervasive mood in the House is low.

We won't make our deadline.

Right after opening formalities, we advance to the 11th order of business — announcements — and among the measures sent us by the Senate is my bill on open space property tax adjustments and administration: Amended. Upon review, we deem it acceptable and pass it 82-8. We also send the oil spill bill to the governor. With the exception of a Shoreline Management Act, which still concedes too much to developers, the environmental package is falling into place.

I finally lead two protracted floor debates on those bills we've deferred for days on end in favor of simpler legislation. We can avoid them no longer. As a House we discuss the property tax mill bill (which seems fine), and then our bill on the local sales tax, which the Senate has substantially changed. We cannot concur and send it back: Please recede therefrom.

The Senate, meanwhile, accepts our changes to their thermonuclear power plant bill and their county assessment bill. These two get signed all around, along with the bill to expedite court cases that deal with pollution control.

Near the end of Day 30, we're closing in on our session goals, but time is running out. We call a quick recess and the leadership group meets in the Speaker's office, where we quickly draft House Concurrent Resolution 8 to limit our special session to 32 days. We pass it, send it to the Senate, and they return it without argument. We have forty-eight hours more.

But we are caught up on the Department of Ecology Bill.

The Senate refuses to concur with our House amendments — my scalp that returned the governor's oversight. We take it into conference committee, and there we get nowhere at all.

We overflow into Day 31 and then into Day 32.

By now, even the governor's much-debated supplemental budget has passed.

Some version of agreement has been struck on nearly every major bill, and most have collected the requisite set of leadership signatures to become new law. The cities and counties have their sales tax — half a cent — which we finally settled, after the governor, the legislature, the public and even the press pressured Seattle Mayor Wes Uhlman: Please accept less than 1 percent, for the sake of passing this bill. Unemployment compensation is in good shape. Our young people's voting-age change is ballot bound. Our revenue reforms are ready, our environmental protections in place, and we now have a new Department of Social and Health Services to streamline myriad agencies that serve the people.

Only one item remains: Senate Bill 1, the Department of Ecology.

The conference committee having failed to reach consensus, we move into a free conference committee, take a deep breath, swallow political pride, and finally agree on a bill we know will pass muster with our legislative colleagues, with the governor and with our voters back home. We write it up, send it first to the Senate, and then it arrives in the House. It is ready.

We bring this final bill to its final vote in the House of Representatives, and ninety percent of us dare to take one last stand: We pass the Department of Ecology bill 89-1, with nine not voting.

IN THIRTY-TWO DAYS WE HAVE APPROVED AND PASSED into law 115 measures, an incredible feat considering that by Day 20 not one was yet complete. More remarkable, however, is the nature of each. These were no small laws, no pet bills of minimal significance, but major reforms — dramatic, sweeping, complex change that will fashion a better state, to the benefit all of the wonderful people who call this beautiful corner of the country home.

I could not be more proud.

I watch from my seat in the House as the sergeant at arms swings wide the doors to our chamber. I rise with my colleagues and turn to face the spacious rotunda, past the glimmer that dances from the grand chandelier, past the bronze medallioned George in the marbled floor with his nose rubbed snubby, and beyond, through those other doors swinging wide to the Senate, where the senators rise and greet us in return at the end of this whirlwind month-long Extraordinary Session. Our two leaders raise their gavels, and in unison we are resolute in our final legislative pronouncement of othe 41st Session: *Sine die!*

Our voices echo, then fade to silence.

WITHOUT A DOUBT, THIS EXTRAORDINARY SESSION is the 'crown jewel' of my legislative career. Not only did we meet our goal of a swift, efficient session, but we did so with immense civility and great care for the people of this state. Our list of accomplishments and trend-setting legislation is truly extraordinary — well in advance of the national curve, and bold in tackling sticky issues that languished too long in legislative neglect.

The status quo governs us no more.

Thanks to our determination and persistence, this behemoth ship of state has finally changed course. We've provided our state a positive, progressive stance from which it can act: Today to battle a declining economy, and from here on out to ably respond to our citizens' needs.

In just thirty-two days, we have passed:

- The nation's first governmental department devoted entirely to environmental protection, preceding even Congress's contemplated protection agency for the whole U.S.

- Protection of air and water quality, open spaces and wilderness areas, and regulation of oil spills, effluent standards, strip mining and nuclear power plants, all in the national forefront.

- A revolutionary system of unemployment compensation that includes our innovative 'earned credit' system of graduated pay-in for stable industries, cost-of-living adjusted benefits, and — perhaps most importantly — an end to both partisan bickering and the feuding between business and labor that kept our system grossly inefficient and costly for more than a decade.

- Abortion legalization, subject to voter approval — potentially the first in the nation. We join a half dozen other states at the forefront of this issue's expanding national debate.

- A lowered voting age, to nineteen while the national age is twenty-one. We also granted these young people majority status, linking increased-citizen responsibilities to increased citizen rights.

- A complete reorganization of the social and health services in our state by pulling together under a single departmental roof programs, resources and expertise. In the same vein, we passed such complementary measures as licensing standards for nursing home administrators and more productive programs for the adoption of children, for convicts, for the developmentally disabled and for the mentally ill.

- The innovative authorization of a local government sales tax — a nod to local control and in progressive recognition of the increasing needs of our state's densely populated urban areas, which had been ignored by prior legislatures during two decades of tremendous growth.

- Other legislation of major significance for the health and welfare of our state's citizens: A broadened consumer protection act, an improved retirement system for our law enforcement officers and firefighters, regulation of factory-built housing, an extension of the B & O tax to all financial institutions, a revised criminal code, a new drug control agency, millage limits and other adjustments to how we administer property tax.

For this extraordinary month we managed to successfully set aside partisan politics. The spirit of cooperation we established worked miracles. So many major groundbreaking accomplishments in so short a time — these are the fruits of a legislature that sought to serve the people's interests first.

Our House leadership, in particular, kept our eye on the statewide ball. We set aside 'pet' bills, kept our committee system unclogged by these and therefore free for those matters of most importance. We also willingly allowed the Senate (and that meant mostly Democrats — not only the other legislative body but the other party as well!) to sponsor our most important bills, if it meant a speedier passage. Our meticulous pre-planning paid off: Setting priorities, setting a schedule, sticking to it and working so closely in tandem with the Senate. The first week's joint House and Senate committee hearings in particular really helped us set the rapid pace, allowing us to dive deep into the major issues (many of them familiar from our previous work), with the entire legislature working from the very same page, right from the start.

Undoubtedly, we also benefited from being together a third time running, drawing on relationships we forged during two previous sessions last year. All told, we were able to operate as a finely tuned legislative body — perhaps our state's finest ever.

The governor is due some credit for this session's elevated character and success, even though he is not an official component of the legislature. His respect for the legislative process, his clear agenda, and his willingness to listen and cooperate all played a role in our accomplishments. Governor Evans consciously spent much of his hard-earned political capital to convene us, undaunted by the risk of his very public appeal for statewide support of our time-critical work.

Several items do remain incomplete, ready for the next legislature to address anew: A cohesive Department of Transportation, tighter gambling controls and an effective Shoreline Management Act, to name three. But as a whole, we've made tremendous strides.

We took charge as elected leaders, we met our state's many challenges, and we demonstrated to doubters that with the combination of a clear agenda and a proper arena for civil debate, this representative government of ours is capable of responding to needs, particularly when the people's interest supersedes individual politicking or party political play.

I won't claim there was no partisan pull in these 32 days, but partisanship played a subdued second fiddle — its rightful role.

THIS 1970 SESSION OF THE 41ST LEGISLATURE of Washington State serves as a modern model — living proof that a trio of our most fundamental legislative elements really can work: Cooperation, public service and good will.

I join many others in the belief that this Extraordinary Session of 1970 was extraordinary in every sense of the word, and perhaps the most productive in the history of our state. I am thrilled and honored to have played a part.

This time, at *sine die*, each one of us can go home satisfied. We've silenced the skeptics, astonished the press, and the citizens of our state can no longer doubt we are capable of truly serving them... or that we truly care.

With the closing of the Special Session of the Washington State Legislature, it is safe to say it was an historic session — historic in that the most effective pressure group in operation was the general public...

The legislators found they must give the public what it wants... that merely responding to the special interests will not substitute for acting in the public interest.

EDITORIAL, FEBRUARY 15, 1970
THE SEATTLE POST-INTELLIGENCER

EPILOGUE

THE CALIBER OF OUR GOVERNMENT — its integrity, its relevance, how well it responds to our needs — really is up to us, as citizens.

We singled out this slice of political history because it provides us a perfect microcosm for taking a good, close look at how many ways we may each insert our voice. Rarely has a government transformed so thoroughly in so few years. Rarely have citizens accomplished change so swiftly, and to such enduring effect. By viewing this decade through a real legislator's lens, we've been able to share the experience of a government operating at its optimum.

Politics of the Possible confirms our government is powered by the people. And yet, while relationships drive our governmental process, this human element is far too often absent from what we learn in civics class or glean from the news.

We focused on the relationships within the process to show what works: Teamwork. Courage. Bi-partisanship. Citizen input. A responsible eye on the future. A realistic eye on the day. Serious study. Earnest problem solving. Fiscal pragmatism. Durable solutions.

Governing is extremely serious work.

We also showed what doesn't work — public servants forgetting they've been elected to solve problems, combined with a public that is apathetic or unaware, and therefore not holding our leaders to task.

Finally, we showed the demands of a family person serving in public office, a public servant working on behalf of American families.

Some things are admittedly different since the 1960's:

- **Technology** has created both boon and confusion — a whole new world of instant communication, but also information overload, insufficient sound bites and increasingly fuzzy facts.

- **Political campaign budgets** are exorbitant, calling into question whether a run for political office is really open to all, or whether greater voice is available to the moneyed.

- **Our media is less neutral**, increasingly reporting on government from the fringes of the political spectrum, and increasingly blurring the line between opinion and fact.

- **Our media is also diverting us** from our state and local governments by covering almost exclusively what's going on in Washington, D.C. Our states govern the bulk of what affects our daily lives. Too much federal focus robs us of a valuable connection — the elected and electorate working together locally to preserve our quality of life, closer to home.

What hasn't changed in forty years, or in the two hundred years-plus since its founding, is our governmental process — our hero. When we understand how this process works, or should work, we have the power and the tools to keep it on course, to productively lead and legislate real change.

TO UPDATE THE HISTORIC DECADE IN *Politics of the Possible*, we took a quick look at this state's legislature forty years forward and found some encouraging new gems amid the familiar.

On day two of the 2010 session, school buses lined the capitol drive and the galleries were packed to hear the governor deliver her State of the State address in the full House chamber: Senators seated in extra chairs among the ninety-nine representatives' desks — the newer members in the back near the water fountains, focused and taking notes, while the nine robed state supreme court justices sat up front (four women, five men — the chief justice female).

Let's make 'good business decisions, not political ones,' said the governor. State citizens didn't have to be at the capitol to hear her. Technology, in its positive mode, has amplified public access to what's going on here:

- TVW, Washington's Public Affairs TV station dedicated to capitol news, broadcasts floor sessions, events and committee hearings we can view live or later, via streaming video on either of two websites — the station's or the legislature's — as well as on cable channels throughout the state. (Or you can still actually, versus virtually, attend.)

- We can also use the legislature's website to easily track bills — by topic, sponsor, title, number, status, or we can flag certain measures for instant updates. We can click on cross-referenced legislative rosters: House members, Senate members, Republicans, Democrats, specific commit-tees or districts. The site posts calendars and agendas daily and in advance. Other legislatures have similar Internet access.

- Email, cell phones, all versions of device and transmission now known and forthcoming make staying in touch with legislators today easy. One-on-one contact has never been easier.

Though the state capitol press corps has shrunk, symptomatic of a news industry in transition, a push for a non-profit corps of legislative journalists—to keep state news flowing to local communities—is in the works: Something for citizens here to contemplate. As for the campaign dollar question, many legislators here continue to rely on 'one-on-one'. Doorbell campaigning is not extinct, nor is the coffee-hour, although it's no longer coffee centric.

IN SO MANY WAYS, IT'S EASIER TODAY to stay in touch and involved. But we can just as easily ignore what's going on in government. The choice is ours. The challenge is real.

How do we navigate the tidal wave of unfiltered, often uncorroborated Internet reports when we want to learn more about a candidate or issue? How can we comprehend complex matters with only sound bite or tweet? What's the best way to gather facts in full detail? And how do we find enough time to weigh the crucial, when new facts and slants bombard us 24/7, and we're already working full time and caring for our families?

The answer is both simple and demanding: Since we cannot fully participate as citizens if we have only partial or partisan understanding, we must take an active role in informing ourselves. We must seek out alternate views, consider each source, filter the false or distracting, weigh all sides, weigh today against the long term, and then... make up our own minds.

Ours is not a passive citizenship.

When we understand the design, intent and process of our government, then we know the distinctions between federal, state and local, and can see to it each governs as prescribed, neither shirking nor usurping: Each has a role. We respect and expect the separation of powers, and safeguard the freedoms and equalities we're all guaranteed. When we're knowledgeable about government, we can't be manipulated or misled. We know what to do when we're not being served.

"There is but one element of government and that is the people. From this springs all government," said John Adams.[1]

Thomas Jefferson agreed, but with qualification: "Whenever the people are well-informed, they can be trusted with their own government."[2]

Abigail Adams added a pragmatic truth, as cogent then as now: "Learning is not attained by chance, it must be sought for with ardor and attended to with diligence."[3]

Freedom remains a big responsibility.

A quick follow through on tax reform.

After all the ballots were counted following Washington State's general election in 1970, the tally showed the voters had approved the proposed constitutional amendment to allow for a state income tax... in only a single district: 32A. This is where Representative McCaffree had continued to conduct a steady dialogue with her constituents on the details of the novel tax reform plan — every consequence and benefit, every merit and potential demerit, answering each question, explaining each unclear point. The people were an integral part of this process of reforming the state revenue base. Mary Ellen, as a leader, kept them in the loop and followed through. We need more such dedicated public servants.

To this day, Washington State continues to struggle with its tax structure minus an income tax, as does its neighbor Oregon without a sales tax, both hobbled by two-legged revenue stools, especially when economies drag. The word 'tax' remains politically precarious, but taxation — ideally intelligent and fair — is how our governments fund their function, which is serving us. Tax study may be dry, but it is essential. And tax we must. Our leaders need to acknowledge this frankly, and as a public we need to, too.

JUST AS EVERY EPOCH OF UNREST BECKONS our best and brightest into action — from our founding revolution, through civil war, the Great Depression, civil rights fights and 1960's revolt — the range of change demanded here during the decade of *Politics of the Possible* attracted problem solvers to public office. They entered politics to make a difference.

The main players from both parties were true public servants and continued to serve — all have impressive public resumés well beyond 1970 to confirm this. A most recent example is Mary Ellen's ninth decade, devoted to writing this book aimed at nudging newer generations of Americans to engage.

We hope every new era of change continues to attract Americans to contribute their best. The system of government in place in our country is pure genius in its design. It can bend and flex and change with the times and allows us to explore bold solutions. Our challenge is this: If we want our government to continue to respond to our changing needs as they evolve, we must be involved. Our citizenship doesn't end with our vote. It doesn't end with complaint.

As they watched their grandmother work on this manuscript, and as they read her words, Mary Ellen's grandchildren have grown less detached from their government... and ours. While they feel no obligation to mimic their grandmother's footsteps precisely, they are searching out citizen pathways of their own, integral to their daily lives.

Paige put her law degree to work in a lower income community: Widely traveled, she was touched by the globe's impoverished, and specialized in international law, but then, following her grandmother's advice, she put passion into practice closer to home. Shayna, a mental health counselor for adolescents at risk, lobbies for public support for better mental health services for urban teens. Stacey, too, lobbies for support for the educational marine biology program she manages at a municipal zoo. Carey, the geologist-turned-mom who proclaimed no time for politics and government, is nevertheless adding quality to her local public schools as a volunteer science teacher in her children's classrooms. Jessica has combined her interest in photojournalism and global concerns into her freelance work for the Gates Foundation and its mission of global health. Ryland's work with his church serves his community in multiple manners. Leif is a municipal firefighter. Ingrid, now involved in children's health care in her hometown, had an epiphany when she read in our prologue, 'Many confuse capitalism with democracy'. During three extended trips to China, she'd seen the clear distinction: Capitalism is rampant there, democracy largely non-existent. Until she read her grandmother's words, however, the twain hadn't clicked.

As for Alison, recipient of her grandmother's long ago letter on the two-party system — Alison took a break between jobs to provide legwork and some research for our book. By the time she was done, she knew the difference between a legislature and Congress, between a Call for the Previous Question and a Call of the House. She accepted the helm of a local non-profit that provides technology to other non-profits, a post that led her to climb those same marbled steps her grandmother first ascended fifty years earlier. She was at the capitol to testify at a legislative hearing on community technology funding. Every day thereafter, she used the Internet to trace the technology bill through the legislative process. As the bill journeyed through the Senate and House — in and out of committees and onto the floor — she lobbied legislators via email each step of the way, targeting those who were best positioned to keep the bill alive.

"How do you know so much about how this all works?" a colleague asked, impressed.

Alison confided the truth: "I learned it all from my grandmother."

It's your turn to serve, Mary Ellen tells her grandchildren today.
It's up to us all.

NOTES

Throughout this book, proceedings described on the floor of the House on specific days within each legislative session have been adapted uniformly from the records of each session's House Journal, including actual statements made on the floor. Accordingly, we have cited by page only extended or key statements. In addition, the Legislative Manual of the State of Washington, published each of the four sessions, confirmed House and Senate session rules, leadership posts, and committee memberships and chairmanships. We also consulted each session's legislative member directory (with photos and bios), published by the Office of the Secretary of State. And finally, as a source of general information throughout, we consulted the oral histories of Joel M. Pritchard, James M. Dolliver, Don Eldridge, R.R. Greive, Thomas L. Copeland and Robert Goldsworthy, each published as part of the Washington State Oral History Program, under the direction of the Office of the Secretary of State.

CHAPTER ONE: THE GAVEL

1 *House Journal of the 38th Legislature of the State of Washington* (Olympia, 1963), 3.

2 Ibid.

3 Robert R. Greive, *R.R. Greive: An Oral History*, interviewed and edited by Sharon Boswell, Washington State Oral History Program, Office of the Secretary of State (Olympia, 2001), 131.

4 *Legislative Members Log, State of Washington*, roster of the members of the state legislature by district from 1889 to 1999, revised and published by Mike O'Connell, Secretary of the Senate, Timothy A. Martin, Chief Clerk of the House of Representatives (Olympia, 1997, 2001), 11.

5 Gordon E. Baker, *The Politics of Reapportionment in Washington State; Case Studies in Practical Politics* (New York: Holt, Rinehart and Winston, 1960). Variations in population and representation by district for 1930, 1950 and 1957 are charted in this book.

6 *Thigpen v. Meyers*, 211 F. Supp. 826, 830 (W.D. Wash. 1962). Population and representation data for the 1960s are presented in the text and appendices of the decision written by Judge William T. Beeks.

7 "How The Proposed Initiative Improves Legislative Representation In Your State," pamphlet, League of Women Voters of Washington, Seattle, 1964.

8 Norman J. Johnston, *Washington's Audacious State Capitol and Its Builders* (Seattle: University of Washington Press, 1988).

9 Daniel J. Evans, "Some Reflections on My 39 years in Washington State Politics and Governments," *Washington Comes of Age: The State in the National Experience*, ed. David H. Stratton (Pullman: Washington State University Press, 1992).

10 Daniel J. Evans, interview by Anne McNamee Corbett, author's notes, Seattle, October 2006.

11 Joel M. Pritchard, *Joel M. Pritchard: An Oral History*, interviewed by Anne Kilgannon, Washington State Oral History Program, Office of the Secretary of State (Olympia, 2000), 98.

12 Gordon E. Baker, *Rural Versus Urban Political Power* (New York: Random House, 1955), 4. The original citation is from a letter from Thomas Jefferson to William King, November 19, 1819, Jefferson Papers, Library of Congress, Vol. 216, 38616.

13 *Legislative Members Log*, ibid.

14 Office of Financial Management, State of Washington, "Population by City and County: 1890 to 2000," http://www.ofm.wa.gov/databook/population/pt01.asp

15 *Greive Oral History*, 114, 123.

16 Baker, *The Politics of Reapportionment*, 4.

17 Baker, *The Politics of Reapportionment*, ibid. A detailed description and analysis of the writing and certification of Initiative 199 for the 1956 election, as well as its political and legislative consequences.

18 Baker, *Rural Versus Urban Political Power*, 26.

19 *Baker v. Carr*, 369 U.S. 186 (1962).

20 *Thigpen v. Meyers*, 211 F. Supp. 826 (W.D. Wash. 1962).

21 Ibid., 833

22 Ruth Pelz, *The Washington Story: A History of Our State*, Revised Edition (Seattle: Seattle Public Schools, 1979), 137-9.

23 *House Journal of the 38th Legislature*, ibid., 5.

24 Ibid., 6, 7, 8.

25 Ibid., 9, 10.

26 Ibid., 10, 11, 12.

CHAPTER TWO: COALITION

1 *1963 Legislative Manual of the State of Washington*, Joint Rules, Rules of the Senate and Rules of the House of the 38th Legislature (Olympia, 1963), 342.

2 *House Journal of the 38th Legislature*, ibid., 20.

3 Ibid., 23.

4 *Senate Journal of the 38th Legislature of the State of Washington* (Olympia, 1963), 22.

5 *House Journal of the 38th Legislature*, ibid., 45.

6 Editorial: "GOP's Showing At Olympia Dismal," *Daily Chronicle* (Spokane), January 15, 1963.

7 John Komen, "O'Brien Sees Demo Victory Next Time Out," *Tacoma News Tribune*, January 15, 1963.

8 *Senate Journal of the 38th Legislature*, ibid., 38.

9 C.E. Johns, "Dissident Democrats of Spokane Area, North Idaho Should Have Formed New State," *Tacoma News Tribune*, January 15, 1963.

10 *House Journal of the 38th Legislature*, ibid., 83-84.

11 Ibid., 111-112.

12 Mary Ellen McCaffree, "Legislative Memo to 32nd District Constituents," author's private collection, January 25, 1963.

CHAPTER THREE: CHANGING TIMES

1 Jack Pyle, "When Good, He Was Very Very Good But When Bad, 'T' Was Horrid," *Tacoma News Tribune*, April 7, 1963.

2 Joe Rigert, "38th Legislature Bit Below Average," *Associated Press*, March 17, 1963.

3 Abigail Adams to John Adams, March 31, 1776, from The Liz Library, "Letters Between Abigail Adams and Her Husband John Adams," http://www.thelizlibrary. org/suffrage/abigail.html.

4 Ibid., John Adams to Abigail Adams, April 14, 1776.

5 *Thigpen v. Meyers*, 231 F. Supp. 938, 939 (W.D. Wash. 1964).

6 Hugh A. Bone, "Washington," *Impact of Reapportionment on the Thirteen Western States*, ed. Eleanor Bushnell (University of Utah Press, 1970), 285, 288.

7 National Governors Association, "1960 - 1969," nga.org, http://www.subnet.nga. org/centennial/timeline/1960.htm.

8 Bone, ibid., 288.

9 "Mrs. McCaffree Honored as Mother of Year in U. District for '63," *University District Herald*, May 8, 1963.

10 Mary Ellen McCaffree to 32nd District Republican Club, speech, Seattle, author's private collection, 1963.

11 Court's Oral Opinion, 5597 federal file, 1 (W. D. Wash. 1964).

12 Bone, ibid.

13 *Thigpen v. Meyers*, ibid.

14 James M. Dolliver, *James M. Dolliver: An Oral History*, interviewed and edited by Norman H. State (Olympia, 1999), 100.

15 *Thigpen v. Meyers*, ibid.

16 *Dolliver Oral History*, 99.

17 C. Montgomery Johnson, "What Shall I Tell My Party About Politics?" Chapter 5: The Engineer and His Blueprint, unpublished manuscript, Accession 5146-1, Box 3, *C. Montgomery Johnson Papers*, Special Collections Division, University of Washington Libraries, Seattle.

18 Ibid.

19 *Dolliver Oral History*, 13.

20 Daniel J. Evans, interview, ibid.

21 Bone, ibid., 288, 289.

22 *Meyers v. Thigpen et al.*, 376 U.S. 902 (1964).

23 *Reynolds v. Sims*, 377 U.S. 533 (1964).

24 *Meyers v. Thigpen et al.*, 378 U.S. 554 (1964).

25 Bone, ibid., 289.

26 *Thigpen v. Meyers*, ibid.

27 Ibid., 939, 940.

28 Ibid., 942.

29 Ibid.

30 Mary Ellen McCaffree to constituents, author's private collection, July 17, 1963.

31 Slade Gorton, interview by Anne McNamee Corbett, author's notes, Seattle, October 2006.

32 Bone, ibid., 290.

33 Daniel J. Evans to Mary Ellen McCaffree, author's private collection, May 5, 1963.

34 Editor, "Dan Evans, That's Who," *Time*, November 13, 1964.

35 Trudy Weckworth, "Mary Ellen McCaffree works for youth, educational needs," *Wallingford Outlook* (Seattle), October 29, 1964.

CHAPTER FOUR: COMPROMISE

1 Editor, "Dan Evans, That's Who", ibid.

2 *House Journal of the 39th Legislature of the State of Washington* (Olympia, 1965), 14.

3 *House Journal of the 39th Legislature*, ibid., 15.

4 Dean Foster to Anne McNamee Corbett, e-mail, December 2, 2009.

5 Ralph Munro, interview by Anne McNamee Corbett, Poulsbo, WA, November 2006.

6 Richard W. Larson, "It Happened One Night - Almost - to Evans," *Seattle Times*, January 10, 1977.

7 *House Journal of the 39th Legislature*, ibid., 43.

8 Poem, private collection of Mary S. McCaffree Johnston.

9 *House Journal of the 39th Legislature*, ibid., 58.

10 Ibid., 60-65.

11 Ibid., 94.

12 *Senate Journal of the 39th Legislature of the State of Washington* (Olympia, 1965), 1601.

13 Charles Dunsire, "In the Year 2015," *Seattle Post-Intelligencer*, January 27, 1965.

14 Adele Ferguson, "Legislators Face Working Weekend," *Bremerton Sun*, January 13, 1965.

15 *House Journal of the 39th Legislature*, ibid., 195-202.

16 *Greive Oral History*, ibid., 167.

17 *House Journal of the 39th Legislature*, ibid., 261.

18 Ibid., 262.

19 *Senate Journal of the 39th Legislature*, ibid., 1602-4.

20 *House Journal of the 39th Legislature*, ibid., 339.

21 Slade Gorton, interview, ibid.

22 *Greive Oral History*, ibid., 164.

23 *House Journal of the 39th Legislature*, ibid., 432.

CHAPTER FIVE: PERSEVERANCE

1 *House Journal of the 39th Legislature*, ibid., 952.

2 Ibid., 999-1000.

3 Bob Houston, "Suddenly It Hit; Big Story Is Here," *Daily Olympian*, April 29, 1965.

4 Dick Lawrence, "Earthquake Closes Legislative Session," ibid.

CHAPTER SIX: THE CHALLENGE

1 The "Team" consisted of varying combinations of people who worked with Dan Evans over the years: Joel and Frank Pritchard, Jim Dolliver, Slade Gorton, Ritajean Butterworth, Mary Ellen McCaffree, Bill Bell (Nancy Evans' brother), Chuck Moriarty, Marshall Neill, C. Montgomery 'Gummie' Johnson, John Hayden,and from time to time and from place to place other individuals such as the Reed family from Spokane, the Fite family in Seattle, Herb Hadley from Longview, Stuart Elway from Olympia, and Helen Rasmussen, Jay Gilmour and Dan and Marilyn Ward in Seattle. Others too numerous to list supported and worked for Dan Evans and shared and promoted his philosophy of progress and desire to change the direction of state government in Washington State.

2 John J. O'Connell to Federal District Court, *Thigpen v. Meyers*, Federal File 5597, 1965.

3 Bone, ibid., 295.

4 Temporary Advisory Council on Public Higher Education, "Report on Higher Education in Washington" (Olympia, October 1966).

5 C. Montgomery Johnson, ibid., Chapter 7: From the beginning... Birch, 20.

6 Sterling Green, "Right-Wingers Marshalling Men and Money for 1966 Elections," *Seattle Post-Intelligencer*, April 4 1965.

7 Roland Evans and Robert Novak, "Inside Report: The Birch Boom," *Philadelphia Inquirer*, August 20, 1965.

8 Daniel J. Evans, "The Winter of Our Discontent," transcript of Port Angeles address, (Olympia: Republican State Central Committee of Washington, September 10, 1965).

9 *Dolliver Oral History*, ibid., 23.

10 Daniel J. Evans, interview, ibid.

11 C. Montgomery Johnson, "The Challenge for Responsible Conservatives," mimeograph, (Olympia: Republican State Central Committee of Washington, September 1965).

12 C. Montgomery Johnson, "Challenge," ibid.

13 Daniel J. Evans, interview, ibid.

14 Herb Robinson, "Courage Shown by Evans," *Seattle Times*, September 12, 1965.

15 Temporary Advisory Council on Public Higher Education, ibid.

16 Mary Ellen McCaffree to campaign school enrollees, Accession 5146-001, Box 26, Folder: "Campaign Advisory Committee 1966," *C. Montgomery Johnson Papers*, Special Collections Division, University of Washington Libraries, Seattle.

17 Nelson Associates, Inc., *Planning for Higher Education Needs in the State of Washington: A Report to the Temporary Advisory Council on Public Higher Education*, (New York, 1966).

18 Trudy Weckworth, ibid.

19 Temporary Advisory Council on Public Higher Education, ibid.

20 Bone, ibid., 284, 302.

21 Betty Hopper, "Mary Ellen McCaffree Is Gal Who Gets Job Done," *Daily Olympian*, January 18, 1967.

CHAPTER SEVEN: LEADERSHIP

1 *House Journal of the 40th Legislature of the State of Washington*, (Olympia, 1967), 15.

2 *Senate Journal of the 40th Legislature of the State of Washington*, (Olympia, 1967), 46.

3 Mike Layton, "No Miracles, But Hints of New Taxes," *Daily Olympian*, January 11, 1967.

4 Shelby Scates, "Evans' Blueprint for State Applauded By Both Sides," *Seattle Post-Intelligencer*, January 12, 1967.

5 *Senate Journal of the 40th Legislature*, ibid. 62.

6 Bobbi McCallum, "Kitchen Kicked for Caucus," *Seattle Post-Intelligencer,* January 12, 1967.

7 Shelby Scates, "Democrats Stiff-Arm Evans' Budget," *Seattle Post-Intelligencer*, January 13, 1967.

8 Betty Hopper, "Mrs. McCaffree Sets Busy Pace for Solons," *Tacoma News Tribune*, January 18, 1967.

9 *House Journal of the 40th Legislature*, ibid., 168.

10 Ibid., 170.

11 Don Burrows, "The Economics and Politics of Taxation in Washington: From Governor Elisha Ferry in 1889 to Governor Christine Gregoire in 2006, Including a Critique of Current Tax Issues and the Income Tax Question," unpublished manuscript, 2006.

12 Don Burrows, interview by Mary Ellen McCaffree and Anne McNamee Corbett, authors' notes, February 9, 2008.

13 Tax Advisory Council of the State of Washington, *Proposals for Changes in Washington's Tax Structure* (Olympia, December 1966).

14 *Senate Journal of the 40th Legislature*, ibid., 107.

15 "Suggested Copy for 'Olympia Report' newspaper columns," (Olympia: House Republican Publicity Office, February 3, 1967).

16 Bobbi McCallum, "Tax Reform is Left in Lady Legislator's Lap," *Seattle Post-Intelligencer*, February 14, 1967.

17 Shelby Scates, "Evans Lectures on Taxes," *Seattle Post-Intelligencer*, February 17, 1967.

18 Shelby Scates, "House Committee Approves Evans' Tax Bill," *Seattle Post-Intelligencer*, February 26, 1967.

19 Shelby Scates, "Tax Reform Bill to Trigger Big Action," *Seattle Post-Intelligencer*, February 23, 1967.

CHAPTER EIGHT: BLUEPRINT FOR PROGRESS

1 *House Journal of the 40th Legislature of the State of Washington* (Olympia, 1967), 858.

2 Ibid., 873.

3 *House Journal of the 40th Legislature*, ibid., 1148.

4 Mike Layton, "Evans Thinks Demos a Drag," *Daily Olympian*, March 10, 1967.

5 Ibid., 1436-37.

6 Ibid., 1436.

7 Shelby Scates, "House Turns Down Evans' Tax Package," *Seattle Post-Intelligencer*, March 18, 1967.

8 *House Journal of the 40th Legislature*, ibid., 1532.

9 Leroy Hittle, "Solons Home to Ponder Tax Bill," *Seattle Post-Intelligencer*, March 26, 1967.

10 Paul Ellis, "Motherhood and Tax Reform," *Seattle Post-Intelligencer*, March 24, 1967.

11 Editorial: "Dreams and Schemes," *Vancouver Columbian*, March 26, 1967.

12 *House Journal of the 40th Legislature*, ibid., 1704.

13 Ibid., 1763.

14 Ibid., 1767-68.

15 Shelby Scates, "Evans' Tax Reform Plan Killed in House: Possibility of Income Tax Fades," *Seattle Post-Intelligencer*, April 5, 1967.

16 Richard D. Lyons, "Banana Peel Smoking Probed," ibid.

17 Craig Smith, "Pro-Hippie Petition in U-District," ibid.

18 "Pike Place Sets Love-Arts Fete," ibid.

19 *House Journal of the 40th Legislature*, ibid., 1796-1804.

CHAPTER NINE: COMMUNITY VOICE

1 Mary Ellen McCaffree to the 32nd District Republican Club, speech notes, author's private collection, 1968.

2 Clifton Daniel and John W. Kirshon, eds., *Chronicle of America* (Farnborough, Hampshire, England: Chronicle Communications Ltd., 1993), 816.

3 Daniel and Kirshon, ibid., 815.

4 Rita Sevcik, notes, http://archives.evergreen.edu/WebPages/sevcik/home.

5 *1969 Legislative Manual of the State of Washington*, Joint Rules, Rules of the Senate and Rules of the House of the 41st Legislature of Washington (Olympia, 1969), 56.

6 Daniel and Kirshon, ibid., 817.

7 Ibid., 818.

8 Tax Advisory Council of the State of Washington, *Proposals for Changes in Washington's Tax Structure: Second Report* (Olympia, December 1968).

9 Robert F. Doherty, Jr., "Report of Campaign Internship, McCaffree for Representative Campaign, District 32-A," unpublished thesis, author's private collection, November 25, 1968.

10 Daniel and Kirshon, ibid., 819.

11 Ibid.

12 Ibid., 820.

13 "Lessons in Leadership: Dan Evans," KCTS-TV series segment produced by the Agora Foundation (Seattle, 1999).

14 Daniel and Kirschon, ibid., 821.

15 Ibid., 822.

16 Tax Advisory Council, *Second Report*, ibid., 51-53.

17 Mary Ellen McCaffree, constituent newsletter, author's personal collection, July 18, 1968.

18 Daniel J. Evans, *Today Show*, NBC, August 7, 1968.

19 "Loner from Olympia," *Time*, August 9, 1968.

20 Daniel and Kirschon, ibid., 822.

21 Ibid., 823.

22 Ibid.

23 C. Montgomery Johnson, "What Shall I Tell My Party About Politics?," Chapter 2: Mary Ellen's Basement, ibid.

24 Ibid.

25 Bobbi McCallum, "A Fighting Chance to Vote," *Seattle Post-Intelligencer*, December 22, 1968.

26 Daniel and Kirschon, ibid.

CHAPTER TEN: TAX REFORM

1 *House Journal of the 41st Legislature of the State of Washington* (Olympia, 1969), 88.

2 Tax Advisory Council, *Second Report*, ibid.

3 Mrs. Leonard G. Wells to Mary Ellen McCaffree, February 15, 1969, Accession 2217-4, Box 4, Folder: "Correspondence - 1969 Session Org. on tax reform," *Mary Ellen McCaffree Papers*, Special Collections Division, University of Washington Libraries, Seattle.

4 Bert Billdt to Mary Ellen McCaffree, February 20, 1969, ibid.

5 Mrs. Janet Austin to Mary Ellen McCaffree, February 26, 1969, Folder: "Out Dist. Teachers supporting tax reform 1969," ibid.

6 Shelby Scates, "Angry Blacks Berate Solons in Eloquent Capitol Lecture," *Seattle Post-Intelligencer*, March 1, 1969.

7 Bill Sieverling, "Tiff Over Olympia 'Invasion'," *Seattle Post-Intelligencer*, March 4, 1969.

8 Cecelia Goodnow, "City Made Great Strides During the Civil Rights Movement," *Seattle Post-Intelligencer,* February 26, 2002.

9 Kurt Schaefer, "The Black Panther Party in Seattle, Part 3: The Panthers and the Politicians," Seattle Civil Rights and Labor History Projects, http://depts.washington.edu/civilr/Panthers1_schaefer.html, 2005.

10 Mary Ellen McCaffree to Mrs. Leonard G. Wells, March 1, 1969, *Mary Ellen McCaffree Papers*, ibid.

11 Mary Ellen McCaffree to Mr. Gregg E. Hals, March 13, 1969, Folder: "Out Dist. Teachers supporting tax reform 1969," ibid.

12 Mrs. Lynne Teevin to Mary Ellen McCaffree, March 16, 1969, Folder: "Correspondence -1969 Session: Letters on Tax Reform," ibid.

13 L. Herlwyn Lutz to All Senators and State Representatives, March, 1969, ibid.

14 Mary Ellen McCaffree to 32nd District constituents, March 27, 1969, ibid.

15 *House Journal of the 42st Legislature*, ibid., 1565.

16 Mary Ellen McCaffree to 32nd District constituents, "Citizens of Washington to Decide Tax Reform Measure," April 25, 1969, Accession 2177-2, Box 4, Folder: "Misc Newsletters on Tax Reform," *Mary Ellen McCaffree Papers*, ibid.

17 Mrs. Mortimer H. Thomas to Senate Committee on Revenue and Taxation, transcript of statement, April 28, 1969, Accession 2177-4, Box 4, Folder: "News clippings - misc on tax reform '69," ibid.

18 Adele Ferguson, "Tax Measure Wends Way Back to House," *Bremerton Sun*, May 8, 1969.

19 Bill Sieverling, "Today is Do or Die for Tax Reform," *Seattle Post-Intelligencer*, May 8, 1969.

CHAPTER ELEVEN: INCOMPLETE

1 Ken Beller and Helen Chase, *Great Peacemakers: True Stories from Around the World*, Chapter 17, "Rachel Carson: The Balance of Nature" (Sedona, Arizona: LTS Press), 139-145.

2 Jack Lewis, "The Spirit of the First Earth Day," *EPA Journal*, January/February, 1990.

3 Associated Press, "Former Wisconsin Senator, Earth Day Founder, Gaylord Nelson Dies," *USA Today*, July 3, 2005.

4 Daniel J. Evans to Washington Environmental Council, transcript of address, Seattle 15, 1969. Provided courtesy of Joan Thomas.

5 "Lessons in Leadership," ibid.

6 *Dolliver Oral History*, ibid., 34-36.

7 Mary Ellen McCaffree newsletter to 32nd District Republican Club, September 24, 1969, Accession 2177-2, Box 4, Folder: "Misc Newletters on Tax Reform," *Mary Ellen McCaffree Papers*, ibid.

8 Mrs. Dale A. McDonald to Mary Ellen McCaffree, December 3, 1969, Kenneth M. McCaffree, *Kenneth M. McCaffree Papers*, Accession 3238-2-87-8, Box 7, Folder 16, Special Collections Division, University of Washington Libraries, Seattle.

9 The Rev. Canon Lincoln to Mary Ellen McCaffree, December 15, 1969, Accession 2177-4, Box 1, Folder: "Abortion Legislation 68/69," *Mary Ellen McCaffree Papers*, ibid.

10 John Britt to Mary Ellen McCaffree, December 8, 1969, Folder 9, *Kenneth M. McCaffree Papers*, ibid.

11 "Legislature Cold to Local Tax - Evans," *Seattle Post-Intelligencer*, January 7, 1970.

12 Gladwin Hill, "Environment May Eclipse Vietnam as College Issue," *New York Times*, September 30, 1969.

13 *House Journal of the 41st Legislature of the State of Washington, Second Extraordinary Session* (Olympia, 1970), 2.

CHAPTER TWELVE: EXTRAORDINARY

1 Mary Ellen McCaffree to Mrs. Dale A. McDonald, January 2, 1970, Folder 16, *Kenneth M. McCaffree Papers*, ibid.

2 Carolyn Rolfs, "Meeting Minutes of Eighteen Year Old Vote Committee of Washington State," January 25, 1969, Folder: "18 yr old vote," *Mary Ellen McCaffree Papers*, ibid.

3 Washington State Coordinating Committee for the 18-year Old Vote, "List of co-chairs, sponsors and steering committee," *Mary Ellen McCaffree Papers*, ibid.

4 *House Journal of the 41st Legislature, Second Extraordinary Session*, ibid., 12-15.

5 Daniel J. Evans, Governor to the Honorable Mary Ellen McCaffree, Chairman, Revenue and Taxation Committee, January 13, 1970, Accession 2177-4, Box 3, Folder: "Public Hearings 1969-70," *Mary Ellen McCaffree Papers*, ibid.

6 Adele Ferguson, "State Legislators Hear City, County Officials Plead For Taxation Rights," *Bremerton Sun*, January 13, 1970.

7 "Boeing Effects Awaited," *Seattle Post-Intelligencer*, January 17, 1970.

8 Shelby Scates, "Environment Turns Foggy in Capitol Bog: After Two Weeks One Begins to Wonder," *Seattle Post-Intelligencer,* January 28, 1970.

9 Terry L. Webb to Mary Ellen McCaffree, author's private collection, January 15, 1969.

10 Rusty Yerxa, "Commitment to Host Evans, State Officials," *University of Washington Daily*, January 9, 1970.

11 *House Journal of 41st Legislature, Second Extraordinary Session*, ibid., 98.

12 "Washington's New Unemployment Compensation Law," *Special Session of 1970: A Record of Achievement*, Washington State Republican Caucus (Olympia, 1970), 26.

13 Bill Lee, "Morrison Feels Business Should Accept Jobless Pay Compromise," *Yakima Herald Republic*, February 22, 1970.

14 *Pritchard Oral History*, ibid.,163.

15 Richard W. Larsen, "100 Demonstrate at Capitol for Legalized Abortion," *The Seattle Times*, January 12, 1970.

16 *Pritchard Oral History*, ibid., p. 161.

17 Henry C. Epps to Mary Ellen McCaffree, telegram, January 25, 1970, Accession 2177-4, Box 1, Folder: "Abortion Correspondence 1970," *Mary Ellen McCaffree Papers*, ibid.

18 Robert Love to Mary Ellen McCaffree, ibid.

19 Mary Ellen McCaffree abortion issue form letters to constituents, ibid.

20 Richard W. Larsen, "No Tax Relief Seen for Boeing," *Seattle Times,* January 27, 1970.

21 Shelby Scates, "Environment Turns Foggy…" ibid.

22 Maribeth Morris, "Save Environment Bills: Governor Issues Appeal to Public," *Seattle Post-Intelligencer,* February 5, 1970.

EPILOGUE

1 John Adams quotation taken from the Washington State Legislature website: www.leg.wa.gov/legislature/Pages/EffectiveParticipation.aspx

2 Thomas Jefferson quote: www.brainyquote.com/quotes/authors/t/thomas_jefferson_9.html

3 Abigail Adams quote from www.quotationspage.com/quote/3072.html

ACKNOWLEDGEMENTS

JUST AS TEAMWORK WAS CENTRAL to the results in this story, the creation of our book has been a team effort. Readers, interviewees, assistants and those who cheered from the sidelines while we focused on this long labor of love all contributed to bringing this essential history to the printed page. Any errors of omission or commission are, of course, ours.

For reading and critique of early and subsequent drafts, special thanks to colleagues Governor Dan Evans and U.S. Senator Slade Gorton and to Anne Kilgannon, former director of the Oral History Program, Secretary of State's Office, Washington State. Many thanks to our additional readers: Ralph Munro, Sam Reed, Steve Excell, Alex Bolton, Jerald Podair, Kerry Mazzoni, Reggie Winner, Kay Read, Mark Jaroslaw, Bill Gates, Sr., Pat Lyon, Brandon Reim, Christen Gregory, Chuck McCaffree, Jim McCaffree, Marty Winner, Joe Clarke, Kevin O'Connor, Dallas Salisbury, Glen Slaughter, Andrea Adams, Sylvie Bokshorn and Corinne Ruokangus.

To Don Burrows, for personally sharing with us his expertise and his manuscript on the history of taxation and tax reform in Washington State, and to Joan Thomas for her recollections of the early days of the Washington Environmental Council, thank you both.

Much appreciation to the staff of the Washington State House of Representatives for information, tours, photo sessions and for audiotape of the floor session of the standing ovation. At the Washington State Archives, thanks to Mary Hammer and Benjamin Helle, and thanks also to the research staff at the Washington State Library, to the Special Collections staff at the University of Washington libraries, and for the assistance of librarians at newspapers throughout the state.

Thank you to Michelle deBeauchamp for early interviews of the McCaffree grandchildren, and to the grandchildren themselves for ongoing commentary: Carey, Leslie, Alison, Stacey, Jared, Jessica, Shayna, Ryland, Paige, Leif, Ingrid, Zelina, Cameron and Veronica (and to each spouse).

Thank you also to the five McCaffree 'kids' and their spouses for sharing memories, scrapbooks, insights and for tremendous ongoing support: James and Ruthann McCaffree, Charles and Lee McCaffree, Nancy and Aubrey Carter, Mary and Jack Johnston, and David and Alex McCaffree.

To Anne's parents, Bob and Mary McNamee, thank you for reading, for discussions and especially for providing Anne an office away from home. Thanks also to Anne's husband Hoyt and to her daughters Christen, Nicole and Catherine for support and understanding.

To Jessica McCaffree Mans and Kobus Mans, great thanks for creating our book's website, **www.politicsofthepossible.com**; and Jessica, we so appreciate your work on the scrapbooks, your photographs of the capitol and bill books for our website and book, and your deep reading of the manuscript.

Thanks to Quinlan Corbett for reading and recording our audio version.

And finally, immense gratitude to the two who round out our central team: To Alison McCaffree, who actively joined us in 2006 and has contributed her enthusiasm, research, legwork and outreach ever since; and to Ken — Dr. Kenneth M. McCaffree, who gracefully accepted a growing role as this project stretched into years, whose dedication to our endnotes deserves special mention, and whose diplomacy, intelligence and care know no bounds. A true partner.

Thank you, all.

ABOUT THE AUTHORS

MARY ELLEN McCAFFREE inadvertently entered political life when she took up the cause of her children's overcrowded and under funded schools. This led the 1950's housewife into work on two statewide redistricting initiatives, four terms as a state legislator, accolades as architect and author of her state's most comprehensive package of tax reform, co-author of legislation that established the state's community college system, author of the constitutional amendment for youth voting rights, and as a sponsor of groundbreaking environmental protections. She served on her state's founding hearings boards for pollution control and shorelines management which wrote the initial regulations for each. The first woman director of the Washington State Department of Revenue, she also served as King County (Seattle) budget director and as administrative assistant to a U.S. Senator in Washington, D.C. Upon her retirement from public life she continued to encourage women's active roles in local and national politics, and served on many local, state and national commissions, committees and boards. She has a degree in home economics from Kansas State University, and has been married 69 years to Dr. Kenneth McCaffree, Professor Emeritus, Economics, University of Washington and her high school sweetheart. The couple has 5 children, 14 grandchildren, 18 great-grandchildren and counting, and together wrote *Piecing Together Our Separate Lives* as a gift to their family on the occasion of their 60th wedding anniversary. She resides with her husband in Snohomish, Washington. As a lifelong gardener and relentless taker-on-of-tasks, Mary Ellen's words back her actions: "You never retire — you just repot and keep growing."

ANNE McNAMEE CORBETT With parallel careers in writing, editing and publication design, Anne has spent her adult life immersed in non-fiction. Her degree is in journalism from the University of Washington, and she worked two sessions at the Washington State Legislature — as a reporting intern for *The Seattle Times* and as a staff writer in the Senate. An initiator, she was founding editor of both a weekly community newspaper and a regional medical center newsmagazine, as well as the co-creator of an annual trade magazine. She also co-founded a community land trust and film development company. Her collective writing spans a variety of fields: education, state and county government, the courts, land use and community planning, legislative reporting and political campaigns, medical advances, pharmaceutical research, alternative heating technology, investments and theater. The mother of three lovely daughters, friend to two stepsons and to a growing circle of daughters- and sons-in-law, she resides with her husband in the U.S. Pacific Northwest.